INTERNATIONAL ECONOMIC LAW SERIES

General Editor: JOHN H. JACKSON

International Law in Financial Regulation and Monetary Affairs

International Law
in Financial Regulation
and Monetary Affairs

Edited by
THOMAS COTTIER,
JOHN H. JACKSON,
and
ROSA M. LASTRA

OXFORD
UNIVERSITY PRESS

OXFORD
UNIVERSITY PRESS

Great Clarendon Street, Oxford, OX2 6DP,
United Kingdom

Oxford University Press is a department of the University of Oxford.
It furthers the University's objective of excellence in research, scholarship,
and education by publishing worldwide. Oxford is a registered trade mark of
Oxford University Press in the UK and in certain other countries

British Library Cataloguing in Publication Data

Data available

ISBN 978–0–19–966819–9

Printed in Great Britain by
CPI Group (UK) Ltd, Crydon, CR0 4YY

General Editor's Preface

The global financial crisis has profoundly affected the lives and lifestyles of a great number of people. This has led individuals in all sections of society—including academia, government, and business—to inquire into the causes and progression of the crisis. It has also prompted reflection on potential reforms that could prevent such a catastrophe from happening in the future.

Motivated by these concerns and mindful of the complexity (as well as the perplexity) of the activities in international financial markets, a number of the *Journal of International Economic Law*'s editors discussed whether the Journal could make a pertinent contribution to the relevant policy debates.

As the Editor-in-Chief of the Journal, I was thrilled when Professors Thomas Cottier and Rosa Lastra agreed to my request to take on the formidable task of Special Editors for this project. Thomas and Rosa accepted the principal responsibility for constructing an appropriate outline of topics as well as selecting and inviting authors to participate. With a few necessary exceptions, the authors discussed these drafts at a fascinating conference held at Georgetown University's Center for Transnational Legal Studies in London on 21 May 2010. A Special Issue of the Journal, published in September 2010, entirely devoted to the issues implicated in the crisis, was the result of these discussions.

Following the publication of the Special Issue it was agreed with Oxford University Press that it would be beneficial to release an updated volume that took into account some of the recent legal developments in international financial regulation and monetary policy. This book is the result with each chapter newly updated, where appropriate, to take into account relevant developments while ensuring that the fundamental concepts raised by each contributor remain intact. In addition the amended introduction and additional conclusion highlight some of the major events that have occurred in the field since the Special Issue was first published.

While the editors decided that they could make a worthy contribution to current discourses, they were cautious not to venture outside of the mission and expertise of the Journal. There is an ever-increasing amount of published material dealing with all facets of the crisis. The editors consciously decided that the contributions would focus (insofar as feasible) on those aspects of the crisis most suited to analysis and study by (international) legal scholars. As a revision of the original Special Issue this volume follows suit and is directed at regulation and how regulatory activity and reform might best be approached. While other major policy problems—such as recession, stimulus, and bail outs—might be better examined by experts from disciplines other than law, the editors also conceded that those issues could not always be detached from the complex and interrelated 'lawyers' agenda'.

The role that international law plays in financial regulation and monetary policy remains at the forefront of governments and international bodies policy agendas and will continue to do so for the foreseeable future. The contributions in this volume will serve as a platform for future analysis and will remain a guide for policy makers, professionals, and academics looking to tackle the complex issues discussed.

John H. Jackson

Contents

IV. TRADE, COMPETITION, AND TAX-RELATED ASPECTS

V. MONETARY REGULATION

VI. CONCLUSIONS

List of Abbreviations

AFM	Authority for Financial Markets
AIFs	Alternative Investment Funds
AIG	American International Group
A-IRB	Advanced Internal Rating-Based approach
BaFin	Bundesanstalt für Finanzdienstleistungaufsicht
BCBS	Basel Committee on Banking Supervision
BIS	Bank for International Settlements
BIT	Bilateral Investment Agreements
CC	Competition Commission
CCMR	Committee on Capital Markets Regulation
CD	Certificate of Deposit
CDOs	Collateralized Debt Obligations
CDS	Credit Default Swaps
CFTC	Commodities Future Trading Commission
CIC	China Investment Corporation
CLS	Bank Contentious Link Settlement Bank
CPI	Consumer Price Index
CPSS	Committee on Payments and Settlements Systems
CTT	Currency Transaction Tax
CVDs	Countervailing Duties
DFM	De Facto Money
DNB	De Nederlandsche Bank (Dutch Central Bank)
EBA	European Banking Authority
ECB	European Central Bank
ECMR	European Community Merger Regulation
ECOFIN	Economic and Financial Affairs Council
EIOPA	European Insurance and Occupational Pensions Authority
EMDCs	Emerging Market and Developing Countries
EMS	European Monetary System
EMU	European Monetary Union
ERISA	Employee Retirement Income Security Act
ESM	Emergency Safeguard Measures
ESMA	European Securities and Markets Authority
ESRB	European Systematic Risk Board
ESRC	European Systematic Risk Council
EU	European Union or Treaty on European Union (after Article number)
FAS	Financial Accounting Standards
FASB	Financial Accounting Standards Board
FAT	Financial Activities Tax
FDIC	Federal Deposit Insurance Corporation
FDICIA	Federal Deposit Insurance Corporation Improvement Act
FINMA	Financial Markets Supervisory Authority
FINRA	Financial Industry Regulatory Authority

FSA	Financial Services Authority
FSAP	Financial Sector Assessment Program
FSB	Financial Stability Board
FSC	Financial Stability Contribution
FSF	Financial Stability Forum
FTC	Federal Trade Commission
FTT	Financial Transactions Tax
FX Market	Foreign Exchange Market
GAAP	Generally Accepted Accounting Principles
GAPP	Generally Accepted Principles and Practices
GATS	General Agreements on Trade in Services
GATT	General Agreement on Tariffs and Trade
GDDS	General Data Dissemination System
GDP	Gross Domestic Product
GFC	Global Financial Crisis
IAIS	International Association of Insurance Supervisors
IAS	International Accounting Standards
IASB	International Accounting Standards Board
ICCPR	International Covenant on Civil and Political Rights
ICESCR	International Covenant on Economic, Social and Cultural Rights
ICMA	International Capital Market Association
IFAC	International Federation of Accountants
IFIs	International Financial Institutions
IFRS	International Financial Reporting Standards
ILO	International Labour Organization
IMF	International Monetary Fund
IMFC	International Monetary and Financial Committee
IOSCO	International Organization of Securities Commissions
IRFSS	International Regulatory Financial Standard Setting
ISDA	International Swaps and Derivatives Association
ISSBs	International Standard-Setting Bodies
ISWF	International Sovereign Wealth Fund
IT	Inflation Targeting
ITO	International Trade Organization
IWG	International Working Group (on sovereign wealth funds)
LBG	Lloyds Banking Group
LCR	Liquidity Coverage Ratio
LTRO	Long-Term Refinancing Operations
LTV	Loan to value
MDGs	Millennium Development Goals
MBE	Management by Exception
MEIP	Market Economy Investor Principle
MFN	Most Favoured Nation
MoU	Memoranda of Understanding
NASD	National Association of Securities and Dealers
NIFA	New International Financial Architecture
NPOs	Non-Profit Organisations
NSFR	Net Stable Funding Ratio
OECD	Organisation for Economic Co-operation and Development

OFT	Office of Fair Trading
OTC	Over The Counter
OTS	Office of Thrift Supervision
POSB	Post Office Savings Bank
PTA	Preferential Trade Agreements
RAP	Regulatory Accounting Principles
RTGS	Real Time Gross Settlement
S&D	Special and Differential Treatment
SCAP	Supervisory Capital Assessment Program
SCM	Subsidies and Countervailing Measures
SDDS	Special Data Dissemination Standard
SDRs	Special Drawing Rights
SEC	Securities and Exchange Commission
SIFIs	Systematically Important Financial Institutions
SIVs	Structured Investment Vehicles
SNB	Swiss National Bank
SPS	Sanitary and Phytosanitary Measures
SRO	Self-Regulatory Organizations
SRR	Special Resolution Regime
STF	Systematic Transfer Facility
SWFs	Sovereign Wealth Funds
SWIFT	Society for Worldwide Interbank Financial Telecommunications
TA	Technical Assistance
TARP	Troubled Asset Relief Program
TBT	Technical Barriers to Trade
TBTF	Too Big To Fail
TFEU	Treaty of Functioning of the European Union
TPRB	Trade Policy Review Board
TPRM	Trade Policy Review Mechanism
TRIMs	Trade-Related Investment Measures
TRIPS	Trade-Related Aspects of Intellectual Property Rights
TSB	Trustee Savings Bank
UCITS	Undertakings for Collective Investment in Transferable Securities
UN	United Nations
UNCTAD	United Nations Conference on Trade and Development
US	United States (of America)
VaR	Value at Risk
WPDR	Working Party on Domestic Regulation
WTO	World Trade Organization

List of Contributors

Kern Alexander, Professor of Banking, Commercial and Financial Market Law, Law Faculty, University of Zürich; Senior Research Fellow, Centre for Financial Analysis and Policy, The Judge Business School, University of Cambridge

Ernst Baltensperger, Professor Emeritus of Economics, University of Berne

Chris Brummer, Professor of Law, Georgetown University Law Centre

Steve Charnovitz, Associate Professor of Law, The George Washington University Law School

Peggy A. Clarke, Partner, Blank Rome LLP, Washington DC

Thomas Cottier, Managing Director, World Trade Institute; Professor for European and International Economic Law, University of Berne; Director, Institute of European and International Economic Law

Panagiotis Delimatsis, Associate Professor of Law at Tilburg University; Co-Director of the Tilburg Law and Economics Center (TILEC); Senior Research Fellow, World Trade Institute, University of Berne

R. Michael Gadbaw, Adjunct Professor, Georgetown University Law Centre; Distinguished Senior Fellow, Institute for International Economic Law

Luis Garicano, Professor of Economics and Strategy, Center for Economic Performance, the London School of Economics; Co-Director, Center for Economic Policy Research

Charles A.E. Goodhart, Member of the Financial Markets Group, London School of Economics

Sean Hagan, General Counsel and Director of the Legal Department of the International Monetary Fund

Gary N. Horlick, Attorney-at-Law, Law Offices of Gary N. Horlick, Washington DC; the first Chair of the WTO Permanent Group of Experts

Gary Hufbauer, Reginald Jones Senior Fellow, Peterson Institute for International Economics, Washington DC

Christine Kaufmann, Professor of Law, Chair for International and Constitutional Law and Head of the Centre of Competence on Human Rights and Business, University of Zürich

Ioannis Kokkoris, Reader, University of Reading, UK; International Consultant on Competition Policy, Organisation for Security and Cooperation in Europe

Markus Krajewski, Guest Professor, Collaborative Research Center (Sonderforschungsbereich) 'Transformations of the State', University of Bremen, Germany

Donald C. Langevoort, Thomas Aquinas Reynolds Professor of Law, Georgetown University of Law Center, Washington DC

Rosa M. Lastra, Professor in International Financial and Monetary Law, Centre for Commercial Law Studies, Queen Mary, University of London

Matthias Lehmann, D.E.A. (Paris II), LL.M. (Columbia); Director, Institute of Economic Law; Professor and Chair for German and European Private Law, Commercial and Business Law, Private International and Comparative Law, Law School of the University of Halle, Germany

Andreas F. Lowenfeld, Rubin Professor of International Law Emeritus, New York University School of Law

Philip Marsden, Senior Research Fellow, British Institute of International and Comparative Law; Director, Competition Law Forum

Joseph J. Norton, James L. Walsh Distinguished Faculty Fellow in Financial Institutions and Professor of Law, SMU Dedman School of Law, Dallas, Texas; former Sir John Lubbock Professor of Banking Law, University of London (1993–2004)

Pierre Sauvé, Deputy Managing Director and Director of Studies, World Trade Institute

Hal S. Scott, Nomura Professor of International Financial Systems, Harvard Law School; Director, Committee on Capital Markets Regulation (CCMR)

Christian Tietje, LL.M. (Michigan); Director, Institute of Economic Law; Director, Transnational Economic Law Research Center; Professor and Chair for Public Law, European and International Economic Law, Law School of the University of Halle, Germany

Joel P. Trachtman, Professor of International Law, the Fletcher School of Law and Diplomacy, Tufts University

Rolf H. Weber, Professor of Civil, European and Commercial Law, Law Department of the University of Zürich; Visiting Professor at the University of Hong Kong

Geoffrey Wood, Professor Emeritus of Economics, Cass Business School, London

Daniel Danxia Xie, Research Analyst, Peterson Institute for International Economics, Washington DC

Introduction

Thomas Cottier and Rosa M. Lastra

The 2007–2009 financial crisis triggered a worldwide recession and a slump in international trade of some 10 per cent in 2008 and 2009. Millions of jobs were lost, savings destroyed and opportunities missed. Governments responded with massive interventions to secure liquidity and solvency and to stimulate investment and consumption in the United States, the European Union and around the world. Future generations will need to live with the debts incurred.

Furthermore, the financial crisis mutated into a sovereign debt crisis in the eurozone in 2010. Spreads between ten-year government bonds of some peripheral euro area countries relative to German bonds started to rise, reflecting market concerns about the sustainability of public finances in the aftermath of the global recession. The sovereign debt crisis was initially seen as a problem of relatively small EU economies such as Greece, Ireland and Portugal. However, the fear that the problems may spread to other larger EU economies such as Italy and Spain did materialise, bringing fresh problems to the banking sector and significantly expanding the magnitude of the crisis. Despite a plethora of official responses (EU- and IMF-led rescue packages, launch of the ECB Securities Markets Programme, the long-term refinancing operations (LTRO) of the ECB, the so-called 'Fiscal Compact' Treaty, etc.) and a new architecture to deal with sovereign debt problems, (comprising a European Financial Stabilization Mechanism or EFSM, a temporary European Financial Stability Facility or EFSF and a proposed permanent European Stability Mechanism or ESM, that will replace the EFSM and ESFS once their terms expire), the problems remain, compromising the stability and future of the euro.

This book deals with the financial crisis, rather than with the subsequent sovereign debt crisis. While the causes of the financial crisis remain controversial and manifold, one factor clearly deserves our attention: the lack of substantive principles and 'hard law' rules at the level of international or global law in the field of financial regulation and monetary affairs. The regulatory hands-off approach, which has dominated recent decades of international relations in these fields, contrasts with other areas of international economic law. International trade regulation witnessed an increased number of international rules and the reinforcement of a rule-oriented, if not rule-based, approach. Judicial dispute settlement and retaliation exclusively based upon international ruling and authorization was reinforced. The recession, so far, and due to such evolutions, has not led to a return to protectionism comparable to the reactions in the 1930s in the absence of a multilateral trading system. Likewise, rules on investment have been reinforced and the network of international agreements has greatly increased in the process of globalization. The crisis has evidenced the need for financial and monetary regulatory reform on the one hand, and for the establishment of appropriate mechanisms for the settlement of financial disputes and for the regulation of cross-border financial institutions, on the other.

The purpose of this book, which builds upon the papers that were published in the Special Edition of the *Journal of International Economic Law* on 'The Quest for International Law in Financial Regulation and Monetary Affairs' (Volume 12, Number 3, September 2010) is to raise some of these basic questions and to work towards answers possibly filling the black holes in international law in this area. It includes twenty-two succinct commissioned papers addressing the issues mentioned above. Most of the papers were discussed at an informal conference in London on 22 May 2010, sponsored by Georgetown University Washington, and jointly organized with the World Trade Institute, University of Bern, and with the Centre for Commercial Law Studies, Queen Mary, University of London.

The papers of this book deal with general, cross-border topics, and topics focusing on financial regulation on the one hand, and monetary policies and regulation, on the other hand. Given the importance of trade regulation and World Trade Organization law, they seek to establish linkages and make comparisons wherever suitable. We hope to lay some foundations with these contributions and to encourage much needed debate.

We are aware that these are fields of immense complexity and technicalities, and it is far from clear what role the law, in particular international law, can and should play in stabilizing financial and monetary affairs around the globe. The system, it seems, has been operating under the assumption that such a role is inherently limited, that it is not suitable for per se rule in order to enhance stability, predictability and legal security. The issue goes to the heart of the relationship of law and economics which, of course, is not limited to finance and monetary affairs, but equally shapes trade and competition rules and policies. Yet, while the lawyers would at least seem to know more about this relationship in the field of trade, investment and competition, a black hole still confronts us in financial and monetary affairs. Conventional wisdom has often suggested that these matters are best left to markets and economics, and that a policy of setting per se rules is to be avoided. Financial institutions pursuing this course of action were successful in shielding their activities from the intrusion and disciplines of international economic law, let alone international dispute settlement. International law was simply called upon to support market access and liberalization, but the matter was otherwise left to the private sector and to domestic regulation which the sector is able to shape in accordance with its own and nationally varying needs. The globalization of operations of banks and financial companies had little or no impact on regulating the industry or on allocating regulatory powers. They have remained under the national jurisdictions of central banks or national supervisory and regulatory authorities. Likewise, monetary affairs have been included under the broad and exclusive responsibilities of national banks and reserve boards, deliberately detached from government influence, in order to pursue monetary policies mainly focusing on the problem of inflation. This field, conventional wisdom holds, is not really suitable for a rule-oriented or even-rule based approach. Once the gold standard was abandoned, the International Monetary Fund (IMF) lost its regulatory monetary functions and the Bank for International Settlements (BIS) operated as a coordinating network controlled by national banks and reserve boards without any regulatory powers on their own. The same, it would seem, is true for other organizations in the field: the Financial Stability Forum, the International Accounting Standards Board, the Financial Accounting Standards Board and the International Organization of Securities Commissions.

We do not exclude the possibility that the predominance of economics and the lack of international law in the two fields could, in the end, prove to be the right approach and answer. It may well be that these fields do not lend themselves to rule-based policies in international relations, comparable to those which have emerged in international trade regulation. Rules may always come too late, given the dynamics of the fields. Yet, such findings cannot be assumed, and we need to address the issues carefully. No longer can we leave this matter as a black hole in terms of research and thinking in international economic law. International law may need to play a stronger role, and we are called upon to examine to what extent this proposition makes sense. The relationship of law and economics needs to be revisited in light of past disruptions. Clearly, it has never been a matter of simply leaving finance to markets or economics. Markets cannot exist without legal foundations and regulation, even under conditions of perfect information. As a matter of fact, finance is strongly regulated in domestic or regional law, and the issue is one of finding a more appropriate relationship between law and economics, in particular in regulating capital, liquidity, and bank-like institutions, credit rating agencies and remuneration. What is the current and potential contribution of law towards overcoming market irrationality? What is the potential role of fundamental principles of international economic law, in particular non-discrimination and transparency? What measures can be designed to make markets more transparent, liquid and efficient? The quest inherently entails an examination of the relationship between hard and soft law, and other regulatory approaches, such as informal networks. Moreover, it is a matter of finding a more appropriate relationship between domestic, regional and international law. The same questions as apply to law and economics arise here too. The quest also introduces the relevance of analysis in terms of the theory of multilevel governance henceforth applied to other fields of international economic law, in particular trade regulation. The doctrine of constitutionalization of international law and multilayered governance as a means to bring about greater coherence between the different layers of governance, offering guidance in allocation of powers and in matching them with the requirements of legitimacy, may further assist in exploring the black holes.

The financial crisis has triggered a revolution in regulatory thinking. Once relegated to the obscure universe of the specialist, financial regulation has come to the forefront of economic and policy debate. The crisis has shown that markets cannot always be trusted to deliver what is good for society, since the pursuit of the private interest has proven at times to be greatly misaligned with the pursuit of the common good. Markets need rules and international financial markets need international rules.

In the absence of 'formal' international rules, soft-law rules fill the vacuum. This is an ongoing process, in which new developments can soon render some of the existing rules obsolete. This is the case, for instance, with regard to the so-called Basel III, i.e., the new capital and liquidity standards adopted by the Basel Committee on Banking Supervision in December 2010. The Basel Committee subsequently conducted a review that resulted in a small modification of the credit valuation adjustment, and published the revised version of the Basel III capital rules in June 2011. The core aspects of Basel III are scheduled to be implemented into national law by 1 January 2013; certain aspects of the new standards are slated to become effective upon implementation while others will be phased in over several years in between 2013–2019. In terms of liquidity standards, after an observation period beginning in 2011, the Liquidity Coverage Ratio (LCR) will be introduced on 1 January 2015 and Net Stable Funding Ratio (NSFR) will move to a minimum standard by 1 January 2018. Both the Basel Committee and the Financial Stability Board have been busy issuing new soft-law rules. For example, new 'Core Principles for Effective Banking Supervision' were issued for consultation in December 2011, addressing issues such as corporate governance, the treatment of Systemically Important Banks, recovery and resolution plans, which were not included in the original 1997 document. For its part, the Financial Stability Board has also been publishing a number of principles and documents, the most relevant being the 'Key Attributes of Effective Resolution Regimes for Financial Institutions' (published on 4 November 2011). These key attributes—which are the result of work undertaken by the FSB jointly with its members including the IMF, World Bank and the standard-setting bodies—are considered new internationally agreed standards that lay out the responsibilities, instruments and powers that national resolution regimes should have to resolve a failing SIFI (systemically important financial institutions). They also establish the requirements for resolvability assessments and recovery and resolution planning for global SIFIs, as well as for the development of institution-specific cooperation agreements between home and host authorities. They are aimed at solving the too-big-to-fail problem by making it possible to resolve any financial institution in an orderly manner and without exposing the taxpayer to the risk of loss, protecting essential economic functions through mechanisms for losses to be allocated between shareholders and unsecured and uninsured creditors.

The twenty-two papers of this book treat these issues in their own way. They all offer important and interesting building blocks, reflecting a wide range of views. Many inherently focus on domestic regulation. With a view to stimulating debate no attempt to eliminate overlaps and contradictions has been made. We also refrain from drawing specific conclusions, at this stage. This work will entail an in-depth analysis of the different papers which, for reasons of timing alone, cannot be undertaken at the moment. Yet, on substance, it would be equally premature to draw general conclusions as to the proper regulatory functions of international law in financial and monetary affairs. The papers do, however, offer a solid foundation for further thought on the relationship between markets and law and between domestic and international regulation, the pros and cons of hard law and soft law, of fundamental principles, and of different regulatory models available under the broad umbrella of public international law. The quest for international law in financial regulation presents complex and difficult challenges. Yet, as Einstein famously remarked: 'We can't solve problems by using the same kind of thinking we used when we created them.'

The editors are most grateful to the authors of this volume who agreed to produce their contributions in a remarkably short time. We should like to thank Clifford Hudson for his generous financial assistance to this project, which particularly enabled us to have the London conference last May. We also thank Christine Washington and Maike Kotterba, Georgetown University, for support in organizing the London conference. We are most grateful to the editorial support staff at the World Trade Institute. Rachel Liechti coordinated the editing process, supported by research fellows, Ronald Abegglen, Tetyana Payosova, Ruth Peterseil, Maria Schultheiss and Christian Steiger, IT support. Susan Kaplan, the science editor of WTI and the NCCR, reviewed all the manuscripts before they reached the *Journal of International Economic Law*. We particularly thank Nicolas Lamp and Jennifer Hawkins, editorial assistants at the Journal, and Jack R. Williams, who assisted in the review of the papers ahead of their publication as a book. Finally, our thanks extend to Oxford University Press for agreeing to expand the volume of the special edition and to publish this book.

PART I

THE CRISIS OF 2007–2009: NATURE, CAUSES, AND REACTIONS

1

The Crisis of 2007–09: Nature, Causes, and Reactions

*Rosa M. Lastra and Geoffrey Wood**

I. Introduction

Financial crises are of two types: liquidity crises and capital crises. One type rapidly merges with the other, so that beyond the initial stage of a crisis there are both liquidity and capital problems, but it is useful to start with a sharp distinction. That will help us to examine the numerous explanations given for the crisis of 2007–09.[1]

A. A liquidity crisis

A liquidity crisis is what might be described as the classic type of banking crisis: a bank for some reason cannot meet all its payment obligations. Given the imperfect knowledge that customers have of their banks, and the links through the interbank market and the payment system, other banks experience runs. These other banks get into difficulties because, by the nature of fractional reserve banking, they cannot immediately pay out on all deposits. In the extreme the entire banking system collapses like a row of dominoes.[2]

---

* The authors are indebted to Charles Goodhart, David Westbrook, and Philip Wood for their insightful comments.

[1] This does not mean that the crisis ended in 2009, but that financial sector difficulties ceased to be acute. That said, in 2009 and 2010, the crisis eventually mutated into a sovereign debt crisis in some countries.

[2] Gary Gorton believes that it was the [wholesale] run on the sale-and-repurchase market (the repo market) during 2008, a bank run not so much on depository institution, but on the shadow banking system, which caused the crisis. In Gary Gorton and Andrew Metrick, 'Securitized Banking and the Run on the Repo', National Bureau of Economic Research Working Paper No w15223, August 2009, <http://papers.ssrn.com/sol3/papers.cfm?abstract_id=1454939> (visited 9 August 2010), the authors argue that the panic of 2007–08 was a run on the repo market which is a very large short-term market that provides financing for a wide range of securitization activities and financial institutions. Repo transactions are collateralized, frequently with securitized bonds. They refer to the combination of securitization plus repo finance as securitized banking, and argue that these activities were at the nexus of the crisis. Concerns about the liquidity of markets for the bonds used as collateral led to increases in repo haircuts—the amount of collateral required for any given transaction. With declining asset values and increasing haircuts, the US banking system was, the authors suggest, effectively insolvent.

It is a liquidity crisis that is modelled in the famous Diamond and Dybvig paper.[3] It could not be otherwise, for their model of a bank is of a bank without capital (and, incidentally, in a world without money). Nevertheless that model does describe one of the most famous banking crises in history—that which occurred in England at the outbreak of the wars with France in 1793. That crisis has become famous partly because, thanks to Francis Baring, it led to the emergence of the term 'lender of last resort' or *dernier resort*.[4] The concept was developed by Henry Thornton (1802)[5] and further explained by Walter Bagehot, notably in his book *Lombard Street* (1873)[6] but also in his journalism in *The Economist* and elsewhere. How a lender of last resort operation by the central bank can stop a liquidity crisis and, indeed, what constitutes a liquidity crisis, is best clarified by two quotations. In 1802, Thornton explains that: 'If any bank fails, a general run upon the neighbouring banks is apt to take place, which if not checked in the beginning by a pouring into the circulation of a very large quantity of gold, leads to very extensive mischief'.[7]

Bagehot in 1873 explained why this policy worked: 'What is wanted and what is necessary to stop a panic is to diffuse the impression that though money may be dear, money is still to be had. If people could really be convinced that they would have money...they would cease to run in such a herd-like way for money'.[8] A liquidity crisis, then, originates with a sudden demand for cash—for central bank money, to use the modern term. Fractional reserve banks by their nature cannot meet this demand. So unless the central bank meets it, many, perhaps all, banks in a system may fail.

B. A capital crisis

The second type of crisis is when there is a sharp decline in the value of a bank's capital. This could come about if one large loan suddenly collapsed in value. As bank balance sheets are opaque to customers (and apparently often to management too, judging by recent experience), this leads to fears about the solvency of other banks, runs take place on them, and again in the extreme the whole system fails.[9]

Although the authors single out the repo market, other markets, such as the commercial paper market, also suffered a run.

[3] Douglas W. Diamond and Philip H. Dybvig, 'Bank Runs, Deposit Insurance and Liquidity', 91 (3) *Journal of Political Economy* 401 (1983).

[4] See Francis Baring, *Observations on the Establishment of the Bank of England and on the Paper circulation of the Country*, 1797 ed. (New York: A.M. Kelly, facsimile reprint 1967) 19–23. Baring both imported the term *dernier resort* and used it in a new, metaphorical way—in France, *dernier resort* referred to the final court of appeal. It is truly remarkable how accurately Baring's description of the 1793 crisis also describes that of 1929–33 in the USA. That latter episode is discussed further below.

[5] Henry Thornton, *An Enquiry into the Nature and Effects of the Paper Credit of Great Britain* (London: J. Hatchard and F. and C. Rivington, 1802).

[6] Walter Bagehot, *Lombard Street: A Description of the Money Market* (London: Henry S. King & Co., 1873).

[7] See Thornton, above n 5, at 182.

[8] See Bagehot, above n 6, at 63–4.

[9] These runs may well, in modern circumstances, be what are called 'silent runs'. We set out this concept later, and also propose that a better name might be 'private runs'.

The archetypal capital crisis also occurred in England, but this time in the nineteenth century. This episode was confined to one bank, and thus was not a banking-system crisis, but it could easily have spread to the entire system and perhaps beyond. This was the 'Baring Crisis' of 1890.

Barings was a bank of high reputation. Driven by competition from newer banks, it had invested substantially in Argentina. In April 1890, the Argentinian government defaulted. Next, and partly in consequence, the Argentinian national bank suspended interest payments on its debts. This precipitated a run on the Argentinian banking system. By November 1890, its directors realized that Barings could not survive unaided, and on 8 November, they revealed this to the Bank of England. The Bank was horrified, fearing a run on the British banking system, and perhaps on sterling, if Barings defaulted. After a hurried inspection of the books of Barings, it was decided that the situation could be saved by an injection of capital. A consortium was organized—the Bank was too small to have sufficient funds on its own—and Barings was saved.

That is a perfect example of a capital crisis. A firm is short of capital and cannot pay its debts. If this brings down other banks, or if depositors in the original bank lose their deposits, a system-wide liquidity crisis may start. But the injection of capital can stop the crisis short. Note that central bank provision of liquidity would not suffice, because, to continue with the example of Barings, Barings did not have the assets to offer in exchange for the capital.

Until the twentieth century, only problems in the banking system were regarded as crises. Even the failure of merchant banks (the traditional term in the UK for what are now called investment banks) was not regarded as a crisis unless the event led to a run on the banks whose liabilities were part of the money stock. This view was restated in the twentieth century by Anna Schwartz.[10] She distinguished between 'real' and 'pseudo' crises. A real crisis she defined as follows: 'Such a crisis is fuelled by fear that means of payment will be unavailable at any price, and in a fractional reserve banking system leads to a scramble for high powered money'.[11] These real crises are often referred to as 'banking crises'. Pseudo crises, meanwhile, involve 'a decline in asset prices, of equity stock, real estate, commodities; depreciation of the exchange value of the national currency; financial distress of a large non-financial firm, a large municipality, a financial industry, or sovereign debtors'.[12] A common term for such pseudo crises is 'financial crises'.

This might seem to suggest that, if we accept Schwartz's definition of a crisis, the failure of investment banks or insurers (such as AIG) is of no importance.[13] But the definition most certainly does not suggest that. Failures of institutions whose liabilities are not part of *any* measure of the money stock matter if they trigger

---

[10] Anna J. Schwartz, 'Real and Pseudo-Financial Crises', in Forrest Capie and Geoffrey Wood (eds), *Financial Crises and World Banking Policy* (New York: St. Martin's Press, 1986).

[11] Ibid, at 11.

[12] Ibid, at 24.

[13] The whole range of definitions of financial stability is reviewed in William A. Allen and Geoffrey Wood, 'Defining and Achieving Financial Stability', 2(2) *Journal of Financial Stability 152* (2006). They conclude by essentially concurring with the Schwartz definition.

alarm or threats to the stability of the core banking system. For if they do, they can lead quickly to a banking crisis in the strict, Anna Schwartz, sense. They therefore fall within the scope of the present discussion.

With the distinction between the two types of crisis, banking and financial, and the two types of cause, capital and liquidity, clearly in mind, we can proceed to an examination of the 2007–09 crisis.

II. 2007–2009: Liquidity or Capital?

A comparison between the 2007–09 crisis, the first major banking crisis of the twenty-first century, and the crisis of 1929–33, the first major banking crisis of the twentieth century, helps answer the question.

What was the main cause of the crisis of 1929–33?[14] The US economy started to decline after the 1929 Stock Market Crash. The decline continued until 1933, by which time money income in the USA had fallen by 53 per cent and real income by 36 per cent. There had been wave after wave of bank failures. These did not end until the closure of all banks by President Roosevelt and the suspension of gold shipments abroad on 6 March 1933. Why did these waves of bank failures occur?

There are two primary, competing explanations: (i) banking practices of previous years which saw banks getting into securities dealings; and (ii) the behaviour of the Federal Reserve. The first explanation has been examined by Peach,[15] Benston,[16] and Kroszner and Rajan,[17] among many others. All found that securities dealing did not bring the banks down. The cause was substantial pressure on bank liquidity, unrelieved by Federal Reserve action. Banks were forced to sell their holdings of government bonds at a big discount, thus adding shortage of capital to shortage of liquidity.

That was manifestly a liquidity crisis in its origin.[18] How did it spread? As the monetary approach to the balance of payments suggests, the monetary squeeze in the USA affected those countries pegged to the US dollar (through gold, at this time) but left countries without such a link substantially unaffected. Countries such as Sweden and the UK, which broke early from the gold standard, escaped the US

---

[14] A brief overview of these years can be found in the introductory essay to Forrest Capie and Geoffrey Wood (eds), *Critical Writings on the Great Depression* (Oxford: Routledge, 2010).

[15] William N. Peach, *The Security Affiliates of National Banks* (Baltimore: Johns Hopkins Press, 1941).

[16] George J. Benston, *The Separation of Commercial and Investment Banking: the Glass-Steagall Act Revisited and Reconsidered* (New York: Oxford University Press, 1990).

[17] Randall S. Kroszner and Raghuram G. Rajan 'Is the Glass-Steagall Act Justified? A Study of the U.S. Experience with Universal Banking Before 1933', 84(4) *The American Economic Review* 810 (1994).

[18] This is certainly not to deny that the banks also had other problems. Many banks were heavily involved in call loans to the New York Stock Exchange (NYSE), and when the NYSE broke many of these loans would have gone bad. Thus they would certainly have experienced considerable losses on their earning assets.

problems, while those which stayed with the gold standard, such as France, experienced banking strains and severe recessions.

How did the recent crisis spread? The contrast with 1929–33 could not be sharper. The recent crisis spread between countries whose exchange rates were floating (the USA and the UK, for example). And it did not spread across all areas that used a single currency—the extreme case of fixed exchange rates—for the banking systems of some countries in the Eurozone were either unaffected or only slightly affected (for example, Finland). The crisis was not triggered by a scramble for liquidity. We can conclude that *the first crisis of the twenty-first century was a capital crisis, not a liquidity crisis.*[19]

There have been numerous explanations given for this recent crisis. We consider them in turn, and discuss in conclusion some of the consequences of the crisis, the increase in moral hazard and the reduction in competition that the policy response to the crisis has produced. Our starting point is a comparison of the recent crisis with some notable earlier ones. Time has allowed some firm conclusions about the origins of many previous crises, and this can help in understanding the most recent crisis.

III. A Brief Historical Account

First, we examine the seasonal and cyclical pattern of early crises. It is widely accepted that in the nineteenth and early twentieth centuries there was a seasonal pattern to banking crises.[20]

The still-accepted explanation for this seasonality is that given by Jevons in 1866. He observed a seasonal pattern, associated with the agricultural cycle, in asset demand. Reserve/deposit ratios for banks fell in the spring and the autumn when there was a seasonal upturn in the demand for both currency and credit. So it was in spring and autumn that banking systems were at their most vulnerable.[21] These were therefore manifestly all liquidity crises. In contrast, there was little cyclical regularity; Gary Gorton[22] found that crises usually occurred at business-cycle peaks, but not by any means at every business-cycle peak.

---

[19] Happily, in the twenty-first century, world trade rules ensured there was no outbreak of protectionism to make the situation worse. The role of protection in spreading the 1929–33 recession has been discussed many times—an outstanding and brief overview can be found in Forrest Capie, *Protection and Depression* (London: Macmillan, 1993). How it impeded recovery in the USA is set out clearly in Allan Meltzer, 'The Smoot Hawley Tariff and Economic Recovery', in Karl Brunner (ed), *The Great Depression Revisited* (London: Nijhoff, 1981, 1982) 148–63. Chapter 2 by Michael Gadbaw in this volume, considers the role of trade regulation in detail.

[20] Jeffrey A. Miron, 'Financial Panics, the Seasonality of the Nominal Interest Rate, and the Founding of the Fed', 76(1) *The American Economic Review* 125 (1986).

[21] The seasonal pattern in interest rates largely vanished when central banks started smoothing the interest-rate cycle. They could do this only after 1914, with the founding of the Federal Reserve, as it was a worldwide cycle.

[22] Gary Gorton, 'Banking Panics and Business Cycles', 40 *Oxford Economic Papers* 221 (1988).

The East Asian crises of the mid-1990s were certainly not all identical, but they did have common features. There were asset-price booms, followed by crashes, problems in banking systems, and flight from currencies.[23] The build-up of foreign currency indebtedness was encouraged by the pegged exchange-rate regime. Because of the guarantees, there was both undiversified lending and undiversified borrowing by banks. In addition, again because of the guarantees, the problem was large in scale.

None of the crises so far discussed necessitated an injection of capital.[24] Even the East Asian banks required liquidity, albeit in many cases in a currency their central banks could not supply. But Japan's problems of the 1990s were different and were on an altogether greater scale than those so far discussed. In the Great Depression, US banks lost capital equal to about 3–4 per cent of the 1930 US gross national product (GNP). In the 1990s, Japanese banks lost capital equal to about 15–20 per cent of the 1990 Japanese GNP.[25] Accordingly, the first point to emerge from the historical comparison is that while the recent crisis was not unprecedented, the Japanese crisis would appear to be the only precedent.

The Japanese crisis started with the bursting of an asset bubble at the end of the 1980s and culminated in 1997 with the failure of several major financial institutions. In the second half of the 1980s, Japan had experienced above-trend growth and near-zero inflation. The resulting optimism led to a surge in the prices of most assets. There was financial market deregulation, and credit standards were eased. The stock market boomed, peaking at the end of 1989. Then the Ministry of Finance introduced limits on bank lending to the real estate sector. There was a fall in property prices and in the stock market. These damaged Japanese banks, since the fall in property prices undermined the real estate companies to which they had lent, and the decline in the value of banks' equity holdings also put pressure on their capital. The entire system was weakened. Then, in November 1997, Sanyo Securities declared bankruptcy. This resulted in Japan's first interbank loan default. Two weeks later Hokkaido Tokushoku was unable to borrow in the interbank market and had to declare bankruptcy—the first failure of a major Japanese bank since World War II. Only a week later Yamaichi Securities, one of the four biggest security dealers in Japan, failed. It soon emerged that the rumours of fraud that had led to its failure were true. Next, before the end of the month, Tokuyo City Bank failed. The three-month Eurodollar Tokyo Interbank Borrowing Rate rose sharply above its London equivalent. Spreads sharply widened in the domestic interbank market, and by late November 1997 some banks were finding even overnight borrowing difficult. By the end of 1997 the government decided that 'something must be done'. They decided to inject taxpayers' funds, and also approved accounting changes which would allow banks to use either market or book value, whichever

---

[23] Ronald I. McKinnon and Huw Pill, 'Exchange-Rate Regimes for Emerging Markets: Moral Hazard and International Overborrowing', 15(3) *Oxford Review of Economic Policy* 19 (1999).

[24] The same is true of the numerous nineteenth-century banking crises in France, and those in Italy from the middle of the nineteenth to the early twentieth century.

[25] We are indebted to Charles Calomiris of Columbia University for these noteworthy data.

they wished, when valuing their share and real estate portfolios. There is plainly much in common between the background circumstances of the Japanese crisis and the recent, more widespread one.[26]

IV. Why the Recent Crisis?

It is possible to divide the explanations for this crisis into ten groups. These are not mutually exclusive; all may have played a part: (a) macro-economic imbalances; (b) lax monetary policy; (c) regulatory and supervisory failures; (d) too-big-to-fail (TBTF) doctrine and distorted incentives; (e) excesses of securitization; (f) unregulated firms, lightly regulated firms, and the shadow banking system; (g) corporate governance failures; (h) risk-management failures, excessive leverage, and excessive complexity; (i) the usual suspects: greed, euphoria, and others; and (j) faulty economic theories.

The first four groups of explanations put the blame mainly on the authorities (governments, regulators, central bankers). Groups (e)–(i) blame mainly the markets (financial products, managers, risk, greed, poor lending, leverage). The last group (faulty theories) blames economists.

A. Macroeconomic imbalances notably between the USA and China

The linkage to trade liberalization and the trade imbalances (the so-called China factor) have been cited as causes of the crisis. 'Credit expansion in the US was financed by countries with sizable current account surpluses, notably China and oil exporting nations'.[27] Although there is nothing unusual about one country wanting to borrow and another to lend, large and persistent imbalances should prompt examination. Accordingly, the role of the IMF in the surveillance of macroeconomic policies has come under greater scrutiny since the crisis.

B. Lax monetary policy in the USA and other countries

Easy money and cheap credit fuelled the boom. Interest rates in the USA were for some years below what the Taylor Rule (the rule which has the central bank's policy rate set according to deviations from trend of nominal GNP) implied. The measurement of inflation essentially ignored asset prices, in particular house prices. This led in turn to the ignoring of the 'elephant in the room', the large asset-price bubble, including in particular a nationwide surge in house prices, which eventually

---

[26] There is also much in common between the official responses to the episodes, but that is not a concern of this Chapter.

[27] See House of Lords' European Union Committee, 'The Future of EU Financial Regulation and Supervision', 14th Report of Session 2008–09, 17 June 2009, at 7, <http://www.publications.parliament.uk/pa/ld200809/ldselect/ldeucom/106/106i.pdf> (visited 9 August 2010).

burst in August 2007.[28] 'An asymmetric approach to managing interest rates, whereby policy is loosened when asset prices plunge but policymakers remain indifferent to asset prices until they burst' has been cited as a cause of the crisis.[29] In the phrase of the longest-serving chairman of the Federal Reserve (from 1951 to 1970), William McChesney Martin, 'the role of the central bank is to take away the punch bowl just when the party is going'. Not, let it be emphasized, when the hangover has taken hold.

C. Failures of regulation and failures of supervision

There were plenty of regulatory and supervisory failures (as well as a degree of regulatory capture or, at the very least, excessive group-think). Rules regarding capital proved inadequate; accounting rules exacerbated problems; and the absence of rules on liquidity was unfortunate. Indeed, capital and accounting regulations actually made things worse by being procyclical, with rules on risk-weighting capital combining with mark-to-market accounting to reduce requirements in good times and raise them sharply in bad.[30] And the most glaring mistake and omission is that there was no appropriate legal framework to deal with cross-border financial crises. Supervision failed at the level of individual institutions (AIG being a notable example) and at the systemic level, where systemic risk considerations were not properly taken into account.

D. The TBTF doctrine and distorted incentives

The belief that some institutions were too-big-to-fail (and belief too in its variants, too interconnected to fail, too complex to fail, too many to fail) and other distorted incentives (a system that rewards short-term profits at the expense of long-term stability) triggered—and continue to trigger—huge moral hazard incentives. Huertas[31] has pointed out that the sudden and unpredictable reversal in resolution policy that marked the failure of Lehman Brothers profoundly changed market expectations and led to a general flight to quality. As straight after AIG was bailed out and a couple of weeks before Lehman Brothers failed, Fannie Mae and Freddie Mac had received support, and TBTF expectations were inflamed. The sudden

---

[28] This may be a variant of 'Goodhart's law': that any observed statistical regularity will tend to collapse once pressure is placed upon it for control purposes. See Charles Goodhart, *Monetary Theory and Practice: The UK Experience* (London: MacMillan, 1984) 96. See also Charles Goodhart, 'What Weight Should be Given to Asset Prices in the Measurement of Inflation?', 111(472) *The Economic Journal* F335 (2001), <http://www.jstor.org/stable/2667880> (visited 9 August 2010).

[29] See John Plender, 'Just Targeting Symptoms of the Crisis is too Neat', *Financial Times*, 25 February 2010.

[30] The combination of Basel II and mark-to-market fair value accounting was almost a dooms day machine in itself—both reducing capital requirements under the wrong assumption that the system was extremely strong at the end of the asset price boom, and then reversing horribly during the crash.

[31] Thomas Huertas, 'Resolution as a Source of Contagion', presented at the Financial Markets Group and Bank of England conference on Sources of Contagion, 25–26 February 2010, London. See also Thomas Huertas, *Crisis: Cause, Containment and Cure* (Basingstoke: Palgrave Macmillan, 2010).

change exacerbated instability in the financial system. This illustrates the need to remove or properly price the implicit guarantee that TBTF institutions (both banks and 'systemically significant' financial institutions) at the moment enjoy.[32]

E. Excesses of securitization

This was the 'causa proxima' of the crisis. The securitization market grew, encouraged by: accounting and capital rules, financial innovation, government housing and lending policies to encourage home ownership amongst the poor or less prosperous (sub-prime), mortgage policies and mortgage regulation (in the USA and in the UK) that proved inadequate given what some institutions did, the ratings method that ratings agencies applied to securitized products, and the reliance on those ratings both for regulatory purposes and as a substitute for due diligence by the financial institutions themselves. The term 'securitization' is often used as a shorthand for all these various factors—government policies, regulatory actions, and behaviour of the private sector—that combined to cause the securitization bubble. Much has been written about this, since the problems that commenced in the summer of 2007 were clearly related to the securitization market. But it would be wrong to describe securitization—a technique needed to bring market liquidity—as 'the cause' of the crisis. The mortgage market in the USA and its associated credit ratings were premised on the fact that there had been no significant fall in house prices *nationwide* in fifty years of data, and such a decline occurred.

F. The part played by derivatives markets, unregulated firms, lightly regulated firms, and the shadow banking system

The common denominator of these firms, markets, and products that now constitute a major part of the financial system is their lighter regulatory, clearing, and accounting structure. Unregulated firms (such as credit-rating agencies), lightly regulated firms (such as hedge funds), and the shadow banking system, generally, have also been blamed for the crisis. While credit-rating agencies have received much negative publicity,[33] hedge funds and other alternative investment funds have been relatively unscathed. According to Ken Scott, 'CDS or derivatives in general . . . created none of the losses. . . . They are an instrument for transferring,

---

[32] Some authors have warned about the systemic impact of 'too-safe-to-fail' transactions (such as repo transactions), suggesting that macro-prudential supervision should be more concerned about 'seemingly fail-safe assets' which are typically beyond the radar of micro-prudential supervision. See Viral Acharya, 'Why Bankers Must Bear the Risk of "Too Safe to Fail" Assets', *Financial Times*, 18 March 2010: 'If a financial activity is viable only if its systemic risk must be borne by society while its profits in good times remain privatised in the financial sector, then it is time to revisit the desirability of the activity in the first place'.

[33] A recent US Senate investigation into the role of the credit rating agencies (CRAs) in the financial crisis has exposed the conflicts of interest that riddle their business model. See 'Rating Agencies' Nixon Moment', *Financial Times*, 24 April 2010.

and thereby spreading, some of the risk, and they worked as designed'.[34] However, naked credit default swaps (CDS) have come under a great deal of scrutiny (with calls for their regulation) following the crisis in Greece. The expression 'shadow banking system' is imprecise and its contours are not clearly defined. According to Roubini,[35] broker-dealers, hedge funds, private equity groups, structured investment vehicles and conduits, money market funds, and non-bank mortgage lenders are all part of this shadow system. Other commentators relate the shadow banking system to the growth of the securitization of assets.[36] Gary Gorton and others believe that it was the (wholesale) run on the repo market during 2008—the bank run not so much on depository institutions as on the shadow banking system—that caused the crisis. Gorton explains that, while in the past depositors ran to their banks and demanded cash in exchange for their checking accounts, the 2008 panic involved financial firms 'running' on other financial firms by not renewing repo agreements or increasing the repo margin, thus forcing sudden deleveraging and leading to many banking insolvencies. Earlier banking crises have many features in common with the current crisis. History can help understand the current situation and guide thoughts about regulatory reform, by making the shadow banking system less vulnerable to panic.[37]

G. Corporate governance failures

The misaligned incentives between the short-term interests of bankers (due to their compensation/bonus pay structure) and the long-term interest, and indeed the very survival, of their firms must be addressed. Pay structures, relationships between managers and shareholders, the relationships with other stakeholders and the

---

[34] See Kenneth Scott, 'Criteria for Evaluating Failure Resolution Plans' (Mimeo presented at 'Ending Government Bailouts as We Know Them' Policy Workshop, Stanford University, 10 December 2009, on file with authors).

[35] See Nouriel Roubini, 'The Shadow Banking System is Unravelling: Roubini Column in the Financial Times. Such Demise Confirmed by Morgan and Goldman Now Being Converted into Banks', <http://www.roubini.com/roubini-monitor/253696/the_shadow_banking_system_is_unravelling_roubini_column_in_the_financial_times_such_demise_confirmed_by_morgan_and_goldman_now_being_converted_into_banks> (visited 9 August 2010).

[36] See Tobias Adrian and Hyun Song Shin, 'The Shadow Banking System: Implications for Financial Regulation', Federal Reserve Bank of New York Staff Report No 382, 1 July 2009, <http://papers.ssrn.com/sol3/papers.cfm?abstract_id=1441324> (visited 9 August 2010). In this article, they argue that although securitization was intended as a way to transfer credit risk to those better able to absorb losses, instead, it increased the fragility of the entire financial system by allowing banks and other intermediaries to 'leverage up' by buying one another's securities.

[37] See Gorton, above n 2, at 13. Gorton observes that the 'great panic' which commenced in August 2007 is no different from the panics of 1907 or 1893, except that in 2007 'most people had never heard of the markets that were involved, did not know how they worked, or what their purposes were. Terms like subprime mortgage, asset-backed commercial paper conduit, structured investment vehicle, credit derivative, securitization, or repo market were meaningless'. And just like deposit bank runs earlier, the securitized banking system, which is in essence a real banking system, 'allowing institutional investors and firms to make enormous, short-term deposits', was vulnerable to a panic. What should be more troubling is that the events commencing with the August 2007 waterfall were not a retail panic involving individuals, but a wholesale panic involving institutions, where large financial firms 'ran' on other financial firms, making the system insolvent.

respective responsibilities of each need to be reassessed. Crucial here is that shareholders acknowledge and act on their responsibilities.[38]

H. Risk-management failures, bad lending, excessive leverage, and excessive complexity

Banks and the shadow banking system built up extraordinary leverage, which reached a historical maximum in June 2007. Over the preceding years, bank credit expansion was on average much faster than the growth rate of bank deposits. Banks achieved this through reducing their liquid assets, borrowing (massively and short term) in wholesale markets, securitizing, and increasing leverage. All these factors left them more exposed to any fall in asset prices. (The parallels with the Japanese crisis are particularly striking here.) The decline in lending standards also contributed to the crisis.[39] Lord Turner (then and currently Chairman of the Financial Services Authority in the UK)[40] has claimed that some trading activities are socially useless.[41] Management failed to conduct appropriate due diligence, in particular with regard to subprime decisions, and relied unthinkingly on ratings. Complexity and opacity are risks per se, and were not properly priced in the build up of the crisis. In the words of Buchheit: 'When history looks back on this crisis, a big culprit will be the astonishing complexity of modern financial instruments and the drafting of their contracts'.[42] Scott and Taylor, who blame the toxic assets on banks' balance sheets as one of the causes of the crisis, emphasize how 'maddeningly complex' securitization was and suggest that 'mandated transparency is the only solution'.[43] One intriguing issue is the extent to which certain financial operations or vehicles are Ponzi schemes or other types of quasi-fraudulent transactions intended to mislead or to conceal losses.[44] While fraud is clearly a crime, and

[38] Martin Wolf, 'The Challenge of Halting the Financial Doomsday Machine', *Financial Times*, 21 April 2010: 'The combination of state insurance (which protects creditors) with limited liability (which protects shareholders) creates a financial doomsday machine'.

[39] Conrad Voldstad (Chief Executive of the International Swaps and Derivatives Association, ISDA), 'We Have Failed to Address the Real Cause of the Financial Crisis', *Financial Times*, 7 July 2010: 'Bad lending, driven by poor underwriting standards and awful risk management, created and drove the crisis'.

[40] Interview of Lord Turner, 'How to Tame Global Finance', *Prospect*, 27 August 2009.

[41] Ibid. Lord Turner asserts that many of the financial activities which had proliferated in the City of London over the past ten years were 'socially useless'. He neither defined the term nor provided any evidence for the assertion.

[42] Lee Buchheit, 'We Made it Too Complicated', 27 *International Financial Law Review* 24 (2008), at 24, <http://www.iflr.com> (visited 9 August 2010): 'We . . . reached the point where some financial engineers have managed to baffle even themselves. Along the way though, they seem to have befuddled their boards of directors, risk management committees, lawyers, accountants, customers and regulators'.

[43] See Kenneth Scott and John Taylor, 'Why Toxic Assets Are so Hard to Clean Up', *Wall Street Journal*, 20 July 2009, <http://online.wsj.com/article/SB124804469056163533.html> (visited 2 October 2010).

[44] William White, 'Modern Macroeconomics is on the Wrong Track', 46(4) *Finance and Development* 15 (2009), at 17, quoting Minsky: 'Minsky (1982) also spoke of stages of credit growth, with the horizon of the credit getting ever shorter, culminating into what was essentially Ponzi finance. Loans would, in the last stage of the boom, be made to pay the interest on previous loans.'

individuals such as Madoff should have been caught and prosecuted much earlier, there are other complex transactions or schemes which may be intended to obfuscate or disguise the real financial position of a firm. In this 'murky terrain', firms may sometimes exploit opportunities for regulatory arbitrage or 'forum shopping'. At other times they may be playing on the fringes of the law.[45] The report published by Anton Valukas on his investigations of Lehman Brothers raises eyebrows about the questionable use of the so-called Repo 105 transactions:

Lehman's Repo 105 practice consisted of a two-step process: (1) under-taking Repo 105 transactions followed by (2) the use of Repo 105 cash borrowings to reduce liabilities, thus reducing leverage. A few days after the new quarter began, Lehman would borrow the necessary funds to repay the cash borrowings plus interest, repurchase the securities, and restore the assets to its balance sheet. Lehman never publicly disclosed its use of Repo 105 transactions, its accounting treatment for these transactions, the considerable escalation of its total Repo 105 usage in late 2007 and into 2008 or the material impact these transactions had on the firm's publicly reported net leverage ratio.[46]

The use of an accounting artifice that allowed Lehman Brothers to move assets off the balance sheet to improve its results suggests that in some cases complexity and opacity can be intended to misrepresent the true financial implications of certain transactions or to conceal financial distress.

I. 'The usual suspects'—greed, euphoria, etc.

Human frailty is always a factor in both crisis and non-crisis situations. Furthermore, excessive 'group-think' and 'herd behaviour' were also to blame. What was surely partly at fault is 'unbridled greed'—a system of incentives that rewarded the pursuit of excessive profits, while not appropriately internalizing the costs of losses. 'Too-big-to-fail' plainly contributed to this; but again, shareholders in institutions must surely take some responsibility for the contracts that they sign with their employees.

J. Faulty economic theories

In the decades that preceded the great crash of 2008, some relied with almost unquestioning faith on the efficient market theory—markets as self-correcting

---

[45] See Gillian Tett, 'Global Harmony a Distant Prospect Despite Lehman Outrage', *Financial Times*, 16 March 2010: 'The conditions which gave rise to the kind of regulatory arbitrage that Lehman exploited—namely a fragmented global regulatory and accounting regime—do not seem to be on their way out.... What drove Repo 105 ... was a form of "forum shopping"'. Michael Lewis, *The Big Short: Inside the Doomsday Machine* (London: Allen Lane, 2010) 43, suggests that the line between gambling and investment is artificial and thin.

[46] See Lehman Brothers Holdings Inc. Chapter 11 Proceedings Examiner's Report, 11 March 2010, at 733–4, <http://lehmanreport.jenner.com> (9 August 2010). For press coverage see *Financial Times*, 13–14 March 2010.

mechanisms with rational expectations.[47] The existence of transaction and information costs was neglected, and it was forgotten that theory as well as much evidence says that markets tend to display these admirable efficiency properties *on average*, not all the time. Further, a certain belief in the superiority of mathematics, game theory and modelling over what were perceived as less rigorous disciplines—law, political science, psychology, sociology, history—permeated much research and teaching in economics and finance departments.[48] Utopian interpretations of economic theories can be construed as a 'causa remota' of the crisis. At times, a crude reliance on modelling with insufficient or incomplete data proved catastrophic. Particularly damaging was the neglect (and not just in the above-noted case of the housing market) of all but recent history. Any institution which based its risk modelling on even the preceding ten years of daily data was drawing its data from what a longer perspective would have shown to be an unusually benign period; and many of those who looked at a longer perspective nonetheless behaved as if the change in the environment over the preceding few years would last forever. Cottier, in his excellent analysis of the challenges ahead for international economic law, suggests that the financial crisis 'epitomizes the failures of a strictly disciplinary tradition of fragmentation and specialization, and the lack of truly interdisciplinary research', and suggests the need to deepen the relationship between international economic law, economics, and other social sciences, such as international relations theory.[49] Very few economists—with White[50] and Borio, at the Bank for International Settlements (BIS), and Roubini[51] as some of the most notable exceptions—predicted the magnitude of the crisis. In a visit to the London School of Economics (LSE) in November 2008, Queen Elizabeth II asked Luis Garicano why no economist had seen the crisis coming. Some had, but no one appeared inclined to listen. Westbrook wrote:

Why was orthodox finance[52] so convincing, for so long, and yet so wrong? One might start by noting that finance has been oddly insensitive to law. Financial markets are essentially

[47] See White, above n 44, at 16: 'The recent crisis has demonstrated the inadequacy of models based on the assumption of rational expectations. . . . [T]he simplifying assumptions on which much of modern macroeconomics is based were not useful in explaining real world developments'.

[48] See generally Financial Services Authority, 'The Turner Review: A Regulatory Response to the Global Banking Crisis', March 2009, <http://www.fsa.gov.uk/pages/Library/Corporate/turner/index.shtml> (visited 9 August 2010).

[49] Thomas Cottier, 'Challenges Ahead in International Economic Law', 12 *Journal of International Economic Law* 3 (2009), at 12.

[50] William White was Economic Adviser and Head of the Monetary and Economic Department of the Bank for International Settlements from May 1995 to June 2008. His speeches and the BIS Annual Reports which included numerous warnings about the perils of the bubbles that were emerging in international financial markets were all but ignored.

[51] Nouriel Roubini, known in some circles as Dr Doom, predicted the crisis as far back as 2006. See generally his archived articles on his website 'Roubini Global Economics' at <http://www.rge.com>. See e.g. Nouriel Roubini, 'Revisiting My July/August 2006 Prediction of a US Recession in 2007', *Roubini Global Economics*, <http://www.roubini.com/roubinimonitor/160927/revisiting_my_-july_august_2006_prediction_of_a_us_recession_in_2007> (visited 9 August 2010).

[52] See generally David A. Westbrook, *Out of Crisis: Rethinking our Financial Markets* (Boulder: Paradigm Publishers, 2009). Westbrook explains that financial markets are like networks and that no firm should be too big to be resolved without substantial interruption to the trading operations of

legal. Collateral is a form of property; derivatives are contracts; corporations and fiat money are creatures of law. Economics, however, has always aspired to be a natural science, and so has considered the social as if it were natural. This fundamental ontological error has led to fanciful pricing models, as if we could model the movements of legal instruments like we model the movements of the stars. When times are good, or trading intervals are very short, such conceits may be overlooked. But when times are bad, it becomes obvious that legal phenomena deform under political and social stresses, as holders of Greek debt or Lehman Brothers collateral ought to be amply aware.

V. A Longer Perspective

While *financial crises* ('pseudo' crises in Schwartz's terminology) are a fairly common feature of the economic cycle, *banking* crises ('real' crises) are much rarer. Banking crises are a subset of financial crises distributed differently in time and in space. Financial crises may well be inherent to the business cycle, or to human nature itself. Kindleberger[53] and Minsky[54] have both argued that they are an inevitable part of the business cycle, and result from irrational reactions and myopia. Some banking theorists have argued, in a somewhat similar manner, that the structure of bank balance sheets makes panics inevitable.[55] If we are persuaded by one argument or the other (or both), then we should expect crises always to be with us. Perhaps we should have that expectation so far as financial crises are concerned; but the evidence is that we should not hold that expectation for banking crises.

Banking crises tend to occur (if they occur) around the time of cyclical down-turns, and are closely associated with large declines in the value of bank loans, reflecting declines in the fortunes of the borrowers. Second, they have become more common in recent years, despite government interventions (such as government insurance of deposits) intended to achieve the opposite. Third, panics can happen without failures and failures without panics—the panic of 1907 in the USA was not associated with a rise in the bank failure rate, and the wave of agricultural bank failures in the USA in the 1920s was not accompanied by a systemic panic. This suggests that uncertainty about small losses can cause panic without failure, while large losses with clear incidence cause failure without causing widespread panic. Most notable of all is that there are substantially different 'propensities' for crises at different times and places. The US banking system has historically been crisis prone. Britain too was crisis prone, but that changed in the middle of the

counter-parties. He also draws an analogy between financial markets and eco- systems. Economics, he argues, should abandon its claim to be like physics.

[53] Charles P. Kindleberger, *Manias, Panics and Crashes: a History of Financial Crises* (London: Macmillan, 1978).

[54] Hyman P. Minsky, 'The Financial Instability Hypothesis' (reprint), The Jerome Levy Economics Institute Working Paper No 74, May 1992.

[55] See e.g. James Tobin, 'Financial Intermediation and Deregulation in Perspective', 3(2) *Bank of Japan Monetary and Economic Studies* 19 (1985).

nineteenth century. After 1866 there was no crisis—even the outbreak of World War I did not provoke one. In the years 1875–1913, only four countries experienced severe waves of bank insolvency. This diverse pattern shows clearly that there must be more to banking crises than the inevitable features of human nature or bank balance sheets.

Changes in the fragility of banking systems usually result from changes in the 'rules of the banking game'. Such changes can be stability promoting, as was the Bank of England's adoption of and commitment to a lender of last resort role after 1866, or risk promoting, as were the pre-1893 Italian guarantees of the property lending of the Banca di Roma. The same story continues up to the present. Restrictions on structure have often proved perverse—for example, the protection of unit banking in the USA. In contrast, Canada's early allowing of nationwide branch banking contributed to stability. Getting the rules of the banking game wrong readily makes the game go wrong.

Did that happen this time? Looking at the USA, we certainly see a repetition of previous mistakes. There was pressure from Congress on banks, on Fannie Mae, and on Freddie Mac, to promote house ownership by taking on more high-risk mortgages. There was Federal Housing Administration subsidy of high mortgage leverage. Foreclosures were discouraged. The legislation of 2006 encouraged rating agencies to relax standards on the rating of securitizations. Unsurprisingly, the US housing market boomed.

Banks elsewhere, some already caught up in their own housing booms, were drawn into the US boom. Regulators were defective. Preoccupied with individual banks, they did not see, or ignored, that securitization was simply spreading risk around the system, and focused instead on the illusory reduction in individual bank risk which it produced.[56] Problems spread round the world and systemic risk expanded.

In addition, it should be noted that the recent crisis was remarkably like the Japanese one. Easy money and steady growth followed by ill-thought-out regulatory policies were sufficient to cause the Japanese crisis. They were also present in the run-up to the present one.

VI. The Regulatory Responses

We now turn to the flurry of regulatory responses, which can be divided into five groups.[57] The first looks at the substance of regulation, at the 'what to regulate', with new rules (or proposed rules) for capital, liquidity, and other indicators of banking and financial soundness. In this we can include the new Basel proposals

---

[56] See Geoffrey Wood and Ali Kabiri, 'Firm Stability and System Stability: the Regulatory Delusion', in John Raymond LaBrosse, Rodrigo Olivares-Caminal and Dalvinder Singh (eds), *Managing Risk in the Financial System* (Cheltenham: Edward Elgar, 2011).

[57] See Rosa M. Lastra, 'The Check Book that the Banks Cannot Bounce', *Parliamentary Brief*, 2 March 2010, 27–8, <http://www.parliamentarybrief.com/articles/1/new/mag/83/1066/the-%20check-book-that.html> (visited 9 August 2010).

(sometimes referred to as Basel III)[58] and others that look at ways of enhancing the quality or quantity of regulation (from dynamic provisioning and rules to prevent excessive leverage to rules regarding bonuses or compensation schemes, rules on insolvency and early intervention) at the national, European, or international level. With regard to the scope of institutions to be regulated, Andrew Crocket advocates the need to 'widen the net' beyond the three pillars upon which financial regulation has traditionally rested (i.e. banking, securities, and insurance) to a wider range of institutions that are now central to financial stability. In particular, he cites the players involved in the originate-to-distribute model of credit intermediation, service providers such as clearing and settlement systems, credit-rating agencies, auditing firms, and private pools of capital such as hedge funds and private equity funds.[59] Perhaps the answer in some cases—for example, with regard to derivatives markets—is not more regulation, but more transparency and accountability, a well-functioning clearing system, and on-balance-sheet accounting treatment.

The second group of proposals looks at the structure of supervision and regulation, at the 'how' and the 'who', and the intensity of supervision. It should be noted though that all national 'architectures', whether one authority, twin-peak, or many regulators, failed to prevent the crisis.[60] Further, many of these proposals are nationally based. An 'international architecture' may have to be an essential part of any reform.

One of the major 'breakthroughs' in the response to the crisis is that a distinction is now made between macro-prudential supervision and micro-prudential supervision. According to the House of Lords' report on the Future of EU Financial Supervision and Regulation:[61]

macro-prudential supervision is the analysis of trends and imbalances in the financial system and the detection of systemic risks that these trends may pose to financial institutions and the economy.... Micro-prudential supervision is the day-to-day supervision of individual financial institutions.... The same or a separate supervisor can carry out these two functions.[62]

---

[58] The Basel Committee on Banking Supervision formally adopted reforms, known as Basel III, to require banks to hold more and better capital in September 2010, with the G20 endorsing these reforms at the Seoul Summit in November 2010. Basel III also introduced two international minimum standards for liquidity risk supervision Liquidity Coverage Ratio (LCR) and Net Stable Funding Ratio (NSFR). The implementation of the Basel III reforms allow for various periods of transition. See <http://www.bis.org/bcbs/basel3/b3summarytable.pdf> (visited 17 January 2012).

[59] See Andrew Crocket, 'Rebuilding the Financial Architecture', 46(3) *Finance & Development* 18 (2009), at 18.

[60] See the paper by Luis Garicano and Rosa M. Lastra in this issue for further elaboration on this point, in particular with regard to the EU proposals. In the USA, President Obama signed the new financial legislation on 21 July 2010. The Dodd–Frank Wall Street Reform and Consumer Protection Act of 2010, H.R. 4173, Public L. 111–203, is the major financial reform in the USA since the New Deal legislation in the 1930s. In the UK, the new Government launched a consultation document spelling out the proposals that the Chancellor had outlined in his Mansion House Speech: 'A New Approach to Financial Regulation: Judgment, Focus and Stability', 26 July 2010, <http://www.hm-treasury.gov.uk/d/consult_financial_regulation_condoc.pdf> (visited 9 August 2010).

[61] House of Lords' European Union Committee, above n 27.

[62] Ibid, at para 27 and 28.

The third group of proposals concerns the behaviour of the banking industry and bank managers and the need to internalize the costs of protection. Here one can include the proposal by Deutsche Bank CEO Josef Ackermann (set out at Davos in January 2010) to establish a European Rescue and Resolution Fund largely financed by the banking industry and the proposal of then IMF Managing Director Dominique Strauss-Kahn (on 19 March 2010) for a 'European Resolution Authority', an agency pre-financed by the banking industry as far as possible, to deal with failing cross-border banks in the EU.[63] Acknowledging the lack of adequate rules in this area, the European Commission published a Communication on 20 October 2009 proposing an EU framework for cross-border crisis management and a further Communication on bank resolution funds on 26 May 2010.[64]

A fourth group focuses on the fiscal side. In particular, 'extracting rents' (rather than merely profit taking) in a banking and financial market, which has been largely subsidized by governments' rescue packages and monetary and fiscal policies, raises controversy.[65] Acute moral hazard problems persist. The UK Government targeted compensation by imposing a one-off 50 per cent tax on the bonus pools of a number of financial institutions in the UK. Some economists have advocated the imposition of a (global) tax on financial transactions, akin to the Tobin tax (a tax on the value of foreign exchange transactions). This has been a divisive issue among EU member states with the UK Prime Minister David Cameron threatening to veto any EU wide Tobin tax while French President Nicolas Sarkozy declared that he would press on with a Tobin tax unilaterally regardless of his EU partners support.[66] The IMF issued a report on 27 June 2010 recommending that countries consider adopting two taxes: a Financial Stability Contribution and a Financial Activities Tax.[67]

A fifth group of proposals are bank structural reforms which aim to change the structure of the banking industry and the balance-sheet structure of commercial banks and other financial institutions so as to circumscribe the scope of institutions that receive governmental protection, to separate 'utility banking' from 'casino banking'. These proposals range from narrow banking to a full-scale mutualization

---

[63] See 'IMF Seeks Bank Crisis Agency', *Financial Times*, 20 March 2010.

[64] See European Commission, 'Communication from the Commission to the European Parliament, the Council, the European Economic and Social Committee and the European Central Bank: Bank Resolution Funds', COM(2010), 26 May 2010, <http://ec.europa.eu/internal_market/bank/crisis_management/index_en.htm> (visited 22 July 2010).

[65] See Plender, above n 29: 'Bankers in the boom were being paid bonuses not for brilliance but for excessive risk taking via leverage and for oligopolistic super-profits. Now they have been offered a state safety net and a steep yield curve, whereby they borrow at low cost to invest in higher yielding assets. This guarantees easy, low risk profits, on which they nonetheless expect bonuses'.

[66] See 'France to push ahead with "Tobin tax" proposal', *Financial Times*, 4 January 2012 and 'Fresh clashes brew over Tobin tax', *Financial Times*, 5 January 2012.

[67] International Monetary Fund, 'A Fair and Substantial Contribution by the Financial Sector', Final Report for the G-20, 27 June 2010. The IMF's recommended financial stability contribution is similar to the financial stability fee that Sweden adopted in 2009, a direct levy on Swedish banks based on bank liabilities and equity. For a discussion of financial taxes generally see Kern Alexander in this volume at Ch 19.

of the financial industry.[68] The so-called Volcker rule adopted by the Dodd–Frank Act is also a structural reform, albeit more limited.[69] The Volcker rule prohibits federally insured 'banking entities' from engaging in proprietary trading (subject to certain exceptions) and restricts their relationships with hedge funds and private equity funds.

Given the multiplicity of proposals, it might be sensible to implement a simple approach that considers what is essential to maintain financial stability while preserving competition on the one hand, and what is desirable and feasible in the longer term on the other hand. The establishment of a robust and well-understood framework for the resolution of cross-border financial institutions, a framework which includes rules on burden sharing, is an essential policy priority.[70] The alternatives to an orderly resolution—either a chaotic resolution or a bail-out—would be disastrous. Capitalism relies on the lure of wealth (privatization of gains) and the discipline imposed by the fear of bankruptcy (privatization of losses). It is imperative to reinstate a credible fear of bankruptcy for banks and other systemically significant financial institutions so as to ensure that banks once more play their proper role in a market economy.

VII. Concluding Observations

In this chapter, we have tentatively analysed the causes of the financial crisis of 2007–09 and outlined some of the responses. Following a distinction between liquidity crises and capital/solvency crises, we draw on the lessons of history to present the various culprits of the recent crisis. This is not the final story, since only with the benefit of hindsight will anyone be able to write an account of what happened akin to Milton Friedman and Anna Schwartz's authoritative Monetary History of the United States, which in 1963, three decades after the New Deal legislation introduced in the USA by President Roosevelt, provided the definitive analysis of that Depression.

This was a solvency/capital crisis, not a mere liquidity banking crisis. As for the culprits, the observation with which we conclude is that it is remarkable how people tend to side with 'one side of the story'. *Laissez-faire* proponents tend to argue that it is an unfettered free market that encourages virtue and government regulation

---

[68] The narrow banking proposals have been again endorsed by John Kay, 'Narrow Banking: The Reform of Banking Regulation', Centre for the Study of Financial Innovation, 15 September 2009, <http://www.johnkay.com/wp-content/uploads/2009/12/JK-Narrow-Banking.pdf> (visited 9 August 2010); while Lawrence J. Kotlikoff has made a case for the mutualization of the financial industry in his book: Lawrence J. Kotlikoff, *Jimmy Stewart is Dead: Ending the World's Ongoing Financial Plague with Limited Purpose Banking* (Chichester: John Wiley & Sons, 2010).

[69] Dodd–Frank Wall Street Reform and Consumer Protection Act of 2010, H.R. 4173, Public L. 111–203, x 619.

[70] See generally The International Monetary Fund, 'Resolution of Cross Border Banks—a Proposed Framework for Enhanced Coordination', Report of the Legal and Monetary and Capital Markets Departments, 11 June 2010 (to which one of the authors, Professor Rosa M. Lastra, contributed), <http://www.imf.org/external/np/pp/eng/2010/061110.pdf> (visited 22 July 2010).

that destroys it; markets are the solution, and government is the problem. In contrast, those who believe that markets are principally to blame advocate more intrusive and extensive regulation and intervention. Where both groups tend to agree is that finance needs to go back to being an instrument directed towards improved wealth creation and development.[71] To ensure this, the fear of failure needs to return to the business of banking.

---

[71] See Speech of Lord Turner, 'What Do Banks Do, What Should they Do and What Public Policies are Needed to Ensure Best Results for the Real Economy?', CASS Business School, 17 March 2010: 'A critical issue is...whether this increased financial intensity has delivered value added for the real economy—whether it has improved capital allocation, increased growth or increased human welfare and choice...And whether it has made the economy more or less volatile to shocks'. See also <http://www.vatican.va/holy_father/benedict_xvi/encyclicals/documents/hf_ben-xvi_enc_20090629_caritas-in-veritate_en.html> (visited 18 March 2010).

PART II

ARCHITECTURE AND CONCEPTUAL ISSUES

2

Systemic Regulation of Global Trade and Finance: A Tale of Two Systems

*R. Michael Gadbaw**

I. Trade and Finance: The Twin Pillars of Systemic Regulation of the Global Economy

A. Nature or nurture?

The interplay of two global regulatory systems—finance and trade[1]—deserves scrutiny in our thinking about the crisis of 2007–09 with respect to what happened, the underlying causes, and how to identify and implement reforms that will mitigate or prevent crises of this magnitude in the future. Parallels to the Great Depression have been drawn as analysts, policymakers, regulators, politicians, and the general public try to develop a narrative to explain the events that reverberated across national borders to virtually every corner of the globe, utilizing the channels of globalization to spread the impact and threatening to undo many of the benefits (wealth, economic growth and asset values) to which trade and capital flows have been so instrumental. This chapter seeks to contribute to this dialogue by comparing and contrasting the way the global financial system and the global trading system performed as systemic regulators through the crisis. The argument will be made that the dramatic differences in the way each of these performed, with the collapse of the financial system while the trading system experienced only a

* In the interest of full disclosure, note that this chapter draws on the author's experience working in international economic law: in the White House (summer of 1973); in the Treasury Department and the Office of the US Trade Representative (1975–80); in private law firms (1980–1990) representing, among others, the semiconductor and computer industries; as Vice President and Senior Counsel of General Electric (1990–2008).

[1] The interplay of trade and finance is as old as economic history itself. See William J. Bernstein, *A Splendid Exchange; How Trade Shaped the World* (New York: Atlantic Monthly Press, 2008) 18: 'First, trade is an irreducible and intrinsic human impulse, as primal as the needs for food, shelter, sexual intimacy, and companionship. Second, our urge to trade has profoundly affected the trajectory of the human species'. See also Niall Ferguson, *The Ascent of Money: A Financial History of the World* (New York: The Penguin Press, 2008) 2: 'Despite our deeply rooted prejudices against "filthy lucre", however, money is the root of most progress'.

minor disruption, can be attributed to important differences in their underlying regulatory systems as reflected by their respective institutions, the rules, dispute settlement and enforcement mechanisms. Ultimately, we find two profoundly contrasting regulatory paradigms for trade and finance, reflecting underlying differences in market dynamics and policies regarding the interaction of markets and rules. How did these mutually interdependent systems evolve side by side in such dramatically different directions?

The importance of this debate should not be underestimated. Although the global economy is recovering from the worst of the asset declines in housing, household wealth and financial institution solvency, the question remains whether the global economy can recover in the absence of a greater sense of confidence among investors, consumers, employers and employees that comparable crises can be avoided or at least mitigated in the future. Moreover, can the global economy function properly when the two systems of trade and finance seem so out of synch in terms of the quality of their regulatory frameworks and the strains that must be absorbed by one when the other fails to carry its weight in maintaining the stability of the overall system.

B. Systemic performance—finance and trade—crisis to crisis

The totality of the collapse in our global economy, attributed in part to economic policies and regulatory failures, has led us to take a system wide view of causes and effects. Systemic failure and its counterparty systemic risk have entered our public policy lexicon. This kind of top-down preoccupation has its historical parallels. The Great Depression prompted a rethink of our economic policies and the adoption of Keynesian intervention to promote full employment and economic growth. Internationally, Lord Keynes and his colleagues seized the opportunity in the aftermath of World War II to create the Bretton Woods triumvirate, comprising the International Monetary Fund (IMF), the World Bank, and the General Agreement on Tariffs and Trade (GATT), to bring countries together in a comprehensive set of international institutions based on the rule of law and the principles of free trade and economic integration.[2] The series of financial crises over the ensuing decades— starting with the US decision to abandon the gold standard in the early 1970s,[3] followed by the Russian and Latin American crises of the 1990s, and the Asian crisis of 1998—actually reinforced the view that the system, as it had evolved at those

---

[2] For an excellent review of the origins of Bretton Woods and the challenges facing the system in the aftermath of the financial crisis, see Richard N. Gardner, 'The Bretton Woods-GATT System after Sixty-five Years: A Balance Sheet of Success and Failure', 47 *Columbia Journal of Transnational Law* 26 (2008), at 27; see also the paper by Andreas Lowenfeld in this issue at 575–595.

[3] One of the key linkages between trade and finance has been the use of trade measures for balance of payments reasons, the most significant case of which was the 10 per cent import surcharge imposed by President Nixon in 1971. See John H. Jackson, William J. Davey and Alan O. Sikes, Jr, *Legal Problems of International Economic Relations* (5th edn, St. Paul, MN: Thomson West, 2008) 1098–109.

times, was sound and could be managed, by the likes of the Committee to Save the World,[4] to handle the occasional crisis.

Now we find ourselves thinking once again about systemic failure, systemic risk and systemic regulation. Systemic risk is generally used only in connection with financial regulation to refer to 'a problem with payment or settlement systems or...some type of financial failure that induces a macroeconomic crisis'.[5] For reasons explained more fully below, the concept is used here more broadly to encompass a failure of any major pillar of our global economy, including trade and finance, which leads to a macroeconomic crisis. Including the trading system as a source of systemic risk is consistent with our historical experience in the 1930s when protectionism was an important factor in the cause, depth, and length of the Great Depression. Moreover, this perspective allows us to consider the policies and institutions that have led us, perhaps too easily, to take for granted the notion that trade cannot be a source of macroeconomic failure.

In the 1930s, what started as a financial crisis with a run on the banks, also turned into a full-blown economic crisis and more than a decade of depressed economic growth, notwithstanding a complete shift in the paradigm for government intervention from *laissez faire* to Keynesian intervention. The critical point for our purposes is the way the trading system performed as a result of the passage in 1930 of the Smoot–Hawley Tariff Act,[6] which erected insurmountable tariff barriers on goods coming into the USA and reduced both the value and the volume of international trade with the USA by as much as 50 per cent. Not only did this intervention account for a very high percentage in the decline in trade, as distinct from the fall in demand, but this intervention was mimicked by other countries that erected similar barriers around the globe, the cumulative result of which was to exacerbate the depression and block a critical avenue for post-crisis recovery.

The contrast with the crisis of 2007–09 is striking. While there was a decline of around 18 per cent in the peak-to-trough value of international trade in the first year of the crisis, that decline was virtually entirely the result of a decline in demand, not of government intervention.[7] Under the scrutiny of global institutions and private trackers, the government interventions were of minor consequence; less than 1 per cent of global trade by some accounts.[8] In the second year after the crisis (2011), global trade is expected to grow at a rate of over 9 per cent; and for many

---

[4] This reference comes from the cover of *Time*, 15 February 1999, <http://www.time.com/time/covers/0,16641,19990215,00.html> (visited 3 August 2010) which featured Robert Rubin, Lawrence Summers and Alan Greenspan for their work in the aftermath of the Asian financial crisis.

[5] Kern Alexander, Rahul Dhumale and John Eatwell, *Global Governance of Financial Systems: The International Regulation of Systemic Risk* (Oxford: Oxford University Press, 2006) 24.

[6] United States: Tariff Act of 1930, Act of 17 June 1930, 46 Stat. 685.

[7] The performance of the WTO in the course of the crisis has been ably analyzed in Brendan Ruddy, 'The Critical Success of the WTO: Trade Policies of the Current Economic Crisis', 13(2) *Journal of International Economic Law* 287 (2010) 475–95. Ruddy looks at the economic literature and the tracking systems that document and measure the effect of protectionist measures and concludes: 'unlike the trade restrictive measures of the Great Depression, measures taken during the current economic crisis have not materially contributed to the decline in trade volume and GDP'. This conclusion is also supported by the WTO's own analysis.

[8] Ibid, fn 48 and accompanying text.

countries, not least the USA, international trade is seen as one of the critical channels for economic recovery.[9]

In contrast to the trading system, which performed well throughout the crisis, the financial system seems to have failed in fundamental ways across the spectrum of monetary policy and prudential supervision.[10]

There is a growing consensus that regulators individually—and the regulatory system as a whole—should have anticipated some of the consequences of the behavior of the market and market participants and responded to counter those effects before they led to the collapse of the financial system.[11] It is this systemic

---

[9] For a very thorough analysis of the failure of protectionism to manifest in the course of the recent crisis, with a very low-key endorsement of the WTO's role, see Simon J. Evenett, Bernard M. Hoekman and Olivier Cattaneo (eds), *Effective Crisis Response and Openness: Implications for the Trading System* (Washington, DC: World Bank and Center for Economic and Policy Research, 2009), at 5. The countries that were most protectionist in their responses were not at the time members of the WTO (Algeria and Russia) (p. 5).

[10] To assist the reader, the primary sources for this description of the crisis are collected here. For a first-hand account of the collapse of Lehman Brothers and the ensuing collapse of the financial markets, see Andrew Ross Sorkin, *Too Big to Fail* (New York: Viking, 2009). Michael Lewis has looked at the small group of hedge fund managers who saw the coming crisis and took advantage of it by betting against it in Michael Lewis, *The Big Short: Inside the Doomsday Machine* (London: Allen Lane, 2009). Nassim Nicholas Taleb has looked at the role of financial models for valuing assets and risks and how these models miscalculated the probability of events with catastrophic consequences in Nassim Nicholas Taleb, *The Black Swan: The Impact of the Highly Improbable* (New York: Random House, 2007). Richard A. Posner documents his own conversion from a Chicago school critic of excessive financial regulation to a more pragmatic advocate for the proper balance of regulations and the market in a capitalist system, first in Richard A. Posner, *A Failure of Capitalism: The Crisis of '08 and the descent into Depression* (Cambridge, MA: Harvard University Press, 2009) and Richard A. Posner, *The Crisis of Capitalist Democracy* (Cambridge, MA: Harvard University Press, 2010). Simon Johnson has analyzed the concentration of the banking industry and the role of campaign contributions in shaping the regulatory framework for finance in Simon Johnson, *13 Bankers: The Wall Street Takeover and the Next Financial Meltdown* (New York: Pantheon Books, 2010).

[11] Some of the major regulatory failings cited as causes of the crisis: the failure of the monetary system to deal with global imbalances which facilitated the lax monetary policy of the Federal Reserve and the unwillingness to recognize the systemic risk of excessive credit leading to excessive risk taking; the role of Fannie Mae and Freddie Mac in subsidizing home ownership and the role of their implicit government guarantee in excessive risk taking, the role of the Community Reinvestment Act of 1977 (Codified to 12 USC 2901 note; Section 801 et seq. of title VIII of the Act of 12 October 1977, Pub. L. No. 95–128; 91 Stat. 1147, effective 12 October 1977) in requiring federal regulatory agencies to encourage banks to take on excessive risks in subprime mortgages; the Securities and Exchange Commission's (SEC) decision to loosen the leverage requirements on investment banks, failure of the SEC to identify the burgeoning fraud in regulated financial institutions; the repeal of the Glass–Steagell Act (The Banking Act of 1933, 48 Stat. 162) restrictions on the separation of investment and commercial banking, the authorization in Gramm–Leach–Bliley Act (The Financial Services Modern-ization Act of 1999, 113 Stat. 1338, Public Law 106–2) for financial holding companies to enter into a wide array of activities including banking insurance and securities while still enjoying federal deposit insurance; the failure to regulate over the counter derivatives later confirmed by legislation, the failure to see flaws in the AAA ratings that the rating agencies were giving to securitized mortgages, the failure of the Fed to regulate predatory lending of non-bank financial institutions, the failure to see how AAA-rated, mortgage-backed securities would undermine bank balance sheets, the failure to see the inadequacy of the risk assessment models of financial institutions and the failure to regulate the size of financial institutions leading to the too-big-to-fail problem. See generally Howard Davies and David Green, *Global Financial Regulation: The Essential Guide* (Cambridge: Polity Press, 2008); James Barth, Gerard Caprio, Jr and Ross Levine, *Rethinking Bank Regulation: Till Angels Govern* (New York: Cambridge University Press, 2006) which presents a comparative study of bank regulation across 150 countries; Viral V. Acharya and Matthew Richardson, *Restoring Financial Stability: How to Repair a Failed System* (New Jersey: John Wiley & Sons, 2009).

character of the collapse that lends the most credence to the conclusion that the regulators failed, because it appears that quite a number of factors had to work together to create an overall system-wide failure. What began as an asset bubble in the housing market[12] was fed by the availability of easy money (caused in part by global imbalances involving high saving countries like China and India exporting capital to low savings countries like the USA and UK) and was exacerbated by the ability of banks to securitize mortgages and move risk from their balance sheets to the broader markets, which in turn responded by creating insurance policies against the failure of these mortgage-backed securities and the institutions that held them. The volume of insurance policies on mortgage-backed securities, allowing investors to bet for and against their failure, by far exceeded the amount of underlying mortgages. The appetite for these mortgage-backed securities and their related insurance policies spread across the global financial system. Because many of these securities were rated AAA by the credit-rating agencies, some institutions could originate the instruments and sell them for a handsome fee while others could buy them as part of their underlying capital structure, allowing them to leverage themselves further to do more and more lending.

What regulators and market participants missed were the inherent risks of this interaction, which in hindsight have become all too clear. When housing prices started to decline, institutions at the center of the mortgage origination and securitization process started to fail. These failures tipped the balance in the market, undermining the value of mortgage-backed securities and in turn the institutions that held them. Because the mortgages were so much a part of the capital structure of many financial institutions, what started as a liquidity crisis quickly turned into a solvency crisis, which very quickly implicated institutions so interconnected that their failure (or impending failure) brought to a halt the entire system by which financial institutions perform their functions of clearing payments, intermediating investment, and allocating risk and capital. Compounding all of these market interactions are allegations of lack of transparency, fraud and misrepresentation at both the transactional and institutional level, together with complicity on the part of regulators who were mandated to oversee risk management, consumer protection, institutional integrity, and the proper functioning of markets.

At the end of the day, the numbers tell a story but cannot capture the full impact. In the USA alone, $11 trillion in household wealth and eight million jobs were lost as the economy hit an annualized rate of decline in gross domestic product (GDP) of 6.2 per cent in the fourth quarter of 2008.[13]

---

[12] In California, in 2007, over 90 per cent of the securitized mortgages were so-called thin file mortgages, that is, there was no verification of the income of the borrower; most of the mortgages insured by Freddie Mac and Fannie Mac were subprime mortgages since only 12 per cent of the Californian population could afford a median priced home (See Howard Savage, Current Housing Reports: 'Who Could Afford to Buy a Home in 2004', US Census Bureau, Issued 9 May 2009).

[13] Catherine Rampell, 'GDP Revision Suggests a Long, Steep Downfall', *New York Times,* 27 February 2009, <http://www.nytimes.com/2009/02/28/business/economy/28econ.html> (visited 10 September 2010).

The contrast in the performance of the global trade and financial systems in the course of the recent crisis leads to an important conclusion for policymakers: while systemic failure was the chief characteristic of the global financial system, the trading system, judged on its face solely by its performance in the course of this crisis, has emerged as a candidate for the most successful systemic regulator in the history of humankind.[14] The next section of this chapter analyzes this characterization by comparing the regulatory systems governing trade and finance in an attempt to identify those aspects of the two systems that seem to play the most important roles in protecting against systemic risk.

II. Characteristics of the Trade and Financial Systems: Bretton Woods Revisited

A. From a common origin to different paths

In the course of the recent crisis, trade did not exacerbate the crisis by translating the shock of the stock market crash into a contagion fed by chain reactions throughout the global economy. Instead, countries heeded the call in the G-20 statement of November 2008 that all economies refrain from protectionist interventions in their markets.[15] Meanwhile, the capital markets ground to a halt as the credit markets froze when banks and other financial institutions were unwilling to lend to all but the most creditworthy borrowers. This leads to the questions: Why do these regulatory systems look so different? How did they evolve in such different directions? What were the aspects of the trading system that helped protect it from systemic failure? How do these characteristics compare to the financial system?

In considering this question, it is helpful to remind ourselves what a 'political miracle'[16] the Bretton Woods system was.[17] The American Bankers Association claimed that the IMF would amount to 'handing over to an international body the power to determine the destination, time, and use of our money ... abandoning, without receiving anything in return, a vital part of American bargaining power'.[18] The National Foreign Trade Council, the National Association of Manufacturers

---

[14] See R. Michael Gadbaw, 'The WTO as a Systemic Regulator?', *The Globalist*, 16 February 2010, <http://www.theglobalist.com/storyid.aspx?StoryId=8214> (visited 3 August 2010).

[15] Paragraph 48 of the Pittsburgh Summit Communique, 25 September 2009.

[16] See Gardner, above n 2, at 28–32. Gardner points out the changes to the world order that have occurred since 1948, particularly:

> the 'money bags', the 'brains', the economic weight and the political influence are all more evenly distributed today than they were.... Yet the old and difficult issues that confronted the founding fathers of the Bretton-Woods system are still with us—how to reconcile freedom of international trade and payments with full employment and social justice at home, how to balance the need for effective international economic institutions with still-powerful demands for national economic sovereignty, and how to relate regional and bilateral economic arrangements to a global economic order.

[17] Powerful political and intellectual currents on both sides of the Atlantic opposed the creation of these institutions. Ibid, at 28.

[18] Ibid, at 31.

and the US Chamber of Commerce were staunchly opposed to the proposed International Trade Organization (ITO) and helped to kill it in the US Congress. In the end, the vision of the founding fathers prevailed:

> They conceived of a postwar economic system ruled by law. They wanted it to be a universal system ... rather than a collection of trading blocs. They wanted permanent international institutions to promote cooperation on monetary, trade, and development problems. And they wanted somehow to reconcile the concept of maximum possible freedom in trade and payments at the international level with the domestic pursuit by governments of progressive economic and social policies.[19]

'Monetary questions had to be dealt with before trade questions ... because countries would not be willing to commit themselves to tariff reductions if the conditions of competition could be completely altered by large and unforeseen changes in exchange rates'.[20] A fixed exchange rate system based on gold and special drawing rights was adopted when the Keynes proposal for a Clearing Union with global overdraft facilities proved too ambitious and the founders anticipated that there would be a high degree of voluntary coordination of economic policy. From a systemic perspective, the critical issue that the Bretton Woods founders faced was how to reconcile an open international trading system with the free movement of capital. In the end, the importance of open trade took preeminence over capital movements. Finally, there was a fight over whether to authorize, encourage or prohibit capital controls that ultimately led to a compromise in which capital controls were allowed, even encouraged, but countries were not required to cooperate in their application.

For our purposes, the fight over capital controls was the most important because it pitted the New York bankers against the founders in a fight that led to the triumph of finance ministries over the New York bankers and their central bank allies[21] and prompted Henry Morgenthau to proclaim that one of the goals of Bretton Woods was to 'drive the usurious moneylenders from the temple of international finance'.[22] In this respect, the founders backed away from a total commitment to an open, liberal international economic order and, instead, institutionalized the view that 'a liberal financial order would not be compatible, at least in the short run, with a stable system of exchange rates and a liberal trading order'.[23] Underlying this position were complementary economic and strategic views. On the economic side, 'capital controls were necessary to prevent the policy autonomy of the new interventionist welfare state from being undermined by speculative and disequilibrating international capital flows'.[24] On the strategic side, the US foreign policy establishment believed that a benevolent attitude toward

---

[19] Ibid, at 32.
[20] Ibid, at 36.
[21] Eric Helleiner, *States and the Reemergence of Global Finance: From Bretton Woods to the 1990s* (Ithaca and London: Cornell University Press, 1994) 45.
[22] Cited in Gardner, above n 2, at 38.
[23] Ibid, at 5.
[24] Ibid, at 4.

the interventionist policies of Europe and Japan was the most effective means of promoting economic growth and sustaining the Cold War alliance.[25]

Ironically, the importance of international trade to the policymakers ran headlong into political reality. When the over ambitious ITO project was unable to overcome political opposition, the GATT was forced to survive on life support through most of its early years. Compared to its sister organizations, the IMF and the World Bank—which were busy through the decades of 1950s and 1960s building up a sizable staff, planting a dramatic bricks-and-mortar physical footprint in Washington, DC and spending their considerable resources—the GATT, or more accurately, the Interim Commission for an ITO, had to struggle in political obscurity until 1968 when the US Congress took the modest step of providing permanent authorization for contributions to the GATT Secretariat.[26] The GATT took on the challenge of proving itself as an effective international regulatory framework. Aided by the US willingness to lead with open markets and Marshall Plan assistance and some exceptional leadership within the organization from individuals like Eric Wyndham White, the GATT ultimately concluded eight major rounds of trade negotiations. 'Pragmatic accommodation, good practical sense, and important leadership led a weak "birth defected" GATT to become an important part of the world's international economic institutional landscape'.[27]

Europe was the critical partner throughout this period. European support for the GATT was affirmed politically and economically as the European Communities transposed the basic framework of the GATT into the core principles for their economic union and the very identity of Europeans became associated with economic integration through the elimination of internal barriers to trade among European countries and eventually the single European market.

The 1970s proved to be a watershed decade for both the trade and the international financial system. By the end of the decade, the USA had abandoned the dollar's link to gold, imposed an import surcharge on Japan to force currency realignment, and launched the modern era of flexible exchange rates. Treasury officials decided to reverse their benevolent attitude toward capital controls and began to adopt policies encouraging the flow of capital, teaming up with the banks to use commercial leverage to affect the economic policies of other countries.[28] Meanwhile, the GATT concluded the Tokyo Round. It was the most ambitious trade negotiation round in history with agreements to lower tariffs, codes on such nontariff barriers as subsidies, government procurement, valuation and standards, and the elimination of some sacred cows (e.g. the American Selling Price system, Wine-Gallon Proof-Gallon valuation of imported spirits) that had been grandfathered in the GATT and were a longstanding source of tension with US trading partners. Approval of this liberalizing package by an overwhelming vote in Congress, even in the face of a recession, was made possible by a US fast-track

---

[25] Ibid, at 5.
[26] See Gardner, above n 2, at 50–1.
[27] John H. Jackson, *Sovereignty, the WTO, and Changing Fundamentals of International Law* (New York: Cambridge University Press, 2006) 261.
[28] Helleiner, above n 21, 112–15.

legislative approval scheme that was nothing short of a revolution in the political economy of trade.[29] In short, the table was set for the globalization of the global economy driven by trade and capital movements that would be the dominant economic story of the following three decades.

Also important in the 1970s was the emergence of an alliance of right and left around the theme of regulatory efficiency. Contrary to the views of some that this was principally a conservative phenomenon, Eduardo Canedo has argued that the movement that became associated with deregulation had its roots in the convergence of views from the Chicago School of Economics (on the right), under the intellectual leadership of George Stigler, and from the left, under the intellectual and political instigation of Ralph Nader.[30] Both Stigler and Nader were highly skeptical of the role of government regulation, Stigler out of an innate faith in the market, Nader from the perspective that regulatory agencies were more likely to be captured by those they were intended to regulate. While these movements diverged over the issue of social regulation, they were extremely influential in the initiatives to deregulate a number of areas, from aviation and trucking to natural gas and power generation.

It was the resurgence of US competitiveness in the 1980s and the confidence that it gave to Americans that helped support the extreme monetary policies that Paul Volcker introduced in the early 1980s to break the grip of inflation on the US economy. The success of this policy in turn helped form the basis for the Washington Consensus, namely that the key to international development lay in the adoption of carefully managed monetary policies, open trade policies and liberalizing financial markets. The strong US economy buttressed the role of the US dollar and overwhelmed any efforts to replace it with the special drawing right or other currencies. It also gave US Treasury officials few incentives to consider new rules for global finance. New rules for the global world of finance were unnecessary because domestic policymakers could oversee the system, and all that was needed were loose

---

[29] For a detailed account of the political history of trade politics, see I.M. Destler, *American Trade Politics* (4th edn, Washington, DC: Institute for International Economics, 2005).

[30] See Eduardo Canedo, 'The Rise of the Deregulation Movement in Modern America 1957–1980' (2009 PhD dissertation on file at Columbia University, Department of History), at 97 (cited with the permission of the author). See also Joshua Green, 'Inside Man', *The Atlantic Monthly*, April 2010 (<http://www.theatlantic.com/magazine/archive/2010/04/inside-man/7992/>) and a description of the defections from the Chicago School in John Cassidy, 'After the Blowup; Laissez-Faire Economists Do Some Soul-Searching—and Finger-Pointing', *The New Yorker*, 11 January 2010, 28. John Cassidy recounts a history lesson from Richard A. Posner, a jurist and intellectual leader of the Chicago School:

> By the late 1980s, with the collapse of Communism, the basic insights of the Chicago School about deregulation and incentives had been accepted worldwide, he recalled, and the bitter enmity between Chicago and its rival economics departments had faded. Eventually, many of the founders of the Chicago School died, and were replaced by more moderate figures, such as Thaler and Levitt. Now, largely as a result of misguided efforts to extend deregulation to the finance industry, we have experienced the biggest economic blowup since the nineteen-thirties. Posner, who appeared to be enjoying his role as a heretic, paused, then said, 'So probably the term "Chicago School" should be retired'.

Available at: <http://mfs.uchicago.edu/pastworkshops/capitalisms/readings/After_the_Blowup.%20pdf> (visited 3 August 2010).

confederations of regulators whose objective would be the exchange of ideas on collective problem-solving.

It is said that nothing succeeds like success, and this unfettered model of regulation marked an era of unprecedented growth in the financial sector and the proliferation of financial instruments. While global trade grew steadily over the past 50 years, exceeding GDP growth rates and reaching $14 trillion by 2007, financial assets saw explosive growth from being about equal to global GDP in 1980 to over three times GDP by the end of 2005. By 2007, financial services accounted for over one third of corporate profits in the USA and an estimated 5.9 per cent of US GDP, up from 3.5 per cent of GDP in 1978 depending on how you calculate it.[31] This explosion in the markets for financial services was accompanied by the globalization of those markets and the combination of size, complexity, growth and global scope beyond the grasp, if not the reach, of national regulators set the stage for what some predicted would be a systemic crisis of global proportions.[32]

Somewhat ironically, the financial community was one of the most ardent supporters of the emerging rules of the international trading system, even as they resisted regulation as it would be applied to finance. Moreover, financial interests, through their associations, sought new rules in the context of the international trading system but their focus was on limiting restrictions that countries could use to constrain the operations of financial institutions across borders. These new rules were developed in what eventually became known as the General Agreement on Trade in Services (GATS), incorporated with the World Trade Organization (WTO) in 1995, and subject to further negotiations in the Doha Round.[33]

Meanwhile, as predicted, the floating exchange rate system did lead to crises, but these were successfully managed on an ad hoc basis with governmental and IMF bailouts that were seen as confirmation of the importance of implementing more rigorously the Washington Consensus, particularly in emerging markets. The importance of crisis management in preparing individuals and their mindset for the latest crisis is well described by Joshua Green in his profile of Timothy Geithner:

---

[31] Johnson, n 10, at 60–1.
[32] See Alexander et al., above n 5, at 7:

> The recent history of capital market liberalization has coincided with a swing in the balance of intellectual influence from a postwar theory of economic policy that urged national governments to limit international capital movements to the present-day theory that encourages free capital movements and the abdication of national regulatory powers. So financial stability is largely a matter of convention.

Written in 2006, these authors make one of the most compelling predictions at page 9: 'Recent crises suggest the current international efforts to regulate financial systems lack coherence and legitimacy and fail to effectively manage systemic risk'.

[33] The Financial Service portion of the GATS deals narrowly with measures that limit the cross-border establishment and operation of financial institutions but the obligations are implemented not on a generalized basis but country by country and measure by measure, depending on the willingness of countries to incorporate the obligation into their schedule. The prudential exception [General Agreement on Trade in Services, Annex on Financial Services, para 2(a)] could be a framework for incorporating rules on prudential supervision and this exception is subject to WTO dispute settlement, however, there has been little interest in this possibility to date. For the most part, countries have simply incorporated into their schedules their existing framework of regulations.

Geithner came of age in Washington just after the Cold War ended, when the country's preoccupation with wealth and the long bull market made Treasury a nerve center of the government. It helps explain Geithner to think of him as someone whose formative experience was in figuring out how to contain the series of upheavals that swept the international financial community in the 1990s, from Japan to Mexico to Thailand to Indonesia to Russia, and threatened the boom. Toward the end of the Clinton administration, a view emerged that the government had more or less figured out how to manage the global financial system. Those at the helm won extraordinary renown. The era's time-capsule-worthy artifact is a *Time* cover touting Alan Greenspan, the Federal Reserve chairman, Robert Rubin, the Treasury secretary, and Lawrence Summers, Rubin's deputy, as 'The Committee to Save the World'. Geithner was an aide de camp.[34]

It was roughly during this same period from 1980 to 1995 when the trading system made its most extraordinary evolution into a global systemic regulatory system. The great debate—whether the GATT should be a rule-based system with a juridical function or an essentially diplomatic facilitator where trade issues could be resolved through negotiations—was resolved in favor of converting soft law into hard law or hard-hard law. It is nothing short of revolutionary that the Uruguay Round was concluded with a single undertaking that every country in the world was required to take or leave and a dispute settlement understanding that gave any country the right to challenge the practices of any other country, no matter how big or small. Whether this system would work or not was unclear but the history since then is clear; the enforcement record of the institution is singular and the stress test of the Great Contraction has confirmed at least to date that the system is still holding.[35]

By the dawn of 2007, these two systems that started life from a common conception had evolved two very different regulatory and institutional structures. The WTO became a member-driven, rule-oriented, unitary, comprehensive and nearly universal system where the obligations run *horizontally* from members to other members, decisions are made by consensus, and obligations are interpreted and enforced through a dispute settlement mechanism with a highly developed juridical function having the power to determine violations and authorize sanctions. The international financial regulatory system became a fragmented, complex, multi-tiered, multi-dimensional, resource-oriented system[36] that accommodates

---

[34] Joshua Green, 'Inside Man', *The Atlantic Monthly*, April 2010, <http://www.theatlantic.com/magazine/archive/2010/03/inside-man/7992/> (visited 3 August 2010).

[35] See WTO Appellate Body, 'Annual Report for 2009', WT/AB/13, 17 February 2010.

[36] There is an interesting view that the IMF started as a rule-based system while the GATT started on a more flexible, 'ideas-based' system but they reversed their characters over time. See Barry Eichengreen and Peter B. Kenen, 'Managing the World Economy under the Bretton Woods System: An Overview' in Peter B. Kenen (ed), *Managing the World Economy: Fifty Years After Bretton Woods* (Washington, DC: Institute for International Economics, 1994) 3–57, at 7:

> The International Monetary Fund was a formal structure intended to enforce an explicit set of rules; its Articles of Agreement contained a detailed list of international monetary do's and don'ts and established enforcement capabilities. Some of the rules were not enforceable, however, and they failed to anticipate all the subsequent problems. The [GATT], by contrast, was an ad hoc agreement intended mainly to provide a framework for pursuing nondiscriminatory, multilateral trade liberalization. Many observers would now conclude that the GATT was the more effective arrangement. The strength of a formal arrangement

the different domains and regulatory prerogatives of finance officials, central bankers, and bank regulators as well as the private financial community by creating a variety of different organizations from treaty-based to intergovernmental to cooperative arrangements among functional regulators.

B. Contrasting regulatory philosophies

The philosophical principles underlying the global trading system will be explored in some detail in the next section, so it is sufficient here to set up in contrast some of the core thinking around the financial system through the views of two of the major operational and intellectual leaders (Alan Greenspan and Robert Rubin) reflecting on why they did not anticipate the crisis.

It is helpful to start with the October 2008 testimony of Alan Greenspan, former Chairman of the Federal Reserve, which posed the question: 'What went wrong with global economic policies that had worked so effectively for nearly four decades?'[37] He goes on to focus on the failure of the market in subprime mortgages:

subprime mortgages pooled and sold as securities became subject to explosive demand from investors around the world. These mortgage backed securities being 'subprime' were originally offered at what appeared to be exceptionally high risk-adjusted market interest rates. But with US home prices still rising, delinquency and foreclosure rates were deceptively modest. Losses were minimal. By the most sophisticated investors in the world, they were wrongly viewed as a 'steal'.[38]

In an exchange with Henry Waxman, Chairman of the House Oversight Committee and Government Reform, former Chairman Greenspan is asked about the responsibility of regulators: 'You had the authority to prevent irresponsible lending practices that led to the subprime crisis. You were advised to do so by many others. . . . Do you feel that your ideology pushed you to make decisions that you wish you had not made?'[39]

---

such as the IMF is its rigidity; that of an informal, ideas-based institution such as the GATT is its adaptability. The greater success of the GATT thus illustrates the importance for postwar economic performance of an adaptable institutional framework.

[37] Alan Greenspan, Prepared testimony to the House Committee on Oversight and Reform, 23 October 2008, <http://oversight.house.gov/index.php?option=com_content&view=article&id=3470&-catid=42:hearings&Itemid=2> (visited 6 October 2010).

[38] Ibid. <http://oversight.house.gov/index.php?option=com_content&view=article&id=3470&catid=42:hearings&Itemid=2> (visited 6 October 2010).

[39] Ibid. In his prepared testimony, Greenspan concentrates on the market for securitized subprime loans:

It was the failure to properly price such assets that precipitated the crisis. . . . The modern risk management paradigm held sway for decades. The whole intellectual edifice, however, collapsed in the summer of last year [2007] because the data inputted into the risk management models generally covered only the past two decades, a period of euphoria. Had instead the models been fitted more appropriately to historic periods of stress, capital requirements would have been much higher and the financial world would be in far better shape today, in my judgment. <http://oversight.house.gov/index.php?option=com_content&view=article&id=3470&catid=42:hearings&Itemid=2> (visited 6 October 2010).

In response, Chairman Greenspan concedes: 'Yes, I've found a flaw. I don't know how significant or permanent it is. But I've been very distressed by that fact'. In explaining his excessive faith in the self-correcting power of free markets and his failure to anticipate the collapse of the mortgage lending system, he states: 'Those of us who looked to the self-interest of lending institutions to protect shareholders' equity, myself included, are in a state of shocked disbelief'.[40] Finally, in his prepared comments, he made reference to the power of regulation relative to the impact of market discipline: 'Whatever regulatory changes are made, they will pale in comparison to the change already evident in today's markets.... Those markets for an indefinite future will be far more restrained than would any currently contemplated new regulatory regime'.[41]

This picture is filled out further by the testimony of Robert Rubin, Chairman of the Board of Citibank, to the Financial Crisis Investigatory Commission in questioning by Douglas Joltz-Eakin:

Mr. Rubin, you said no one could have foreseen this crisis and that was a universally held belief.... The question is... could you have foreseen the spark that lit the crisis,... the poor standards in underwriting, the poor assessment of risks associated with mortgages, the inadequate hedging and capital provisions...?... In your experience, we have seen crises in Mexico, in Thailand and in the Far East, wouldn't there be grounds to be suspicious at some point?[42]

Rubin responds:

It's a good question.... I didn't say no one could have foreseen [the crisis], some people did foresee. What I said was that very few people foresaw the full combination.... You had a large combination of forces that came together.... I think it was this extraordinary combination of many factors that came together and you can say well you can see some of these and why didn't that suggest that this could be a problem.... I actually did worry about the excesses and talked about them in speeches in 2005 and 2006.... What I didn't see, and virtually nobody saw, was that it wasn't only those excesses but it was so many other factors coming together at that time and I think it's that combination that led to this crisis.... As long as we have had capital markets, we have had crises and then when you look back... you say those were some obvious warning signs but they weren't obvious at the time. They were only obvious in hindsight. I personally think unfortunately that market-based systems which I believe in strongly, will have periodic down cycles and that is why this financial reform effort is so extremely important.[43]

[40] See Edmund L. Andrews, 'Greenspan Concedes Errors on Regulation', *New York Times*, 23 October 2008, <http://www.nytimes.com/2008/10/24/business/economy/24panel.html> (visited 30 September 2010).
[41] Ibid.
[42] See n 43 below.
[43] Robert Rubin Testimony to the Financial Crisis Investigative Commission, 8 April 2010, transcribed from the audio available at <http://www.cspan.org/Watch/Media/2010/04/08/HP/R/31560/Govt+officials+testifying+Frmr+Citi+execs+apologize.aspx> (visited 3 August 2010).

C. Characteristics of the robust regulatory system governing trade

While systemic risk is typically associated with financial systems and crises, it seems to be applicable to the trading system and, indeed, provides a perspective from which all regulatory systems should be evaluated. As we saw in the case of the Great Depression, the trading system failed in a systemic way, that is, a shock resulted in reactions in one country that then triggered a chain reaction throughout the global economy causing a breakdown in the entire framework for international trade. This pattern did not repeat itself some 80 years later when the global economy went through a very similar experience to that in 1929, namely a banking crisis that put enormous pressure on governments to mitigate the impact of the crisis in their individual markets by erecting barriers to international trade. While the G20 governments called on one another[44] to refrain from such measures, it does not seem that this hortatory call explains the fact that governments responded very differently this time around, any more than hortatory calls for countries to maintain the safety and soundness of their financial institutions preserved the financial system from systemic failure. What then explains this difference?

Let's start with Paul Blustein who, judging by the title of his recent book, has quite a different view of the state of the international trading system: *Misadventures of the Most Favored Nations: Clashing Egos, Inflated Ambitions, and the Great Shambles of the World Trade System*. Blustein takes a somewhat more measured view in the book itself: 'The trading system is at risk of joining the financial system in crisis. That is the central message of this book, and the story of how the system reached this parlous state will unfold in chapters to come'.[45] Blustein provides an insightful and readable account of the difficulty trading nations have had concluding the Doha Round of trade negotiation and in doing so points out the most fundamental weakness of the international trading system, namely that the rule-making or legislative side of the system is not nearly as developed as the juridical and rule-enforcement side.[46] One can juxtapose this view with the one widely held among finance experts commenting on the WTO, that the system is simply not enforcing its rules:

The WTO operates without any international enforcement powers and relies on consensus among all member nations to establish policies consistent with the agreed rules. Lack of enforcement often makes compliance problematic, and agreements to reduce trade barriers

---

[44] Paragraph 48 of the Pittsburgh Summit Communique, 25 September 2009.

[45] Paul Blustein, *The Misadventures of the Most Favored Nations: Clashing Egos, Inflated Ambitions, and the Great Shambles of the World Trading System* (New York: Public Affairs, 2010) 8. Ultimately, Blustein comes to the conclusion that the question is not how to save the Doha Round, but, in the words of Ernesto Zadillo, 'How can the WTO be saved from the Doha Round?' (at page 281). The answer, says Blustein, seems to belie his characterization of the system: 'The most important goal is to ensure the survival of the rules-based trading system. It is unwise to devote a lot of energy to opening markets more than they already are; after eight rounds, global trade is already reasonably free. The focus should be on keeping protectionism, and quasi-protectionism, from becoming long-lasting features of the international economy, so that globalized trade can help the world recover and prosper anew' (at page 286).

[46] Ibid, at 280.

can only be reached after endless rounds of negotiation such as the currently ongoing Doha round. Progress has been made but, in the absence of any supranational authority, it relies on the very gradual consensus building.[47]

In contrast, other finance experts see the WTO's success in dispute settlement and enforcement as the model for the international financial system.[48]

Those who measure the success of the trading system entirely against its success in achieving the next generation of free trade objectives fail to appreciate the value of preserving the gains of over three-quarters of a century of negotiations; what the European Union would call the *acquis,* the body of rules to which all members must adhere. Indeed, it would be more accurate to talk about the benefits of a well-regulated system of trade rather than free trade because that is what we have. People who condemn the WTO solely for its failure to deliver on the Doha Round agenda make the same mistake as those who measured the success of the financial regulatory regime against its ability to facilitate financial innovation by opening markets to ever more exotic (and sometimes toxic) financial instruments. There is great merit in pursuing a Doha Round deal to the extent that it can truly contribute to global growth and recovery, but failure in this regard does not make the existing rules outmoded or irrelevant. On the contrary, for all those who earn their livelihood from trade, the WTO operates to reduce risk and thereby cost, eliminate uncertainty and provide a critical source of stability for the global economy. Moreover, that is why the WTO has become a magnet for global regulatory issues from climate change to currency manipulation.

These views provide an appropriate set of cautions as we look with a critical eye at what aspects of the trading system contributed most to its ability to withstand the stress test of the Great Contraction. Even more importantly, they form an integral part of the perception of this institution and, as we have learned from the financial crisis, perceptions can play a large role in influencing the market. George Akerlof and Robert Shiller have criticized traditional economics for its failure to understand the importance of animal spirits in the functioning of the economy, namely 'confidence, fairness, corruption and antisocial behavior, money illusion and stories'.[49] They explain that economic theory has failed to appreciate that economic crises 'are mainly caused by changing thought patterns. . . . It was caused precisely by our changing confidence, temptations, envy, resentment, and illusions—and especially by changing stories about the nature of the economy'.[50]

The public, and the regulators who were supposed to act on their behalf, had failed to understand a fact of life that is totally obvious to everyone who has played a serious team

---

[47] Viral V. Acharya, Paul Wachtel and Ingo Walter, 'International Alignment of Financial Sector Regulation', in Viral V. Acharya and Matthew Richardson (eds), *Restoring Financial Stability: How to Repair a Failed System* (New Jersey: John Wiley & Sons, 2009) 365–76, at 372.

[48] See Evenett, above n 9, at 218.

[49] George A. Akerlof and Robert Shiller, *Animal Spirits: How Human Psychology Drives the Economy and Why it Matters for Global Capitalism* (Princeton and Oxford: Princeton University Press, 2009) 5.

[50] Ibid, at 4.

sport: there have to be rules and there has to be a referee who enforces them—and a good and conscientious referee at that.[51]

There are a number of characteristics of the GATT/WTO system that appear relevant in explaining why the system performed so well as a systemic regulator.

1. Rule-oriented system

The very essence of the WTO is what John Jackson has christened the 'rule-oriented approach' that focuses on the importance of predictability and stability for those who must function within the international trading system and for whom the size and nature of the 'risk premium' inherent in international transactions can be the critical determinant for their long-term decisions regarding investment. Ultimately, this predictability and stability when institutionalized creates the base of a pyramid upon which many private decisions are grounded and the larger and more secure that base, the higher the pyramid can be built. The confidence that this set of rules can withstand even exogenous shock like a financial crisis must be seen as the ultimate validation for the role that rules can play.[52]

2. Alignment of incentives with the public good

Rules alone are not enough to protect a system from systemic risk. We know that systemic risk is created when the actions of an individual may be rational and advance the individual's interest but if everyone acts in the same way the system may collapse. The rules must serve an overall objective with incentives for behavior that is best for the overall public interest. Kenneth Dam talks about the theory of the second best, that in a world of second bests, it is not always clear whether the elimination of a particular barrier will lead to greater efficiency.[53] The GATT confronted the problem of how to reconcile differing views of the function of international trade. While the USA saw trade as critically important to the promotion of international efficiency, other countries, especially in the developing world, saw economic development as their top priority. What the GATT and WTO have been able to do through successive rounds of negotiations is focus the attention of Members on the common good that comes from the accumulation of individual concessions. In this respect, the GATT/WTO has followed Dam's advice of 1970 that it 'attempt not only to resolve this conflict in values but to aid governments in

[51] Ibid, at xiii.
[52] See Jackson, above n 27, at 88: The phrase 'rule orientation' is used here to contrast with phrases such as 'rule of law', and 'rule-based system'. Rule orientation implies a less rigid adherence to 'rule' and connotes some fluidity in rule approaches which seems to accord with reality (especially since it accommodates some bargaining or negotiations). Phrases that emphasize too strongly the strict application of rules sometimes scare policy makers, although in reality they may amount to the same thing.
[53] Kenneth W. Dam, *The GATT: Law and International Economic Organization* (Chicago: The University of Chicago Press, 1970) 6.

clarifying the common interest of all members of the international trading community. Neither rules nor mere pragmatic improvisations can do that'.[54]

The question is how negotiations can orient countries with essentially mercantilist attitudes toward trade to serve the public good. Economic theory (known as the market access or terms of trade theory) now tells us that the principle of reciprocity which, although not required as a principle of negotiations by any provision of the GATT/WTO agreements, provides a critical incentive, particularly for large countries, to lower their trade barriers.[55] Reciprocity is operationalized in the GATT Article XXIII:1 provision which provides members recourse in the event that they feel the benefits to which they are entitled are being 'nullified or impaired' whether by a violation of the agreement, any measure, or any other situation.

Whether there is a counterpart in finance to the set of rules and an internal dynamic that ties those rules to the public good is a prime question for public policy and is at the heart of the national legislative efforts for financial regulatory reform.[56] One way to replicate the benefit of the nullification or impairment provision of the GATT/WTO would be to adopt, as a first principle in an international financial agreement, the concept of systemic failure and the concept that countries must regulate in such a way as to protect against global systemic failure. Thus, as an analogy to GATT Article XXIII, a global financial agreement would ensure that any member has recourse if it faces the risk of a systemic crisis as a result of the actions of another member, including a violation of any provision of the agreement, any other measure (including the failure to regulate), or any other situation.

3. Dispute settlement and self-enforcement

While there are many examples of international agreements with elaborate sets of rules, the WTO is unique in the scope and importance of its juridical system for interpretation of the rules and the concentration of peer pressure on a violator. The success of the dispute settlement mechanism as a means of managing trade disputes—large and small, and between developed and developing countries—is the crown jewel of the global economic regulatory order. Moreover, the rate of adherence to the WTO rules, both in general and in response to disputes brought, is a singular achievement for the system and is at the heart of its success as a systemic regulator in the face of the recent crisis.

The counterpart to the market access theory is the commitment theory that holds 'without the threat that . . . foreign market access will be taken away if one

---

[54] Ibid, at 7.

[55] See Chad P. Bown, *Self-Enforcing Trade: Developing Countries and WTO Dispute Settlement* (Washington, DC: Brookings Institution Press, 2009) 16: 'There is nothing in the GATT texts that requires countries to reciprocally negotiate market access liberalization'.

[56] Financial reform legislation has been enacted in the United States which creates a Financial Services Oversight Council to go with its European counterpart, the European Systemic Risk Board. The focus of these regulatory bodies could well be the source of international initiatives to strengthen the international regulatory system as advocated in this paper. Dodd–Frank Consumer Protection and Financial Reform Act, Public Law 111–203, 21 July 2010.

country deviates from the agreement by imposing new trade barriers, market access openings could not be sustained through renegotiations either'.[57] Critical to the WTO model is that it does not involve an imperial international bureaucracy that imposes its will on the Member but rather 'the GATT/WTO is a set of self-enforcing agreements: member countries enforce trading partners' commitments embodied in the agreements by challenging each other's missteps through forced dispute settlement'.[58]

4. Regulatory capture and the political economy underlying effective global regulation

Rules and alignment with the public good still do not ensure that the system will not be captured by those interests it seeks to regulate. In the case of the WTO, 'the rule system shelters national governments from the power of protectionist groups within individualized economies. . . . The WTO has been likened to a mast to which—like Odysseus—governments can tie themselves to escape the siren-like calls of domestic interest groups and even, to some extent, of their voters'.[59]

5. Comprehensive coverage—the domain of the regulatory system is coextensive with the domain of the problem

The WTO rules are comprehensive in their coverage geographically as well as functionally. WTO obligations cover 153 Members 'comprising 93 per cent of world trade, and 87 per cent of world population'.[60] In geographical and demographic terms, the major breakthrough came with the admission of China on 11 December 2001, validating the WTO's claim to be the 'world' trade organization.[61] From a functional perspective, the WTO has a comprehensive approach to the regulation of international trade for it covers explicitly any measure that a country may use to regulate trade. Moreover, the WTO incorporated the GATT concept that a 'nullification or impairment' of the benefits of the agreement could come from 'the application by any Member of any measure, whether or not it conflicts with the provisions' of one of the constituent agreements or 'the existence of any other situation'.[62] While no case of a non-violation nullification complaint has ever been successful and the clause has been characterized as 'of little practical significance',[63] the provision takes on significance from a systemic

---

[57] Bown, above n 55, at 19.

[58] Ibid, at 20.

[59] Horst Siebert, *Rules for the Global Economy* (Princeton: Princeton University Press, 2009) 76.

[60] See Jackson, above n 27, at 135.

[61] Russia had been the last major hold-out but its membership was approved by the Ministerial Conference on 16 December 2011 with ratification expected in 2012: see Ministerial Conference approves Russia's WTO membership, 16 December 2011, <http://www.wto.org/english/news_e/news11_e/acc_rus_16dec11_e.htm> (visited 24 January 2012).

[62] Article XXIII:1(c) of the GATT 1994 and Article 26.2 of the Understanding on Rules and Procedures Governing the Settlement of Disputes.

[63] Peter Van Den Bossche, *The Law and Policy of the World Trade Organization* (New York: Cambridge University Press, 2008) 185.

perspective. For one, it precludes the possibility that parties might engineer a measure outside the scope of the agreement. Furthermore, it acts as a kind of magnet, drawing issues into the trade regulatory system that could emerge as the perception regarding the scope of international trade versus domestic policy changes[64] along with the responsibility of trading nations to their partners in maintaining the integrity of the regulatory system.

6. Transparency

A critical element in the success of the GATT/WTO is the use of transparency as a regulatory device. Members are required to disclose the measures that they use to regulate trade and to include them in their Schedules of Concessions.[65] Transparency plays two roles: it enables the Members to enforce one another's commitments by directly monitoring them and it forces Members to confront their own domestic constituencies with the reality and substance of measures that end up imposing a cost on their domestic economies. This transparency has worked over time to help forge the constituencies of interest that then lobby for the elimination of barriers to trade.[66]

Transparency as a device for financial regulation is a subject of considerable interest and complexity. Ken Rogoff cites transparency as one of the most important roles for international institutions but points out how difficult it can be to obtain accurate data on things like government debt and the composition of the Federal Reserve's assets.[67] A culture of nontransparency seems to be a characteristic of the financial system, even though some analysts see this as even more effective than supervision and limits on leverage.[68] Complicating the picture is the view that the more transparency, the more information is homogeneous which leads to markets reacting in the same way to information and thereby creating systemic risk.[69]

[64] See C. Fred Bergsten, 'Managing the World Economy of the Future' in Peter Kenan (ed), *Managing the World Economy: Fifty Years after Bretton Woods* (Washington, DC: Institute for International Economics, 1994) 3–57, at 342: 'International economic negotiations now routinely address, and even sometimes alter, policies traditionally viewed as "purely domestic"'.

[65] GATT Article II.

[66] See generally Bown, above n 55 for the view that these constituencies did not develop in those developing countries that were given special and differential treatment and were not required to offer concessions in negotiations.

[67] See Carmen M. Reinhart and Kenneth S. Rogoff, *This Time is Different: Eight Centuries of Financial Folly* (Princeton and Oxford: Princeton University Press, 2009) 282: 'One has only to look at how opaque the United States government's books have become during the 2007 financial crisis to see how helpful an outside standard would be.... The task of enforcing transparency is easier said than done, for governments have many incentives to obfuscate their books'.

[68] See Barth et al., above n 11, at 312.

[69] See discussion of the importance of heterogeneity in markets and the problem created by equal information in Alexander et al., above n 5, at 261: 'But the attainment of equal information is bought at a cost—increased homogeneity and, hence, potentially reduced liquidity'.

7. Governance

The consensus-based system of the WTO has been its most widely criticized dimension because of the obstacles it creates to the rule-making process. Yet, when looked at from a systemic point of view, the legitimacy of the WTO is grounded in this rule. China's adherence to the WTO is in part attributable to the legitimacy it gets from a principle of governance that contrasts to that of the IMF (and other international financial institutions) where voting power is allocated according to an economic formula that is static and resistant to revision, even in the face of changes in underlying economic alignments.

Ultimately, the sustainability of the trading system in the face of the real world stress of the Great Contraction must stand as the highlight of an extraordinary history. The story is far from over and enormous pressures on the system continue to be felt, but the structure held with the ongoing support of the Members. The so-called bicycle theory of the international trading system—which holds that without forward progress on trade liberalization, the system would lose its balance and fall over—has not been proven, at least in this recent crisis.

III. Conclusion—The Quest for Coherence

At the heart of this chapter is the idea that we need to pull the covers back and face the real challenges of regulation in our globalized world. Coherence can only be achieved by adopting a mindset, tools and analytical frameworks that enable us to look at the 'nuts and bolts' as well as at the way the entire system fits together. If all economics is global and all politics are local, then regulators work in that space where the two come together and can only be reconciled by making economics work for the community and ensuring that all political decisions are taken with an eye to their impact on the global community. What Jack Welch called a culture of 'boundarylessness'[70] is a necessary component of our regulatory culture, by which he meant that one must respect the limits of one's own responsibility while being mindful of the impact and need to share across functions and organizations.

We have just lived through the most dramatic economic event of our generation and, while there is an air of normalcy to this recovery, we have yet to digest the real consequences and implications of this crisis for the global economy.

From the perspective of the past 80 years and through the prism of global regulation, it appears that the worlds of trade and finance have evolved in two dramatically different directions, with the world of finance characterized by an almost pathological antipathy to regulation while the trade world has developed through trial and error an extensive set of rules, adjudication and dispute settlement mechanisms and sanctions which together have ensured a high degree of enforce-

---

[70] Jack Welch was the CEO of General Electric from 1981 to 2001. See Jack Welch, *Straight From The Gut* (Warner Books Inc., 2001).

ment and compliance. This difference has consequences and helps to explain the relative performance of the two systems in the course of the real world crisis.

So the question can legitimately be posed: does the trading system deserve a voice in efforts to ensure global stability? The reason for an affirmative response is twofold. First, the trading system has experience in designing and operating a successful systemic regulatory system that for all the claimed differences between regulating trade and finance has in fact confronted many of the same problems facing the world of finance, such as rule-making, sovereignty, political economy, reconciling conflicting values, economic theories and governance to name but a few. Second, the trading system has a huge stake in the outcome of the financial reform process for the same reason that the financial system was created, namely to facilitate payment and finance of international trade transactions. In fact, it is fair to say that trade started out as the weak sister in the Bretton Woods system and now it is the tent-pole holding up a system in which the other two pillars are showing signs of extreme distress.

This reality leads to the question: why does the WTO not have a seat on the Financial Stability Board? Have we not learned that taking a fragmented approach to the regulation of the global economy is flawed? Is it not possible that the next systemic risk could come from the inability of the trading system to hold up the global economy while the world of finance works its way through the political obstacles to reform? And is there not some chance that a representative of arguably the most successful systemic regulator in the history of humankind might have something to offer to an attempt to fundamentally restructure the regulatory system of finance?

This analysis raises a host of other questions that deserve further examination. Do we need a greater convergence in the global regulatory regimes governing trade and finance? Do we need a new paradigm for understanding global regulation that gets beyond the polarized debate over regulation versus deregulation? What are the implications for how we view the Doha Round and other efforts at the further liberalization of trade? How do we look at the interplay of rules and governance? What stake does the private sector have in the outcome of this debate and is the private sector playing an effective role in proposing solutions to the underlying problem of how to harness the benefits of globalization while managing the risks that are inevitably a part of making it work?

3

The International Monetary System: A Look Back Over Seven Decades

Andreas F. Lowenfeld

I. Introduction

For three weeks in July 1944, nine months before the signing of the United Nations Charter, 10 months before the end of World War II in Europe, and more than a year before the end of the war in the Pacific, representatives of 44 nations assembled at a grand hotel in Bretton Woods, New Hampshire, to create the organization and draft the rules for the post-war international financial system. Seven decades later the International Monetary Fund (IMF) created at Bretton Woods still exists, and so do some of the rules, for instance, prohibition of discrimination and restriction on exchange controls. But the main organizing principle, fixed exchange rates linked to gold through the US dollar, broke down in the 1970s, and the law-giving function has changed drastically.

As the world longs for a return to stability in the wake of chaos and recession, it is enlightening to recall what the IMF founders attempted, where and why they succeeded, and where and why they failed. For readers who have kept up with the ups and downs of the international monetary system, much of what follows will be a review, but with some forward looking at the end. For those who have not followed the story closely—which includes many observers and participants in other aspects of the international economy—what follows may hold a fascination of its own.

II. Creating an international Monetary System

A. Before Bretton Woods

It would not be accurate to say that before 1945 there was no international monetary system. States and their enterprises traded with one another, currencies were exchanged, and states held monetary reserves in gold, in silver, and in foreign currencies. But prior to the end of World War II no international legal regime governed the conduct of states with respect to monetary affairs.

For about 35 years prior to the outbreak of World War I, the major Western countries—the UK, France, Germany, and the USA—all tied their currencies to gold, so that the rate of exchange among the principal currencies was essentially fixed.[1] Those years, in the minds of the builders at Bretton Woods, were the good old days. In contrast, the years between World War I and World War II were years of unemployment and depression, of chaos and manipulation. Currencies went on and off a link to gold, and countries imposed a variety of subsidies, regulations and controls designed to increase their holdings of gold—each nation for itself and beggar thy neighbor. Nazi Germany appeared to be particularly skillful and ruthless in using tariffs, quotas, barter, and discriminatory exchange controls to its advantage.

Looking at the years leading up to World War II, while the war was still in progress, the architects of the post-war system were determined: Never again! The post-war system would encourage trade in goods, full employment, and stable currencies in a peaceful world. It would also include an institution to oversee achievement of these goals.[2]

B. The IMF

On the basis of drafts prepared for over two years under the leadership of the great John Maynard Keynes for the UK and Harry Dexter White, a senior official in the US Treasury, for the USA, the Bretton Woods Conference produced Articles of Agreement for an International Monetary Fund (as well as for a sister institution, the World Bank), designed to carry out the objectives set out above. Pursuant to separate international treaties, each institution would be governed with a three-tier structure, designed as far as possible to be insulated from political pressures.[3] The Articles provided for a Board of Governors consisting of the Finance Ministers or Central Bank governors of each member state, who would meet at least twice a year; a Board of Executive Directors, who would be in continuous residence at the institutions' headquarters in Washington; and a staff headed by the President of the World Bank and the Managing Director of the Fund, respectively. Under a tradition not stated in the Articles of Agreement of either institution, the President

---

[1] Thus if 20 dollars equal 1 ounce of gold, and 4 pounds sterling equal 1 ounce of gold, as long as the respective currencies were freely convertible, 1 pound sterling would equal 5 dollars, and say 50 francs could be exchanged for 12.5 dollars (i.e. 4 francs = $1) or £2.50 (i.e. 20 francs = £1). Of course, if any issuing country placed restrictions on use or transfer of its currency exchange for gold, the 'system' would break down.

[2] See the closing statements of the American Secretary of the Treasury Henry Morgenthau, Jr, in *Proceedings and Documents of the United Nations Monetary and Financial Conference*, Vol. I (Washington: US GPO, 1947) 117–18.

[3] For the USA, the Articles of Agreement were submitted to both Houses of Congress and were adopted by implementing statutes. Once adopted, however, the Articles of Agreement function under the US Constitution just like a treaty.

of the World Bank has always been an American, and the Managing Director of the IMF has always been a European.

Unlike the United Nations and later the General Agreement on Tariffs and Trade (GATT), which provided for one country, one vote, the Bretton Woods institutions provide for voting strength based on member states' quotas in the Fund or shares of stock in the Bank. The charter of each institution provides for five appointed Executive Directors, representing the states with the largest quota or number of shares, plus non-Executive Directors which represent groups of countries with common interests grouped by geography, language, or economic development. There is no provision for veto, but major decisions require super majorities, so that either the USA or the members of the European Union voting together can block approval of most important proposals. While the substantive code of conduct reflected in the Articles of Agreement has undergone major changes as described below, the organization and governance of the Fund and the Bank remain (as of 2010) essentially unchanged.

This fact has provided stability to an organization in the midst of storms all around it, but there is general agreement that quotas in the Fund, which were supposed to represent strength and importance in the international economy, are seriously out of line. Despite an agreement being reached by G20 Finance Ministers and Governors in October 2010 which saw a doubling of IMF members' quotas and a shift of more than 6 per cent to emerging market and developing countries (EMDCs) quotas are still a contentious issue.[4] This is primarily due to the USA, the European Union, the developing countries, and the least developed countries all having different proposals and different priorities regarding quota realignment. The quota formula will again be reviewed by January 2013 in an attempt to reach a broader consensus. A related controversy concerned resentment over the fact that the European Union—itself not a member of the IMF—has been represented by seven Directors on the Executive Board, compared with one for the USA and 12 for the 161 developing countries.[5]

C. The code of conduct

Keynes and White agreed that the Articles of Agreement stated law. Each state, upon joining the Fund, was required to certify that it had taken all steps necessary to enable it to carry out all of its obligations under the Agreement.[6] Thus, it would

---

[4] See IMF Factsheet 'IMF Quotas', <http://www.imf.org/external/np/exr/facts/quotas.htm> (visited 6 March 2012) and 'G20 Agreement on Quotas and Governance', <http://www.imf.org/external/np/exr/faq/quotasgov.htm> (visited 6 March 2012).

[5] As part of the reforms that saw the quota realignment in 2010 the Executive Board also underwent changes with an agreement where there became two fewer directors from advanced European countries and a move where all Executive Directors where no longer appointed, see 'G-20 Ministers agree "historic" reforms in IMF governance', <http://www.imf.org/external/pubs/ft/survey/so/2010/new102310a.htm> (visited 6 March 2012).

[6] Articles of Agreement (original version), Art XX(2)(a); amended Articles, Article XXXI(2).

be no defense to a charge of conduct inconsistent with the Agreement that an action required by the Agreement would be contrary to the member state's domestic law.

The overriding obligation of member states under the original Articles of Agreement was stated in Article IV (4)(a): 'Each member undertakes to collaborate with the Fund to promote exchange stability, to maintain orderly exchange arrangements with other members, and to avoid competitive exchange alterations'.

Members were to fulfill this obligation primarily by maintenance of par values—that is, they were to see to it, if necessary by intervention by their central bank, that exchange transactions taking place with their territory shall not differ from parity by more than 1 per cent in either direction.[7] If a member had difficulty meeting that obligation on its own, that is, if it was running out of reserves, it could apply to the Fund for assistance, subject to the conditions described below. The goal was to reestablish equilibrium. The Articles of Agreement stated that 'a member shall not propose a change in the par value of its currency except to correct a *fundamental disequilibrium*'.[8] That term was not defined in the Agreement, but was understood as something to be avoided if at all possible.

D. Transactions with the Fund

The basic plan for the IMF—reflected in its name—was to create a pool of resources based on mandatory contributions by member states. This pool could be drawn on by member states for balance of payments purposes—that is, to fulfill the obligation to maintain the par value of their currencies. Member states entered the Fund with a quota designed roughly to reflect their importance in the world economy, but subject to negotiation on both economic and political grounds. The larger a state's quota, the greater its required contribution and the greater its entitlement to draw on the Fund's resources. Contributions to the Fund were payable one-quarter in hard assets (gold under the original articles, special drawing rights (SDRs) under the amended Articles of Agreement) and three-quarters in their own currencies.[9] As it turned out, only a few members' currencies were generally acceptable for settlement of international accounts—the so-called 'freely usable' or 'freely convertible' currencies. Typically, a member state needing resources to settle its accounts would draw US dollars from the Fund and use these to redeem its own currency—say pesos—held by a creditor country.

In effect, the transaction with the Fund was a loan, subject to interest while it was outstanding and subject to repayment within a stated period. In form, however, Article V of the original Articles provided for purchase by the members of dollars (or other freely usable currency) with the member's own currency. The relevant state was subject to an obligation to repurchase its own currency within a given time

---

[7] Article IV(3) of the original Articles of Agreement, no longer in force.

[8] Note the similarities between this system and the several efforts of the European Community to establish a system of exchange stability, all of which broke down, to be replaced eventually, by the common currency.

[9] Article III(3) of the original Articles of Agreement.

and subject to stated charges (comparable to interest) payable to the Fund, based on the amount of that currency held by the Fund at any given time.

III. The Fund in Operation: 1946–71

A. Drawing rights

The critical question—and the subject of major disagreement between the American and British delegations at Bretton Woods—was whether a member state had a *right* to draw on the Fund's resources, or whether the Fund could impose conditions on use of the resources. Lord Keynes, on behalf of the UK, which was likely to be a debtor country, had urged that members be given an automatic entitlement to draw on the Fund—no questions asked. Thus the country in deficit could use the resources drawn from the Fund to support a general wage increase, or a tax reduction, or an enhanced national health service, and it would not owe an explanation to the Fund as to its intentions. The analogy would be a consumer drawing on a credit card issued by a bank or department store, which could not ask whether a drawing was to be used for food for the drawer's children, or gifts for a mistress, or for gambling at a casino.

The USA, expecting to be a creditor or surplus country, took the view that the Fund resources should be available only upon an undertaking to comply with conditions decided upon by the Fund. In the original Articles, the controversy was left unsettled.[10] In the event, the American position prevailed. In a series of resolutions adopted by the Executive Directors, it became clear that a member state seeking to draw on the Fund would have to answer questions put by the Fund, and that the answers would be subject to verification or negotiation.[11]

Applicants for a drawing were supposed to demonstrate that they could cure the problem—that is, return to equilibrium—within the period of the drawing, at first within six months, later generally within a year. Applicant countries responded to the Fund through a Letter of Intent signed by the Minister of Finance or the Central Bank Governor setting out the policies that the country would follow. Although in form a Letter of Intent is a unilateral declaration, in practice it is a document resulting from negotiation between the Fund and the applicant country. Letters of Intent are considered binding on the country involved, even though they

---

[10] Article V(3)(a) stated that a member 'shall be entitled to buy the currency of another member[if]:
  (i) The member desiring to purchase the currency represents that it is presently needed for making in that currency payments which are consistent with the provisions of this Agreement. Article V(5), however, provided that, subject to procedural safeguards:

  Whenever the Fund is of the opinion that any member is using the resources of the Fund contrary to the purposes of the Fund. . . . the Fund may limit the use of its resources by the member. . . . or may, after giving reasonable notice to the member, declare it ineligible to use the resources of the Fund.

[11] See Executive Board Decision No 71–2, 26 September 1946; Executive Board Decision No 284–4, 10 March 1948.

have not been submitted to its parliament and even when the administration in office has changed during the period of the drawing.[12]

For many years, the text of Letters of Intent was kept confidential; as the content of the letters tended to leak out, often amid public claims of betrayal, the practices changed and Letters of Intent are now usually published and posted online.

B. Standby arrangements

One of the main attractions of drawing rights as described above was that they were to have the function of reserves, that is, the resources drawn could be used to settle accounts with creditor countries. Indeed, if a creditor country knew that the debtor country had the right to draw from the Fund up to a stated amount, it might well prolong the credit and not insist on immediate settlement. But if the right to draw depended on successful negotiation of a Letter of Intent, this function of drawing rights would lose much of its value. The solution, developed in a series of resolutions by the Executive Directors, was the Stand-by Arrangement.[13] In consideration of the commitment set out in a Letter of Intent, which could be negotiated well before the member state in question needed to apply for a drawing, the Fund agreed to permit the purchase of its resources within a stated period without further questioning.

From 1952 on, the Letter of Intent and Stand-by Arrangement became the principal instruments for transactions with the Fund, including the development of conditionality.

C. The demise of the par value system

For a full quarter-century, from 1946 to 1971, the Bretton Woods scheme based on fixed par values enhanced by drawing rights, stand-by arrangements, and conditionality succeeded surprisingly well. A major hitch in the system occurred in 1967, when pressure on the British pound, still used as a reserve currency, became irresistible and the British government announced a devaluation of 14.3 per cent 'with the concurrence of the IMF'. President Johnson immediately issued a statement declaring that '[t]he nations of the free world are united in their determination to keep the international monetary system strong', and that:

The USA will continue to meet its international monetary responsibilities. I reaffirm unequivocally the commitment of the USA to buy and sell gold at the existing price of $35 an ounce.[14]

---

[12] But failure to honor the commitments in a drawing is not considered a breach of international law, so that the penalties for breach of obligations to the Fund (amended Articles XXVI(2)(a)–(c)) are not applied. It was understood, however, that failure to meet the commitments set forth in a Letter of Intent would make it difficult for the member concerned to negotiate a new drawing or Stand-by Arrangement (discussed in Section III:B).

[13] See Executive Board Decision No 155, 1 October 1952; Executive Board Decision No 270, 23 December 1953.

[14] 3 Weekly Compilation of Presidential Documents 1599, 18 November 1967.

The Managing Director of the Fund declared that:

in concurring with the UK proposal the Fund has indicated its agreement that the change is needed to deal with a fundamental disequilibrium.

... The United Kingdom has stressed the importance of rebuilding confidence in sterling, and in this connection has requested a new stand-by of $1.4 billion.[15]

The stand-by was approved and, for a time, Britain's balance of payments moved toward equilibrium as its exports rose and imports declined. Meanwhile, concern shifted to sustainability of the US dollar at its 1934 rate.

By 1971, the Vietnam War had been going on for six years, and Japan had maintained an exchange rate of 360 yen to 1 US dollar set in 1949, notwithstanding the growth of its economy at an annual average growth rate of over 10 per cent, well in excess of the growth of any other developed country.[16] The reserves of the USA (i.e. gold) were approaching the symbolic level of $10 billion, as contrasted with $13 billion in 1967 and $25 billion in 1949. On 15 August 1971, in a dramatic Sunday night broadcast—the 'Nixon shock', as it was called in Japan—President Nixon announced that the USA would no longer convert foreign-held US dollars to gold or other reserve assets, or intervene in exchange markets to maintain the par value of the dollar against gold. Effectively, the par value system was over.

D. The par value system on life support (1971–73)

For two years following the Nixon shock, the Fund, the major European countries and Japan, as well as the USA, attempted to preserve the system through realigned exchange rates and commitments by the participants to maintain 'central rates' (i.e. not 'par values') within wider margins than prescribed in the Articles of Agreement. But the UK dropped out of the first realignment in the summer of 1972 and, over the next year, several efforts by the USA to establish a new value for the dollar failed. By July 1973 all the major currencies were floating, that is, central banks were not intervening in the markets at all or in any event were not endeavoring to maintain any particular exchange rate. It had become clear that it was no longer possible to design a fixed rate system with sufficient accuracy to accommodate global volatility, not only in exchange markets but in interest rates, rates of inflation, capital movements, trade flow, and political expectations. In the meantime, however, that realization was less and less viewed as a catastrophe.

---

[15] 19 *International Financial News Survey* 381, 18 November 1967.

[16] Note that the Fund had no authority to order Japan to alter the value of its currency, that being one of the indicia of sovereignty that countries had not been willing to give up at Bretton Woods or later.

IV. Toward a New Fund Agreement

If the Fund Agreement no longer described, let alone controlled, the international monetary system, then it seemed reasonable that the Articles should be rewritten to align the law as much as possible to the actual situation, while recording as far as possible the consensus of the member countries. Had the second generation of architects—or rather the countries that employed them—wanted to build or rebuild a rule-based regime, they might have focused on gains or loss of reserves by member countries within a prescribed margin, as was in fact suggested, though not proposed, by a high-level study group within the Fund. They might have followed the suggestion that the objective of equilibrium fell on surplus as well as deficit countries, with pressures (not to use the word sanctions) on surplus countries such as Japan in the 1970s (and more recently China) to increase domestic demand and imports, with or without intervention in the currency market. The institution was preserved—that is, the skeleton; but the fundamental rule was replaced by a non-rule, and the mission gradually changed.

A. The amended Articles of Agreement

The principal decisions reflected in the amended Articles were reached at a summit conference at the Chateau de Rambouillet outside Paris in November 1975, attended by the Presidents or Prime Ministers of what came to be known as the Group of Seven or G7—France, West Germany, Italy, Japan, the UK, Canada, and the USA. By the time of the Rambouillet Conference, the international economy had experienced, and on the whole survived, the massive shift in resources caused by the embargo and fourfold increase in the price of oil imposed by the Arab oil-producing states in the wake of the Yom Kippur War of October 1973. It seemed clear that the oil-importing countries could not have adhered to an obligation to maintain a fixed exchange rate for their currencies. With no such obligation in place, the perception was that floating had enabled oil-importing countries to 'roll with the punch'. While a return to a fixed parity system was preserved as a distant contingency, the G7 and subsequently the entire membership of the IMF agreed on a system (if it could be called that) based on floating exchange rates.[17]

Under Article IV of the original Articles of Agreement, entitled 'Par Value of Currencies', each member state had been required to maintain its currency within a narrow band around its stated par value in terms of gold or the US dollar tied to gold. Under the amended Articles, Article IV was renamed 'Obligations Regarding Exchange Arrangements', but in fact imposed no obligations other than to avoid

---

[17] Declaration of Rambouillet, Rambouillet, 17 November 1975, 4 IMF Survey 350, 24 November 1975. With some more details added to meet the concerns of the developing countries in particular, the Declaration was turned into the Second Amendment of the Articles of Agreement, submitted to a meeting of the so-called Interim Committee in Jamaica in January 1976 and approved by the Executive Directors in March 1976. The amended Articles entered into force on 1 April 1978 upon approval by 78 member states having four-fifths of the total voting power.

manipulating exchange rates. The member states were authorized to maintain the value of their currency (i) in terms of another currency or the Fund's own currency, the SDR (but not gold); (ii) in cooperative arrangements with other members; or (iii) using any other exchange arrangements of the member's choice.

A number of developing countries chose option (i), typically with a link to the US dollar or to the currency of the former colonial power. Members of the European Community attempted over three decades to build a European Monetary System (EMS) comparable within the Community to the Bretton Woods system— but without a central authority or a system of sanctions none of the efforts could be maintained for more than a few years.[18] From time to time the G7 or the G5 (i.e. the G7 without Italy and Canada) held conferences designed to achieve a common response to an unexpected event, such as the rapid rise (or fall) of the yen or the dollar. None of these meetings led to a long-term coordinated strategy, and indeed it appears that none of the major participants desired such an outcome. In effect, they all chose option (iii), 'free play'.

Reacting to a suggestion for a coordinated strategy, Prime Minister Thatcher said: 'No one is going to tell me how to run economic policy'.[19] A spokesperson for the US Secretary of the Treasury responded: 'We wouldn't want to have the IMF order us around...either'.[20] Thus all the major currencies floated against each other. While countries occasionally intervened in the market, except within the EMS, none announced or sought to maintain a consistent value of its currency in relation to any other.

B. Surveillance

The amended Articles did retain one area in which the international community acting through the Fund could exercise influence, if not control, over the economic policies of member states. Article IV(3)(a) of the amended Articles says that the Fund 'shall oversee the international monetary system in order to ensure its effective operation, and shall oversee the compliance of each member with its obligations under Section 1 of this Article'. Moreover, according to Article IV(3)(b) each member, '*shall* provide the Fund with the information necessary for such surveillance, and when requested by the Fund, *shall* consult with it...' (italics added).

---

[18] For a book-length discussion of both the technical and the political hurdles of the EMS see e.g. Peter Ludlow, *The Making of the European Monetary System: A Case Study of the Politics of the European Community* (London: Butterworths, 1982); Jacques van Ypersele, *The European Monetary System: Origins, Operation and Outlook* (Luxemburg: Commission of the European Communities, 1985). For a briefer account, including the takedown of the pound and lira in 1992 and the collapse of the franc in 1993, see Andreas Lowenfeld, *International Economic Law*, 2nd ed. (Oxford: Oxford University Press, 2008) 771–819.

[19] Quoted in Joseph Gold, 'Strengthening the Soft International Law of Exchange Arrangements', 77 *American Journal of International Law* 443 (1983), at 477, footnote 97.

[20] *Washington Post*, 30 May 1982, A1, quoted in Joseph Gold, 'Strengthening the Soft International Law of Exchange Arrangements', 77 *American Journal of International Law* 443 (1983), at 477, footnote 97.

In a Decision on Surveillance even before the amended Articles, the Executive Directors set out a number of contingencies—not limited to exchange rates—that 'might indicate the need for discussion' between the Fund and a member state.[21] It was understood that while such discussions would cover movements in exchange rates, the Fund's appraisal of a member's exchangerate policies shall be made 'within the framework of a comprehensive analysis of the general economic situation and economic policy strategy of the member, and shall recognize that domestic as well as external policies can contribute to timely adjustments of the balance of payments'.[22] Could an activist IMF, supported by the USA and other major countries, have built on the authorization in Article IV and the accompanying Principles of Fund Surveillance over Exchange Rate Policies (Principles) to undertake some affirmative regulation of countries that were not seeking loans— that is, the industrial countries of the West? This may seem an idle question, given the attitude of the leaders of the developed world reflected in the preceding paragraphs. But I raise the question here with the thought that perhaps if the attitude changes some four decades later, the legal authorities can be found in Article IV of the amended Articles and the accompanying Principles to prevent actions at cross purposes, at a minimum. For instance, as these lines are written, it is reported that the German Chancellor is raising interest rates and curbing government spending to guard against inflation, the French President is urging greater government expenditures to increase employment, and the US President is urging Americans to spend more on consumer goods.[23] But I am getting ahead of the story, and of my assignment.

Coming back to the historical account, Article IV did not accomplish the objectives that the drafters had in mind. Governments were reluctant to answer inquiries put by the Fund, and had no real incentive to do so. When information was disclosed to staff of the Fund, it was often subject to confidentiality.[24] Surveillance pursuant to the new Article IV was conducted for both developed and developing countries, but in practice resources were generally only made available to developing countries pursuant to Article V.[25] The idea that the IMF, or the international community through the IMF, could prescribe conduct under amended Article IV comparable with what the Fund prescribed under Article V did not prove viable, if indeed it was ever seriously considered.

[21] Executive Board Decision No 5392-(77/63), 29 April 1977, reprinted as amended in Selected Decisions and Selected version repealed by Executive Board Decision No 13919-(07/51), 15 June 2007, see Selected Decisions and Selected Documents of the International Monetary Fund, 33rd Issue, Washington, 31 December 2008, 31.

[22] *Principles of Fund Surveillan over Exchange Rate Policies*, annexed to Executive Board Decision No 5392-(77/63), 29 April 1977, para 3.

[23] See e.g. Steven Erlanger, 'Two Competing Visions of a European Economy: One French, One German', *New York Times*, 2 July 2010, A8.

[24] For a description of how a surveillance mission is organized and extracts from sample reports, see Lowenfeld, above n 18, at 640–4 and sources there cited.

[25] The last industrial countries to draw on the Fund were Italy and Great Britain in 1977; Russia drew on the Fund in 1998 in the midst of a major crisis.

V. A Different IMF

From the late 1970s on, the IMF did not have a major role in the international monetary system. Each of the principal currencies floated freely against each of the others, and accumulation or depletion of reserves by developed countries took place without approval or disapproval by the Fund. It is also worth remarking that the prediction of many economists that—under a floating regime balance of payments would become irrelevant did not come to pass. Leadership in legislation concerning the international economy passed to the GATT and subsequently to the World Trade Organization (WTO) as new rules were being negotiated and drafted by trade ministries and not by finance ministries. Meanwhile, nearly all the former colonies had gained their independence and all joined the IMF, most with very small quotas and great need. *De facto*, the IMF became essentially a foreign aid agency. The IMF did not engage in sponsoring major long-term infrastructure projects, that was the role of the World Bank, but in tiding over member states in need of reserves to balance their domestic budgets or international accounts.

The form of assistance remained Article V of the amended Articles, with purchases of hard currency pursuant to stand-by arrangements subject to repurchase within a stated period. But the Article V(3)(c) of the amended Articles now said clearly that the Fund 'shall examine a request for a purchase to determine whether the proposed purchase would be consistent with the provisions of the Agreement and the policies adopted under them'. This Article, as agreed in Jamaica in 1976, provided that drawings could not cause the Fund's holdings of a member's currency to exceed 200 per cent of its quota. In other words, the member could draw up to 125 per cent of its quota.[26]

But Article V(4) provided that the Fund may in its discretion waive the limits on a drawing. In crisis situations, the Fund regularly granted waivers up to 4000 times quotas. The higher the amount of a proposed drawing, and the longer its proposed repurchase time and the stricter the conditions that the Fund would impose.[27]

---

[26] This follows because the Fund already holds 75 per cent of a member's quota in its own currency unless it has been subject of a drawing by another member country.

[27] Jacques de Larosière, the Managing Director of the IMF in the 1980s, said this was the wrong way to look at conditionality:

> For instance, if a country runs a balance of payments current deficit amounting to let's say 8 percent of its gross domestic product, and if in that particular case its sustainable deficit is considered to be in the order of 2 percent of its GDP, an adequate three-year adjustment program would imply an adjustment of some 2 percentage points a year in the deficit of that country. But suppose now ... that this same country has moved into a worse balance of payments position. For instance a deficit of 12 percent instead of 8 percent of GDP because of an irreversible deterioration in its terms of trade or/and because of a slippage in its domestic financial policies. Its long-term sustainable financable position has not by the same token changed and is still, in my example, at 2 percent of GDP. The necessary adjustment would imply a reduction of a little more than 3 percentage points a year in the course of the three-year program. Now, in such a situation ... the perception might have arisen that conditionality has tightened. But what has really happened is not a tightening of conditionality per se, it is the worsening of the external conditions of the country in question and the need for more adjustments.

A Conversation with Mr de Larosière, 19(2) Finance and Development (June 1982), at 4–5.

To reiterate, all of this funding, and law-giving via conditionality, has taken place only under Article V which governs drawings. With one significant exception, all drawings have been by developing and emerging market countries.

VI. The International Monetary System and Regional Crises

The governments of most developing countries sought as far as possible to avoid applying to the IMF for credit. Private credit, when available, came without instructions and monitoring, while the requirement for submitting a Letter of Intent to the Fund was often regarded as humiliating. Only when a crisis did break out, typically with a run on a country's currency, did it become necessary to seek support from the major countries who were generally led by the USA as well as the IMF.

More than a dozen countries in nearly every continent fell into the debtors' crisis of 1982–83. The details varied from country to country but all were affected by the same overall factors—excessive public sector borrowing, floating interest rates that reached unexpectedly high levels, recession in the developed countries, and a contagious loss of confidence by private lenders and investors in the developed countries. The first, and most-watched, country was Mexico. I have set out the facts in some detail, not for the sake of completeness or historical record, but to illustrate how the international monetary system brought its rules and facilities to bear on the debtor countries, with the IMF as catalyst, coordinator, law giver, and scapegoat.[28]

A. Mexico 1982–83

Following a major discovery of oil in 1978, Mexico's economy grew by more than 8 per cent per year in the period 1978–81 and employment increased by more than half a million jobs per year. But by year-end 1981, price inflation had reached an annual rate of 28.7 per cent and the current account deficit almost doubled to about 15 per cent of gross domestic product (GDP). Even as both price and demand for oil were falling, Mexico's cumulative foreign debt stood at nearly $70 billion, with about $18 billion due to be repaid in 1982 unless it could be rescheduled.

The Mexican peso had been pegged to the US dollar; as inflation in Mexico exceeded that of the dollar, the peso became increasingly overvalued. Mexico did not maintain exchange controls and conversion of pesos into dollars—that is, capital flight—took place on a massive scale. When the Bank of Mexico ceased to support the peso in February 1982, it dropped by 40 per cent in a few days. The government ordered wage increases to compensate for the loss in value of the peso, but capital flight continued.

---

[28] This section is abridged and adapted from Lowenfeld, above n 18, at 667–80.

Paul Volcker, the Chairman of the US Federal Reserve, repeatedly advised Mexico's financial officials to apply to the IMF for a stand-by and to use the conditions that would be attached as a way to introduce necessary reforms into the Mexican economy.[29] But Mexican officials always refused. Having freed itself from a tough and unpopular IMF program in the 1970s, Mexico was determined never to submit to another such program. As to the Fund, its surveillance teams must have known the situation in Mexico; but without a request for a stand-by, it had no authority with respect to Mexico's policies (either domestic or international) and it made no public statement.

On 1 August 1982, the government of Mexico announced major price increases for electricity and gasoline, as well as for bread and tortillas. On 5 August, as capital flight continued without let up, the government imposed exchange controls. On 12 August all dollar-denominated pesos were ordered to be converted to pesos at a rate 20 per cent below the market rate. On Friday 13 August, the Minister of Finance announced that Mexico would be unable to make the payments on its debt due two days later.

The announcement came as a shock to the international community. It turned out that many of the loans made to Mexico (and now threatened with default) had been made through a web of reciprocal deposits, guarantees, and participation loans; it was feared that if one strand broke—if the loans to Mexico had to be charged off on the books of the major money-centre banks—the system might well unravel. Before a thorough examination of Mexico's economy could be undertaken, the first task was to keep the international system of payments in operation.

Within five days in August, the USA came up with an advance payment of $1 billion from the US Petroleum Reserve for oil from Mexico, and another $1 billion line of credit from the US Commodity Credit Corporation for purchases of agricultural products by Mexico. The Bank for International Settlements (the central bankers' bank) put together a bridging credit of $1.85 billion, half on behalf of the USA, the other half on behalf of central banks of 10 other states, to be repaid as soon as a more permanent credit could be arranged with the IMF. That, of course, would require a stand-by arrangement which would have to be negotiated. At Mexico's request, the commercial bank creditors agreed to a 90-day stand-by pending negotiation with the Fund. The Fund, in turn, would not agree to a stand-by arrangement without (i) a commitment from all the commercial bank creditors (i.e. not merely a majority) to deferral of principal repayment so long as interest was kept up, and (ii) an application by Mexico to the IMF for a stand-by arrangement supported with the kind of program of reform that Mexico could have sought six or nine months earlier, but had chosen not to.

Negotiating the second phase of the rescue operation took longer than anticipated as the government sought to protect its standing with the people of Mexico, but eventually agreement was reached. Again, each of the affected parties had to

---

[29] Paul A. Volcker and Toyoo Gyohten, *Changing Fortunes: The World's. Money and the Threat to American Leadership* (New York: Times Books, 1992) 199.

participate and each of the participants had to give up something, in reliance on all the others doing so as well:

- Mexico had to submit to the economic discipline demanded by the Fund in return for which Mexico would be permitted to make the drawing described below;

- the commercial lenders not only had to give up the ability to withdraw their funds upon the stated maturity, but were required to contribute to a package of new loans, roughly in proportion to the amount of their outstanding credits;

- the US government had to offer additional medium-term credits of about $2 billion; and

- one-third of the amount—which Mexico was permitted to draw upon— would come from its own resources, with the other two-thirds borrowed under the so-called General Arrangements to Borrow.

Only the IMF could point to a legal instrument on the basis of which it could demand fundamental reforms, such as a negotiated formula governing the relation between wage increases and inflation targets. No deal was done until all deals were in place, formalized by a resolution of the Executive Directors of the Fund reciting the respective commitments, and a press release asserting 'sufficient assurance that the needed amounts were being made available'.

No Mexican loans were charged off on the balance sheets of commercial banks, no banks became insolvent, and export–import trade between Mexico and the rest of the world continued. The system, one could say, had survived and shown its strength, based on a principle which not everyone accepted: that if a credit transaction requires restructuring or default, both (or all) sides are in part responsible, or in any event must share the burden.

Each case was, of course, somewhat different but a Brazilian crisis arose while the Mexican crisis was still in phase I, and was addressed substantially along the same lines as the crisis in Mexico. The debtor country, the creditor banks, the USA, and the IMF all realized that they needed one another, and that if the strategy failed, no one could predict what global consequences would follow. Altogether 39 countries rescheduled around $140 billion in commercial bank debt in the 1980s, substantially following the precedent set in the Mexican case. Like the report of Mark Twain's death, the reports of the demise of the international monetary system and the lapse of the IMF into irrelevance were exaggerated. But the system looked quite different in 1990 from what Keynes and White had designed in the 1940s.

VII. Recent Adventures

If you wanted to fast-forward through a quarter-century before resuming this narrative, you would be missing several exciting events, each showing the international monetary system, and in particular the IMF, in a different light.

A. South-East Asia 1997–98

In the summer of 1997, a cascade of South-East Asian countries—first Thailand, then the Philippines, then Indonesia, then South Korea—found themselves with large debts in foreign currencies, declining gross domestic product, and an inability to maintain the ties of their currencies (formal or otherwise) to the US dollar. Each time an IMF mission was quickly dispatched, a bridge loan was arranged, and a Letter of Intent and stand-by arrangement were negotiated.

A major innovation was what came to be known as 'structural reform'. South Korea, for instance, committed in its Letter of Intent not only to address the traditional macroeconomic factors, but made commitments about regulation of banks, including capital adequacy standards and rights of shareholders. Furthermore, commitments included accounting standards, competition law, rights of foreign investors, and also conditions for hiring and laying off workers. Thailand and Indonesia made similar commitments, covering not only strictly economic subjects, but also improved medical and maternity benefits as well as HIV/AIDS facilities.[30]

Critics said that in going into these and comparable areas, the Fund was exceeding both its legal authority and its credibility as a neutral international agency. The Fund's position, backed strongly by the USA and expounding the so-called Washington Consensus, was that such factors as 'crony capitalism', corruption, and weakness in regulation had been major causes of the Asian crisis and its unexpectedly rapid spread from country to country. Its position suggested that 'there is neither point nor excuse for the international community to provide financial assistance to a country unless that country takes measures to prevent future such crises'.[31] The controversy is not finally resolved, and the results of the rescue packages were uneven. But clearly, structural reform marked another stage in the evolution of the IMF.

B. Russia 1996–99

Bringing Russia into the international financial economy after the collapse of the Soviet Union would, of course, be a major achievement. To accomplish the integration of Russia into the Fund and the World Bank, the Western countries led by Germany and the USA were prepared to gather nearly $18 billion in credits, loan guarantees, and debt deferrals, plus a $6 billion fund to stabilize the ruble, all subject to agreement between Russia and the IMF. In May 1992, less than half a

---

[30] The information in this paragraph comes from South Korea's Letter of Intent and Accompanying Memorandum, 7 February 1998; Thailand's Letter of Intent and Memorandum on Economic Policies, 24 February 1998; Indonesia's Memorandum of Economic and Financial Policies, 15 January 1998. All available on the IMF website, <http://www.imf.org> (visited 3 August 2010).

[31] Stanley Fischer, 'The IMF and the Asian Crisis', Forum Funds Lecture, Los Angeles, 20 March 1998, reproduced on the IMF website and excerpted in 27 IMF Survey 97, (6 April 1998). Mr Fischer was First Deputy Managing Director of the IMF. His remarks were made in reply to Martin Feldstein, *Refocusing the IMF*, 77 *Foreign Affairs* 20 (March/April 1998).

year after it had become independent, Russia (along with 13 former constituent states of the Soviet Union) was admitted to the IMF as well as to the World Bank.[32] However, Russia and the IMF did not reach agreement on a stand-by arrangement until August, and then only with a further deferral on Russia's official debt.

In the event, Russia did not meet its commitments calling for reduction of its budget deficit and reduction of inflation. Western countries sought to strengthen democracy in Russia against threats to Boris Yeltsin, who had led Russia out of the Soviet Union and had stood on top of a tank in resistance to antidemocratic elements threatening his regime. More than in any prior case and contrary to its tradition, the Fund took sides in an election. In order to keep Russia in good standing, even when it was not complying with interest payments or domestic reforms, the Fund invented a Systemic Transformation Facility (STF). The STF was tailored especially to Russia or possibly to other states emerging from the Soviet Union, but not designed as a precedent for other states that might not keep up with their obligations under present or future stand-by arrangements. The idea was that a member would be allowed to make a drawing—even when conditions for a regular drawing under a stand-by arrangement were not available—based on a declaration of its intention to reach an understanding with the Fund as soon as possible. Russia took advantage of this facility to make an initial drawing, but as inflation continued to run at 1000 per cent in the fall of 1993, a second tranche under the STF was withheld.

Yeltsin won the 1996 election, but a new problem faced the Fund as the ruble kept losing value notwithstanding on-again, off-again disbursements under stand-by arrangements of varying kinds. Reports of funds flowing out of Russia into a series of offshore havens such as the Cayman Islands and the Isle of Man had been circulating for years. In the late 1990s, it appeared that such funds came not only from oligarchs who had grown rich from privatization of state enterprises, but also from the Central Bank itself, possibly including funds supplied by the IMF. The IMF withheld disbursements for a year, and meanwhile Russia declared a 90-day moratorium on foreign commercial debt and the ruble was permitted to float, in effect a default and a devaluation of about 30 per cent.

When Russia again came to the IMF in the summer of 1999, with a new and contrite Letter of Intent, it received a new loan, but in the form of SDRs that could be used only to pay off prior drawings from the Fund. In announcing the new loan, the Fund issued a press release stating: 'Directors expressed strong disapproval of the finding that ... the transfer of assets in the books of the Central Bank to FIMACO [a financial management company incorporated in the Channel Islands] meant that the balance sheet of the Central Bank had given a misleading impression of the true state of reserves and monetary and exchange policies'.[33] No doubt the

---

[32] Note that, in contrast, it took until December 2011, 18 years after Russia had started the accession process, for it to gain approval to become a member of the WTO with ratification expected in 2012. see Ministerial Conference approves Russia's WTO membership, 16 December 2011, <http://www.wto.org/english/news_e/news11_e/acc_rus_16dec11_e.htm> (visited 24 January 2012).

[33] IMF Press Release No 99/35, 28 July 1999, reprinted in 28 IMF Survey 241 (2 August 1999).

Fund was angry, and permitting new credits would (as many observers thought) reinforce the moral hazard program. Mr Fischer replied:

[The Russians] were allowed to fail. It was very controversial last August, but the moral hazard play, as you recall, was Russia. It was actually the one case where I thought the markets might have a point. But when push came to shove, the official sector did not go along with that.

So I don't see, in the Russian case, how the moral hazard argument can be sustained at present. And yes, we are trying to help them; but yes, they are members of the IMF, they have a program, they are doing reasonably well on implementing it, they have a right to assistance. I would say that the Russians have shown enormous determination to stay in the international financial system, and to find, after August, a consensual way of dealing with their creditors.[34]

C. Argentina 2000–07

When President Carlos Menem took office in 1989, the Argentine economy was in a state of decline. Menem embarked on a program of economic expansion, based on privatization of state enterprises and the parity, by law, of the Argentine peso and the US dollar. The value of the peso would be guaranteed also by a so-called currency board, which would hold an amount in dollars equal to the pesos in circulation. For the first-half of the 1990s, the policy was successful as capital flowed in, inflation was halted, exports increased, and unemployment was reduced. In the second-half of the decade, however, the model ceased to work. Unemployment rose to 15 per cent, public sector debt rose to 46 per cent of GDP, and the risk premium on Argentine bonds (public and private) increased sharply.

As inflation in Argentina steadily ran ahead of the movement of its anchor currency, the US dollar, its pegging policy became unsustainable. In other countries, devaluation might have been an option, but that would be incompatible with the currency board.

With monetary policy precluded and tax increases hard to obtain, Argentina turned both to commercial loans at increasing interest rates and to the IMF. In March 2000 the Fund approved a three-year stand-by arrangement with precise performance targets, replacing an earlier arrangement approved in 1998 and based on a projected growth in domestic product of 3.5 per cent. In fact, growth in GDP was close to zero and borrowing costs exceeded 10 per cent. In November 2000, after some doubts, the Fund approved an augmented stand-by arrangement on top of the previous one. This arrangement was based on projections that the Fund did not believe—for example, an increase in investment of 6 per cent and various structural reforms—and preservation of the currency board. Argentina did not meet the targets for the first quarter of 2001, asked for a waiver, and the Fund went along. The same scenario was repeated in the summer of 2001, with Argentina

---

[34] Press Conference Call with Stanley Fischer First Deputy Managing Director International Monetary Fund on the Russian Federation, 29 July 1999, IMF External Affairs Department, <http://www.imf.org/external/np/tr/1999/tr990729.htm> (visited 24 September 2010).

making proposals not grounded in reality and the Fund (as well as the US government) concerned that 'pulling the plug' on support for Argentina would be worse.

In late November 2001, the IMF sent one last mission to Buenos Aires to tell the government that no more resources could be made available. There would be no release of the fourth-quarter installment under the augmented stand-by arrangement. In the last week of November, deposits were being withdrawn from Argentine banks at a billion dollars a day. The government closed the banks, then reopened them with a limit on cash withdrawals. On 19 December 2001, following a number of riots and looting throughout the country, President de la Rúa declared a state of siege. On the following day he resigned. On 23 December, a provincial governor, Adolfo Rodriguez Saá, was elected interim president and immediately declared a default on Argentina's public debt. One week later, President Rodriguez Saá resigned.[35]

On 1 January 2002, Eduardo Duhalde, who had lost to de la Rúa in the 1999 election, assumed the Presidency and he remained in office until a popular election was arranged in May 2003. Congress passed an Emergency Law repealing the legal requirement of equivalence of the peso and the dollar, and delegating constitutional authority to the President to take the necessary measures to reorganize the banking, financial and exchange market regimes. For a while, the government attempted to fix a new exchange rate of 1.4 pesos to 1 US dollar. That rate did not hold; further efforts to fix an exchange rate were abandoned and the peso was allowed to float. A 'pesification' program was introduced, whereby persons who had borrowed from banks could pay back their debts in pesos at the nominal rate contracted in dollars; persons who had lent in dollars—for example with a savings bank deposit—could convert their holdings to pesos at an artificial, more favorable rate. Detailed regulations on implementation of the Emergency Law were issued almost daily.

Overall, Argentina's GDP declined by about 11% in 2002, bringing the cumulative decline since 1998 to about 20 per cent. Unemployment stood at over 20 per cent; by September 2003, more than half of the population of Argentina was living below the poverty line.

The IMF maintained a mission in Argentina throughout this period, but did not participate in the various measures and did not resume disbursement under the stand-by arrangement suspended in 2001. Eventually, in January 2003, the IMF and the Duhalde administration reached agreement on an eight-month transitional agreement, designed to avoid default by Argentina to the Fund. No net new funding was provided, but (as with Russia) the funds released would be kept in Argentina's account with the Fund to be used for payments as they became due.

In the spring of 2003, Argentina held a presidential election. Originally 18 candidates entered the race. Carlos Menem, the president during most of the 1990s, finished first, but with less than a quarter of the vote. Four days before the scheduled run-off, Menem withdrew and the run-off was cancelled. The

---

[35] For a day-by-day chronology of these and other measures, see Daseking, Ghosh, Lane, and Thomas, 'Lessons from the Crisis in Argentina,' Appendix II, IMF Occasional Paper No 236 (2004).

second-place finisher from the first round, Nestor Kirchner, was declared the winner. In his inaugural speech, Kirchner promised that his government would not make debt repayments 'at the price of the hunger and exclusion of Argentines'. Argentina had kept up its payments to the Fund throughout the crisis, but a payment of $2.9 billion was due in September 2003. President Kirchner announced that he would not make the payment until agreement on a new stand-by arrangement was reached. The Fund held up the stand-by arrangement, and on Tuesday, 9 September 2003, Argentina defaulted on its payment to the Fund. On the next day, the Fund gave in. The Managing Director announced that a Letter of Intent had been signed, and that once Argentina's arrears were cleared, he would recommend approval of the proposed three-year arrangement. On Thursday, 11 September, Argentina paid back the $2.9 billion loan. To the local population, and to much of the rest of the world, it appeared that Argentina had won the exchange.

Over the next two years, while the government and the IMF continued to negotiate, the Argentine economy continued its recovery as exports increased, the peso remained highly depreciated, and Argentina began to replenish its reserves. On 15 December 2005, President Kirchner announced that by year-end, Argentina would pay back all of its outstanding debt to the IMF—about 9.9 billion dollars— thus ending its decades-long status as a debtor to the Fund, and subject in varying degrees to the Fund's conditionality. 'With this payment,' the President told the Argentine people, 'we are burying a significant part of our ignominious past'. On the day before, President Lula da Silva of Brazil had made essentially the same statement, announcing that Brazil would pay off its debt to the IMF two years ahead of schedule.

Inside and outside the Fund, questions were raised about its continuing role in the world economy. President Kirchner, as well as President Chávez of Venezuela and others, declared that the Bretton Woods institutions had now become irrelevant. Writing just at the end of 2007, before the full force of the Great Recession of 2008–09 could be felt, I disagreed with this assessment:

This writer is not persuaded by those who follow President Kirchner and others in asserting that the Bretton Woods institutions have become irrelevant. Surely the Fund is changing, perhaps not quickly enough for some, but in the present writer's view, it remains an indispensable organization, as coordinator, law-giver, and *crisis manager*, if not necessarily as lender.[36]

VIII. Conclusions

If it is indeed true that the IMF is an institution searching for a mission, that its role as a lender/lawgiver to developing and emerging market nations is no longer vital. Could it not step onto the big stage for which Keynes and White and the other Founding Fathers intended it? Could it not act as a forum for the principal

---

[36] See Lowenfeld, above n 18, at 733.

participants—the major players, if you will—with respect to the issues that affect all aspects of the international financial community, public and private?

Consider the many agenda items when one looks for the causes and cures for the crises of the past three years: investment banks and bank-holding companies, national versus international regulation and the race to the bottom, disclosure, insider trading, proprietary trading, securitization, CDOs, capital adequacy, definition of assets, risk management, derivatives, credit swaps, the role of rating agencies and insurance, and so on. True, many of these subjects have not been at the top of the list for the IMF surveillance teams or semiannual forecasts. But we have seen that they matter, and are hard to understand, let alone to achieve common understanding across party lines and frontiers. I submit that the narrative here presented (albeit selective) has shown that the IMF is capable of evolving and improvising, and that it possesses unique legitimacy as a treaty-based international organization of 65 years standing.[37] Some, including the current Managing Director, have questioned whether the IMF has the needed energy and imagination.[38] I hope that the present symposium will contribute to a reinvigorated and, if necessary, reinvented IMF.

---

[37] It is worth recalling that Article I (i) of the Fund's Articles of Agreement, unchanged in the amended Articles, provides:

The purposes of the International Monetary Fund are:
(i) To promote international monetary cooperation through a permanent institution which provides the machinery for consultation and collaboration on international monetary problems.

[38] See Speech of Managing Director Dominique Strauss-Kahn, 'Multilateralism and the Role of the International Monetary Fund in the Global Financial Crisis', School of Advanced International Studies, Washington DC, 23 April 2009, <http://www.imf.org/external/np/speeches/2009/042309. htm> (visited 23 July 2010).

4

Towards a New Architecture for Financial Stability: Seven Principles

*Luis Garicano and Rosa M. Lastra**

I. The Financial Crisis and the Organization of Supervision

Policy-makers have concluded that the recent financial crisis resulted in part from an insufficient focus on systemic risks. To deal with such a problem, the Group of 20 (G-20) decided to push for the creation of systemic risk supervisors. In this chapter, we discuss the optimal organization of such authority in light of the organizational economics literature. We then use our analysis to discuss current reform proposals. These include, in Europe, the establishment of a European System of Financial Supervision with three authorities (revamped Lamfalussy Level 3 committees)[1] and the creation of a European Systemic Risk Council (ESRC) under the aegis of the European Banking Authority (EBA), based upon the recommendations of the De Larosière Report.[2] In the UK, the Financial Services Act[3] introduced a Council for Financial Stability and the new Government is proposing a radical overhaul of the regulatory structure that will see the powers of the Bank of England substantially expanded and the Financial Services Authority (FSA) ceasing to exist in its current form.[4] In the USA, the new financial legislation

* The authors thank seminar participants in Stockholm SIFR, the LSE FMG, the Central Banking Annual Conference in Cambridge, and Thomas Baxter, Douglas Diamond, Charles Goodhart, Raghu Rajan, Hyun Shin and Thomas Cottier for their valuable comments.

[1] For a summary of the tasks of these Committees see Appendix 9 of the report of the House of Lords' European Union Committee, 'The Future of EU Financial regulation and Supervision', 17 June 2009, <http://www.publications.parliament.uk/pa/ld200809/ldselect/ldeucom/106/106i.pdf> (visited 3 August 2010) (House of Lords' Report).

[2] Report of the High Level Group on Financial Supervision in the EU, Brussels, 25 February 2009, (de Larosière Report), <http://ec.europa.eu/internal_market/finances/docs/de_larosiere_report_en.pdf> (visited 3 August 2010).

[3] On 19 November 2009 the Chancellor of the Exchequer, Alistair Darling, introduced the Financial Services Bill into Parliament, and received Royal Assent in April 2010. The Financial Services Act 2010, <http://www.opsi.gov.uk/acts/acts2010/pdf/ukpga_20100028_en.pdf> (visited 3 August 2010).

[4] See Speech by The Chancellor of the Exchequer, The Rt Hon George Osborne MP, The Lord Mayor's Dinner for Bankers and Merchants of the City of London, Mansion House, 16 June 2010, <http://www.hm-treasury.gov.uk/press_12_10.htm> (visited 3 August 2010). On 26 July 2010, the UK Government launched a consultation document spelling out the proposals that the Chancellor had

establishes *interalia* a Financial Services Oversight Council and gives the Federal Reserve System (the Fed) responsibility for the regulation of systemically significant firms.[5] The focus of the article is on the architecture of the system and its reform (a fast-moving target) and *not* on the content of the specific regulations concerning liquidity, risk taking, capital requirements and other rules that have been addressed by several reports,[6] national legislative initiatives, EU and international proposals.

We are mindful that all existing architectures, independently of their specific characteristics, performed poorly at their mission. Whether twin peaks (like in the Netherlands), fragmented (like in the USA), unitary (like in the UK with the FSA), or separated (like in France), most advanced countries suffered a severe hit to their financial systems. While to some extent that may mean that the architecture does not matter, since it was not a cause of the crisis, we do believe, however, that the institutional design is important for the resolution of the crisis and for the establishment of a more effective framework of supervision, systemic risk control and crisis management.

The terms supervision and regulation are conceptually different, even though many commentators use them interchangeably. Supervision has to do with monitoring and enforcement, and regulation with rule-making. Crisis management refers to the instruments available to the authorities to confront crisis, in particular, lender of last resort assistance, deposit insurance, and insolvency proceedings.

In designing a new architecture (nationally as well as internationally), we must take into account the goals it is expected to achieve. Financial stability is the ultimate goal of supervision, regulation and crisis management. Yet, supervision is also designed to meet other goals, such as consumer protection, market integrity and prevention of fraud (depending on the type of financial institution subject to oversight). Regulation is also driven by these 'supervisory objectives' and other considerations such as fair competition or the needs of a single market. And crisis management also has objectives of its own, which tend to vary from country to country (e.g. minimization of costs to the Federal Deposit Insurance Corporation (FDIC)/taxpayers is a goal in the USA) and across institutions (with differential treatment of debtors and creditors in the case of bankruptcy).

The relationship between national structures and the international architecture is of particular relevance to our study. Restrictions imposed by one jurisdiction often

---

outlined in his Mansion House Speech. See Her Majesty's Treasury, 'A New Approach to Financial Regulation: Judgment, Focus and Stability', CM 7874, July 2010, <http://www.hm-treasury.gov.uk/d/consult_financial_regulation_condoc.pdf> (visited 3 August 2010).

[5] Dodd–Frank Wall Street Reform and Consumer Protection Act, Pub. L. 111–203 (2010) (the Dodd–Frank Act). The Act, named after Senator Christopher Dodd and Congressman Barney Frank, was signed by President Obama on 21 July 2010.

[6] See e.g. Markus Brunnermeier, Andrew Crockett, Charles Goodhart, Avinash D. Persaud and Hyun Song Shin (eds), *The Fundamental Principles of Financial Regulation* (11th Geneva Report on the World Economy) (Geneva: International Center for Monetary and Banking Studies and Centre for Economic Policy Research, 2009); Group of 30, Financial Reform Working Group, 'Financial Reform—A Framework for Financial Stability', Washington, DC, 2009 (Volcker's Report), <http://www.group30.org/pubs/recommendations.pdf> (visited 3 August 2010); and the Report of the High Level Group on Financial Supervision in the EU, above n 2.

result in regulatory arbitrage, providing business opportunities for other jurisdictions that do not impose such restrictions. This is clearly sub-optimal, a case of 'good intentions and unintended consequences'. Hence the need to advance towards adequate international financial regulation and supervision.

II. Regulatory Environment and Background

The principles for a new financial architecture that we propose affect three very different realities in the USA, UK and EU; realities which we describe below.

A. USA

The USA is a single monetary area with a single currency, combined with an extremely fragmented supervisory landscape and a complex regulatory system based upon federal law (financial laws enacted by Congress), state law (laws enacted by state legislatures, particularly relevant in terms of insurance companies), regulation by agencies (the Fed and the Securities and Exchange Commission (SEC) have rule-making powers), and self-regulation (in the field of securities, the rules of the self-regulatory organizations (SROs)), features which remain in the new financial legislation.

Decentralization in the USA runs deep within the fabric of the country and its constitutional tradition. It is both geographical—under its federalist structure, the powers of the states are very important—and functional, with the allocation of authority to narrowly focused agencies. The existence of multiple regulators, with sometimes overlapping roles, often allows firms to choose their regulator. Banking in the USA is subject both to federal law and to state law, with several supervisory authorities at the federal level (the Fed, the Office of the Comptroller of the Currency and the FDIC),[7] and at the state level. The securities industry is subject to a combination of federal law and self-regulation (with some elements of state law). The SEC is a federal agency that oversees the exchanges and administers the federal system for the registration of new issues of securities.[8] The exchanges are self-regulatory organizations with powers to promulgate rules for member firms and listed companies. The Financial Industry Regulatory Authority (FINRA) was

---

[7] The FDIC has 'three hats' as supervisor, insurer and receiver of failed banks. The Dodd–Frank Act extends the resolution powers of the FDIC with regard to systemically important financial institutions.

[8] The Securities Act of 1933 established a federal system for the registration of new issues of securities, and the Securities Exchange Act of 1934, created a new federal agency, the Securities and Exchange Commission. Following the stock market crash of 1929, these pieces of legislation were enacted to promote stability and confidence in capital markets and to protect investors in view of the shortcomings and inadequacies of the state 'blue sky' laws. The reason why state securities statutes were known as 'blue sky' laws is because some lawmakers believed that 'if securities legislation was not passed, *financial pirates would sell citizens everything in the state but the blue sky*'. See Howell E. Jackson and Edward L. Symons, *Regulation of Financial Institutions* (St. Paul, Minn.: West Group, 1999) 655–62 and 751–5.

created in July 2007 through the consolidation of the National Association of Securities Dealers (NASD) and the member regulation, enforcement, and arbitration functions of the New York Stock Exchange. It also performs market regulation under contract for the NASDAQ Stock Market, the American Stock Exchange, the International Securities Exchange, and the Chicago Climate Exchange.[9]

The Sarbanes–Oxley Act of 2002—which introduced sweeping reforms with regard to corporate governance—did not much change the regulatory structure of US securities markets. Investment companies (including mutual funds) have been regulated almost exclusively at the federal level by the SEC since the enactment of the 1940 Investment Company Act and the 1940 Investment Advisers Act.[10] Insurance in the USA has remained a matter of state law since the McCarran–Ferguson Act of 1945, although pension funds have been subject to federal law since the enactment of Employee Retirement Income Security Act (ERISA) in 1974. The US financial regulatory landscape also comprises other regulators, such as the Commodities Future Trading Commission (CFTC) for financial derivatives (commodity futures and options).

The failure to provide adequate supervision over large sectors of the financial market triggered a process of legislative reform. Amongst the 'architectural' issues included in new legislation[11] (a somewhat watered-down version of some earlier proposals) are: the powers to the Fed with regard to the supervision of the largest bank-holding companies and other systemically significant financial firms, the extension of the resolution authority of the FDIC (a new resolution process to unwind failing systemically important financial institutions), the creation of a Bureau of Consumer Financial Protection, the establishment of a Financial Services Oversight Council, some modest consolidation (the Office of Thrift Supervision (OTS) is abolished),[12] and more coordination between the SEC, the CFTC and others.[13]

---

[9] FINRA is involved in registering industry participants, examining securities firms, regulating markets and writing rules. For summary of its activities, see 'About the Financial Industry Regulatory Authority', <http://www.finra.org/AboutFINRA/index.htm> (visited 3 August 2010).

[10] Hedge funds are not required to register with the SEC as investment companies under the Investment Company Act of 1940. In the past, hedge fund advisers were not required to register under the Investment Advisers Act of 1940. However, in December of 2004, the SEC issued a final rule and rule amendments requiring certain hedge fund managers to register as investment advisers under the Act. See <http://www.sec.gov/rules/final/ia-2333.htm> (visited 3 August 2010).

[11] Dodd-Frank Wall Street Reform and Consumer Protection Act.

[12] Some academics—such as Howell Jackson—advocated the need for greater consolidation of the regulatory agencies. See Howell E. Jackson, 'A Pragmatic Approach to the Phased Consolidation of Financial Regulation in the United States', Harvard Public Law Working Paper No 09–19, 12 November 2008, <http://papers.ssrn.com/sol3/papers.cfm?abstract_id=1300431> (visited 10 May 2010). See also Howell E. Jackson, 'Regulatory Reform in the New World', Remarks at the Hart Seminar, London, 16 June 2009.

[13] One of the most controversial aspects of the new legislation is the so-called 'Volcker rule' (named after Paul Volcker). The Volcker rule (Section 619 of the Dodd-Frank Act, which takes the form of a new Section 13 of the Bank Holding Company Act of 1956 and new Section 27B of the Securities Act of 1933) prohibits federally insured 'banking entities' from engaging in proprietary trading (subject to certain exceptions) and restricts their relationships with hedge funds and private equity funds. Although the Dodd–Frank Act 2010 deals with many issues, it does not tackle the very severe problems of Fannie Mae and Freddie Mac.

However, following the enactment of the Dodd–Frank Act on 21 July 2010, the US financial architecture remains fragmented and 'multi-peaked'. *Plus ça change?*

B. UK

From 1997 to 2010, the UK presented a unified picture in terms of supervision, following the transfer of supervision away from the Bank of England and the establishment of a single supervisory agency, the FSA, governed by the Financial Services and Markets Act 2000. However, the relationships between the Bank of England (which provides lender of last resort assistance), the FSA (the supervisor) and the Treasury (responsible for the fiscal costs of bail-outs), which had been spelt out in a Memorandum of Understanding in 1997, became the subject of much criticism following the Northern Rock episode in September 2007.[14] The inadequacy of the UK system to confront financial crisis led to the new Banking Act of 2009 and to the establishment of the Special Resolution Regime (SRR) to deal with troubled and failing banks in which the Bank of England plays a key role. The structure of supervision remained intact under the Labour Government. It took the election of a new Government in May 2010 to change this and to abolish the tripartite regime. In a policy reversal, the new Conservative–Liberal Democrat (Con–Lib) coalition Government has condemned the model of the single regulator, a regulatory model which has inspired reforms in many other jurisdictions, to history. The new Chancellor, George Osborne, announced a radical redrafting of financial regulation on 16 June 2010, which was followed by the publication of a consultation document on 26 July 2010.[15] The Bank of England will be the key institution in the new financial architecture, while the FSA will cease to exist in its current form. The Governor of the Bank of England will chair a new Financial

---

[14] See Financial Services Authority, 'The Turner Review: A Regulatory Response to the Global Banking Crisis', March 2009, <http://www.fsa.gov.uk/pages/Library/Corporate/turner/index.shtml> (visited on 14 February 2012).

[15] See The Chancellor of the Exchequer, above n 4. In the words of the Chancellor:

> I can confirm that the Government will abolish the tripartite regime, and the Financial Services Authority will cease to exist in its current form. We will create a new prudential regulator, which will operate as a subsidiary of the Bank of England. It will carry out the prudential regulation of financial firms, including banks, investment banks, building societies and insurance companies. We will create an independent Financial Policy Committee at the Bank, which will have the tools and the responsibility to look across the economy at the macro issues that may threaten economic and financial stability and take effective action in response. We will also establish a powerful new Consumer Protection and Markets Authority. It will regulate the conduct of every authorised financial firm providing services to consumers. It will also be responsible for ensuring the good conduct of business in the UK's retail and wholesale financial services, in order to preserve our reputation for transparency and efficiency as well as our position as one of the world's leading global financial centres. I can also confirm that we will fulfil the commitment in the coalition agreement to create a single agency to take on the work of tackling serious economic crime that is currently dispersed across a number of Government departments and agencies.... We will handle the transition carefully, consult widely and get this right. The process will be completed in 2012. And I have asked Hector Sants to remain at the FSA to oversee the transition and become the first new deputy governor and chief executive of the new prudential regulator.

Policy Committee within the Bank and a new Prudential Regulatory Authority, which will operate as a subsidiary of the Bank of England. A new Consumer Protection and Markets Authority and an Economic Crime Agency will be created. Furthermore, the Government is also setting up an independent banking commission to look at the structure of and competition in the banking industry and at ways to reduce systemic risk. This supervisory and regulatory overhaul is expected to be completed in 2012.[16]

The Bank of England has a clear mandate with regard to monetary policy, and since the Banking Act of 2009, it has also had a mandate for financial stability as well as crisis management responsibilities—the SRR—to deal with troubled banks. With the new Government proposals, the supervisory powers of the Bank of England will be further expanded both with regard to macro-prudential supervision and to micro-prudential supervision.

C. EU

The 'architecture' of financial supervision in the EU is currently characterized by three principles: decentralization, co-operation, and segmentation. These principles which inform the Lamfalussy structure (see Fig. 4.1) also characterize the new structure, based upon the proposals outlined in the De Larosière Report (see Fig. 4.2), further analysed below. In the EU, prudential supervision remains decentralized at the level of the Member States, based upon the principle of home-country control, combined with mutual recognition on the basis of prior regulatory harmonization. The fact that some EU Member States have adopted the euro, while others retain their national currencies and national monetary policies, has significant implications for the purposes of our article. In the eurozone, the abandonment of the coincidence between the area of jurisdiction of monetary policy and the area of jurisdiction of supervision is a major novelty brought about by the advent of European Monetary Union (EMU).[17] Since the launch of the euro in January 1999, the European Central Bank (ECB) has been in charge of the monetary policy of the countries which have adopted the single currency, while responsibility for supervision remains decentralized, which means that each EU country (eurozone or non-eurozone) organizes supervision as it wishes. Some (like the Czech Republic) rely on their central banks to do everything, some others (like Sweden) have a single supervisory authority different from their central banks. Others (like Spain or Switzerland) have separate authorities for banking, securities, and insurance, and there are 'permutations', like the Dutch twin peaks approach of having the central bank (De Nederlandsche Bank, DNB) as the institution

---

[16] See FSA Press Release, 'FSA Chairman Welcomes Chancellor's Plans for Regulatory Reform', 16 June 2010, <http://www.fsa.gov.uk/pages/Library/Communication/PR/2010/100.shtml> (visited on 14 February 2012).

[17] Tommaso Padoa-Schioppa, 'EMU and Banking Supervision', Lecture at the London School of Economics, 24 February 1999, <http://fmg.lse.ac.uk/events/index.html> (visited on 14 February 2012), also published in Charles Goodhart (ed), *Which Lender of Last Resort For Europe?* 13–29 (London: Central Banking Publications, 2000) 13–29.

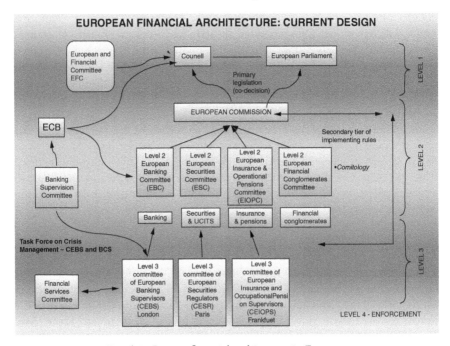

Fig. 4.1 Current financial architecture in Europe

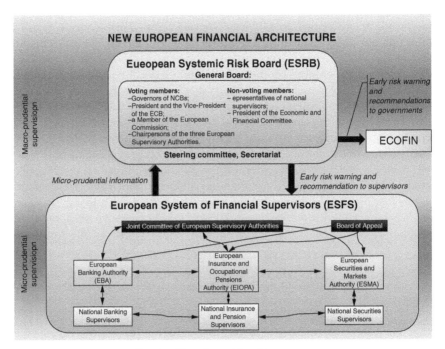

Fig. 4.2 New financial architecture

responsible for prudential supervision in the pursuit of financial stability and a separate Authority for Financial Markets (AFM) as the authority responsible for conduct of business supervision.[18] (Both supervisory authorities cover the full cross-sector width of financial markets, i.e. all institutions in banking, securities, insurance and pensions.)

In Europe, the basis of the reform proposals is the so-called de Larosière Report, a Report by a high-level group on financial supervision in the EU, chaired by Jacques de Larosière, presented to the European Commission, on 25 February 2009.[19] The report was endorsed by the European Commission in May 2009 and by the European Council in June 2009. On 23 September 2009 the EU Commission presented legislative proposals to implement its recommendations (illustrated in Fig. 4.2). These included proposals for regulations establishing a EBA, a European Insurance and Occupational Pensions Authority (EIOPA) and a European Securities and Markets Authority (ESMA), as well as a European System Risk Board (ESRB) and a decision entrusting the ECB with specific tasks concerning the ESRB.[20] In October 2009 the Commission proposed a directive amending a number of directives in respect of the EBA, the EIOPA and the ESMA. The Economic and Financial Affairs Council (ECOFIN) reached a broad consensus regarding the main features of the ESRB at its meeting on 20 October 2009 and on 2 December 2009, ECOFIN approved the creation of the new European Supervisory Authorities.[21] Following approval by the European Parliament the legislation establishing the ESRB came into force on the 10 December 2010.[22] The ESRB will have to identify risks to financial stability and, where appropriate, issue warnings or recommendations of a general or specific nature concerning the Community as a whole, individual Member States, or groups of Member States. Although ESRB recommendations will not be legally binding, it is expected that the addressees of recommendations will not remain passive towards a risk which has been identified and are expected to react in some way. The ESRB might decide on a case-by-case basis whether warnings or recommendations should be made public.

---

[18] See 'Recent Developments in Supervisory Structures in EU and Acceding Countries', *ECB Monthly Bulletin*, October 2006, <http://www.ecb.int/pub/pdf/other/report_on_supervisory_structuresen.pdf> (visited 10 May 2010).

[19] See de Larosière Report, above n 2.

[20] The legal basis of the regulations is Article 114 of the Treaty on the Functioning of the European Union (TFEU), which was Article 95 of the EC Treaty and the legal basis of the decision granting certain tasks to the ECB is Article 127(5) TFEU, which was Article 105(5) EC Treaty.

[21] See Press Release, 'Commission Adopts Legislative Proposals to Strengthen Financial Supervision in Europe', IP/09/1347, 23 September 2009, <http://europa.eu/rapid/pressReleasesAction.do?reference=IP/09/1347&type=HTML> (visited 10 May 2010). The ECOFIN Council on 2 December 2009 approved the creation of the three new European Supervisory Authorities, which together with the ESRB (for which broad political agreement was reached on 20 October 2009) form the new EU supervisory structure. See Council of the European Union Press Release, Economic and Financial Affairs, 16838/09 (Presse 352), 2 December 2009, <http://www.consilium.europa.eu/uedocs/cms_Data/docs/pressdata/en/ecofin/111706.pdf> (visited 10 May 2010).

[22] See 'Establishment of the ESRB', <http://www.esrb.europa.eu/about/background/html/index.en.html> (visited 17 January 2012).

Having described the existing structures, as well as the issues being discussed in Europe, the USA and the UK, we proceed to answer the key questions on the table concerning a set of principles that, in our view, should govern the reform of the architecture of supervision.

III. Seven Regulatory Principles

The principles outlined in this section should be observed by countries in their domestic law and should also be considered as principles of multilevel governance in this area.

A. Principle 1: The supervision of banking, securities and insurance should be further integrated

The key argument in favour of separate supervisors for several problems is one of specialization and division of labour. The main source of the gains from specialization is that knowledge costs are fixed costs, and thus the average cost decreases with utilization. Single focused agencies are likely to utilize their knowledge more intensively and thus will be able to acquire deeper expertise in their domain.[23] However, coordination costs increase with the proliferation of specialized agencies. Specifically, in the context of financial supervision and regulation, there are two main issues to consider. First, the proliferation of specialized agencies may increase the likelihood of a particular firm having multiple supervisors. This may leave unregulated gaps.[24] Moreover, as financial institutions continue to diversify into a broader range of activities, a single regulator will be more efficient at monitoring these activities (e.g. by operating a single database for licensing firms).[25]

This type of coordination cost is non-trivial as exemplified by the AIG supervision system. In the words of Fed Chairman Bernanke 'AIG built up its concentrated exposure to the subprime mortgage market largely out of the sight of its functional regulators',[26] The AIG–Financial Products exposure was mainly

---

[23] The existing literature (Clive B. Briault, 'The Rationale for a Single National Financial Services Regulator', UK FSA Occasional Paper 2, 1999; David Llewellyn, 'The Economic Rationale for Financial Regulation', UK FSA Occasional Paper 1, 1999; Richard K. Abrams and Michael W. Taylor, 'Assessing the Case for Unified Sector Supervision', London School of Economics Financial Markets Group Special Papers 134, 2001) tends to emphasize the economies of scale advantage from the perspective of IT, support, etc., of a single supervisory agency. While there are undoubtedly some utilization gains of that kind, those are likely to be small compared with the knowledge gains of having a group of subject specialists dealing repeatedly with matters within their domain.

[24] See Llewellyn, above n 23; Charles Goodhart 'The Organisational Structure of Banking Supervision', Financial Stability Institute Occasional Papers No 1, Bank for International Settlements, 2000.

[25] See Briault, above n 23, and see Llewellyn, above n 23.

[26] 'Second, the AIG situation highlights the need for strong, effective, consolidated supervision of all systemically important financial firms. AIG built up its concentrated exposure to the subprime mortgage market largely out of the sight of its functional regulators. More effective supervision might have identified and blocked the extraordinarily reckless risk-taking at AIG–FP.' Ben Bernanke, Testimony to the Committee on Financial Services, US House of Representatives, 24 March 2009.

handled from London, hidden from its insurance regulators and the Fed, and essentially only supervised by the OTS. Thus the OTS, a small regulator in charge of the Savings and Loan industry was tasked with supervising what was a key cog in the global financial system.[27] The ability of AIG to conduct a large-scale scam makes most clear the risks of multiple competing regulators with overlapping responsibilities: a sophisticated financial institution may engage in a particularly insidious type of regulatory arbitrage, whereby it 'chooses' its own regulator, one that is unlikely to have the relevant knowledge and expertise.[28]

Thus the coordination costs derived from having multiple authorities are likely to be large. How large are the gains from specialization? These gains are unlikely to be large in the financial knowledge domain, as the substantive valuation, risk analysis, liquidity and solvency issues are the same in insurance, securities and banking. Thus, on grounds of division of labour, the balance is strongly in favour of an integrated authority.

A second possible argument for diversity is to encourage innovation. Having multiple regulators is like having several independent screens, where behaviours are accepted as long as they are accepted by at least one screen. In contrast, a centralized structure is like one with successive (not alternative screens) where only projects or ideas accepted by those successive screens are accepted.[29] If innovation matters, a decentralized structure will be preferred.[30] Conversely, the centralized system generates too little innovation, and leads to fossilization.[31] In our view, recent events show that financial innovation is of limited value relative to the risk engendered. A more centralized and hierarchical system is needed.

A final argument for multiple agencies is adaptation to change. If there are multiple regulators, some of them may prove better adapted to a change in the environment. On the other hand, if a coordinated radical change through the system is needed, a single regulator will be better able to implement it.[32]

---

[27] AIG had bought a savings and loan—this was the reason the OTS was the regulator.

[28] The literature argues that a single, large supervisory authority is better able to attract, develop and maintain professional staff expertise. See Briault, Llewellyn, and Abrams and Taylor, all above n 23. This has not been found to be the case in other domains, where specialized agencies can offer a congenial environment to the experts in that field irrespective of size (consider the CIA and NSA in intelligence, with clearly differentiated domains and different structures), and we do not expect it to be the case here.

[29] Raaj K. Sah and Joseph E. Stiglitz, 'The Architecture of Economic Systems: Hierarchies and Polyarchies', 76(4) *American Economic Review* 716 (1986).

[30] See Edward J. Kane, 'Regulatory Structure in Futures Markets: Jurisdictional Competition between the SEC, the CFTC and Other Agencies', 5 *Journal of Futures Markets* 367 (1984); Roberta Romano, 'The Political Dynamics of Derivative Securities Regulation', 14 *Yale Journal on Regulation* 279 (1997); Roberta Romano, 'The Need for Competition in International Securities Regulation', Mimeo, Yale International Center for Finance, 30 June 2001, <http://icf.som.yale.edu/working_papers/papers/2001/X.pdf> (visited 10 May 2010); Paul H. Kupiec and Patricia White, 'Regulatory Competition and the Efficiency of Alternative Derivative Product Margining Systems', 16 *Journal of Futures Markets* 943 (1996).

[31] A variant of this argument would consider learning—multiple supervisory authorities may adopt different approaches to supervision which can yield valuable information that would not be generated by a single supervisor. See Llewellyn, above n 23.

[32] The existing literature has also argued that a single regulator may be preferred in other areas such as conflict resolution (a single regulator is better able to resolve conflicts that emerge between different

The empirical evidence on the question is small. Barth, Dopico, Nolle and Wilcox[33] find that countries with multiple supervisors tend to have lower capital-adequacy ratios and hence higher insolvency risk (they take this as evidence of the 'competition in laxity').

Our discussion here suggests that there are some limited pluses to a system with multiple agencies, but these pluses are in this case clearly overwhelmed by the coordination costs that we have identified. Both the USA and the EU area have a large multiplicity of actors already, particularly given the 'federal' structure of both areas. Given that many supervised financial institutions operate in all of those areas, the argument suggests that insurance, securities and banking supervisors should be further integrated.[34]

B. Principle 2: Systemic supervision must be under the purview of the central bank

The role of the central bank is *the* major issue at stake in this organizational structure, in particular, whether supervision should be a responsibility of the central bank. With or without direct supervisory responsibilities, a central bank has a responsibility for financial stability, because of its lender-of-last-resort role.

The debate about the supervisory responsibilities of central banks is linked to the discussion of the goals and history of central banks. The Federal Reserve System was set up in 1913 'to establish a more effective supervision of banking',[35] following the banking crises of the 19th and 20th centuries. The Fed conceives of its monetary policy as having been largely grafted onto its supervisory functions, and regards its supervisory and regulatory functions as a prerequisite and complement to its monetary policy responsibilities. These origins, as well as the experience

---

regulatory goals because of lower 'frictions' in deciding and implementing resolutions, see Briault, above n 23, and see Llewellyn, above n 23, and Larry D. Wall and Robert A. Eisenbeis, 'Financial Regulatory Structure and the Resolution of Conflicting Goals', 16(2) *Journal of Financial Services Research* 223 (1999), accountability (a single regulator will be more transparent and accountable than multiple regulators, and may find it more difficult to 'pass the buck' if it makes a mistake), see Briault, above n 23, see Llewellyn, above n 23, and see Abrams and Taylor, above n 23 and transparency (a system with a single regulator is simpler for financial institutions and consumers to understand, see Llewellyn, above n 23); while worrying that a single regulator may have excessive power (Michael Taylor, 'Twin Peaks: a Regulatory Structure for the New Century', Centre for Financial Innovation, London, 1995, Edward J. Kane '*De Jure* Interstate Banking: Why Only Now?', 28(2) *Journal of Money, Credit and Banking* 141 (1996); see Briault, above n 23, and see Llewellyn, above n 23).

[33] James R. Barth et al., 'An International Comparison and Assessment of the Structure of Bank Supervision', Working Paper, February 2002, <http://ssrn.com/abstract=306764> (visited 10 May 2010).

[34] Our recommendations in this regard have found support in recent proposals of the Economic and Monetary Affairs Committee of the European Parliament, suggesting that the EBA, the EIOPA and the ESMA, working together through an improved joint coordinating committee, should all be located in Frankfurt so as to achieve much closer collaboration among them. See Press Release of the Economic and Monetary Affairs Committee, 'MEPs Vote to Beef up Financial Supervisory Package', <http://www.europarl.europa.eu/news/expert/infopress_page/042-74361-130-05-20-907-20100510IPR74360-10-05-2010-2010-false/default_en.htm> (visited 10 May 2010).

[35] See Introduction to the Federal Reserve Act of 23 December 1913.

of the Great Depression, help explain the decisiveness and extensiveness with which the Fed has reacted to the financial crisis from the summer of 2007 to date.

The more recent emphasis on stable money as the primary objective of monetary policy—the driving force of central bank independence in many countries around the world in the 1980s and 1990s—was often accompanied in some countries (such as the UK and Australia) by a move away from supervisory functions. While there are important grounds for the creation of a separate agency, we believe that the reasons for combining both functions are more important.

First, and most importantly, the lender-of-last-resort function can only be undertaken by a central bank. The involvement of central banks in financial stability originates in their role as monopolist suppliers of fiat money and in their role as bankers' banks.[36] Only the ultimate supplier of money can provide the necessary stabilizing function in a nationwide scramble for liquidity, as the financial crisis has amply evidenced, with conventional and non-conventional monetary policy operations (quantitative easing and others). This is a clear lesson of the crisis in the UK, where the problems of Northern Rock caught the Bank of England by surprise: having timely information is particularly crucial during financial crises and the best way to ensure access is to have daily supervision by the central bank, as the literature has noted.[37]

Second, we have learned in this crisis that monetary policy not only affects inflation rates, but the price (and thus the amount) of risk-taking. An excessively accommodating Fed convinced actors that they would be saved from their folly (the famous 'Greenspan put') and led to excessive risk-taking. Thus, those in charge of monetary policy need to know the amount of risk and instability in the system. Moreover, the absence of stable prices harms the stability of the financial system, while financial fragility, in turn, negatively affects monetary stability.

Third, the prestige and independence of central banks enhances their ability to enforce actions,[38] as well as to recruit and retain the best staff.

Of course, extracting synergies never comes without organizational costs. One key problem with combining tasks has to do with the difficulty in providing adequate incentives and measurement on the stability task. The measurement of the success of a bank on its central banking functions is pretty straightforward. There is one goal, price stability, one instrument, monetary policy. There are also a

---

[36] Cf. Baltensperger and Cottier in Ch 20 of this volume.

[37] See Charles Goodhart and Dirk Schoenmaker, 'Institutional Separation between Supervisory and Monetary Agencies' in Charles Goodhart (ed), *The Central Bank and the Financial System* (Cambridge, MA: MIT Press, 1995) 333–414 and Charles Goodhart, 'Price Stability and Financial Fragility' in Charles Goodhart (ed), *The Central Bank and the Financial System* (Basingstoke: MacMillan Press, 1993) 263–303. Joseph G. Haubrich, 'Combining Bank Supervision and Monetary Policy', Federal Reserve Bank of Cleveland Economic Commentary, November 1996. See Briault, above n 23, see Llewellyn, above n 23, and see Abrams and Taylor, above n 23. Joe Peek, Eric S. Rosengren and Geoffrey M. B. Tootell, 'Is Bank Supervision Central to Central Banking?', 114(2) *Quarterly Journal of Economics* 629 (1999).

[38] Ian H. Giddy, 'Who Should be the Banking Supervisors?' (Paper presented at the seminar on Current Legal Issues Affecting Central Banks, International Monetary Fund, 10 May 1994, on file with authors); Rosa M. Lastra, 'The Independence of the European System of Central Banks', 33(2) *Harvard International Law Journal* 475 (1992); and See Abrams and Taylor, above n 23.

relatively small number of people (the governor/chairman and the members of the executive board/monetary policy committee)[39] in charge of that task. In contrast, regulation and supervision try to achieve multiple goals (financial stability, protection of investors and consumers, conduct of business and others), with a wide range of instruments: licensing requirements, macro- and micro-prudential supervision, financial stability reviews, lender-of-last-resort operations and other crisis-management procedures, and there are multiple agencies involved: the central bank, the ministry of finance or treasury, the supervisory agency or agencies. Moreover, supervision typically relies on a large number of staff to perform examinations and other tasks.

The clarity of the metrics used to measure success by central banks in their inflation-fighting mission makes it hard to combine these tasks with the supervisory task. As Holmstrom and Milgrom[40] have pointed out, in an environment with multiple tasks that are observable with different levels of difficulty, the setting of clear performance criteria in the tasks that are easily measurable deflects agents' efforts away from the tasks that may be valuable but are more difficult to measure. That is, we can expect a central bank with a clear inflation-target objective to subordinate success on its financial supervision mission to its inflation targeting performance. Conversely, a financial system without a target, but with political pressure on stability, may pursue monetary policy that is too expansionary in order to minimize the adverse effects on bank earnings and credit quality.[41] A final negative spillover between both tasks is reputational. If the central bank is responsible for bank supervision and bank failures occur, public perception of its credibility in conducting monetary policy could be adversely affected. A related reputational risk concerns its independence, the wider the role of the central bank, the more subject it could become to political pressures, thus threatening its independence.[42]

Early empirical research into these questions generally supported the argument that there were important organizational and incentive costs of combining both tasks and suggested that central banks should adopt a narrow focus and not undertake bank supervision.[43] The recent crisis, however, decisively shifts the

---

[39] Although the central bank also needs a team of economists to do the forecasting, to study the transmission mechanisms of monetary policy, etc.

[40] Bengt Holmstrom and Paul Milgrom, 'Multitask Principal-Agent Analyses: Incentive Contracts, Asset Ownership, and Job Design', 7 *Journal of Law, Economics, & Organization* 24 (1991) (special issue) and Bengt Holmstrom and Paul Milgrom, 'The Firm as an Incentive System', 84(4) *American Economic Review* 972 (1994).

[41] See Goodhart and Schoenmaker, above n 37. Charles Goodhart and Dirk Schoenmaker, 'Should the Functions of Monetary Policy and Banking Supervision be Separated?', 47 *Oxford Economic Papers* 539 (1995). See Haubrich, above n 377 See Briault, above n 23, and Abrams and Taylor, above n 23.

[42] See Haubrich, above n 37. See Briault, above n 23, and Abrams and Taylor above n 23. Indeed, one of us [Rosa M. Lastra, *Central Banking and Banking Regulation* (London: FMG, 1996)] has argued that the Bundesbank (German Central Bank) was not given direct responsibility for prudential banking supervision in order to remove any possible threat to the credibility of its price-stability target.

[43] For instance, see Goodhart and Schoenmaker, above n 41, 'Should the Functions of Monetary Policy and Banking Supervision be Separated?' and Carmine Di Noia and Giorgio Di Giorgio, 'Should

argument against the previous consensus. We saw, again, in the Northern Rock debacle which caught the Bank of England completely unprepared, that the central bank's absence from supervision or closer involvement in the pursuit of financial stability has enormous costs. The problem is, however, that extracting the clear synergies between supervision and monetary policy requires finding solutions that reduce these organizational costs.

The recent consensus points to an intermediate solution, which bundles macro-prudential supervision with monetary policy and segregates micro-prudential supervision. According to the House of Lords' Report on the Future of EU Financial Regulation and Supervision:[44]

> macro-prudential supervision is the analysis of trends and imbalances in the financial system and the detection of systemic risks that these trends may pose to financial institutions and the economy. The focus of macro-prudential supervision is the safety of the financial and economic system as a whole, the prevention of systemic risk. Micro-prudential supervision is the day-to-day supervision of individual financial institutions.

In our view, splitting macro-prudential supervision and allocating it to the central bank makes it possible to capture the main synergies while avoiding most of the organizational costs.[45] The multitasking, informational economies of scope and reputational issues that we have discussed above apply typically to micro-prudential supervision.[46] On the other hand, the arguments against separation, namely the central bank's lender-of-last-resort role (especially in the case of systemic failure), its oversight function concerning the payment system and the need for consistency

---

Banking Supervision and Monetary Policy Tasks be Given to Different Agencies?', Universitat Pompeu Fabra Department of Economics and Business Working Papers 411, October 1999, <http://www.econ.upf.edu/docs/papers/downloads/411.pdf> (visited 10 May 2010), use cross-country data to find a positive correlation between the rate of inflation and the central bank having responsibility for both monetary policy and supervision. Goodhart and Schoenmaker, above n 41, 'Should the Functions of Monetary Policy and Banking Supervision be Separated?', note that independent central banks, which are generally better at fighting inflation, are also more likely to not have responsibility for banking supervision. Vasso Ioannidou, 'Does Monetary Policy Affect the Central Bank's Role in Bank Supervision', 14(1) *Journal of Financial Intermediation* 58 (2005), focuses solely on the USA, where the central bank is one of three federal-level bank supervisors. Using data on formal actions taken by federal bank supervisors against banks, this article suggests that the Federal Reserve's monetary policy responsibilities affect its supervisory behaviour. In particular, when the federal funds rate increases, it relaxes its supervisory posture as a form of compensation to the banks. Ron J. Feldman, Jan Kim, Preston J. Mille and Jason E. Schmidt, 'Are Banking Supervisory Data Useful for Macroeconomic Forecasts?', 3(1) *Contributions to Macroeconomics*, Article 3 (2003), use data for the US banking system to test the hypothesis that a central bank with direct access to confidential supervisory data can enhance its macroeconomic forecasting ability, and thereby bolster its monetary policy efforts. However, they find little empirical support for the 'access to information' argument.

[44] Above n 1. One of the authors, Rosa M. Lastra, acted as Specialist Adviser to the House of Lords during the inquiry and contributed to the writing of the Report.

[45] The distinction between macro-prudential supervision (the supervision of the financial system at large) and micro-prudential supervision (the supervision of individual financial institutions) has been adopted *inter alia* by the de Larosière Report, above n 2; and by Brunnermeier, Crockett, Goodhart, Persaud and Song Shin (eds), *The Fundamental Principles of Financial Regulation* (11th Geneva Report on the World Economy), above n 6.

[46] See Goodhart and Schoenmaker, 'Should the Functions of Monetary Policy and Banking Supervision be Separated?', above n 41.

between monetary policy and prudential supervision, are more related to macro-prudential supervision. Thus combining only the macro-prudential supervision tasks with central banking seems to provide important benefits while avoiding the main costs identified above.

There are two initial difficulties with this combination. First, the critical question is the extent to which this 'macro' role would be sufficient to avoid the next financial crisis. This crisis is also a micro-crisis, after all—knowing how AIG and some of the mono-line insurers were operating required an intimate knowledge of their behaviour that could only come from being their (micro-prudential) supervisor. On the other hand, there may be some tools (such as extended monetary type aggregates, the volume of repurchase agreements outstanding, the amount of short-term commercial paper), that could give advanced warning of 'frothy' conditions.

Second, there is a specific problem in Europe: that of jurisdictional domain. Not all the countries in the EU belong to EMU.[47] The purview of any EU financial supervisor must be Europe wide, but the European Central Bank only includes some of the countries in Europe. The recently created ESRB responsible for macro-prudential oversight follows the recommendation of the de Larosière Report and includes on its General Board the Governors of the national central banks of all EU Member States. The jurisdictional issue, however, continues to effect European efforts to implement systemic supervision. The UK as Europe's key financial centre is particularly important and relations between the UK and the rest of the EU have become increasingly strained following Prime Minister Cameron's veto of a new EU Treaty in 2011.[48]

C. Principle 3: Management by Exception should govern the relation between micro- and macro-supervision

The problem with the 'vertical specialization' between macro- and micro-prudential supervision is articulating this relationship. This involves two problems: making sure that the right type of problems goes to the right authority and making sure that the decisions of the macro authority are in fact executed—giving teeth to these proposals.[49]

On the first issue, the standard solution in the business world (analysed by Garicano)[50] is Management by Exception (MBE). Essentially, the idea is that every problem (e.g. a bank decision or a bank portfolio) arrives initially at the micro-

---

[47]　See de Larosière report, above n 2, and the House of Lords' Report, above n 1.

[48]　The veto by Prime Minister David Cameron on a new EU treaty and the subsequent abstention of the UK in joining almost all Member States (the Czech Republic is the only other member not to ratify but has indicated it may) in ratifying the 'treaty on stability, coordination and governance in the economic and monetary union', see <http://www.european-council.europa.eu/media/579087/treaty.pdf> (visited 6 March 2012) has led to concerns that the UK may have caused a split in the union see *Financial Times* 'Cameron Frozen out after wielding veto', <http://www.ft.com/intl/cms/s/0/9cd5f4b6-2232-11e1-923d-00144feabdc0.html#axzz1odMAvt4J> (visited 6 March 2012).

[49]　Both of these issues are avoided in the de Larosière Report, above n 2.

[50]　Luis Garicano, 'Hierarchies and the Organization of Knowledge in Production', 108(5) *Journal of Political Economy* 874 (2000).

authority and is dealt with by it unless it is classed as exceptional. If it is an exception, then the problem (a risk or the bearer of the risk) must be passed up to the next authority (the macro-prudential supervisor). Of course, the difficulty, both in firms and in this context, is ensuring that the 'lower level' agent (or agency, here) is willing to pass 'upwards' the problems that are not truly in his domain. Financial incentives may be used for this purpose in firms or even in markets,[51] but not in this context.

Authority is also needed in the case of the enforcement of the actions of these supervisors. In the particular context of the European architecture, it is necessary that the European financial supervisory authority or authorities be endowed with authority to overrule and direct the national supervisors, as well as to determine the allocation of problems to each level. This is how the antitrust system currently works, with (i) independent agencies in each country as well as (ii) a central agency for cases that reach across borders, the Directorate General for Competition and (iii) a clear hierarchical system of allocation of cases as well as a (iv) direct enforcement authority of the EU institution that directly applies in each Member State.

Beyond the allocation of decision-making, it is necessary to ensure good communication between micro- and macro-supervision. But there are two main obstacles to information sharing among agencies. First, bounded rationality, resulting in misunderstandings due to the use of different languages or 'codes' by the different agencies, and conflicting incentives.[52] Organizations choose (evolve) different languages or codes as a result of the specific issues they deal with[53]— evolving specialized codes allows them to improve communication within the organization but tends to isolate it from other organizations. Consider the AIG fiasco. As Ben Bernanke has put it: 'There was no regulatory oversight because there was a gap in the system.' Insurance activities were subject to regulation from state insurance regulators, and the way such activities are 'coded' is as insurance. As a result, the form of the earnings and financial statements reported by AIG was inadequate for non-insurance regulators to understand its exposure; since the provision of financial products was one of its main activities, this miscommunication proved extremely important.

Second, there are usually strong disincentives to information sharing across organizations. A turf war is an extreme instance of this. In a turf war, agencies shift resources from productive activities to influence activities. This may enable the less productive agency to obtain more resources in the future.[54]

---

[51] Referral payments are used in the law with this purpose, see Luis Garicano and Tano Santos, 'Referrals' 94(3) *American Economic Review* 499 (2004).

[52] Information flows also present the challenge of the jurisdictional domain, since supervisors must exchange information across national boundaries. They failed to do this with regard to the size and riskiness of the securitized market and the credit derivatives market, to cite two glaring examples.

[53] See Jacques Cremer, Luis Garicano and Andrea Prat, 'Language and the Theory of the Firm', 122(1) *Quarterly Journal of Economics* 373 (2007).

[54] Stergios Skaperdas, 'Cooperation, Conflict, and Power in the Absence of Property Rights', 82(4) *American Economic Review* 720 (1992).

We propose three ways to facilitate information sharing. First, the communication advantages of single organizations can be obtained through the use of centralized and common databases (common codes) together with horizontal (rather than hierarchical) communication.[55] Second, organizations, even if separate, should be housed in close proximity to facilitate the creation of bonds that facilitate informal sharing. This should be complemented with encouraging an '*esprit de corps*' and identification with the ultimate aim. Third, while explicit monetary incentives are unlikely to be used, agents should be rewarded as a function of the 'impact' that their recommendations have on final decisions.

D. Principle 4: The supervisor must build a strong culture and rely on subjective performance, rather than quantitative incentives, to motivate its agents

How should jobs, decision rights, incentives and accountabilities be established for employees in a supervisory agency? The key issue is that performance in these tasks is hard to measure. Moreover, these tasks have many downsides and few upsides so that little credit is received if things go well, and a great deal of scrutiny and criticism are given if things go badly.[56] That means the biases of employees are towards taking actions that look good and that can be easily explained. The job is made particularly difficult by the pro-cyclical nature of some of the rules supervisors must enforce. In a falling market, capital rules and market-value accounting rules may bring to their knees institutions that would otherwise be considered sound, and may force the supervisor to take unnecessarily tough decisions.

Thus using explicit performance objectives is hard, and likely to distort that performance towards easy to measure but meaningless tasks.[57] Instead, agents must be rewarded through low-powered incentives and little 'objective' performance measurement, using instead the employees' career to provide long-term incentives, and subjective evaluation of their performance by their hierarchical superiors.

This, of course, also creates distortions, since distinguishing the part of the performance that is due to random errors or noise from the part that is due to good or bad decisions by the agent may be difficult, and this in turn results in a wedge being driven between self-interest and agency interest. First, career concerns can provide a spur to herding behaviour. As Sharfstein and Stein[58] have argued, an agent who discovers that his opinion does not coincide with that of his colleagues may infer that his information is bad, and prefer to copy what others say rather than offer his own view. Also, public employees typically compete against each other for

---

[55] See Cremer, Garicano and Prat, above n 53 for a study of the cost and benefits of horizontal communication through common codes.

[56] That supervision is a thankless task is a point made by Charles Goodhart, 'The Organizational Structure of Banking Supervision', LSE Financial Markets Group Special Paper 127, 2000, at 30–1.

[57] George Baker, Robert Gibbons and Kevin J. Murphy, 'Subjective Performance Measures in Optimal Incentive Contracts', 109(4) *The Quarterly Journal of Economics* 1125 (1994).

[58] David S. Scharfstein and Jeremy C. Stein, 'Herd Behavior and Investment', 80(3) *American Economic Review* 465 (1990).

pay and promotion and they may try to sabotage each other[59] by concealing information or providing false information. Or they may squander resources on 'influence activities' that seek to manipulate the perception of their performance by superiors or otherwise gain the favour of those superiors.[60]

Avoiding this kind of careerist behaviour is important if there is to be a well-functioning supervisory agency. Creating a sense of identification of employees with the agency can help to align individual and organizational incentives and thus reduce this type of principal–agent conflict.[61] Military organizations, for example, endeavour to create an *esprit de corps* that substitutes good performance for financial incentives.

E. Principle 5: The macro-supervisor should be less independent than central banks are now in their monetary policy responsibilities

Over the past two decades, the establishment around the world of independent regulatory agencies has ignited a debate on how to reconcile technocratic independent institutions with the demands of democratic legitimacy. How can giving freedom (i.e. independence) to unelected officials be reconciled with a society remaining democratic? The answer is: through accountability.

Performance accountability requires that there are objectives or standards (criteria of assessment) according to which an action or decision might be assessed. The extent to which a particular type of accountability may be preferred can be a function of the type of supervision that is at stake.[62] In the case of supervision, input or process monitoring should be preferred, because as discussed above, performance or outputs on the supervisory activity are hard to measure. The fact that inputs, rather than output monitoring should be chosen also suggests that providing a monetary authority (with a clear performance objective) with independence is not the same as providing independence to a supervisor: if delegation and output measurement cannot be used, then independence must be more restricted with regard to financial supervision than with regard to monetary policy.

Transparency is a complement of accountability—information needs to be observed for the agent to be made accountable.[63] However, the provision of information is hardly ever a neutral account of what happened or of what is happening, as the agent is likely to provide it in a self-serving way. Essentially, as

---

[59] Edward P. Lazear, 'Pay Equality and Industrial Politics', 97(3) *Journal of Political Economy* 561 (1989).

[60] Paul Milgrom and John Roberts, 'An Economic Approach to Influence Activities and Organizational Responses', 94 *American Journal of Sociology*, Supplement, S154–S179 (1988) and Paul Milgrom and John Roberts, 'Bargaining Costs, Influence Costs and the Organization of Economic Activity' in James E. Alt and Kenneth A. Shepsle (eds) *Perspectives on Positive Political Economy* (Cambridge: Cambridge University Press, 1990) 57–89.

[61] George A. Akerlof and Rachel E. Kranton, 'Identity and the Economics of Organizations', 19(1) *Journal of Economic Perspectives* 9 (2005).

[62] See Canice Prendergast, 'The Tenuous Trade-Off between Risk and Incentives', 110(5) *Journal of Political Economy* 1071 (2002).

[63] See also Kaufmann and Weber in this volume at Chapter 13.

Prat[64] has argued, if the action is transparently observable, the risk is that agents will behave in a conformist way by doing what is expected of them.[65] A related theoretical argument has been made by Amato, Morris and Shin[66] who argue that too much transparency can actually reduce policy effectiveness. If the central bank signal is noisy relative to private signals, they show that attaching too much weight to the noisier signal may distort the quality of the market's treatment of information. While this argument is of unclear validity for monetary policy where most relevant information is public,[67] it may be very relevant to supervision, where private information is important.

A second downside of transparency concerns panics. While the macroeconomics literature[68] argues that transparency in the decision making of central banks is useful, the need for covert assistance in the case of lender-of-last-resort operations (which is recognized in the new Banking Act of 2009 in the UK) is crucial to a crisis, since the belief in a panic is self-fulfilling. These considerations put transparency for supervisory decisions in a different category from transparency for monetary policy decisions, where the arguments are overwhelmingly in favour of disclosure.

Thus our review of the organizational economics and macro-literature on independence and accountability leads us to three conclusions. First, that the difficulty in making supervisory performance measurable means independence of supervisors should be limited with regard to certain supervisory decisions. Second, that input (or process) monitoring rather than output monitoring should be preferred. In other words, accountability cannot simply rely on whether or not crises are taking place; instead, mechanisms must be put in place that ensure that supervisors have to explain the actual decisions and the process leading to them. Third, transparency, itself a complement of accountability, must be minimized with regard to certain crisis-sensitive decisions in a supervisory agency to avoid career-based decisions by experts, informational distortions by the market and bank panics.

F. Principle 6: The macro-supervisor must limit its reliance on self-regulation

Market supervision and regulation, i.e. self-regulation, exercised by market institutions, has played a role in the financial system.[69] The idea is that financial firms

---

[64] Andrea Prat, 'The Wrong Kind of Transparency', 95(3) *The American Economic Review* 862 (2005).

[65] This is arguably the case also for monetary policy tasks: if minutes of the meetings were published, then board members would be more likely to take the actions that are expected of them, such as acting in their national interest rather than the common interest.

[66] Jeffery D. Amato, Stephen Morris and Hyun Song Shin, 'Communication and Monetary Policy', 18(4) *Oxford Review of Economic Policy* 495 (2002).

[67] Alan Blinder and Charles Wyplosz, 'Central Bank Talk: Committee Structure and Communication Policy', Mimeo, Prepared for the session 'Central Bank Communication' at the ASSA Meeting in Philadelphia, 9 January 2005, <http://www.aeaweb.org/annual_mtg_papers/2005/0109_1015_0702.pdf> (visited on 14 February).

[68] Alan S. Blinder, *The Quiet Revolution: Central Banking Goes Modern* (New Haven: Yale University Press, 2004).

[69] Rosa M. Lastra, *Legal Foundations of International Monetary Stability* (Oxford: Oxford University Press, 2006), ch 3.

are subject to continuous monitoring by their competitors, institutional investors, customers, counter-parties, rating agencies and other private agents. In fact, there is some evidence to support this view: Barth, Caprio and Levine[70] find evidence (pre-crisis!) that countries with government policies that promote the private monitoring of banks tend to have better bank performance and more stability.[71]

This was, however, not the case during this crisis. As Alan Greenspan stated in the US Congress:

> Those of us who have looked to the self-interest of lending institutions to protect shareholders' equity, myself included, are in a state of shocked disbelief.... Yes, I've found a flaw. I don't know how significant or permanent it is. But I've been very distressed by that fact.[72]

Why would self-interested agents not self-regulate adequately? The problem is moral hazard: that banks are not the ones determining these self-regulatory decisions, it is their agents, the human beings who work at banks. It is by now clear that the bonus system, combining short-run horizons for executives at the banks (bonuses are awarded annually) together with the enormous sums at stake, means that executives do not have an incentive to self-regulate, but rather to take on excessive risk. It is an asymmetric system of 'heads I win, tails you lose'. This system puts the managers' own interests ahead of the long-term interests of the institution (including its very survival as a viable entity). Moreover, even taking into account the institution's interest would not be sufficient, as, given the lender-of-last-resort protection afforded by the state, a manager *acting in the interest of the institution* could still act in ways contrary to the financial system as a whole. Essentially, the state insurance against losses is an incentive not just for the manager, but for the institution itself to gamble. *Better corporate governance is thus not a solution to these problems.* There is little reason a priori to expect self-interested managers to have any incentive to worry about the long-term consequences of their actions for their own institution and no reason to expect them to worry about the financial system as a whole.

G. Principle 7: International supervision must move from a loose network to a hierarchical structure

The international dimension of supervision adds another layer of complexity to the reform of the supervisory structures, which require a new 'international architecture'. This suggests that the issues of jurisdictional domain are likely to dominate the debate regarding the future of the architecture of financial stability. Calls for the creation of an international financial authority (whose powers, relationships with

---

[70] James R. Barth, Gerard Caprio and Ross Levine, 'Bank Regulation and Supervision: What Works Best?', 13 *Journal of Financial Intermediation* 205 (2004).

[71] Also Richard Ferguson, 'Alternative Approaches to Financial Supervision and Regulation', 16(2) *Journal of Financial Services Research* 297 (1999), suggests that market information (contained in either bond ratings or equity performance) tends to be a better predictor of future banking performance than supervisory information, indicating that there is an important role for market self-regulation.

[72] Edmund L. Andrews, 'Greenspan Concedes Error on Regulation', *The New York Times*, 23 October 2008.

national authorities, legitimacy, and accountability would need to be debated carefully *ex ante*) have been made in response to the current plethora of informal bodies, standard-setters (of soft law) and inadequate institutional structure. Colleges of supervisors address some problems of co-ordination and co-operation, but they are not enough to respond to the challenges of global institutions and markets governed by national regulation and supervision.

The current actors in the international financial architecture are organized as a loose network of 'formal' international financial institutions [International Monetary Fund (IMF), Bank for International Settlements (BIS), World Trade Organization (WTO) to the extent that it is engaged in trade in financial services]; regional financial institutions (notably the ECB); international *fora* meeting under the auspices of a formal international organization (such as the Financial Stability Forum—renamed Financial Stability Board following the G20 meeting in London in April 2009—and the Basel Committee on Banking Supervision); other international *fora* (such as the International Organization of Securities Commissions); 'informal' international groupings where international financial issues are discussed (such as the Group of Seven (G7), Group of Ten (G10), G20; national central banks and ministries of finance or treasuries (which can play a role individually or collectively meeting in an international forum of a formal or informal character); and private financial institutions acting on a global scale. This multiplicity of actors and the mushrooming of international fora create a very complex network structure.

In our view, given the rise in systemic risks noted by all the reports on the current system and the interconnectedness of the global financial system the way forward must involve the substitution of this loose network with a hierarchical structure more akin to the one used in the WTO.[73] That is, in the same way as the governance of trade has required a new multilateral organ with a clear, hierarchical structure that has superseded the previous morass of bilateral relationships, the evolution of the financial system requires the creation of a new multilateral financial body with authority to settle disputes and to impose its decisions.[74]

A move from a loose network to a hierarchical structure is not without costs. Network structures are generally based on informal relationships, enforced by reciprocity, by relational contracts where each agent takes his actions in the knowledge that the relationship will continue.[75] These networks tend to support very thick exchanges of information, as agents develop trust; the absence of hierarchical relationships limits the downside of honesty and truthful reporting and the scope for 'yes-men' type behaviour. On the other hand, networks have limited ability to enforce decisions. Precisely, this absence of hierarchical authority limits the extent to which agents can compel each other to comply with decisions

---

[73] See also papers dealing with multilevel governance in this volume by Weber, Brummer and Norton. More sceptical of the WTO model is Charnovitz, in this volume.

[74] See the contribution by Michael Gadbaw in this volume.

[75] On this comparison between networks and hierarchies, see Walter W. Powell, 'Neither Market nor Hierarchy: Network Forms of Organization', 12 *Research in Organizational Behavior* 295 (1990).

not strictly in their own interest. True, relational contracting (the expectation of future cooperation) can do a lot; but the more agents involved in the relational contract, and the more complex the structure, the less likely such a structure is to compel this behaviour.

A hierarchy is preferable in this financial context for precisely this reason. Loose coordination works only in imposing decisions that are win–win, but will never succeed at imposing decisions that are better for all but leave one party worse off. A hierarchical authority, one that, like the WTO, is perceived as representative, may be able to do this. The IMF, for reasons discussed elsewhere,[76] is the institution best placed to adopt the role of 'global sheriff' with regard to international financial stability.

IV. Conclusions: A New EU Architecture

We are mindful that any reform proposal for the EU must contend with what is an inevitable tension in the current EU structure: a national mandate in prudential supervision, combined with a single European currency (which affects all eurozone Member States) and a European mandate in the completion of the single market in financial services, which affects all EU Member States. Moreover, reformers have to contend with the different jurisdictional areas of the EU (27 Member States) on the one hand and the eurozone (16 Member States) on the other. None of those issues fall within the purview of our analysis.

The system until now is quite clear: only monetary policy has been centralized (and only for those Member States that have adopted the euro); supervision and crisis management have remained for the most part a national competence (the ECB does provide market-emergency liquidity assistance, but assistance to individual institutions whether via collateralized lines of credit, recapitalization or other forms of support is a national competence).[77] Regulation is both national and European, with a large amount of Directives and Regulations providing a unifying picture with regard to banking and financial regulation in the EU (although some rules, notably with regard to insolvency proceedings are yet to be harmonized). Padoa-Schioppa has referred to the current approach as one based on 'European regulation with national supervision'.[78]

Such a system has the advantages of specialization, creativity and innovation, but the lack of synergies and coordination may prove costly, especially in a crisis. In this

---

[76] See Rosa M. Lastra, 'The Role of the IMF as a Global Financial Authority' in *European Yearbook of International Economic Law*, Vol. 2 (Berlin: Springer Verlug, 2011) 121–36. See also the article by Michael Gadbaw in Chapter 2 of this volume.

[77] In accordance with [strict] Treaty provisions, the Commission is advancing the need for European solutions both with regard to supervision and crisis management. See e.g. Commission Communication COM(2009)561 on an EU Framework for Cross-Border Crisis Management in the Banking Sector of 20 October 2009, <http://eur-lex.europa.eu/LexUriServ/LexUriServ.do?uri=-COM:2009:0561:FIN:EN:PDF.> (visited 10 May 2010).

[78] See Tommaso Padoa-Schioppa, *Regulating Finance* (Oxford: Oxford University Press, 2004), 121ff (Chapter 8 on 'Central Banks and Financial Stability').

chapter, we have suggested that the set of seven principles discussed above that must govern the redesign of the system.

Although the new European financial architecture (outlined in Fig. 4.2) is a step forward in the project of European integration it falls short of the needs of a single market in financial services. What Europe needs in banking is what Europe has in football: national rules and supervision for national teams and players, and European rules and supervision for pan-European players. In short, what we need is a Champions League for Europe's pan-European financial institutions, governed by the principles that we have presented in this chapter, in particular, consolidated and integrated supervision, Management by Exception, and a hierarchical structure.

Finally, in order to succeed in the long run, EU initiatives must both consider the international dimension and be aligned with international efforts.

5

Why Soft Law Dominates International Finance—and not Trade

Chris Brummer

Introduction

International financial law is in many ways a surprising instrument for establishing a global economic order. Unlike international trade and monetary affairs, where global coordination efforts are led by formal international organizations, international financial law is promulgated by inter-agency forums with (at best) ambiguous legal status. Furthermore, the commitments made by participating regulatory agencies have no legal effect, but are instead non-binding as a matter of international law. This divergence is perplexing both from a comparative perspective and from the standpoint of international legal theory, especially when comparing international financial law to international trade. Both trade and finance are clearly key areas addressed by 'international economic law', and their rules have important consequences for global markets. In addition, they relate to market access, embrace non-discrimination and potentially have asymmetric distributive implications for special interests in affected jurisdictions.

Why then are most instruments used for the promulgation of international regulatory standards 'non-binding' and thus 'soft'? This chapter suggests that in order to understand soft law's implications as a coordinating mechanism, it is necessary to undertake an institutional assessment of the way that law is enforced. Specifically, it builds on more recent scholarship demonstrating that international financial law departs from traditional public international law notions of informality, and is in fact 'harder' than its soft-law quality suggests. This feature, the chapter suggests, helps explain why international financial rules, though soft, are often relied upon even where commitments may have steep distributional implications for parties. The predominance of international soft law in finance does not, however, imply its perfection, particularly with regard to its 'compliance pull', and the chapter highlights important structural deficiencies in the international financial regulatory system that the global trading system, as embodied by the World Trade Organization, largely avoids.

I. Hard Law and International Economic Affairs

International treaties have long occupied a special place in global economic affairs, especially in trade matters. Part of their popularity lies in their overt democratic trappings: unlike customary law, where international law is deducted from the consistent practice of states, treaties specifically memorialize agreement between countries and often require approval by national legislatures.[1] As a result, treaties are not only able to express commitments in more precise terms than customary international law, but they are also imbued with legitimacy and imply the 'consent of the governed'.[2]

As species of 'hard law'—that is, as recognized sources of international law—treaties are additionally viewed as especially well positioned to address what can be considered the distributive challenges inherent to international trade. Trade, like many areas of international economic law, is not always an area in which agreement can be reached between parties and sustained. To the extent to which they open barriers to goods and services, trade agreements inherently involve a redistribution of wealth or market share to more efficient industries. As a result, where markets are opened, some businesses will find themselves potentially losing market share to new, more efficient competitors and will lobby their national government to back-pedal on liberalization efforts even if consumers benefit from lower-priced goods and services.[3] Trade liberalization is, as a result, an inherently fragile activity, and is difficult to achieve on a sustained level even where countries express their intent to liberalize markets and open their borders to one another's goods.

Treaties help respond to these domestic pressures both by making commitments to liberalization more credible and by developing institutions that make defections from commitments more costly. Because treaties require significant levels of governmental involvement, including leadership by heads of state and usually ratification by legislatures, states may face considerable reputational costs where they do not honor their treaty obligations. Simply put, states that tend to honor their commitments develop strong reputations that help them coordinate with

---

[1] Customary international law is, as a result, generally regarded as a vaguer and less specific form of international law. See Janet Koven Levit, 'A Bottom-Up Approach to International Lawmaking: The Tale of Three Trade Finance Instruments', 30 *Yale Journal of International Law* 125 (2005), at 179 (noting that customary international law norms must remain vague to ensure that they envelop enough 'state practice' to constitute international law).

[2] John O. McGinnis, 'The Comparative Disadvantage of Customary International Law', 30 *Harvard Journal of Law and Public Policy* 7 (2006), at 10, <http://www.law.harvard.edu/students/orgs/jlpp/Vol30_No1_McGinnisonline.pdf> (visited 14 June 2010).

[3] The argument here stems from the fact that the political costs incurred by alienating domestic manufacturers will likely outweigh the political favor curried from domestic consumers. This is because those benefitting in the aggregate most from liberalization—namely individual domestic consumers—will often not be as effective as producers at promoting their interests. See Warren F. Schwartz and Alan O. Sykes, 'Toward a Positive Theory of the Most Favored Nation Obligation and Its Exceptions in the WTO/GATT System', 16 *International Review of Law & Economics* 27 (1996), at 28. Furthermore, the domestic political process often assigns disproportionate weight to the interests of domestic producers as compared to those of individual domestic consumers, though of course consuming industries may still wield significant political influence.

parties when they need to advance their national interests.[4] On the other hand, where countries fail to honor their commitments, they send a signal that they cannot be trusted, and thus gain reputations that hamper their future prospects for cooperation from and with others.[5]

International treaties additionally enable the creation of institutions that can enhance compliance themselves.[6] Because of the costs involved in establishing hard legal orders, participants want to make sure signatories live up to their commitments. As a result, treaties often create or enable the creation of institutional structures that increase the transparency of parties' activities with regard to the issues memorialized in the treaty—and thus make it easier to identify and punish cheaters.[7] Institutions, furthermore, often serve as the forums where disputes between members as to the terms of the agreement are elaborated and potentially solved.

The paradigmatic institution cited as evidence for such institutional evolutionary dynamics is the World Trade Organization (WTO) and its predecessor treaty, the General Agreement on Tariffs and Trade (GATT).[8] In 1948, the USA and its principal economic partners created the GATT to promote freer and fairer trade, primarily through negotiated reductions of formal tariffs. Over time, the GATT evolved, through successive rounds of treaty negotiations spurred by the USA, to include the deeper substantive commitments assumed by its signatory countries to reduce trade barriers as well as important institutional characteristics including dispute panels and a secretariat. This evolutionary process culminated with the creation of the WTO in 1995, a true international organization with a distinct legal personality and an almost universal membership of nearly 150 countries.[9] As well as enjoying the authority to interpret laws, it enjoys more efficient and formalized disciplinary mechanisms than the GATT, whose dispute resolution mechanisms were often delayed and altogether sidelined due to the ability of disputants to block proceedings and the frequent failure of members to implement decisions.[10]

Perhaps most importantly, the WTO can, through its panels, authorize states that are harmed by uncured rule violations by other states to retaliate by suspending equivalent concessions or other obligations under the covered agreements.[11] As a

[4] This idea has been articulated by a variety of theorists, but for a comprehensive assessment see Andrew Guzman, *How International Law Works* (Oxford: Oxford University Press, 2007) 71–111.
[5] Ibid.
[6] Gregory C. Shaffer and Mark A. Pollack, 'Hard vs. Soft Law: Alternatives, Complements, and Antagonists in International Governance', 94 *Minnesota Law Review* 706 (2010), at 718 (noting that hard law treaties create mechanisms for the interpretation and elaboration of legal commitments over time).
[7] Kenneth W. Abbott and Duncan Snidal, 'Hard and Soft Law in International Governance', 54 *International Organization* 421 (2000), at 429 (noting that treaties establish monitoring provisions to detect noncompliance with the commitments).
[8] For an authoritative history of the WTO, see John H. Jackson, *Sovereignty, the WTO and the Changing Fundamentals of International Law* (Cambridge: Cambridge University Press, 2006).
[9] Joost Pauwelyn, 'The Transformation of World Trade', 104 *Michigan Law Review* 1 (2005), at 25.
[10] Robert Gilpin, *Global Political Economy, Understanding the International Economic Order* (Princeton: Princeton University Press, 2001) 223.
[11] Jide Nzelibe, 'The Credibility Imperative: The Political Dynamics of Retaliation in the World Trade Organization's Dispute Resolution Mechanism', 6 *Theoretical Inquiries in Law* 215 (2005), at 215.

result, the WTO's enforcement strategy employs what Jide Nzelibe rightly describes as a robust tit-for-tat approach: 'if state A is found to breach its obligations to state B and state A refuses to remedy the breach, state B can suspend an equivalent measure of its market access obligations to state A.'[12] The WTO also enjoys an Appellate Body to oversee the work of the dispute panels, accept a decision of the dispute panel, and in doing so permit strong monitoring and enforcement of commitments made by Member States.[13]

II. The 'Soft' Sources of International Financial Law

Still, hard law institutions and instruments play a very limited role in the regulation of finance, especially at the global multilateral level. The International Monetary Fund (IMF) and World Bank do not generally create regulatory standards, even though they can serve as monitors of regulatory activity. Moreover, the WTO's only commitment that touches on financial services, the General Agreement on Trade and Services (GATS), is not prudential in nature. Instead, like trade agreements, it relates to the treatment of foreign investment by national authorities and does not so much coordinate specific regulatory actions as define the limits of regulatory authority. Indeed, the GATS, like most of its bilateral and regional counterparts, has explicit prudential exceptions from country commitments and permits measures 'for the protection of investors [and] depositors... or to ensure the integrity and stability of the financial system'.[14] National authorities face, as a result, few limitations with regard to how they oversee their national markets. Only the European Union wields what is commonly viewed as supervisory authority in financial services—though its influence is only regional, not multilateral, and even here its power is fragmented among federal (regional) authorities and Member States.[15]

Instead, most of the sources of international financial law are informal, intergovernmental institutions that set agendas and standards for the global regulatory community. These institutions are generally not grounded by treaty, but instead usually operate according to consensus and non-binding by-laws.[16] Furthermore, coordination is not dominated and led by heads of state, but instead by central banks, regulatory agencies and supervisors, and finance ministries.

---

[12] Ibid, at 216.

[13] Susan D. Franck, 'The Legitimacy Crisis in Investment Treaty Arbitration: Privatizing Public International Law Through Inconsistent Decisions', 73 *Fordham Law Review* 1521 (2005), n 466 (discussing the mandate of the WTO Appellate Body).

[14] GATS Annex on Financial Services Paragraph 2(a).

[15] For a discussion of the shortcomings of the institutional framework in the European Union with regards to financial supervision and its role in the recent financial crisis, see Eilis Ferran and Kern Alexander, 'Soft Institutions and Hard-Edged Power: What Role for the European Systemic Risk Board?', at 29 (Unpublished manuscript, 3 March 2010, on file with author).

[16] For a description of the soft law basis of international standard setting bodies, see generally David Zaring, 'Informal Procedure, Hard and Soft, in International Administration', 5 *Chicago Journal of International Law* 547 (2005); David Zaring, 'International Law by Other Means: The Twilight Existence of International Financial Regulatory Organizations', 33 *Texas International Law Journal* 281 (1998).

Perhaps the best known of these groups is the G20, the only institution where heads of state do participate directly (if somewhat irregularly) and which now largely determines the broad agenda for international standard setting, and the Financial Stability Board which is charged with oversight of systemic risk. Other important bodies include the Basel Committee on Banking Supervision, the International Organization of Securities Commissions (IOSCO), and the International Association of Insurance Supervisors (IAIS), responsible for setting international standards for banking, securities regulation, and insurance, respectively. Finally, alongside these primary regulators are other important standard-setting bodies that enjoy much more limited mandates and tackle very specific domains of finance. To name a few, the International Accounting Standards Board (IASB), with participation from the International Federation of Accountants (IFAC), promulgates international guidelines on how particular types of transactions and other events should be reflected in financial statements.[17] Meanwhile payment systems are addressed primarily by the Committee on Payments and Settlements Systems (CPSS),[18] while the Financial Action Task Force promulgates rules to combat money laundering and terrorist financing.

III. Key Species of (Soft) International Financial Law

Just as the sources of international financial law are informal, so are the legislative products that they promulgate. International financial law is, in short, legally non-binding, and as such is characterized (and analyzed) as international 'soft law'. Although the forms in which soft law arises are myriad, they can be categorized according to three basic genres.

A. Best practices

First, international financial law often takes the form of best practices that promote sound regulatory supervision through rules of thumb.[19] Often, best in a softer version, 'generally accepted' practices, concern discrete issue areas, like capital adequacy, optimal disclosure rules, and due diligence techniques for preventing

---

[17] The first-generation set of rules, promoted under the organization's predecessor organization, The International Accounting Standards Committee, were called the International Accounting Standards (IAS). Later, when the organization changed its name and reorganized in 2001, the IASB incorporated the IAS but now promulgates new rules called international financial reporting standards (IFRS). These standards have gained prominence and now rival the US Generally Accepted Accounting Principles (GAAP), especially since the European Union adopted IFRS in 2001, though they are generally viewed as more flexible—and lenient—than US standards. See William W. Bratton and Lawrence A. Cunningham, 'Treatment Differences and Political Realities in the GAAP-IFRS Debate', 95 *Virginia Law Review* 989 (2009), at 997–9.

[18] For further information on the CPSS, see Bank for International Settlements, 'CPSS History, Organization, Cooperation', <http://www.bis.org/cpss/cpssinfo01.htm> (visited 14 June 2010).

[19] Best practices have not been much analyzed from the standpoint of international law, but have been the subject of insightful scholarly examination in the domestic US context. See David Zaring, 'Best Practices', *81 New York University Law Review* 294 (2006), at 294–350.

money laundering. They may be transmitted by coalitions of wealthy regional bodies[20] and even private legislatures comprising professional associations and industry groups.[21] In other instances, best practices have broader scope, touching on the general features of sound oversight in a particular financial sector. Particularly important in this regard are the standards comprising 'core principles' of regulation promulgated by the Basel Committee, IOSCO, and IAIS.[22] As opposed to focusing on one discrete area, they provide an overview of what qualities are necessary for sound supervisory and prudential oversight. Best practices can also be articulated through codes of conduct addressed directly at private parties. IOSCO in particular has issued guidance aimed at minimizing conflicts of interest among credit ratings agencies, as well as promulgating implementation advisories to boost its effectiveness.[23]

B. Regulatory reports and observations

Though rarely acknowledged as such, the data collected, assessed and ultimately utilized by national regulators to craft policy serve as a second important form of international financial law. Reports create an official record of fact, as well as institutional opinions and perspectives as to financial data and their implications for the broader global economy. In doing so, reports help establish a basis for policymaking and often generate normative undercurrents that help define the appropriateness of national regulatory approaches. They also, by extension, help establish tacit commitments by national authorities. Where, for example, reports identify certain regulatory practices as deficient or ineffective, sponsors of the report are, at least tacitly, committing to not adopting such practices. In this way, reports can take on commitment-like qualities because insofar as signatories have wide discretion as to future actions, but are at least expected by one another (and often by outsiders) not to engage in behavior contrary to or conflicting with the values or norms expressed in the reports. They are, for this reason, highly debated and negotiated instruments. Reports can similarly identify alternative policies that, at least implicitly, regulators commit to following or developing in their home jurisdictions.

---

[20] See, for example, the G20, which represents the economies of leading developed and emerging economies.

[21] Perhaps the most important private legislatures include IASB and IFAC, the international standard-setters for accounting and auditing services (noted above).

[22] See e.g. Basle Committee on Banking Supervision, 'Core Principles for Effective Banking Supervision', Basle, September 1997, <http://www.bis.org/publ/bcbs30a.pdf> (visited 14 June 2010); International Association of Insurance Supervisors, 'Insurance Core Principles and Methodology' 2003, <http://www.iaisweb.org/temp/Insurance_core_principles_and_methodology.pdf> (visited 14 June 2010); IOSCO, 'Objectives and Principles of Securities Organization', May 2003, <http://www.iosco.org/library/pubdocs/pdf/IOSCOPD154.pdf> (visited 14 June 2010).

[23] The Technical Committee of the IOSCO, 'Code of Conduct Fundamentals for Credit Rating Agencies', December 2004, <http://www.treasurers.org/node/3134> (visited 14 June 2010).

C. Information-sharing and enforcement cooperation

Finally, many international financial agreements spell out, often in the form of memoranda of understanding (MoU), the procedural means by which greater information sharing and enforcement cooperation can be achieved. Information-sharing agreements address, at both regional and global levels, the reality that many financial institutions are themselves globally active, and have a span that reaches around the world. It is often difficult to gain adequate, relevant information in order to assess the risk exposures of banks, or the possibility of transnational fraud or money laundering. Consequently, authorities of both banking and securities markets routinely enter into information-sharing agreements whereby national authorities commit to better coordination with one another to enhance their prudential oversight and monitoring at home.

Meanwhile, enforcement cooperation agreements spell out the terms by which different countries agree to provide one another with assistance with regard to the enforcement of their domestic rules and obligations abroad. Perhaps not surprisingly, securities regulators have been especially active in this space, and have enacted scores of enforcement MoU geared toward more effective cross-border cooperation. Through such agreements, gaps arising in transnational cases are narrowed; where, for example, a Swiss conman perpetrates a fraud concerning the sale of a security against a person in the USA, the existing enforcement agreement between Switzerland and the USA would provide a formal process by which witnesses, evidence, or the proceeds of fraud can potentially be accessed by US regulators with the help of officials in Switzerland.

IV. Dominant Explanations of Soft Law's Popularity

The ubiquity of informal agreements in international financial affairs has been noted frequently in both political science and legal literature, although few comprehensive theoretical explanations have been proffered to explain the phenomenon. Instead, it is commonly viewed as the product of power relations between countries, and usually cast as a dependent variable or signpost of power positions, as opposed to an independent variable informing the behavior of a host of regulatory and financial actors.

In many ways, this realist framing is not surprising, especially in light of the 'soft law' character of international financial regulation. The absence of any formal obligation enables a cheap exit from commitments, and by extension permits opportunism wherever it suits a country. As a result, international relations theorists do not view international financial law as an independent variable possessing any disciplining power; instead, international financial regulation is largely posited as the product of more rudimentary forces of political or economic (and for some, military) power. Simply put, in the absence of a forceful legal regime, it is 'power', not law, which promotes the promulgation of international standards.[24]

Nevertheless, scholars have put forward two explanations that help, to a degree, clarify soft law's popularity from the standpoint of negotiation costs. Contractarian interpretations of soft law, articulated most famously by Kenneth Abbott and Duncan Snidal, and later by Charles Lipton, view soft law's primary merits as lying in the value of lowering the costs of contracting.[25] States, they note, not only seek to generate credible commitments and norms to following certain policies, but they also seek to do so quickly and efficiently. From this perspective, hard law is at times unattractive. Treaty-making often entails months—if not years—of negotiation between heads of state, their representatives, and domestic legislatures. And once created, they are hard to change, increasing the risk that rules generated through treaties fall out of step with practice.[26]

Soft law, by contrast, provides a decisively cheaper means of agreement-making.[27] It carries what can be thought of as low bargaining costs due to its informal status. Perhaps most important, it does not necessarily require extensive participation by heads of state or lengthy ratification procedures. Instead, agreements can be entered into between administrative agencies and technocrats—with relatively little interference by outsiders. As a result, the universe of interests becomes more finite, easing negotiation. Parties can also, because of the flexibility afforded by soft law, amend accords relatively easily, so long as agreement among parties exists.[28]

Soft law additionally involves far fewer 'sovereignty costs' or constraints that may limit the ability of a state to follow its own national prerogatives. Sovereignty costs arise, at a most basic level, any time countries are no longer able to follow their national prerogatives.[29] Hard law is, as discussed above, often extremely restrictive; retaliation, reciprocal noncompliance, and reputation act as important disciplines for most countries. Together, or on their own, each of these consequences can affect a country's ability to secure its policy preferences once a treaty is signed. Treaty signatories thus find themselves more constrained with regards to the range of conduct practically available to them and their ability to secure their own policy preferences and welfare.

---

[24] This realist interpretation of international affairs was first articulated by Kenneth Waltz. See generally Kenneth Waltz, *Theory of International Politics* (Reading: Addison-Wesley, 1979).

[25] Abbott and Snidal, above n 7 at 434; Charles Lipson, 'Why Are Some International Agreements Informal?', 45 *International Organization* 495 (1991), at 518 (noting that it is less costly to abandon informal commitments).

[26] Levit, above n 1, at 171.

[27] Jacob E. Gersen and Eric A. Posner, 'Soft Law: Lessons from Congressional Practice', 61 *Stanford Law Review* 573 (2008), at 589 (discussing 'cheap talk' theories).

[28] Lipson, above n 25, at 500 (noting that although treaties often contain clauses permitting renegotiation, the process is slow and cumbersome).

[29] David Epstein and Sharyn O'Halloran, 'Sovereignty and Delegation in International Organizations', 71 *WTR Law & Contemporary Problems* 77 (2008), at 89 (defining sovereignty costs as the distance between the policy a country would implement if it were not a member of an international organization and the policy it enacts once it has joined).

Sovereignty costs will be particularly steep where, as is often the case, hard law involves the acceptance by countries of an external authority over significant political or economic decisions.[30] International agreements may implicitly or explicitly empower international or supranational authorities—many of which are neither elected nor otherwise subject to domestic forms of accountability—to act in ways that may limit the ability of states to govern entire classes of issues.[31] Indeed, in some cases, such delegations of authority may even inform and determine the relations between a state and its own citizens and domestic market participants, as the famous *Metalclad* case demonstrated.[32]

Soft law's informal status allows parties to avoid such unexpected sovereignty costs, scholars note.[33] Where organizations are informal, no delegation of power is made to independent supranational authorities. And because agreements are not legally binding, financial regulators can choose not to adopt certain elements of the international legislation. This of course applies not only to policy suggestions proffered by reports, but also to more prescriptive terms spelled out in instruments laying out best practices. Additionally, even where they may signal intent to pursue a particular course of action, they may defect from such soft commitments if later circumstances suggest that compliance would not be in the best interests of the signatories. These defections from their commitments will not, international theorists predict, carry reputational consequences insofar as no 'legal' obligations exist. Simply put, most soft law agreements are usually framed in conditional language ('parties intend to' or 'strive to achieve') and are not legal instruments as a matter of international law; parties have thus not committed to anything that could harm or erode a state's national reputation. Regulators retain flexibility in managing their own affairs since no legal obligations are assumed and parties are given the opportunity to learn about the impact of certain policy choices over time.[34]

Finally, soft law also helps facilitate agreement by lowering the risk of uncertainty that frequently pervades policy issue areas. Frequently, there is considerable skepticism or angst concerning the adoption of any particular approach. 'The underlying problems may not be well understood, so states cannot anticipate all possible consequences of a legalized arrangement.'[35] The wrong standard can, in principle, not only disadvantage domestic firms, but could also prove to be inefficient by either overburdening firms or not being stringent enough with regard to oversight

---

[30] Michael C. Dorf, 'Dynamic Incorporation of Foreign Law', 157 *University of Pennsylvania Law Review* 103 (2008), at 133–8 (describing the costs arising when organizations incorporate the laws of foreign or international bodies).

[31] Abbott and Snidal, above n 7, at 421 (defining hard law as legally binding obligations that delegate authority for interpreting and implementing the law to international actors).

[32] *Metalclad Corp. v United Mexican States*, ICSID Case No ARB(AF)/97/1 (ICSID AF) (30 August 2000).

[33] Ibid, at 438 (noting that hard law can lead to unanticipated costs because states cannot predict all possible contingencies); Shaffer and Pollack, above n 6, at 719 (noting that soft law allows states to limit the risk of uncertainty).

[34] Abbott and Snidal, above n 7, at 423.

[35] Ibid, at 441.

of financial activities. There is, as a result, considerable uncertainty attached to entering into longstanding or durable agreements. This can especially be the case with regard to financial regulation which can address novel products, vehicles for investment, or investment strategies, and thus full information as to the impact of any particular rule may be unavailable.

Hard law deals with this problem by leaving contentious terms imprecise or vague.[36] In doing so, however, it reduces the usefulness of coordination in the sense that without a full or comprehensive agreement, uncertainty can still undermine agreements. Alternatively, treaties may incorporate reservations or, more importantly, allow signatories to exit from commitments.[37] However, even then, treaty exit can take decades to execute. As a result, hard law instruments frequently delegate authority to an international organization or special tribunal, which would then be charged with implementing and interpreting the agreement as circumstances unfold. This latter approach, however, not only involves high sovereignty costs, but it may also do little to assuage the basic risks of uncertainty that ultimately pervade international economic agreements.

In comparison, soft law provides an attractive alternative to these approaches by employing non-legal obligations that allow participants to avoid any unpleasant surprises.[38] By avoiding formal legality, parties to agreements are able to see the impact of rules in practice in order to better assess their benefits; at the same time, they retain the flexibility to avoid any unpleasant surprises the rules may hold.[39] Thus, from this perspective, soft law affords strategies for both individual and collective learning whereby parties can work out problems over time.[40] Especially in the financial regulatory context, soft law allows parties to experiment, and, if necessary, change direction when new information and costs arise. Additionally, soft law serves as a communicative mechanism whereby countries can signal to one another their intention to take a particular regulatory action or to adopt a particular regulatory approach.

It is worth adding that the value of soft law has also been extolled by scholars of both international relations and international law who have come to view soft law as a power or a persuasive force in its own right. For nearly a decade, most scholars, guided by the pioneering work of Anne-Marie Slaughter, have described the international financial system as consisting of collegial 'networks' that foster collective problem-solving and innovation through interactions of regulatory peers.[41]

---

[36] Ibid, at 442. Indeed, for some scholars, such vagaries render hard law 'soft'. Donald Langevoort notes, however, that other regulatory strategies are possible, including the targeting of new overlapping areas of interest among jurisdictions. See 'Global Securities Regulation after the Financial Crisis', *Journal of International Economic Law* (2010) (noting how the institutionalization of securities markets in both the USA and Europe creates new opportunities for international regulation).

[37] Laurence R. Helfer, 'Exiting Treaties', 91 *Virginia Law Review* 1579 (2005), at 1641–2 (analyzing the unilateral exit from international agreements).

[38] Abbott and Snidal, above n 7, at 442.

[39] Ibid.

[40] Ibid, at 443.

[41] See generally Anne-Marie Slaughter, 'Governing the Global Economy through Government Networks', in Michael Byers (ed), *The Role of Law in International Politics, Essays in International Relations and International Law* 202 (Oxford: Oxford University Press, 2000) 177–206.

Key to the success of networks has been the idea that within these networks, decision-making is not so much vested in the hands of uninformed political elites, but is instead guided by a stable of skilled technocrats who develop shared expectations and trust allowing them to dispense with time-consuming treaties and formal international organizations.[42] Regulators instead execute and rely on less formal instruments that permit them to make rapid responses that keep pace with rapidly evolving financial markets.[43]

V. Filling the Gaps in Existing Theory

The above theories offer welcome starting points for helping to evaluate the predominance of soft law in international affairs. But when applied to financial regulation, they overlook two important points. First, the above theories overlook perhaps the most obvious structural dynamic encouraging soft law at the international levels—the fact that administrative agencies of some variety, and not heads of state, are primarily involved in fashioning international rules. That is, because regulatory authorities are responsible for oversight in their home jurisdictions, in part due to their technical expertise, they take the lead internationally as well, often in order to fulfill domestic legislative mandates. Regulatory agencies and bureaucracies do not, however, have authority to enter into treaties by themselves, so one would and should expect a certain informality in their dealings.

Yet even this is, by itself, an ultimately inadequate explanation for soft law's predominance, as is evident from the second important shortcoming of the dominant explanatory models. Although existing theories differ considerably in terms of both their methodological and normative starting points, all ultimately assume a considerable consonance of interests between different regulatory players. For network theorists, soft law is largely envisaged as a means of power in a world animated by similarly situated, albeit decentralized parties engaged in a cooperative joint venture. Meanwhile, contractarians, though acknowledging the possibility of conflicting interests, often imply that interests are sufficiently congruent that soft law can paper over the cracks and constitute a suitably robust instrument for future coordination purposes.

Both presumptions are often difficult to support in international financial regulation. Many, if not most, coordination challenges in international finance are undermined by significant distributive problems. One rule may have, in short, significant positive economic effects in one country, whereas in another, the implications may be far from beneficial. The possible canonical example is capital

---

[42] See generally Pierre-Hugues Verdier, 'Transnational Regulatory Networks and Their Limits', 34 *Yale Journal of International Law* 113 (2009) (highlighting the limits of networks); see also Charles K. Whitehead, 'What's Your Sign?—International Norms, Signals, and Compliance', 27 *Michigan Journal of International Law* 695 (2006), at 704.

[43] Kal Raustiala, 'The Architecture of International Cooperation: Transgovernmental Networks and the Future of International Law', 43 *Virginia Journal of International Law* 1 (2002), at 30 (exemplifying widespread use of MoU as a cooperation tool).

adequacy, where banks may find themselves in a less competitive position vis-à-vis their international competitors if they are required to satisfy the same capital positions as competitors. Numerous other examples are, however, available: mark-to-market rules can impact some financial institutions more negatively than others depending on their current accounting practices and balance sheet assets; money laundering rules may make some countries less attractive destinations for capital; and even corporate governance reforms may force some countries to more dramatic reforms of firm organization than others.

This observation holds serious implications for soft law as an instrument of international financial regulation. At the most basic level, even if soft legal agreements can be achieved between parties, aided presumably by the informality of the rules, asymmetric distributional effects undermine the durability of informal international agreements as backtracking on commitments is possible. A state may, for example, recognize an opportunity to attract new business or transactions to its borders by offering less onerous disclosure requirements. Or, similarly, implementing a particular standard may be more costly (economically or politically) than what authorities expected when entering the agreement. Resources may have to be diverted to regulatory activities that are more valued by legislators or the general population, or the volume of financial transactions taking place in a country may unexpectedly suffer after entering into a particular international regime that imposes certain limitations on securities firms or banking institutions.

In such circumstances, soft law provides, at least as traditionally conceived, few disciplining mechanisms to prevent noncompliance with commitments. Indeed, the availability of cheap exit enables opportunism for parties if circumstances change or if they identify, perhaps at a later time, more advantageous regulatory options. First, and perhaps most obvious, countries can choose not to implement any international rule. Instead, they can choose to continue on their current course, and in so doing avoid the adjustment costs of moving to a new standard. Alternatively, regulators may choose another regulatory approach that still departs from the path implied by existing international best strategies or agreements.

Alternatively, authorities can cherry-pick certain aspects of international agreements without embracing them comprehensively. If a particular global agreement, say on core standards, contains fifteen best practices, a country may choose to comply with only those that promote its own competitive position or financial market strength. In doing so, it may ultimately adopt in practice only a handful of the principles expressed in international agreements.

Finally, countries can adopt regulations in name, but can under-enforce the rules on their books, effectively leading to soft defections from commitments. This is frequently a problem where, as in the case of many regulations, commitments to international reforms involve not only the adoption of new laws, but also new domestic regulatory structures that may prove costly to domestic governments with other priorities. In such circumstances, signatories may agree in principle to certain kinds of conduct *ex ante* but may be incapable of, or institutionally incompetent with regard to, carrying out or executing the terms of the agreement *ex post*.[44]

We are, therefore, left with a puzzle when integrating these options into existing cheap law theories: Why is soft law relied on so frequently to express global standards than treaties, which dominate the international trade arena? Although soft law may make agreement more likely on the front end, the availability of easy exit enables opportunism for parties when circumstances change or if they identify superior individual gains to be made by abiding to possibly (globally) suboptimal regulatory strategies. Insofar as regulatory choices and compliance with particular standards begin to resemble zero-sum games, as opposed to win–win collaborations, international legal theory predicts that international financial regulations will be unable to achieve deep and lasting convergence.

A. Stable versus unstable issue—area equilibria

At least one explanation can be found in what can be roughly acknowledged as the differing states of equilibrium states that trade and finance agreements imply. As the dominant theory predicts, informality lowers bargaining costs, not only because of presumably lower stakes, but also because of the possibility of leadership by lower-level non-political regulatory actors. This advantage can be particularly important where the underlying object of regulation is constantly evolving. The regulation of financial markets, for example, is difficult since financial markets are constantly evolving due either to innovations in the trading strategies or technological capabilities of market participants, and because of the changing macroeconomic and regulatory environment in which markets operate. As a result, 'the prudential regulation and supervision of financial markets requires continuous adaptation as markets themselves evolve'.[45] In such a reiterative bargaining context, which often requires swift regulatory responses, leadership by administrative agencies holds considerable advantages. Not only do regulators enjoy technical expertise, but rules and standards can be devised without necessarily jumping the political procedural hurdles associated with treaty ratification.[46]

By comparison, trade has historically been a more stable object of regulation and it is here where treaties are more prominent. Goods are less fungible than financial products, and there are fewer means to evade core provisions of trade agreements. Instead, countries generally attempt to exploit existing (as opposed to new) loopholes to support domestic special interests such as longstanding exemptions (like

---

[44] Though not addressed specifically in this context, Howell Jackson surmises similar possibilities with regard to the under-enforcement of even domestic rules. See Howell Jackson, 'Variation in the Intensity of Financial Regulation: Preliminary Evidence and Potential Implications', 24 *Yale Journal on Regulation* 253 (2007), at 286–7 (discussing rational under-enforcement and inefficient under-enforcement).

[45] Ferran and Alexander, above n 15, at 1.

[46] See Roberta S. Karmel and Claire Kelly, 'The Hardening of Soft Law in Securities Regulation', 34 *Brooklyn Journal of International Law* 883 (2009), at 885 (noting that soft law is relied upon 'because of the need for speed, flexibility and expertise in dealing with fast-breaking developments in capital markets').

agriculture) and non-tariff trade barriers (like currency manipulation). And it is particularly where trade lawyers have attempted to address those issue areas involving constant change and innovation such as intellectual property issues and services that treaties have been noticeably less robust and comprehensive.

B. Reputational disciplines

Institutional design also plays an important role in explaining the dominance of soft law in international financial regulation. Specifically, international financial law, though formally a species of soft law, is 'harder' than traditional public international law anticipates, a topic I have discussed elsewhere.[47] First, soft law, although informal, can express 'commitments' made by parties. In some cases, commitments may be relatively weak, since soft law comprises a set of observations made by members at international forums and, as such, may operate as way stations to a more elaborate regime or expressions of limited consensus among regulators as to the causes, and not the solutions, to emerging challenges.[48] In such cases, agreements take on qualities of broad 'negative covenants',[49] where signatories or sponsors of the legislation may have wide discretion as to future actions, but are at least expected not to engage in behavior contrary to or conflicting with the values or norms expressed in the agreements. In other circumstances, international financial law may express specific actions that parties to agreements intend to take, and in doing so constrain self-serving autonomy as kinds of 'affirmative covenants' or regulatory contracts.[50] In these circumstances, international financial law may be operationalized through bilateral or even multilateral MoU or codes of conduct and best practices. Moreover, precise commitments may be spelled out under these agreements, along with explanatory methodologies or supporting documentation addressing the implementation of agreed-upon standards and principles.[51]

That the agreements are not legally binding like trade treaties does not detract from the fact that they are often made with great solemnity.[52] International financial agreements often have important consequences for counterparties, and this makes them intrinsically important. To use a simple example, one regulator may rely on another in order to gain access to witnesses or evidences concerning a domestic violation that may be located in another jurisdiction. Where regulators fail to live up to their commitments to provide assistance, the counterparty will

[47] Chris Brummer, 'How International Financial Law Works (and How It Doesn't)', *Georgetown Law Journal* 99 (2011), at 33 and 58, <http://papers.ssrn.-com/sol3/papers.cfm?abstract_id=1542829> (noting that international financial regulation is often buttressed by a range of reputational, institutional and market disciplines that render it more coercive than traditional theories of international law predict).

[48] Abbott and Snidal, above n 7, at 423.

[49] Ibid, at 425 (discussing how some international agreements are viewed as covenants).

[50] Ibid, at 424, 427 (discussing how rationalists view international agreements as expressing contractual commitments, usually between states).

[51] Gersen and Posner, above n 27, at 573.

[52] Chris Brummer, above n 47, at 13.

often internalize the costs of the defection. As a result, noncompliance with key international standards, if discovered by the parties, will cause counterparties and allies to rethink or reevaluate their expectations concerning the regulator's future behavior, and undermine its incentives to cooperate with the regulator in the future.

C. Market disciplines

Alongside the reputational dynamics presaged by classic international law is what can be considered an array of possible market disciplines that can inform both firm preferences, and by extension, the decisions of regulators. Simply put, where capital markets are operating efficiently, they will reward a firm for its adherence to practices that are viewed by investors as making the firm more profitable.[53] If, for example, a firm discloses clear and useful information concerning its profits, shareholders should reward the company with higher share prices that reflect lower investment risk.[54] Similarly, where firms like banks and insurance companies set aside large capital cushions, shareholders will generally have more faith in the financial health of the company, contributing to higher valuations of the firms, just as potential counterparties to financial transactions will be more eager to transact with them.[55]

What precisely constitutes 'efficient' rules or standards is, however, often debatable.[56] That said, market participants frequently perceive adherence to major international standards as a mark of good regulatory practice. The law and finance literature has long argued that some firms seek to become subject to the laws and supervision of major financial centers (and especially those in the USA) so that they can signal their strong corporate governance and disclosure for investors, and enjoy lower costs of capital.[57] Similar market reputational effects can take place with

[53] This point perhaps enjoyed its most famous articulation in corporate law scholarship, especially regards to the 'choice' of states under domestic US corporate law. See Roberta Romano, *The Genius of American Corporate Law* (Washington, DC: AEI Press, 1993) (arguing that firms that choose states with inefficient corporate laws should have lower stock prices); Ralph K. Winter Jr, 'State Law, Shareholder Protection, and the Theory of the Corporation', 6 *Journal of Legal Studies* 251 (1977).

[54] See David Easley and Maureen O'Hara, 'Information and the Cost of Capital', 59 *Journal of Finance* 1553 (2004) (showing that differences in the composition of information between public and private information affect the cost of capital, with investors demanding a higher return to hold stocks with greater private information).

[55] In this case, the reverse is, not surprisingly, equally applicable. Specifically, where banks (or for that matter any financial institution embedded in financial systems as intermediaries) are viewed as having insufficient capital to meet their operational requirements or credit obligations, 'runs' on those banks are likely. For a recent description of bank runs over time, see Carmen M. Reinhart and Kenneth S. Rogoff, *This Time is Different: Eight Centuries of Financial Folly* (Princeton: Princeton University Press, 2009) 144–5.

[56] Indeed, the very concept of market efficiency is often difficult to discern. Randall S. Thomas and James F. Cotter, 'Measuring Securities Market Efficiency in the Regulatory Setting', 63 *SUM Law & Contemporary Problems* 105 (2005), at 122.

[57] See John C. Coffee Jr, 'Racing Towards the Top?: The Impact of Cross-Listings and Stock Market Competition on International Corporate Governance', 102 *Columbia Law Review* 1757 (2002), at 1763.

regard to international regulatory standards: banks, for example, and even some insurance companies, often seek to adopt the Basel Committee's capital standards to signal that they are solvent and well-capitalized, as well as to signal to investors that they meet the most stringent regulatory oversight.[58] Moreover, where firms ignore or do not comply with well-regarded international standards, investment analysts will at times attempt to evaluate the risk embodied by the compliance gap—even where firms are still abiding by (less rigorous) national hard law obligations.

D. Institutional sanctions

Finally, alongside reputational and market costs, particularly egregious instances of non compliance with international standards can trigger sanctions by and from international organizations and financial institutions. Compliance with international standards is often the basis upon which loans are granted by the IMF and the World Bank.[59] If recipient countries take the loans and then renege on these commitments, they theoretically risk not being able to take out loans in the future. Moreover, where loans can be made in installments, they can be used as policy tools whereby subsequent extensions are made on the basis of steps taken to comply with the standards.

International standard-setting bodies themselves may have institutional mechanisms that make compliance more likely. Although many institutions are universal organizations, and thus open to all countries, institutions can adopt membership standards and punish those that fail to comply.[60] For more exclusive organizations that often operate as governmental 'clubs', organizational mechanisms may additionally provide for expulsion as the ultimate sanction for bad behavior and non compliance with the group's standards.[61]

Finally, institutions can publicly signal a member's failure to comply with particular rules or standards. Conventionally, this 'name and shame' strategy is associated with public international law institutions like the United Nations where states ignore widespread international law standards such as those relating to human rights or security. However, these institutional affects can also be employed in the financial regulatory arena as a means of isolating regulators both institution-

---

[58] Daniel W. Drezner, *All Politics is Global: Explaining International Regulatory Regimes* (Princeton: Princeton University Press, 2007) 147.

[59] Kern Alexander, Rahul Dhumale and John Eatwell, *Global Governance of Financial Systems: The International Regulation of Systemic Risk* (Oxford: Oxford University Press, 2006) 89; see also Joseph Stiglitz, *Globalization and Its Discontents* (New York: W. W. Norton & Company, 2002) 44 (discussing conditionality loans via the IMF); Rosa Lastra, *Legal Foundations of International Monetary Stability* (Oxford: Oxford University Press, 2006).

[60] See Abram Chayes and Antonia Handler Chayes, *The New Sovereignty: Compliance with International Regulatory Agreements* (Cambridge, MA: Harvard University Press, 2007) 70–1.

[61] Drezner, above n 58, at 75–7 (discussing clubs, standards, and the possibility of expulsion); see also Chris Brummer, 'Post-American Securities Regulation', 98 *California Law Review* 327 (2010), at 364–72.

ally (and at times, personally) in the international community. Regulators can be viewed as second-class citizens within their own larger regulatory body.[62] Additionally, regulators can face social opprobrium from counterparts in the relatively close-knit regulatory community for failing to deliver on the group's regulatory program.

Shaming can also, importantly, carry costs beyond institutional and professional reputations. By publicly identifying jurisdictions that do not comply with their standards, institutions can create new market costs by implying or arguing that non-cooperative jurisdictions suffer from poor domestic over-sight and market supervision and thus are somehow risky or dishonorable places to do business. As a result, any firm operating in a jurisdiction that is not compliant with the standards of the organization can potentially incur higher costs of capital, and targeted countries may find it more difficult to attract firms to enter their borders.

VI. Why Predominance is not Perfection

For all its popularity, international financial regulation has not been without its own serious structural flaws and shortcomings, especially when compared to the law and institutions of international trade. Hard law, at least as operationalized under the WTO, allows members to police for compliance from their trading partners and fellow signatories. It then leverages the capabilities and incentives of members to enforce its decisions, thereby making its decisions (and underlying treaty commitments) directly applicable to members. Such design innovations have not historically characterized the international financial architecture. For one, monitoring of compliance with international regulatory standards is not always robust. Although the IMF and World Bank are the primary actors tasked with the lion's share of surveillance responsibilities with regard to compliance with international regulatory standards, only those countries that are recipients of loans from the World Bank and the IMF have faced the prospect of surveillance by the two institutions. And even here, the data provided to international institutions are self-reported by national authorities—and can depend on information often provided by regulated financial entities that are themselves subject to little supervisory oversight.[63] Additionally, the information gained by surveillance is often published only with the permission of the country that is inspected.[64] Important changes

---

[62] Embarrassment caused by deviating from network norms operates, for some, as a kind of social tax. Adhering to network-based standards may encourage praise, and deviation may cause embarrassment or shame that results in a loss of prestige or influence among peer regulators as the violation becomes known to others. See Whitehead, above n 42, at 705.

[63] World Bank, 'Financial and Private Sector Development—Financial Sector Assessment Program', <http://lnweb90.worldbank.org/FPS/fsapcountrydb.nsf/FSAPexternalcountryreports?OpenPage&count=5000> (visited 14 June 2010).

[64] International Monetary Fund, 'Factsheet: The Financial Sector Assessment Program (FSAP)', <http://www.imf.org/external/np/exr/facts/fsap.htm> (visited 14 June 2010) (noting that the voluntary nature of FSAPs is necessary for 'buy-in' among participants).

have, however, recently been announced,[65] including commitments by G20 countries to undertake assessments by the IMF and World Bank, but the degree to which this will be sustainable and effective remains unclear.

Ironically, it is where soft financial law 'is' effective, and overcomes these challenges, that another second important problem arises—that of legitimacy.[66] Many international standard-setting bodies, though informal, are nonetheless 'exclusive' clubs generally constituted by wealthy countries, which effectively export their rules to the rest of the world, or 'open-membership' organizations administered by a tight policy core. Some outsiders to the policy process believe that rules and standards are devised to protect the interests of key players (especially developed countries) and in the process block legislation that is globally welfare-enhancing. As a result, international financial regulation, even where effective, can be exposed to charges of being unrepresentative (even more so than the WTO) and lacking in transparency and accountability—charges that in themselves can diminish the compliance pull of international financial regulation.[67]

These observations suggest that in the long term, despite the predominance of soft law, reforms will likely have to be made as international financial law becomes an increasingly critical element of the global financial system. I have in my other writings suggested some good starting points.[68] For one, more robust monitoring of regulatory rules is necessary. Here, existing institutions can be improved—by making compliance with global inspection and surveillance processes mandatory, and by making the information gained from monitoring more useful and utilizable for investors and regulators alike.

Additionally, the legitimacy challenges facing the existing system suggest that more basic changes will likely have to be introduced at an organizational level to the existing regulatory architecture. Although it is unlikely that a 'WTO' can be created with the moral authority or mandate to supersede existing organizational arrangements, less dramatic reforms that enhance legitimacy may still be possible in existing soft law organizations. Most importantly, expanded or reformed membership in key standard-setting bodies may have to be introduced. Already, international financial institutions are beginning to adopt structural changes. The G20 itself represents a displacement of the G7, the erstwhile and more exclusive venue of policy-making that dominated economic decision-making during the 1990s, and voting rules and decision-making in leading international financial institutions are making way to include leading emerging markets.[69] Similarly, emerging markets are

---

[65] IMF, 'IMF Expanding Surveillance to Require Mandatory Financial Stability Assessments of Countries with Systemically Important Financial Sectors', Press Release No 10/357, 27 September 2010, <http://www.imf.org/external/np/sec/pr/2010/pr10357.htm> (visited 18 October 2010).

[66] Ferran and Alexander, above n 15, at 11, 18, 37–54 (discussing the legitimacy concerns regarding the Financial Stability Board, the IMF, and European Systemic Risk Board).

[67] Ibid, at 12.

[68] Brummer, above n 47, at 65 (suggesting improvements in the monitoring and information utility to the existing structure of international financial system).

[69] Ibid, at 80.

gaining, albeit slowly, both clout and voting power in international financial institutions like the World Bank and the IMF.[70] Further institutional innovations will, however, perhaps inevitably be necessary in these and other standard-setting bodies as these countries come to wield more financial power and regulatory significance.

---

[70] Ibid.

6

The 'Santiago Principles' for Sovereign Wealth Funds: A Case Study on International Financial Standard-Setting Processes

*Joseph J. Norton**

I. Introduction

Since the fall of 2008, there have been four 'historic' 'summit meetings' of the Leaders (Heads of State) of the G20 'countries', representing 80 per cent of the world's population and 90 per cent of the world's gross domestic product (GDP).[1] What elevates these G20 Leaders' summits is that they were the first gatherings the G20 convened in the Leaders format, with the Leaders coming to confirm this new grouping as now the 'permanent' and 'premier' 'council for international economic cooperation',[2] a new and fundamentally different geopolitical 'steering committee'

* The topic of this essay arose from one of a series of ten lectures on 'Global Financial Market Regulation' delivered by the author at the SMU Dedman School of Law during the Spring Semester 2010. The author is expanding this topic into a more extensive work-product, and (when completed) it will be posted on SSRN. I express my appreciation to Professor Cottier and to Professor Lastra, for their kind invitation to participate in this Symposium issue, and also to Professors Brummer and Weber (whose respective contributions give rise to many of the ideas contained in my essay). I especially thank Professor John H. Jackson for his many kindnesses to and support of me over the years.

[1] The first G20 Leaders' Summit on 'Financial Markets and the World Economy' was hosted by former President Bush from 14–15 November 2008 in Washington, DC. The second Leaders' Summit was held in London on 2 April 2009, and resulted in a 'Global Plan for Recovery and Reform'. On 24–25 September 2009, President Obama hosted a third G20 (Leaders) Summit in Pittsburgh on 'Creating a 21st Century International Economic Architecture'. This Summit launched the new 'G-20 Global Growth Framework' mentioned below. The fourth G20 (Leaders) Summit was held in Toronto from 26–27 June 2010 on 'Recovery and New Beginnings'. Since the writing of this chapter a fifth G20 (Leaders) Summit took place in Seoul from 11 to 12 November 2010, with a sixth (Leaders) Summit held between 3–4 November 2011 in Cannes in France. These summits resulted respectively in the Seoul and Cannes Action Plans. A seventh is planned for June 2012 in Mexico. For the Communiqués of the first six Summits, see <http://www.g20.org/en/g20/previous-leaders-summits> (visited 13 February 2012).

[2] The G20 was established in 1999 as a global policy forum by the G7 Heads of State for Finance Ministers and Central Bank Governors of the G20 countries, along with the Financial Stability Forum [since 2009 the Financial Stability Board (FSB)] to deal with the series of emerging market crises that occurred during the 1990s and other global issues affecting the international financial system and financial stability. For the G-20 website, see <http://www.g20.org/index.aspx> (visited 20–21 July 2010). The G20 comprises 19 countries and other members: Argentina, Australia, Brazil, Canada,

for global economic policy determination and management has been put in place. These G20 Leaders' summits were convened, in part, to develop, on a comprehensive and coordinated basis, a 'global response' to the current Western country-generated global financial crisis (GFC).[3] In developing this global response, the G20 countries would be bonded by five agreed 'common principles for reform': (i) strengthening transparency and accountability, (ii) enhancing sound regulation, (iii) promoting integrity in financial markets, (iv) reinforcing international cooperation, and (v) reforming international financial institutions (IFIs).[4] These common principles serve as overarching 'core principles' within which the subject matter of this essay (i.e., the Santiago Principles) might be evaluated and might evolve over time.

But, these summits were intended not simply to be about the GFC and global financial sector reform, but also, in the longer term, a new governance structure for the 'global economic order'.[5] In this context, the Leaders have agreed to launch a 'Framework for Strong, Sustainable and Balanced Growth' ('G20 Global Growth Framework').[6] Under this new 'governance' model, each G20 member country would set out its objectives and put forward policies to achieve them. Collectively, the Leaders would periodically assess the progress, with input from a range of international bodies. The G20 countries agreed to work together 'to ensure that [their] fiscal, monetary, trade, and structural policies [including macro prudential and regulatory policies] are collectively consistent with more sustainable and balanced trajectories of growth'.[7] If this framework proves viable over time, this would be a major qualitative advance in global economic governance and management of the globalization processes.

Part of this new global governance framework is the reform of financial markets and their regulation by establishing 'a global architecture to meet the needs of the twenty-first century'.[8] But, this 'new architecture' is not to be made of 'whole cloth'. In the mid-1990s, the G7 Heads of State and their Finance Ministers had already begun to put into place a 'new international financial architecture' (NIFA-I) centered

China, France, Germany, India, Indonesia, Italy, Japan, Mexico, Russia, Saudi Arabia, South Africa, the Republic of Korea, Turkey, the UK and the USA with the European Union represented by the rotating Council presidency and the European Central Bank (ECB) as the 20th member of the G20. In addition, there are three *ex officio* representatives from the IMF and one from the World Bank. The Leaders' level of the G-20, as mentioned, was added in the fall of 2008.

[3] On the GFC see, *inter alia*, Rosa M. Lastra and Geoffrey Wood, Chapter 1 in this volume.

[4] See G20, 'Declaration of the Summit on Financial Markets and the World Economy', 15 November 2008, Washington, DC, <http://www.g7.utoronto.ca/g20/2008-leaders-declaration-081115.html> (visited 20–21 July 2010). This global response and its implementation would be guided by a detailed 'Action Plan' setting out a series of 47 short-term and medium-term objectives, this Plan can be found at the end of the aforesaid First Summit Declaration.

[5] See e.g. Remarks after First Summit by German Chancellor Merkel and her former Finance Minister Steinbrück, 'On the Way to a Global Economic Order', 15 November 2008, <http://www.g7.utoronto.ca/g20/2008/2008merkel-en.html> (visited 20–21 July 2010).

[6] See 'Leaders' Statement: The Pittsburgh Summit', 24–25 September 2009, <http://www.g20.org/Documents/pittsburgh_summit_leaders_statement_250909.pdf> (visited 20–21 July 2010). The 'Framework' comprises paras 2–9 of the main body of the Statement, an Annex on 'Core Values for Sustainable Economic Activity', and an attached four-paragraph framework.

[7] Ibid.

[8] Ibid, Preamble, para 1.

around the overarching policy objective of 'financial stability' and an institutional configuration comprising the G20 Finance Ministers and Central Bank Governors, the Financial Stability Forum (FSF), a series of international standard-setting bodies (ISSBs), a recast IMF, and, to a lesser extent, a specifically directed World Bank Group and Organisation of Economic Co-operation and Development (OECD). By 2008, NIFA-I was largely developed, unknowingly awaiting its subsequent revamping under the G20 Leaders' 'architecture'—that is, a NIFA-II.[9]

Given the above context, this article is a narrow-focused case study, related and complementary to the subject-matter of the 'multi-level governance' dimensions of 'international, regulatory financial standard-setting' (IRFSS) and the NIFA-II. Although this study uses a random and idiosyncratic example of IRFSS—the formulation of the October 2008 'Santiago Principles' ('best practices'; hereinafter, *Principles*) and the related establishment of the International Forum of Sovereign Wealth Funds (ISWF Forum)—it suggests that these *Principles* are unearthing a type of international 'rule-oriented' process and set of 'best practices' which are having an ongoing impact on the operation, governance and decision-making of sovereign wealth funds (SWFs).[10] Although *sui generis*, this saga of the formulation of 'best practices' for SWFs and of these entities acting more collectively as a new, significant component of our changing global financial system provides a different window for better evaluating NIFA-II and the new 'G20 Global Economic Growth Framework'.

II. The Beginnings of the SWF Multi-Governance, Rule-Oriented Processes

Policy interests and concerns respecting SWFs[11] surfaced at a multi-governance level in the latter part of 2007[12] when it became apparent that China[13] and

---

[9] See, *inter alia*, Joseph J. Norton, ' "NIFA-II" or "Bretton Woods- II"?: The G-20 (Leaders) Summit Process on Managing Global Financial Markets and The World Economy—Quo Vadis?', 11 *Journal of Banking Regulation* 261 (2010).

[10] For a classic statement on 'rule-orientation' as to the international economic order, see John H. Jackson, 'Global Economics and International Economic Law', 1 *Journal of International Economic Law* 1 (1998).

[11] The International Working Group of Sovereign Wealth Funds (IWG) (see below, n 15) definition is:

> SWFs are . . . special purpose investment funds or arrangements, owned by the general government. Created . . . for macroeconomic purposes, SWFs hold, manage, or administer assets to achieve financial objectives, and employ a set of investment strategies which include investing in foreign financial assets. [They] are commonly established out of balance of payments surpluses, official foreign currency operations, the proceeds of privatizations, fiscal surpluses, and/or receipts resulting from commodity exports.

By 2010, there were over 50 SWFs owned by over 30 countries/jurisdictions with total assets of around $3.8 trillion, with the potential to increase to $6–10 trillion by 2013. See, *inter alia*, IMF, 'Sovereign Wealth Funds—A Work Agenda', 29 February 2008), <http://imf.org/external/np/pp/eng/2008/022908.pdf> (visited 20–21 July 2010) (IMF Work Agenda).

[12] In terms of timeline, this was prior to the full unfolding of the GFC in 2008.

[13] On 29 September 2007, the People's Republic of China Ministry of Finance established the China Investment Corporation (CIC), which is to maintain a 'strict commercial orientation'. On CIC

Russia[14] would be separately setting up such state-owned international investment vehicles and that the largest SWFs were from the Middle East Gulf Region (a post-9/11 reflexive concern).[15] While SWFs had been known to governments and the financial world for some time and their number and size had substantially increased since the end of the twentieth century, governmental interest in these entities had previously been minimal. But, within the European Union (EU), there arose heightened governmental concerns vis-à-vis the aggressive economic power of Russia and its implications for EU energy security.[16] In the USA, there were imbedded Congressional and political lobby groupings that are anti-China and that were likely to interpret matters as a pernicious rise of global state capitalism.[17]

A. The domestic starting point: the US treasury

This contentious environment for SWFs was not lost on the US Secretary of the Treasury, Henry Paulson. The first public sign of the Treasury's position on SWFs came in June 2007 when, for the first time, a pending Treasury proposal for developing 'best practices' for SWFs that would involve some form of 'joint task force' through the IMF and World Bank was disclosed.[18] The Treasury had gained an appreciation that the SWFs were becoming a 'systemically significant' component of the international capital markets and could be a constructive force in global economic policies and global financial stability objectives. The Treasury's position aligned with President Bush's preference for a strong 'open market' foreign policy,[19] along with his position of developing stronger and more constructive relationships with China during his second term. Complementing President Bush's

see generally Hong Li, 'China Investment Corporation: A Perspective on Accountability', 43(4) *International Lawyer* 1495 (2009).

[14] See Andrew E. Kramer, 'Russia Creates $32 Billion Fund for Foreign Investment', *New York Times*, 1 February 2008, C2.

[15] On SWFs generally, see the IWG website at <http://www.iwg-swf.org> (visited 20–21 July 2010). The first modern SWF was created by Kuwait in the 1950s. Historically, SWFs have operated on a discrete, long-term perspective and on a non- or low-leveraged, commercial-investment basis: there appears to be no common investment strategy or collective collaboration among the SWFs. There has been no evidence that SWFs have ever brought mischief to the inter- national financial system.

[16] See e.g. Sylvia Pfeifer, 'Gazprom Flexes Its Muscles in Europe', *Telegraph*, 15 April 2007, <http://www.telegraph.co.uk/finance/migrationtemp/2807346/Gazprom-flexes-its-muscles-in-Europe.html> (visited 20–21 July 2010); and French President Sarkozy referring to non-European SWFs as 'predators', see 'Sarkozy Outlines "Refoundation" of Capitalism', EurActiv, 22 October 2008, <http://www.euractiv.com/en/financial-services/sarkozy-outlines-refoundation-capitalism/article-176571> (visited 20–21 July 2010).

[17] See generally, 'Implications of Sovereign Wealth Fund Investments for National Security': Hearing Before the US–China Economic and Security Review Commission, 110th Congress, 2008.

[18] See e.g. Press Release, US Department of the Treasury, 'Remarks by Acting Under Secretary for International Affairs Clay Lowery on Sovereign Wealth Funds and the International Financial System', 21 June 2007, <http://www.ustreas.gov/press/releases/hp471.htm> (visited 20–21 July 2010).

[19] See Press Release, President George W. Bush, 'Open Economies Policy Statement', 20 May 2007, <http://georgewbush-whitehouse.archives.gov/news/releases/2007/05/20070510-2.html> (visited 20–21 July 2010).

policy positions were the views of Paulson, the former head of Goldman Sachs, who for many years had been a fervent promoter of stronger ties with China.[20]

Yet, notwithstanding strong support from the executive branch, it became clear that China/China Investment Corporation (CIC) could become a controversial matter in the US Congress, particularly as a number of major US global financial institutions were in search of significant injections of fresh capital from CIC and other foreign SWFs.[21] Congress, in the summer of 2007, was to begin to debate an amendment of the Foreign Investment and National Security Act of 2007; and, as in November 2007, there would be the national political election, during which China-bashing and protectionist sentiments would be 'fair political game'.

Thus, the first hurdle for Treasury was to have a solid sense by the fall of 2007 that the SWF would get through the domestic US legislative and political 'quicksand' largely unscathed. With supportive Congressional testimony from a number of senior Treasury, Federal Reserve Board and Securities Exchange Commission officials, Treasury was able to gain this comfort level, although Congressional hearings on the topic were to continue through the end of 2007 and into early 2008.

B. The international level: commandeering the IFIs

The 2007 joint Annual Meeting of the IMF and World Bank was to be held on 20–22 October 2007.[22] Immediately beforehand, the G7 Finance Ministers were to meet among themselves and then with the IMF's International Monetary and Financial Committee (IMFC).[23] At the ministerial meeting on 19 October 2007, Paulson had put on the G7's agenda the issue of the SWFs and the related, suggested roles of the IFIs. After this meeting, Paulson hosted an 'outreach dinner' with finance ministers and heads of major SWFs from eight countries. Paulson confirmed that there should be openness to SWF investments, provided these funds were not used for political objectives.[24] He further proposed that the countries having SWFs should be opening up their home markets to foreign investment also.[25] Paulson then addressed the IMFC the following morning: the IMFC

---

[20] See Henry M. Paulson Jr., *On The Brink: The Race To Stop The Collapse Of The Global Financial System* (New York: Business Plus, 2010) 32–3 and 52–5; and his '2006 Speech on the International Economy', 11 September 2006, <http://www.ustreas.gov/press/releases/hp95.htm> (visited 20–21 July 2010).

[21] See, e.g. 'Citigroup Abu Dhabi Deal Signals Trouble Ahead', *Reuters,* 27 November 2007, <http://www.reuters.com/article/idUSN2752968520071127> (visited 20–21 July 2010).

[22] See '2007 Annual Meetings: World Bank Group International Monetary Fund', <http://www.imf.org/external/am/2007/index.htm> (visited 20–21 July 2010).

[23] On the IMFC, see <http://www.imf.org/external/np/exr/facts/groups.htm> (visited 20–21 July 2010).

[24] See Robert M. Kimmitt, 'In Praise of Foreign Investment', *The International Economy*, Spring 2008, 71ff.

[25] See Pete Kasperowicz, 'Paulson Sets Tough Goals for IMF on Sovereign Wealth Funds, Currency, Spending', *Forbes.com*, 20 October 2007, <http://www.forbes.com/feeds/afx/2007/10/20/afx4242119.html> (visited 20–21 July 2010).

supported Paulson's SWF agenda.[26] As such, Paulson had 'nudged' the IMF/ IMFC, along with the OECD (from the foreign direct investment perspective) and the World Bank, to take on the task of overseeing the development of the SWF 'best practices' project.[27]

Subject to the G7 Finance Ministers' guidance and the IMFC's direction, the IMF convened a 'roundtable of sovereign asset and reserve managers' from 28 countries on 15–16 November. The IMF also embarked upon a comprehensive survey of the main SWFs. It began formulating a work plan ('Work Agenda') for developing best practice guidelines for SWFs, and undertook broader, related, international collaborative efforts to better evaluate the possible beneficial and negative implications of the growing presence of SWFs. Issues to be considered included the relation of SWFs (i) to financial stability and currency exchange rate impact, (ii) to possible geo-political issues, such as the likelihood of government policy direction of these funds and a rise of protectionism among home or target countries and (iii) to risk management issues, including matters of transparency, accountability and governance.[28] On 29 February 2008, the IMF set out a 'Work Agenda', under which the International Working Group (IWG) would be established and a SWF proposal as to 'principles' or 'best practices' would be presented to the IMF's Executive Board at its Annual Meeting in Fall 2008. The final proposal was to be based upon consultations with various officials of the SWF host countries and with other bodies—such as the OECD, the EU Commission and ECB, the US Treasury and other concerned finance ministries.[29] As the senior IMF official heading this working group surmised: 'Best practices and principles could also help ease concerns about SWFs... and contribute to an open global monetary and financial system... [T]he key to a successful result is one that is based on an inclusive, collaborative, and evenhanded effort.'[30] These sentiments reflect a true change in 'culture' of the IMF and other IFIs, under NIFA-I and now NIFA-II, as to notions of inclusivity, openness, legitimacy, ownership, institution-underpinning, accountability and the bottom-up development of rule-oriented global principles/best practices.

---

[26] See Press Release, US Treasury Department Office of Public Affairs, 'Statement by US Treasury Secretary Henry M. Paulson, Jr., at the International Monetary and Financial Committee Meeting', 20 October 2007, <http://www.imf.org/External/AM/2007/imfc/statement/eng/usa.pdf>, (visited 20–21 July 2010).

[27] See Press Release, International Monetary Fund, 'Communiqué of the International Monetary and Financial Committee of the Board of Governors of the International Monetary Fund', 20 October 2007, <https://www.imf.org/external/np/sec/pr/2007/pr07236.htm> (visited 20–21 July 2010). This SWF assignment seems compatible with the IMF's multilateral consultation on global imbalances and perceived mandate to foster global financial stability; however, as the IMF has been 'assigned' a range of new tasks over the past decade or so, IMF mandate issues have become of fundamental concern to the Fund.

[28] See IMF Work Agenda, above n 11, at 10–16.

[29] Ibid, at 21–2.

[30] See 'IMF Board Endorses Work Agenda on Sovereign Funds', *IMF Survey online,* 21 March 2008, <https://www.imf.org/external/pubs/ft/survey/so/2008/NEW032108A.htm> (visited 20–21 July 2010).

The G7 and IMFC tasked the OECD with developing a related and complementary voluntary SWF investment 'code' for the recipient countries, so that free
flows of global capital and foreign investment are not impaired by undue reactions
of the recipient or targeted investment countries.[31]

C. The covert trilateral track

Paulson was pursuing discretely another track, apparently not fully known to the
non-involved members of the IWG. On 20 March 2008, Paulson, the heads of the
Abu Dhabi SWF and one of the two Singapore SWFs (GIC), along with the Abu
Dhabi and Singapore governments, agreed that their SWF investments would be
based solely on commercial grounds and that they would work toward increasing
the disclosure of information and making sure that they have strong risk management and governance controls. They also agreed that countries receiving investments should not set up protectionist barriers and should have consistent, non-
discriminatory investment rules.[32] It appears Paulson was attempting to 'prime' in
advance the direction of the IMF–OECD efforts. A subsequent Treasury Release
indicated that the Singapore Principles would 'support' the IMF–OECD efforts.[33]

D. The IFIs at work

By March 2008, the IMF was moving forward with its 'Work Agenda'. The IWG,
comprising senior officials from 25 SWFs, was constituted in May 2008.[34] Con-
temporaneously, considerable background research was being conducted by the
IMF, World Bank and OECD, while the US Treasury continued to engage in
bilateral discussions with selected major SWFs.[35] In addition, the European
Commission worked with the concerned EU countries to arrive at a common
EU position.[36] The IWG met on three occasions: the Group agreed preliminarily
on a set of 24 'principles and practices' at its third meeting held in Santiago on

---

[31] See G7/8, G7 Finance Ministers and Central Bank Governors, G7/8 Finance Ministers Meeting,
19 October 2007, <http://www.g8.utoronto.ca/finance/fm071019.htm> (visited 20–21 July 2010).
[32] See Government of the Republic of Singapore, 'Joint Release of Policy Principles for Sovereign
Wealth Funds and the Countries Receiving Sovereign Wealth Fund Investment by the United States,
Abu Dhabi and Singapore', at app. A, 21 March 2008, <http://www.channelnewsasia.com/annex/
210308swf.pdf> (visited 20–21 July2010) ['Singapore Principles'].
[33] Press Release, US Department of Treasury, 'Treasury Reaches Agreement on Principles for
Sovereign Wealth Fund Investment with Singapore and Abu Dhabi', 20 March 2008, <http://www.
ustreas.gov/press/releases/hp881.htm> (visited 20–21 July 2010).
[34] See Press Release, 'International Monetary Fund, International Working Group of Sovereign
Wealth Funds is Established to Facilitate Work on Voluntary Principles' (1 May 2008), <http://www.
imf.org/external/np/sec/pr/2008/pr0897.htm> (visited 20–21 July 2010).
[35] See Singapore Principles, above n 32.
[36] See e.g. Commission of the European Communities, 'Communication from the Commission to
the European Parliament, the Council, the European Economic and Social Committee and the
Committee of the Regions: A Common European Approach to Sovereign Wealth Funds' (2008), at
3, <http://ec.europa.eu/internal_market/finances/docs/sovereign_en.pdf> (visited 20–21 July 2010).

2 September 2008 (the 'Santiago Principles').[37] These *Principles* covered the SWFs' legal, institutional and macro-economic setting, the SWFs' governance and accountability arrangements, and the SWFs' investment policies and risk management.[38] The IMF and IWG completed their survey of SWFs on 15 September 2008.[39]

Having secured the approval of the governments of the IWG member countries, the IWG presented the *Principles* to the IMFC on 11 October 2008 in Washington, DC. Immediately following this meeting, the IWG met with a range of officials from major recipient countries. The *Principles* were published promptly thereafter.[40]

At this IMFC meeting, the IWG also announced the creation of a 'Formation Committee' to explore the establishment of a permanent SWF 'Standing Group'.[41] The objective of this Standing Group would be 'to facilitate dialogue with official institutions and recipient countries on developments that affect SWF operations'.[42] Thus, inherent to the creation of the Santiago Principles was the distinct possibility that there would be some ongoing organizational mechanism to further study and to monitor the implementation of these *Principles*.

On 8 October 2008, the OECD presented to the IMFC its final package of 'guidance' for countries receiving SWF investment.[43] The OECD's approach subsumed the SWF issue under its 'Freedom of Investment and National Security' process. In light of the GFC, this process was enhanced to provide a forum for intergovernmental dialogue on how governments can reconcile the need to preserve and expand an open international investment environment with their duty to safeguard the essential security interests of their people and to take action to recover from the crisis. They responded with a series of investment policy reports issued to date and issued throughout 2010. This enhanced process extended and intensified

[37] IWG, 'Sovereign Wealth Funds: Generally Accepted Principles and Practices "Santiago Principles"' (2008), at 1, <http://www.iwg-swf.org/pubs/eng/santiagoprinciples.pdf> (visited 20–21 July 2010).

[38] Press Release, IWG, 'International Working Group of Sovereign Wealth Funds Reaches a Preliminary Agreement on Draft Set Generally Accepted Principles and Practices—"Santiago Principles"', 2 September 2008, <http://www.iwg-swf.org/pr/swfpr0804.htm> (visited 20–21 July 2010).

[39] See Cornelia Hammer, Peter Kunzel and Iva Petrova, 'Sovereign Wealth Funds: Current Institutional and Operational Practices', IWG Working Paper No 08/254, 2008, <http://www.iwg-swf.org/pubs/eng/swfsurvey.pdf> (visited 20–21 July 2010).

[40] See Press Release, IWG, 'International Working Group of Sovereign Wealth Funds Presents the "Santiago Principles" to the International Monetary and Financial Committee: Promotes Operational Independence in Investment Decisions, Transparency, and Accountability', 11 October 2008, <http://www.iwg-swf.org/pr/swfpr0806.htm> (visited 20–21 July 2010).

[41] See Statement of H.E. Hamad Al-Hurr Al-Suwaidi, Co-Chair of the International Working Group of Sovereign Wealth Funds, Meeting of the International Monetary and Financial Commission', Washington, DC, 11 October 2008, <http://www.iwg-swf.org/pubs/eng/imfciwg.pdf> (visited 20–21 July 2010).

[42] See 'SWF Principles Will Help Cross-Border Investment—Lipsky,' *IMF Survey Online*, 3 September 2008, <https://www.imf.org/external/pubs/ft/survey/so/2008/NEW090308B.htm> (visited 20–21 July 2010).

[43] See Organisation for Economic Co-Operation and Development, 'Message by the OECD Secretary-General to the International Monetary and Financial Committee', 11 October 2008, at 1, <http://www.oecd.org/dataoecd/0/23/41456730.pdf> (visited 20–21 July 2010).

the OECD tradition of ongoing 'dialogue' beyond its member countries—its efforts being made to promote progressive investment practices of non-discrimination, liberalization, and transparency—strengthened the 'peer monitoring' of country development.[44] The OECD SWF Report to the IMFC was based upon input from the 30 OECD members, and from a broader group of non-members including Brazil, China, Russia and South Africa.[45]

In the G7 Finance Ministers' mandate of October 2007, the World Bank was specifically included as one of the IFI collaborators in the SWF best practices process, although (unlike with the IMF and the OECD) the Bank was given no specific task. The Bank's involvement makes sense as many of the SWFs are from developing countries; a number of SWFs have been and will be investing in developing countries; the Bank has extensive technical assistance (TA) expertise (including providing TA to SWFs) and over the past decade there has been a trend for greater IMF–World Bank collaboration in the areas of TA, country consultations and program assessments.[46]

Although, in this process, the World Bank stayed on the sidelines a 'permanent observer' to the IWG, the Bank's President was promoting a 'One-percent Solution', whereby SWFs would commit to invest 1 per cent of their equity holdings in Africa.[47]

Unlike the OECD SWF Report, which was built largely upon pre-existing OECD reports, practices and processes, the IMF–IWG's efforts were made afresh, but not in isolation. There was input from 29 SWFs, 26 countries, which were members of the IMF, a group of key recipient countries, the World Bank, the OECD and the European Commission.[48] The IWG 'Secretariat' (i.e. the IMF acting informally) sought to gain as much knowledge as it could about the existing practices of the SWFs and about recipient country concerns, and to build the 'best practices' on this substantial knowledge base. Additionally, the IWG–IMF wanted to avoid the perception of a top-down process: it engaged the SWFs and recipient countries in a collaborative manner.[49]

---

[44] Ibid, the umbrella component of the OECD SWF Report was a 'Declaration on Sovereign Wealth Funds and Recipient Country Policies' that had been issued previously by the OECD Ministerial Council on 5 June 2008.

[45] OECD, 'Guidance on Sovereign Wealth Funds', <http://www.oecd.org/document/19/0,3343, en_2649_34887_41807059_1_1_1_1,00.html> (visited 20–21 July 2010).

[46] See e.g. International Monetary Fund and World Bank, 'Strengthening IMF–World Bank Collaboration on Country Programs and Conditionality', 2001, <http://siteresources.worldbank.org/ PROJECTS/Resources/imf-wb-conditionality08-22-01.pdf> (visited 20–21 July 2010). See OECD Directorate for Financial and Enterprise Affairs, 'Protection Freedom of Investment at the OECD', <http://www.oecd.org/document/7/0,3343,en_2649_34887_37363207_1_1_1_1,00.html> (visited 20–21 July 2010).

[47] See e.g. World Bank Press Release, 'The World Bank, Sovereign Wealth Funds Should Invest in Africa, Zoellick Says', 2 April 2008, <http://go.worldbank.org/50LXBPOUM0> (visited 20–21 July 2010).

[48] See 'Santiago Principles', above n 38, at 2.

[49] See IMF Work Agenda, above n 11, at 4.

III. The Santiago Principles as 'International Best Practices'

The Santiago Principles[50] were conceived of as a 'voluntary set of principles and practices'[51] for a variety of reasons. The formulating IWG itself is a 'voluntary' body, being an informal, ad hoc and partially self-generated body with no formal legal authority. Furthermore, the SWFs involved are creatures of domestic governmental bodies and are subject to the law and practical control of the home country.[52] In addition, this bringing together of the SWFs within an international forum and subject to 'best practices' was totally 'new territory' for the IMF, the SWFs and the other 'stakeholders' involved (including the rapidly changing global capital markets). Goodwill and mutual benefit, and not formal rules, would need to be the main drivers respecting the integration of participating parties and their home countries. Once the SWFs were brought into the overall IWG process and became more comfortable with the other parties involved, a sense of 'club law' began to develop, or at least an aura of influencing peer/group pressure.[53] While recognizing differences in the stages of evolution of the various SWFs and the need to allow for transitional arrangements and some necessary variances, the end goal of the process was not a 'cafeteria style' set of principles and practices but rather a common set of 'generally agreed' principles derived from the practices of the SWFs and embraced by all the endorsing parties.[54] As a corollary, the Santiago Principles process does not create a conventional 'self-regulatory' regime, system of private-regulation or a code of conduct due to the mix of participants and due to the complex set of overriding pressures referred to above. At best, the environment would be quasi-self-regulatory or self-regulatory in a very constrained manner.[55]

Although designed as 'principles' and not as detailed rules, the document is intended to serve as a 'framework' within which greater 'rule-orientation' would evolve over time; that is, a work in progress but with a direction.[56] Second, the Generally Accepted Principles and Practices' (GAPP) 24 main 'principles'[57] cover the key SWF areas in a relatively comprehensive manner: Part A covers 'Legal

[50] See 'Santiago Principles', above n 38. Sometimes referred to by the acronym 'GAPP' (Generally Accepted Principles and Practices).
[51] Ibid, at 5. Yet, as discussed above, the process was never fully voluntary, as it was to operate within a complex of considerable overt and latent pressures.
[52] Ibid.
[53] The concept of 'peer group review' is implied in the Santiago Principles, Principle 24, as developed in the Kuwait Declaration. See IWG, ' "Kuwait Declaration": Establishment of the International Forum of Sovereign Wealth Funds', <http://www.iwg-swf.org/mis/kuwaitdec.htm> (visited 20–21 July 2010).
[54] See 'Santiago Principles', above n 38, at 6: ('[T]he GAPP is formulated broadly enough so that underlying principles and practices can be accommodated in different institutional, constitutional, and legal settings in various countries').
[55] Compare Olaf Dilling et al. (eds), *Responsible Business: Self Governance and Law in Transnational Economic Transactions* (Oxford: Hart Publishing, 2008).
[56] See 'Santiago Principles', above n 38, at 4–6.
[57] Ibid, at 7–9 (listing the Principles, some of which have Subprinciples).

Framework, Objectives and Coordination with Macroeconomic Policies';[58] Part B addresses 'Institutional Framework and Governance Structure';[59] Part C touches upon 'Investment and Risk Management Framework';[60] and the 24th Principle speaks to ongoing issues regarding 'Implementation'.[61] In addition, in Appendix 1, the GAPP present an agreed definition of an SWF with explanatory notes; Appendix II identifies the list and the representatives of the IWG members (including permanent observers) and of the participating recipient countries; Appendix III presents summary information of each of the participating SWFs; and a list of key SWF references is set forth at the end of the document.[62] The two core elements of disclosure and accountability permeate the *Principles*.

Significant about the GAPP is that each of the *Principles* is accompanied by an 'Explanation and commentary' that endeavors to develop and to interpret the substantive issues related to each Principle. This approach is intended to provide general principles and practices that 'are potentially achievable by countries at all levels of economic development'. As such, the GAPP should not be considered a final product, but rather a starting point in an ongoing dialog concerning SWFs and their role in the international financial and economic systems. The primary 'purpose of the *Principles* is to identify a framework of generally accepted principles and practices that properly reflect appropriate governance and accountability arrangements as well as the conduct of investment practices...on a prudent and sound basis'.[63] Moreover, the GAPP 'aims to contribute to the stability of the global financial system, reduce protectionist pressures, and help maintain an open and stable investment climate'.[64]

IV. The IWG–ISWF Forum as 'Soft Regulatory Process'

The efficacy of law ('hard' or 'soft') is dependent on the quality of the related procedures and processes.[65] Certainly, it is premature to denote the Santiago Principles as 'soft law' or 'soft administrative regulation'. But it is clear that these *Principles* and the attendant creation of the ISWF Forum and a permanent Forum Secretariat are generating an ongoing procedural construct within which the Santiago Principles and the OECD SWF 'best practices' can be further developed, monitored and assessed.

At its meeting in Kuwait City on 6 April 2009, the IWG announced in the so-called Kuwait Declaration the formation of the ISWF Forum as a 'voluntary' group of SWFs whose primary purpose is 'to meet, exchange views on issues of common interest, and facilitate an understanding of the Santiago Principles and SWF activities'.[66] This Declaration stressed the 'voluntary character' of this new

---

[58] Ibid, at 11 (Principles 1–5).   [59] Ibid, at 15 (Principles 6–17).
[60] Ibid, at 20 (Principles 18–23).   [61] Ibid, at 20 (Principle 24).
[62] Ibid, at 27–49.   [63] Ibid, at 4.   [64] Ibid.
[65] Compare the classic article: Edson R. Sunderland, 'An Inquiry Concerning the Functions of Procedure in Legal Education', 21 *Michigan Law Review* 372 (1923).
[66] IWG, ' "Kuwait Declaration" ', above n 53.

Forum, and also that '[t]he Forum shall not be a formal supranational authority and its work shall not carry any legal force'.[67] Yet, the reality is that the Forum does represent a 'global community' of SWFs that have come about through the mandate of the G7, G20 and IMFC, and that remains accountable to the G20 and IMFC. Furthermore, though SWFs are commercial investors, they remain controlled, directly or indirectly, by their home-country governments, and these governments maintain some level of accountability through the G20 and/or IMFC. Moreover, as a 'club' and as subject to a form of internal peer review and other forms of periodic assessment, there are obvious built-in structures to help ensure that the member SWFs do not 'back-pedal' but actively contribute to the agreed objectives of the group. In addition, the SWFs, as new significant financial players in the global capital markets, will be subject to greater market scrutiny so maintaining a good reputation or brand will probably become more important to them. Buying into externally respected 'best practices' should help in this respect.

The SWF Forum is to be developed as an 'inclusive' body, open to all SWFs agreeing to accept and foster those *Principles*.[68] Furthermore, the Forum continues its predecessor IWG's practice of offering 'permanent observer' and other forms of 'associate' status.[69] Thus, the Forum facilitates communication and exchange of views among its members and their respective governments, and fosters communication among recipient country officials, representatives such as the OECD and World Bank and even with the private market sector.[70]

The ISWF Forum maintains a professional secretariat, with the IMF agreeing to serve initially in this capacity. The head of the Australian SWF serves as the initial Chair of the Forum, with Deputy Chairs drawn from the Chinese and Kuwaiti funds.[71] The Forum has three 'subgroups' of Forum members and recognized external experts:[72] one will work on the application of the Santiago Principles; a second on investment and risk management practices and, the third on the international investment environment and recipient country relationships.[73] Additionally, the IMF confers regularly with the major SWFs on a bilateral basis as part of its 'surveillance' role in the global economy.[74]

It is suggested that the Santiago Principles are based on 'an innovative, postmodern approach to global governance'.[75] Initially what this refers to is a system of 'peer review' to which member SWFs have committed themselves.[76] How this 'self-

[67] Ibid.   [68] Ibid.   [69] Ibid.
[70] See Jukka Pihlman, 'Sovereign Funds Set Up Permanent Representative Forum,' *IMF Survey Online*, 6 May 2009, <http://www.imf.org/external/pubs/ft/survey/so/2009/NEW050609A.htm> (visited 20–21 July 2010).
[71] Ibid.
[72] See IWG website, above n 15.
[73] See Pihlman, above n 70.
[74] See IMF Work Agenda, above n 11, at 5 and 17.
[75] IWG Press Release, 'Working Group Announces Creation of International Forum of Sovereign Wealth Funds', 6 April 2009, note particularly remarks therein of H.E. Mustafa J. Al-Shimali, Chairman of the Kuwaiti SWF and Kuwait's Minister of Finance, <http://iwg-swf.org/pr/swfpr0901.htm> (visited 20–21 July 2010).
[76] Ibid.

regulatory' process will work remains to be seen, but this sort of process is not without precedent in the international financial arena.[77] However, this ISWF Forum 'peer-review' process will not be a purely internal process but, instead, will be part of a process that includes the 'global community' of SWF interests. In this context, the ISWF Forum is an incipient framework of legitimacy, account-ability and transparency (the trilogy of criteria by which SWF regulation should be evaluated) that is capable of maturing over time. In this maturation, the ISWF Forum framework should consider the relevant 'constituencies' or 'stakeholders' as they assess these three criteria.[78]

Purely on a preliminary observational basis, it appears that there is a broad and complex array of possible constituents and stakeholders who, ideally, may need to be accommodated by seeking input from such parties and, more generally, by having the ISWF Forum provide a viable, ongoing, administrative-type process for monitoring, evaluating and supporting the SWFs as to the *Principles*.[79] In light of this, without any real, encompassing and coordinated policy forethought, a number of these possible constituents appear already to have been interconnected in some manner with the enhanced ISWF Forum process (e.g. the major SWFs and their governments, the key recipient countries, the G20, IMF/IMFC, OECD and World Bank). Also, with the global accounting, investment banking and consulting firms' involvement with the major SWFs, an indirect connection with the actual financial markets and their evolving standards, requirements and practices is being forged, although this connection to the financial markets remains tenuous and incomplete.

V. Concluding Observations

In the ad hoc saga to date involving the SWFs and the IWG–ISWF Forum processes, one sees a curious, initially unplanned and largely disjointed pattern of incipient 'multi-level global governance' among major national and regional actors

---

[77] See generally Douglas W. Arner and Michael W. Taylor, 'The Global Financial Crisis and the Financial Stability Board: Hardening the Soft Law of International Financial Regulation?', Asian Institute of International Financial Law, Working Paper No 6, 2009, <http://papers.ssrn.com/sol3/papers.cfm?abstract_id=1427084> (visited 20–21 July 2010).

[78] On the basis of his 33 element assessment scheme, Truman evaluated the Santiago Principles, giving them a 'score' of 74 (within rating of the top-half of the 46 SWFs that he originally assessed). Edwin R. Truman, 'Real Time Economic Issues Watch: Making the World Safe for Sovereign Wealth Funds', Peterson Institute for International Economics, 14 October 2008, <http://www.petersonin-stitute.org/realtime/?p=105> (visited 20–21 July 2010).

[79] For example, constituents/stakeholders, in addition to the SWF members of the Forum and the 'permanent observers', might include: the respective controlling and funding governmental bodies; private, public and quasi-public parties as to which the SWFs might have significant commercial/investment/financial/counterparty relationships (each of which probably will have differing expect-ations and risk-protection requirements); the recipient countries; private and public bodies responsible for the orderly and sound functioning of the global capital markets; international bodies that might see the SWFs as having a relationship to the global goals of sustainable financial stability and sustainable and balanced economic growth and development; non-Forum member SWFs and, even possibly the SWF home-country citizenry.

(e.g. the US Treasury and the European Commission) triggered by a concern regarding a possible NIFA-II subject-matter (i.e. the rise of the SWFs).[80] The USA largely dealt with this concern domestically through the pragmatic efforts of its Treasury Secretary, who in turn placed this issue squarely on the agendas of the G7 Finance Ministers and Heads of State level (and subsequently the G20 Finance Ministers level) and the IMF's IMFC. The G7/G20 Ministers and the IMFC provided the direction and delegated follow-up responsibilities to the IMF, the World Bank and the OECD.[81] In this initial process, the concerns for the SWFs were brought within (or at least to the edges of) the G20's NIFA-II 'Action Plan' for restructuring the global financial architecture in light of the GFC.[82] From the US Treasury's initial attempts to achieve rather limited and immediate objectives, the IWG–ISWF Forum process has evolved into a maturing (although still evolving) scheme that entails broad micro- and macro-economic objectives that have come to the forefront as a result of the GFC. What this ad hoc, *sui generis* process generated, in addition to the Santiago Principles, is a working 'global policy network' that in the form of the IWG– ISWF Forum comprised 26 SWFs (23 as members and three as permanent observers). This group of SWFs collaborate with the IMF, the OECD, the World Bank and the key recipient countries in formulating a set of international standards/best practices—a 'global public good'[83]—in the form of Santiago Principles and in establishing the structure of the ISWF Forum as a nascent, ongoing vehicle and process for continuing communication, interpretation, monitoring, assessment, implementation and further development of the *Principles* and the SWF grouping process. What is unique in this situation is that this emerging 'global policy network' not only affects the relevant SWFs, but also the home-government entities (most often accountable to the respective Ministries of Finance and Central Banks, some of whom are themselves also members of the G7 Ministers and/or the IMFC) that effectively control these SWFs. The network now centers around the agreement/consensus arrived at with respect to their own operational and governance 'international standards' (the Santiago Principle-GAPP). Tangentially, the OECD, in collaboration with this grouping, has com-

---

[80] For those familiar with the historical informal and random 'network' development of International Financial Reporting Standards (IFRSs) over the past three to four decades, one sees ISSB bodies such as the G10, Basel Committee, IOSCO, Financial Action Task Force (FATF) and International Association of Insurance Supervisors (IAIS), along with the global policy determinant G7 to have been initially created in a random, ad hoc manner. It was not until the mid- and late-1990s when NIFA-I evolved that one could see any overarching policy or practical coherence. See Norton, above n 9.

[81] As mentioned elsewhere in this chapter, Secretary Paulson's concerns for the SWFs (and more specifically the CIC) do not appear to be systemic in nature or truly global in policy scope. He was more concerned with heading off probable domestic resistance to the SWFs and their investment in the USA and in US financial institutions and corporations.

[82] See above 'Introduction'.

[83] See Press Release, IWG, 'Statement by the European Commissioner on the Santiago Principles', 11 October 2008, <http://www.iwg-swf.org/pr/swfpr0808.htm> (visited 20–21 July 2010): 'The principles and practices of the GAPP amount to a global public good that can help foster trust and confidence between sovereign wealth funds, their originating countries, and the recipient countries. This is what we need in these turbulent times: a strong commitment to enhance mutual trust and maintain and preserve an open investment environment'.

piled its own complementary 'Guidelines' for the recipient countries as to their treatment of SWF investments.

So where does this 'global policy network' go from here, as the 'heat' appears to have been taken away from the SWF phenomenon and as the GFC appears possibly to be bottoming out? There are several possibilities. The SWF issue may become marginalized as the G20, the IMF, Financial Stability Board (FSB) and others involved in the new 'global architecture' cope with broader and more fundamental matters dealing with restructuring the global economy and the financial system. Alternatively or concurrently, the SWFs (or certain of them) may retract from moving the ISWF Forum process forward and return to 'business as usual'.[84] More hopefully, the ISWF Forum process will continue to mature, and become a proactive, contributory component to the new NIFA-II global financial architecture and to global capital markets.

In his 2010 Spring Semester lectures,[85] the author made a series of modest suggestions, including the following: (i) the ISWF Forum needs to inculcate a serious institutional and individual member commitment to ensure that it becomes a more inclusive body and that its members adopt enhanced standards of greater transparency, better corporate governance and higher levels of accountability for the global SWF community; (ii) the Forum needs more fully to appreciate that the SWFs' position as to the global capital markets and to the broader global financial system will be magnified in coming years; (iii) the Forum should seek further links to the financial markets and to the global policymakers responsible for global financial stability including 'affiliate' status[86] with the International Organization of Securities Commissions (IOSCO), the ISSB in the securities law area;[87] (iv) the Forum should consider being more openly and actively involved with the private players in the capital markets by associating and exchanging views with the major private international capital markets bodies such as the private, self-regulatory International Capital Market Association (ICMA),[88] the Hedge Fund Association[89] and the International Investment Fund Association;[90] (v) the Forum and its members need to be tied into and committed to the IMF's bilateral surveillance initiatives of financial stability analyses and should explore ongoing technical assistance programs for its members through the IMF, the World Bank and the OECD as to upgrading their governance structures and as to some form of voluntary periodic assessments; (vi) there should be some form of substantive

---

[84] The SWFs were never viewed as contributing to the causes of the GFC. Furthermore, certain SWF home countries such as Saudi Arabia have never been over enthusiastic about the IWG– ISWF Forum process and remain only 'permanent observers'.

[85] See author's acknowledgment at the beginning of this chapter.

[86] See IOSCO Membership and Committees Lists, <http://www.iosco.org/lists> (visited 20–21 July 2010).

[87] Part of IOSCO's mandate is: 'to unite their efforts to establish standards and an effective surveillance of international securities transactions'.

[88] See <http://www.icmagroup.org> (visited 20–21 July 2010).

[89] See <http://www.thehfa.org> (visited 20–21 July 2010).

[90] See International Investment Funds Association Statement of Principles, <http://www.iifa.ca/about/objectives.aspx> (visited 20–21 July 2010).

'associate' linkage between the Forum and the FSB inasmuch as a 'public good' related to global financial stability and a set of *de facto* international standards are involved;[91] and (vii) perhaps (in the long term) the G20 and the IMFC, in consultation with the Forum, should consider a way to fit the ISWF Forum within the revised NIFA-II framework involving the IMF and FSB[92] and more generally within and contributing to the G20 Leaders' new 'Global Growth Framework'.[93]

The Forum's ultimate success will depend in part upon it internally developing as a quasi-global administrative body with a sound basis of legitimacy as to its numerous constituents and stakeholders and with heightened institutional transparency, good governance and accountability. While not precipitated by the GFC, the ISWF Forum process has the capacity to become a key component to the NIFA-II overall approach to global financial stability, market integrity and economic openness.

---

[91] See generally <http://www.financialstabilityboard.org/about/overview.htm> (visited 20–21 July 2010).

[92] See G20 Declaration, above n 4.

[93] A number of the aforementioned linkages might be achieved through a series of particularized (but coordinated) Memoranda of Understanding (MoU) between the ISWF Forum and the relevant bodies/authorities. In part, it would be these MoU that might form the foundation for the Forum's successful and effective evolution into a responsible participant in the global financial markets, the international investment environment and the global financial stability policymaking processes of NIFA-II.

PART III

FINANCIAL MARKET
REGULATION

7

The Role and Prospects of International Law in Financial Regulation and Supervision

Christian Tietje and Matthias Lehmann

I. Introduction

The global financial crisis of 2007–09, which is more than symbolically tied to the breakdown of Lehman Brothers on 15 September 2008, resulted in challenges for governments and markets alike. Governments—both providing the framework for market activities and having the capacity to intervene in a market if necessary—and the market as a self-regulatory mechanism are trying to cope with the problem of how to prevent a future global economic crisis. For governments, both on the national level and with regard to efforts in international cooperation and coordination, 'better' regulation and supervision of financial markets are called for. Modified and/or new models of regulation and supervision are a central element in providing for stable domestic and international financial markets in the future. It is thus not surprising that G20 leaders at the London Summit of 2 April 2009 listed '[s]trengthening financial supervision and regulation'—right after '[r]estoring growth and jobs' as a priority in reviving financial markets.[1]

Strengthening regulation and supervision is always in potential conflict with the essential freedom of financial markets. There is always a necessity to seek an equilibrium between the two components. The tension between regulation or supervision and market freedom is not a new phenomenon in financial law. What is new, however, is that in strengthening regulation and supervision today, one has also to take into account—at least partially—the need for international regulatory and supervisory cooperation and coordination.

This chapter sketches some conceptual aspects of the ongoing domestic and international debate on strengthening financial regulation and supervision. This is primarily done from a legal perspective; it does not go into the details of economic theory. We understand 'regulation' broadly in terms of the legal framework shaping

---

[1] G20, 'Global Plan for Recovery and Reform: *The Communiqué from the London Summit*', London, 2 April 2009, <http://www.londonsummit.gov.uk/en/summit-aims/summit-communique> (visited 4 August 2010). The decisions made by the leaders of the world's largest economies at the London Summit are recorded in this communiqué which all leaders signed.

financial services and transactions. 'Supervision' is distinct from regulation as it refers only to the enforcement of regulatory standards. Neither with regard to regulation nor to supervision is this chapter concerned with questions of liberalization of financial services.[2] We will thus only discuss measures which are applied on the basis of non-discrimination[3] after market entry has occurred.

This chapter is divided into three main parts. Section II describes and discusses different systems and methods of domestic regulation and supervision as well as related conceptual challenges. Section III discusses new areas and methods of regulation and supervision in reaction to the crisis of 2007–09. Section IV, based on findings in sections II and III, looks into the question of optimal harmonization of financial markets. Section V draws the conclusions.

II. Areas, Systems and Methods of Domestic Regulation of Financial Markets

A. Classical areas of financial law

Financial regulation is not complete. It does not cover the entire reality of financial markets. There have always been some areas willingly left unregulated by states in order not to hamper the innovative talents and potential of financial actors. In other areas, there was concern and the need for regulation and supervision was recognized and dealt with. Whether or not areas have been regulated largely depends upon historical antecedents: it is accidental. Most often, financial legislation was enacted after innovative dealings got out of hand and created a crisis. As a result, the matters that are covered by financial legislation do not in any way form a logical or consistent system. The same applies to the content of the legislation: sometimes it addresses the quality of financial actors, sometimes information asymmetries, sometimes market behaviour, and sometimes the infrastructure of the market.

The typical way to regulate financial markets is to demand that actors comply with certain defined conditions. These actors are different financial intermediaries, such as banks, fund managers, brokers, or investment advisers. Underlying their regulation and supervision may be varying concerns. Chief among them is the risk that they might embezzle the funds of their clients or give false advice. Traditional instruments by which financial intermediaries are controlled include the requirement to register and the obligation to turn over certain information to the supervisory authorities.

For some actors, the legal requirements go further, cutting deeply into their organizational structure. This is particularly true for banks. Although banks are in some ways the archetypal financial actors, definitions vary as to what legally makes a bank a bank. There is an abundance of different activities that may constitute

---

[2] On this topic, see the paper by Panagiotis Delimatsis and Pierre Sauvé in this volume at Chapter 16.
[3] See Chapter 15 by Thomas Cottier and Markus Krajewski in this volume.

'banking'.[4] Nevertheless, it can be said that the central reason why banking is regulated in modern societies lies in the risk of the bank not being able to return the funds of its customers when requested to do so. This concern has led to the requirement of obtaining a licence in order to enter the banking business, and to stringent prudential requirements such as those on capital adequacy and liquidity.[5] Since these measures alone are not sufficient to create the necessary trust in credit institutions, most states have added guarantees partly securing the deposits of customers; these deposit insurance schemes exist in various legal systems.[6] Often they are state-sponsored, but are partly supplemented by voluntary or mandatory private guarantees.

The regulation regarding information asymmetry is designed to counter the marked difference between the two sides of the market, i.e. between the issuers of financial products on one side, and the buyers of financial products on the other. In order to balance such asymmetries and to provide both sides with a fair amount of information, different measures have been adopted. Chief among them is the requirement to make a prospectus available to the client.[7] Accounting and auditing rules pursue similar goals: they aim at providing the investor with accurate information about the issuer. Another measure that pursues a similar purpose is to impose specific fiduciary duties on intermediaries who sell financial products.

Financial regulation of market behaviour sets the basic rules on what is and what is not allowed in the marketplace. Remarkably, these rules are applicable to everyone, not only those who offer financial products, but also the buyers. Examples of behavioural rules are provisions on insider trading and other fraudulent practices.[8]

Finally, the regulation regarding the financial infrastructure addresses the technical basis of the market, e.g. exchanges or trading platforms. Mostly, this technical

---

[4] See e.g. European Parliament and Council Directive 2006/48/EC on the taking up and pursuit of the business of credit institutions, OJ 2006 L 177/1, art 4(1) (defining a credit institution as an 'undertaking whose business is to receive deposits or other repayable funds from the public and to grant credits for its own account' or an 'electronic money institution'). Contrast this with the definition of banks in US case law, see e.g. *Exchange Bank of Columbus v Hines*, 3 *Ohio St.* 1 (1953) (holding that 'the business of banking, in its most enlarged signification, includes the business of receiving deposits, loaning money, and dealing in coin, bills of exchange, etc., besides that of issuing paper money'); *Brenham Production Credit Association v Zeiss*, 153 *Tex.* 132, 264 S.W.2d 95 (Tex., 1953) (holding that 'the primary function of a bank is to serve as a place for safe keeping of depositors' money'); *City National Bank v City of Beckley*, 579 S.E.2d 543 (W.Va., 2003) (holding that 'having a place of business where deposits are received and paid out on checks, and where money is loaned upon security, is the substance of the business of a banker').

[5] See e.g. in the USA: Bank Holding Company Act 1956, 12 USC xx1841ff, Annex A; in the EU: Directive 2006/48/EC, above n 4, arts 9 and 10.

[6] For a comparative overview, see Asli Demirgüç -Kunt and Edward J. Kane, 'Deposit Insurance Around The Globe—Where Does It Work?', World Bank Policy Research Working Paper No 2679, 2001.

[7] See e.g. in the USA: Securities Act 1933, 15 USC x77e(2)(b), Section 5(2)(b); in the EU: European Parliament and Council Directive 2003/71/EC on the prospectus to be published when securities are offered to the public or admitted to trading, OJ 1003 L 345, at 64, art 3(1).

[8] See e.g. for the USA: Rules 10b-5 and 10b5-1, 17 CFR x240.10b-5; for the EU: European Parliament and Council Directive 2003/6/EC on insider dealing and market manipulation (market abuse), OJ 2003 L 96/16.

basis is the product of private initiatives. Individual actors also contribute to the creation of the norms and standards that are vital for the functioning of the market's infrastructure. However, since a breakdown would create considerable risk for the stability of the whole financial system, modern legislation has set up some minimum requirements as to the operation of these mechanisms. One example is the regulation of exchanges or clearing houses.[9] A number of these requirements concern the qualities and the organizational structure of the entities themselves in their quality as financial intermediaries and can therefore be considered actor-specific legislation. However, one can also find provisions that govern their transactions, such as clearing and settlement.

B. Systems and mechanisms of regulation and supervision

Supervision of the financial markets and its actors can be organized in different ways. The traditional method is the sectoral model: for each sector of the financial industry, one supervisor is installed. For these purposes, the industry is typically divided into banks, insurance companies, and securities firms. Often, the regulation is split into these three different parts.

Sectoral supervision and regulation has, however, been called into question by a major development in the financial industry: cross-sectoral financial intermediation. Starting in the 1980s, the once clear-cut lines between banks, insurance companies and securities firms blurred. Due to innovative products, the respective business models increasingly overlapped. As a consequence, the organization of supervision was outdated due to the new realities of the industries. Inefficiency and lack of transparency were the results.

Such development led to the search for new models of supervision. One alternative would be an operational model which distinguishes not according to the supervised institution but according to the types of products that are offered. Another alternative is the so-called institutional model. In principle, it follows the sectoral model in that the different financial intermediaries are supervised by different agencies. The new feature extends the functions of the supervisor to all activities of the institutions under its supervision, no matter in which market they take place.[10] An obvious problem for this approach is presented by hybrid intermediaries, which are truly in-between and hard to categorize, such as bank and insurance conglomerates.

Under a functional approach, the competences would be divided among different supervisors according to the supervisory task to be fulfilled. For instance, licensing could be overseen by one supervisor, prudential supervision by another, and standard setting by a third. Such a system was installed in France[11] and, to

---

[9] See e.g. in the USA: Securities Exchange Act 1934, Sections 5 and 6, 15 USC xx78 e and f; in the EU: European Parliament and Council Directive 2004/39/EC on markets in financial instruments (MiFID), OJ 2004 L 145/1.

[10] See Enrico Cervellati and Eleonora Fioriti, 'Financial Supervision in EU Countries', Working Paper, <http://ssrn.com/abstract=873064> (visited 4 August 2010).

[11] Ibid, at 10–11 for a discussion of the French system.

some extent, also in Germany, where the *Bundesanstalt für Finanzdienstleistung-saufsicht* (BaFin)[12] and the *Bundesbank* are jointly responsible for supervision.

The model that has proliferated the most in recent years is integrated financial supervision. Under this model, one supervisor covers the whole financial industry. This 'one-for-all' approach was first adopted in the Scandinavian countries. The UK later followed with the creation of the Financial Services Authority (FSA), and then Germany where the BaFin was charged with supervising banks, insurance companies and securities intermediaries. The advantage of this approach is that it lays the foundation for a one-stop shop system for authorizations and also—possibly—for a single regulatory regime. The drawback of integrated supervision, however, is that it creates gigantic bureaucracies which may not have close contact with financial actors in the different parts of the industry, nor a sufficient under-standing of their specific needs.[13]

C. Conceptual transnational challenges

As the previous section indicates, both the classic areas of financial regulation or supervision and the systems and mechanisms applied are characterized by a certain degree of complexity. One reason for this, and an important aspect of any attempt to strengthen and/or reform financial regulation and supervision, is that 'form follows function' in this context.[14] This means that financial regulation and supervision follow the market so that the legal form and substance of financial regulation or supervision is to a large extent dependent on the factual situation of the markets for financial services.[15]

The obvious problem of retaining 'policy space',[16] in the face of the dominant market power, is not at all new in the context of financial regulation and supervi-sion. What is new in the current situation, however, is that the determining factual situation is not one single market any more (if it ever was). Instead, the complexity of the financial market instruments that have been invented and that are being invented with increasing speed has led to a multitude of markets. Moreover, those markets are not exclusively domestic financial markets, but inherently and comprehensively also global financial markets. The necessarily global functional

[12] German Federal Financial Supervisory Authority.

[13] For a comparison of the advantages and disadvantages of the dominant models of supervision, see Karel Lannoo, 'Supervising the European Financial System', Centre for European Policy Studies Policy Brief No 21, May 2002, at 4.

[14] The famous quotation 'form follows function' is from an article written by the architect Louis Sullivan, 'The Tall Office Building Artistically Considered', *Lippincott's Magazine*, March 1896; 'form follows function' is used in our context as a classic description of a functional approach to law (functionalism).

[15] Klaus J. Hopt, 'Auf dem Weg zu einer neuen europäischen und internationalen Finanzmark-tarchitektur', 12 *Neue Zeitschrift für Gesellschaftsrecht* 1401 (2009), at 1402.

[16] On the concept and implications of 'policy space' see e.g. Jörg Mayer, 'Policy Space: What, for What, and Where?', UNCTAD Discussion Papers, No 191, October 2008; Kevin P. Gallagher, 'Policy Space to Prevent and Mitigate Financial Crises in Trade and Investment Agreements', UNCTAD, G-24 Discussion Paper Series, No 58, May 2010.

approach towards financial regulation and supervision implies complex conceptual challenges.

Even though any strengthening and/or reform of regulation and supervision of financial markets has to cope with the challenges of globalization, it is equally important to take note of the 'domestic embeddedness' of financial market products. Financial market products are always, and necessarily so, linked to a specific domestic legal order. They are, in other words, children of domestic jurisdiction. An investor buying, for instance, shares in a Luxemburgian investment fund not only trusts the issuer, but also the well-known quality of Luxemburg's legislation and administrative practices in the area of finance. This is a unique feature of financial market products. Unlike physical products and most services, financial market products always feature a particular jurisdiction. They are thus products that are deeply rooted in one specific domestic legal order on the one hand, and increasingly traded on global markets on the other. They are offered not only on their domestic market, but also on a worldwide basis, and in this sense they are 'international' or, more precisely, 'transnational'. Therefore, one may speak of transnational financial products and markets in order to highlight the above-described double character of products and markets, being always both domestic and international.

The transnational character of financial products and markets directly affects financial regulation and supervision. The main consequence in this regard is that international cooperation and coordination of financial regulation and supervision is not primarily about 'levelling the playing field'. As domestic embeddedness is a key feature of financial products, international financial markets need to be characterized by at least some degree of regulatory competition (that is, competition of regulatory systems). Even though regulatory competition is a general feature of economic law-making and enforcement, it has a special importance in the context of financial markets. The basis of financial products—capital—is intangible and may thus be relocated easily to any other jurisdiction. Thus, even though the relocation of financial products always depends on a rearrangement of the legal foundations of the respective product in domestic law, capital (as the basis of financial market products) can be characterized as having a high 'exit' potential. As Hans-Werner Sinn convincingly observed: '[c]apital, except possibly for corporate capital trapped by divided taxes, will be the big winner of systems competition'.[17] The importance of regulatory competition in the area of financial products, already dominant from a theoretical perspective, can also be proven by empirical evidence. Some examples include: the rivalry between Frankfurt and London over being the number one financial market-place in Europe, and the current struggle as to where the next offshore hub for hedge funds will be.

This, however, does not mean that one should leave the issue of financial regulation and supervision exclusively to domestic jurisdictions in order to score the highest possible positive results of systems competition. As the concept of

---

[17] Hans-Werner Sinn, *The New Systems Competition* (Malden/Oxford: Blackwell, 2003) 60.

regulatory or systems competition is based on the idea of a generally functioning 'international regulatory market', it is important to provide all legal rules which are necessary for the functioning of the market. These rules may be called 'meta norms'.[18] In the present context, it is thus an important task of international law to provide the meta norms necessary to enable regulatory competition among domestic jurisdictions that produce financial market products. Moreover, it is also important to ensure respect for and the effective enjoyment of certain public goods. The most important public good in this regard, and in the present context, is the stability of the international financial system.[19] Other important public goods may be those classically identified in economic theory, such as the environment. Overall, it is thus necessary to establish principles and rules of an international competition order[20] so that regulatory competition in financial regulation and supervision may function comprehensively and well, and create positive effects.[21] All current efforts towards strengthening and reforming financial regulation and supervision by international cooperation and coordination, i.e. by international law, have to be seen from this perspective.

In addition, it is important to realize that domestic financial regulation and supervision inherently tends to have extraterritorial reach and effect. This is mainly because, as indicated, financial products are embedded in domestic legal orders on the one hand and increasingly traded on globalized markets on the other. Extraterritoriality may thus be seen as an inherent characteristic of modern financial products and the law governing them. This in turn causes problems in the same way that extraterritorial jurisdiction causes conflicts more generally.[22] It is therefore important to find solutions to these jurisdictional problems on the basis of the principle of cooperation in international economic law.[23]

---

[18] For an overview of different aspects of regulatory competition with regard to financial regulation see e.g. Mahmood Bagheri and Chizu Nakajima, 'Optimal Level of Financial Regulation under the GATS: A Regulatory Competition and Cooperation Framework for Capital Adequacy and Disclosure of Information', 5 *Journal of International Economic Law* 507 (2002).

[19] On the stability of the financial system as a (global) public good, see e.g. Heribert Dieter, 'The Stability of International Financial Markets: A Global Public Good?', in Stefan A. Schirm (ed), *New Rules for Global Markets—Public and Private Governance in the World Economy*, (Basingstoke Palgrave MacMillan, 2004) 23 ff; Michel Camdessus, 'International Financial and Monetary Stability: A Global Public Good', in Peter B. Kenen and Alexander K. Swoboda (eds), *Reforming the International Monetary and Financial System* (Washington, DC: International Monetary Fund, 2000) 9 ff; Geoffrey Underhill, 'The Public Good versus Private Interests and the Global Financial and Monetary System', in Daniel Drache (ed), *The Market and the Public Domain? Global Governance and the Asymmetry of Power*, (London: Routledge, 2001) 274 ff.

[20] On the notion of competition order (Wettbewerbsordnung in German), see Walter Eucken, *Grundsäätze der Wirtschaftspolitik*, 6th ed. (Tübingen: Mohr Siebeck, 1990) 245–50.

[21] On the importance of a meta order with regard to systems competition from a legal perspective see e.g. Anne Peters and Thomas Giegerich, 'Wettbewerb von Rechtsordnungen', in *Veröffentlichungen der Vereinigung der Deutschen Staatsrechtslehrer* 69 (2010) 38 ff.

[22] On jurisdiction and extraterritorial jurisdiction in general see Robert Jennings and Arthur Watts, *Oppenheims International Law, Volume 1: Peace*, 9th ed. (Oxford: Oxford University Press, 2008) para 139.

[23] For a comprehensive study on the principle of cooperation in international economic law, see Christian Tietje, 'The Duty to Cooperate in International Economic Law and Related Areas', in Jost

Furthermore, while discussing challenges to strengthening financial regulation and supervision, it is necessary to keep certain differences between financial regulation and supervision in mind. There are no specific obstacles in the way of any attempt to harmonize rules and principles of financial regulation by international instruments. Different harmonization strategies may be applied, namely full harmonization or minimum harmonization. While minimum harmonization would leave states the freedom to regulate in areas not covered and with respect to standards not defined by the relevant international instrument, full harmonization would oblige states to implement an international standard without any space for discretion. However, disregarding whether full harmonization, minimum harmonization or—as frequently happens—a mixture of both approaches is applied, states always have discretion over how to implement the respective international standards, i.e. they may find ways and means to smoothly adjust their national legal order to accommodate the new international standard.

As experience in the European Union shows, harmonization is often more complicated with regard to supervision. Supervision is, like all forms of law enforcement, deeply rooted in domestic legal systems and traditions. Moreover, states are very reluctant to allow 'foreign' (i.e. also international) law and/or authorities to influence, let alone to determine, domestic supervision. Any attempt to establish some kind of international financial supervisory authority is currently utopian.[24]

None of these conceptual problems of financial regulation and supervision is entirely new. On the contrary, there has been widespread discussion on these and related issues for several years within the larger framework of the globalization debate.[25] The political (and public) reaction to the financial market crisis of 2007–09, however, ignored, at least to some extent, these conceptual problems. Any attempt at strengthening financial regulation and supervision will have to take conceptual problems and issues into account in order to have a chance of success.

III. The Extension of Areas of Supervision and Regulation and New Methods after the Crisis

A. New areas

After the financial crisis had reached its climax in 2008, a number of changes to the existing state of financial supervision and regulation were suggested. Some of them have already been adopted.

Delbrück (ed), *International Law of Cooperation and State Sovereignty* (Berlin: Veröffentlichungen des Walther-Schücking-Instituts für Internationales Recht an der Universität Kiel Nr. 139, 2002) 45–65.

[24] Creating a central supervisory authority on a supranational level proves difficult, even in the European Union. For details on the *status quo* and the current reform debate, see Matthias Herdegen, *Banking Supervision within the European Union* (Berlin/New York: de Gruyter, 2010).

[25] See e.g. Kern Alexander, Rahul Dhumale and John Eatwell, *Global Governance of Financial Systems: The International Regulation of Systemic Risk* (Oxford: Oxford University Press, 2006).

One central change is to bring previously unregulated financial intermediaries under supervisory control. This applies, for instance, to hedge funds and private equity funds. It is often said that they constitute a 'shadow banking system' next to the traditional—supervised and regulated—banking system.[26] Although no direct causal link between these funds and the outbreak of the financial crisis has been demonstrated, in both the US and the EU efforts are being made to require registration by fund managers, to impose capital requirements, and to prescribe or prohibit certain fund activities.[27]

Other players in the new financial architecture that will be subject to tighter regulation are the credit rating agencies. The EU has adopted a regulation that requires them, *inter alia*, to register with the authorities of the Member States.[28] In the USA, measures to improve the accountability and transparency of nationally recognized statistical rating organizations have been taken.[29]

Furthermore, states seek to render financial supervision more efficient. In the USA, an effort was made to concentrate the supervisory function, which previously had been very fragmented.[30] Nonetheless, a new agency in the form of a Bureau of Consumer Financial Protection has been added.[31] In the EU, besides reform efforts in the Member States, the main direction is to strengthen the supervisory function at the Union level.[32]

It is remarkable that on both sides of the Atlantic, the traditional control of financial intermediaries will be supplemented by macro-prudential supervision.[33] In the USA, the Federal Stability Oversight Council was created by the Dodd–Frank Act.[34] In the EU, the Commission suggested installing a 'European Systemic Risk Board'.[35] This implies that the traditional focus on the individual institutions will be supplemented by a concern for systemic stability. The institutional setting of this macro-prudential supervision and its interaction with the other supervisors is not yet fully elaborated. In the USA, for instance, much will depend on the regulations that are yet to be enacted.

---

[26] See e.g. Financial Services Authority, 'The Turner Review: A Regulatory Response to the Global Banking Crisis', March 2009, at 21; The High Level Group on Financial Supervision in the EU ('de Larosière Report'), 2009, at 8.

[27] See, for the USA: Dodd–Frank Wall Street Reform and Consumer Protection Act of 2010, Public L. 111–203 (Dodd–Frank Act), Title IV, Sections 401 ff. For the EU: see Draft Alternative Investment Fund Managers Directive, COM(2009) 207 final.

[28] European Parliament and Council Regulation (EC) No 1060/2009 on credit rating agencies, OJ 2009 L 302/1.

[29] See Dodd–Frank Act, Title IX, Subtitle C, Sections 931 ff.

[30] See the improvements to supervision and regulation of federal depository institutions proposed by the Dodd–Frank Act, Title III, Sections 300 ff.

[31] Dodd–Frank Act, Title X, Sections 1001 ff.

[32] See the European Commission's drafts suggesting the establishment of 'European Supervisory Authorities' for banks, insurance companies, and securities firms: COM(2009), 501, 502 and 503 final.

[33] For further details on the micro/macro perspective, see Section III:C below.

[34] See Dodd–Frank Act, Title I, Subtitle A, Sections 111 ff.

[35] See European Commission, Proposal for a Regulation of the European Parliament and of the Council on Community macro prudential oversight of the financial system and establishing a European Systemic Risk Board, COM(2009) 499 final.

As to the reform of the substantive requirements of banking regulations, discussions are under way. They mostly concern enhanced capital adequacy and/or liquidity requirements.[36] So far, transatlantic agreement on these reforms has not been reached. What is clear, however, is that micro-prudential standards will be changed in such a way as to take into account macro-prudential concerns: more anti-cyclicality shall be obtained by requiring banks to build up buffers of resources during good times, which they can draw on when economic conditions deteriorate.[37]

One new area that has appeared on the political agenda since the crisis, and seems set to stay, is the regulation of bankers' remuneration. The former Financial Stability Forum (FSF, now Financial Stability Board) asked for changes in its 'Principles for Sound Compensation Practices'.[38] Underlying the changes is the idea that the current remuneration scheme has induced short-term thinking and risk-prone behaviour of bank managers. Efforts to regulate the problem are being made on the national level.[39] However, it is hard to tell whether they are really inspired by the FSF's principles or—which seems at least equally probable—by the public outrage over huge bonuses.

A further area that has attracted the interest of legislators since the crisis is the restructuring of credit institutions. It is a well-known aphorism that 'banks live globally and die nationally'. Bail-outs have required taxpayers to put up staggering amounts in guarantees and cash. No wonder that governments are increasingly looking for alternatives. Although it is still totally unclear whether and how the 'too big to fail' logic and moral hazards can be escaped, there is an apparent endeavour for the 'juridification' of bail-outs.[40] The goal is to remove the topic from the political scene and bring it under a legal framework.

States are also resolved to reform accounting. At a meeting in Washington, DC, in April 2010, finance ministers and central bank governors agreed that a single set of high-quality global accounting standards shall be reached.[41] The aim is to increase transparency for investors and supervisors.

Impending regulations increasingly impinge upon the activities that financial institutions may undertake. The Volcker rule as contained in the Dodd–Frank Act prohibits proprietary trading and other capital market activities for banks.[42] Restrictions are also foreseen for other new techniques. Take, for example, secur-

---

[36] See Chapter 12 by Hal S. Scott, in this volume.

[37] See G20, above n 1.

[38] Financial Stability Forum, 'Principles for Sound Compensation Practices', 2 April 2009, <http://www.financialstabilityboard.org/publications/r_0904b.pdf> (visited 10 October 2010).

[39] See e.g. the draft for a Management Remuneration Act by the German Federal Government, 'Entwurf eines Gesetzes über die aufsichtsrechtlichen Anforderungen an die Vergütungssysteme von Instituten und Versicherungsunternehmen', 31 March 2010, BT-Drucks. 17/1291.

[40] See e.g. Dodd–Frank Act, Title II, Sections 201 ff. See Gesetz zur Einführung eines Reorganisationsplanverfahrens für systemrelevante Kreditinstitute und zur Abwehr von Gefahren für die Stabilität des Finanzsystems (German Reorganization Procedure and Financial Stability Protection Bill), 26 August 2009, published in WM (Wertpapier-Mitteilungen) 2009, p. 913.

[41] See G20, 'Communiqué: Meeting of Finance Ministers and Central Bank Governors', Washington, DC, 23 April 2010, para 4.

[42] See Dodd–Frank Act, Section 619.

itizations: the Group of 30 demanded that banks shall keep a 'meaningful' part of the credit risk on their books in order to align their interests with those of the purchasers of collateralized debt obligations (CDOs) or other asset-backed securities.[43] This so-called minimum risk retention, or 'skin in the game', has been fixed on both sides of the Atlantic at 5 per cent.[44]

The infrastructure of the financial system is under equally enhanced scrutiny. Particular attention is being paid to the way that credit default swaps (CDS) are traded. While traditionally they have been sold over the counter, an international consensus has emerged that they shall be brought to exchanges and electronic platforms and cleared through central counter-parties.[45] Moreover, individual transactions shall be reported to trade repositories.[46] The goals are to prevent counter-party risk from concentrating in a few private institutions and to bring more transparency to the market. National plans exist to put these agreements into practice.[47]

B. New methods

The methods used for international cooperation and coordination of financial regulation and supervision are basically known. As there is almost no 'hard' international law on regulation and supervision, different categories of 'soft' law are commonly used.[48] The typical international soft law instrument in this regard is standardization. The best known example for such soft law standardization with regard to financial regulation is probably the International Convergence of Capital Measurement and Capital Standards, the so-called Basel Accord.[49] While the Basel Accord is essentially a non-binding instrument, in other areas of financial regulation a strategy of incorporation is used in order to give non-binding instruments some legal force. This mechanism is used, for example, with regard to accounting standards, which are initially non-binding but are incorporated into domestic legislation.[50]

---

[43] Group of 30, 'Financial Reform—A Framework for Financial Stability', 15 January 2009, at 8, Core Recommendation I, Recommendation 1 b.

[44] See for the USA: Securities Exchange Act 1934, above n 9, Section 15G(c)(1)(B) as amended by the Dodd–Frank Act, Section 941; for the EU: Directive 2009/111/EC, OJ 2009 L 302/97, art 1, No 30.

[45] See G20, 'Leaders' Statement: The Pittsburgh Summit', Pittsburgh, 24–25 September 2009, at 9, para 13.

[46] Ibid.

[47] See for the USA: Dodd–Frank Act, Titles VII and VIII, Sections 701 ff; for the EU: Communication from the Commission, Ensuring efficient, safe and sound derivatives markets, COM(2009) 332 final; Future policy actions, COM(2009) 563 final.

[48] See Chapter 5 by Chris Brummer, in this volume.

[49] Basel Committee on Banking Supervision, 'International Convergence of Capital Measurement and Capital Standards: A Revised Framework', June 2004, <;http://www.bis.org/publ/bcbs107.pdf? noframes=1> (visited 4 August 2010).

[50] See e.g. European Parliament and Council Regulation (EC) No 1606/2002 on the application of international accounting standards, 19 July 2002 OJ 2002 L 243, at 1.

The general strategy of international cooperation and coordination by soft law instruments was not changed after the financial market crisis of 2007–09. However, G20 leaders at the London Summit on 2 April 2009 made it clear that the applicable principles for financial market reforms '[a]re strengthening transparency and accountability, enhancing sound regulation, promoting integrity in financial markets and reinforcing international cooperation'.[51] All of these principles not only refer to domestic financial markets, but also per se to the international financial system. This is due to the simple fact that there was a rapidly emerging consensus that the crisis of 2007–09, at least to some extent, revealed evidence of 'insufficient coordination among regulators and supervisors and the absence of clear procedures for the resolution of global financial institutions'.[52] So far, the main response of the international community to this insight was the establishment of the (international) Financial Stability Board (FSB), succeeding the FSF. The FSF was established in 1999 as a reaction to the Asian financial crisis of that time. The FSF was composed of the finance minister, the central bank governor, and a supervisory authority from each of the G7 states and a few other developed countries together with representatives of the most important international financial institutions.[53] This composition, i.e. the exclusion of emerging markets and of developing countries, and the rather limited political mandate and support of the FSF, created obstacles in the work of the FSF. Faced with the obvious challenge of strengthening international cooperation and coordination in financial regulation and supervision, there was a pressing need to decide on, and implement, institutional reforms in the international financial system as a reaction to the Asian crisis. The most natural candidate for a more prominent role in this regard was, of course, the IMF. However, the mandate of the IMF was restricted with regard to financial regulation and supervision.[54] Moreover, voting rights in the IMF are limited and cannot be opened up to react convincingly to the demands for increased participation of emerging markets and developing countries.[55] Thus, similar to the situation in 1998–99, the FSF was chosen as the more appropriate institution or 'regime' for effective international cooperation and coordination.[56]

---

[51] G20, above n 1.

[52] Stijn Claessens, Giovanni Dell'Ariccia, Deniz Igan and Luc Laeven, 'Lessons and Policy Implications from the Global Financial Crisis', IMF Working Paper, WP/10/44, 2010, at 7.

[53] For details, see Enrique Carrasco, 'Global Financial and Economic Crisis Symposium: The Global Financial Crisis and the Financial Stability Forum: The Awakening and Transformation of an International Body', 1 *Transnational Law & Contemporary Problems* 19 (2010), at 203 ff.

[54] Regarding the mandate of the IMF, see e.g. IMF, 'The Funds Mandate: An Overview', 22 January 2010, <http://www.imf.org/external/np/pp/eng/2010/012210a.pdf> (visited 19 October 2010); IMF, 'The Funds Mandate—The Legal Framework', 22 February 2010, <http://www.imf.org/external/np/pp/eng/2010/022210.pdf> (visited 4 August 2010); Independent Evaluation Office of the IMF, Biagio Bossone, 'Integrating Macroeconomic and Financial Sector Analyses within IMF Surveillance: A Case Study on IMF Governance', BP/08/11, May 2008 <http://www.ieo-imf.org/eval/complete/pdf/05212008/BP08_11.pdf> (visited 4 August 2010).

[55] Following the G20 (Leaders) Summit in Seoul 2010 a 6 per cent shift in quota shares to emerging and developing countries was agreed upon. However there continues to be debate on the appropriate quotas with the next General Review of Quotas brought forward to January 2014, see <http://www.imf.org/external/np/exr/facts/quotas.htm> (visited 22 February 2012).

[56] See Carrasco, above n 53.

In this regard, the main purpose of establishing the FSB as the successor of the FSF was to form 'a stronger institutional basis' for cooperation with and assistance of national and international financial authorities and institutions so as to help to ensure financial stability.[57] More specifically, as well as extended membership, the mandate of the (new) FSB was—in addition to the tasks which had been assigned to the (old) FSF—extended to:

a) monitor and advise on market developments and their implications for regulatory policy;
b) advise on and monitor best practice in meeting regulatory standards;
c) undertake joint strategic reviews of the policy development work of the international SSBs to ensure their work is timely, coordinated, focused on priorities and addressing gaps;
d) set guidelines for and support the establishment of supervisory colleges;
e) manage contingency planning for cross-border crisis management, particularly with respect to systemically important firms; and
f) collaborate with the IMF to conduct Early Warning Exercises.[58]

The FSB is not only a 'new' international financial institution with a broad mandate with respect to coordination and cooperation in the area of financial regulation and supervision, it is also a reaction to the important lesson learnt from the crisis that financial macro- and micro-policy need to go hand in hand.[59] Moreover, the establishment of the FSB may be seen as the interesting evolution of an international regime from a 'very soft' forum to—albeit still non-binding—a more rule-based institution. Certain similarities with the evolution of the General Agreement on Tariffs and Trade 1947 may emerge in the future.[60] Finally, the existence of the FSB as the key institution for international cooperation and coordination in the areas of financial regulation and supervision indicates that the dominant strategy remains soft-law oriented. One could thus gain the impression that the entire international approach towards financial regulation and supervision is more or less exclusively power-oriented,[61] i.e. not based to any great extent on legal principles and rules. This impression, however, would not be accurate. It is important to realize that the G20 process since Autumn 2008, namely the estab-lishment of the FSB, offers evidence of increasing reliance on legal principle and rules in order to provide international financial stability. Even though what has been agreed by G20 leaders is not a treaty of public international law and is actually not legally binding at all, the developments described offer evidence that a similar evolution to that which followed the Asian crisis of 1998–99 has occurred. At that

---

[57] Ibid, at 218.
[58] FSF, 'Financial Stability Forum Re-Established as the Financial Stability Board', Press Release, 2 April 2009, <http://www.financialstabilityboard.org/press/pr_090402b.pdf> (visited 4 August 2010).
[59] For further details, see the discussion at Section III:C below.
[60] See also Chapter 12 by Michael Gadbaw in this volume, and see e.g. John H. Jackson, *The World Trade Organization—Constitution and Jurisprudence* (London: Routledge, 1998) 12 ff.
[61] On the notion of 'power-oriented' versus 'rule-oriented' approaches in international economic law, see John H. Jackson, 'The Birth of the GATT-MTN System: A Constitutional Appraisal', *Law & Policy in International Business* 21 (1980), at 27 ff.

time, the international community reacted to a major crisis of the international financial system by strengthening the rule of law, i.e. by moving towards a more legalized international financial system.[62]

C. Conceptual transnational challenges

Despite strong political willingness—at least when the crisis was at its peak in 2008–09—to accept internationally coordinated reforms of financial regulation and supervision, as expressed by the establishment of the FSB, it is questionable whether we have seen truly substantive moves to this effect so far. One reason for this might be that it is much easier to produce an internationally acceptable general paper, such as the Communiqué from the London Summit of 2 April 2009, than to reach consensus on detailed and to a large extent technical questions of financial regulation and supervision. Moreover, one may argue that even though some successful reforms have been initiated in the area of financial regulation, this is not true of supervision. Financial supervision seems to have been utilized in some countries during the crisis in order to pursue protectionist interests.[63]

The observations above lead back to the question of conceptual transnational challenges for reforming financial regulation and supervision. Based on the arguments presented above on regulatory competition and the need for international meta norms, it is clear that globalized financial markets have to cope with a prisoner's dilemma: even though it is evident that the greatest welfare gains will be achieved by a strategy of internationally harmonized rules and principles in some core areas of regulation and supervision combined with regulatory competition, states tend to deviate from this model by pursuing national interests, i.e. acting in a protectionist way. This not only negatively affects welfare gains, but inherently poses risks to international financial stability. Even though this is known by the relevant actors, namely states, their protectionist behaviour may very well be explained by rational choice theory.[64] Thus, at least to some extent, the international financial system faces similar problems to those faced by the international trading system.[65] However, what is different is the inherently extraterritorial character of measures concerning financial markets. As with any extraterritorial measure, this raises additional legal problems and transaction costs. The situation is thus similar to competition law as an area of economic law in which there is also insufficient international harmonization and coordination in regulatory and super-

---

[62] Nicholas Bayne and Stephen Woolcock, 'Economic Diplomacy in the 2000s', in Nicholas Bayne and Stephen Woolcock (eds), *The New Economic Diplomacy. Decision-Making and Negotiation in International Economic Relations* (Aldershot: Ashgate, 2005) 291.

[63] See Hopt, above n 15, at 1401.

[64] For details on the public/rational choice theory and the international economic system, see e.g. Ernst-Ulrich Petersmann, *Constitutional Functions and Constitutional Problems of International Economic Law* (Fribourg: University Press, 1991) 116 ff.

[65] On the prisoner's dilemma in the international trading system, see e.g. Bernard Hoekman and Michel Kostecki, *The Political Economy of the World Trading System*, 3rd ed. (Oxford: Oxford University Press, 2009) 34 ff and 146 ff.

visory matters and thus a high level of extraterritorial measures with negative effects and severe legal problems.[66]

The substantive conceptual problem of insufficient international meta norms on financial regulation and supervision also has an institutional perspective. Despite the existence of the newly established FSB and a somewhat strengthened role of the IMF, financial regulation and supervision is almost completely dominated by domestic regulatory and supervisory institutions. Attempts to establish international (or supranational) authorities have failed, even in the EU.[67] Thus, as financial markets are not only characterized by domestic embeddedness, but also by international (or global) interdependence, the institutional design is not aligned with the scope of financial regulation and supervision, i.e. the domain of the regulator is not the same as the domain of the financial market(s).[68]

A further challenge to international financial market stability is the classic differentiation between a micro and a macro perspective. The criticism on this differentiation and thus the call for a more integrated approach towards financial regulation and supervision is not new. It was articulated with regard to the Asian crisis of 1997–98[69] and the IMF actually shifted at that time towards more microeconomic financial regulation. Yet, the capacity of the IMF to follow an integrated approach in this regard is limited by the restrictive mandate of the Fund (IMF Article IV).[70] For this reason, and because of the cumbersome procedure for changing the founding treaty of the IMF, the establishment of the FSB and the reasonably broad mandate given to it have to be seen as a soft law approach towards better integrated financial regulation and supervision. It remains to be seen whether this new approach will be successful.

IV. What Level of Harmonization is Optimal for Financial Markets?

The basic question that is still open is on which level financial markets would be optimally supervised and regulated. There are at least three different levels available: the local, regional, and international.

At first sight, the international level seems the most appropriate. Regulation by public international law and/or international soft law responds to the existence of a truly global financial market. As the crisis has shown, national financial systems are not only interdependent, but also integrated. International regulation would fit

---

[66] See e.g. Dietmar Baetge, 'The Extraterritorial Reach of Antitrust Law between Legal Imperialism and Harmonious Coexistence', in Eckart Gottschalk, Ralf Michaels, Gisela Rühl and Jan von Hein (eds), *Conflict of Laws in a Globalized World* (Cambridge: Cambridge University Press, 2007) 220 ff.

[67] For details, see Herdegen, above n 24.

[68] See Alexander, Dhumale and Eatwell, above n 25, at 15: 'The domain of the regulator should be the same as the domain of the financial market'.

[69] See e.g. Alexander, Dhumale and Eatwell, above n 25, at 208: '[a] weak macroeconomic environment is often associated with emerging banking crises'.

[70] Above n 54.

with this reality. It would avoid disparities of national rules and reduce opportunities for regulatory arbitrage.

However, an internationally harmonized financial system would have a major drawback: it eliminates, to a large extent, the competition of states for the best regulatory regime. As mentioned above, financial products are domestically embedded, meaning that their quality and content is determined to a large extent by the domestic legal system under which they are created.[71] This creates a competition of systems. The important point is that such competition plays a crucial role in the efficiency of financial markets because no one knows what kind of regulation and supervision is best. Reforming and adapting financial legislation to new needs is therefore a process of discovery. The 'consumers' ultimately decide what balance between public oversight and private liberty they think is most appropriate to the risks involved. Total harmonization of regulation and supervision obviously would stall this discovery process because it would eliminate the competition between systems.

There is more: instead of reducing the probability of financial fallout, a uniform global financial regime would increase the risk of global failures. This counter-intuitive claim can be proven by a parallel to the problems resulting from the 'herd behaviour' of investors: if all state regulators and supervisors were to work in the same way, any unknown risk hidden in the financial markets would have disastrous consequences. While, nowadays, it only affects those states whose legislation and administration is ignorant of or ill-adapted to the risk, under a globally harmonized regime it would affect *all* countries in the world. No longer would there be islands and safe havens that are less affected, such as Spain or Italy who were doing well despite the financial crisis in 2007–09—until it turned into a sovereign debt crisis in 2010. Moreover, it would no longer be possible to empirically determine the performance of different systems and compare their results in real life. We would all be chained to one method of financial regulation, for better or for worse. Improvements could only be suggested in a theoretical way, without testing their viability in practice.

One can thus see that a certain degree of decentralization or localization of financial law has inherent advantages. It works as a permanent laboratory in which different degrees and methods of legislation and supervision are tested. Moreover, it sets the stage for a system of multilayered or multilevel governance in the financial area.[72] Under this system, regulation and supervision can be better adapted to the peculiarities of local markets and at the same time comply with the need for a uniform framework.

On the other hand, the harmful effects that divergences between national regimes and practices are producing cannot be denied. One only needs to remember the negative externalities created by extra-territorial effects of financial legislation or the over-regulation of domestic markets that may be inspired by

---

[71] See Section II:C above.
[72] See Chapter 8 by Rolf Weber in this volume.

protectionist instincts.[73] Hence, the relationship between international harmonization and regulatory competition cannot be an 'either/or' one: it has to be an 'at the same time' one. The focal point of the discussion on a meta-norm for international finance therefore must be to find the right balance between global harmonization and the possibility for states to create new regulatory and supervisory techniques, so that possible welfare gains are not lost and competition between different systems is not stalled. The question is thus not whether we need international cooperation— we certainly do—but what is the optimal *degree*.

In answering this question, it should be noted that competition of systems is not always beneficial. Instead, differentiation is needed. In some areas, divergences between national laws make no sense when seen from an overall viewpoint. This is true, for instance, for bail-out regimes. Peculiar national rules on saving financial institutions can often only be explained by protectionist motives. Differences between restructuring regimes thus serve no useful purpose. Indeed, the rules for restructuring banks should be globally harmonized or it will never be possible to achieve a fair and equitable framework in which financial institutions can operate. Similar arguments could be made for rules on the infrastructure, for instance CDS clearing. Here again, divergent national rules have only limited usefulness, and the advantages of a global regime seem to outweigh the benefits of competition. Thus, these topics could be addressed by a meta-norm without any damage to the efficiency of financial markets. On the contrary, a global regime would provide the necessary framework for efficient competition of legal systems.

On the other hand, there are areas in which different regimes will be useful. For example, capital requirements for credit institutions may be better regulated on a national level. There is no agreement on how much equity a bank needs to run its business safely. It may thus be a good idea to have states fixing different rules for their institutions. Although at first sight, this might go against the idea of a 'level playing field', its creation is not the major goal of financial law. There are other aims that are of greater importance.[74] Moreover, some banks might see the imposition of stricter capital requirements by their law not as a comparative disadvantage but as an edge over their competitors because they breed trust in the minds of the clients. Therefore, some form of competition between states should be allowed with regard to this issue. Similar considerations may apply for bankers' remuneration schemes.

It is apparent that when determining the optimal level of global coordination, it is indispensable to consider this according to the practical problem that has to be solved. Of course, there are no predetermined rules as to which matters should be left to states and which should be dealt with by global fora or institutions. This does not exclude, however, the use of some rules of thumb. For instance, areas which by their very nature lend themselves to extra-territorial legislation should, as a matter of principle, be dealt with on the international level. A case in point is the registration and supervision of credit rating agencies. Since the business model of these intermediaries is global, it makes little sense to entrust their regulation to the

---

[73] See Sections II:C and III:C above.
[74] See Section II:C above.

whims of the national legislator in the jurisdiction of which they happen to be located. At the same time, the efficient functioning of the rating agencies would be threatened if each state or region were to operate its own registration process for these intermediaries. Rather, what is needed is a transnational regime. The same is true for hedge funds and other lightly regulated masses of capital. The reason why they have become an area of concern is the potential domino effects their breakdown could have on the financial system. As these effects would spill over national boundaries, it is clear that efforts to achieve closer regulation and control of such funds should in principle be globally coordinated.

V. Conclusion

The role of international law in financial regulation and supervision cannot be determined by an all-embracing formula. There are different levels on which financial problems can be dealt with. Each of them has its purpose and function. For a particular matter, it might be advisable to choose one level, while a different issue would better be left to another.

There can thus be no one-size-fits-all approach. In particular, it would be misplaced to think that global harmonization would offer a magic cure for all of the financial system's ills. Under some circumstances, it can indeed lead to an increase in overall efficiency and welfare. But since it is unknown what kind and degree of oversight and regulation is optimal, in some areas competition between states for the best regulatory regime must be maintained. These findings coincide with arguments put forward under the doctrine of multilayered or multilevel governance, seeking to properly allocate powers and functions to different regulatory levels. This article has offered some indications as to the forms which international financial legislation can take and the areas it should cover. They can serve as yardsticks for the research on individual issues that still needs to be done.

8

Multilayered Governance in International Financial Regulation and Supervision

*Rolf H. Weber**

I. Introduction

In the past few decades, financial markets have become increasingly international in scope. The recent financial crisis has demonstrated that the interlinkages between financial institutions and markets within and across borders are even more distinct than previously assumed and that disturbances in the financial sector of one country have the potential to culminate in global financial turmoil threatening international financial stability. Simultaneously, however, the focus of financial regulation and supervision—even with respect to major, internationally active financial groups and conglomerates—has largely remained limited to the domain of national jurisdictions.[1] The recent financial crisis has shown that measures and initiatives taken by nation states can be insufficient to tackle major systemic instabilities. They need to be accompanied by internationally coordinated efforts to combat evolving crises.

Addressing the discrepancy between international financial activities and nationally oriented financial regulation and supervision, this chapter looks at new theoretical concepts underlying international financial regulation and supervision. During recent years, scholars have sought to identify the characteristics of what constitutes an 'international regulation' and have explored how its context affects its success. The discussions encompass issues such as why the delegation of powers to international bodies in order to achieve international regulation faces opposition and how regulatory and supervisory powers should be allocated among the different authorities on the domestic, regional and international levels. At the core of these debates is the quest for appropriate criteria which could and should be developed and applied in making such determinations.

International regulation and supervision is not 'naturally superior' to regional or national rules and supervisory practices or vice versa. It is necessary to take into

* The author wishes to thank Seraina Gruenewald for excellent research assistance.
[1] For a more extensive discussion of the effects of financial globalization on sovereignty see Goodhart and Lastra, Chapter 9 of this volume.

account the structure of the financial industry and the particular regulatory concern in order to establish whether international, regional, supranational, national or even local rules are most appropriate to address the concern.[2] With the goal of establishing criteria on how regulatory and supervisory responsibilities should be allocated to the different layers of governance, this chapter applies the doctrine of multilayered governance to regulation and supervision of financial markets.

II. The Starting Point: Existing Milestones in Financial Markets

This section evaluates the *status quo* of regulation and governance in the area of financial markets. It does so by defining the structure of financial regulation, outlining the limits of international law in regulating financial markets and highlighting the effects of the fragmentation of law that results from the multiplicity of possibly conflicting regulatory regimes.

A. International financial regulation

International financial regulation assumes a wide range of functions. Mostly, the normative intervention of a competent body in the economic activities of individuals and firms, including the concessions of public services and direct rulemaking, is at the regulatory heart of the matter.[3] The supervisory function encompasses—whether mandatory or not and whether institutionalized or not—different aspects of financial markets.[4] Another task relates to organizational and behavioral norms as well as the rules of sanction.[5]

Financial regulation can be enacted both by governmental authorities such as parliaments, executive bodies and public institutions, and by self-regulatory agencies. The latter either have a delegated competence to devise regulations or to impose such regulations on the members of a specific market sector in a non-mandatory way.[6] International financial regulation can be divided into three subsets of rules:[7] (i) systematic or institutional rules, regulating the performance of financial institutions; (ii) rules ensuring institutional safety, systemic stability and market conduct; and (iii) rules pertaining to supervision in the form of self-supervision, industry supervision or public supervision. Usually, the focus of

---

[2] See also Joel P. Trachtman, in this volume at Chapter 10.
[3] Rolf H. Weber, 'Mapping and Structuring International Financial Regulation—A Theoretical Approach', 20(5) *European Banking Law Review* 651 (2009), at 652.
[4] Jan H. Dalhuisen, *Dalhuisen on International Commercial, Financial and Trade Law* (Oxford and Portland: Hart Publishing, 2004) 908.
[5] Peter Nobel, 'Zur Regulierungsarchitektur im Finanzmarktbereich', in Hans Caspar von der Crone et al. (eds), *Fragen des Bank- und Finanzmarktrechts* (Zurich: Schulthess, 2004), 105–29 at 106, 125.
[6] Weber, above n 3, at 653.
[7] Roy C. Smith and Ingo Walter, *Global Banking* (New York: Oxford University Press, 2003) 336–7.

financial regulation lies on crisis prevention and maintenance of financial stability, meaning the safety and soundness of the financial system.[8]

B. Limits of traditional international law

Structurally, international regulation is an appropriate response to global developments since it is able to govern transboundary technical, economic and legal issues. It should not be forgotten, however, that international law currently consists of a patchwork of different legal instruments. It is limited to minimal rules which nation states have been willing to agree on, following tough negotiations. It therefore tends only to address a limited and fragmented field.[9] Furthermore, international law lacks a constitution as a fundamental source and basis of law. It possesses neither legislative nor administrative agencies to produce regulations and does not have a general judiciary in place with plenary jurisdiction over disputes that arise.[10]

Contemporary international law tends to acknowledge a wider definition of international law, according to which it is no longer limited to relations between nation states, but generally accepts the increasing role of other international players such as individual human beings, international organizations and juridical entities.[11] Indeed, history and present experience show that general principles of international law can be developed under different social circumstances, as the enormous number of non-state ('private') regulations that shape and rule transnational banking relations, issued by private standard-setting bodies and business associations, clearly demonstrate.[12]

C. Fragmentation of law

International financial institutions as well as business associations have been very active in adopting regulatory rules in the past few decades. Their number is growing, implying a risk of incoherent rulemaking in the financial markets.[13] This risk is amplified by the fact that some regulatory institutions have expanded their activities far beyond their original mandates. In particular, the mandates of the Bretton Woods Institutions no longer reflect their actual scope of operation.[14]

---

[8] Rolf H. Weber and Douglas Arner, 'Toward a New Design for International Financial Regulation', 29(2) *University of Pennsylvania Journal of International Law* 391 (2007), at 416–17.

[9] Thomas Cottier, 'Multilayered Governance, Pluralism, and Moral Conflict', 16(2) *Indiana Journal of Global Legal Studies* 647 (2009), at 648.

[10] Ibid, at 648–50.

[11] Samantha Besson, *The Morality of Conflict: Reasonable Disagreement and the Law* (Oxford and Portland: Hart Publishing, 2005) 534–5.

[12] Rainer Nickel, 'Participatory Transnational Governance', in Christian Joerges and Ernst-Ulrich Petersmann (eds), *Constitutionalism, Multilevel Trade Governance and Social Regulation* (Oxford and Portland: Hart Publishing, 2006), 157–98 at 157, 162.

[13] See Weber, above n 3, at 682.

[14] See Weber and Arner, above n 8, at 393–404.

The increasing role of different stakeholders in international law, such as cross-border financial organizations, companies, and professional associations, inevitably leads to a certain fragmentation of regulation since societal processes and contradictions are necessarily reflected.[15] As a result of fragmentation of knowledge, power, and control,[16] increased specialization and diversification occur and lead to multiple variations of regulatory types or regimes of relationships and arrangements.[17] If epistemic communities and networks are involved in the rulemaking processes, different actors start to play a role not only as decision-makers but also as intermediaries and brokers.[18]

In the meantime, international legal scholars have developed theories about the process of fragmentation and constitution of autonomous regimes: (i) *Ruggie* analyzed the functions of the manifold epistemic communities and their role in the rulemaking processes, arguing that collective awareness and attention may be mutually beneficial.[19] Epistemic communities are created when no state goes out of its way to construct international collective arrangements.[20] The processes of international regime formation result from the interactions between science and politics on the one hand and collective response on the other hand.[21] However, these procedures leading to disintermediation could Balkanize public discourse.[22] (ii) *Koskenniemi* highlighted the structural conflicts between various regimes and addressed possible approaches for a harmonization of the rulemaking processes.[23] In particular, although states may be prepared to participate in hybrid forms of regimes (possibly through delegated experts or by exercising their influence otherwise), they are often also inclined to transpose transnational rules into their legal framework.

Nevertheless, the multiplicity of regulatory regimes does not per se cause incoherence but is an inherent characteristic of the global governance of financial systems. What must be mitigated, however, are substantial conflicts of law resulting from the fragmentation; this is the basic notion of several new theoretical concepts which emphasize the necessity of inclusive and coherent regulatory processes at all levels of global governance.

---

[15] Martti Koskenniemi, 'Fragmentation of International Law: Difficulties Arising from the Diversification and Expansion of International Law', United Nations Report of the Study Group of the International Law Commission, A-CN.4/L682, 13 April 2006, at 11–12.

[16] Myriam Senn, 'Decentralisation of Economic Law—An Oxymoron?', 5(2) *Journal of Corporate Law Studies* 427 (2005), at 442.

[17] See Koskenniemi, above n 15, at 30–4; see also Rolf H. Weber, 'New Rule-Making Elements for Financial Architecture's Reform', 10 *Journal of International Banking Law and Regulation* 512 (2010), at 515.

[18] Peter N. Grabosky, 'Using Non-Governmental Resources to Foster Regulatory Compliance', 8(4) Governance 527 (1995), at 545.

[19] John Gerard Ruggie, 'International Responses to Technology: Concepts and Trends', 29(3) *International Organization* 557 (1975), at 562.

[20] Ibid, at 570.

[21] Ibid, at 559.

[22] See also Rolf H. Weber, *Shaping Internet Governance: Regulatory Challenges* (Zurich: Schulthess, 2009) 92–3.

[23] See Koskenniemi, above n 15, at 30–67 and 99–101.

III. The Ongoing Process: Development of New Theoretical Concepts

The experience of the financial crisis and the present situation in financial market law requires rethinking the theoretical concepts underlying international financial regulation and supervision. This section looks at three closely related theoretical concepts, which offer a valuable framework for analysis without predetermining how regulatory responsibilities should be allocated.

A. Concept of networkism

New theoretical concepts emerged by contrasting the notion of decentralized government networks at the international level contrasting with unitary world state visions. These concepts point to the flexibility, problem-solving capacity and efficiency of the networkism approach by arguing that normative voluntarism would be replaced by a functionalist concept.[24]

Raustiala assessed the viability of transgovernmental networks and evaluated their relationship to liberal internationalism.[25] Transgovernmental cooperation is exemplified in the fields of securities regulation, competition policy and environmental regulation.[26] A special focus on the 'informal' information exchanges among the competent authorities for the sectoral legal rules is based on sets of direct interactions among sub-units of different governments which are not controlled by the decision-making bodies of the respective states. This kind of cooperation leads to a disaggregation of states in favor of the established networks, i.e. to a 'disaggregated sovereignty';[27] thereby, actual cooperation and achievement of a solution could be improved.[28] Even treaty compliance might gain greater attention in a system of transgovernmentalism.[29] Nevertheless, the weakness of this approach consists in the lack of political control and the democratic deficit as well as the normative concerns regarding the missing (formal) legal framework.[30]

In *A New World Order*, Slaughter attempted to offer a solution to the 'governance dilemma' by referring to 'governmental networks'. These are set out as 'relatively loose, cooperative arrangements across borders between and among like agencies that seek to respond to global issues'[31] and that manage to close gaps

---

[24] See Nickel, above n 12, at 167; see also Rolf H. Weber, 'New Sovereignty Concepts in the Age of Internet?', 14(2) *Journal of Internet Law* 12 (2010), at 16–18.

[25] Kal R. Raustiala, 'The Architecture of International Cooperation: Transgovernmental Networks and the Future of International Law', 43(1) *Virginia Journal of International Law* 1 (2002), at 17–26.

[26] Ibid, at 26–51.

[27] Ibid, at 11.

[28] Ibid, at 23–4 and 55–6.

[29] Ibid, at 76–83.

[30] Raustiala, above n 25, does not address the democratic elements of a liberal state; however, allocation of power is important as the subsequent considerations explain in more detail.

[31] Kenneth Anderson, 'Book Review: Squaring the Circle? Reconciling Sovereignty and Global Governance through Global Government Network', 118(4) *Harvard Law Review* 1255 (2005), at

through coordination among governments from different states, 'creating a new sort of power, authority, and legitimacy'.[32] This model presupposes disaggregated states; in other words, it sees governments as a collection of disparate institutions, each with its own powers, mandates, incentives, motivations, and abilities, similar to the term 'government' which can be understood as the various activities of the courts, the parliaments, the regulatory agencies, and the executive itself.[33] This approach is contrary to the perception of unitary states according to traditional international law. In Slaughter's view, national governments cannot effectively address every problem in a networked world and should therefore delegate their responsibilities and 'actual sovereign power to a limited number of supranational government officials',[34] who would then have to engage in intensive interactions and in the elaboration and adoption of codes of best practice and agreements on coordinated solutions to common problems.

B. Concept of multilayered governance

Traditionally, a clear distinction is made between international relations and domestic polities. Notions of federalism have been constrained to domestic law. Globalization and regionalization increasingly call into question the traditional divide, and notions of federalism are extended beyond the classical constitutional realm, encompassing different layers of governance (supranational, regional, national, intranational, and local). Legal scholars and political scientists increasingly focus on the interaction and the allocation of powers among different levels of governance as well as on the problem-solving capacity of multilayered governance.[35] The allocation of regulatory powers to, and the balance within, different levels of governance has become a key topic in the most recent discussions on sovereignty; it features in the nation-state context (due to the widely applied subsidiarity principle) and even more so in an international setting. According to Cottier, the definition of the proper interaction of the different levels has a direct impact on an ideally coherent regulatory architecture of multilayered (or multilevel) governance; in other words, 'multilayered governance proposes a process and direction'.[36]

The concept of multilayered governance requires common foundations applicable to all relevant layers, while at the same time it must respect diversity and pluralism in order to be commensurate with the respective level of integration.[37]

1257; see also Anne-Marie Slaughter, *A New World Order* (Princeton and Oxford: Princeton University Press, 2004) 14.

[32] Anderson, ibid, at 1257.

[33] See Slaughter, above n 31, at 12–13.

[34] Ibid, at 263.

[35] For a general overview see Cottier, above n 9, at 655–73; Fritz W. Scharpf, 'Introduction: The Problem-Solving Capacity of Multi-Level Governance', 4(4) *Journal of European Public Policy* 520 (1997).

[36] See Cottier, above n 9, at 656.

[37] Ibid, at 656–7.

Consequently, multilayered governance needs to develop normative guidance as to how relations between different layers of governance should be framed in a coherent and not fragmented manner, encompassing both analytical and prospective issues in building upon observations of legal phenomena. In a nutshell, multilayered governance relies upon a common and shared body of underlying constitutional values and legal principles, which penetrate all layers of governance.[38]

Given that such multilayered governance seeks to identify core values to be shared by the international community, the discussion needs to be directed towards the legal rights and obligations accepted by all or most nation states.[39] If such legal rights and obligations can be identified, the ensuing legal framework possesses special legitimacy, which is essential for the operation and effectiveness of law. Social scientists refer to universalism, stressing the existence and the normative potential of shared values on the one hand, and to cosmopolitanism, including the moral and political doctrine which extends to legal and institutional dimensions on the other hand.[40]

C. Concept of polycentric regulation

In all regulatory segments, the institutional actors play a key role in the process of rulemaking. North points out that institutions structure incentives in terms of human exchange, whether political, social, or economic.[41] Furthermore, institutional change shapes the way that societies evolve; hence, it is important to understand historical change. Actors also institute processes by producing and disseminating rules that determine the behavioral patterns of the 'participants'.[42]

In the context of financial regulation, Black refers to polycentric regulations occurring in multiple sites, shaped by practical issues and events.[43] Comparatively speaking, polycentric regulations, reflecting a federalism approach,[44] conform to the multi-stakeholder approach[45] as the information exchanges and the decision-making processes are moved to the most concerned 'participants' of a specific market segment or regulatory regime.

From an institutional point of view, the actors such as organizations and public institutions adopting regulatory rules are quite numerous in the financial markets.

---

[38] Ibid, at 657; for a discussion of rights-based constitutionalism see also Ernst-Ulrich Petersmann, 'Multilevel Trade Governance in the WTO Requires Multilevel Constitutionalism', in Christian Joerges and Ernst-Ulrich Petersmann (eds), *Constitutionalism, Multilevel Trade Governance and Social Regulation* (Oxford and Portland: Hart Publishing, 2006), 5–58, at 5.

[39] See Cottier, above n 9, at 659–60.

[40] Ibid, at 660; see also Joseph H.H. Weiler, 'Democratic or Technocratic Governance?', Jean Monnet Working Paper No 6/01 (2001), at 5–6.

[41] Douglass C. North, *Institutions, Institutional Change and Economic Performance* (Cambridge: Cambridge University Press, 1990), at 3.

[42] See Weber, above n 3, at 682.

[43] Julia Black, 'Constructing and Contesting Legitimacy and Accountability in Polycentric Regulatory Regimes', 2(2) *Regulation & Governance* 137 (2008), at 139–41.

[44] Rolf H. Weber and Thomas Schneider, *Internet Governance and Switzerland's Particular Role in its Processes* (Zurich: Schulthess, 2009) 17, 29.

[45] See Weber, above n 22, at 88–9.

The main drivers are the financial institutions, incorporating a considerable amount of regulatory authorities and powers. Even if, over the years, several important institutions and organizations have expanded their activities to new levels, the multi-stakeholder approach invites the adoption of a more cooperative attitude towards the inclusion of non-governmental organizations and interest groups in the rulemaking process. While it is clear that the multiplicity of regulatory actors carries the substantial risk of incoherent rulemaking in the field of financial regulation,[46] such an approach would not necessarily entail an additional fragmentation of regulatory powers. In fact, the aim of a more balanced allocation of powers could be achieved by mandating the regulatory actors to cooperate and consult with the various stakeholders.

IV. The Future Prospects: Global Coherence Based on Multilayered Governance?

The theoretical concepts described above are similar insofar as they emphasize the different layers of governance and shared responsibilities of different stakeholders in the rulemaking processes. Financial regulation and supervision are increasingly tackled in both international and national law, and the ongoing integration and globalization of financial markets will further increase the importance of cooperation and interacting regulatory regimes. A core question that remains is how regulatory and supervisory responsibilities and powers should be allocated to the different levels of global governance.

A. Characteristics and elements of global governance

In recent years, the notion of global governance has attracted increased attention. The legal doctrine refers to contemporary global governance as a new 'order, characterized in part by porous borders and power sharing amongst states, non-state actors, and new geographic and/or functional entities'.[47] It encompasses collective efforts which enable the individuals concerned to identify, understand and address worldwide problems going beyond the capacity of single states to solve.[48] Some authors consider global governance as a (possible) successor to the Treaty of Westphalia,[49] which is treated as the benchmark for the emergence of the modern system of national sovereignty.

---

[46] See Weber, above n 3, at 682.

[47] N. Brian Winchester, 'Emerging Global Environmental Governance', 16(1) *Indiana Journal of Global Legal Studies* 7 (2009), at 22.

[48] For a further discussion see Thomas G. Weiss and Ramesh Thakur, *The UN and Global Governance: An Idea and Its Prospects* (Bloomington: Indiana University Press, 2006).

[49] Richard Falk, 'Revisiting Westphalia, Discovering Post-Westphalia', 6(4) *Journal of Ethics* 311 (2002), at 345.

While the elements which define global governance seem diffuse, some core themes can be distilled, partly from other sources:[50]

(i) Future regulatory problems by their nature will require broader and more collective decision-making than in traditional state affairs as envisaged by the multi-stakeholder approach. Global interactions encompass not only states' exchanges but also the involvement of non-governmental organizations,[51] private businesses, and members of civil society. The different interests and needs necessitate the establishment of multilayered mechanisms which allow the voices of all stakeholders to be heard.[52]

(ii) The absence of hierarchical structures and the fact that responses to the new problems are complex on the international level should be acknowledged. Flat structures on different sub-levels facilitate decision-making by including the relevant persons and organizations in the process at the actual point of their respective concern.

(iii) Global governance is not simply a new way of understanding the operation of society. Recent developments call for new concepts, such as that of multilayered governance.

(iv) The ongoing processes of globalization and integration necessarily lead to an altered perception and notion of state sovereignty and, at least partly, to a reduction of its importance in favor of numerous other authorities and actors. Nevertheless, under certain circumstances, the legitimacy of sovereign state action could be enhanced by leveraging it through joint action, for example, by including non-governmental agencies, technical communities and academics into the decision-making process.

B. Importance of common core values

The concept of multilayered governance is based on the notion of 'shared values upon which common structures and procedures can be solidly built'.[53] Some core values, such as the non-discrimination and equal treatment principles, provide the fundaments for governmental action and rule-making processes at all layers of governance on an equal basis. They offer a joint framework for decision-making in multilayered governance based on the principles of inclusive participation from a material perspective, as well as procedural fairness and legal protection through courts from a formal perspective.[54] Even if international agreements are not

---

[50] See Timothy William Waters, '"The Momentous Gravity of the State of Things Now Obtaining": Annoying Westphalian Objections to the Idea of Global Governance', 16(1) *Indiana Journal of Global Legal Studies* 25 (2009), at 33.

[51] For further details see Maria Ludovica Murazzani, 'NGOs, Global Governance and the UN: NGOs as "Guardians of the Reform of the International System"', 16(2) *Transition Studies Review* 501 (2009); see also Waters, above n 50, at 40–1.

[52] See Peter Newell, 'Civil Society, Corporate Accountability and the Politics of Climate Change', 8(3) *Global Environmental Politics* (2008), 122–53, at 122.

[53] Cottier, above n 9, at 650.

[54] Ibid, at 673.

reached, the shared values can help establish global coherence in conditions of reasonable pluralism.

To identify common core values in the financial markets is not an easy task. Unlike the field of monetary policy, where nation states have sought international agreement for many years, international cooperation with regard to financial regulation and supervision is still in its infancy. Nevertheless, some principles— beyond that of non-discrimination—are widely acknowledged within the international community and can serve as common grounds for establishing a system of multilayered governance.

   (i) *Financial stability*: Financial stability is generally accepted as constituting an important (perhaps even the most important) objective of economic and regulatory policy. Since it affects the functioning and performance of the economy as a whole and it is so inherently linked to sustainable economic growth,[55] the achievement of financial stability is even considered a public good.[56] However, there is no commonly agreed positive definition of what constitutes financial stability as most scholarly attempts have confined themselves to describing its absence. With this caveat, it will remain difficult to develop a widely accepted model or useful analytical framework for examining regulatory and supervisory issues based on the notion of financial stability.[57]

   (ii) *Trust/confidence in systems and persons*: To safeguard confidence in the financial system and financial services providers, regulators and supervisors share the mandate of ensuring appropriate conduct of business. Besides being aimed at the proper functioning of financial systems and providing for financial institutions to fulfill their functions appropriately, prudential regulation and supervision also contribute—at least collaterally—to the protection of investors and consumers.[58]

  (iii) *Market integrity*: The integrity of financial markets is a basic premise for their functioning; market integrity requires the abatement of corruption, money laundering and terrorist financing in order to avoid a loss of public confidence.[59]

The development of fundamental values is also important in view of the fact that the democratic deficit in the emerging supra-national systems of political authority

---

[55] See Rolf H. Weber, 'Financial Stability—Structural Framework and Development Issues', 6(4) *International and Comparative Corporate Law Journal* 1 (2008), at 8; Garry Schinasi, *Safeguarding Financial Stability: Theory and Practice* (Washington, DC: International Monetary Fund, 2006) 100; Douglas W. Arner, *Financial Stability, Economic Growth, and the Role of Law* (Cambridge: Cambridge University Press, 2007) 136.

[56] See, for example, Marc Quintyn and Michael W. Taylor, 'Regulatory and Supervisory Independence and Financial Stability', IMF Working Paper, WP/02/46, 2002, at 8.

[57] See Garry J. Schinasi, 'Defining Financial Stability', IMF Working Paper, WP/04/187, 2004, at 3.

[58] See Weber, above n 3, at 669.

[59] See Arner, above n 55, at 181–2; Weber, above n 3, at 670–1.

cannot be overlooked.[60] Obviously, state powers must arise from the collective decisions of the society's members who are governed by that power[61] as civil society constitutes the 'guarantor of collective identity'.[62] The members of civil society represent the values of certain cultures that must be reflected in any regulatory approach, including financial regulation. Common values help overcome national barriers in regulating financial markets on the upper levels of global governance while maintaining and respecting the will of civil societies. Thereby, the problem of a lack of legitimacy related to rulemaking by more powerful economies and international organizations is partly mitigated.

C. Development of standards applicable at different levels

1. Historical developments

In recent decades, financial markets have undergone an extensive integration process and thus become international in scope and impact. In the meantime, financial regulation and supervision have remained largely limited to the domain of national jurisdictions. With the establishment of the Bretton Woods Institutions after World War II, the first step was made towards international cooperation in monetary—and later in financial—matters. A number of more or less widespread financial crises since the early 1970s (including the most recent financial meltdown) have led to the creation of an impressive number of regulatory actors (state actors, networks and self-regulatory bodies) on the global, regional, and national levels.[63] Policy-makers as well as private industry have acknowledged that a solely national approach towards financial regulation is no longer viable in the modern world of global finance.

At the core of these developments is the realization that financial activities in one country may directly or indirectly affect other countries. Related to the increasing interconnectedness of global financial markets is the fear that local financial problems (sometimes even when confined to a small number of financial institutions) may spread to other parts of the financial system and eventually bring it to a halt.[64] The channels of contagion—whether on the domestic, regional or global level—are multifaceted, with the interbank market, payment and settlement systems and capital markets being the most obvious. Financial stability has become

---

[60] See Patrizia Nanz, 'Democratic Legitimacy and Constitutionalisation of Transnational Trade Governance: A View from Political Theory', in Christian Joerges and Ernst-Ulrich Petersmann (eds), *Constitutionalism, Multilevel Trade Governance and Social Regulation* (Oxford and Portland: Hart Publishing, 2006), 59–82, at 59, 67.

[61] See Joshua Cohen, 'Procedure and Substance in Deliberative Democracy', in Seyla Benhabib (ed), *Democracy and Difference: Contesting the Boundaries of the Political* (Princeton: Princeton University Press, 1996) 95–119, at 95.

[62] See Nanz, above n 60, at 70.

[63] For an overview, see Weber and Arner, above n 8, at 401–27.

[64] See Rosa Maria Lastra, *Legal Foundations of International Monetary Stability* (Oxford: Oxford University Press, 2006) 138.

a common concern in the process of globalization as it is so directly linked with economic prosperity and human welfare.

Historically, international financial regulation has been significantly influenced by the more powerful economies, in particular by the USA and major European countries. Their regulatory and supervisory actions have affected other jurisdictions not only by means of extraterritorial application of law in the traditional sense, of which the US Sarbanes–Oxley Act of 2002[65] was probably the most prominent example in the recent past. They also more indirectly—due to the sheer importance of these countries' financial markets and economies—exert pressure on other countries to act accordingly. Given their powerful position within the international community, these countries have been able to translate their ideas and regulatory traditions into international regulations, which is another 'modern' form of extra-territorial application of law. Other means by which domestic regulation is made applicable outside the national jurisdiction are less problematic from a legitimacy perspective. Transnational laws, such as the EU single passport for financial insti-tutions and the principle of mutual recognition with regard to the free movement of capital,[66] may in fact facilitate the interaction of different regimes, thereby reducing the potential of conflicts of law. Nevertheless, they remain exclusive and may thus increase existing imbalances in both a financial and political sense. Integration and globalization of financial markets, however, increasingly refute regulatory exclusivity and provide a basis for a more balanced financial system.

Independent of their level of action, the financial regulators' response to the threat of systemic risk and financial instability is quite straightforward: the goal is to increase the safety and soundness of financial institutions and infrastructure (crisis prevention) and to improve the instruments available to handle a crisis once it has occurred (crisis management and resolution). As a result, a rather extensive and multilayered set of financial regulations has emerged.[67] But how should the different regulatory layers interact? What criteria could determine the allocation of regulatory and supervisory responsibilities in the dynamic and ever-changing reality of financial markets?

2. *Financial regulation at different levels*

The above-mentioned common values[68] may serve as a starting point for defining what constitutes international financial regulation as they provide a basis for financial regulation on all layers of governance and decision-making. The scope of regulation on the particular layers then depends on the structure of international financial markets and the financial industry, which is of course not static but is in a constant process of innovation and globalization.

---

[65] Available at <http://www.sec.gov/about/laws/soa2002.pdf> (visited 11 July 2012).
[66] George Alexander Walker, *European Banking Law*, Vol. 6 (London: Walker, 2007), 314–24.
[67] See Weber, above n 3, at 674.
[68] See above Section IV:B.

The layers of international financial regulation differ in their regulatory object-ives and in the level of flexibility and detail. Not all regulatory objectives are considered important enough to be tackled at the global level. Regulatory objectives thus undergo a process of selection when it comes to establishing solutions in international law. This is determined by two inter-related factors:

(i) Nationally oriented regulation appears problematic in the context of finan-cial activity that has become global in scope. Due to the widespread phenomenon of financial disintermediation, capital markets have expanded their scope to a global level. Similar developments can be observed with regard to the emergence of large cross-border groups, which have become global players with assets in various countries around the world. In these cases, national regulation or—perhaps even worse—non-regulation in one country may have a direct impact within foreign jurisdictions. International laws help establish a 'common ground' for the proper handling of these challenges by the nation states, mitigating potential conflicts between na-tional regulators and increasing the potential for mutual reliance and trust.

(ii) In order to establish a level playing field in financial services, basic prudential regulatory requirements must apply (in one form or another) on a global scale, meaning that financial activities must be subject to minimal standards of prudence and safety independent of their place of exercise. As such prudential restrictions always come at certain costs for financial institutions, their effectiveness can only be ensured if they are not confined to particular jurisdictions. In an incoherent system of regulatory objectives the danger prevails that regulations are circumvented by simply moving the targeted activities from the original jurisdiction to more lenient jurisdictions. Such circumvention again abets the undesired possibility of a regulatory 'race to the bottom'.

Which regulatory objectives are so essential that they need a 'common ground' across jurisdictions as to treat them in a non-coherent way would jeopardize the level playing field? Most importantly, a common approach is necessary to the extent that regulation directly restricts the risk taking of financial institutions. Direct restrictions are particularly prone to being circumvented and they favor financial institutions that are not subject to such a regime. This is, first and foremost, the case with regard to capital standards. The Basel Committee on Banking Supervi-sion (BCBS) has thus, since its implementation in 1974, promoted an internation-ally applicable capital measurement system, commonly referred to as the Basel Capital Accord (Basel I, II and III). The aim of the framework is 'to secure international convergence on revisions to supervisory regulations governing the capital adequacy of internationally active banks'.[69] Similar conclusions can be drawn with regard to the regulatory handling of liquidity risk that was established

---

[69] Basel Committee on Banking Supervision, 'International Convergence of Capital Measurement and Capital Standards: A Revised Framework', June 2004, at 1.

by the BCBS in Basel III.[70] The envisaged implementation of the minimum levels of liquidity for financial institutions operating on an international scale, set out in Basel III, will require obedience by all countries with large cross-border financial institutions.

Related to the argument that risk-taking restrictions should be coordinated through an international regulatory layer on top of national regulations is the problem of how to treat bank insolvencies. The current lack of means to deal with large and interconnected financial institutions in distress has led certain institutions that are considered 'too big to fail' to take unduly high risks. Due to their global scope of activities, national initiatives to establish resolution mechanisms for systemic financial institutions are limited in their efficiency and, again, undermine the level playing field. It is fair to say that finding 'common ground' with regard to major cross-border bank insolvencies is one of the most challenging tasks that the international financial community will have to meet in the future.[71]

Transparency is another regulatory objective that requires attention at an international level of global governance. If financial activity is made transparent, the market is able to evaluate and compare the performance of financial institutions and the financial services they offer; transparency therefore promotes the common value of consumer protection as it contributes to mitigating information asymmetries.[72] Another focal aspect of transparency is the availability of information on regulatory and supervisory actions. The disclosure of relevant information to regulators (and the public) provides for early warning and efficient correction in cases of financial distress. Which information has to be made transparent by financial institutions must be understood across jurisdictional borders; it should thus follow internationally agreed patterns with regard not only to its informational content but also to its format. Besides establishing 'common material grounds' it is necessary to find a 'common language' in financial disclosure on the international level. For these reasons, the International Accounting Standards Board (IASB), in particular, has made a substantial effort to standardize disclosure rules for financial institutions.

3. Standards as a means of establishing an architecture of multilayered governance

Beyond the question of objectives, the second main difference in the layers of financial regulation consists, as mentioned above, in its level of detail and flexibility. Regulation can obviously 'only' identify the main objectives and define the baseline for regulatory action. At the same time, however, international financial

---

[70] See Basel Committee on Banking Supervision, 'Basel III: International Framework for Liquidity Risk Measurement, Standards, and Monitoring', December 2010.
[71] See Basel Committee on Banking Supervision, 'Report and Recommendations of the Cross-Border Bank Resolution Group', March 2010; International Monetary Fund, 'Resolution of Cross-Border Banks—A Proposed Framework for Enhanced Coordination', 11 June 2010.
[72] See Weber, above n 3, at 665.

regulation should not be exclusive or unduly restrict regulatory action at the sub-layers of global governance. International financial regulation must leave room for adaptation to particularities within the individual regions or nation states and concretization with regard to the needs identified by regional and national regulators. Importantly, national and regional authorities are more familiar with the characteristics and problems of the financial markets within their jurisdiction than any international body.

The dynamics of standardization may be key in the endeavor to establish multilayered governance. The Financial Stability Board (FSB) defines standards as a set of 'widely accepted . . . good principles, practices, or guidelines in a given area'.[73] The standardization of international financial activities constitutes an important element in the process of regulating financial markets. Standards help to provide a level playing field in financial services and to ensure that important financial activities meet widely recognized levels of performance and safety.[74]

Most standards will qualify as soft law because of their non-binding, recommendatory character. However, even if they lack an enforcement regime, standards have the potential to exert substantial influence on the 'target group' by defining behavioral benchmarks.[75] Standards represent the common denominator with respect to a particular regulatory field while leaving room for concretization and adaptation to the specific environment and circumstances on sub-layers of governance. They allow for a streamlined and coherent reaction to financial innovation and developments across the governance system.

By identifying regulatory objectives and outlining principles for their implementation at the global level, international standards influence regulation at regional and national levels. Albeit perhaps imperfectly compared to hard law,[76] standards facilitate the establishment of a common ground within a system of multilayered governance. Compliance with international standards, however, takes various channels: Some standards exert pressure to comply on market participants without or before being implemented in national or supranational laws. This may be the case if market participants assume that the transformation of standards into binding laws is only a matter of 'when' and not 'if' (e.g. Basel I, II and III). Voluntary compliance with international standards may also derive from their powers of persuasion, leading to market participants' firm conviction that regulation in the area concerned is needed and is efficient.

The main caveat regarding international standards relates to the problem of enforcement which remains a key challenge at the international level. By transformation into supra-national or national laws, international standards may be given the status of mandatory and enforceable regulation.[77] However, standing

---

[73] Financial Stability Board, 'What are Standards?', webpage about the Compendium of Standards, <http://www.financialstabilityboard.org/cos/standards.htm> (visited 13 June 2010).

[74] See Weber, above n 3, 661.

[75] Vera Schreiber, 'What Are International Standards?', in Peter Nobel (ed), *International Standards and the Law* (Bern: Stämpfli, 2005), 1–15, at 10.

[76] See Brummer, in this volume at Chapter 5.

[77] See Schreiber, above n 75, at 10.

alone, standards must rely on their 'natural pressure' on and their acceptance among market participants, as there is no international system of enforcement in existence and such a system is unlikely to be established in the near future.[78]

D. Allocation of supervisory powers in a multilevel approach

In contrast to the increasing importance of international standards in financial regulation, financial supervision has remained a function that is largely executed and determined on the national level. While regulation captures the notion of rulemaking, supervision can be referred to as the monitoring of compliance by financial institutions (and other market participants) with the rules, i.e. while the regulators create the rules, the supervisors implement and enforce them.[79]

1. Supervision as a national concept in an international context

Not only is the scope of financial supervision nationally oriented, but also the institutional organization of the supervisory function varies across borders and is often considered a display of national sovereignty. Among the most contentious aspects of the design of financial supervision is the question of whether monetary and supervisory functions should be institutionally separated.[80] While some countries have transferred supervision away from their Central Banks, others regard the supervisory functions of their Central Bank as a precondition and supplement to its monetary policy mandate. Others involve the Central Bank in the supervision of banks but have established separate supervisory authorities, outside the Central Bank, to oversee the insurance and capital markets sectors.

Similarly controversial is the optimal model of financial supervision. Should the supervision of the banking, insurance and capital markets sectors be consolidated in a single authority or be subject to multiple authorities? Historical and political considerations are likely to be the determining factors in a country's choice of supervisory model.[81] Even though in recent years a trend towards the unification of financial supervision has been observed (examples are the creation of the UK Financial Services Authority in 1997 and the Swiss Financial Market Supervisory Authority in 2009), there seems to be no particular model that has proved superior to the others.

In a field that is rooted so deeply in the political and historical intricacies of individual nation states it is difficult to establish a common ground at the upper

---

[78] For the relationship between soft and hard law see Lastra, above n 64, at 473–4; unfortunately, the enforcement issue cannot be addressed in more detail in this chapter but deserves further examination.

[79] See Rosa Maria Lastra, *Central Banking and Banking Regulation* (London: Financial Markets Group, London School of Economics, 1996) 108–10; Lastra, above n 64, at 84–9.

[80] See e.g. Charles A. E. Goodhart and Dirk Schoenmaker, 'Should the Functions of Monetary Policy and Banking Supervision be Separated?', 47 *Oxford University Papers* 539 (1995); see also Lastra, above n 64, at 90–2.

[81] See Lastra, above n 64, at 96.

layers of global governance. Not even within the EU has an agreement on the optimal institutional structure of financial supervision been reached as Member States have each implemented their own wide range of different supervisory arrangements,[82] although the most recent reform debates suggest more harmonious developments.[83] However, even though nation states disagree on numerous organizational aspects of financial supervision, they may be able to reach a consensus with regard to the responsibilities and powers granted to financial supervisors. The acknowledgement of the need for so-called 'macro-prudential' supervision is a recent example of such agreement on material aspects of financial supervision that is being shared among numerous nation states. Macro-prudential supervision aims to identify sources of systemic risk (such as contagion), links with the real economy, and the collective behavior of financial institutions, and to outline actions to contain such risk.[84] The concept of macro-prudential supervision implies that financial supervisors adopt a system-wide perspective in performing their duties, leaving the monitoring of individual financial institutions to a micro-prudential supervisor.

Sources of systemic risk in one country may have implications in other countries; the danger of systemic risk has thus crossed national borders and become a common concern. While many aspects of macro-prudential supervision remain challenging and controversial, it is fair to say that the concept itself has found broad acknowledgement in the international community. Such 'informal' agreements may lay the basis for future coherence in supervisory practices.

2. International standard-setting

Since financial supervision is often considered a feature of national sovereignty, the national orientation of its execution has not been challenged substantially in the past. This is partly because of the notion that national supervisors are most familiar with the individual financial institutions and markets that they oversee and thus they must be given substantial flexibility in their judgment of risk and compliance.

Nevertheless, growing cross-border activities of financial institutions have increased the need for universally applicable, common principles of sound supervisory practices. Ineffective national supervisory systems can threaten financial stability both within the country and internationally. The BCBS has thus defined 25 Core Principles that are considered necessary for a supervisory system to be effective.[85] In particular, they include recommendations with regard to objectives,

---

[82] See e.g. Karel Lannoo, 'Challenges to the Structure of Financial Supervision in the EU', in George G. Kaufmann (ed), *Bank Fragility and Regulation: Evidence from Different Countries* (New York: Elsevier, 2000) 121–60, at 130, for an overview of Member States' supervisory arrangements.

[83] For example, both the UK and German governments have proposed to (re-)integrate the monetary and supervisory functions under the roof of their Central Banks.

[84] Speech by Jean-Claude Trichet, 'Macro-prudential Supervision in Europe', The Economist's 2nd City Lecture, London, 11 December 2009, <http://www.bis.org/review/r091218b.pdf?noframes=1> (visited 13 June 2010).

[85] Basel Committee of Banking Supervision, 'Core Principles for Effective Banking Supervision', October 2006.

independence, powers, transparency and cooperation of supervisory authorities (Principle 1); methods of ongoing banking supervision (Principles 19 to 21); corrective and remedial powers of supervisors (Principle 23); and consolidated and cross-border banking supervision (Principles 24 and 25).

The Principles do not imply any particular institutional approach to supervision but outline overriding goals that national supervisors are expected to achieve. Furthermore, the Principles are not designed to tackle all the intricacies of national financial systems, implying that country-specific circumstances may be considered at the nation state level.[86] They allow nation-states the flexibility to adapt the benchmarks to their particular needs and to the characteristics of their financial and political systems.

While providing a concise material framework for financial supervision, the Principles only deal rudimentarily with the procedural side of financial supervision. Mutual assistance and collaboration in the supervision of financial groups with subsidiaries and branches located in different jurisdictions are addressed more explicitly in the Financial Stability Forum's work on cross-border cooperation in crisis management[87] and supervisory colleges; however, they do not provide a general procedural framework for supervisory cooperation. A more process-related approach in international standard-setting, like that taken in the EU's multilateral Memorandum of Understanding,[88] would facilitate international cooperation in both 'normal' times and in financial crisis situations.

3. Supervisory colleges as an additional level of governance

The (current) acknowledgement of the leading part taken by nation states in executing financial supervision and the simultaneous establishment of international standards leaves a rather fragmentary pattern of governance in financial supervision. The gap between the layers of international principles and nationally based financial supervisory operations is impressive and does not reflect the current status of increasingly regionally and globally integrated financial markets. The current governance arrangements in particular appear to neglect the increasing emergence of large cross-border financial groups with multiple stakeholders in various countries.

A means of filling this gap, and adding an additional layer of governance to the current arrangement, can be seen in the establishment of supervisory colleges. Supervisory colleges are generally understood as multilateral working groups of all supervisors involved in the supervision of an international banking group and these colleges are formed for the collective purpose of enhancing effective, consolidated

---

[86] Basel Committee of Banking Supervision, 'Core Principles for Effective Banking Supervision', October 2006, para 7.

[87] Financial Stability Forum, 'Principles for Cross-border Cooperation on Crisis Management', 2 April 2009. The Financial Stability Forum is the successor to the Financial Stability Board.

[88] 'Memorandum of Understanding on Cooperation between the Financial Supervisory Authorities, Central Banks and Finance Ministries of the European Union on Cross-Border Financial Stability', 1 June 2008.

supervision of the group on an ongoing basis.[89] They establish bilateral or multi-lateral structures for supervising individual financial institutions, including moni-toring their potential threat to the stability of the system as a whole. Without implications for existing, wider bilateral or multilateral cooperation, supervisory colleges formalize their cooperation with regard to the financial institutions that they cover and provide an institutional framework for cross-border financial supervision. They neither dispossess national financial supervisors of their supervis-ory responsibilities or powers, nor should they be considered a surrogate for national supervision. They constitute an additional supervisory layer with the goals of balancing multilateral interests and informing decision-making.

In the light of the recent global financial crisis, the G20 has stressed the importance of supervisory cooperation and has identified colleges of supervisors as a viable instrument to enhance the supervision of large financial institutions. In their Action Plan, the product of the Washington Summit, the G20 leaders state that supervisors are asked to collaborate to 'establish supervisory colleges for all major cross-border financial institutions, as part of the efforts to strengthen the surveillance of cross-border firms'.[90] Following this call by the G20 leaders, the BCBS has issued a consultative document on Good Practice Principles with respect to supervisory colleges.[91] The Principles outline expectations in relation to college objectives, governance, communication and information as well as identifying potential areas for collaborative work.

V. Conclusion

This chapter explores the dynamics of multilayered governance in the context of financial regulation and supervision. Due to the continuing integration and global-ization of financial markets, the financial landscape has become increasingly multi-faceted, ranging from local retail banking institutions to large financial conglomerates operating in various business sectors and on an international scale. The rapid increase in cross-border financial activity demands a reassessment of the nationally based regulatory and supervisory system, which has developed based on nation states' individual historical and political backgrounds and which fails in many ways to respond to the regional and international dimensions of today's financial reality.

The acknowledgement that financial markets are to be regulated and supervised at different levels of global governance inevitably raises the question of allocation of responsibilities. Focusing on the concept of multilayered governance, the chapter identifies core values which influence and shape financial regulation and supervi-

---

[89] Basel Committee on Banking Supervision, 'Good Practice Principles on Supervisory Colleges—Consultative Document', March 2010, at 1, footnote 1.
[90] G20, 'Washington Action Plan', Summit on Financial Markets and the World Economy, Washington, DC, 15 November 2008, para 35.
[91] See BCBS, above n 89.

sion internationally. These common core values, including financial stability as well as trust and integrity of financial markets and actors, form a 'common ground' for the evolving global regulatory and supervisory system. By means of standard-setting, the different layers of governance can be dynamically interlinked to enable them to address developments in the ever-evolving financial markets. The chapter suggests that the allocation of regulatory responsibilities to the different layers of governance should be based on the (geographic) scope of the underlying financial activities and the importance of the regulatory objectives by reference to the common core values. As for financial supervision, which has largely remained a national concept, it will be helpful to create additional layers of governance to fill the gap between nationally based supervision and international standards. The implementation of supervisory colleges and peer review procedures is a first step in this direction.

The global financial crisis has given a boost to the idea of an international approach to establishing sound financial systems. The G20—previously the G8—has been unexpectedly successful in agreeing on several important common reactions to the crisis, and with several initiatives in the areas of cross-border supervision and bank resolution, international cooperation has entered uncharted territory. With this in mind, there is reason to believe that these developments are contributing to a regulatory and supervisory system with responsibilities allocated to multiple layers of global governance.

9

Border Problems

Charles A.E. Goodhart and Rosa M. Lastra

I. Introduction

As with territorial waters and the exclusive economic zone in fishing disputes between countries, where to draw the line of regulation, protection and government assistance is contentious. Calls either to widen the net of regulation (and related protection) or to limit protection, e.g. to some set of 'narrow banks', have proliferated in response to the crisis.[1] The dichotomy between international (global) markets and institutions and national rules, exposing the limitations of the principle of national sovereignty, adds yet another layer of complexity to the design of effective financial regulation. In this chapter, we explore these two boundaries.

II. The First Boundary Problem

The first boundary problem was examined at some length in the National Institute Economic Review (2008)[2] and in the Appendix to the so-called Geneva Report (2009),[3] focusing on cases where the non-regulated can provide a (partial) substitute for the services of the regulated.[4] The unregulated frequently depend on

---

[1] While in fisheries, it is a matter of defining jurisdiction—the basis of regulation—and the actual amount of regulation, including subsidies, is left to the particular jurisdiction, in finance the issues are more complex for a number of reasons including the border problems analysed in this chapter.

[2] See Charles Goodhart, 'The Boundary Problem in Financial Regulation', 206(1) *National Institute Economic Review* 48 (2008).

[3] See Charles Goodhart, 'The Boundary Problem in Financial Regulation', Appendix A, in Markus Brunnermeier, Andrew Crockett, Charles Goodhart, Avinash D. Persaud and Hyun Song Shin (eds), *The Fundamental Principles of Financial Regulation* (11th Geneva Report on the World Economy) (Geneva: International Center for Monetary and Banking Studies and Centre for Economic Policy Research, 2009) Appendix A.

[4] The very definition of what constitutes financial regulation is contentious. While all companies are subject to some rules (general law concerning torts, contracts, property, etc.), some financial entities—notably commercial banks—are subject to more stringent 'financial rules' (concerning licensing, capital and liquidity requirements, lending limits, etc.) than others. It is in this context that the dichotomy between the regulated and non-regulated becomes significant. There is always concern that financial activities will migrate from banks to other kinds of companies (non-regulated or

services, e.g. payment services, and on back-up lines of credit from the regulated. In the build-up to the crisis, there are plenty of examples of unregulated entities that were structured as 'associates', or off-shoots, of the regulated ones.

If regulation is effective, it will constrain the regulated entities from achieving their preferred, unrestricted position, often by lowering their profitability and their return on capital. So the returns achievable within the regulated sector are likely to fall relative to those available on substitutes outside it. There will be a switch of business from the regulated to the non-regulated sector.[5] In order to protect their own businesses, those in the regulated sector will seek to open up connected operations in the non-regulated sector to enable them to catch the better opportunities there. The example of commercial banks setting up associated conduits, structured investment vehicles (SIVs), and hedge funds in the last credit bubble is a case in point.

But this condition is quite general. One of the more common proposals, at least in the past, for dealing with the various problems of financial regulation has been to try to limit deposit insurance and the safety net to a set of 'narrow banks', which would be constrained to hold only liquid and 'safe' assets. The idea is that this would provide safe deposits for the orphans and widows. Moreover, these narrow banks would run a clearing-house and keep the payment system in operation, whatever happened elsewhere. For all other financial institutions outside the narrow banking system, it would be a case of *caveat emptor*. They should be allowed to fail, without official support or taxpayer recapitalization.

In fact, in the UK something akin to a narrow banking system was put in place in the nineteenth century with the Post Office Savings Bank (POSB) and the Trustee Savings Bank (TSB). But the idea that the official safety net should have been restricted to the POSB and TSB was never seriously entertained. Nor could it have been. When a narrow bank is constrained to holding liquid, safe assets, it is simultaneously prevented from earning higher returns, and thus from offering high interest rates, or other valuable services (such as overdrafts), to its depositors. Nor could the authorities in good conscience prevent the broader banks from setting up their own clearing house. Thus the banking system outside the narrow banks would grow much faster under normal circumstances; it would provide most of the credit to the private sector, and participate in the key clearing and settlement processes in the economy.

Taking legal steps to prohibit broader banks from providing means of payment or establishing clearing and settlement systems of their own might be prevented by law. There are, at least, four problems with such a move. First, it runs afoul of

---

less regulated) to avoid the crackdown of more stringent financial rules, such as those of the US Dodd–Frank Act 2010 [Dodd–Frank Wall Street Reform and Consumer Protection Act, Pub. L. 111–203 (2010)] and of the new Basel Committee proposals. 'Defining the perimeter of regulation will continue to be a challenge, given the growing number of tax and regulatory incentives for firms to establish businesses in the shadows outside the regulated sector'. See Francesco Guerrera, Tom Braithwaite and Justin Baer, 'Report on Financial Regulation', *Financial Times*, 1 July 2010, quoting Charles Randell of the law firm Slaughter and May.

[5] Although, in some cases, legal security will be preferred over higher profits.

political economy considerations. As soon as a significant body of voters has an interest in the preservation of a class of financial intermediaries, they will demand, and receive, protection. Witness, for example, money-market funds and 'breaking the buck' in the USA. Second, it is intrinsically illiberal. Third, it is often possible to get around such legal constraints, e.g. by having the broad bank pass all payment orders through an associated narrow bank. Fourth, the reasons for the authorities' concern with financial intermediaries, for better or worse, go well beyond ensuring the maintenance of the basic payment system and the protection of small depositors. Neither Bear Stearns nor Fannie Mae had small depositors, or played an integral role in the basic payment system.

When a financial crisis does occur, it usually first attacks the unprotected sector, as occurred with SIVs and conduits in 2007. But the existence of the differential between the protected and unprotected sector then has the capacity to make the crisis worse. When panic and extreme risk aversion take hold, the depositors in, and creditors to, the unprotected, or weaker sector seek to withdraw their funds, and place these in the protected, or stronger sector, thereby redoubling the pressures on the weak and unprotected sectors, which are then forced into fire sales of assets. The combination of a boundary between the protected and the unprotected, with greater constraints on the business of the regulated sector, almost guarantees a cycle of flows into the unregulated part of the system during cyclical expansions with sudden and dislocating reversals during crises.

The institutional criterion that typically governs financial regulation divides firms into banks, securities firms, and insurance firms, among others, and then generally applies a separate set of rules for each type of institution (with banks bearing the heaviest regulatory cost), while leaving entities that perform similar services (e.g. the 'shadow banking system') outside the regulatory loop; and this approach has proven deficient during the crisis. The example of the shadow banking system, which played a key role in the growth of the securitization market, and is considered by many as one of the causes of the crisis, is an example of this boundary problem.[6] While we mostly know what a bank is, the very expression 'shadow banking system' is imprecise and its contours are not clearly defined. According to Roubini, broker-dealers, hedge funds, private equity groups, SIVs and conduits, money market funds and non-bank mortgage lenders are all part of this shadow system.[7] Gary Gorton and Andrew Metrick believe that it was the (wholesale) run on the sale-and-repurchase market (the repo market) market during 2008, a run not so much on depository institutions as on the shadow banking system, that caused the crisis, and suggest that new regulation could improve the functioning of

[6] See Rosa M. Lastra and Geoffrey Wood, 'The Crisis of 2007–2009: Nature, Causes and Reactions', in this volume at Chapter 1.

[7] See Nouriel Roubini, 'The Shadow Banking System is Unravelling: Roubini Column in the Financial Times. Such demise confirmed by Morgan and Goldman now being converted into banks', Roubini Global Economics, <http://www.roubini.com/roubini-monitor/253696/the_shadow_banking_system_is_unravelling_roubini_column_in_the_financial_times_such_%20demise_confirmed_by_morgan_and_goldman_now_being_converted_into_banks> (visited 4 August 2010).

the shadow banking system by making it less vulnerable to panics and crises of confidence.[8]

Today's financial markets are characterized by the proliferation of financial conglomerates and complex financial groups and by the blurring of the frontiers between the types of business that financial firms undertake, thus rendering institutional classifications less meaningful. Supervision has traditionally been organized by institution, irrespective of the business function or range of functions that the institution undertakes. Inter-industry affiliation and inter-industry competition in the financial sector have suggested the need for enhanced consolidated supervision, and increased reliance on regulation by business function rather than by institution. Under a system of supervision by business function, supervisors focus on the type of business undertaken, regardless of which institutions are involved in that particular business. The Dutch supervisory model, introduced in the second half of 2002, provides an example of a functional model based on the objectives of supervision. The Dutch Central Bank (De Nederlandsche Bank or DNB) is the institution responsible for prudential supervision in the pursuit of financial stability. The Authority for Financial Markets (AFM) is the authority responsible for conduct of business supervision. Both supervisory authorities cover the full cross-sector width of financial markets (all institutions in banking, securities, insurance, and pensions).[9] Notwithstanding this functional–institutional boundary problem, whether we need to circumscribe government protection to a specified set of regulated institutions remains an issue of great importance. If regulation is to differ in intensity between the systemically important and those less so, then there is a need for (legal) clarity as to which falls into each camp. But the systemic importance of any financial intermediary may vary depending on circumstances. The definition of 'systemic importance' is fuzzy.

However, the recent crisis has shown that we must make a much greater effort to understand the emergence and existence of such systemic risks. We need greater transparency to be able to identify systemic risk in the first place. It is clear that some non-banks are systemically significant and that the potential provision of government assistance justifies the widening of the regulatory net. The problem is how to do it.

The issue of drawing boundaries for regulation protection is not new. For instance, the Glass–Steagall Act of 1933 (Glass–Steagall, named after its legislative sponsors, Carter Glass and Henry B. Steagall) established a clear boundary between commercial banks and investment banks in the USA, with government assistance typically confined to the former (even though there were some emergency provisions, such as section 13(3) of the Federal Reserve Act, which permitted the Federal Reserve to act as lender of last resort to non-depository financial institutions, a

---

[8] See Gary Gorton and Andrew Metrick, 'Securitized Banking and the Run on the Repo', National Bureau of Economic Research Working Paper No w15223, August 2009, <http://pa-%20pers.ssrn.com/sol3/papers.cfm?abstract_id=1454939> (visited 4 August 2010).

[9] See Rosa M. Lastra, *Legal Foundations of International Monetary Stability*, (Oxford: Oxford University Press, 2006) Ch 3.

provision that became handy since it was activated in the rescues of Bear Stearns in March 2008 and of AIG in September 2008). Many provisions of Glass–Steagall were repealed by the passage of the Financial Modernization Act of 1999 (Gramm–Leach–Bliley Act).[10] Interestingly, this repeal, although hailed at the time as a major achievement, has been blamed by a few politicians and commentators for some of the problems that led to the financial crisis.[11] Indeed, among the structural reforms suggested to deal with crises, some have proposed a return to Glass–Steagall, while narrow banking or mutual fund banking has been advocated by others.[12]

Given the link between regulation and government protection, financial institutions are somewhat reluctant to accept more intensive regulation as the price for protection. This explains why Goldman Sachs and Morgan Stanley did not apply to become bank holding companies until after the collapse of Lehman Brothers in September 2008. But regulation is costly and banks and other regulated financial institutions often try to game or circumvent the regulatory system, so as to reduce this cost. There often appears to be a trade-off between safety and profitability, with financial institutions willing to sacrifice safety in good times in order to enhance their profitability.[13]

How in a regulatory system can we combine the need to protect safety and soundness with the need to make a profit, and therefore to take risks? What is the difference between normal risk and excessive risk, and who defines it? These are perennial questions in financial regulation. While regulators—in a free market economy—should not be unduly concerned about profits (unless the lack of profits should threaten a desirable function) they should, however, worry about risks. As acknowledged, a regulator can always claim: 'If I am going to assist you on a rainy day, I need to oversee you on sunny day.' Safe and sound banking and finance rests

[10] Pub. L. 106–2, 113 Stat. 1338, enacted 12 November 1999.

[11] Ten years ago, the revocation of Glass–Steagall drew few critics. One of the leading voices of dissent was Senator Byron L. Dorgan, Democrat of North Dakota. He warned that reversing Glass–Steagall and implementing the Republican-backed Gramm–Leach–Bliley Act was a mistake whose repercussions would be felt in the future. 'I think we will look back in 10 years' time and say we should not have done this, but we did because we forgot the lessons of the past, and that that which is true in the 1930s is true in 2010', Mr Dorgan said 10 years ago. 'We have now decided in the name of modernization to forget the lessons of the past, of safety and of soundness.' Senator Richard Shelby of Alabama, now the ranking Republican on the Senate Banking Committee, voted against the Gramm–Leach–Bliley Act because of his concern that repealing Glass–Steagall would threaten the safety and soundness of the banking system. Mr Dorgan's views were echoed by then-Senator Barack Obama in 2008 as he campaigned for presidency. For details of all of these views, see '10 Years Later, Looking at Repeal of Glass–Steagall', *New York Times*, 12 November 2009, <http://dealbook. blogs.nytimes.com/ 2009/11/12/10-years-later-looking-at-repeal-of-glass-steagall> (visited 10 May 2010).

[12] The narrow banking proposals have been again endorsed by John Kay, 'Narrow Banking: The Reform of Banking Regulation', Centre for the Study of Financial Innovation, 15 September 2009, <http://www.johnkay.com/wp-content/uploads/2009/12/JK-Narrow-Banking.pdf> (visited 4 August 2010), while Lawrence Kotlikoff has made a case for the mutualization of the financial industry in his book Lawrence Kotlikoff, *Jimmy Stewart is Dead: Ending the World's Ongoing Financial Plague with Limited Purpose Banking* (Chichester: John Wiley & Sons, 2010).

[13] See Charles Goodhart, 'How Should We Regulate the Financial Sector?', in Richard Layard and Peter Boone (eds), *The Future of Finance: The LSE Report* (London: The London School of Economics and Political Science, 2010) 153–76.

first upon good risk management and second on good risk control (by both the regulated and the regulators). In principle, only if management fails to control risks adequately should regulators intervene. However, it is difficult for regulators to know whether the institution has been or is being irresponsible unless they monitor it on a regular basis. Any risk can grow to systemic proportions when its negative impact extends beyond an individual institution, affecting or threatening to affect by contagion many other institutions, often creating a disruption in the monetary system and an associated economic paralysis. Systemic risks seldom occur alone; they usually spread to other risks like wildfire and undermine confidence. Confidence and trust play an essential role in the financial system. Henry Thornton wrote in 1802:

Commercial credit may be defined to be that confidence which subsists among commercial men in respect to their mercantile affairs. . . . In a society in which law and the sense of moral duty are weak, and property is consequently insecure, there will, of course be little confidence or credit, and there will also be little commerce.[14]

Historical experience suggests that regulation, and more specifically governmental banking regulation, was often a by-product or reaction to crises or conflicts. In the UK, for instance, the shift from self-regulation to legal regulation in the field of financial services was prompted by a series of crises: the enactment of the 1979 Banking Act[15] followed the secondary banking crisis, and the 1987 Banking Act[16] was enacted following the Johnson Matthey Bankers failure. This is also the case in the USA, where both the creation in 1913 of the Federal Reserve System (acting as lender of last resort) and the Federal Deposit Insurance Corporation in 1933 were responses to financial crises. Similarly, in Spain the creation of the guarantee insurance funds (Fondos de Garantía de Depósitos) for banks and thrifts in 1977 was motivated by a banking crisis. At an international level, regulation has also been prompted by financial failure and crises. Regulation after crisis is a constant in the history of finance.[17]

   In some instances, there are regulated and unregulated entities doing similar types of business. This is the case, for instance, with investment companies (pools of funds), where the legislation in the USA (and other jurisdictions) distinguishes the 'ins', i.e. mutual funds falling in the USA under the Investment Company Act of 1940, from the 'outs', such as hedge funds, which are not subject to the stricter requirements of the Act and other securities laws. In the EU, Alternative Investment Funds (AIFs) are defined as funds that are not harmonized under the

---

[14] Henry Thornton, *An Enquiry into the Nature and Effects of the Paper Credit in Great Britain* [1802] (London: George Allen & Unwin, 1939), reprinted in (Fairfield, NJ: A.M. Kelley, 1978) 75–6.

[15] Banking Act 1979, <http://www.opsi.gov.uk/acts/acts1979/pdf/ukpga_19790037_en.pdf> (visited 30 August 2010).

[16] Banking Act 1987, <http://www.opsi.gov.uk/acts/acts1987/pdf/ukpga_19870022_en.pdf> (visited 30 August 2010).

[17] See Rosa M. Lastra, *Central Banking and Banking Regulation*, (London: Financial Markets Group, London School of Economics and Political Science, 1996) Chs 2 and 3.

Undertakings for Collective Investment in Transferable Securities (UCITS) Directive.[18]

Another twist in the boundary problem is the interaction that some unregulated (or lightly regulated) institutions have with regulated ones. For instance, rating agencies exert an extraordinary influence and power over financial institutions and their regulators (not to mention politicians in countries where sovereign debt is downgraded, with the example of Greece in 2010 providing ample evidence on this point).

The boundary problem has particular implications with regard to capital requirements. Why should capital requirements be strictly imposed upon commercial banks (credit or depositary institutions) when the shadow banking system is engaged in similar types of risky activities? Moreover, emphasis on capital, important as it is as an indicator of soundness, should not be the sole tool in the regulators' armoury. As Robert Litan insightfully stated in the 1980s, regulators focus so much upon capital requirements because it is difficult to assess and control the quality of the asset portfolio, and, of course, potential mismatches between the duration of liabilities and assets provide a cause for concern about liquidity management and controls.[19]

The boundary problem is also present with regard to lending limits, a traditional tool in banking regulation. We need to devise effective leverage limits that fulfil the same function that traditional lending limits have fulfilled in the past with regard to banks' overall exposures (including lending limits to insiders, to subsidiaries, to shareholders and limits on large credit exposures).

Insofar as regulation is effective in forcing the regulated to shift from a preferred to a less desired position, it is likely to set up a boundary problem. It is, therefore, a common occurrence, or response, to almost *any* regulatory imposition. An example of this has been the proposal to introduce additional regulatory controls on systemically important financial institutions (SIFIs).[20] If SIFIs are to be penalized, there needs, on grounds of equity and fairness, to be some definition of and some criteria for what

---

[18] The UCITS III framework consists of two directives that regulate funds sold across the European Economic Area: (i) Directive 2001/107/EC of the European Parliament and of the Council of 21 January 2002 amending Council Directive 85/611/EEC on the coordination of laws, regulations and administrative provisions relating to undertakings for collective investment in transferable securities (UCITS) with a view to regulating management companies and simplified prospectuses; and (ii) Directive 2001/108/EC of the European Parliament and of the Council of 21 January 2002 amending Council Directive 85/611/EEC on the coordination of laws, regulations and administrative provisions relating to undertakings for collective investment in transferable securities (UCITS), with regard to investments of UCITS. See also the proposed European Parliament and Council Directive on Alternative Investment Funds, 30 April 2009, <http://ec.europa.eu/internal_market/investment/docs/alternative_investments/fund_managers_proposal_en.pdf> (visited 4 August 2010).

[19] See Robert E. Litan, 'Taking the Dangers Out of Bank Deregulation', 4(4) *The Brookings Review* 3 (1986), at 5: 'Examinations are costly and time-consuming, and the most important aspect of a bank's balance sheet, the quality of its asset portfolio, is difficult to assess at any given time. Perhaps in recognition of those limitations, federal regulators are increasing capital requirements.'

[20] This proposal has already been endorsed at the global level by G20 Leaders who agreed to implement FSB proposals that targeted Global SIFIs with 'more intensive and effective supervision', see point 28 of Cannes Summit Final Declaration, <http://www.g20-g8.com/g8-g20/g20/english/for-the-press/news-releases/cannes-summit-final-declaration.1557.html> (visited on 8 March 2012).

constitutes a SIFI—a complex exercise. But once such a definition is produced and a clear boundary established, there will be an incentive for institutions to position themselves on one side or another of that boundary, whichever may seem more advantageous. Suppose that we started, say in a small country with three banks, each with a third of deposits, and each regarded as too big to fail (TBTF), and the definition of a SIFI was a bank with over 20 per cent of total deposits. If each bank then split itself into two identical clones to avoid the tougher regulation, with similar portfolios and interbank linkages, would there have been much progress? Similarity can easily generate contagion. Indeed, regulation tends to encourage and to foster similarity in behaviour. Does it follow then that regulation thereby enhances the dangers of systemic collapse that its purpose should be to prevent? Does the desire to encourage all the regulated to adopt, and to harmonize with, the behaviour of the 'best' actually endanger the resilience of the system as a whole?

One extreme solution to the first boundary problem is either to regulate all financial entities alike or none at all.[21] *Laissez faire* proponents of free banking have long advocated this system, suggesting a minimalist approach in which the only acceptable rules are those that promote competition (entry or licensing, bankruptcy rules to govern exit and others) or anti-fraud provisions. Such a laissez-faire system, however, is unrealistic, while the alternative—regulate all alike—is not feasible. This means that the boundary problem is likely to remain, and that any new rule will bring with it new boundary problems.

What should the regulators and supervisors then do? Again we quote from the Geneva Report:

> They should start by trying to list the key financial markets and systems in their own country. Having done so, they should review whether and which financial institutions are so important to the functioning of that market, or system, that their downfall, whether in the form of bankruptcy or major deleveraging, would seriously disrupt the operations of that market or system. . . . In essence the financial supervisors have got to ask themselves, which financial institutions can be allowed to fail, and which cannot. Those that they claim cannot be allowed to fail, should be specifically regulated. . . . Besides occasions of institutional downfall, regulators need to be concerned with such market failures as may lead to resource misallocations, e.g. in the guise of asset bubbles and busts.[22]

A criterion that divides institutions into those that can be allowed to fail and those that cannot (a criterion that draws on the TBTF doctrine and its variants, such as too interconnected to fail), needs to be well known and publicized *ex ante*, since only those institutions that cannot be allowed to fail (because of the need to protect essential functions such as the smooth functioning of the payment system) are to be protected and regulated. And since licensing is the first stage in the supervisory process, which acts as a filter in subsequent stages, the licensing requirements would be a relatively straightforward way to deal with this problem.[23] Of course, if

---

[21] See Goodhart, above n 3. [22] Ibid.

[23] With regard to the four stages of the supervisory process: licensing, supervision *stricto sensu*, sanctioning and crisis management, as well as the difference between supervision and regulation, see Lastra, above n 17, Ch 2.

enacted, any such rule dividing institutions into those that are allowed to fail and those that are not, is likely to lead a legion of lawyers to look at it in microscopic detail so as to find loopholes.

The more effective regulation is, the greater the incentive to find ways around it. With time and considerable money at stake, those within the regulatory boundary will find ways around any new regulation. The obvious danger is that the resultant dialectic between the regulator and the regulated will lead to increasing complexity, as the regulated find loopholes which the regulators then move (slowly) to close. Basel I metamorphosed into Basel II [and now into Basel III]. So the process becomes ever more complex, almost certainly without becoming less porous.[24]

The above consideration suggests that any prescriptive rule-based approach needs to be complemented with more generic principles that respect the spirit of the law. Furthermore, national regulation alone will not suffice. Global problems require global solutions, which leads us into the next section.

III. The Second Boundary Problem

The second boundary of critical importance to the conduct of regulation is the border between states or jurisdictions (such as the EU), each with their own legal and regulatory structures, i.e. the cross-border problem, which is rooted in the limitations of the principle of national sovereignty. Sovereignty as a supreme power is typically exerted over the territory of the state: the principle of territoriality.[25] So, the ongoing process of globalization and the frequency of cross-border movement of persons, capital, goods or services has major implications for the scope of unfettered sovereignty, which continues to shrink.[26]

Financial markets and institutions have grown international in recent years. However, supervision and crisis management generally remains nationally based, constrained by the domain of domestic jurisdictions. The cross-border expansion of banks (via mergers and acquisitions, joint ventures or the establishment of branches and subsidiaries) and the effective supervision of institutions operating in various

---

[24] See Goodhart, above n 3.

[25] See Rosa M. Lastra, *Legal Foundations of International Monetary Stability*, (Oxford: Oxford University Press, 2006) Ch 1. Sovereignty is the supreme authority within a territory. The state is the political institution in which sovereignty is embodied. Sovereignty in the sense of contemporary public international law denotes the basic international legal status of a state that is not subject, within its territorial jurisdiction, to the governmental (executive, legislative or judicial) jurisdiction of a foreign state or to foreign law other than public international law. It forms part of the fundamental principles of general international law and it is considered to be one of the principal organizing concepts of international relations. Monetary sovereignty is a particular attribute of the general sovereignty of the state under international law. Some authors argue that the concept of monetary sovereignty predates by thousands of years the concept of political sovereignty that was developed in the Renaissance, since the authority to create money had been proclaimed by the rulers or priesthood of ancient civilizations (Sumer, India, Babylon, Persia, Egypt, Rome and others). However, the modern understanding of the attributes of sovereignty is rooted in the political thought that was developed in the Renaissance. Politics operated without this organizing principle in the Middle Ages.

[26] See Helen Stacey, 'Relational Sovereignty', 55 *Stanford Law Review* 2029 (2003), at 2040–51.

jurisdictions present numerous challenges for financial regulators and supervisors. Although progress has been made with regard to the regulation and supervision of cross-border banks, notably via soft law rules (Basel Committee on Banking Supervision and others) and regional rules (EC rules), the cross-border resolution of banking crises remains a matter of intense policy and legal debate. Despite the many difficulties involved, efforts to develop international standards on cross-border bank resolution are currently under way.[27]

In a global financial system with (relatively) free movement of capital across borders, most financial transactions that are originated in one country can be executed in another. This means that any constraint, or tax, that is imposed on a financial transaction in a country can often be (easily) avoided by arranging for that same transaction to take place under the legal, tax and accounting jurisdiction of another country, sometimes, indeed often, under the aegis of a subsidiary, or branch, of exactly the same bank or intermediary as was involved in the initial country.

This tends to generate a race to the bottom, although not always since the parties to a contract will prize legal certainty and contract reliability. (In this latter regard, Howell Jackson, drawing on the 'race to the bottom' versus 'race to the top' debate that has been a feature of corporate law scholarship in the USA—through the work of Roberta Romano and others—over the past twenty-five years, discusses the merits of regulatory competition in securities markets.)[28] Another aspect of this same syndrome is the call for 'a level playing field'. Any state which seeks to impose, unilaterally, tougher regulation than that in operation in some other country will face the accusation that the effect of the regulation will just be to benefit foreign competition with little, or no, restraining effect on the underlying transactions.

Moreover, the cross-border concern may constrain the application of counter-cyclical regulation. Financial cycles, booms and busts, differ in their intensity from country to country. Housing prices rose much more in Australia, Ireland, Spain, the UK and the USA than in Canada, Germany and Japan in the years 2002–07. Bank credit expansion also varied considerably between countries. But if regulation becomes counter-cyclically tightened in the boom countries, that will, in a global financial system, just lead to a transfer of such transactions offshore; and London has been at the centre of arranging such cross-border financial operations.

---

[27] The Basel Cross-border Resolution Group issued a report and recommendations, see Basel Committee on Banking Supervision, 'Report and Recommendations of the Cross-border Bank Resolution Group', March 2010, <http://www.bis.org/publ/bcbs169.htm> (visited 4 August 2010). The International Monetary Fund issued a paper (to which one of the authors contributed), see 'Resolution of Cross Border Banks—a Proposed Framework for Enhanced Coordination', 11 June 2010, <http://www.imf.org/external/np/pp/eng/2010/061110.pdf> (visited 22 July 2010). See generally Rosa M. Lastra (ed), *Cross Border Bank Insolvency* (Oxford: Oxford University Press, 2011).
[28] Howell Jackson has advocated the advantages of legal certainty and reliability and the role of securities laws in creating strong capital markets. See, *inter alia*, Howell E. Jackson, 'Centralization, Competition, and Privatization in Financial Regulation', 2(2) *Theoretical Inquiries in Law* (Online Edition) Article 4 (2001), <http://www.bepress.com/til/default/vol2/iss2/art4> (visited 3 July 2010).

More generally, financial globalization, and the cross-border activities of SIFIs in particular, mean that the level-playing-field argument is advanced to oppose almost any unilateral regulatory initiative. The main response to this, of course, is to try to reach international agreement, and a whole structure of institutions and procedures has been established to try to take this forward, with varying degrees of success. Inevitably, and perhaps properly, this is a slow process.[29] Those who claimed that we were losing the potential momentum of the crisis for reforming financial regulation simply had no feel for the mechanics of the process. Moreover, any of the major financial countries, perhaps some three or four countries, can effectively veto any proposal that they do not like; so again the agreements will tend to represent the lowest common denominator, and perhaps desirably so.

Finally, there can be circumstances and instances when a regulator can take on the level-playing-field argument and still be effective. An example can be enforcing a margin for housing loan to value (LTV) ratios by making lending for the required down-payment unsecured in a court of law. Another example is when the purpose of the additional constraint is to prevent excessive leverage and risk-taking by domestic banks, rather than trying to control credit expansion more widely (as financed by foreign banks).

There is no easy solution to the second boundary problem. The doctrine of multilayered governance, which discusses the allocation of regulatory powers at the national, regional (e.g. European) and international level, provides a template to address some of these issues.[30] We need an inter-jurisdictional approach to financial regulation. Some rules and supervisory decisions must remain at the national level, while rules for a regional area, such as the EU, ought to be regional. Yet, a global banking and financial system requires some binding international rules and an international system for the resolution of conflicts and crises. An analogy with football could be instructive in this regard. There are domestic leagues, ruled by national football associations, there is in Europe a Champions League of the best football clubs governed by UEFA and, finally—although this is a competition among countries, not clubs—there is FIFA and the World Cup. The challenge is to identify the criteria under which financial regulatory powers should be allocated and the different layers (including private mechanisms) that are needed. Effective enforcement remains the greatest challenge at the international level, since enforcement mechanisms have traditionally been nationally based. The conditioning of market access on the basis of compliance with some international rules could be an effective way of tackling some of these difficult cross-border issues.

Globalization and regionalization (in particular in the EU) have challenged the traditional law-making process, a development which is particularly relevant for the future of financial regulation.

---

[29] The problem is a general one and in EU law outside of finance, e.g. in goods, it has been a matter of harmonizing only key points, but not entire areas. A level playing field in international finance calls for some international rules. Given the difficulties inherent in the regulation and harmonization of asset quality, the focus so far has been on capital, although in the aftermath of the crisis, attention has also turned to other areas, such as liquidity and resolution.

[30] For a more extensive discussion of this doctrine, see Chapter 8 by Rolf H. Weber in this volume.

International financial soft-law is often a 'top-down' phenomenon with a two-layer implementation scheme. The rules are agreed by international financial standard setters and national authorities must implement them in their regulation of the financial industry. The financial intermediaries are the 'final' addresses of those rules. Standards and uniform rules, however, can also be designed by the financial industry itself. Self-regulation, by definition, has a 'bottom-up' character.

International lawmaking relies upon a variety of sources. It is in the confluence of 'hard law' (legally enforceable rules), soft law of a 'public law' nature (which can complement, co-exist or turn into hard law) and soft law of a 'private law' nature (comprising rules of practice, standards, usages and other forms of self-regulation as well as rules and principles agreed or proposed by scholars and experts) where the future of international financial and monetary law lies.[31]

IV. Concluding Observations

To conclude, border problems are pervasive, and complicate the application of regulatory measures both within and between countries. The prospective regulator will always need to be alert to the likely effect of shifts of business across such borders, and seek to mitigate them. But to some extent such cross-border business transfers are generic and the regulator or supervisor will just have to monitor and, up to a point, to live with them. The perimeter issue remains a major challenge for regulators and supervisors, one that resurfaces again and again in the debate about derivatives, hedge funds, rating agencies and others. Progress towards an effective framework for cross-border crisis management and resolution is hampered by the two boundaries that we have discussed in this chapter. Regulation is most needed in good times, when rapid credit expansion and exuberant optimism cloud the sound exercise of judgement in risk management, yet regulation is typically designed in bad times, in response to a crisis. We need appropriate counter-cyclical regulation, bearing in mind the biblical story of Joseph, in which provisions were gathered in good times to be used in bad times. Regulation and supervision should aim at protecting the interests of society (by identifying, preventing and containing systemic risk as well as by guaranteeing the functioning and access to critical banking and financial functions), rather than the interests of individuals or institutions. Notwithstanding the porous borders of financial regulation, we have to continue to make progress in redesigning finance so as to restore the faith in the financial market as an instrument for the wealth and development of nations.

---

[31] See Rosa M. Lastra, *Legal Foundations of International Monetary Stability* (Oxford: Oxford University Press, 2006) 500–1.

10

The International Law of Financial Crisis: Spillovers, Subsidiarity, Fragmentation and Cooperation

Joel P. Trachtman

I. The International Dimension of Domestic Regulatory Reform: Opportunity and Constraint

International law should generally play a subsidiary role to domestic law. The principle of subsidiarity in its most rational, and economic, form, is best understood as a principle of efficiency. It holds that the state should intervene in civil society—should regulate—only where its involvement improves welfare, and that in turn international law and organizations should be established only where they improve welfare.[1] It is appropriate to adopt a subsidiarity- or efficiency-based method, examining first the circumstances in which it appears that states should regulate, and second the separate and different reasons why international law of regulation may be appropriate.

Thus, domestic regulation may be needed when firms do not bear all the risks of their actions or when the managers who are delegated control of firms do not bear all the risks of their actions. The recent crisis illustrates both types of problem. Building on the subsidiarity concept at a higher level of organization, international regulation is needed when states do not bear all the risks of their regulatory actions, where states acting individually would otherwise under-invest in a global public good, or where states may regulate more efficiently by working together.

A. Externalities

Actions or inactions of states may have positive or negative 'effects' on other states. Thus, the financial regulation (or deficiencies therein) in one state may be associ-

[1] For my more general analysis of this topic, see Joel P. Trachtman, *The Economic Structure of International Law*, (Cambridge, MA: Harvard University Press, 2008). See also Thomas Cottier, 'Multilayered Governance, Pluralism, and Moral Conflict', 16 *Indiana Journal of Global Legal Studies* 647 (2009). See also the paper by Rolf H. Weber, in this volume at Chapter 8, and equally addressing regulatory competition, the paper by Christian Tietje and Mathias Lehmann, in this volume at Chapter 7.

ated with adverse or beneficial effects (negative or positive externalities) in other states. Externalities may be addressed through rules of jurisdiction that accord the affected state control over the injurious behaviour.

Domestic financial regulation may also 'cause' adverse effects in other states by being too strict with respect to the entry of foreign financial services into the national market, or too lax with respect to domestic financial institutions, resulting in competitiveness effects (pecuniary externalities). Externalization through regulation that fails to protect foreign interests (or that implicitly subsidizes by failing to protect local or foreign interests), pecuniary externalization through strict regulation that has protectionist effects or through lax regulation that may be viewed as a subsidy and subsidization itself may all be viewed as questions of prescriptive jurisdiction: which state—or international body—will have power to regulate which actions?

An example of a principle of international financial regulatory jurisdiction that seems problematic from this standpoint is contained in a January 2009 proposal from the Group of Thirty, entitled 'Financial Reform: A Framework for Financial Stability'.[2] This report recommends, with respect to private pools of capital such as hedge funds, that 'the jurisdiction of the appropriate prudential regulator should be based on the primary business location of the manager of such funds'.[3] However, the jurisdiction assigned responsibility under this principle might not include the primary location of investors, or of others who might be harmed by actions of the funds. Under these circumstances, the affected state might be denied control over the injurious behaviour.

The externalization problem is accentuated by the diversity of states' positions. Some states may be regulatory 'havens' that impose lax regulation because the adverse effects of the lax regulation will largely be felt externally, while the positive effects in terms of tax revenues and employment can be enjoyed by the regulatory haven. Certain jurisdictional rules, such as rules of regulatory recognition, might allow such externalization. On the other hand, jurisdictional rules of national treatment, or of managed recognition,[4] can reduce the possibility for such negative externalization.

Furthermore, one state's strict regulation might provide positive externalities to other states, both in terms of avoidance of contagion and avoidance of consequent economic disruption. Because this is a positive externality, the first state would require some incentive—in terms of some type of narrow or diffuse reciprocity—as compensation. International cooperation can set the terms of such reciprocity.

---

[2] Group of Thirty, 'Financial Reform: A Framework for Financial Stability', Washington, DC, 2009, <http://www.group30.org/pubs/recommendations.pdf> (visited 16 July 2010).

[3] Ibid, at 9.

[4] See Kalypso Nicolaidïs and Joel P. Trachtman, 'From Policed Regulation to Managed Recognition: Mapping the Boundary in GATS', in Pierre Sauvé and Robert Stern (eds), *GATS 2000: New Directions in Services and Trade Liberalization* (Washington, DC: The Brookings Institution, 2000).

B. Public goods

One type of cooperation problem in international financial regulation arises from the fact that international public goods exist.[5] Public goods are non-excludable and non-rival in consumption. Relevant examples include the international financial and payments system, international financial stability, and global economic growth. Financial stability and the resultant economic growth may be viewed not just as a domestic public good, but also as a global public good, due to contagion and systemic effects. That is, the benefits of stability are available to all states, and the enjoyment of stability by one state does not reduce its availability to others. At the financial level, under interconnectedness, regulatory cooperation may reduce the scope of systemic risk that each state's financial institutions experience. The 1974 Herstatt Bank crisis was an early example of this type of international contagion risk. At the economic level, a US economic slump has repercussions around the world through the mechanism of trade and investment.

Public goods result in the problem of underinvestment. If a particular good is a public good, then because those who invest in its production may not capture all of the benefits, a collective action problem may arise and the public good may be underproduced. This is a problem of a positive externality. Alternatively, a public bad involves adverse effects that are non-excludable and inexhaustible. Those who produce public bads may not internalize all of the detriments, and the public bad may be overproduced. This is a type of negative externality.

States affected by externalities, including public bads, or states that observe the possibility of under-produced international public goods, may thus determine to seek to alter other states' activities, through their own regulation or by seeking changes in the first state's regulation. There are two main ways to do this. The first is bilateral persuasion. The second is through institutionalization. Bilateral persuasion may involve inducement by force, exchange or implicit reciprocities (either specific or diffuse);[6] it occurs in the 'spot market'. Institutionalization involves the 'wholesale' transfer of power over time through a treaty or an international organization.

C. Economies of scale and scope, and network externalities

Additional potential sources of gains from cooperation may arise from economies of scale and economies of scope, as well as network externalities. Given the increasingly global nature of society, and of problems such as the international financial crisis, it seems likely that there would be economies of scale, under some circum-

---

[5] See Scott Barrett, *Why Cooperate? The Incentive to Supply Global Public Goods* (Oxford: Oxford University Press, 2007); Inge Kaul et al. (eds), *Providing Global Public Goods: Managing Globalization* (Oxford: Oxford University Press, 2003).

[6] See Robert O. Keohane, 'Reciprocity in International Relations', 40 *International Organization* 1 (1986).

stances, in the regulation of these matters.[7] There may be institutional economies of scale and scope: development of institutions may make it more likely that more issues will be addressed by those institutions. Network externalities may increase savings with increases in the number of states that are party to an institution or a rule.

Economies of scale have a number of components. First, states may enjoy economies of scale in contexts where they regulate transnational actors. For example, there may be efficiencies gained through coordinated rulemaking, surveillance and enforcement activities. In the absence of these transactions, states face heightened risks of evasion, detrimental regulatory competition (which can be driven by externalization) and unnecessary regulatory disharmony, all resulting in inefficiencies.[8] Second, there may be technological economies of scale, relating to equipment, acquisition of specialized skills, or organization. Certainly, as finance has become more complex, there may be greater economies of scale in developing the necessary regulatory capacities. Economies of scale may provide motivation for integration, in the sense that the economies of scale tilt the cost–benefit analysis in favour of integration.

D. Regulatory competition

Technological advances, globalization, innovation and growth have combined to make finance both actually and virtually rather footloose. Mobility exists both on the producer and on the consumer side of the equation. On the other hand, Joseph Stiglitz has argued that the part of the financial system that is critical to the real economy—the part that lends to main street business—is not as footloose as the more speculative part of the financial system.[9] Prior to the crisis, there had been some evidence of movement away from US capital markets, arguably due to increasingly stringent regulation. However, no one has identified a move from the USA as being motivated by a desire for *more* onerous regulation. Indeed, the crisis may prove that we cannot trust private actors to leave a jurisdiction with inadequate financial regulation: the class of persons protected by regulation seemed, in this case, to lack the ability to evaluate and identify inadequate regulation.

The greater a financial institution's powers, the lower its capital requirements, and the greater the government safety net, the more profitable it is likely to be. Therefore, a financial institution exclusively regulated by a jurisdiction that is more liberal in connection with capital or powers regulation, or that provides a stronger safety net, can be expected to be more competitive, all else being equal, than a more constrained or less supported financial institution. So there is definitely a competi-

---

[7] Of course, the fact that it is efficient to regulate activity from a global perspective does not mean that only one regulator should exist; rather, it is a problem of contracting and establishing the most efficient institutional structure in response to technical or contextual factors. A similar caveat applies with respect to 'economies of scope'.

[8] See Joel P. Trachtman, 'International Regulatory Competition, Externalization and Jurisdiction', 34 *Harvard International Law Journal* 47 (1993).

[9] Joseph Stiglitz, 'Watchdogs Need Not Bark Together', *Financial Times*, 9 February 2010.

tive, or pecuniary, externality arising from certain types of financial regulation. Moreover, this externality will often involve non-pecuniary elements, where the relevant financial institution may operate internationally and the risk of its failure may be detrimental to people outside its home jurisdiction.

Thus, unilateral action alone, perhaps by use of national market-access restrictions that might prevent an inadequately regulated bank from doing business in a more vigilant jurisdiction, does not appear to be sufficient to establish appropriate rules. Furthermore, it may be difficult to distinguish such unilateral action from protectionism, raising fragmentation issues between regulation and trade. Therefore, discourse based on regulatory expertise, towards multilateral essential harmonization, seems appropriate in this area, again, assuming that we are able to overcome uncertainty as to the appropriate regulatory action. Of course, there is another type of uncertainty that is more difficult to overcome: uncertainty regarding the appropriateness of a particular regulatory rule across different legal, financial, and social systems. However, under circumstances of increasing globalization, greater homogenization and greater mobility of abuse will militate towards essential harmonization of financial regulation rules in this area.

To the extent that we continue to operate under uncertainty regarding the appropriate structure of regulation, diversity may allow for us to learn from further experience. On the other hand, where we believe that diversity is driven more by externalization or protectionism than by good faith regulatory views, there can be no assurance that diversity will be beneficial.

The utility of regulatory competition is recognized to be dependent on the question of regulatory jurisdiction, in the form of questions of positive and negative externalities that may limit the utility and domain of the Tiebout model. (The Tiebout model suggests that under certain strong conditions, regulatory competition would result in efficient provision of governmental services. The conditions include no spillovers, costless movement of citizens, and an infinite variety of local packages of public services.)[10] The Tiebout model depends on a number of assumptions, including the absence of externalities, and so in order to assess its applicability, we must evaluate the match between regulatory jurisdiction and effects.

In the regulatory context, proponents of greater competition in some areas, notably securities regulation, argue that there is a 'joint' jurisdictional decision made by producers and consumers. Thus, analysis must examine the degree to which consumers are able to make an informed choice. The economic theory of

---

[10] See e.g. Robert P. Inman and Daniel L. Rubinfeld, 'The Political Economy of Federalism', in Dennis C. Mueller (ed), *Perspectives on Public Choice: A Handbook* (New York: Cambridge University Press, 1997) 73–105, 85. After stating that current empirical evidence is suggestive that competitive local governments can provide an efficient level of congestible (local) public goods, Inman and Rubinfeld offer the following caveat, at 86:

> What is not assured is the efficient allocation of public goods with significant spillovers. In this case, a subsidy is needed to internalize the externalities. But any such policy to control interjurisdictional spillovers would require the agreement of the competitive city-states. For such agreements we must look to more encompassing political institutions. In Madison's compound republic this is the representative central government.

regulation would suggest that at least some regulation is motivated by the inability of consumers to make an informed choice. It is difficult to imagine that consumers who are unable to make an informed choice regarding the regulated subject matter would be able to make an informed choice regarding the regulatory law governing this subject matter. Given that it is probably more difficult to grapple with issues of applicable law than direct issues of policy, it is unrealistic to say that consumer choice of mandatory regulation is an improvement.

Furthermore, there are substantial concerns as to whether the Tiebout model can result in a stable equilibrium.[11] The stability of intergovernmental competition is separate from its efficiency: an unstable market for regulation might be characterized by 'price wars' or a race to the bottom.[12]

Externalities can be a source of instability.[13] Breton points out that centralization may not be the best way to provide stability, but the existence (without necessarily the assertion) of central authority appears necessary to address problems of instability.[14] The central government may set minimum standards of regulation, as has been done in the European Union's (EU's) essential harmonization technique.

Breton concludes that 'in the area of international competition, it would be impossible to prevent an unstable competitive process from degenerating, unless, in the language of international relations "realists", a hegemonic power undertook to prevent the debacle.'[15] There appears to be no reason in theory why the hegemonic power in this type of context must be a state; we have seen the EU emerge as just such a power in Europe, and it might be argued that the Basel Committee on Banking Supervision (BCBS), the World Trade Organization (WTO), or another functional organization, may play such a role also. Alternatively, perhaps the US or EU exercises, or shares, hegemony through these organizations.

Perhaps, a dynamic governance structure along the lines of 'cooperative federalism' or managed mutual recognition may provide a kind of contingent hegemony or centralization that can maintain stability. Within the US federal system, stability is provided by the ability of the federal government to intervene; this is an important distinction between regulatory competition in the US domestic context and regulatory competition in the international context, and may be an important distinction between corporate law, where the federal government has not intervened, and securities law or banking law, where it has chosen to intervene.

E. Fragmentation and Cooperation

At the international level, we observe a set of overlaps with other functional areas, or fragmentation issues. These fragmentation issues are in addition to those relating to

[11] Edward M. Gramlich, 'Cooperation and Competition in Public Welfare Policies', 6 *Journal of Policy Analysis and Management* 417 (1987). See also Albert Breton, 'The Existence and Stability of Interjurisdictional Competition', in Daphne A. Kenyon and John Kincaid (eds), *Competition Among States and Local Governments: Efficiency and Equity in American Federalism* (Washington, DC: The Urban Institute Press, 1991).
[12] See Breton, ibid, at 43.   [13] Ibid, at 51.
[14] Ibid, at 49.   [15] Ibid, at 51–2.

functional separation, for example, among commercial bank regulation, securities regulation, insurance regulation, corporate governance, bankruptcy, consumer regulation, and commodities regulation. Of course, the resolution of fragmentation issues at the international level is made more difficult by the fact that there is not a single institution that serves as forum or legislator for all of the relevant issues.

1. Macroeconomic management

If the root cause of pressure on domestic regulatory mechanisms, and their eventual failure, is macroeconomic imbalances, then it may be more efficient to address these imbalances rather than to make certain changes to regulation. It is likely to be necessary to do both. The correct balance would depend on an overall cost–benefit analysis of each mechanism. Macroeconomic imbalances might be caused, in turn, by savings rate differentials, or might result from distorted exchange rates, or from other factors.

2. Trade

As is well known, one of the important pressures on the USA to relax its powers regulation, allowing its banking organizations to engage in insurance, investment banking and other activities, came from demands by European and other states for reduced impediments to access to the US market. Of course, this pressure operated under uncertainty, or at least disagreement, regarding the utility of these components of powers regulation. Putting that political pressure aside, a state was nevertheless free to engage in unilateralism regarding powers criteria for market access. At least in the general international system, as opposed to, say, in the EU, there is no rule of exclusive regulation by the home country. So, a potential host country could block market entry by the laxly regulated foreign financial institution. On the other hand, however, states like the USA found their financial institutions disadvantaged in terms of operations in more lax foreign markets, where the US financial institutions were subject to extraterritorial home-country restrictions, while native or other foreign financial institutions enjoyed a broader range of powers.

So, cross-national regulatory differentials will have some distortive effect on trade, and may cause some states to close their borders to market access from other states that have less onerous regimes.

On the other hand, liberalization and globalization generally may change our definition of 'too big to fail' (TBTF). If there are low barriers to market access, then a foreign firm may stand ready to acquire or to supplant a failing domestic firm.

3. Development

Different states have different needs at different times. A developing state might need the 'right to regulate' in order to promote growth under circumstances in which the risk of a resulting banking crisis is small in relation to the benefits of resulting development. So, there may be cross-national diversity as to the ideal level of regulation. Therefore, in any international regulatory response that includes some degree of harmonization, recognition or enforcement cooperation, there may be some need to create a mechanism that recognizes appropriate diversity for development purposes. The International Monetary Fund (IMF), in its role as development agency, and the World Bank, have established a significant body of semi-soft financial law. States that seek access to IMF and World Bank facilities are required to demonstrate a satisfactory level of compliance with these standards and codes.[16]

II. Future Change and its Impact on Regulatory Reform

Of course, it is not possible to anticipate all aspects of the future stresses on financial institutions, but it will be important to do so as far as possible. This chapter cannot engage in a detailed exercise in futurology, but can identify some broad trends, and suggest how these may affect the themes of financial regulation discussed above. We focus on globalization, technological advance, financial innovation and economic growth.

A. Globalization

A simple and effective definition of globalization for our purposes involves greater mobility of the four economic factors: goods, services, money and workers. Globalization in finance and financial services has grown dramatically, in large measure due to technological advances. Since we have historical instances of globalization being reversed in the early part of the twentieth century, it is not possible to predict that globalization will continue to increase. However, enhanced technology over time and the expected economic benefits of globalization are likely to continue to drive increasing globalization.

Practically by definition, globalization results in greater competition, potentially reducing margins and thereby making local financial institutions more vulnerable to the risk of commercial failure. Reduced margins might indicate a need for closer supervision, greater capital requirements or perhaps even the imposition of restrictions on competition in order to maintain the stability of financial institutions. This is the concept of 'overbanking' that in some states has been used as a basis to limit market access for newcomers. Furthermore, globalization, by increasing the mobility of firms, would be expected to accentuate regulatory competition, depending on how globalization is structured. Regulatory competition could be benevolent or malevolent, as discussed above, depending on whether it is a race to externalize in which the regulating state is imposing costs on outsiders, or whether it is a race to efficiency in which the regulating state is seeking more efficient regulation.

---

[16] See International Monetary Fund and the World Bank, 'The Standards and Codes Initiative—Is it Effective? And How Can it Be Improved?', <http://www.worldbank.org/ifa/ROSC%20review%202005.pdf> (visited 16 July 2010).

This same mobility that allows honest firms to move to reduce costs can allow dishonest operators to seek out under-regulated markets, engaging in a perverse transfer of defalcation technology. This means that, under globalization, states cannot wait for indigenous fraudsters to appear, but must protect against imported fraud.

Greater competition due to globalization, combined with a safety-net doctrine for companies TBTF, is a dangerous combination. Thus, under globalization, at the same time that regulatory competition may have induced reductions in regulatory stringency, increased cross-border, inter-firm competition has reduced margins, driving financial institutions to seek more profitable, and more risky, activities. Developing countries may consider this phenomenon as they determine to open their markets to competition in financial services. The risk of imported defalcation suggests a greater role for imported regulatory structures.

In other dimensions, globalization provides opportunities both for greater stability and risks of contagion, depending on the structure of financial institutions and of risk. Globalization may provide opportunities for greater stability by increasing the size of the market and reducing barriers to entry. If a firm is TBTF in a smaller market, it may not be TBTF given the readiness of foreign competitors to enter the market and acquire the firm or otherwise to take over its market niche. This readiness may be enhanced by liberalization of trade in financial services, especially in connection with commercial establishment by foreign financial service providers through acquisition.

On the other hand, globalization increases the risk of contagion,[17] with the result that a firm that might not be too interdependent to fail from a purely national perspective might be so from a global perspective. This could occur where the firm has few local obligations, but greater foreign ones. This effect raises increasing problems of externalities and collective action. In the crisis, the collapse of Lehman Brothers destabilized many other financial institutions, and American International Group (AIG) raised the spectre that its failure could damage European banks and insurance companies, as well as money market funds.

Globalization can also increase risk by making the process of regulation, including supervision and enforcement, more difficult. Increasing globalization places pressure on regulators to coordinate, and to assist one another in surveillance and enforcement. In order to encourage such assistance, it may be useful to harmonize rules.

Finally, the very mobility of capital that is a hallmark of globalization could be damaging in a pro-cyclical way, or even in an inaccurate way, where a 'run' on particular financial institutions, or on financial institutions in a particular country, might be precipitated with the result that those financial institutions or that country is destabilized.

---

[17] See Jorge A. Chan-Lau, Donald J. Mathieson and James Y. Yao, 'Extreme Contagion in Equity Markets', IMF Staff Papers, Volume 51(2), 2004; Olivier De Bandt and Philipp Hartmann, 'Systemic Risk: A Survey', Working Paper No. 31 (2000), Frankfurt, European Central Bank.

B. Technological advance

Finance, of course, is completely dependent on information and communications, as well as on information processing. As technological advance proceeds, it not only contributes powerfully to globalization, but also contributes to greater efficiency and competition by reducing transaction costs, reducing information asymmetry and increasing effective market access. This effect would be expected to reduce margins and, along with globalization, to make finance not only systematically cheaper but also more homogeneous in price. Technology and globalization promote the effectiveness of the 'law of one price'.

One approach to financial regulation would take advantage of decentralized technologically structured networks to procure, organize and disseminate information.[18] This might help to address information asymmetries in connection with bank regulation, as well as in connection with securities offerings.

C. Financial innovation

It is true that the crisis has given financial innovation a bad name, and it may be that certain types of innovation have increased risk, but it is important to remember that financial innovation has increased welfare broadly and deeply by allowing worthwhile projects, which could not have been developed prior to financial innovation, to be financed after innovation, and by broadly allowing more efficient financial markets. It is tempting to say that we have already innovated enough and that all future innovation would only add to excessive complexity and uncompensated risk. However, just as with innovation in physical technology, it is to be expected that innovation in financial services will improve our lives in the future. Consider, for example, the rise of microfinance, which is still to some extent a frontier, but which holds promise for the alleviation of poverty.

What are the dangers of innovation? Innovation often involves increased complexity, making each step of the regulatory process more difficult, and making it more and more difficult for different types of market intermediaries or consumers to evaluate financial services products. Innovation in investments will require intellectual suitability standards that forbid sale to investors who lack the ability to evaluate the relevant complexity, or alternatively will necessitate prospectuses to explain the complexity in a usable fashion. Greater innovation will therefore put greater pressure on regulation.

Innovation, through swaps, derivatives and other devices, has already had significant impacts on globalization. Globalization, in turn, has resulted in greater need for innovation in order to allow companies to reduce the risks involved in international payments flows: the development of the swaps market was initially

---

[18] See e.g. 'Rethinking Financial Regulation: Simple Transparency, Open Source, and XML', <http://nextbigfuture.com/2009/03/rethinking-financial-regulation-simple.html> (visited 16 July 2010).

driven by the desire for arbitrage across markets. Furthermore, advances in information technology allow for greater innovation.

The availability of a government safety net is deeply problematic from an incentive standpoint, and gives rise to problematic regulatory efforts, such as capital requirements and powers regulation. However, the rise of information technology and financial innovation has moved us far beyond the days of banks as principally depository institutions and payments facilitators. It may be that technology and innovation have made deposit insurance less important, while making it easier to apply market disciplines that were not operative under the shadow of government safety nets for financial institutions. Under these circumstances, it may be time to wean most of the financial architecture off governmental support, while providing for narrow banks or even something akin to a postal savings system to allow consumers who require governmental support to obtain it, at reduced returns. Obviously, the implementation of such a solution would need to be evaluated separately, and customized, for each adopting state. But if some states were to withdraw their safety nets, while others did not, this might raise issues of externalization of risk and regulatory competition.

D. Economic growth

Economic growth can be expected broadly to increase demand for financial services. It can also be expected to increase globalization, increase education and enhance information infrastructure. Thus, economic growth can be expected to increase the need for enhanced regulation in emerging market states, and also to increase the need for international cooperation. Greater homogenization in the economic position of states, and in their needs for financial markets, may make harmonization of financial regulation more attractive.

III. Applying the Subsidiarity Methodology to International Financial Regulation Cooperation

In this section, I examine how the reasons for international cooperation, issues of fragmentation, and expected future developments, all discussed above, affect possible regulation of (i) executive compensation; (ii) capital regulation; (iii) powers regulation; (iv) safety nets, bailouts and resolution; (v) disclosure; and (vi) rating agencies. Here, given an understanding about national policy in light of what we now know about the crisis and expected changes, we are able to evaluate the possible utility of international cooperation.

A. Corporate governance and compensation

In connection with existing and proposed caps on bankers' pay, banks have argued that caps in one jurisdiction will cause highly skilled personnel to move to jurisdictions that lack caps. Given the competition among financial centres for the tax revenues, economic growth benefits and prestige that comes with dominance as a financial centre, it is not difficult to imagine that states would find it difficult to impose pay caps unilaterally, at least over the long term. Failure of states to coordinate with respect to pay caps would be a test of whether the market, supplemented by corporate governance systems, is capable of providing adequate discipline with respect to compensation.

If it were possible to devise compensation systems that provide adequate incentives for performance, without the incentives for taking on excessive risk, then, assuming effective corporate governance or market mechanisms, we would expect investors to discipline firms using these mechanisms and to avoid excessive compensation.[19] Market disciplines by virtue of investor voice or exit seem to have failed to prevent corporate governance problems. Nor has regulatory competition provided an effective response.

It might be argued that if it is impossible for the market to devise such systems, then it is likely to be equally impossible for governments to square that particular circle. Therefore, this argument would run, governmentally imposed caps are likely to provide inefficiently low incentives for performance. Whether compensation restrictions are, nevertheless, valuable because they also avoid offering excessive incentives to take on risk would depend on the magnitude of each effect. An opposing argument would point to information asymmetries that make it difficult for shareholders to evaluate the effects of compensation arrangements, or broader social externalities that would not be taken into account by shareholders in policing compensation arrangements. Corporate governance problems might have prevented the development of systems under which leading executives would have been required to bear risk, such as systems providing for deferred payment of bonuses in the form of equity or subordinated debt, with retention obligations.[20] Finally, the correct blend of incentives would depend to some extent on the social, legal and financial context in which each firm operates. There is, therefore, likely to be some cross-national diversity in the optimal response.

So, in order to craft an appropriate international response, it would be necessary to balance the utility of cross-national diversity, plus the utility of beneficial regulatory competition and experimentation that might yield a superior solution, against the possibility of adverse regulatory competition that might yield insufficient discipline on compensation. The process of negotiating an international regime would help to establish the right balance, most likely in terms of essential harmonization allowing a degree of national diversity.

To the extent that the financial crisis can be understood as a failure of corporate governance, or of other national financial regulation, it suggests that mere market

---

[19] But see George Akerlof and Rachel Kranton, 'It is Time to Treat Wall Street Like Main Street', *Financial Times*, 24 February 2010 (arguing that incentive compensation is less likely to improve performance than is commonly thought).
[20] See Financial Stability Board, 'Financial Stability Board Principles for Sound Compensation Practices', 2 April 2009, <http://www.financialstabilityboard.org/publications/r_0904b.pdf> (visited 16 July 2010).

forces harnessed to regulatory competition are insufficient to ensure a good result. In a very real sense, we have now experienced the results of a laissez-faire approach to regulatory competition, and have found them starkly unattractive. After all, in the run-up to the crisis, investors did not broadly migrate from US to Canadian mortgage-backed securities, nor did they migrate to investments in firms that had sufficient capital or that avoided risky investments.

B. Capital

In the field of capital regulation, we already have an international regime, but there is broad agreement that it requires further revision.[21] Revised Basel requirements were agreed too late to be included in this chapter.[22]

There are important international regulatory aspects of capital regulation. First, since financial institution stability and broader market stability are global public goods, we would expect them to be undersupplied without a cooperative arrangement. Second, we have some experience of states engaging in competitive reductions of capital requirements in order to promote their own financial services firms. There is broad agreement here also that unrestrained regulatory competition would result in inadequate capital requirements. Indeed, all of our observations with respect to powers regulation also apply to capital regulation. Therefore, it seems important to coordinate capital requirements for financial institutions. The BCBS, acting under the auspices of the Bank for International Settlements (BIS) has done so since 1988, although the degree to which it has created a level playing field is still uncertain.[23] Indeed, we might understand the Basel process as a technique of essential harmonization, which will develop a degree of harmonization, but which has left and will leave significant latitude for national regulatory diversity. At its Pittsburgh summit in September 2009, the G20 committed itself to develop 'by end-2010 internationally agreed rules to improve both the quantity and quality of bank capital and to discourage excessive leverage'.[24] But we have also found an increasing need to take account of broader types of risks. Most recently, the BCBS has found the need to focus on risk arising from choice of counterparties and magnitude of relationships with counterparties.

Furthermore, in the current crisis, we have found that financial institutions that were not subject to the Basel capital requirements were able to engage in activities in competition with financial institutions that were subject to these requirements: the so-called 'perimeter' issue.[25] In addition, not all states have accepted the Basel

---

[21] See the contribution by Hal S. Scott, Chapter 12 of this volume to this symposium.

[22] See Bank for International Settlements, 'International Regulatory Framework for Banks (Basel III)', <http://www.bis.org/bcbs/basel3.htm> (visited 24 September 2010).

[23] See Patricia Jackson et al., 'Capital Requirements and Bank Behavior: The Impact of the Basle Accord', Basel Committee on Banking Supervision Working Paper No 1, April 1999; Hal S. Scott and Shinsaku Iwahara, 'In Search of a Level Playing Field: The Implementation of the Basel Accord in Japan and the United States', Group of Thirty Occasional Paper No 46, 1994.

[24] G20, 'Leaders' Statement: The Pittsburgh Summit', 24–25 September 2009, <http://www.pittsburghsummit.gov/mediacenter/129639.htm> (visited 18 October 2010).

[25] See Chapter 9 by Goodhart and Lastra in this volume.

capital requirements. So, there is a dual problem of regulatory competition, or leakage, by virtue of competition from entities subject to less stringent regulation, either because of functional distinction or because of jurisdictional differences.

Leakage may be addressed by further harmonization or by restrictions on competition. That is, where unregulated entities seek to compete, they can be subjected to regulation—this is harmonization. The USA and other states have used national restrictions on foreign bank entry to limit the ability of weakly regulated entities to compete in the US market.[26] Unilateral restrictions on competition would evidently be inconsistent with globalization, and with the liberalization of trade in financial services sought at the WTO. On the other hand, internationally sanctioned restrictions on competition might be understood to thereby be 'laundered' of protectionist intent, and may serve as an appropriate 'line of equilibrium' between prudential regulation and liberalization.[27]

In the EU context, essential harmonization is often combined with mutual recognition; that is, under EU single market arrangements, essential harmonization is structured as a predicate for agreements to open the markets of Member States to competition from firms in other Member States.

Any level of harmonization will raise the question of implementation, and whether national supervision and enforcement of capital requirements will yield a sufficient level of effective harmonization. Different states might supervise and enforce, and fill in the details of regulation, in different ways. These differences could undermine efforts to harmonize. One institutional response to this question would be to provide for an international supervisory and enforcement mechanism that would be structured to act independently of domestic political concerns.

Finally, but by no means least important, capital requirements, leverage ratios, loan-to-value ratios and liquidity requirements may be utilized by regulators to reduce the possibility and magnitude of asset bubbles. It is important to note that this macroeconomic rationale is a distinct function for these types of regulation, but that these types of regulation seem well- designed for this function.[28] Furthermore, this rationale and function suggests that within particular governments, it may be appropriate for monetary policymakers to be in charge of at least these components of regulation. However, the dual function of these types of regulation might suggest a dual responsibility, with the minimum requirements being set as the higher of the requirements laid down by the prudential regulator or monetary policymaker.

C. Powers

Putting aside for a moment corporate governance problems and perverse incentives that may derive from a safety net and compensation schemes, the greater a financial

---

[26] See e.g. the Foreign Bank Supervision Enhancement Act of 1991, 12 United States Code xx 3101–11 (Supp IV 1992).

[27] WTO Appellate Body Report, *United States—Import Prohibition of Certain Shrimp and Shrimp Products (US—Shrimp)*, WT/DS58/AB/R, adopted 6 November 1998.

[28] Stijn Claessens et al., 'Lessons and Policy Implications from the Global Financial Crisis', IMF Working Paper, WP/10/44, February 2010, at 17.

institution's powers the more profitable it is likely to be. This is because one would not expect a fully market-disciplined financial institution to exercise powers that are not profitable, taking full account of risk. So the powers that would be exercised absent regulatory restrictions are likely to increase profits. Conversely, under these assumptions, regulatory restrictions decrease profits and financial resilience.

Therefore, under these assumptions, a financial institution exclusively regulated by a jurisdiction that is more liberal in connection with powers regulation can be expected to be more efficient, and more competitive, than a more constrained financial institution. What is more, even where we relax the assumption of full market discipline by allowing for a governmental safety net, we can expect the beneficiary unconstrained financial institutions to be more competitive. This is because they benefit from an implicit subsidy by virtue of the government absorption of risk. So there is definitely a competitive, or pecuniary, externality arising from lax powers regulation. Moreover, this externality will often involve non-pecuniary elements, where the relevant financial institution may operate internationally and the risk of its failure may be detrimental to people outside its home jurisdiction. So, a race to the bottom may be fuelled by the possibility of externalizing adverse consequences.

Of course, at least in the general international system, as opposed to say the EU, there is no rule of exclusive regulation by the home country. So, a potential host country could block market entry by the laxly regulated foreign financial institution. On the other hand, however, there are incentives for states to reduce inefficient or even merely uncompetitive regulation. As noted above, states like the USA that formerly imposed greater limits on the powers of their institutions found them disadvantaged in terms of operations in more lax markets, where the US financial institutions were often subject to extraterritorial home-country restrictions, while native financial institutions enjoyed a broader range of powers. Thus, unilateral action alone, by virtue of market-access rules, does not appear to be sufficient to establish appropriate rules. Furthermore, it may be difficult to distinguish such unilateral action from protectionism.

Therefore, discourse based on regulatory expertise, towards multilateral essential harmonization, seems appropriate in this area, again, assuming that we are able to overcome uncertainty as to appropriate regulatory action. Of course, there is another type of uncertainty that is more difficult to overcome: uncertainty regarding the appropriateness of a particular regulatory rule across different legal, financial, and social systems. However, under circumstances of increasing globalization, greater homogenization and greater mobility of abuse will militate towards essential harmonization of financial regulation rules in this area.

To the extent that we continue to operate under uncertainty regarding the appropriate extent of powers regulation, diversity may allow us to learn from further experience. On the other hand, where we believe that diversity is driven more by externalization than by good faith regulatory views, then there can be no assurance that diversity will be beneficial.

By contrast, if there were no uncertainty that principal trading by financial institutions that benefit from a safety net is in theory and in practice highly likely to cause such financial institutions to take on excessive risk, then there would be a strong argument for international harmonization of a restrictive rule.

D. Safety nets, bailouts, and resolution

Deposit insurance is a critical part of a government safety net, and would obviously reduce financing costs for beneficiary banks. During the crisis, modifications of deposit insurance by Ireland provoked concerns regarding regulatory competition, and speedy coordination within Europe.

As we have seen, much of the need for bank regulation stems from the fact that banks in many contexts benefit from a government safety net. If government, either legally or practically, cannot allow a bank to fail, then there is a critical incentive problem that must be addressed. In addition, governments find themselves in a time inconsistency bind, in which they may wish to say *ex ante* that they will not bail out a bank, but *ex post* are unable to avoid doing so. Of course, to the extent that banks or their owners understand this bind, they will take advantage of it.

Strangely, in the crisis, only a handful of major US financial institutions had their equity holders wiped out—the equity holders of Citigroup and Goldman Sachs, for example, were bailed out when the government might instead have decided to take over full equity ownership. But even if equity holders were wiped out when their banks fail, this would not fully address the incentive problem. As long as they have the opportunity to profit from risk, where there are external losses—such as to the financial system in general or the economy—they will not have sufficient incentives to take care. So, it is not just a corporate governance problem, but a regulatory problem to determine how to ensure that bank owners take full account of the social cost of bank operations.

During the crisis, questions arose in Europe regarding the extent to which government bailouts of their financial institutions might be considered illegal subsidies. In an open letter to the *Financial Times*, dated 22 April 2009, the EU Directorate General for Competition made the following statements:

> We are applying the tried and tested code of good economic governance that the EC Treaty's state aid rules represent to ensure four things: 1) that banks receive sufficient support to avoid financial meltdown; 2) that Member States' cures for their own banks do not put those banks in an artificially advantageous competitive position that would kill off banks in other Member States; 3) that banks are restructured to ensure their future long-term viability so that the mistakes of the past are not repeated, that taxpayers' money does not disappear down a black hole and that lending to the real economy is secured; 4) that the Single Market is preserved, with no discriminatory conditions attached to aid and no barriers to entry for cross-border banking. This is because the Single Market is crucial to ensuring Europe's economic recovery.

Resolution or bankruptcy proceedings for multinational financial institutions present special cooperation problems.[29] During the crisis, we saw the examples of

---

[29] IMF and World Bank, 'An Overview of the Legal, Institutional, and Regulatory Framework for Bank Insolvency', 17 April 2009, <http://www.imf.org/external/np/pp/eng/2009/041709.pdf> (visited 18 October 2010) (mentioning a forthcoming report on the issue); G20, Working Group

UK authorities 'ring-fencing' assets of Icelandic banks available in the UK, for the benefit of UK depositors, of German authorities ring-fencing Lehman Brothers' assets in Germany, and of Lehman Brothers' insolvency being addressed in both US and UK courts. Few bailouts, resolutions or bankruptcy proceedings were internationally coordinated, and there were often powerful political incentives to secure local assets in order to maximize returns to domestic claimants.

On the other hand, we saw the US bailout of AIG confer a remarkable positive externality on Europe, by virtue of the fact that it prevented many European banks from failing.

In resolution and bankruptcy proceedings, the classic tension between territoriality and universality will continue to play itself out, representing the tension between local public policy preferences and local claimants, on the one hand, versus cross-border fairness and comity on the other hand. This tension has been difficult to address in ordinary bankruptcy, and will raise similar issues in financial institution resolution. At the London Summit in April 2009, the G20 leaders welcomed action by the IMF, Financial Stability Board (FSB), World Bank and BCBS to develop an international framework for cross-border bank resolutions.

E. Securities disclosure regulation

Because issuers and underwriters located in one jurisdiction might be able to sell securities to investors located in another, there are significant issues of externalities and public goods in connection with securities law reform. For example, if the USA were to establish a disclosure rule requiring detailed information regarding loan-level data,[30] including analysis of the probability of default and the magnitude of default that would exceed the applicable credit support, financing costs for US issuers might be higher or lower. They might be higher if this information is not valued in the market, and the requirement provides only costs without benefits to the issuers. They might be lower to the extent that this information is valued in the market and the resolution of relevant uncertainty allows for cheaper financing.

If the financing costs are higher, but the social value of this disclosure is greater than the incremental costs, then the USA would be conferring a positive externality on foreign beneficiaries. On the other hand, another state that did not establish this type of regulation would be conferring a negative externality on foreign securities' purchasers. If the financing costs are lower, then it might be possible for US issuers to capture a sufficient amount of the benefits to compensate them for the increased costs of preparing the disclosure.

on Reinforcing International Cooperation and Promoting Integrity in Financial Markets (WG2), 'Final Report 19', 27 March 2009, <http://www.g20.org/Documents/g20_%20wg2_010409.pdf> (visited 16 July 2010); Bank for International Settlements, 'Basel Committee on Banking Supervision Cross-Border Bank Resolution Group', <http://www.bis.org/bcbs> (visited 16 July 2010).

[30] Committee on Capital Markets Regulation, 'The Global Financial Crisis: A Plan for Regulatory Reform', 26 May 2009, at E22–24 (recommending that issuers of mortgage-backed securities be required to provide loan-level data).

Economies of scale or network externalities might arise from a uniform standard worldwide, allowing investors to compare and evaluate securities without experiencing the costs of dealing with different disclosure regimes. The stability that might arise from better information might be a global collective good, and therefore might be under-supplied without a cooperative agreement to supply it in concert.

Future globalization, economic growth and financial innovation will all militate towards greater cooperation in securities disclosure regulation.

F. Rating agencies

Prior to the crisis, the conventional wisdom was that rating agencies would be adequately disciplined by market forces: after all, the only thing they had to sell was their reputation for integrity and diligence. For the rating agencies, it is difficult today to choose between being perceived as knaves or fools. During the boom in mortgage-backed securities, the rating agencies appear to have suffered from conflicts of interest, and perhaps competitive pressure, as well as a lack of financial foresight, that allowed them to rate these securities as investment-grade with insufficient regard for their dependence on prices in the housing market. But is there an international dimension to this problem? Regimes of registration, liability rules and limitations on conflicts of interest, may be somewhat useful. And here, one would expect that there would be a race to the top: any rating agency that can establish a good reputation should be able to sell its services, and it may be that appropriate government regulation would assist in the development of a good reputation. So it does not seem that international coordination is necessary.[31]

IV. Selecting Structural Features in International Law and Organization

The above analysis suggests a number of areas in which international law might be useful to establish cooperative solutions to regulatory problems. There are a number of parameters of choice in connection with the structuring of international law and organization. This section is intended to review some of the basic issues and describe some of the existing organizations that address the regulation of finance.[32]

---

[31] For an opposite view, see Committee of European Securities Regulators Press Release, 'CESR Advises the European Commission to Take Steps and Offers Its Proposals to Enhance the Integrity and Quality of the Rating Process', 19 May 2008, <http://www.cesr.eu/popup2.php?id%20=%205050> (visited 16 July 2010).
[32] For a useful extended analysis, see Eric J. Pan, 'Challenge of International Cooperation and Institutional Design in Financial Supervisions: Beyond Transnational Networks', Cardozo Working Paper No 300, April 2010.

A. Hard law, soft law and networks

There are many who believe that soft law is the best tool for international financial regulatory cooperation.[33] By 'soft law', many refer to rules that are specifically made non-binding in formal terms. However, soft law can only be appropriate where its net benefits after costs exceed those of hard law. We would expect this to be the case where soft law can be legislated with sufficient coverage, and where there are sufficient reputational or retaliatory tools available to generate a sufficient degree of compliance.

As to the question of the ability to generate a sufficient degree of compliance, we would have to assess the magnitude of possible incentives to defect in comparison to the magnitude of incentives to comply. There certainly may be circumstances where soft law would do the trick. Networks of regulators with diffuse reciprocity and temporally linked reciprocity may provide powerful incentives. But we would also expect to be able to identify circumstances where the incentives to defect are great enough to overcome the incentives to comply—for example, in circumstances where by doing so a state can ring-fence a sufficient portion of a failed financial institution's assets to be able to avoid a political disaster at home. It is likely that 'hard' or formal law would carry greater incentives to comply, placing the integrity of the legal system at stake. Furthermore, with formal law, it is more natural to be able to establish formal penalties, and of course the remedies under the customary international law rules of state responsibility would operate by default.

B. Specificity

The advantage of the EU technique of essential harmonization is that it seeks an optimum level of specificity that will allow appropriate national diversity while sufficiently addressing the relevant cooperation problem. The Basel Accord also left significant room for national diversity, and in some ways this may have diminished the utility of the Basel Accord as a tool of cooperation.

C. Surveillance

If states are serious about compliance, regardless of whether soft law or hard law is to be used, then it is necessary to have mechanisms by which to observe whether other states comply. Reporting requirements may be sufficient, or more involved mechanisms may be necessary. Much would depend on the relative incentives to defect. Furthermore, with greater penalties, less surveillance is necessary. Surveillance may be carried out directly by an international organization, it can be done by individual states acting on their own, or it can be effected through a process of peer review, as recently suggested by the FSB.[34]

---

[33] See Chris Brummer's contribution to this volume at Chapter 5, as well as his broader work.

[34] FSB, 'FSB Framework for Strengthening Adherence to International Standards', 9 January 2010, <http://www.financialstabilityboard.org/publications/r_100109a.pdf> (visited 16 July 2010).

D. International dispute settlement

Experience in certain other areas where states can externalize costs to other states, such as the regulation of trade and foreign investment, shows that dispute settlement can be necessary to clarify what are necessarily incomplete international law obligations, and to establish the predicate for, and limit the scope of, retaliation. So, if German banks examine the way that Japan applies international capital requirements or powers regulation, or the way it distributes assets in a resolution, and finds a violation of international legal obligations, it would seem appropriate to give the German government, or the European Commission, a formal forum for complaint and dispute settlement.

E. Adaptation to change

In order to avoid holding a Maginot Line, and allowing the causes of future crises to evade regulation, it will be necessary to continue to be vigilant regarding growing risks, as well as having the adaptability to address them. Thus, international law or organization in this area must have the capacity to observe, analyse and adapt as necessary. Normal methods of making international law by custom or treaty are likely to be too slow, and too politically charged, to be feasible. Rather, some degree of delegation to a regulatory agency appears necessary, combined with the resources and tools to promote effective action.

F. Economies of scale and scope

There may be important benefits that can be obtained by sharing regulatory capacity among states in particular areas. For example, smaller countries may benefit from economies of scale by sharing regulatory capacity among themselves, or with larger countries. Insofar as financial services operations are increasingly global, while the default structure of regulation is national, modifications to regulation to make it more international may yield important benefits. One significant benefit is in the ability to engage in coordinated international surveillance and audit, in order to identify accounting irregularities, other violations of rules, or defalcation.

There may be important economies of scope that can be obtained from combining different financial services regulatory functions. Not only would this allow more coordinated regulation of financial conglomerates, but it would also make it easier to identify perimeter problems and leakage. Furthermore, to the extent that identification of fragmentation shows relationships and synergies between prudential regulation of financial services and macroeconomic regulation, development policy, investment regulation or trade, it may be possible to capture further economies of scope.

G. Organizations

Once states determine which types of commitments for cooperation would be appropriate, they will be able to determine which organizational features are appropriate to support those commitments. They will be able to determine whether to 'house' the commitments within an existing international organization, whether to establish a new organization, or, alternatively, to split responsibilities among different international organizations.

There are a number of international organizations with responsibilities relating to prudential regulation of finance. It is worthwhile to consider the existing responsibilities of these organizations, as well as their capacities and competences, in connection with an assessment of the possibilities for international cooperation with respect to prudential regulation.

V. Conclusions

It will take some time for economic historians to sort out the causes of the recent crisis. Yet, some major themes of possible national reform are emerging. States must review carefully the scope of their commitment to bail out financial institutions. They must make firm commitments not to bail out certain financial institutions. Those financial institutions that benefit from the safety net must be firmly regulated as to corporate governance, capital, and powers. Corporate governance must be structured to ensure that managers manage in the best interests of the firm, including its strict compliance with regulatory requirements. Capital requirements must be restructured to minimize their pro-cyclical effects in downturns. Securities offerings of complex financial products must be accompanied by reasonably accessible disclosure that addresses risks with specific analysis, and not simply boilerplate warnings. Similarly, rating agencies must incorporate specific risk analysis into their ratings.

Because of the existing extent of globalization, and because of future increases in globalization, financial innovation, information technology and growth, these reforms will require greater international coordination. The international coordination is necessitated by increasing capacity to externalize risk, as well as increasing scope of financial global public goods.

We have an increasingly global society. This society must recognize the role of government regulation in providing and protecting efficient capital markets that will allow us, individually and together, to save and invest efficiently for important projects. There is no evidence yet of a beneficial regulatory competition in the case of the crisis. Shareholders and creditors do not seem systematically to have identified regulatory inadequacies, and migrated to stronger regulatory environments. So, competition-based discipline on lax regulation seems not to have worked. Further research will be needed in order to determine whether just the opposite occurred: a race to inappropriate laxity. In order for each state to make its citizens better off, and to reduce risk, we must work together to avoid cross-border harm that is not fully taken into account in national decision-making, and to avoid detrimental regulatory competition. We must work together to make rules, but we must recognize that our vision of the future is limited, and so we must establish institutions that will allow us to revise our rules, and our institutions, as necessitated by unfolding change.

11

Addressing Government Failure through International Financial Law

Steve Charnovitz

In the course of years—in the course of a century—economic lines, drawn ever tighter, have been tied among the peoples. National economies have become more and more independent. Beside and above them, or, to put it better, among them, a world economy has been formed. And the common problem in which are united these various problems may be stated in these terms: give to world economy its fundamental law (ILO, 1923).[1]

I. Introduction

As the International Labour Organization (ILO) observed in 1923, a world economy needs appropriate law. Recognition of the importance of economic law harks back to antiquity,[2] and yet each era strives to establish and nurture the optimal norms and institutions required for contemporary and anticipated future problems. As the visionary economist Eugene Staley once explained: 'Economic problems can never be "solved" once and for all. The very essence of economic problems is change, readjustment to new conditions'.[3]

The world financial crisis that began in 2007 has revived the attention of policymakers and citizenry as to the need for more effective public and private governance of financial markets. In 2009, world output fell by 0.6 per cent and world trade fell by 10.7 per cent.[4] Since the financial crisis began, the number of unemployed people in the world has risen by about 34 million.[5]

---

[1] Wallace McClure, *World Prosperity as Sought Through the Economic Work of the League of Nations* (New York: The Macmillan Company, 1933), 279, note 38, translating ILO, Enquête sur la Production, Rapport général, Tome V, Deuxiè me volume (Geneva: ILO, 1923) 1592.

[2] See generally Benn Steil and Manuel Hinds, *Money, Markets and Sovereignty* (New Haven: Yale University Press, 2009) Ch 2.

[3] Eugene Staley, *World Economy in Transition* (New York: Council on Foreign Relations, 1939) 300.

[4] International Monetary Fund, 'World Economic Outlook', April 2010, 155, 170.

[5] ILO, 'Global Employment Trends', January 2010, 47.

The governmental response to the financial crisis has occurred at all levels, from the local to the global. In considering how to improve such policy responses, analysts should proceed from a perspective that distinguishes the national from the international and market failures from government failures. Below is a brief overview of the relevant policy matrix.

At the national level, governments respond to market failure, such as pollution, using instruments of regulation, tax, and subsidy. These interventions are complemented by private standard-setting mechanisms that improve information and seek efficiencies. As yet, no one has invented a cure for the business cycle, and governments use fiscal and monetary policy to boost weak economies.

The problems of government failure are more inchoate. Inefficient and counterproductive regulation, subsidies to politically favoured special interests, and wasteful government spending are corrected on an ad hoc basis through elections, so-called reform legislation, and public law litigation. To some extent, the market can also be a corrective as jurisdictions compete for investment and governmental reputation.

At the international level, the problems of market and government failure become more acute, and as John H. Jackson has noted, 'the kinds of government responses possible at the nation-state level differ dramatically from those at the international level'.[6] The world 'ecolonomy' encompasses all of the problems within each country, but then is also challenged by conflicting sovereign regulation of transborder problems and by governmental policies that seek to externalize costs onto other countries. The classic examples of the latter are beggar-thy-neighbour trade policies, currency depreciation, and expropriation of foreign assets. The provision of global public goods, such as public health, is also a major challenge in governance beyond the nation-state.

Governance of transborder market failure has historically been weak, but has been strengthened in recent decades by the Organisation for Economic Co-operation and Development (OECD), the International Competition Network, the Basel Committee on Banking Supervision, the International Organization of Securities Commissions, and the Financial Stability Board. In contrast to the thick international lawmaking for dealing with the effects of market failure on the environment, there is little hard law in the financial arena.[7] As Thomas Cottier has noted: 'It seems paradoxical that financial services are among the most regulated businesses in domestic law, but that no rules of such significance exist on the global level for the most advanced global players'.[8]

The market failure of inadequate capital for investment (particularly public investment and adequate liquidity) is addressed through the regular lending programmes of the International Monetary Fund (IMF) and the World Bank.

---

[6] John H. Jackson, *Sovereignty, the WTO, and Changing Fundamentals of International Law* (Cambridge: Cambridge University Press, 2006) 221.

[7] See Brummer, Chapter 5 in this volume.

[8] Thomas Cottier, 'Challenges Ahead in International Economic Law', 12 *Journal of International Economic Law* 3 (2009), at 7–8.

When a sovereign debt crisis occurs, which has happened recently in Greece, the international lending that ensues is more precisely termed a response to government failure than to market failure. A classic government failure occurs when a government overspends to propitiate special interests, runs up high deficits, and mismanages the domestic economy so badly that the only way for the government to dig itself out of debt is via induced inflation, currency depreciation, and financial default.

The oversight of transborder government failure exists in some areas but not others. The earliest international law of that sort was the ILO Constitution, enacted in 1919, which is premised on the view that 'the failure of any nation to adopt humane conditions of labour is an obstacle in the way of other nations which desire to improve the conditions in their own countries'.[9] The IMF, established in 1944, has as one of its purposes 'to promote exchange stability, to maintain orderly exchange arrangements among members, and to avoid competitive exchange depreciation'.[10] The IMF influences governments through rules and through conditional loan agreements.[11] Much more so than the World Trade Organization (WTO), the IMF has a strong bureaucrat-driven economic surveillance capacity. Recently, the IMF has sought more harmonization of financial regulation.[12]

The WTO and the preceding General Agreement on Tariffs and Trade (GATT) have been successful in managing the transborder government failure of protectionism. For public choice reasons, governments are prone to protecting a domestic economy from foreign competition either directly through tariffs or quotas or indirectly through nontariff barriers and subsidies. WTO law hardly eliminates these practices, but it does make governmental measures more transparent and outlaws (or limits) the most egregious practices, such as export subsidies.

The international economic order does not contain an institution, analogous to the ILO, the IMF, or the WTO, to supervise and prevent government failures that lead to transborder financial problems. This lacuna has been filled over the past 11 years by the G20, which has had some success in addressing market failure but less in addressing government failure. The role of the G20 continues to be amorphous. WTO Director-General Pascal Lamy has explained that the G20 is 'an embryo of consensus building' but that the G20 itself 'does not decide', leaving the making of 'internationally binding decisions' to member-driven international agencies.[13] Given the state of play, the purpose of this chapter is to propose improvements in international economic law and its institutions so as to prevent a repeat financial crisis in the USA and around the world.

---

[9] Constitution of the ILO, Preamble.
[10] IMF Articles of Agreement, Article 1.
[11] See Baltensberger and Cottier, Chapter 20 in this volume.
[12] Marcus Walker and Stephen Fidler, 'IMF Chief Urges Coordinated Finance Rules', *Wall Street Journal*, 30–31 January 2010, A11.
[13] Speech of Director-General Lamy, 'The Global Trading System and the World Economy', Seoul, 7 December 2009, <http://www.wto.org/english/news_e/sppl_e/sppl144_e.htm> (visited 12 September 2010).

The remainder of the chapter has four parts: Part II examines the causes of the recent crisis; Part III proposes substantive policy changes to enhance recovery; Part IV examines the role and techniques of international institutions; Part V concludes.

II. Causes of the Crisis

The conventional narrative is that the US financial crisis was caused by excessive and risky speculation on Wall Street, greedy bankers, industry capture of the regulation on derivatives and swaps, and abuses in the mortgage markets whereby banks took advantage of innocent homeowners. Although all of that may have occurred to some extent, that narrative is incomplete at best because it suggests that the cause of the crisis originated in an unregulated market. That view is naïve because it confuses symptoms with causes and misses the role of government in causing and exacerbating the crisis. In my view, the financial meltdown was at least as much a product of government failure as it was of market failure.[14] One of the core government failures was the breakdown in the long-time regulatory and supervisory distinctions between investment and depositary banking.[15]

The US crisis started with large asset bubbles fed by lax monetary policy[16] and ill-advised government subsidies in the housing sector. The proximate cause of the crisis may have been the declining value of mortgage bonds and collateralized debt obligations (the misnamed 'toxic assets'), but the real cause was the government policy of buying mortgages through the off-budget entities Fannie Mae and Freddie Mac and hence guaranteeing payment. No wise government would guarantee that home investors would repay a mortgage without some method of collecting from derelict homeowners.[17]

Nonetheless, the US government did so, and compounded the error by making it easier for home investors to walk away without any tax consequences and by discouraging banks from foreclosing in a timely fashion. For years, risk watchers had pointed out the dangers as Fannie and Freddie grew bigger, but US politicians refused to take serious measures to rationalize housing lending.[18] Indeed, Senate Banking Committee[19] Chairman, Christopher Dodd, took part in a preferential deal on mortgage refinancing from Countrywide, one of the banks that collapsed

---

[14] See Allan H. Meltzer, 'Market Failure or Government Failure?', *Wall Street Journal*, 19 March 2010, A19.

[15] Cynthia Crawford Lichtenstein, 'Lessons for the 21st Century Central Bankers: Differences between Investment and Depositary Banking', in Mario Giovanoli and Diego Devos (eds), *International Monetary and Financial Law: The Global Crisis* (Oxford: Oxford University Press, 2010) 217–33s.

[16] See Hufbauer and Xie, Chapter 21 in this volume.

[17] See Nick Timiraos, 'Why Hasn't Canada's Housing Market Blown Up?', *Wall Street Journal*, 7 December 2009.

[18] Robert G. Wilmers, 'What About Fan and Fred Reform?', *Wall Street Journal*, 4 May 2010.

[19] US Senate Committee on Banking, Housing, and Urban Affairs.

during the crisis.[20] Even worse, Congressman Barney Frank famously opined that he wanted to 'roll the dice a little bit more' in the interest of expanding federal subsidies for homeowners.[21] Ironically, such subsidies do not help and may even hurt the 33 per cent of American families who are not homeowners, often because they cannot afford to be. The federal government bailout of Fannie and Freddie has now cost the federal government over $145 billion in direct aid, and many tens of billions more have been given in direct and indirect aid to homeowners whose mortgages are under water. Unfortunately, the ironically named Dodd–Frank Wall Street Reform and Consumer Protection Act of 2010[22] contains no reforms of the mess at Fannie and Freddie.[23]

The 'too big to fail' commitment to large investment banks and insurance companies by the Federal Reserve and the US Treasury led to massive loans which undermined confidence in the US economy. Although Warren Buffett's loan to Goldman Sachs in September 2008 provided a template for how the US government could make a smart loan to a bank that needed liquidity, the US Treasury acted to demand that large banks take 'cheap capital' government loans even when they did not request it,[24] and then later by using the loans to justify heavy-handed regulation of investment strategies and vilification of Wall Street investment and compensation practices.[25] In my view, allowing the investment bank Bear Stearns to fail would have sent the right signal to Wall Street. The same is true for AIG, which received credit infusions of about $182 billion from the Treasury and the Federal Reserve.

After the Congressional conference committee completed negotiations on the Dodd–Frank bill in June 2010, President Barack Obama extolled the then-pending legislation saying: 'The reforms making their way through Congress will hold Wall Street accountable so we can help prevent another financial crisis like the one that we're still recovering from'.[26] Yet it is hard to see how this legislation, had it been in effect four years ago, would have made much difference. The central regulatory thrust of Dodd–Frank is to establish a Financial Stability Oversight Council (Council) composed of 10 voting members, nine from the federal government and one independent expert with insurance expertise. The Council also has five non-voting members including two federal officials and three state government officials. The statutory purpose of the Council is to 'identify risks to the

[20] 'Dodd and Countrywide', *Wall Street Journal*, 10 October 2008, <http://online.wsj.com/article/SB122360116724221681.html> (visited 26 June 2010).

[21] 'What They Said About Fred and Fan', *Wall Street Journal*, 2 October 2008, <http://online.wsj.com/article/SB122290574391296381.html> (visited 26 June 2010).

[22] H.R. 4173, Public L. 111–203, <http://financialservices.house.gov/Key_Issues/Financial_Regulatory_Reform/Final_conference_titles/T1_FINAL.pdf> (visited 26 June 2010).

[23] John B. Taylor, 'The Dodd-Frank Financial Fiasco', *Wall Street Journal*, 1 July 2010, A19.

[24] Henry M. Paulson, Jr, *On the Brink: Inside the Race to Stop the Collapse of the Global Financial System* (New York: Business Plus, 2010) 364–6.

[25] James R. Hagerty and Ruth Simon, 'For Financial Engineers, A New Risk: Washington', *Wall Street Journal*, 2 February 2010, C1; Michael R. Crittenden, 'Treasury Makes Banks Pay a TARP Premium', *Wall Street Journal*, 20 January 2010, C3.

[26] Remarks by the President on Wall Street Reform, 25 June 2010, <http://www.whitehouse.gov/the-press-office/remarks-president-wall-street-reform-1> (visited 26 June 2010).

financial stability of the United States that could arise from the material distress or failure . . . of large, interconnected bank holding companies . . .',[27] to respond to such emerging threats with regulation, and 'to promote market discipline, by eliminating expectations on the part of shareholders, creditors, and counterparties of such companies that the Government will shield them for losses in the event of failure'.[28] The Council is exempt from the normal transparency requirements in the Federal Advisory Committee Act.[29]

Identifying unanticipated risk is hard and there is no reason to think that the same busy federal officials, who apparently overlooked these risks in 2006 and 2007, will become more prescient simply because they serve together on an elite Council. The presence of the one independent expert is helpful, but there was no lack of experts in the late 2000s who warned of an impending financial collapse. There were also some savvy investors and economists who anticipated the collapse,[30] but the financial regulators and the US intelligence community apparently took no notice of that.

The inescapable conclusion is that a Council dominated by government bureaucrats is unlikely to be able to predict and manage systemic risk. This is particularly so when the mandate of the Council does not include oversight of the government-induced sources of risky behaviour such as huge, uncontrolled budget deficits, lax monetary policy, and corrupt relationships between federal legislators and banks.[31] The omission from the Council of foreign regulators, academic economists, and consumer watchdog groups and other independent voices suggests that risk regulation in the US government will not be fundamentally different after the new law than it was before. Indeed, the chair of the new Council is the Secretary of the Treasury who presumably already has a full-time job.

The new US model of risk management by wise guardians is misguided. The best way to avoid risks to US financial stability is to use markets to identify the risk and put prices and values on it. Indeed, that was the beauty of the over-vilified and now-to-be heavily regulated credit default swaps because they showed in hard numbers how the market was valuing distressed debt. The same is true of short selling which helps to purify prices in an uncertain market. The notion embedded in the legislation that this new Council can 'promote market discipline' is risible because, in fact, only markets can establish market discipline.[32] If there was an expectation by shareholders, creditors, and counterparties that the federal

---

[27] Title I, Section 112(A) of the Dodd–Frank Act.

[28] Title I, Section 112(B) of the Dodd–Frank Act.

[29] 5 U.S.C. Appendix, Public L. 92–463, Aproved 6 October 1972 (86 Stat. 770).

[30] See Lastra and Wood, Chapter 1 in this volume.

[31] Earle B. Hammond Jr, 'Risk? Let Congress Look in a Mirror', *Wall Street Journal*, 9 December 2009, A26.

[32] See Robert E. Litan, 'Economics: Global Finance', in P.J. Simmons and Chantal de Jonge Oudraat (eds), *Managing Global Issues: Lessons Learned* (Washington: Carnegie Endowment, 2001) 196–233 at 226 ('Hence one challenge that should be uppermost in the minds of financial policy makers is to find ways of harnessing the forces of the market to help ensure the stability of the financial system. . . . I believe that a superior approach to incorporating the views of the market into capital standards would rely explicitly on the judgments of the market itself').

government would bail them out, that expectation was justified because many of them did get bailed out, as did the debtors. Those bailouts were wrong, but future expectations will not be changed by government officials giving minatory speeches.

It was not expectations that caused the bailouts; the bailouts were caused by the government officials who chose to gratify those expectations. The way to avoid future bailouts is to repeal government power to use tax dollars or borrowing to provide more bailouts. Moreover, the time has come to end the federal subsidy programmes that have created an entitlement mentality among the American people.[33] For example, the Dodd–Frank Act provides a *retroactive* increase in bank deposit insurance to socialize the losses for individuals with large sums of money in banks that failed.

The low point of the financial crisis came in mid-September 2008 when financial markets appeared 'frozen' and close observers thought that 'the wheels were coming off the financial system'.[34] At that moment, emergency actions were needed to provide liquidity, and such actions were taken. As Anatole Kaletsky has explained: 'There are times, perhaps once in every generation, when the financial oscillations of greed and fear get out of control. At times like this, a political force from outside the market economy must intervene to moderate the financial cycle'.[35] Several years on and the US economy has remained weak with economic growth falling throughout 2010 to just 0.4 per cent in the first quarter of 2011 and showing only modest signs of recovery in the following three quarters.[36] This suggests that the US government has been more adept in managing the worst of the crisis than in devising policies to generate new economic growth.

III. Enhancing Economic Recovery and Resiliency

In thinking about how to respond to the financial crisis, there are two distinct policy responses that need to be fine tuned. One is to put in place preventive and cleanup measures. The other is to make the economy stronger and more resilient so that it can recover from the effects of a credit crunch and recession. Specific suggestions for the USA are made in Section III.

A. Boost competitiveness

Since the crisis unemployment has remained stubbornly high, output has been weak, and budget discipline nearly non-existent. As the US Competitiveness Policy Council explained in its first annual report, the components of a national competitiveness strategy (for any country) are attention to: saving and investment,

---

[33] See Peter G. Peterson, *Running on Empty* (New York: Farrar, Straus, and Giroux, 2004); Peter Eavis, 'No End to U.S. Housing Handouts', *Wall Street Journal*, 24 March 2010, C16.

[34] See Paulson, above n 24, at 243.

[35] Anatole Kaletsky, 'The Benefits of the Bust', *Wall Street Journal*, 19–20 June 2010, W3.

[36] 'Gross Domestic Product: Fourth Quarter and Annual 2011 (Second Estimate)', <http://www.bea.gov/newsreleases/national/gdp/2012/pdf/gdp4q11_2nd.pdf> (visited 6 March 2012)

education, worker training, critical technologies, corporate governance, trade, public infrastructure, and manufacturing.[37] Unfortunately, this recipe for economic growth is not being followed in Washington. Space does not permit a full examination of the economic policies of the Obama Administration, but two areas (manufacturing and trade) will be briefly discussed below.

Instead of policies that promote manufacturing in general, the Bush and Obama Administrations settled on a strategy of bailing out GM, GMAC, and Chrysler with over $50 billion in direct aid supplemented by millions of dollars in indirect aid through the 'Cash for Clunkers'[38] program. 'Cash for Clunkers' soon became the leitmotif for a panoply of new, highly leveraged federal spending by the Obama Administration as money was channelled to pork-barrel projects that were too wasteful for local governments to fund themselves, a new alphabet of homeowner subsidies, and dubious job creation initiatives. The huge aid to the US automobile industry was especially troubling given that it undermined the long-held US policy stance that governments should not subsidize domestic automobile industries. The USA had participated in cases in the WTO against small automobile subsidies by Canada, Indonesia, and Australia. Yet now, the USA was signalling to the rest of the world that the US opposition to automobile subsidies had been opportunistic rather than principled.

Weak US trade policy is another factor exacerbating a lingering pain since the Great Contraction. Despite the welcome signing of three long-delayed free trade agreements by President Obama in late 2011[39] there seems to have been no serious efforts to complete the Doha Development Round or to launch any new trade negotiations, suggesting that the Obama Administration treats trade as a third rail of economic policy. Rather than a positive trade agenda of market opening, the Administration argues that the top priority should be enforcing trade agreements. Yet when the time comes for the USA to comply in the *US—Zeroing*[40] cases and in the *US—Upland Cotton*[41] cases, respect for the rule of law disappears in the White House.[42]

---

[37] U.S. Competitiveness Policy Council, *Building a Competitive America* (March 1992).

[38] Car Allowance Rebate System program, <http://www.cars.gov> (visited 27 September 2010).

[39] 'Statement by U.S. Trade Representative Ron Kirk on Presidential Signature of Trade Legislation', October 2011, <http://www.ustr.gov/about-us/press-office/press-releases/2011/october/statement-us-trade-representative-ron-kirk-preside> (visited on 6 March 2012)

[40] WTO Appellate Body Report, *United States—Measures Relating to Zeroing and Sunset Reviews—* Recourse to Article 21.5 of the DSU by Japan, WT/DS322/AB/RW, adopted 31 August 2009; WTO Appellate Body Report, *United States—Laws, Regulations and Methodology for Calculating Dumping Margins* ('"Zeroing"')—Recourse to Article 21.5 of the DSU by the European Communities, WT/DS294/AB/RW, 11 June 2009.

[41] Decision by the Arbitrator, United States Subsidies on Upland Cotton—Recourse to Arbitration by the United States under Article 22.6 of the DSU and Article 4.11 of the SCM Agreement, WTO Doc WT/DS267/ARB1, 09-4009; Decision by the Arbitrator, United States—Subsidies on Upland Cotton—Recourse to Arbitration by the United States under Article 22.6 of the DSU and Article 7.10 of the SCM Agreement, WTO Doc WT/DS267/ARB2, 09-4015, 31 August 2009.

[42] 'World Tariff Wars: U.S. Protectionism is Hurting American Exports', *Wall Street Journal*, 9 April 2010, A18.

B. Revive trade liberalization

Completing the Doha Agenda would give a boost to the world economy and enhance the recovery from the financial crisis. As WTO Director-General Pascal Lamy has explained, the Doha Round can 'deliver a very welcome stimulus package to the world economy... [o]ne that does not have to be financed out of national treasuries'.[43] Unfortunately, US Trade Representative Ron Kirk has not skillfully engaged in unblocking the current impasse at the WTO.

One possible approach would be to transform the Doha Agenda into a true development round,[44] and have the advanced economies swear off any expectation of obtaining liberalization among themselves. Instead they could join together in offering significant concessions to help low-income countries. In my view, it would be easier to ratify a trade negotiation in the USA that delivers little to US exporters because it is not intended to do so, than to ratify a trade negotiation that is advertised as helping US exporters when in fact it would not.

C. Eradicate domestic content subsidies

Although it has been many years since the USA was truly able to lead the world on trade, the Buy American policies championed by the Obama Administration and Congress have seriously undermined the reputation of the USA. While it is true that the USA is hardly the only country that has championed economic nationalism since the financial crisis,[45] the fact that the USA was willing to do something so blatantly protectionist without evincing much embarrassment showed the world how little other countries could depend on the USA for leadership at a time of economic crisis. The American Recovery and Reinvestment Act[46] of 2009 was unprecedented in size ($787 billion) and scope of subsidy ambition. The Act's Buy American provision prohibits state and local governments from using newly provided federal aid for a public works project unless all of the iron, steel, and other manufactured goods used are produced in the USA.[47]

Much of the literature on this provision assumes that it is WTO-legal,[48] but that hypothesis is questionable when one looks closely at the WTO law of subsidies, in

---

[43] Speech of Director-General Lamy, 'Drivers of Sustainable Growth', G-20 Business Summit, Toronto, 26 June 2010, <http://www.wto.org/english/news_e/sppl_e/sppl160_e.htm> (visited 17 September 2010).

[44] See Faizel Ismail, *Reforming the World Trade Organization: Developing Countries in the Doha Round* (Jaipur: CUTS, 2009) 120–1, 154.

[45] A recent study by Global Trade Alert lists the buy-national provision in the US stimulus package as being the second largest of 22 jumbo protectionist measures enacted since November 2008. Simon J. Evenett and Johannes Fritz, '"Jumbo" Discriminatory Measures and the Trade Coverage of Crisis-Era Protectionism', in Evenett (ed) *Global Trade Alert, Unequal Compliance: The 6th GTA Report*, <http://www.globaltradealert.org/sites/default/files/GTA6.pdf> (visited 27 June 2010) 49–58 at 55.

[46] Public L. 115–5, approved 17 February 2009.

[47] Section 1605, <http://frwebgate.access.gpo.gov/cgi-bin/getdoc.cgi?dbname=111_cong_bills&do%20cid=f:h1enr.pdf> (visited 27 June 2010).

[48] For example, see Jagdish Bhagwati, 'Defending an Open World Economy', in Terry L. Anderson and Richard Sousa (eds), *Reacting to the Spending Spree: Policy Changes We Can Afford* (Stanford: Hoover Institution Press, 2009) 139–47, at 141–4.

particular Articles 1 and 3 of the Agreement on Subsidies and Countervailing Measures (SCM Agreement). The key question is whether a grant from the US federal government to subnational governments qualifies as a 'subsidy'. If it is a subsidy under the SCM Agreement, then this measure would seem to be a violation of SCM Article 3.1(b) because it would be a subsidy contingent upon domestic content.

The SCM Agreement does not clearly indicate whether a financial contribution from one WTO Member to another or a subsidy from one level of government to another is covered by the definition of subsidy in SCM Article 1. Obviously, there is a benefit to the recipient,[49] since a subnational government gets a direct transfer of funds. Consequently, the only definitional question is whether grants that go to individuals or to other governments, rather than to enterprises, are covered. In my view, US federal aid to states is not excluded from being a 'financial contribution' under the SCM Agreement and is distinguishable from funding movements that occur between agencies of the federal government. When the federal government gives budget aid to a state contingent on the use of domestic over imported goods, the goal of the federal government is to exert influence not only on how the federal dollars are spent but also on how the matching state dollars are spent. By using the lure of federal dollars, the Obama Administration was able to pressure states into not purchasing foreign-made goods even when states would have preferred a more cost-effective approach to building public works.[50] To argue that no prohibited subsidy has occurred because the recipient is a government agency rather than an enterprise would be to confound both the purpose and the letter of the SCM Agreement.

D. Avoid demagoguery

Finally, let me note one other dangerous aspect of the US President's economic policies, which is the constant anti-business rhetoric from the White House. By fomenting public hatred of business, the government makes it harder for banks and businesses to engage in new investment and job creation. While there was certainly considerable unprincipled behavior by some banking executives who were at the centre of the financial crisis, I have seen no evidence that the private sector acted more irresponsibly than the public sector. In that regard, one can recall how during the Great Depression, John Maynard Keynes chided President Franklin D. Roosevelt for his criticism of businessmen with the sage advice that 'it is a mistake to think they are more immoral than politicians'.[51]

---

[49] See Joseph Francois, 'Subsidies and Countervailing Measures: Determining the Benefit of Subsidies', in Kyle W. Bagwell, George A. Bermann and Petros C. Mavroidis (eds), *Law and Economics of Contingent Protection in International Trade* (Cambridge: Cambridge University Press, 2010) 103–15.
[50] Jay L. Eizenstat, ' "Buy America": A Regrettable Step Toward Protectionism', *BNA International Trade Reporter*, 9 July 2009, 938.
[51] John Maynard Keynes, Letter to Franklin D. Roosevelt, 1 February 1938. As quoted in Amity Shlaes, 'How to Make a Weak Economy Worse', *Wall Street Journal*, 2 February 2010, A19.

IV. Improving International Institutions in Financial Regulation

The success of the world trading system in knocking down trade barriers and in providing a robust system of enforcement has led some analysts to consider whether the WTO could take on a greater role in financial regulation. This section considers that option and also examines the role of other international institutions toward correcting what went wrong during the financial crisis. A comparative institutional perspective will be used to make organizational design proposals by first examining the WTO, then the G8 and G20, and then the ILO model.

A. The role of the WTO

Pascal Lamy has opined that:

> The primary vocation of the WTO is to regulate, not to deregulate trade as is often thought. By putting in place rules to regulate trade flows and remove trade distortions, the WTO aims to create a global level playing field, where fairness is the rule and where the rights of individual members are safeguarded.[52]

These are weighty thoughts that deserve unpacking and response.

Because the WTO is aimed at the problem of government failure not market failure,[53] the WTO has no general role in creating a global level playing field in the regulation of labor markets, antitrust, financial markets,[54] and environmental protection. Nor does the WTO have a role in regulating trade flows of oil, endangered species, conflict diamonds, armaments, or many other commodities in which there is substantive international law. The only level playing field at issue in the WTO is the use of measures that distort trade such as subsidies, tariffs, and nontariff barriers.

While the WTO has some authority to promote a level playing field through regulation and harmonization,[55] little of that nature has been accomplished. The

---

[52] Speech of Director-General Lamy, 'Toward Shared Responsibility and Greater Coherence: Human Rights, Trade and Macroeconomic Policy', Geneva, 13 January 2010, <http://www.wto.org/english/news_e/sppl_e/sppl146_e.htm> (visited 17 September 2010). In an earlier speech, Lamy had declared: 'The WTO encourages, and will continue to encourage, its members to abide by international norms'. Speech of Director-General Lamy, 'Global Problems, Global Solutions: Towards Better Global Governance', WTO Public Forum, Geneva, 28 September 2009, <http://www.wto.org/english/news_e/sppl_e/sppl136_e.htm> (visited 17 September 2010).

[53] It is sometimes suggested that the Agreement on Trade-Related Aspects of Intellectual Property Rights (TRIPS) is an exceptional WTO agreement in addressing market failure because it mandates that governments protect intellectual property (IP) rights. Although TRIPS does not require that a government give IP rights to its nationals (see TRIPS Agreement, Article 1.1), TRIPS does require the provision of IP rights to foreign nationals. One can look at this as a response to transborder market failure or as a response to a government failure of economic nationalism.

[54] See Cottier and Krajewski, Chapter 15 in this volume, for a discussion of the deregulatory approach of General Agreement on Trade in Services (GATS).

[55] For example, see GATS, Article VI; General Agreement on Tariffs and Trade (GATT), Articles XVIII, XXVIII bis (3), XXXVI:1(e), XXXVII:3, XXXVIII:2; Agreement on Technical Barriers to Trade (TBT Agreement), Articles 2.4, 12.6.

WTO rules on accountancy[56] are sometimes given as an example of how the WTO can legislate on financial services. An examination of these rules shows that they do not contain any international requirements for licensing accountants with regard to minimum qualifications, but they do repeat the admonitions in the General Agreement on Trade in Services (GATS) regarding the creation of unnecessary barriers to trade. It is interesting to note that the GATS Council has not enacted similar legislation for other services. And even with all the mistakes that US regulators admit that they made in the US financial crisis, no one has argued that the insufficient US regulation constituted a violation of the GATS Annex on Financial Services.

In my view, seeking to assign the WTO the role of the super-regulator in financial services would be a mistake for many reasons. To start with, the WTO already has a critical role in promoting economic growth and sustainability. If the WTO were doing that more effectively, the world economy could be recovering more quickly from the financial crisis. Moreover, the pathologies of WTO decision-making, which have prevented the WTO from completing new agreements, would also prevent the WTO from acting to require better financial regulation.

The attractiveness of the WTO is that it contains hard law and accountability mechanisms for governments including the possibility of trade sanctions against a scofflaw. But this model cannot be used in other fields unless there is a similar agreement on what the hard law should be. In the field of trade, the hard law needed is to head off government failure. In the field of financial markets, the hard law needed is to address both government failure and market failure. Although there has been progress in the past few years (outside the WTO) in getting government agreement towards harmonizing financial regulation to address market failure, there has been little progress towards addressing government failure because major governments, like that of the USA, are not willing to give up their powers to borrow, subsidize, and redistribute income to favoured interests. Governments are also not willing to take responsibility for how their fiscal and regulatory practices affect other countries and to compensate other countries for the harm caused by transboundary financial pollution. So at present, hard law international solutions can only be pursued on limited facets of the problems that led to the financial crisis.

In contrast to using the WTO itself, it would be possible to borrow some of its techniques and employ them in other regimes. For example, the WTO's Trade Policy Review Mechanism (TPRM) could be adapted more broadly to deal with issues beyond trade. Already, climate change negotiators have been looking to replicate some aspects of the TPRM model. The current model features a report by the WTO Secretariat, a report and presentation by the government being reviewed, a commentary from a discussant, and then a discussion by WTO Members on the report followed by a response from the government being reviewed. Since the TPRM is not connected to the WTO dispute process, the government being reviewed does not have to defend whether it is complying with

---

[56] Disciplines on Domestic Regulation in the Accountancy Sector, S/L/64, 14 December 1998.

WTO law. Also, the topics to be discussed can go outside WTO rules. The benefit of this model is that each government's policy is reviewed individually based on analyses that have been prepared beforehand, and then documentation of this review is posted on the WTO website. The disadvantage of this model is that there is no opportunity for business or civil society to participate in the TPRM reviews. Grafting the TPRM model on to financial regulation would provide an opportunity for the review of the practices of key governments on a regular basis. No doubt, governments can ask each other questions in bilateral meetings, but on matters of interest to the world community, it would be better to have an organized process in place than to rely on normal diplomacy.

B. The G8 and G20

The G8 Summit of June 2010 produced the Muskoka Declaration: Recovery and New Beginnings.[57] The Declaration begins by noting that the annual summit 'takes place as the world begins a fragile recovery from the greatest economic crisis in generations',[58] but then curiously veers away from any substantive statement about the crisis in the remainder of the Declaration. Instead, the first issue treated in the Declaration is 'maternal health' and the G8 leaders report that progress in improving it has been 'unacceptably slow'.[59] Curiously, the Declaration does not explain exactly why maternal health is an international issue and certainly does not explain why it should be the top issue in the 2010 Declaration. International trade appears in one paragraph on page 6 of the Declaration wherein the Leaders pledge to 'continue to resist protectionist pressures, and to promote liberalization of trade and investment under the WTO, through the national reduction of barriers, as well as through bilateral and regional negotiations'.[60] Free traders may be cheered, but it is unfortunate that G8 leaders did not explain how they could 'continue to' resist protectionist pressures when a major Report prepared for the Summits in Ontario found that 13 of 22 jumbo protectionist measures put in place since 2008 had been enacted by G8 countries.[61]

By contrast, the G20 (which includes all G8 Members) did promulgate a Declaration over the same weekend that does address the recovery from the financial crisis.[62] For example, the Declaration states:

We agreed that the core of the financial sector reform agenda rests on improving the strength of capital and liquidity and discouraging excessive leverage. We agreed to increase the

---

[57] G8 Muskoka Declaration, Muskoka, 25–26 June 2010, <http://www.whitehouse.gov/sites/default/files/g8_muskoka_declaration.pdf> (visited 27 June 2010).
[58] Ibid, para 1.
[59] Ibid, para 8.
[60] Ibid, para 26.
[61] Evenett and Fritz, above n 45, at 55–7.
[62] G20, 'Toronto Summit Declaration', Toronto, 26–27 June 2010, <http://g20.gc.ca/toronto-summit/summit-documents/the-g-20-toronto-summit-declaration/> (visited 28 June 2010). The Declaration characterizes the G20 as the 'premier forum' for international economic cooperation (para 1).

quality, quantity, and international consistency of capital, to strengthen liquidity standards, to discourage excessive leverage and risk taking, and reduce procyclicality.[63]

We agreed the financial sector should make a fair and substantial contribution towards paying for any burdens associated with government interventions, where they occur, to repair the financial system or fund resolution, and reduce risks from the financial system.[64]

In addition, the Declaration memorializes numerous other agreements in parallel language.

In my view, this G20 Declaration fails to give law to world finance. In a Declaration of about 10,600 words, the word 'law' appears only twice and neither time in an international context. At no point does the Declaration read as a code or a binding instrument. The Declaration contains no indication that any of the agreements reached are to be enforced. Although the leaders say that they are 'committed to international assessment and peer review',[65] no details are given. Another omission from the Declaration is any acknowledgment of state responsibility and liability for the impact of trans-boundary financial pollution.

The publication of a declaration of platitudes not moored to any accountability mechanism was made more likely when the summiteering governments failed to provide for nongovernmental participation, apart from a working session between the G20 finance ministers and a conclave of senior business executives from G20 countries. To be sure, there were some other parallel events, such as a Young Entrepreneur Summit with participation from each G20 country, a meeting of 80 senior leaders of the world's religions and faith-based organizations, and a dialogue between the Canadian Sherpa and the transnational civil society delegation. Nevertheless, one can see no evidence that any of those ideas arising out of the parallel event were brought into the Summit itself. The business leaders did not make any formal proposals, but did post a summary of points made to the governments.[66] Among the points made were that '[the] biggest worry shared by the business people in this room is the growing burden of government debt.... The next big worry for business is the continuing uncertainty about what governments are going to do on a number of important issues'.[67]

The G20 Summit organizers did not host a sidebar meeting with international labour unions, which is a shame since the worker groups had been thoughtful enough to prepare and send a detailed 12-page list of recommendations in advance.[68] The labour unions offered a number of interesting observations and recommendations, including, for example, that: (i) governments give priority to

---

[63] Ibid, Annex II, para 5.
[64] Ibid, para 21.
[65] Ibid, para 16.
[66] G20 Business Summit, 'Chairman's Summary', 26 June 2010, <http://www.ceocouncil.ca/publications/pdf/test_b02eacab85823e18b154cc630e0bf3d0/G20_Business_Summit_June_2526_Chairman_s_Summary.pdf> (visited 27 June 2010).
[67] Ibid, at 1.
[68] International Trade Union Confederation, 'Take Action on Jobs to Sustain the Recovery, Global Unions' Statement to the G8/G20 Summits', June 2010, <http://www.ituc-csi.org/IMG/pdf/Final-Trade_Union_Statement_to_G20_Toronto.pdf> (visited 27 June 2010).

developing new sources of finance and support the development of a financial transactions tax (FTT) as a fair and practical means of paying for the crisis; (ii) the Financial Stability Board has not led to any concrete change and its reports reveal the extent to which supervisory authorities have lost control over global finance; (iii) the IMF proposals to reform the Basel II Framework represent too little too late; (iv) the Financial Stability Board needs to adopt formal consultation processes, and to publish documents for comment; (v) the ILO should help the OECD implement its new Declaration on Propriety, Integrity and Transparency in the Conduct of International Business and Finance. Although I do not agree with all of these points, note should be taken of how substantive the labour union recommendations are and how ministers agreed to meet with the business leaders but not the labour leaders. The Canadian Prime Minister, however, did receive the global union delegation which presented him with the vœu.

Although I am sure that the G20 Summit of politicians and bureaucrats was interesting, this Summit would surely have been better if there had been organized input from business, labour, legal analysts, environmentalists, and others. The G20 Declaration offers normative guidance, and yet one wonders whether the authoring bureaucrats drew from a wide enough range of data and ideas. As Thomas Cottier has noted: 'Theories alone cannot serve as a basis for the operation of markets and the exercise of discretionary powers in the real world'.[69] Cottier further reminds the reader of how economic models need to be supplemented by input from the lawyer and in particular the relevance of values and justice, human experience and psychology, expertise in institutional design and in due process decision-making with fairness and transparency. The importance of a vibrant, open marketplace of ideas has been noted by social scientists for centuries.[70]

If it proves impractical for the G20 to be more open to public input when drafting Declarations, then such policymaking should occur in other institutions which provide space for interdisciplinary analysis and public debate. The modern OECD is one such institution that could be tasked with serving as a forum for ideas on financial regulation, but the OECD is handicapped in its limited governmental membership. Another approach would be to establish an apparatus in the Financial Stability Board for public input, public participation, and multi-stakeholder dialogues. Ideally, the transnational labour unions and business leaders could have hashed out their conflicting views in public in Toronto in front of global leaders. In addition, whenever dialogues are prepared for the edification of financial regulators, there should be an economist or other participant designated to make the case in favour of free markets which often find themselves unrepresented at intergovernmental meetings.

Public input is also important to obtain at the national level. Indeed, it may be even more important at that level.[71] Thus, the G20 could usefully call on governments to improve their administrative law public disclosure and notice and

---

[69] Cottier, above n 8, at 12.
[70] Thomas Butterworth, 'The Openness Elixir', *Wall Street Journal*, 19–20 June 2010, W8.
[71] See Weber, in this volume at Chapter 8.

comment processes and to require national regulators to consult with regulated entities, investors, consumers, and civil society.

C. The ILO model

Another international model that can be drawn upon is the annual review by the ILO of the reports submitted pursuant to the ILO Declaration on Fundamental Principles and Rights at Work.[72] Under this arrangement, now a decade old, each government submits its own report on the status of relevant domestic rights relating to the core ILO conventions that it has *not* ratified. The reports are then reviewed by the Committee of Independent Expert Advisers. In turn, their observations are considered by the ILO's Governing Body where employers and workers organizations are given an opportunity to comment on these reports. This process, which has received much less international attention than the TPRM, is more progressive in providing for comment by employer and worker organizations.

V. Conclusions

It was already evident by 1923 that the world economy needed better law. The ensuing decades have crystallized the perceptiveness of that early insight. Yet as this chapter points out, none of the international institutions overseeing financial regulation operates through the rule of law in a similar style to that of the WTO. But that situation is not intolerable as leading governments and publics are probably not ready to legalize international financial rules in the same way that they have legalized international trade rules. Because the best approach to building law is from the bottom up, the proper degree of authoritative decision-making for international financial matters remains at the stage of best practices and soft law standards.[73]

Although this article does not criticize the lack of hard law and hierarchy in international financial market oversight, it does raise two other criticisms. First, the *problématique* in much of the literature is to assume that all social problems stem from market failure. In my view, the problem of government failure is at least as serious.[74] The US financial crisis did not ensue because there was too much speculation. Rather, speculation increased because the value of many widely held assets became uncertain. Because government policies had artificially inflated housing prices, hundreds of billions of dollars of securities were being misvalued. Because government policies had built-in expectations of welfare state and bailout, the phenomenon of moral hazard expanded. When financial

---

[72] ILO Governing Body, 'Review of annual reports under the follow-up to the ILO Declaration on Fundamental Principles and Rights at Work', GB/307/3, March 2010.

[73] See Brummer, in this volume at Chapter 5.

[74] Gerald P. O'Driscoll Jr 'The Gulf Spill, the Financial Crisis and Government Failure', *Wall Street Journal*, 14 June 2010, A17.

legislation responds only to the symptom of a problem and not to its cause, such legislation will not succeed in promoting economic growth and in preventing future financial calamities.

Second, the optimal international institutions to manage financial markets will be transparent and deliberative.[75] Although there can be a need for national regulators to act in secrecy, the international level should be open in order to bring a broad array of views to bear and to expose government actions that seek to impose costs on other countries. Transnational civil society and business should have an opportunity to participate in dialogues with regulators so that the problems of government failure can be exposed. Just as market failure has to be corrected through intervention from outside the market, government failure has to be corrected through intervention from outside bureaucrats and politicians. In 2009, at the UN Conference on the World Financial and Economic Crisis and its Impact on Development, the General Assembly suggested the possibility of establishing an ad hoc panel of experts to provide independent technical expertise in order to inform better international action and policy decision-making.[76] Such an independent panel has not yet been set up within the UN Economic and Social Council.

In summary, the world economy needs a better law of financial markets and such law needs to be responsive to the problems of both market and government failure. The regulation of financial markets is a transnational problem because markets overlap political borders, but is also a transnational problem because sovereign governments need positive reinforcement from global institutions. Optimal global institutions will not merely comprise the governments to be overseen. Rather, international institutions can benefit from systematic input from international civil servants, business, and civic society.

---

[75] Daniel C. Esty, 'Good Governance at the Supranational Scale: Globalizing Administrative Law', 115 *Yale Law Journal* 1490 (2006), at 1520.
[76] A/Res/63/303, 13 July 2009, para 56.

12

Reducing Systemic Risk through the Reform of Capital Regulation

Hal S. Scott

I. Introduction

This chapter concentrates on the central problem for financial regulation that has emerged from the 2007–2009 financial crisis—the prevention of systemic risk. It is largely based on the work and recommendations of the Committee on Capital Markets Regulation (CCMR) in its May 2009 Report entitled 'The Global Financial Crisis: A Plan for Regulatory Reform'.[1] This chapter addresses what I regard as two of the most important policies for dealing with systemic risk: the imposition of capital requirements (or limits on leverage) and the use of market discipline in calibrating, enforcing and regulating these requirements.

II. Defining the Central Problem: Systemic Risk Reduction

The central objective of financial regulation (conceived as the prescription of rules, as distinct from supervision or risk assessment) is to reduce systemic risk.[2] Systemic risk can be defined in many ways. Most broadly, it is the risk that a national, or the global, financial system will break down. But this can occur for a variety of reasons, ranging from a broad external shock resembling 9/11 or war, to narrower causes more closely related to the financial system, such as lending failures. In a narrower context, systemic risk can arise because of broad lending mistakes affecting many banks, as was the case with the US banking system during the sovereign debt and thrift crises in the 1980s, or the Japanese financial crisis beginning in the 1990s and extending into the turn of the century. These crises occurred as a result of the highly correlated activities of many important institutions—e.g. all lending to Latin

---

[1] Committee on Capital Markets Regulation, 'The Global Financial Crisis: A Plan for Regulatory Reform' (2009) (CCMR CCMR Plan for Regulatory Reform). The CCMR is an independent, nonpartisan research organization with 32 members, founded in 2005 to improve the regulation of US capital markets.

[2] See Hal S. Scott, 'The Reduction of Systemic Risk in the United States Financial System', 33 *Harvard Journal of Law and Public Policy* 671 (2010).

America (sovereign debt crisis) or to affiliated companies (Japan). Now in the subprime crisis, many banks that made subprime loans or invested in derivatives based on such loans experienced significant losses. A growing body of literature seeks to measure overall risk in the financial system, principally on the basis of the degree of correlation risk among financial institutions.[3]

Financial crises can also arise from the problem of interconnectedness and the ensuing risk of contagion.[4] That is, the failure of one institution could lead to the failure of others. For example, at the time of the AIG bailout, it was thought that the failure of AIG could cause the failure of its in-the-money counterparties on credit default swaps (CDS). Also, the failure of one institution could trigger a financial system run, particularly on institutions lacking the support of a deposit insurance system or the assurance that central banks would be lenders of last resort (even if solvent). The most dramatic examples during the subprime crisis were liquidity runs on US money market funds, which were only stopped by a combination of new types of federal lending and government guarantees.

In all these cases of systemic risk, the ability of financial institutions to withstand losses is crucial. With the first line of defense against losses being capital, this chapter focuses on capital requirements in light of the financial crisis.

III. Current Capital Requirements: Basel and Leverage Ratios

The highly regulated nature of capital requirements is not a new phenomenon. Since 1988, the requirements have been adopted for large international banks of the G10 countries by the Basel Committee on Banking Supervision (Basel Committee or BCBS), and have been adopted by more than 100 other countries outside the G10.[5] The USA implemented Basel I and is in the process of implementing the Basel II advanced internal-rating-based approach—known as A-IRB—for 20 or so of its largest banks and their holding companies, with implementation scheduled for April 2011.[6] But US implementation of the A-IRB regime requires minimum capital floors during transition and higher levels of

---

[3] See e.g. Monica Billio, Mila Getmansky, Andrew Lo and Loriana Pelizzon, 'Measuring Systemic Risk in the Finance and Insurance Sectors', (MIT Sloan School, Working Paper 4774-10, 17 March 2010); V. Acharya, Lasse Pedersen, Thomas Philippon and Matthew Richardson, 'Measuring Systemic Risk' (10 March 2010), <http://ssrn.com/abstract=1573171> (visited 5 March 2010); see also 'Systemic Regulation, Prudential Matters, Resolution Authority and Securitization: Hearing Before the House Committee on Financial Services', 111th Congress (29 October 2009) (statement of Andrew W. Lo, Director, MIT Laboratory for Financial Engineering), <http://papers.ssrn.com/sol3/papers.cfm?abstract_id=1497682> (visited 5 March 2010).
[4] See Jan Lorenz, Stefano Battiston and Frank Schweitzer, 'Systemic Risk in a Unifying Framework for Cascading Processes on Networks', 71 *European Physical Journal* 441 (2009) for an attempt to model chain reaction failures. Nodes of a network are exposed to failure as a result of their fragility and the thresholds that determine their failures.
[5] See BCBS, 'International Convergence of Capital Measurement and Capital Standards' 3 (1988), <http://www.bis.org/publ/bcbsc111.pdf?noframes=1> (visited 5 March 2010).
[6] See Federal Reserve Board Of Governors, 'U.S. Implementation of the Basel Accords', <http://www.federalreserve.gov/generalinfo/basel2/USImplementation.htm> (visited 2 April 2010).

capital than Basel would otherwise have required, because of concerns that Basel II's required capital levels were too low. Unlike the European Union (EU), the USA has rejected applying the Basel II Agreement to the rest of its banking system.[7] The standardized approach, designed for most banks, was found to be too complicated for small US banks—with the Foundation IRB alternative to A-IRB judged not to be a useful middle ground.

The Securities and Exchange Commission (SEC) implemented a version of Basel II for securities firms' holding companies, on a voluntary basis, in 2004, before the onslaught of the credit crisis.[8] This was the result of the enactment of the EU Conglomerate Directive requiring all conglomerates, including investment banks, to be regulated at the holding company level by the EU unless the conglomerates were subject to 'equivalent' regulation elsewhere.[9] US investment banks were free of any holding company regulation at the time, being subject only to SEC regulation of their broker-dealers or investment company affiliates. The US investment banks convinced the SEC to allow them to be regulated on a voluntary basis to escape EU regulation, and capital was a key part of that regulation. Since the EU was adopting Basel II, the SEC applied Basel II to its investment banks, thus all but assuring that the equivalence requirement would be satisfied.

These capital requirements proved inadequate. The SEC's Basel II-based rules permitted the top five major investment banks to achieve leverage of over 30 to 1.[10] Insufficient capital was a significant cause of the failure of Lehman Brothers and Bear Stearns,[11] and also played a major role in forcing Merrill Lynch to sell itself to Bank of America.[12]

One of the interesting features of capital regulation is that the leverage of depository banks turned out to be much lower than the leverage of investment banks, which do not take deposits. This was because depository banks were subject to leverage ratios in addition to their Basel I requirements. Indeed, the top five depository banks were leveraged at 13 to 1, compared to the leverage of over 30 to 1 of the investment banks.[13] While Basel II imposed a minimum 8 per cent capital requirement on risk-weighted assets (which the USA increased to 10 per cent for banks seeking to engage in riskier non-banking activities),[14] the USA also imposed its own leverage requirement of 5 per cent on all assets, without risk-weighting, for

---

[7] The Basel II Agreement only requires applying the standards to large international banks, so this decision of the US does not actually violate the Agreement.

[8] 17 C.F.R. xx 200.30-3, 240.3a4-2 to -6, 240.3a5-1, 240.3b-17 to -18, 240.15a-7 to -9 (2004).

[9] Directive 2002/87/EC of the European Parliament and of the Council on the Supplementary Supervision of Credit Institutions, Insurance Undertakings and Investment Firms in a Financial Conglomerate and Amending Council Directives 73/239/EEC, 79/267/EEC, 92/49/EEC, 92/96/EEC, 93/6/EEC and 93/22/EEC, and Directives 98/78/EC and 2000/12/EC of the European Parliament and of the Council, OJ 2003 L 35.

[10] CCMR Plan for Regulatory Reform, above n 1, at 60.

[11] Joint Economic Committee Majority Staff, 'From Wall Street to Main Street: Understanding How the Credit Crisis Affects You', 2008, at 4 <http://jec.senate.gov/index.cfm?FuseAction=Files. View&FileStore_id=b2087603-5883-4777-b13e-6b30845d4265> (visited 5 March 2010).

[12] Ibid.

[13] CCMR Plan for Regulatory Reform, above n 1, at 60.

[14] 12 C.F.R. x 208.43(b)(1)(i).

consideration as a 'well-capitalized' bank.[15] The leverage ratio, which was not applied to investment banks, turned out to be a more binding constraint on banks than the more 'sophisticated' Basel approach. European and Asian banks, which were not subject to leverage ratios, were more exposed to failure, but the subprime crisis had a more dramatic impact in the USA than elsewhere.

IV. Basel II Revisions

The Basel Committee[16] is in the process of revising Basel II capital requirements and adding liquidity requirements in light of the financial crisis. First, in July 2009, the Basel Committee adopted new capital requirements for 'resecuritizations'[17] and increased capital required to support institutions' trading books.[18]

As for securitization, the basic reforms, effective from December 2010, increased the risk-weightings of Basel II, which will require more capital against such exposures. Under the A-IRB, estimates of the risk of holding most assets have been generally left to bank credit models; but in the case of securitizations and resecuritizations, most of which are externally rated, Basel II specifies the risk-weights for securities with different seniority and diversification. These risk-weight revisions raise the general question as to whether we can expect the Basel Committee to appropriately determine risk-weights, particularly when these weights are geared off credit ratings whose reliability must be severely questioned in light of the financial crisis. Indeed, a provision of the recently enacted Dodd–Frank Wall Street Reform and Consumer Protection Act[19] (Dodd–Frank Act) prevents US regulators from relying on credit ratings in any regulation—thus making the implementation of these revisions in the USA impossible. Not only is the risk-weighting process methodologically suspect, it is also subject to political pressure. Can there be any other reason why all residential mortgages (prime or subprime) were risk-weighted at 50 per cent in Basel I, while all other secured debt to the private sector was risk-weighted at 100 per cent? Indeed, Basel II was even worse, dropping the risk-weight on residential mortgages to 35 per cent. Clearly, assigning low risk-weights for residential mortgages was part of the strategy of the USA to promote home ownership, using risk-weights as a means of credit allocation.

In addition, the latest revision to Basel II in July 2009, also effective in December 2010, increased capital for market risk (changes in value) of a bank's trading book. These changes also include a stressed value-at-risk (VaR) requirement, which the Committee believes will help dampen the cyclicality of the

[15] 12 C.F.R. x 208.43(b)(1)(iii).
[16] The Committee was first established by the central bank governors of the G10 countries in 1975. It is now composed of banking supervisory authorities and central banks of 27 jurisdictions.
[17] Resecuritizations include collateralized debt obligations (CDOs), in which existing asset-backed securities are repackaged into new securities.
[18] BCBS, Enhancements to the Basel II Framework', July 2009, <http://www.bis.org/publ/bcbs157.pdf> (visited 5 March 2010).
[19] Pub. L. 111–203 (21 July 2010), x 939A(b) (Dodd–Frank Act).

minimum regulatory capital framework.[20] Again, the issue is whether regulators can get these capital charges right. While in the past capital requirements seem to have been too low, the risk for the future may be that they are too high, which would unnecessarily dampen economic recovery. An impact study conducted on 43 banks in 10 countries by the Basel Committee found that changes in market risk requirements alone would require an average increase in capital holdings by 11.5 per cent and a median increase of 3.2 per cent. Similar increases were reported for stressed VaR.[21] Are these too little, just right, or excessive? Who knows?

V. Basel III Proposals on Capital and Liquidity

The capital and liquidity standards first proposed by the Basel Committee in December 2009 have come to be referred to as Basel III. At its meeting in December 2010, the Committee issued *Basel III: A global regulatory framework for more resilient banks and banking systems* which detailed the required capital ratios and phase-in arrangements. Implementation of the capital proposal of the basic capital framework is planned to begin in 2012, while the leverage proposal should be implemented in 2018. The liquidity requirements are subject to a longer observation period with the Liquidity Coverage Ratio not set to be introduced until 2015 and the minimum standard for the Net Stable Funding Ratio looking to begin in 2018.[22]

A. Capital

The Basel III capital proposal begins by narrowing the definition of Tier 1 capital to engender more reliance on pure equity (which remained unchanged in Basel II from Basel I). In particular, it provides that unrealized gains or losses on available-for-sale assets, which result from the use of fair value accounting, should be reflected in equity for regulatory purposes.[23]

This may be resisted by the EU, and particularly France, where many banks and policymakers oppose fair value accounting on the grounds that it is inappropriate to use mark-to-market accounting for unimpaired debt.[24] Indeed, it may not be

[20] BCBS, above n 18.

[21] BCBS, Analysis of the Trading Book Quantitative Impact Study', October 2009, <http://www.bis.org/publ/bcbs163.pdf?noframes=1> (visited 5 March 2010).

[22] BCBS, 'Basel III: A global regulatory framework for more resilient banks and banking systems', <http://www.bis.org/publ/bcbs189.pdf> (visited 6 March 2012).

[23] BCBS, 'Strengthening the Resilience of the Banking Sector', at 23 para 96, (Consultative Document, December 2009), <http://www.bis.org/publ/bcbs164.pdf> (visited 5 March 2010).

[24] In his report to the President of the French Republic, French General Commissioner for Public Investment, René Ricol described fair value accounting as having a 'detrimental effect on market information and the comparability of financial statements' which, 'when markets break down and become illiquid [may result in] a vicious circle, in which massive sales of impaired assets with insufficient buy-side counterparties drive prices downwards until the assets are worth little or nothing'. René Ricol, 'Report to the President of the French Republic on the Financial Crisis' 30, 52 (September 2008). The response of the EU has been more muted, calling for flexibility in the use of fair value.

appropriate for regulatory and accounting measures of capital to be the same, as discussed further below.

The second part of the capital proposal is to require more capital for counterparty risk where over-the-counter derivatives are not centrally cleared, while concurrently setting a 'modest' 1 per cent to 3 per cent risk-weight on those that are centrally cleared. This system would strongly promote central clearing. Further, the Committee proposes to increase the risk-weights on derivative exposures of banks to financial institutions as compared to exposures to the non-financial sector on the ground that correlation risk is higher for the former. This is to be supplemented by improved collateral risk management practices. While the overall thrust of this approach is sensible, it is questionable whether there should be a low risk-weight on centrally cleared derivatives, as clearinghouses are not impervious to risk and may have to issue a capital call on clearinghouse participants.

The third part of the capital proposal is an international leverage ratio. The December leverage proposal focuses on what assets should be counted in the denominator while using the new capital measures in the numerator. Although there is strong support for using Tier 1 capital as the base for the leverage ratio, the July revision indicated that 'the Committee also will track the impact of using total capital and tangible common equity'. A minimum Tier 1 leverage ratio of 3 per cent will be tested during the 'parallel run period' of 2013–2017.[25] While it is true that the leverage ratio helped to protect the US banking system during the crisis more than the Basel requirements, this is more an indictment of the Basel methodology than grounds for endorsing crude leverage ratios. Indeed, dissatisfaction with the leverage ratio as a measure of capital adequacy was a major impetus in the development by Basel of a risk-weighted approach.[26] If there is to be a leverage ratio, however, it would clearly best be done internationally through Basel, rather than through disparate national requirements.[27]

Charlie McCreevy, 'Keynote Address: Financial Reporting in a Changing World' (7 May 2009), <http://europa.eu/rapid/pressReleasesAction.do?reference=SPEECH/09/223&format=HTML&aged =0&language=EN&guiLanguage=en> (visited 5 March 2010). Also, the Chairman of the UK Financial Services Authority, Adair Turner, has questioned the use of fair value for banks. Adair Turner, Chairman, UK Financial Services Authority, 'Remarks to the Institute of Chartered Accountants in England and Wales' 21 January 2010, <http://www.fsa.gov.uk/pages/Library/Communication/ Speeches/2010/0121_at.shtml> (visited 5 March 2010).

[25] Bank for International Settlements, BCBS, Annex (26 July 2010), <http://www.bis.org/press/ p100726/annex.pdf> (visited 16 September 2010).

[26] In a statement before the Senate Banking Committee, Federal Deposit Insurance Corporation (FDIC) Chairman, Sheila Bair, stated 'It is highly likely that the advanced approaches of Basel II would have been implemented much more quickly and with fewer safeguards, and banks would have entered the crisis with much lower levels of capital. In particular, the longstanding desire of many large institutions for the elimination of the leverage ratio would have been much more likely to have been realized in a regulatory structure in which a single regulator plays the predominant role. This is a prime example of how multiple regulators' different perspectives can result in a better outcome'. See 'Strengthening and Streamlining Prudential Bank Supervision: Hearing before the Senate Committee on Banking, Housing & Urban Affairs', 111th Congress, 4 August 2009 (statement of Sheila Bair, Chairman, FDIC).

[27] See Dodd–Frank Act, above n 19, x 1103(g)(3) which limits 'systemically important' financial institution holding company leverage ratios to 15–1.

   The fourth part of the capital proposal would promote counter-cyclical capital requirements—that is, a system in which more capital would be raised and held in good times than in bad times.[28] The CCMR has also recommended the adoption of techniques to ensure that capital ratios are counter-cyclical, with ratios being higher when markets are rising than in times of falling valuation and liquidity.[29] One element of this approach is to allow an expected, rather than an actual, loss approach to provisioning. Counter-cyclical ratios could be implemented through an expected loss model of provisioning, as in Spain.[30] The CCMR has suggested that this could be accomplished without violating current accounting standards and securities regulation rules by providing that estimated losses do not run through the income statement.[31] Under current accounting rules, premised on the incurred loss model, only known impairments, but not expected future losses, are provided for and reflected in an institution's financial reporting.[32] In addition, the CCMR has argued that financial institutions should be required to maintain some form of contingent capital to address the cyclicality that is characteristic of existing requirements.[33] Two promising proposals for contingent capital should be explored—one

---

[28] BCBS: Countercyclical Capital Buffer proposal (6 July 2010), <http://www.bis.org/publ/bcbs172.pdf> (visited 16 September 2010).

[29] CCMR Plan for Regulatory Reform, above n 1, at 81.

[30] See Financial Services Authority, 'The Turner Review: A Regulatory Response to the Global Banking Crisis' 63 (March 2009), <http://www.fsa.gov.uk/pubs/other/turner_review.pdf> (visited 5 March 2010) (discussing the Spanish dynamic provisioning system).

[31] CCMR Plan for Regulatory Reform, above n 1, at 81. Financial Accounting Standards Board (FASB) Chairman Bob Herz has also endorsed this approach. Robert H. Herz, 'Remarks to AICPA National Conference on Current SEC and PCAOB Developments' 8 December 2009, at 15 <http://www.fasb.org/cs/ContentServer?c=Document_C&pagename=FASB/Document_C/DocumentPage&cid=1176156571228> (visited 5 March 2010).

[32] Both US (GAAP) and IFRS accounting rules operate according to an incurred loss model (embodied, for example, in Financial Accounting Standards or FAS 5 and FAS 114) under which a financial institution records an impairment only after the associated financial asset is known to have incurred a loss. This principle governs even when the exact amount of the loss is not known with specificity and must be estimated based on past experience (for example, in the case of receivables, losses on which may be known to have been incurred but not identified specifically). Expected future losses, by contrast, are not reserved against under the incurred loss model and thus are not deducted from income. Financial Accounting Standards Board, 'Statement of Financial Accounting Standards 5, Accounting for Contingencies'; 'Statement of Financial Accounting Standards 114, Accounting by Creditors for Impairment of a Loan, Amendment to FASB Statements No. 5 and 15'. The incurred loss model is a staple of both US GAAP and IFRS accounting, but has been subject to recent criticism and challenge, for example, in the International Accounting Standards Board's November 2009 exposure draft outlining a proposed expected loss model to replace the incurred loss model in connection with financial asset reporting. IASB Press Release, International Acting Standards Board (IASB) publishes proposals on the impairment of Financial Assets 5 November 2009, <http://www.iasb.org/News/Press+Releases/IASB+publishes+proposals+on+the+impairment+of+financial+assets.htm> (visited 5 March 2010); IASB, 'Financial Instruments: Amortised Cost and Impairment' (Exposure Draft, November 2009), <http://www.iasb.org/NR/rdonlyres/9C66B0E5-E177-4004-A20B-C0076FCC3BFB/0/vbEDFIImpairmentNov09.pdf> (visited 5 March 2010).

[33] CCMR Plan for Regulatory Reform, above n 1, at 81; see also Anil K. Kashyap, Raghuram G. Rajan and Jeremy C. Stein, 'Rethinking Capital Regulation', (prepared for Federal Reserve Bank of Kansas City symposium on 'Maintaining Stability in a Changing Financial System', Jackson Hole, Wyoming, 21–23 August 2008); Mark Flannery, 'No Pain, No Gain? Effecting Market Discipline via Reverse Convertible Debentures', in Hal S. Scott (ed), *Capital Adequacy Beyond Basel: Banking Securities and Insurance* (Oxford: Oxford University Press, 2005).

for catastrophic insurance based on a systemic trigger, and another for reverse convertible debentures based on a bank-specific market value trigger.[34] All contingent capital proposals are crucially dependent on what triggers a conversion or call, and specifying appropriate triggers has proved difficult.[35]

The fifth part of the capital proposal envisions the building of 'capital buffers' through 'capital conservation'. This proposal envisions that banks should hold capital above the regulatory minimum in good times and that, when capital has been drawn down, discretionary distributions of earnings—through dividends or share buybacks, for example—should be restricted. First, a capital conservation range, of an unspecified amount, would be established above the minimum requirement. Then, for example, if a bank's capital fell to a level above the minimum requirement equal to 30 per cent of the capital conservation range, a bank might be required to conserve 80 per cent of its earnings.

B. Liquidity

In 2008, the Basel Committee issued 'Principles for Sound Liquidity Risk Management and Supervision' focusing on management of liquidity.[36] While this included the principle that banks should maintain a sufficient cushion of high quality liquid assets to meet contingent liquidity needs, no methodology was presented for making this determination. A similar process-oriented approach was adopted by US regulators in 2010.[37]

In its liquidity proposal of December 2009, such a methodology was put forward for internationally active banks.[38] Two objectives are formulated: (i) that banks should have sufficient high quality liquid resources to survive an acute stress scenario lasting one month, formalized in a Liquidity Coverage Ratio; and

---

[34] CCMR Plan for Regulatory Reform, above n 1, at 81; Kashyap et al., above n 33; Flannery, above n 33.

[35] Standard & Poor's research on contingent capital draws out these criticisms. It states that since bank capital ratios are typically not comparable, any specific ratio (such as a 5 per cent Core Tier 1, for example) would not apply equally to all banks. Standard & Poor's capital analysis, for example, would take account of how likely a conversion would be to happen in a time of stress—this depends on what type of financial stress scenario the trigger ratio would represent. For contingent capital to be effective in a time of stress, the conversion would need to happen quickly, which may be difficult depending how often the trigger ratio is monitored. Expectations about the likelihood of a conversion may also negatively affect the share price and market confidence. If the conversion trigger is set at a level that would lead to a con- version occurring too late, then Standard & Poor's treats the contingent capital security as having minimal equity credit. Standard & Poor's Research, Contingent Capital is not a Panacea for Banks 10 November 2009, at 2–3 <http://www2.standardandpoors.com/spf/pdf//FITcon1110Article4.pdf> (visited 5 March 2010).

[36] BCBS, 'Principles for Sound Liquidity Risk Management and Supervision', (June 2008), <http://www.bis.org/publ/bcbs138.pdf> (visited 5 March 2010).

[37] Department of the Treasury, Federal Reserve System, FDIC, National Credit Union Administration, Interagency Policy Statement on Funding and Liquidity Risk Management, 75 Fed. Reg. 13656 (22 March 2010), <http://www.federalreserve.gov/boarddocs/srletters/2010/sr1006a1.pdf> (visited 5 March 2010) 2010.

[38] BCBS, International Framework for Liquidity Risk Measurement, Standards and Monitoring, (Consultative Document, December 2009), <http://www.bis.org/publ/bcbs165.pdf> (visited 5 March 2010).

(ii) that banks should have stable funding in the longer term, formalized in a Net Stable Funding Ratio.[39] The Liquidity Coverage Ratio, on which I focus here, requires that the stock of 'high quality assets' is 100 per cent of net cash outflows over the 30-day time period, where outflows are predicated on a stress scenario.

This scenario covers 'both institution-specific and systemic shocks' modeled on circumstances encountered in the global financial crisis. The scenario entails: (i) a significant downgrade of the institution's public credit rating; (ii) a partial loss of deposits; (iii) a loss of unsecured wholesale funding; (iv) a significant increase in secured funding haircuts; and (v) increases in collateral calls for derivatives and substantial calls on contractual and non-contractual off-balance sheet exposures. The methodology goes on to specify what instruments qualify as high quality liquid assets, e.g. cash or sovereign debt, and what haircuts should be given to other instruments (corporate bonds would receive a 20–40 per cent haircut depending on quality). Net cash outflows would be assumed to occur at different rates for different liabilities—e.g. at least 5 per cent for stable retail deposits and 75 per cent for unsecured wholesale funding provided by non-financial corporate customers, and other unsecured whole-sale funding at 100 per cent.

These particular quantitative standards are untested and no clear justification of them is provided in the proposal. They are sure to have a major impact on financial institutions. Given the poor track record for capital requirements, is there any reason to believe the Basel Committee can do better on liquidity, which is, if anything, a more difficult subject? One significant issue in the methodology is its failure to factor in the role of central banks as lenders of last resort. Traditionally, we have not required a solvent bank to have sufficient liquidity to survive a run on banks caused by the insolvency of other banks. Of course, with a deposit base and deposit insurance, such runs are much less likely than for institutions with more wholesale funding. The Basel proposal quite properly recognizes this, even if it is hard to justify particular run-off percentages. But runs on banks with a high percentage of liabilities in deposits can still occur either because deposit insurance is limited in amount or because depositors are irrational. In such circumstances, central banks have acted as lenders of last resort to banks that can post adequate collateral. Put another way, the system is dependent, and should be dependent, on liquidity coming from central banks in certain circumstances—a fact that the Basel Committee does not address or factor into its calculations. Of course, we witnessed this at work in the crisis where central banks met the liquidity needs of banks and other financial institutions that were able to supply adequate collateral. In my view, this was perfectly proper.

One major overall problem in the Basel Committee's approach to both capital and liquidity is that its requirements are only focused on banks. As we saw in the crisis, these are not the only institutions that can trigger or be the victims of

---

[39] In a tacit acknowledgement of the difficulty of setting liquidity standards, the proposal made in December 2009 for a Net Stable Funding Ratio (ibid) was initially abandoned by the Basel Committee in its July 2010 revisions before being reinstated in the final Basel III text with implementation envisioned at the beginning of 2018. See above n 22.

a liquidity crisis. The assisted acquisition of Bear Stearns, the conservatorship of AIG, and the failure of the Reserve Primary Fund, a money market fund, triggered liquidity runs whose victims included, but were not limited to, banks. While the conversion of US investment banks to banks serves to diminish the scope issue with the Basel rules, future runs could still be caused by liquidity problems experienced at non-banks, including hedge funds (c.f. Long-Term Capital Management). The G20 and Financial Stability Board, together with the Basel Committee, need to address this problem.

VI. The Need for Additional Approaches to Capital Adequacy

A. The determination of the proper amount of capital

The most fundamental issue—how much capital banks or other financial institutions should be required to maintain—has gone largely unaddressed. Basel I 'back-solved' into an 8 per cent requirement in 1988 to prevent an increase in bank capital as a result of implementing the new regime.[40] Basel II basically adopted the same approach following several quantitative impact studies.[41] So the general question is, regardless of how capital is measured, how much capital should be required? More fundamentally, can regulation really determine what the right amount of capital is? This is unlikely, based on the poor experience with the somewhat analogous endeavors to regulate prices of goods and services in the USA and elsewhere.[42] Even more daunting is the determination of the correct capital 'price' on risk.

Not surprisingly, regulatory capital requirements (including leverage ratios) have not acted as a binding constraint on the amount of capital banks actually hold, given the lack of a solid foundation.[43] In 2007, before the crisis, the regulatory capital ratio for the top 20 US banks (accounting for almost two-thirds of the

---

[40] BCBS, above n 5; CCMR Plan for Regulatory Reform, above n 1, at 62.

[41] See: Bank for International Settlements (BIS), Quarterly Review, 2 (September 2009); see also BCBS, Results of the Second Quantitative Impact Study (November 2001), <http://www.bis.org/ bcbs/qis/qishist.htm> (visited 5 March 2010); BCBS, Results of the Quantitative Impact Study 2.5 June 2002, <http://www.bis.org/bcbs/qis/qis25results.pdf> (visited 5 March 2010); BCBS, Quantitative Impact Study 3, Overview of Global Results (May 2003), <http://www.bis.org/bcbs/qis/qis3. htm> (visited 5 March 2010); BCBS, Results of the Fourth Quantitative Impact Study (March 2005), <http://www.bis.org/bcbs/qis/qis4.htm> (visited 5 March 2010); BCBS, Results of the Fifth Quantitative Impact Study (June 2006), <http://www.bis.org/bcbs/qis/qis5.htm> (visited 5 March 2010).

[42] See H. Boissevain et al, 'The Effectiveness of Phase II Price Controls', 5 Interfaces 33 (1975); Fiona M. Scott Morton, 'The Problems of Price Controls', *Regulation* 50, Spring 2001, 50, <http:// www.cato.org/pubs/regulation/regv24n1/morton.pdf> (visited 5 March 2010); Dwight R. Lee and Richard B. McKenzie, *Failure and Progress: The Bright Side of the Dismal Science* (Washington, DC: Cato Institute, 1993), 56.

[43] Andrew Kuritzkes and Hal Scott, 'Markets are the Best Judge of Bank Capital', FT.COM, 23 September 2009, <http://www.ft.com/cms/2ca160b0-a870-11de-9242-00144feabdc0.html> (visited 5 March 2010).

nation's banking assets) averaged 11.7 per cent.[44] This figure was nearly 50 per cent above the minimum regulatory requirement of 8 and 17 per cent above the 'well-capitalized' standard of 10 per cent.[45] As a result, banks held more capital than regulation required due to the constraints of their own internal economic models and market demands.[46]

On the other hand, new proposals for more capital risk being excessive, as the regulatory pendulum swings in the direction of being more constraining in light of the financial crisis. The calls for more capital are not restricted to Basel. The G20 and US regulatory reform call for capital above Basel levels for systemically important institutions to combat the too-big-to-fail problem.[47] But the actual systemic risk charge and how to assess it, has yet to be determined.[48] Increased capital requirements could dampen economic activity at the very moment when recovery is in the balance. While it is true that the new proposals do not envision implementation until the end of 2012, banks cannot wait that long to alter their businesses and will begin to plan their activities in light of the impending higher capital requirements.[49]

In light of the difficult challenges facing regulators attempting to specify the appropriate amount of capital for a given quantum of risk, governments should explore expanded use of market forces as a complement to regulation to address the capital problem for publicly traded financial institutions.[50] For example, market forces could be harnessed to impose greater discipline and give regulators a market-based warning of bank difficulties (signaled by the spread from a Treasury benchmark on the subordinated debt yield) provided two conditions are met: (i) the market must have better information about the institutions' riskiness; and (ii) investors in institutions must be forced to bear some risk for their failure due to holding 'unbailable' unsecured credit instruments, such as subordinated debt, and the prospect of experiencing eventual substantial losses on 'bailable' instruments, such as unsecured short-term debt or in-the-money derivative positions. The Shadow Financial Regulatory Committee recommended the subordinated debt approach in 2000,[51] although some have criticized this proposal as impractical

---

[44] See also Klaus Schaeck and Martin Čihák, 'Banking Competition and Capital Ratios', IMF, Working Paper No. WP/07/216, 28 March 2010), <http://ssrn.com/abstract=1579625> (visited 5 March 2010).

[45] Kuritzkes and Scott, above n 43.

[46] Ibid.

[47] G20, 'Leader's Statement: The Pittsburgh Summit', 24 September 2009, 13 <http://www.pittsburghsummit.gov/mediacenter/129639.htm> (visited 5 March 2010) 2010. See also Bair, above n 26; Dodd–Frank Act x171(b)(1)–(2).

[48] The IMF has suggested two possible approaches, each with substantial methodological difficulties: using a 'standardized approach' based on an institution's systemic risk rating or assessing an institution's additional contribution to systemic risk and its probability of distress. IMF, 'Global Financial Stability Report', April 2010, Ch. 2. See also: Jorge Chan-Lau, 'Regulatory Capital Charges for Too-Connected-to-Fail Institutions: A Practical Proposal' (IMF, Working Paper WP/1098, April 2010).

[49] See bank criticisms in BNA's Banking Report, 94 BBR 736 (20 April 2010).

[50] CCMR Plan for Regulatory Reform, above n 1, at 27.

[51] US Shadow Financial Regulation Committee, 'Reforming Bank Capital Regulation' 2000 at 42.

given the poorly developed market in the USA for subordinated debt.[52] Hart and Zingales have proposed that market signals could alternatively be provided by the spreads on CDS referencing banks, instruments where payment is triggered when banks default on their debt.[53] This proposal would sidestep the practicalities of banks issuing subordinated debt. However, if creditors of failing or failed banks do not experience losses, CDS spreads will not be accurate. Losses for writers of CDS depend on an event of default and on the value of auctioned debt under International Swaps and Derivatives Association protocols if there is a default because the more the debt is worth, the lower the CDS payoffs.[54] If debt is bailed out, the exposures of CDS writers will be distorted. Thus, as a complement to these market mechanisms, it would be imperative to design a resolution system that imposes losses on debt holders.

Market signaling through benchmark spreads is only as useful as the information on which the signals are based. There are critical inadequacies in the information presently disclosed by banks. The results of supervisory examinations are generally not revealed to the market, and bank disclosures are difficult to compare from bank to bank. However, as part of government rescue efforts during the financial crisis, the US Treasury and the Federal Reserve sought to subject banks to a so-called 'stress-test' (Supervisory Capital Assessment Program, or SCAP) to measure the amount of capital they would need to operate soundly in the near term. Most immediately, the results of these tests were used to determine which banks could safely repay their Troubled Asset Relief Program (TARP) funds. Broadly, the stress tests sought to assess the performance of bank capital for 19 US banks under two scenarios, one based on a consensus economic forecast, the other on a 'worst-case' outcome. The stress test applied a common methodology to all of the banks, modeling patterns of bank earnings, investment losses, and macro-economic conditions. Where certain banks were found to be wanting, the stress tests were used to specify the amount of additional capital that they would be required to raise to place their future operations on a sounder footing.

---

[52] See e.g. Bert Ely, 'Sub debt—Silver Bullet or Big Dud?', 5 *Financial Regulation* 32 (2000), <http://www.ely-co.com/reports/SubDebt.pdf> (visited 5 March 2010).

[53] Oliver Hart and Luigi Zingales, 'A New Capital Regulation for Large Financial Institutions' (Center for Economic Policy Research, Discussion Paper No. DP7298, September 2009), <http://faculty.chicagobooth.edu/luigi.zingales/research/papers/a_new_capital_regulation>.pdf (visited 5 March 2010). There would be significant issues with using these market signals as a basis for federal intervention into the affairs of a bank, as suggested by the authors, due to the unreliability of CDS spreads in a crisis resulting from the lack of liquidity and trading in the instrument. This was the case during the past crisis when, for example, Goldman Sachs and Morgan Stanley saw their CDS spreads shift hundreds of points in a single trading day. J.P. Morgan, too, saw its spreads widen to levels approaching those of junk bonds. See e.g., Alistair Barr, 'Fate of Remaining Big Independent Brokers in Focus', MarketWatch.com, 15 September 2008, <http://www.marketwatch.com/story/fate-of-remaining-big-brokers-in-focus-after-lehman-collapse> (visited 5 March 2010); Ryan Vlastelica, 'Morgan Stanley CDS Spreads Plunge' 183 BPS; Goldman Sachs, Merrill, Wachovia CDS Fall, Forbes.com, 19 September 2008, <http://www.forbes.com/feeds/afx/2008/09/19/afx5446908.html> (visited 5 March 2010); John Beck, 'CDS Spreads Tighten' as Bailout is Revised, Risk.com, 1 October 2008, <http://www.risk.net/risk-magazine/news/1503631/cds-spreads-tighten-bailout-revised> (visited 5 March 2010).

[54] CFA Institute, Derivatives and Alternative Investments G11 (2008).

Most importantly for future policy, the overall results of the stress test were publicly disclosed on a bank-by-bank basis, though the level of the disclosure was fairly general.[55] Rather than spooking the market and triggering bank runs—a common justification for not revealing the results of bank examinations—the disclosure had a calming effect. This may be because the market abhors uncertainty even more than poor results or because the stress test results were generally positive.

We need to explore the feasibility of regularly disclosing stress tests results to improve market information. Apart from the disclosure issue, we need to explore the design of the test. The 2009 test was designed for the specific purpose of determining what institutions should be free to exit TARP by repaying the US government investments.[56] Regular stress tests would be designed for a different purpose, to provide additional information to the market as well as to give regulators notification of potential problem institutions. The design of scenarios is a key component of a stress test, and it can be argued that it is inherently difficult to predict the future, particularly as one departs from market predictions in the form of consensus forecasts. Indeed, as we now know in hindsight (see Table 12.1), the SCAP forecasts were unduly pessimistic.

Table 12.1. Economic scenarious: baseline, more adverse and actual

	2009	2010
Real GDP		
Average baseline	−2	2.1
More adverse	−3.3	0.5
Actual	−2.4	n/a
Civilian unemployment rate		
Average baseline	8.4	8.8
More adverse	8.9	10.3
Actual	9.3[a]	9.7[b]
House prices		
Average baseline	−14	−4
More adverse	−22	−7
Actual	−2.4	n/a

[a] Unemployment hit 10.1% in October 2009, before closing the year at 9.3%.
[b] Through 26 February 2010.
Source: Andru Wall, Paper for International Finance Seminar, Harvard Law School (2010)

[55] Board of Governors of the Federal Reserve System, 'The Supervisory Capital Assessment Program: Design and Implementation' (April 2009), <http://www.federalreserve.gov/newsevents/press/bcreg/bcreg20090424a1.pdf> (visited 5 March 2010).
[56] Daniel K. Tarullo, Governor, Federal Reserve Board, Remarks at the Federal Reserve Board International Research Forum on Monetary Policy (26 March 2010), <http://www.federalreserve.gov/newsevents/speech/tarullo20100326a.htm> (visited 5 March 2010).

Beyond what can be learned from periodic stress tests, there may also be a need for more periodic disclosure by banks of key information that is presently not made available. Such disclosure could include more information from models (including sensitivity assumptions) and inputs, internal loan ratings, positions in risky securities (like CDOs) and large concentrations.

B. Regulatory and accounting measures of capital

Let me return to the issue of the relationship between regulatory and accounting measures of capital. Currently, an important difference between the Basel definition of Tier 1 capital and the accounting measure of capital is that the Basel measure ignores equity losses or gains attributable to mark-to-market available-for-sale assets, as required by the accounting rules of the Financial Accounting Standards Board and the International Accounting Standards Board. This is because bank regulators have traditionally believed that mark-to-market changes do not fairly portray bank capital. As discussed, the Basel Committee is now proposing to include these marks in measurement of capital in order to unite the regulatory and accounting standards more firmly, but this remains highly controversial.

It is puzzling how this difference has survived under current legislation in the USA. Since the thrift crisis, regulatory accounting principles (RAP) have generally had to conform to general accounting principles—the 1991 FDICIA legislation requires that RAP cannot be 'less stringent' than generally accepted accounting principles (GAAP).[57] But, this has placed enormous regulatory and political pressure on accounting standards to accommodate regulatory and political concerns that stem from banks not having adequate capital, and the resulting need for public money. Indeed, at the very time that the Basel Committee is seeking to import more fair value accounting into the measurement of bank capital, many in industry and the EU itself have been trying to diminish the role of fair value accounting for accounting purposes[58] given the general unification between regulatory and accounting measurement. Bifurcation of these two standards may be a better

---

[57] The Federal Deposit Insurance Corporation Improvement Act of 1991, H.R. 3768, 102nd Congress, generally requires that accounting principles applicable to reports or statements required to be filed with US banking agencies 'result in financial statements or reports of condition that accurately reflect the capital of such institutions.' 12 U.S.C. x1831(n)(a)(1)(A) (2006). The Act further provides, in subsection (n)(a)(2)(A), entitled 'Uniform accounting principles consistent with GAAP', that 'reports and statements' required to be filed by depository institutions shall be uniform and consistent with US GAAP. Furthermore, subsection (n)(a)(2)(B), entitled 'Stringency', provides that if a banking agency determines that US GAAP does not accurately reflect capital, it may prescribe a different accounting principle, but one 'which is no less stringent' than US GAAP. US banking regulators apparently take the view that the 'reports and statements' do not apply to regulatory capital requirements. However, since reports and statements required to be filed with the agencies include those reflecting regulatory capital requirements, this interpretation would seem to be quite weak. Furthermore, the legislative history seems to belie this interpretation. The House Conference Report on H.R. 3768 states that the appropriate Federal banking agency or the FDIC is authorized to prescribe accounting principles applicable to insured depository institutions that are more stringent than GAAP. H.R. Rep. No. 102–330 (19 November 1991). There is no statement that they can be more lax.

[58] See above n 24.

solution, while also ensuring that regulators cannot invoke this authority as an excuse for forbearance. A neutral third party—whose identity would have to be decided—would have to determine that a regulatory approach, diverging from GAAP, was reasonable.[59] I do not believe regulators will adopt the same fair value accounting as is presently described under accounting standards, and it would be bad for investors to have their accounting shaped by the concerns of bank regulators.

VII. Conclusion

However elusive a concept 'systemic risk' may be, capital requirements reflecting true balance sheet values and market risks are indisputably necessary to shore up a financial system against the threat of a chain-reaction collapse arising from a bank or large financial institution's inability to meet its obligations.

The ability of the Basel methodology to protect the financial system from future risk without excessive limits on financial (and therefore economic) activity is doubtful. Is there any reason to believe regulators can be more successful in pricing risk than bureaucrats have been in pricing goods? The world is too complicated and fast changing for this to work. We must, therefore, harness market discipline to play a key role in this process. But this has its own set of challenges. Without eliminating all but assured bailouts for systemically important institutions, creditors will not adequately police financial institution's capital. And further, without the right information, the market will be unable to estimate the right amount of capital.

---

[59] Herz, above n 31, at 7.

13

The Role of Transparency in Financial Regulation

Christine Kaufmann and Rolf H. Weber

I. Introduction

Some hundred years ago, Supreme Court Justice Louis Brandeis was concerned about excessive commissions imposed on investors by underwriters of securities issuances for their services. Brandeis strongly believed that making such commissions transparent would give investors the necessary knowledge to better protect themselves: 'Publicity is justly commended as a remedy for social and industrial diseases. Sunlight is said to be the best of disinfectants; electric light the most efficient policeman.'[1]

For Brandeis, the duty to make information available to the public was a necessary companion to the right to privacy, a concept which he had pioneered.[2] At the time, his focus was not only on investors, but also on government actions and business methods in general. 'Publicity' implied many elements of current transparency concepts by shedding light on governments' actions with regard to data collection, meetings and financing, among others. Brandeis saw transparency as a remedy for otherwise illegal or objectionable actions, an approach which has influenced today's anti-corruption strategies: 'If the broad light of day could be let in upon men's actions, it would purify them as the sun disinfects'.[3] Transparency has long been recognized as a key element of governance[4] and is essential in rebuilding and maintaining trust in financial markets especially after a crisis

---

[1] Louis D. Brandeis, 'What Publicity Can Do', in *Other People's Money: And How the Bankers Use It* (Mansfield Centre: Martino Publishing, 2009, first published 1914 by McClure Publications) 92–108, at 92.

[2] First in Samuel D. Warren and Louis D. Brandeis, 'The Right to Privacy', 4 *Harvard Law Review* 193 (1890) and later as Supreme Court Judge in his dissenting opinion in *Olmstead v USA*, 277 US 433 (1929), at 471 (43 S Ct 394).

[3] Letter to Alice Goldmark, 26 February 1891 in Melvin I. Urofsky and David W. Levy (eds), *Letters of Louis D. Brandeis, Volume I, 1870–1907* (New York: State University of New York Press, 1971) 100.

[4] Rosa M. Lastra and Heba Shams, 'Public Accountability in the Financial Sector', in Eilis Ferran and Charles A.E. Goodhart (eds), *Regulating Financial Services and Markets in the 21st Century* (Oxford: Hart Publishing, 2001) 165–88, at 170–1.

which—at least partially—has been attributed to a lack of 'market confidence'. However, if it were that simple and all it took were some reassuring measures, the crisis would have been resolved long ago. In the real world, the fundamentals of market confidence are neither clear or rational, nor necessarily based on economic evidence and they are not carved in stone. The result is a lack of predictability and at the same time a window of opportunity for the state to be creative and regulate proactively rather than merely to catch up with market developments. For such a shaping policy to succeed in building market confidence, clear objectives and principles that can be understood by all stakeholders need to be established.[5] Integrating transparency into regulation will thus enhance legal certainty and confidence.

Not surprisingly, in the aftermath of the financial crisis, transparency has become a priority on the agenda of regulators around the world. Yet, the perspectives from which transparency is addressed vary. Some focus on the 'micro-level' of transparency by emphasizing its function in restoring confidence in markets and establishing rules for financial institutions. Examples are the revision of the Basel II framework[6] issued by the Basel Committee on Banking Supervision (BCBS) or the Report of the Financial Stability Forum (now Financial Stability Board, or FSB) on Enhancing Market and Institutional Resilience.[7] Others pursue a different approach by embedding transparency in the broader context of lawful and ethical behaviour. Examples are the Swiss Code of Ethics[8] or the Islamic Financial Services Board's disclosure rules:

The need for transparency is, above all, an important Shari'ah consideration. Any form of concealment, fraud or attempt at misrepresentation violates the principles of justice and

---

[5] See the recent comment by Dani Rodrik, 'The Market Confidence Bugaboo', Project Syndicate, 7 July 2010, <http://www.project-syndicate.org/commentary/rodrik45/English> (visited 25 July 2010).
[6] Bank for International Settlements, Basel Committee on Banking Supervision (BCBS), 'International Convergence of Capital Measurement and Capital Standards: A Revised Framework' (integrated version) June 2004 with revisions 2005 and 2006, <http://www.bis.org/publ/bcbs107.htm> (visited 20 July 2010). In January 2009, the BCBS announced enhancements, including to transparency issues, to the Basel II capital framework (Basel III). However, on 26 July 2010, the BCBS agreed on less stringent standards than originally envisioned and announced by the G20. This agreement was formally accepted on 12 September 2010 when the Basel Committee announced 'Basel III' as a reform package for higher global minimum capital standards; see BIS Press Release, 'Group of Governors and Heads of Supervision Announces Higher Global Minimum Capital Standards', 12 September 2010, <http://www.bis.org/press/p100912.htm> (visited 27 September 2010).
[7] Financial Stability Forum, 'Enhancing Market and Institutional Resilience', April 2008, <http://www.financialstabilityboard.org/publications/r_0804.pdf> (visited 26 July 2010); the FSB now (July 2010) invites feedback on the new risk disclosure practices, see FSB Press Release, 'FSB Invites Feedback on Risk Disclosure Practices', 21 July 2010, <http://www.financialstabilityboard.org/press/pr_100721.pdf> (visited 26 July 2010).
[8] The Swiss Code of Ethics is a private initiative of renowned representatives of the Swiss economy. Transparency is one of the seven principles of the code. See Swiss Code of Ethics, <http://www.swisscodeofethics.ch/code/prinzipien/transparenz> (visited 26 July 2010). The Code was written by a working group, consisting of Ernest Abouchar, Balz Hösly, Adrian Jäger, Christina Kuenzle and Hans Wehrli.

fairness in Shari'ah as mentioned in the Qur'an in, among others, Surah An-Nisa' verse 135 and Surah Al-Mutaffifin verses 1 to 3.[9]

This chapter argues that the principles for transparency developed in constitutional law are also applicable to financial regulation. It thus proposes a comprehensive, rule-based rather than a purely process-oriented approach and suggests a *three-dimensional concept* of transparency in financial regulation. The first dimension refers to *institutional* aspects, i.e. procedures and decision-making. These two elements have already been identified in a similar way, especially in the context of internet transparency, yet within a conceptually different framework.[10] By providing legal certainty, transparency serves as an *anchor* for financial regulation. It is the basis for establishing trust, which is the key element of any financial system. In its second dimension, transparency is understood as the *substantive* backbone of financial regulation. It lays open the values and goals of financial policy and regulation. The third dimension is *accountability* of actors as an essential element for rebuilding confidence in the financial system. The chapter follows a 'bottom-up approach' by starting with procedural aspects of transparency, then moving on to its substantial values and concluding with situating transparency in the broader framework of international law; thereby preparing the field for further discussions on transparency at an international level.

II. Notion of Transparency

The literal meaning of transparent, according to the Oxford English Dictionary, is 'easily seen through, recognized, understood, or detected; manifest, evident, obvious, clear.'[11]

Historically, transparency in regulation is seen as a constitutional instrument for empowering the people as opposed to entrusting a monarch with absolute sovereignty. Transparency in its early form, therefore, prohibits the interference in the course of justice by the absolute sovereign ('Kabinettsjustiz') and requires the publication of the law in force. As a principle, it replaces to some extent the prerogative of the sovereign prince.[12] Publication, however, will only be efficient if it reaches both the holder of obligations and the holder of rights. Information thus becomes an essential element of transparency, both as a human right—freedom of information—and with its institutional dimension by making information

---

[9] Islamic Financial Services Board, 'Disclosures to Promote Transparency and Market Discipline for Institutions Offering Islamic Financial Services', December 2007, para 2, <http://www.ifsb.org> (visited 17 July 2010).

[10] Rolf H. Weber, *Shaping Internet Governance: Regulatory Challenges* (Zürich: Schulthess and Springer, 2009) 122–3.

[11] *Oxford English Dictionary Online*, Second Edition 1989 (Oxford: Oxford University Press, 2010).

[12] John Locke, *Second Treatise of Government, An Essay Concerning the True Origin, Extent, and End of Civil Government* (London: Awnsham Churchill by Amen-Corner, 1690) Sections 164–5.

public.[13] Similarly, economists identify information and transparency as essential elements for efficient free markets.[14]

Once rules are published and transparent, holding those who are bound by these rules accountable for violations is a logical consequence. Accountability becomes part of the concept of transparency.

This brief account shows that the notion of transparency contains an element of visibility and clarity on the one hand and an element of empowerment and capability on the other. Transparency in regulation thus entails the process of 'seeing through' as well as the 'object' that is being looked at.[15]

III. The Three Dimensions of Transparency in Financial Regulation

A. Transparency and confidence

As illustrated in the contribution by Rosa Lastra and Geoffrey Wood,[16] the recent financial crisis cannot be attributed to one specific cause but rather to a complex web of interacting phenomena. Nevertheless, there is a recurrent theme in all the discussions from investment to monetary policy: the loss of confidence or trust in functioning financial markets.

Confidence means expecting a specific behaviour of people or institutions because they *must* behave in a specific way. Generally, such a 'must' can be based on a variety of reasons, such as rules, conventions or morals.[17]

Confidence as a legitimate expectation can therefore be lost and betrayed. Confidence in the financial system is based on the combination of a regulatory framework and actors' loyalty to both the framework and to each other.[18] Loyalty in financial markets takes different forms: trust among the parties is the basis of any private business relationship in financial services. An investor needs confidence in the financial institution before he or she entrusts it with managing his or her assets. Vice versa, an investment bank benefits from clients who will not lightly withdraw their money in cases of market turbulence.[19]

---

[13] Rolf H. Weber, *Datenschutz v Öffentlichkeitsprinzip* (Zürich: Schulthess and Springer, 2010) paras 18 and 24.

[14] George A. Akerlof, 'The Market for Lemons: Quality Uncertainty and the Market Mechanism' 84 *Quarterly Journal of Economics* 488 (1970). In 2001, George A. Akerlof, Michael Spence, and Joseph E. Stiglitz received the Nobel Prize in economics for their seminal work on markets with asymmetric information. For a legal analysis see John H. Jackson, 'Sovereignty-Modern: A New Approach to an Outdated Concept', 97 *American Journal of International Law* 782 (2003), at 797–8.

[15] See Weber, above n 10, at 132. See also Lastra and Shams who identify five elements of transparency, above n 4, at 171.

[16] Lastra and Wood, in this volume at Chapter 1.

[17] Bernhard Schlink (ed.), 'Wirtschaft und Vertrauen', in Bernhard Schlink *Vergewisserungen über Politik, Recht, Schreiben und Glauben* (Zürich: Diogenes Verlag, 2005) 66, 67.

[18] Christine Kaufmann and Mirja Ciesolka, 'Wann baute Noah die Arche—Vermögensverwaltung als Akteurin einer nachhaltigen Marktentwicklung' in Peter R. Isler and Romeo Cerutti (eds), *Vermögensverwaltung III*, (Zürich: Schriftenreihe Nr. 105 des Europainstitutes an der Universität Zürich, 2010) 1–32, at 3.

[19] Kaufmann and Ciesolka, above n 18, at 2.

Moreover, transparency is the key instrument in preventing market abuse, including insider dealing[20] and market manipulation,[21] money laundering,[22] terrorism financing[23] and corruption.[24]

Transparency is thus a precondition for building confidence since it is the very essence of any expectation.

B. The first dimension of transparency: anchoring financial regulation

1. *Legal certainty, moral hazard and too big to fail*

Legal certainty is essential for creating a stable environment for efficient financial markets. It entails the establishment of rules which are clearly communicated and accessible to the relevant actors both with regard to their substance and the responsible authorities. At first glance, this may seem a trivial and obvious statement. However, in practice, the situation is rather complex. Several specifics of financial markets are often quoted as reasons to limit regulatory transparency.

The first phenomenon is the risk of moral hazard. On the one hand, an investor will undoubtedly have an interest in knowing the consequences in the case that a financial institution becomes insolvent. From his or her perspective, any guarantee that potential losses will be covered by the state or insurance contributes to certainty. In this light, the USA, following the savings and loan crisis of the 1980s, introduced some basic rules on supporting failing banks. On the other hand, from an economic perspective, insolvent—in contrast to 'only' illiquid—financial institutions must not be rescued. Concerns about moral hazard are one of the reasons why many countries and the European Union (EU) decided not to publish, or not even to establish, rules on which an institution would act as a lender of last resort and under what conditions.[25] For the same reasons, in 1998 the International Monetary Fund (IMF) decided to give a signal that states facing bankruptcy could not assume that they would be rescued automatically and delayed financial aid to defaulting Russia.[26]

During the current financial crisis this concept came under pressure. The unprecedented scale of the crisis required state interventions to prevent further

---

[20] The USA enacted the first insider regulation as early as 1934 with the Securities Exchange Act (15 United States Code (USC) xx 78a ff), which is still in force but has been revised several times.
[21] Directive 2003/6/EC of the European Parliament and of the Council of 28 January 2003 on insider dealing and market manipulation (market abuse), OJ L 96, 12 April 2003, at 16.
[22] Directive 2005/60/EC of the European Parliament and of the Council of 26 October 2005 on the prevention of the use of the financial system for the purpose of money laundering and terrorist financing, OJ L 309, 25 November 2005, at 15.
[23] Financial Action Task Force (FATF), 'Special Recommendations on Terrorism Financing' (October 2001 with subsequent amendments), Special Recommendation IV, <http://www.fatf-gafi.org/dataoecd/8/17/34849466.pdf> (visited 30 July 2010).
[24] United Nations Convention against Corruption, 31 October 2003, UNTS 2005, 2349, arts 5(1) and 10 name transparency as one of the building blocks of anti-corruption policies.
[25] Rosa Maria Lastra, 'Lender of last resort, An International Perspective', 48 *International and Comparative Law Quarterly* 340 (1999), at 351.
[26] Abbigail J. Chiodo and Michael T. Owyang, 'A Case Study of a Currency Crisis: The Russian Default in 1998', 84(6) *Federal Reserve Bank of St. Louis Review* 7 (2002), at 12–14.

spread and contagion with disastrous consequences for the whole economy. In many countries, decision-making took unusual forms not least because confidentiality was crucial with regard to market reactions. 'Decide now, act immediately, explain quickly and validate later',[27] which often led to a series of improvisations, became a widespread approach.[28] In the UK, a relatively small group of representatives from the Government (Treasury), the Bank of England and the Financial Services Authority (FSA) decided based on informal arrangements.[29] Similarly, in Switzerland, the Government[30] decided on a rescue package for the largest Swiss Bank based on its constitutional power for emergency situations.[31]

The decisions of the UK and Switzerland, as well as those of many other countries, in favour of state intervention were heavily influenced by the collapse of Lehman Brothers. After the US government, based on moral hazard considerations, decided not to intervene to rescue Lehman Brothers, the already volatile financial markets became even more distressed. It quickly became clear that referring to the concept of moral hazard and denying a bail-out of systemically relevant institutions was no longer an option given the scale of the crisis. However, the phenomenon of some institutions being 'too big to fail' put governments in a paradoxical situation because many of the globally active, systemically relevant institutions have become so big that covering their risks goes beyond the capacity of national economies.[32]

While profits resulted to a large extent from international business and risks were taken globally, the crisis hit nationally. As Mervyn King put it: 'Global banks are global in life, but national in death'.[33]

---

[27] Julia Black, 'Managing the Financial Crisis—The Constitutional Dimension', LSE Law, Society and Economy Working Papers 12/2010, at 38, <http://ssrn.com/abstract=1619784> (visited 20 July 2010).

[28] Richard A. Posner, *A Failure of Capitalism: The Crisis of '08 and the Descent into Depression* (Cambridge, MA: Harvard University Press, 2009) 329.

[29] For a detailed account see Black, above n 27, at 24–5; on the concept of transparency see George A. Walker, 'United Kingdom Regulatory Reform: A New Beginning in Policy and Programme Construction', in Douglas Arner and Jan-Juy Lin (eds), *Financial Regulation* (Hong Kong: Sweet and Maxwell Asia, 2003) 199–239, at 213 ff.

[30] Together with the Swiss National Bank (SNB) and the Financial Markets Supervisory Authority (FINMA).

[31] The rescue measures were framed as 'Verordnung zur Rekapitalisierung der UBS AG' (Federal Ordinance for the Recapitalization of UBS AG), 15 October 2008 (SR 611.055).

[32] An illustrative example is Switzerland: In 2008, the balance sheet of the largest Swiss bank, UBS, reached 2015 billion Swiss francs, compared to the Swiss Gross Domestic Product of 545 billion Swiss francs. See UBS, 'Annual Report 2008' <http://www.ubs.com/1/ShowMedia/investors/annualreporting/2008?contentId=162873&name=UBS_AnnualReport2008_e.pdf> (visited 29 October 2010), Swiss Federal Statistical Office, 'Gross Domestic Product: Production Approach 1990–2008', <http://www.bfs.admin.ch/bfs/portal/en/index/themen/04/02/01/key/bip_gemaess_produktionsansatz.html> (visited 25 July 2010).

[33] Quoted in *The Turner Review: A Regulatory Response to the Global Banking Crisis* (London: Financial Services Authority, March 2009) 36, <http://www.fsa.gov.uk/pubs/other/turner_review.pdf> (visited 25 July 2010).

2. Who is doing what exactly under what circumstances? Responsibilities and procedures

Countries involved in rescue actions have come to realize that there is a need for making the requirements for interventions in favour of systemically relevant banks transparent in order to avoid insecurity and the related negative impact on markets and the economy as a whole. As a result, several initiatives for addressing the too-big-to-fail phenomenon have been launched or are in the process of being launched. One of the controversial issues is whether the size of financial institutions which are considered too big, too interconnected or too complex needs to be limited.[34]

The financial crisis showed that, in many countries, financial regulation is not adequately anchored in the constitutional framework,[35] particularly when urgent measures are necessary. With a view to maintaining a stable financial system, regulation needs to focus on preventing uncertainty by establishing transparent criteria for state actions in financial markets, including interventions in future crises.

Thus, a constitutional decision on the criteria and the process by which these criteria are being assessed in a concrete case are necessary. This includes a clear distribution of responsibilities, both at the national and international level. As the recent crisis indicates, cooperation among the different institutions and their respective roles are not transparent.[36] Attempts to ameliorate this situation are twofold: on the one hand they include the establishment of new institutions for macro-prudential supervision, such as the Financial Stability Oversight Board in the USA[37] or the European Systemic Risk Board in the EU.[38] In the UK, the Bank of England will replace the FSA as supervisory institution.[39] On the other hand, the regulatory framework is being strengthened by replacing informal, non-transparent rules with formal, published regulations. For the UK, the 2009 Banking Act is the first permanent statutory regime to address banks with financial difficulties, and in the USA a comprehensive revision of financial regulation was accepted in July

---

[34] Size limitation is promoted by, *inter alia*, the Governor of the Bank of England, Mervyn King, see Speech by Mervyn King, Lord Mayor's Banquet for Bankers and Merchants of the City of London at the Mansion House, 17 June 2009, at 6–7, <http://www.bankofengland.co.uk/publications/speeches/2009/speech394.pdf> (visited 24 July 2010).

[35] Thomas Cottier, 'Challenges ahead in International Economic Law', 12 *Journal of International Economic Law* 3 (2009).

[36] See also Garicano and Lastra, in this volume at Chapter 4.

[37] Introduced by the Dodd–Frank Wall Street Reform and Consumer Protection Act which was adopted by the US Senate on 15 July 2010 and signed by President Obama on 21 July 2010 (Pub. L. 111–203).

[38] Proposal for a Regulation of the European Parliament and of the Council on Community macro-prudential oversight of the financial system and establishing a European Systemic Risk Board, COM (2009) 499 final, 23 September 2009.

[39] HM Treasury, *A New Approach to Financial Regulation: Judgment, Focus and Stability* (London: Crown, July 2010), <http://www.hm-treasury.gov.uk/d/consult_financial_regulation_condoc.pdf> (visited 30 July 2010).

2010.[40] An initiative for a new institutional framework for supervision of financial markets is currently being discussed in the EU; however, the new institutions will have relatively weak competences for issuing binding rules. An example for specifically addressing the too-big-to-fail issue is provided by Switzerland where several options are currently being evaluated.[41]

In sum, one key role of transparency is to anchor financial regulation within the constitutional framework by establishing clear responsibilities and procedures and thereby reducing moral hazard.[42]

C. The second dimension: defining substantial values and objectives

1. Defining values: what is the goal of financial regulation?

Sound financial regulation is not an objective in itself but a means to an end. Based on Franklin D. Roosevelt's Four Freedom speech and the Atlantic Charter signed by Franklin D. Roosevelt and Winston Churchill in 1941, participants at the Bretton Woods Conference in 1944 agreed that stable monetary and financial systems were one of the pillars for a peaceful post-war order. They shared a common vision of establishing international institutions and mechanisms that would ensure lasting peace and thereby foster human welfare. Transparency was considered essential at the time given that re-establishing trust in stable currencies after the turmoil of the 1930s was a daunting task. The solution was found in anchoring exchange rates to an undisputed value—gold. However, in 1944 the founding fathers of the Bretton Woods Institutions, John Maynard Keynes and Harry Dexter White, were already aware that their ambitious goal would not be achieved with fixed exchange rates alone, but that efficient markets would be equally essential.

Ensuring efficient markets has become a key objective of financial regulation. From the beginning, information has been at the heart of all of these efforts, especially with regard to limiting information asymmetries and establishing information flows among different actors. The development of corporate governance played an important role in this regard by requiring publicly accessible accounts as a condition for limited liability status and stock market listing in the nineteenth century.[43] In order

---

[40] The Dodd–Frank Wall Street Reform and Consumer Protection Act, above n 37, contains a comprehensive financial reform.

[41] A committee of experts appointed by the government is currently drafting proposals. A preliminary report by the 'Too big to fail' Commission of Experts, 'Limitierung von volkswirtschaftlichen Risiken durch Grossunternehmen' (Limiting economic risks induced by big enterprises) was released on 22 April 2010. The report suggests inter alia regulating a bank's equity, liquidity, risk allocation and organizational structure. The final report was published in autumn 2010, see <http://www.sif.admin.ch/dokumentation/00514/00519/00592/index.html?lang=en> (visited 25 July 2010).

[42] Rolf H. Weber, 'Mapping and Structuring International Financial Regulation—A Theoretical Approach', 20 *European Banking Law Review* 651 (2009), at 666.

[43] Christopher Hood, 'Transparency in Historical Perspective', in Christopher Hood and David Heald (eds), *Transparency: The Key to Better Government?* (Oxford: British Academy/Oxford University Press, 2006) 3–23, at 17 and 20.

to reassure the public in the aftermath of several economic crises in the twentieth century, corporate obligations to disclose and publish internal information were extended.[44]

This extension partly reflects the development of theories on 'information asymmetry' by institutional economists working on transaction costs and principal–agent theories.[45] Once an economic need for horizontal transparency and accountability among market participants had been established, regulations were drafted to provide the necessary binding framework. Legal studies focused on developing systems and rules for the quality and flow of information among the different stakeholders.[46] Obviously, accounting standards or systems to disclose relevant financial information to the public, to investors, counterparties, consumers and regulators and supervisors are essential.[47] Ideally, such information would allow supervisors and market actors to develop an early warning system and prevent major financial shocks.[48] In this respect, the most commonly used international standards are the International Financial Reporting Standards (IFRS) as developed by the International Accounting Standards Board (IASB) and supported by the International Organization of Securities Commissions (IOSCO).[49]

With globalized markets, measuring and assessing risks has become a priority for decision making in financial markets. However, highly complex risk-measurement models, such as the Basel Capital Framework,[50] tend to lose sight of their main objective and instead have started to lead a life of their own.

2. Keep it simple: transparency calls for robust, not more, financial regulation

Experience shows that financial crises regularly provoke a call for more transparency. However, 'more transparency' often implies increasing the amount of information rather than its quality. An illustrative example is the US Sarbanes–Oxley Act that was enacted following the collapse of Enron.[51] It imposes detailed disclosure obligations on companies and yet it has not lived up to the expectation of inducing the most substantial change in business practices since Franklin D. Roosevelt.[52]

---

[44] See Hood, above n 43, at 17.
[45] Adolf A. Berle and Gardiner C. Means, *The Modern Corporation and Private Property* (New York: Harcourt, Brace & World, [1932] 1968) 278 ff.
[46] See Hood, above n 43, at 18.
[47] See Weber, above n 42, at 665.
[48] Kern Alexander, 'The Need for Efficient International Financial Regulation and the Role of a Global Supervisor', in Eilis Ferran and Charles A.E. Goodhart (eds), *Regulating Financial Services and Markets in the 21st Century* (Oxford: Hart Publishing, 2001) 273–95, at 290–1.
[49] See generally, <http://www.ifrs.org and http://www.iosco.org/> (visited on 27 July 2010).
[50] See above n 6.
[51] Sarbanes–Oxley Act of 30 July 2002, 116 Stat. 745, 15 USC x 7201.
[52] Bernhard Kuschnik, 'The Sarbanes Oxley Act: "Big Brother is Watching You" or Adequate Measures of Corporate Governance Regulation?', 5 *Rutgers Business Law Journal* 65 (2008).

Similarly, the current financial crisis revealed that highly sophisticated risk-management systems may be transparent but still not provide the people and institutions in charge with the information they need—and understand. In fact, too much transparency may overburden recipients thus making it impossible for them to adequately process information[53] and may even result in the so-called 'Cassandra effect'[54] or in ignoring 'the prospect of future changes about the actual character of which we know nothing'.[55] A striking illustration in this regard is the report of the Swiss Financial Markets Supervisory Authority on the financial crisis, which concluded that the level of complexity of the Basel II model[56] exceeded the capacities of the supervisor, let alone the bank's management.[57]

In order to achieve the goals set in 1941, in the aftermath of the recent financial crisis, transparency needs to be more than a disinfectant and must provide for healing. As a result, transparency as a substantial principle includes defining clear values and standards as well as providing the necessary legal instruments for accessing information. Consequently, standard-setting cannot be left to the market alone but needs to be clearly positioned within a legal framework in order to protect legitimate expectations of market participants. A first step and a conceptual milestone in combining legal rules with self-regulation by market participants is the 'Protect, Respect and Remedy Framework' for corporate responsibility proposed by John Ruggie.[58]

Applied to transparency, it requires states to impose legal obligations for disclosing relevant information on market participants and at the same time to ensure access to that information for all stakeholders. The latter implies nothing less than protecting freedom of information as an element of the human right to free speech.[59] It therefore mirrors the 'two-sided' approach of Article 10 in the European Convention on Human Rights.

Transparency is also critical in assessing the effectiveness of international regimes. This is why the Human Rights Council explicitly refers to transparency in its institutional framework and the Human Rights Committee emphasizes transparency in the submission of reports according to Article 40 of the International

---

[53] For this confusion effect see Rolf H. Weber, 'Kassandra oder Wissensbroker—Dilemma im Global Village', in Jürgen Becker, Reto M. Hilty, Jean Fritz Stöckli and Thomas Würtenberger (eds), *Recht im Wandel seines sozialen und technologischen Umfeldes*, Festschrift für Manfred Rehbinder (Bern and München: Stämpfli Verlag, 2002) 405–21, at 407.

[54] See Weber, above n 53, at 407.

[55] John Maynard Keynes, 'The General Theory of Employment', 51 *Quarterly Journal of Economics* 209 (1937), at 214.

[56] See above n 6.

[57] Swiss Financial Market Supervisory Authority (FINMA), 'Finanzmarktkrise und Finanzmarktaufsicht', 14 September 2009, at 12–13 and 21–2.

[58] 'Protect, Respect and Remedy: A Framework for Business and Human Rights', Report of the Special Representative of the Secretary-General on the issue of human rights and transnational corporations and other business enterprises, John Ruggie, UN document A/HRC/8/5, 7 April 2008 (Protect, Respect and Remedy Framework). For the most recent report see 'Further Steps toward the Operationalization of the "Protect, Respect and Remedy" Framework', UN document A/HRC/14/27, 9 April 2010 (Operationalization of the Framework).

[59] Patrick Birkinshaw, 'Freedom of Information and Openness: Fundamental Human Rights?' 58 *Administrative Law Review* 177 (2006), at 204 and 216.

Covenant on Civil and Political Rights (ICCPR).[60] In the same light, the Committee on Economic, Social and Cultural Rights regularly states that transparency and accountability are standard elements of a state's duty to protect under the International Covenant on Economic Social, and Cultural Rights (ICESCR) when establishing national human rights policies. An illustrative example is the right to health: 'The national health strategy and plan of action should also be based on the principles of accountability, transparency and independence of the judiciary, since good governance is essential to the effective implementation of all human rights, including the realization of the right to health'.[61]

In general terms, enhancing transparency depends on the purpose for which information is sought, on the capacity of and incentives for actors to provide that information and on the strategies adopted to encourage transparency.[62] Obviously, these criteria need to be stated in the regulatory framework and cannot be left to market participants. However, developing specific methods to enable different regimes and organizations to promote transparency has so far been rather neglected.

With a view to promoting market confidence, transparent obligations for market participants are important, both with regard to their content and to regulatory responsibility. Therefore, a regulatory line needs to be drawn between the issues which can be left to the market and those which cannot. This includes, for example, the regulatory decision on whether stress tests need to be mandatory based on given standards and whether bonus systems need to be limited by the regulator. Transparency also requires supervisory authorities to base new obligations on law. Current developments show that there is a tendency to impose new, especially technical rules, such as stricter liquidity and equity requirements on financial institutions without the necessary legal basis and, accordingly, in a rather non-transparent manner. While such an approach may be feasible in the middle of a crisis, a more robust model based on a careful balancing of transparency interests and the necessary discretion for supervisors needs to be established now.

The aftermath of the crisis is also the time to reflect on the values in which confidence should be re-established. Instead of continuing on the same track, the regulatory goals need to be redefined and the new definition needs to be made transparent. This is by no means a call for more regulation, but instead for better, more robust regulation. The recent crisis did not start because financial markets and financial institutions were not regulated enough but rather because regulations were not adequate. An 'overdose' of transparency in the form of over-complex risk-measurement systems or capital adequacy requirements bears the risk of the 'Cassandra and confusion effect' described above and is rarely capable of accommodating developments that are difficult to anticipate or to calibrate as we have just

[60] Human Rights Council, 'Institution-building of the United Nations Human Rights Council', UN document A/HRC/RES/5/1, 18 June 2007, para 21.

[61] Committee on Social, Economic and Cultural Rights, 'General Comment No. 14: The Right to the Highest Attainable Standard of Health (Art. 12)', UN document E/C.12/2000/4, 11 August 2000, para 55.

[62] Ronald B. Mitchell, 'Sources of Transparency: Information Systems in International Regimes', 42 *International Studies Quarterly* 109 (1998), at 109–10.

experienced. Rules are only robust if they focus on the essentials; otherwise, supervisors will be lost in a jungle of domestic regulations and international standards.

For years, the mantra that free market disciplines are essential for prosperity in the longer term—even if painful in the short term—was taught for good reasons. With the recent crisis, some of its fundamentals have been questioned, given that the crisis did not stem from weaknesses in the real economy. The financial world has changed and requires a regulatory response. Trust in the financial system and in its actors necessitates knowing the rules and respecting them. With market disciplines and many states failing to respond adequately to the crisis, international law is called upon to play a corrective and compensatory role.

D. The third dimension: accountability as an element of transparency

1. Governance, trust and accountability

As already outlined, confidence plays an important role in establishing financial markets. While the first dimension of transparency requires the state to anchor financial regulation in its overall constitutional framework and the second dimension defines the key values and procedures, the question of accountability still needs to be addressed.

Accountability of market actors applies to a variety of relationships in the financial sector: the relationship between the state and financial institutions, between the financial institution and its investors and customers and also the relationship between taxpayers and (rescued) financial institutions. No regulation can prevent breaches of rules, inadequate risk management or unethical behaviour. However, regulation can set the stage with transparent rules of the game, first by integrating financial markets in the constitutional framework (first dimension of transparency), second by defining the applicable basic values and procedures (second dimension of transparency) and third by providing mechanisms to hold actors accountable (third dimension of transparency).

Accountability is a concept with many facets.[63] Together with checks and balances, it is a prerequisite for legitimacy and a key element of any governance discussion.

Accountability depends on reliable information. Such information needs to be available, accessible—both logistically and intellectually—and based on known sources. These elements are enshrined in the human right to access information, a right which 'is fundamental in ensuring transparency. In order for democratic procedures to be effective, people must have access to public information. . . . This allows them to take decisions; . . . challenge or influence public policies; monitor the quality of public spending; and promote accountability. All of this, in turn, makes

---

[63] For a comprehensive analysis see Lastra and Shams, above n 4, at 166–9; see also Weber, above n 10, at 133.

it possible to establish controls to prevent the abuse of power'.[64] Without such mechanisms, 'the members of society will not be informed or able to participate, and decision-making will not be democratic'.[65]

While checks and balances take place *ex ante* by providing mechanisms to prevent the abuse of power, accountability steps in *ex post* by assessing actions with mechanisms such as judicial review, or non-judicial remedies.[66]

2. Challenges in holding actors in the financial sector accountable

Challenges in holding actors in the financial sector accountable are manifold. Three are particularly relevant to transparency:

(a) *The institutional challenge:* It relates to the accountability of public actors in financial markets, such as treasury departments of the government, supervisory and monetary authorities towards society. In this regard, the nature of some of the key actors as 'independent' institutions and expert networks is relevant. What has been framed by some commentators as 'governments in crisis'[67] is in fact the result of the legal and institutional set-up of public actors in financial markets.

In the 1990s, economic studies concluded that *inter alia* because of asymmetric information on policy goals, independent monetary authorities with a mandate for maintaining price stability performed much better than those under governmental control pursuing other policies such as keeping unemployment rates low.[68] As a result, many central banks were vested with significant autonomy and shielded from state influence. The prime example is the establishment of the European Central Bank in 1998.

Not least, the recent crisis showed that tensions may arise when an independent monetary or supervisory authority takes decisions which have an impact on the national economy without involving the parliament or other politically responsible bodies. In these situations, economic perceptions on how much transparency is required may collide with legal concepts of involving the respective stakeholders. To overcome this dilemma and compensate for the lack of publicity, accountability mechanisms which provide for *ex post* transparency have been established. In many countries, central banks will inform the public about the details of their decisions on monetary policy only after a time delay; parliaments will conduct hearings with

---

[64] Human Rights Council, 'Report of the Special Rapporteur on the Promotion and Protection of the Right to Freedom of Opinion and Expression', Mr Frank La Rue, 20 April 2010, UN document A/HRC/14/23, para 31.

[65] See Human Rights Council, above n 64, at para 33.

[66] Ruth W. Grant and Robert O. Keohane, 'Accountability and Abuses of Power in World Politics', 99 *American Political Science Review* 29 (2005), at 30–1. For a different concept see Lastra and Shams, above n 4, at 169.

[67] Steven M. Davidoff and David Zaring, 'Regulation by Deal: The Government's Response to the Financial Crisis', 61 *Administrative Law Review* 463 (2009), at 471.

[68] Alex Cukierman, *Central Bank Strategy, Credibility and Independence: Theory and Evidence* (Cambridge, MA: Massachusetts Institute of Technology Press, 1992) 139–60; Alex Cukierman, Steven B. Web and Bilin Neyapti, 'Measuring the Independence of Central Banks and Its Effect on Policy Outcomes', 6 *World Bank Economic Review* 353 (1992).

central bank governors and supervisors of financial institutions. However, most of these mechanisms date back to the 1990s and the first 'wave' of creating independent central banks. They were neither meant for accommodating rescue packages, such as those brought about by the recent crisis, nor for legitimizing a change in paradigm of a public institution pursuing a macro-economic policy being forced into taking on the role of deal-maker or, as some authors phrased it, a 'deal machine'.[69] Recent economic studies confirm that independence of monetary authorities is still important. However, they also highlight that independence-related discretion leads to asymmetric information and may result in uncertainty about the goals of an agency's policy amongst market participants.[70]

Not surprisingly, accountability of public agencies is now on the agenda of the legislator, particularly in countries where substantial state-led rescue actions had been necessary. Transparency is essential with regard to defining the scope of an institution's discretion. In this regard, addressing the problem of the too-big-to-fail phenomenon plays an important role because this doctrine was one of the factors forcing governments and central banks to act without clear guidelines and criteria in existing law. Thus, for example, decisions in the USA to let Lehman Brothers fail, but to nationalize Fannie Mae and Freddie Mac, had to be taken without clear rule-based guidelines.[71] Accountability with regard to institutions means measuring them against their transparent mandate in the political process. Transparency will also have to include cooperation. The financial crisis has produced a series of memoranda of understanding (MoU) between government, central banks and supervisory authorities. Most of these MoU find no basis in existing law but have been established based on the need for a pragmatic solution. Finally, transparency also implies linking up expert networks with politically accountable domestic institutions. Once transparent goals for monetary policy or supervisory actions are defined, these goals are also to be respected by the experts in the relevant networks, such as the FSB or the BCBS. To sum up, addressing the institutional accountability challenge requires transparency at three levels: defining the policy goals of the public institutions involved, setting a framework for cooperation among them, and including activities of public institutions' representatives in expert networks.

(b) *The contractual challenge:* Two of the basic accountability mechanisms with regard to the relationship between customers and financial institutions are a legal remedy to claim compensation for losses and the possibility of sanctioning violations. As a rule, such a remedy will be provided for by the applicable national civil law based on a violation of the contractual agreement between the customer and its financial institution. With the development of complex derivatives combined with sometimes exceedingly high profit expectations by investors, the question whether the potential risks have been sufficiently explained to customers has gained importance

---

[69] See Davidoff and Zaring, above n 67, at 508 ff.
[70] Li Qin, Moïse Sidiropoulos and Eleftherios Spyromitros, 'Robust Monetary Policy under Uncertainties about Central Bank Preferences', 62 *Bulletin of Economic Research* 197 (2010), at 204.
[71] See Davidoff and Zaring, above n 67, at 474 and 488.

in such disputes. From a governance and policy perspective, providing effective grievance mechanisms for those who believe that they have been harmed contributes to restoring trust in the financial system. A recent example is the conflict between investors and their asset managers in the aftermath of the collapse of Lehman Brothers. While some investors have brought lawsuits against the involved banks for not having correctly informed them about the risks involved, others are relying on informal negotiations. Since the respective banks' policies have not been published, investors cannot assess the likelihood of obtaining compensation in non-judicial proceedings. As a result, it is impossible to make an informed decision. With regard to governance, it is not decisive whether the grievance mechanism is judicial or non-judicial, but whether the requirements and procedures are *transparent*.[72] Transparency in this regard implies five elements which are also part of the suggested UN Framework for Corporate Responsibility for Human Rights (the Protect, Respect and Remedy Framework):[73] legitimacy, fair and equitable procedures, accessibility, predictability and openness.

Mechanisms are *legitimate* if they have clear, transparent and sufficiently independent governance structures as a precondition for *fair and equitable procedures*. An example could be an independent ombudsperson. Grievance mechanisms must be *known* to the public and *accessible* in reality. Market participants will only develop trust in such mechanisms if they are *predictable* with regard to potential remedies—including the limits—length of procedures and cost. Finally, such mechanisms need to be *open*, with process and outcome being as *transparent* as possible. In practice, this requires carefully balancing the public and private interests at stake. The mandate of financial regulation is not to fill all the details of these criteria but to provide the overall framework by defining the applicable criteria and their minimum content. Financial institutions could, for example, be required to designate a specific complaint mechanism and provide statistical data on how many complaints have been received and to what extent they were successful. For synergy and consistency purposes, it is essential to link such efforts with the ongoing discussions of the Protect, Respect and Remedy Framework.[74]

(c) *International context:* Financial markets are undisputedly global markets and yet there is no specific legally binding global regulatory framework. Instead, a multitude of standards, codes, best practices and guidelines have been developed over time.[75]

Notable exceptions from this wealth of non-binding instruments are the rules on transparency in the World Trade Organization (WTO) system, notably in the General Agreement on Tariffs and Trade (GATT), the Agreement on Technical Barriers to Trade (TBT) and—especially relevant for financial services—in the General Agreement on Trade in Services (GATS). Under the GATS, transparency

---

[72] As noted in John Ruggie's most recent report, non-judicial mechanisms may serve as early warning systems and prevent conflicts from escalating: See Operationalization of the Framework, above n 58, at para 92.
[73] See Protect, Respect and Remedy Framework, above n 58, at para 92.
[74] See Protect, Respect and Remedy Framework, above n 58.
[75] For a comprehensive overview see Weber, above n 42.

serves two purposes: it is first—and most obviously—a tool to prevent unnecessary barriers to trade by letting market participants know beforehand what requirements apply and thus creating a predictable trade environment for them. Second, as already outlined, it is also an important legal principle in democratic societies that allows for transparent decision making and thus contributes to legitimacy.[76] In contrast to the Bank for International Settlements (BIS) framework, transparency requirements under GATS relate both to the publication and notification of relevant measures on the one hand, and to the application and administration of measures, which include review mechanisms on the other. These requirements are very much in line with the regulatory measures suggested here, with one caveat: if a GATS member decides to adopt regulations on transparency, GATS Article VI:4 on domestic regulation is applicable. While there is consensus that domestic regulations can impede international trade even if there is no discrimination between domestic and foreign suppliers or an explicit restriction of market access, in contrast to the TBT and SPS Agreements, the GATS does not spell out a requirement for WTO members to base their regulations on objective criteria and to make them 'not more burdensome than necessary to achieve the national policy objective'.[77] Instead, Article VI:4 GATS gives a mandate to the Council for Trade in Services to develop disciplines in this respect. So far, no results with regard to financial services have been produced. There are several options which could be explored in developing such disciplines for financial services.[78]

IV. Conclusions

Transparency is understood as a principle which is closely related to governance. It plays a key role in re-establishing confidence in the stability of the financial system. Since financial markets are determined by a variety of actors, regulations and standards both at the domestic and international level, this chapter suggests a three-dimensional, rule-based approach to transparency in financial regulation.

The *first* dimension of transparency refers to anchoring financial regulation in the overall legal framework. This *constitutional* dimension therefore defines the procedures and institutions by which financial markets are being regulated. A key issue and illustrative example in this regard is the too-big-to-fail problem in the aftermath of the financial crisis. Financial regulation needs to define the applicable procedures for addressing this problem as well as the competent institutions. This requires a political decision which, regardless of its content, needs to be made

[76] Markus Krajewski, 'Democratic Legitimacy and Constitutional Perspectives of WTO Law', 35 *Journal of World Trade* 167 (2001), at 169–70.
[77] Such a provision was indeed proposed during the negotiations on the GATS: Article VII:2 of the Draft Agreement, MTN.GNS/35, 23 July 1990, quoted in Markus Krajewski, *National Regulation and Trade Liberalization in Services: The Legal Impact of the General Agreement on Trade in Services (GATS) on National Regulatory Autonomy* (The Hague: Kluwer Law International, 2003) 131.
[78] This analysis lies beyond the scope of this chapter. It is addressed in the contributions of Cottier and Krajewski (Ch 15) and of Delimatsis and Sauvé (Ch 16) in this volume.

transparent. From a transparency perspective, it is thus irrelevant whether a country opts for a 'political' solution by involving parliament or prefers to take a 'technical' approach by engaging supervisory authorities and the central bank. The key is that whatever decision is made it is laid open and thus fosters credibility of the system as a whole.

The *second* dimension of transparency relates to *values and objectives* of financial regulation. It has two aspects: making the objectives and underlying values of public financial policy transparent and at the same time ensuring that information is both accessible and comprehensible. The essential element is quality, not quantity, of information. A current example in this context is transparency of central bank objectives.

The *third* dimension of transparency addresses *accountability* as another important aspect of good governance. Given the variety of actors and the multitude of standards applicable to financial markets, ensuring accountability needs to be addressed from different perspectives. The concept proposed here is based on the distinction between the accountability of states and private actors and their contribution to restoring confidence in the financial system. The result is a threefold matrix for transparent financial regulation, relating to public and private actors and including the international dimension.

Building on the first dimension of *institutional* transparency, responsible public institutions need to be defined together with the objectives and values—thus referring to the second dimension—against which they are to be held accountable.

Given that confidence in financial systems is heavily influenced by the *contractual relationship* between investors or customers and their financial institutions, accountability of private actors needs to be addressed. Adopting some of the concepts proposed by John Ruggie in his Protect, Respect and Remedy Framework, it is argued that the key for financial regulation with a view to restoring confidence is to provide transparency on grievance mechanisms whether they are judicial or non-judicial.

Finally, the concept of transparency as suggested here cannot be isolated from international developments. However, current discussions in the G20 or the BCBS, to name just two examples, show that reaching consensus on what 'an' international standard would imply, is difficult. In this regard, the chapter suggests that turning to the principles applied under the GATS for defining a set of applicable international standards for financial services may be an avenue to pursue and explore in the future.

14

Global Securities Regulation After the Financial Crisis

*Donald C. Langevoort**

I. Introduction

Even though the recent financial crisis may have originated in the subprime mortgage sector of the US housing market, it was plainly global in its contagion and in the severe economic damage it has done.[1] The demand for the kinds of structured financial products containing the unexpectedly high subprime risk was stimulated to a significant extent by foreign financial institutions and government agencies seeking out dollar-denominated debt instruments bearing a bit more than the meagre yields on more old-fashioned debt at a time of extraordinarily low interest rates in the early 2000s. The pipelines for distribution of these instruments—and the credit default swaps and related derivatives that were linked to them—were global as well. The innovators were not just the US-based firms like Citigroup, Goldman Sachs, J.P. Morgan Chase and the like but also Deutsche Bank, Credit Suisse and UBS, all of which had morphed into transnational institutions deeply rooted in many different nations.[2] The UK, in particular, played a key role in the worldwide distribution network. Tellingly, for example, the financial activities of AIG, whereby the firm took on the most risk in insuring counterparties via credit default swaps, were mainly conducted through its London affiliate; when Lehman Brothers was trying to free up its balance sheet to permit more aggressive leveraging, it turned to its London affiliate as well. With respect to the collateralized debt obligations (CDOs) that played such a large role in the meltdown, Ireland was the preferred secondary marketplace.[3]

---

* The author thanks Chris Brummer for helpful comments.
[1] See e.g. Hal S. Scott, *The Global Financial Crisis* (New York: Foundation Press, 2009); David A. Westbrook, *Out of Crisis: Rethinking Our Capital Markets* (Boulder: Paradigm Press, 2009); Charles A.E. Goodhart, 'The Background to the 2007 Financial Crisis', 4 *Journal of International Economics and Economic Policy* 331 (2008).
[2] Kenneth Dam, 'The Subprime Crisis and Financial Regulation: International and Comparative Perspectives', 10 *Chicago Journal of International Law* 581 (2010).
[3] Cormac Kissane, 'Securitization in Ireland', in Patrick Dolan and Davis Van Leer (eds), *Securitization: Legal and Regulatory Issues* (New York: Law Journals Press, 2006), ch 21, 21–15.

Given the global scope of the problems, it seems evident that the re-regulatory response to the crisis must be global as well. There is no real dissent about that—every major country affected by the scandals and meltdown has recognized the lesson in principle, and promised to help develop a unified, cooperative response.

But few commentators today seem to believe that these efforts will in fact lead to serious global convergence on the regulation of financial services. The political obstacles to finding 'hard law' solutions that would allow for both common standard-setting and dispute resolution on sensitive matters of cross-border import-ance seem too great. Cautionary tales abound. Europe has been working for years to try to find a mechanism for centralizing securities regulation in the EU, with limited success, despite the Member States' treaty-based commitment to full economic integration.[4] Canada has been trying for more than a decade simply to create a national securities regulator in place of the provincial authorities that have long existed, with repeated frustration.[5] The US Securities and Exchange Commission (SEC) is as close as there is to a global securities regulator, which is not a particularly stable strategy either economically or diplomatically, and yet it has a very constrained reach.

Given such pessimism about the creation of what is truly needed, ambitions have to be scaled back, and the more realistic hope is to find softer forms of cooperation and convergence. My effort in this chapter, however, is not to discuss the choice of hard versus soft strategies. I agree with those who see some promise for a very gradual 'hardening' of global standardsetting through cooperative efforts under various guises (e.g. G20, International Organization of Securities Commissions, International Monetary Fund (IMF) and Financial Stability Board), especially if the fact-finding and monitoring function of those institutions can be enhanced.[6] However, I have long been convinced that strong enforcement and dispute reso-lution are the most crucial elements of global securities regulation,[7] and we are far from seriously trying to create that capacity.

Hence, my aim here is more moderate, while still trying to be constructive. One thing that the financial crisis has done is to highlight fundamental uncertainty about what we even mean by securities regulation, whether global or domestic. On careful examination, there are different baskets of regulatory strategies that attend

---

[4] Eilis Ferran, *Building an E.U. Securities Market* (Cambridge: Cambridge University Press, 2004).
[5] Anita Anand and Andrew J. Green, 'Why is This Taking So Long? The Move Toward a National Securities Regulator', 60(2) *University of Toronto Law Journal* 663 (2010).
[6] See Chris Brummer, 'How International Financial Law Works (and How it Doesn't)', 99 *Georgetown Law Journal* 257 (2011), <http://papers.ssrn.com/sol3/papers.cfm?> abstract_id= 1542829 (visited 11 October 2010). See also Roberta Karmel, 'The Hardening of Soft Law in Securities Regulation', 34 *Brooklyn Journal of International Law* 883 (2009); Eric J. Pan, 'Challenge of International Cooperation and Institutional Design in Financial Supervision: Beyond Transgovern-mental Networks', 11 *Chicago Journal of International Law* 243 (2010) (criticizing existing soft law solutions and proposing an administrative law-like structure).
[7] Donald C. Langevoort, 'Structuring Securities Regulation in the European Union: Lessons from the US Experience', in Guido Ferrarini and Eddy Wymeersch (eds), *Investor Protection in Europe: Corporate Law Making, the MiFID and Beyond* (Oxford: Oxford University Press, 2006) 485–506, at 496–7.

to very different institutional contexts in terms of both the underlying economics and the prevailing politics. If we 'slice and dice' securities regulation (much the way structured debt instruments were sliced and diced before the crisis, but hopefully with more transparency), we see that certain of these tranches are somewhat more suited to international cooperation and convergence than others. My suggestion, then, is that we focus on trying to build the most solid form of international cooperation and convergence in the domains where that is most practicable— and hold off, for a time at least, on the others so as not to immediately invite the most virulent forms of political resistance. Maybe if the limited domain conver- gence happens, it will set the stage for greater ambition in the other areas—but maybe not. Limiting the scope of the kind of securities regulation on which serious convergence is sought allows it the greatest chance of success, and would be valuable even if it is limited.

The domain in which this is most possible is the institutional (or 'wholesale') capital marketplace, in which global issuers of various kinds of equity and debt securities interact with institutional investors, or in trading markets that are dominated by institutions. In what follows, I will outline why this approach is more amenable to international cooperation—and why the most intractable frus- trations to cooperation have been driven mainly by political and economic issues arising out of two other domains: banking regulation and retail investor protection. While these three domains do not separate cleanly, there are rough divisions that can be used to carve out those areas best suited for joint effort. I am by no means suggesting that the effort will be easy in the institutional investor domain, there are plenty of political obstacles to convergence in the institutional marketplace, as we have seen recently on subjects like hedge fund regulation. My claim is simply that if convergence has any chance of success at all, it will be there.

II. Deconstructing Securities Regulation

After the Glass–Steagall Act of 1933,[8] the USA treated the domains of banking and securities as largely separable. Banks sought deposits, made a portfolio of loans of substantial maturities to commercial and consumer borrowers, and operated the payments system. The key role of banking regulation was safety and soundness, which made depositor (or investor) protection somewhat subsidiary as a goal. Government insurance via the US Federal Deposit Insurance Corporation was a key innovation, and capital adequacy standards and other limitations on risk-taking are crucial in dealing with the resulting moral hazard.

By contrast, the world of securities—'Wall Street'—was different historically, a way of intermediating between the capital needs of issuers and the funds of a largely (though by no means entirely) retail base of wealthy and middle-class investors and the institutions that managed money for them. Stock and bonds were the conven-

---

[8] The Banking Act of 1933, 48 Stat. 162.

tional instruments, but shorter-term debt products (e.g. commercial paper) were important as well. The underlying regulatory philosophy here was primarily truth-telling—full disclosure—as opposed to intrusive conduct or merit regulation.

In retrospect, at least, this distinction was entirely unstable as technology and marketplace conditions evolved. Non-bank institutions emerged—mutual funds and insurance-based products in particular—that competed aggressively with banks for depositor funds. To be sure, their regulation was not just based on disclosure, but it was not banking regulation either. These products offered higher yields with considerable liquidity. At the same time, Wall Street also found ways to offer commercial borrowers alternatives to bank loans—the world of structured finance evolved to allow debt of various sorts to be packaged, sliced and diced, and distributed to investors. For a variety of regulatory and economic reasons, the market for securitized debt was largely institutional, so that these two developments were symbiotic—and enhanced by the evolution of an additional and massive source of investor funds through tax-favored pension plans.

At the risk of gross oversimplification, the presence of such a high level of institutional demand for (especially) short-term debt instruments plus the technological evolution in ways of structuring these products meant that the work traditionally done by the banking system gradually moved to Wall Street—hence it became known as the 'shadow banking system'.[9] What was happening from a regulatory standpoint was product market regulatory arbitrage, although there were other economic reasons for this shift as well. The intense safety and soundness regulation for banks, particularly capital adequacy rules, simply did not apply in the USA to financial products intermediated by securities firms, and so they could take on much more risk in this process if they wanted. Regulation remained largely disclosure-oriented on the sell-side, even as the products increased in complexity. Most were sold in private markets, with no significant mandatory disclosure at all. And regulation of the buy-side by the SEC (e.g. mutual fund regulation) gradually turned away from intrusive monitoring toward an 'outsourcing' model that stressed independent director oversight and credit ratings as substitute controls. During this time, hedge funds (some of which were affiliated with banks and securities firms) took on a massive presence in the marketplace as both traders and investors without any risk-taking restrictions or disclosure obligations, and became especially active players in the derivatives market that developed alongside shadow banking.

With that, conventional banking regulation was thoroughly frustrated. Banks could not compete on an even playing field with the shadow bankers because of the intrusive safety and soundness restrictions, which led regulators—sometimes uneasily—to lighten those restrictions. Not to do so at all would have made conventional banking increasingly obsolete except for smaller depositors and

[9] For example, Charles K. Whitehead, 'Reframing Financial Regulation', 90 *Boston University Law Review* 1 (2010).

borrowers. The Basel II capital adequacy accord[10] was an example of this liberalization at the international level.[11]

The experience was different in Europe. There was never a stark separation of banking and securities, so banking institutions were the main source of securities products too. Arguably, Germany can claim historical primacy in asset securitization.[12] Banking regulation thus addressed the full range of financial services, limiting the opportunity for regulatory arbitrage. For a variety of historical reasons, Europe has never developed a deep retail investing culture,[13] and so the market for investment products has been largely institutional. The UK built a particularly robust market in securities and derivatives, mainly appealing to institutional investors.[14]

With this brief background, we can easily see the points at which regulation broke down in ways that contributed to the financial crisis, especially in the USA. Most obviously, the technology of risk-taking flourished in the securities sector, where regulators had no long-standing commitment to capital adequacy or other reduction-mechanisms. True, the SEC has long insisted on net capital requirements for broker-dealer firms (which investment banks are) but with minimal interest in stringency because as long as customer cash and securities are sufficiently segregated, the risk of insolvency to the customer is not all that great. And investors in securities firms have always been treated as any other investor, entitled to fair disclosure, but little else. Thus, when the EU insisted that the SEC take on a supervisory role for the non-bank securities firms competing in Europe, the SEC did so reluctantly and without anything approaching the knowledge or resources necessary to do the task. It simply followed the deregulatory lead of Basel II, without fully understanding the likely consequences. For these reasons, its handling of Bear Stearns and Lehman Brothers was unsophisticated at best. The SEC was further hobbled, as were all the US regulators, by the fact that customized derivatives were removed completely from regulatory oversight by Congress and—as we have seen—by the ease with which the remaining regulatory constraints could be arbitraged, by using foreign (often London-based) affiliates and running transactions through completely opaque hedge funds around the world.

As a result, restoring some semblance of prudential regulation to the shadow banking system is the key task of global regulatory reform. That takes in a host of challenges, especially in defining the scope of the shadow banking system as it

---

[10] Basel Committee on Banking Supervision, 'International Convergence of Capital Measurement and Capital Standards: A Revised Framework', June 2004 (Basel II).

[11] Daniel K. Tarullo, *Banking on Basel: The Future of International Financial Regulation* (New York: Peterson Institute for International Economics, 2008).

[12] See Dam, above n 2.

[13] Niamh Moloney, 'Building a Retail Investment Culture through Law: The 2004 Markets in Financial Instruments Directive', 6 *European Business Organization Law Review* 341 (2005).

[14] See John Armour, 'Enforcement Strategies in UK Corporate Governance: A Roadmap and Empirical Assessment', European Corporate Governance Institute Working Paper No 106/208 (2008), <http://www.bancaditalia.it/studiricerche/convegni/atti/corp_gov_it/session.pdf> (visited 12 October 2010).

extends beyond the easily identifiable investment banks to hedge funds and other black box components inside the system. And because—as we have discovered so painfully—risk is not just issuer-specific but systemic, the task extends also to understanding, monitoring and controlling how risk is spread throughout the economy in ways that correlate rather than disperse.

As crucial as this is, risk regulation is not my focus here. I hesitate to be optimistic about convergence in this sensitive area because the costs and benefits of risk-taking are distributed so unevenly around the world. The optimal approach to regulation involves trade-offs that, in turn, depend on the particular political ecology of the nation in question. Countries like Germany or the Netherlands, for example, have organized their economies in a highly centralized fashion with liberal government intervention in the social order—what financial risk means there (and the cost–benefit trade-offs) is very different from the USA or other countries with a more laissez-faire attitude. There is also a cultural dimension to risk regulation that is very hard to bridge. And two countries in particular—the USA and the UK— were able to gain immense rents from aggressive financial innovation, with spillover benefits in terms of tax revenue, employment, and real-estate values, by exporting financial risk and returns. They are naturally reluctant to compromise industries that have been crucial to their economic status and growth, especially in an environment of continued economic stress.

Instead, the main point of my contribution here is that this substantive risk regulation function can and should be separated from the rest of securities regulation (including risk disclosure), and that so doing clearly and explicitly might hasten the development of international cooperation and convergence with respect to the latter. But there is one more step that is required, and that is to further separate the institutional and retail domains within securities regulation. Like substantive risk reduction, retail investor protection is based on a set of historical, social and economic variables that vary dramatically around the world, so that no particular strategy is readily transplantable elsewhere.[15] The next section explains what these two forms of separation mean, and why the promise of international regulatory convergence is more plausible in that one sector.

Separation between the domains of securities regulation and substantive risk regulation also has a second, more normative value. Put simply, those two domains are inherently at odds, and whenever combined under one roof, securities regulation tends to lose. Securities regulation is about truth-telling, and under stressful conditions, risk regulators almost always prefer concealing the truth to exposing it. To be sure, it is far from clear that truth-telling is always the right course, but preserving a regulatory capacity that favors transparency is generally preferable to folding it into the risk regulator's task with some vague mandate to value disclosure. This is the so-called 'twin peaks' model of regulation visible in some way or another in the USA, Australia, the Netherlands and a number of other countries, in contrast

---

[15] Donald C. Langevoort, 'The SEC, Retail Investors and the Institutionalization of the Securities Markets', 95 *Virginia Law Review* 1025 (2009), at 1037–42.

to the UK's single consolidated financial services regulator.[16] Disconnecting sub-stantive risk regulation from disclosure regulation leaves 'twin peaks' as a viable strategy within the global reform agenda.

III. The 'Europeanization' of US Securities Regulation

In other work, I have described the gradual 'Europeanization' of US securities law.[17] For some time, US securities regulation has been based heavily on a distinction between those who need the protection of the securities laws and those who do not and can 'fend for themselves' (i.e. are sophisticated and/or wealthy, and have access to the necessary information about the issuer). As the US economy evolved from the 1930s to the 1970s, the vast majority of investment activity fell onto the retail side and US securities regulation adapted accordingly. Its main strategies and assumptions were about retail investor protection. But by the 1970s, and certainly ever since, the high-end securities markets have rapidly become institutional, so that securities regulation needed to change in these areas. The transition has been awkward and incomplete, but—at least until the financial crisis did its damage—it was clear that the SEC's regulatory strategy in the institutional sector was moving closer to that of Europe. Europe has always been primarily, if not almost exclusively, an institutional capital marketplace, and its lighter touch, principles-based philosophy made sense in that context.[18] The USA was following suit.

Although the retail/institutional distinction is not a clean one, its main conse-quences are relatively easy to describe. As to issuer disclosure rules, the principal question is in what market the securities in question are traded; the New York Stock Exchange and Nasdaq Global markets, at least, are highly institutional, so that pricing is dominated by large sophisticated traders. Smaller markets like Nasdaq Capital Market and the pink sheets, as well as financial products custom-ized for the retail trade (e.g. variable annuities), are mainly retail. The regulation of broker-dealers is retail as well. Importantly, mutual fund regulation is retail, even though a mutual fund is an institutional investor, because retail investors make up most of a fund's investor base and its securities are not traded on any secondary market.

[16] John C. Coffee, Jr and Hillary A. Sale, 'Redesigning the SEC: Does the Treasury Have a Better Idea?', 95 *Virginia Law Review* 707 (2009).

[17] Donald C. Langevoort, 'Steps Toward the Europeanization of US Securities Regulation, with Thoughts on the Evolution and Design of a Multinational Securities Regulator', in Michael Tison et al. (eds), *Perspectives in Company Law and Financial Regulation* (Cambridge: Cambridge University Press, 2009) 485–506. In a similar vein, see Steven M. Davidoff, 'Paradigm Shift: Federal Securities Regulation in the New Millennium', 2 *Brooklyn Journal of Corporate, Financial and Commercial Law* 339 (2008).

[18] Eilis Ferran, 'Principles-based, Risk-based Regulation and Effective Enforcement', in *Perspectives in Company Law and Financial Regulation*, 427–48, above n 17.

As I have also described in some detail elsewhere, retail securities regulation is the product of contingent political and economic circumstances.[19] The USA is unique in the degree of retail penetration for the sale of investment products, although Canada and Australia bear some resemblance to it. Just to give one dramatic illustration, in the UK as of 2005 there were approximately 1000 firms authorized to sell investment products, and some 8000 individuals licensed to conduct customer trading in securities. In the USA the comparable numbers at roughly the same time were 5000 firms employing some 658,000 registered representatives, managing over 110 million customer accounts.[20] The USA has developed a retail culture of investing that Europe has sought to emulate with very limited success. Given the differences in history and scope of retail participation, US and European-style regulation of that sector cannot easily be reconciled, so that transplantation of the sort that some had recommended—for example, letting EU-licensed brokers do business in the USA with only European regulatory law supplying the investor protection—simply would not take.[21]

By contrast, the institutional marketplace has been far less heavily regulated in the USA, at least putting aside the interventionist Sarbanes–Oxley Act of 2002. Most notably, the SEC has facilitated the rapid development of the Rule 144A marketplace, where hundreds of billions of dollars have been raised in the USA with almost no regulatory burdens or disclosure rules.[22] What makes this marketplace exempt from regulation is that only qualified institutional buyers are eligible to participate—and most of the world's large institutional investors qualify. The boom in private equity deals in the early 2000s also enhanced the private unregulated market by taking more and more issuers out of the public domain, and hence out of mandatory disclosure and corporate governance rules. The combination of Rule 144A and private equity has made that dominant segment of the market look much more European in both its investment structure (e.g. the increased presence of large block holders as investors) and diminished regulation.[23] Indeed, it is probably fair to say that the evolution of European and Asian markets was the driving motivation behind Rule 144A.[24]

My hypothesis is that international regulatory convergence is more plausible here precisely because US law has already become so Europeanized. Underlying this is another important force: the homogenization of large-scale portfolio management around the world. That is to say, the education, training and network connectivity of those who manage large pools of money are making them think and behave more similarly than differently, and they need the same kinds of information and other services from securities issuers, underwriters, and dealers. Just as norms in corporate

[19] See Langevoort, above n 15, at 1035–6.
[20] See Langevoort, above n 15, at 1036–7.
[21] Ibid, at 1073–4.
[22] See, generally, William Sjostrom, 'The Birth and Evolution of Rule 144A', 56 *UCLA Law Review* 409 (2009).
[23] On the political ecology here, see John C. Coates IV, 'Private vs. Political Choice of Securities Regulation: A Political Cost/Benefit Analysis', 41 *Virginia Journal of International Law* 531 (2201).
[24] 17 C.F.R. section 230.144A (2010).

governance have diffused quickly—albeit incompletely[25]—among a large set of global 'cosmopolitan' securities issuers, so, too, have they diffused among large investors. Because of this, institutional investors can be a strong proponent for improving the global capital markets through cooperation and convergence on questions of mandatory disclosure and the conduct of securities intermediaries. In the aftermath of the financial crisis, where so much damage was done to institutional investors, the demand for reform should be particularly strong. The obvious challenge, however, is that precisely because the institutional space is where the direct damage occurred, we do need to ask whether at least some aspects of the Europeanization of securities regulation were a serious mistake. If there is considerable divergence on that question, then there is less reason to expect cooperation from now on.

IV. The Failure of Securities Regulation in the Institutional Marketplace

There are two points at which securities regulation—as opposed to systemic risk regulation—arguably failed in ways that contributed directly to the financial crisis, and they are related. One has to do with the relative ease with which significant financial institutions like Lehman Brothers and Bear Stearns were able to raise their own capital (both equity and debt) to finance their operations. As we know, these institutions became highly leveraged, largely through short-term borrowing, in ways that may well have concealed their riskiness. Note that much of this financing was through the money market, part of the institutional, largely unregulated marketplace. However, each of these firms was publicly owned, and hence also had duties of candor towards their shareholders and other investors, at least some of which were retail (although as with all large blue-chip stocks, a minority).

The other point involved the sale of structured investment products—mortgage-backed securities, asset-backed commercial paper, collateralized debt obligations and the like—with seemingly inadequate disclosure about the risks embedded in the products themselves. Because these securities were issued not by the originating or underwriting banks but by separate entities created specifically to hold the assets, the financial condition of the banks themselves was not the focus of disclosure—rather it was just the assets. For example, there was a serious deterioration in the creditworthiness of home buyers from 2004 to 2007 but relatively little loan-level information about that went into the disclosures accompanying these sales. Nor was there particularly useful information about the level of correlation risk in these portfolios of loans, which was also changing over time. These securities were sold almost entirely to institutions and to some well-off households. Some of these distributions were registered public offerings with the SEC, others were structured

---

[25] Gerald F. Davis and Christopher Marquis, 'The Globalization of Stock Markets and the Convergence in Corporate Governance', in Richard Swedborg and Victor Nee (eds), *The Economic Sociology of Capitalism* (Princeton: Princeton University Press, 2005) 352–90, at 352.

as exempt offerings so that no particular disclosure was required. Even when done as exempt offerings, US law (and that of most other countries) did afford buyers protection against fraud.

Here we come to the most profound securities regulation question arising from the crisis: why did institutional buyers not do more to 'fend for themselves', regardless of whether they were buying registered securities? This is relevant both to investor protection and systemic risk, because institutions that unwittingly took on more risk than they realized not only subjected themselves and their stakeholders to that risk, but also built up an inflated level of risk that could have spillover effects on the financial system more generally.

This takes us in turn to the 'Greenspan philosophy' that supposedly drove so many of the deregulatory initiatives of recent decades—that institutions would surely be prudent enough in their risk-taking that their collective presence in the market would protect against opportunistic sales efforts, making intrusive regulation in this domain unnecessary. My strong sense is that neither Alan Greenspan nor any of the many others who advocated this approach ever really meant to claim that markets are anywhere close to perfect. While there are strong versions of market efficiency in the finance literature, these tend to be theoretical ideals; nearly all financial economists recognize that reality necessarily falls short. The 'new institutional economics' associated with Nobel Prize winners like Douglas North, George Akerlof and Joseph Stiglitz stresses the transaction costs, adverse selection, agency costs and informational and structural deficiencies that can produce sustained market imperfections. Advances in behavioral economics suggest that even so-called expert agents exhibit biases that affect investment decision-making.[26] No one familiar with contemporary financial economics would ever be all that sanguine about market self-cleansing.

Rather, the Greenspan philosophy owes more to Friedrich A. Hayek and his followers who were convinced, ideologically as well as descriptively, that whatever imperfections exist in markets, regulatory interventions meant to improve them generally fail and instead make things worse. That is to say, marketplace actors have incentives to learn and not repeat their mistakes, and so occasional harsh consequences from collective and individual mistakes arising from market imperfections generally do better than *ex ante* regulation at improving market efficiency.[27] Once we redefine what the deregulatory claim really was, it is not as easy to respond simply by pointing out the imperfections. We have to go a step further and ask whether there is a particular regulatory intervention that we are reasonably sure would generate more benefits than costs, given what we know about institutional investor decision-making, and thereby improve on the market.

Take, for example, disclosure associated with asset-backed securities. The SEC rules that mandated what information was required in registered distributions were

---

[26] See Langevoort, above n 15, at 1062–5.
[27] Richard Posner's take on the financial crisis has this flavor. See generally Richard Posner, *A Failure of Capitalism: The Crisis of '08 and the Descent into Depression* (Cambridge, MA: Harvard University Press, 2009).

extensive but still inadequate to assess individual loan-level effects on correlation risk. To shift to provision of that data would be very expensive and time-consuming and it would leave open the question of whether potential buyers would really do anything with it.[28] The assumption seems to have been that credit rating agencies were vetting that data, not individual buyers, and that the ratings were reliable. Perhaps now that there is a more jaundiced view of the abilities of the rating agencies, there might be a greater willingness to dig through that data, especially if provided in an open-source format.

A different regulatory intervention is to target the rating agencies and make them more reliable. The EU adopted a comprehensive new credit ratings directive in the fall of 2009, while Congress passed similar provisions in the Dodd–Frank Act for US regulation[29]—plainly the result of some cooperation already occurring on this issue. This is a difficult issue to work through. The standard assumption is that institutional investors buying structured finance products were misled about the objectivity of the three major rating agencies (Standard & Poor's, Moody's, and Fitch), and that greater transparency about incentives and methodology is the right response.

That diagnosis is puzzling, however, because the conflict of interest inherent in the 'issuer pays' model (whereby issuers compensate the rating agencies for their work, not the users) was very well known within the investment community. Some institutional investors had former rating agency employees on their staff, and would certainly know about any corner-cutting, but still made no careful inquiry into creditworthiness. Why? One possible answer is that the incentive structure on the buy-side created an indifference to concerns about creditworthiness so long as other institutional investors were behaving similarly—rational herding of the sort observed for money managers generally. In other words, they could take the higher yields associated with these products and not worry about being blamed for taking on too much risk because everyone else was doing the same thing. The flip side of this is that they would suffer competitively in the short run if they passed on those yields. This could be a manifestation of an incentive (i.e. agency cost) problem within the money management business, though we might not blame the portfolio managers too harshly if they were responding to the risk that investors would pull money out of funds if yields fell short of the competition. If this is a reasonable depiction of the institutional investors' behavior, then it is not clear that simply making the ratings process more transparent would accomplish very much. Indeed, a strong version of this view suggests that rating agencies were simply giving so-motivated institutional investors what they wanted: justifications for reaching for higher yields, and thus taking higher performance fees and bonuses, without all that much fear that they would suffer commensurately from the risk.[30] If so, intrusive

---

[28] For an interesting suggestion about an open source code solution, see Erik Gerding, 'Code, Crash and Open Source: The Outsourcing of Financial Regulation to Risk Models and the Global Financial Crisis', 84 *Washington Law Review* 127 (2009).

[29] See, among others, Dodd–Frank Act, Section 939A.

[30] Charles W. Calomiris, 'The Subprime Turmoil: What's Old, What's New and What's Next', 15 *Journal of Structured Finance* 6 (Spring 2009), at 12–16.

rating agency supervision is unnecessary, and the best solution is simply to abolish the regulatory privilege conferred on highly rated debt.

An alternative diagnosis for why institutional investors seemed so willing to buy these products is behavioral.[31] Given the complexity of these products, it would hardly be surprising to find that judgment and decision-making on the part of portfolio managers was highly inferential and prone to bias. Extrapolation from past trends pointed to low levels of risk, and the day-to-day and week-to-week changes in the products were largely imperceptible, and so (in a form of cognitive dissonance) it was difficult for those managers to change their minds about the relative safety of these products at any point before the dramatic onset of the crisis. If this is an apt description, the value of simply forcing greater transparency about the ratings process would be almost nil, especially if we discovered that the rating agencies were also subject to the same biases.

What would be needed, instead, would be to change the underlying behavior at the rating agency level, by creating stronger incentives for accuracy. One possible solution is enhanced civil liability—seriously considered in the USA, less so in Europe. Another option, noted earlier, is to take away the regulatory privilege associated with a high rating, and thereby make rating agencies more concerned with their reputations. In other words, make institutional buyers do their own due diligence and not use investment-grade ratings as the test for eligible investments. This, however, requires some confidence that if left on their own, these institutions would in fact find ways toward greater (costly) diligence, rather than herd more strongly or just open themselves more blindly to the sales pitches of the product distributors.

V. International Institutional Solutions

So does credit rating agency reform—or reform of the disclosures required for asset-backed distributions—lend itself to an international solution? My sense is that both might, depending on which diagnosis for institutional investor behavior we ultimately arrive at. There is a relatively common interest among countries in striking the right balance. Again, the interests of the many institutional investors in every major country are far more similar than different, and the regulatory intervention need not be so deep and intrusive as to provoke strong protectionist impulses from the USA or the UK, if it takes the form of greater transparency and oversight of the credit rating agencies. On the other hand, if we decide that the problems are too deeply embedded in the institutional investor community and need to be solved there rather than simply by reference to the information sources on which investors draw, then there is little hope of convergence. Addressing agency cost and/or cognitive problems inside institutional investors such as mutual funds, pension funds and the like raises a host of thorny issues of concern to retail investors, and

[31] For example, Emilios Avgouleas, 'The Global Financial Crisis, Behavioural Finance and Financial Regulation: In Search of a New Orthodoxy', 9 Journal of Corporate Legal Studies 23 (2009).

because countries vary in the weight they give retail investor interests, the differences would be hard to bridge. My sense, though, is that a combination of better discipline over rating agencies and the painful experience investors have endured recently could lead to improvement for the debt markets worldwide.

Another objective relatively more susceptible to convergence for similar reasons is creating greater transparency for credit default swaps and other derivatives. To the extent that these products can be standardized enough to permit their trading through central counterparty clearinghouses, far greater marketplace discipline (and more efficient pricing) should follow. There has already been significant international cooperation to move more trading onto organized clearinghouses.[32] The reason, no doubt, is again a high degree of homogeneity of interest among the global institutional investors who are the primary counterparties, and the relatively low scale of regulatory intervention needed for day-to-day supervision of these trading platforms. The hard issue here is how much standardization to insist on—investment bankers covet the fees that come from being able to create customized arrangements outside standard models, and the clearinghouses will be bled of products if banks can exit the regime too easily. That is a tough political choice, but not one on which general agreement among the major countries is completely out of the question.

VI. Rules, Principles and Enforcement

Supposedly, one of the substantial differences between US-style and European-style securities regulation is the emphasis in the USA on rules, while Europe is more principles-based.[33] Whether this is really so—rather than being something of an illusory differentiation created largely for marketing purposes—is not entirely clear.[34] In any event, in the aftermath of the financial crisis, we have found ample weaknesses in both approaches.

Hard and fast rules simply do not work in a dynamic setting like financial services, unless the rules are drawn to shut down innovation entirely within certain spaces except with express regulatory approval. The story of how structured finance and credit derivatives evolved was a process of incremental complexity (making it hard for regulators to know whether it was in the rules or not) that—once the regulators were willing to concede one round of innovation as within the rules—made it impossible to find a stopping place. Heavy lobbying of regulators and Congress made it even harder to say no to these first incremental steps, which were then quickly exploited well beyond what was originally contemplated.

---

[32] Anupam Chander and Randall Costa, 'Clearing Credit Default Swaps: A Case Study in Global Legal Convergence', 10 *Chicago Journal of International Law* 639 (2010).

[33] See Ferran, above n 18; Cristie Ford, 'New Governance, Compliance and Principles-based Regulation', 45 *American Business Law Review* 1 (2008).

[34] Lawrence Cunningham, 'A Prescription to Retire the Rhetoric of "Principles-based Systems" in Corporate Law, Securities Regulation and Accounting', 66 *Vanderbilt Law Review* 1411 (2007).

Thus the appeal of a principles-based approach which can set fairly vague standards to which all variations, exclusions and permutations must aspire. But for principles-based regulation to work, two conditions must be satisfied.[35] First, principles-based regulation is much harder to apply, and takes more experience, intelligence and skill than it does to apply simple rules. It requires sophisticated judgment. Second, principles-based regulation requires a strong commitment to enforcement—some form of punishment—when the principles are evaded, especially when the evasion is clever. To be sure, enforcement does not have to be through adjudication—there are more informal means of suasion that can, in the right circumstances, work. But it does have to be strong. The UK's dual commitment to principles-based regulation and 'light touch' enforcement probably failed more because of the latter than the former. As noted earlier, London did seem to be a destination of choice for sensitive transactions by firms like Lehman Brothers and AIG, to which US regulators far too quickly deferred.

As noted earlier, creating a multinational enforcement capacity in securities regulation has been beyond the realm of political possibility (this has been the sticking point even within the EU), and there seems little likelihood that the crisis has changed that to any significant extent. And, leaving enforcement entirely to the domestic regulators, especially in a principles-based environment, is dangerous because of the ease with which regulation can be drained of its substance by under-enforcement or (in extreme cases) corruption.

The interesting question here is whether some kind of private enforcement/dispute resolution system for internationally agreed-upon standards could be created for a largely institutional marketplace. Private litigation is politically contentious, but largely because of class actions on behalf of large numbers of investors. The question is whether it would not be possible to develop a forum that would allow institutional investors (and perhaps governments intervening on behalf of an aggregation of investors) to seek redress for harm caused by another financial institution that violates an internationally agreed upon securities regulation standard. Putting aside the obvious challenges in designing such a system, which are well beyond the scope of this article, this would be a way to compensate for the uneven public enforcement that is likely to plague national-level securities regulation for some time to come.[36]

VII. Limitations and Conclusion

My suggestion here is a simple one. The best (and maybe only) way to move toward semi-hard forms of international cooperation and convergence in securities regula-

---

[35] Julia Black, 'The Death of Credit, Trust—and Principles Based Regulation?', *Risk and Regulation*, December 2008, 8.

[36] Guido Ferrarini and Paolo Guiduci, 'Financial Scandals and the Role of Private Enforcement: The Parmalat Case', in John Armour and Joseph McCahery (eds), *After Enron: Improving Corporate Law and Modernizing Securities Regulation* (Oxford and New York: Oxford University Press, 2006) 158–213, 158.

tion is by focusing on those aspects of securities regulation that are already highly institutional—i.e. where the trading markets in question are dominated by institutional rather than retail investors—and do not involve debates about substantive standards for risk regulation. The virtues here are two-fold. First, there is relative uniformity in what institutional investors need and expect in terms of transparency and accountability, regardless of where in the world they manage their money. In the aftermath of the crisis, regaining the trust and confidence of this global investment sector is crucial to rebuilding the world's capital markets. This creates a fairly strong incentive for cooperation. Second, this is an area where—arguably at least— the optimal intensity of regulation is still somewhat low, even if standards must be raised from where they were previously. The Europeanization of securities regulation therefore remains the base from which improvements can and should be made.

I do not mean to insist that the institutional/retail or the risk disclosure/risk regulation distinctions can bear an immense amount of weight. As we have noted, one diagnosis for the crisis is that the main culprits were the institutional investors themselves—that the excessive risk-taking was mainly a manifestation of agency cost problems on the buy-side, with the sell-side (such as originators and credit rating agencies) being little more than enablers. If this is the dominant story, then the required intervention is in the name of retail investors and probably will require something more than disclosure as a solution. Convergence on that is impracticable. We also have to recognize that even though there is a great deal of homogenization among institutional investors around the world, there are still important differences. Most significantly, governments still have either control or substantial influence over pools of money—not just sovereign wealth, but also pension funds and others—that inevitably leads to a politicization of those investors' preferences. Protectionism remains a problem in the institutional domain, as we are seeing in the current debates on the regulation of hedge funds taking place between the USA and the UK on one hand, and major European countries like France and Germany on the other.

So I am not all that optimistic, even here. However, the needs for global cooperation are pressing and the positive experiences of international economic law with respect to the World Trade Organization, IMF and other institutional arrangements suggest that sometimes cooperation does occur even against formidable odds. Moreover, we do not know for sure what the global political ecology in finance will be in the future—perhaps both Wall Street and London will be weakened politically by global competition that moves the locus of control toward the Asian countries, which might gradually bolster the institutional buy-side interests. A push toward international standard-setting and dispute resolution in securities regulation is worth the effort in the aftermath of the financial crisis, and has its best chance of succeeding if—but only if—its first targets are chosen very carefully.

PART IV

TRADE, COMPETITION, AND TAX-RELATED ASPECTS

15

What Role for Non-Discrimination and Prudential Standards in International Financial Law?

*Thomas Cottier and Markus Krajewski**

I. Introduction

More than a decade ago—in the aftermath of the 1997–99 Asian financial crisis—Hufbauer and Wada asked whether financiers can learn from traders.[1] The opening remarks of their contribution can easily be transferred to the contemporary state of affairs. Even though bankers and finance ministers are apparently 'more sophisticated, better dressed and earn more money' than their trading counterparts, Hufbauer and Wada assert that 'financiers have collectively stumbled, and stumbled badly, over the past decade'.[2] The authors contrasted this perception with the allegedly much better track record of the trading system. While the impression of the performance of the international financial system then and now seems comparable, the protagonists of the world trading system have currently no reason to cheer. The troubled state of the Doha Development Agenda, two failed Ministerial Conferences (in 1999 and 2003), the proliferation of regionalism, and growing fragmentation within the World Trade Organization (WTO) membership, suggest that the international trading system can no longer be perceived as the bright star in the sky of international economic law. Can it still be useful to look for some inspiration from the trading system when navigating through the murky waters of international financial law? Or, should the trade epistemic community keep their heads down, because the WTO's framework of liberalizing financial services may have contributed to the financial crisis as suggested by the UN Commission of Experts on Reforms of the International Monetary and Financial System under the chairmanship of Josef Stiglitz?[3]

* The authors are grateful to Ronald Abegglen, Research Fellow WTI, for his assistance in preparing the Chapter.
[1] Gary Hufbauer and Erika Wada, 'Can Financiers Learn From Traders?', 2 *Journal of International Economic Law* 567 (1999), at 567.
[2] Ibid, at 567.
[3] 'The framework for financial market liberalization under the Financial Services Agreement of the General Agreement on Trade in Services (GATS) under the WTO and, even more, similar provisions

We approach these questions based on the assumption that the crisis of the politics and policies of the world trading system should not obscure the achievements of this system as a rules-and-principles-based legal order.[4] The multilateral trading system has been reasonably successful in fending off outright protectionism in the wake of the crisis. While there have been temporary support and protective measures which may have had protectionist effects, the crisis did not result in a systemic increase of protectionist trade barriers.[5] The situation is completely different from the experience after the Great Depression in the 1930s when no multilateral framework was in place.[6] The principles and rules of the WTO are therefore bound to play an important role in further developing the architecture of the financial system.[7]

One of the cornerstones of this system is the principle of non-discrimination embedded in the world trade order through its two concretizations, the most-favoured nation (MFN) and the national treatment principles. Despite the paramount importance of these principles for WTO law and, indeed, most regional trade agreements, non-discrimination is hardly mentioned as a general principle of the current international financial system.[8] It is not a central element of reform proposals which have been suggested following the most recent financial and economic crisis. The Toronto G20 Summit Declaration of June 2010 mentions non-discrimination only as a requirement for the implementation of measures to improve transparency and regulatory oversight of hedge funds, credit-rating agencies, and over-the-counter derivatives.[9] It is not perceived as a substantive or stand-alone requirement for regulatory measures. Nor has it been identified as a potentially important contribution to a crisis-resistant system.[10]

Non-discrimination is the main principle and instrument with which to bring about level playing fields between domestic and foreign competitors—a key concern in the search for a new financial architecture and one of the main reasons why rules should be partly allocated to the level of regional, international, or global law.

in bilateral trade agreements may restrict the ability of governments to change the regulatory structure in ways which support financial stability, economic growth, and the welfare of vulnerable consumers and investors', United Nations, 'Report of the Commission of Experts of the President of the United Nations General Assembly on Reforms of the International Monetary and Financial System', 21 September 2009, ch 3, para 208.

   [4] Meinhard Hilf, 'Power, Rules and Principles—Which Orientation for WTO/GATT Law?', 4 *Journal of International Economic Law* 1 (2001), at 111.

   [5] WTO, Trade Policy Review Board, 'Report to the TPRB from the Director General on Trade-Related Developments', WT/TPR/OV/W/3, 14 June 2010, para 2.

   [6] See Barry J. Eichengreen and Douglas A. Irwin, 'The Slide To Protectionism in the Great Depression: Who Succumbed and Why?', National Bureau of Economic Research Working Paper No 15142, July 2009, <http://www.dartmouth.edu/~dirwin/w15142.pdf> (visited 3 October 2010).

   [7] See also Chapter 20 by Ernst Baltensperger and Thomas Cottier in this volume.

   [8] See e.g. Rosa M. Lastra, *Legal Foundations of International Monetary Stability* (Oxford: Oxford University Press, 2006); Mario Giovanoli and Diego Devos (eds), *International Monetary and Financial Law: The Global Crisis* (Oxford: Oxford University Press, 2010).

   [9] G20, Toronto Summit Declaration, Toronto, 26–27 June 2010, <http://www.g20.org/Documents/g20_declaration_en.pdf> (visited 7 July 2010).

   [10] Mario Giovanoli, 'The Reform of the International Financial Architecture After the Global Crisis', 42 *New York University Journal of International Law & Politics* 81 (2010), at 122.

This chapter discusses the potential of the non-discrimination principle for international financial law and the potential impact of and role for the development of a more stable system. It seeks to contribute to an agenda for future research and to suggest a few waymarks which could help to develop roadmaps through the landscape of international economic law.[11]

II. Non-Discrimination in International Economic Law

A. A cornerstone of the trade and investment system

Securing equal conditions of competition has been a core goal and concern of, and in, international economic law. The principles of MFN and of national treatment are at the heart of the multilateral trading system of the WTO and date back to bilateral agreements in ancient and modern history, in particular since the end of the eighteenth century. The generation of friendship and navigation treaties in the nineteenth century, bilateral trade agreements, and multilateral agreements on intellectual property enshrined the principle of national treatment long before it was anchored in General Agreement on Tariffs and Trade (GATT) and subsequently the WTO.[12] The obligation to grant treatment no less favourable to like and competitive foreign products or persons, or the same treatment as granted to domestic products, has been a mainstay of liberal policies securing equal opportunities in markets. The same holds true of the principle of MFN, albeit this has been limited to the multilateral trading system and has been paralleled by policies of preferential or regional agreements limiting its scope and effect.

Unlike the principle of sovereign equality of states, and the principle of equality, the two forms of non-discrimination, MFN and national treatment, have been principles of treaty law. They only apply to the extent enshrined in treaty-based rights and obligations. Within the bounds of sovereign equality, nation states in the Westphalian system are entitled to privilege and discriminate in general public international law. Indeed, nations are constituted by privileging their own citizens and constituencies in many respects, often protecting their economic interests. As a corollary, foreigners and foreign products are discriminated against in domestic law and markets. It has been one of the main tasks of international economic law to offset the protectionist effects of such privileges and to limit such discrimination to the extent required by legitimate and internationally recognized policy goals, such as the protection of *ordre public*, fiscal interests, public health, the environment, or,

---

[11] John Jackson, 'International Economic Law: Complexity and Puzzles', 10 *Journal of International Economic Law* 3 (2007), at 7–8.

[12] See generally: William Davey and Joost Pauwelyn, 'MFN Unconditionality: A Legal Analysis of the Concept in View of its Evolution in the GATT/WTO Jurisprudence with Particular Reference to the Issue of "Like Product", in Thomas Cottier and Petros Mavroidis (eds), *Regulatory Barriers and the Principle of Non-discrimination in WTO Law* (Ann Arbor: The University of Michigan Press, 2000) 13–50; and Thomas Cottier and Matthias Oesch, *International Trade Regulation: Law and Policy in the WTO, the European Union and Switzerland* (Berne/London: Stämpfli Publishers/Cameron May, 2005) 346–81.

of particular importance in the present context, consumers and trust in business relations. The respective function of international economic law has been to counterbalance the preponderant influence of protectionist domestic constituencies and to give rights to those not represented in the domestic political process. In return, it has secured market access rights abroad on the basis of overall reciprocal economic relations.

Much of the history of international economic law depicts the tensions inherent to these functions, expressed in the difficulties in achieving agreement, in the defence of Westphalian and traditional perceptions of national sovereignty, and in the struggle towards new models of regional and global governance. The evolution of the European Union since 1951 is a history of reducing and eliminating discrimination and excessive limitations in terms of market access. The core functions of the four (or six) freedoms—in movements of goods, persons, establishment, services, and of investment and payments, and of competition law and policy—have progressively rendered these goals operational in legal terms by secondary regulation, but mainly by the case law of the European Court of Justice.[13] Likewise, albeit to a lesser extent, the law and policies of GATT and the WTO are dedicated to these goals. Overall, the process has been characterized by progressive liberalization. European integration has been characterized by gradual integration, and the GATT and the WTO by progressive reduction of tariff barriers and the taming of non-tariff barriers. Bringing about equal conditions of competition has been the goal both in regional and global law. Yet, it is important to emphasize that the principles of non-discrimination do not bring this about in a simple and automatic manner. They remain subject to qualifications and important exceptions. The most advanced exception being regional free trade and integration whereby non-discrimination inherently excludes the extension of MFN to third parties, not party to the regional agreement, and restricts the operation of national treatment internally. In the global system of multilateral trade, MFN applies across the board, but is subject to regional integration and national treatment of tariff protection and exceptions, all responding to progressive liberalization and the safeguarding of equally legitimate domestic policy goals of nations. The principles of non-discrimination, however, have offered a coherent framework against which domestic trade policies can be assessed, both politically and in international dispute settlement. They are indispensable cornerstones of the overall system. They are the foundation of what has emerged as a rules-based system where legal principles, combined with transparency, bring their own content and value to the table beyond implementing economic policies.

B. . . . and a neglected element of international financial law?

Against this backdrop, it is noteworthy that non-discrimination has not assumed comparable functions in the field of international monetary law nor, for a long

---

[13] Joseph H.H. Weiler, 'The Transformation of Europe', 100(8) *Yale Law Journal* 2403 (1991).

time, in financial regulation. The informal and club-like co-ordination of monetary policies, mainly within and outside the international financial institutions, such as the International Monetary Fund (IMF) and the Bank for International Settlements (BIS), does not operate on the basis of MFN and national treatment principles. Article I of the Articles of Agreement of the IMF, which refers to the purposes of the IMF, does not include non-discrimination as a key objective of the Fund. Likewise, the general obligations of the Member States towards each other as laid down in Article IV Section 1 do not explicitly require non-discriminatory treatment. Similarly, neither the Statutes of the BIS nor the Basel Capital Measurement and Capital Standards explicitly refer to non-discrimination as a guiding principle.

Non-discrimination also does not feature prominently in the current debate about reforming the international financial system. An overview of recent academic writings[14] and current reform proposals from the IMF[15] and the Financial Stability Board[16] reveals a relative absence of the nondiscrimination principle in this discourse. Non-discrimination is, however, a fundamental element of the regime concerning financial services as can be seen in the GATS, the Understanding on Commitments in Financial Services, and regional trade agreements. In the field of financial and monetary law, the central role of the GATS and its enforceable principles and rules have not yet been sufficiently recognized.

There are two possible explanations for the absence of non-discrimination in international financial law, which are both related to fundamental differences between the trade and financial systems. The first concerns the instruments and institutional settings of the two systems. While the trading system is based on a unified multilateral system of international agreements which are adjudicated by a quasi-judicial dispute-settlement system, the international financial system is based on heterogeneous and hybrid systems of policy and soft law instruments administered partly through formal international organizations such as the IMF and partly through more or less formal networks of governmental institutions (central banks) and private business associations.[17] The rights and obligations partly address the relationship between international organizations and states, and are partly developed as guidance for national banking and finance law. The legal relationships

---

[14] See e.g. Rolf H. Weber, 'Mapping and Structuring International Financial Regulation—A Theoretical Approach', 20 *European Business Law Review* 651 (2009). See also Mario Giovanoli, 'The Reform of the International Financial Architecture After the Global Crisis', 42 *New York University Journal of International Law & Politics* 81 (2010), which does not yet include GATS as a main pillar of the financial system. See also the contributions in Rainer Grote and Thilo Marauhn (eds), *The Regulation of International Financial Markets—Perspectives for Reform* (Cambridge: Cambridge University Press, 2006) which were, however, written before the recent crisis.

[15] Stijn Claessens et al, 'Lessons and Policy Implications from the Global Financial Crisis', IMF Working Paper, WP/10/44, February 2010.

[16] Financial Stability Board, Improving Financial Regulation, 'Report of the Financial Stability Board to G20 Leaders', 25 September 2009; Progress since the Pittsburgh Summit in Implementing the G20 Recommendations for Strengthening Financial Stability, 'Report of the Financial Stability Board to G20 Finance Ministers and Governors', 7 November 2009.

[17] See Thomas Cottier, 'Challenges Ahead in International Economic Law', 12 *Journal of International Economic Law* 3 (2009), at 6–7 for further references.

embodied in the international financial system are therefore structurally different from the relationships of the trading system. The world trading system focuses to a larger extent on binding rules and legal principles applying horizontally among Members, while the financial system employs a more diverse and less legalistic set of rules.[18] It is partly built on vertical relations between international organizations and states and on non-binding regulatory standards developed in a club-like atmosphere. Non-discrimination is a hard law principle which might therefore be less applicable in a system built on more flexible instruments and institutions.

The second potential explanation concerns the different functions of the trading and financial systems. While international trade law predominantly aims at liberalization to ensure competitive markets, the international financial system concerns itself mostly with regulation to secure financial stability.[19] Non-discrimination in international trade law is an instrument of trade liberalization, of negative integration in particular.[20] National treatment targets protectionist behaviour of states whereas MFN treatment addresses preferential treatment of certain foreign goods and services compared to others. Non-discrimination is therefore not a principle which supports the establishment of regulations. On the contrary, non-discrimination often has a deregulatory effect. This could be why non-discrimination has been less attractive for the development of the international financial system. Below, we will return to this question in greater detail and will ask what impact the principle of non-discrimination may have on particular approaches towards financial regulation at the international level.

III. Non-Discrimination in the WTO Regime for Financial Services

Multilateral and regional rules on trade in financial services are currently the only area of international financial law in which the principle of non-discrimination plays an important role. This is due to a recent development which only came about in the 1990s, most prominently with the founding of NAFTA and the WTO. The potential of the GATS as a cornerstone of international financial regulation has not been fully recognized by the financial law community.[21] It amounts to the centrepiece of hard law in the field, and the question arises to what extent it and non-discrimination will be able to contribute to financial stability in the future.[22]

---

[18] Chris Brummer, 'How International Financial Law Works (and How it Doesn't)', 99 *Georgetown Law Journal* 257 (2011), <http://ssrn.com/abstract=1542829> (visited 3 August 2010).

[19] Régis Bismuth, 'Financial Sector Regulation and Financial Services Liberalization at the Crossroads: The Relevance of International Financial Standards in WTO Law', 44 *Journal of World Trade* 489 (2010), at 491.

[20] Thomas Cottier and Petros Mavroidis, 'Regulatory Barriers and the Principle of Non-Discrimination in WTO Law: An Overview', in Thomas Cottier and Petros Mavroidis (eds), *Regulatory Barriers and the Principle of Non-Discrimination in World Trade Law* (Ann Arbor: The University of Michigan Press, 2000) 3–10, 4.

[21] See Mario Giovanoli and Diego Devos (eds), *International Monetary and Financial Law: The Global Crisis* (Oxford: Oxford University Press, 2010).

[22] See also Chapter 16 by Panagiotis Delimatsis and Pierre Sauvé in this volume.

Within the GATS, MFN (GATS Article II) and national treatment (GATS Article XVII) require WTO Members to grant treatment no less favourable to foreign services and service suppliers than they accord to like foreign or domestic services and service suppliers.[23] Both principles aim at protecting the competitive relationship between services and service suppliers of different origin. However, they do not apply without restrictions. Members have listed specific exemptions to the MFN principle based on GATS Article II:2 and the Annex on Article II exemptions. National treatment only applies to those sectors for which the WTO Members made specific commitments and only subject to any conditions and limitations set out in these schedules. The financial services sector is among those with the largest number of commitments.

The requirements of GATS Articles II and XVII are extended to monopoly suppliers and exclusive service suppliers by virtue of Article VIII:1 and GATS Article VIII:5, respectively: according to those provisions, Members shall ensure that monopolies and exclusive service suppliers do not act in a manner which would be inconsistent with MFN and national treatment.

The GATS contains further references to the non-discrimination principle. GATS Article V:1(b) requires that economic integration agreements provide for the absence or elimination of substantially all discrimination by eliminating existing discriminatory measures, and/or prohibiting new or more discriminatory measures. The background of this requirement is that regional trade agreements are only considered beneficial, from the perspective of the multilateral trading system, if they lead to an overall reduction of discrimination and protectionism. GATS Article VII:3 prohibits a Member from recognizing education and experience gained abroad or requirements met or licences obtained in another country in a manner which would discriminate between countries. More specifically, GATS Article VII:2 requires a Member which is a party to a mutual recognition agreement to afford adequate opportunity for other interested Members to negotiate their accession to such an agreement or to negotiate comparable ones. Regarding autonomous recognition, a Member shall afford adequate opportunity for any other Member to demonstrate that education, experience, licences, or certifications obtained or requirements met in that other Member's territory should be recognized.

GATS Article XII:2(a) requires that restrictions on trade in services, because of serious balance-of-payments and external financial difficulties, do not discriminate among Members. Similarly, GATS Article X:1 calls for multilateral negotiations on emergency safeguard measures (ESM) 'based on the principle of non-discrimination'. Even though these negotiations have not yet obtained a result, the mandate of GATS Article X:1 clearly indicates that ESM should only be applied on a non-discriminatory basis.

While the provisions mentioned so far apply to all service sectors, the GATS also contains a special regime for financial services which is laid down in the Annex on

---

[23] See Mireille Cossy, 'Some Thoughts on the Concept of "Likeness" in the GATS', in Marion Panizzon, Nicole Pohl and Pierre Sauvé (eds), *GATS and the Regulation of International Trade in Services: World Trade Forum* (Cambridge: Cambridge University Press, 2008) 327–57.

Financial Services (Annex). Despite its importance for the regulation of financial services,[24] the Annex does not contain any additional references to non-discrimination. It replicates the obligation on conditional MFN of GATS Article VII:2 for mutual recognition agreements regarding prudential measures in paragraph 3(b) of the Annex, but does not, for example, specifically require that prudential measures are applied on a non-discriminatory basis. Paragraph 2(a) of the Annex only requires that such measures are not to be used as a means of avoiding the Member's commitments and obligations. This can be interpreted as a good faith obligation.[25]

Unlike the Annex on Financial Services, the Understanding on Commitments in Financial Services (Understanding) includes additional elements of non-discrimination. However, the Understanding is, as such, not part of the single undertaking and of mandatory WTO agreements. It contains a set of rules and disciplines which a group of WTO Members wanted to adopt in addition to the provisions of the GATS.[26] Paragraph B.2 of the Understanding imposes the MFN and national treatment standards on the purchase of financial services by public entities. This is a 'GATS Plus' obligation because the GATS itself exempts public procurement from the application of the non-discrimination principles (GATS Article XIII:1). Furthermore, paragraph C.1 of the Understanding requires national treatment regarding access to payment and clearing systems operated by public entities, and to official funding and refinancing facilities. Paragraph C.2 does the same regarding membership, participation in, and access to any self-regulatory body, securities or futures exchange or market, clearing agency, or any other organization or association.

IV. Potentials and Limits of the Principle of Non-Discrimination in Financial Regulation

We now move to the question of whether the principle of non-discrimination can in the future play a useful role in international financial law in light of the recent financial crisis. An aspect which has already received considerable attention in the public debate and in the literature concerns the application of non-discrimination principles to rescue measures and financial stimuli offered to address the solvency crisis of the banking sector in 2008–09.[27] Support measures which discriminate against foreign banks or foreign enterprises because they are only available to

---

[24] See Chapter 16 by Panagiotis Delimatsis and Pierre Sauvé in this volume.
[25] Eric Leroux, 'Trade in Financial Services under the World Trade Organization', 36 *Journal of World Trade at* 413 (2002), at 431. See also Bart De Meester, 'The Global Financial Crisis and Government Support for Banks: What Role for GATS?', 13 *Journal of International Economic Law* 27 (2010), at 61, who argues that 'if support schemes are discriminatory in the sense that they exclude foreign-owned banks that have a local presence in the market and are of . . . systemic significance, such schemes are not genuinely taken for prudential reasons' and therefore do not benefit from the prudential carve-out.
[26] See Leroux, above n 25, at 433.
[27] Speech of Director-General Lamy, 'The Global Trading System and the World Economy', Conference on the New Global Trading System in the Post-Crisis Era, Seoul, 7 December 2009, <http://www.wto.org/english/news_e/sppl_e/sppl1144_e.htm> (visited on 15 April 2010).

domestic institutions violate the national treatment principle of the GATS if Members undertook specific commitments in financial services.[28] We extend the analysis beyond support measures, because they are of a short-term character and we are more interested in the impact of non-discrimination on the development of a stable regulatory framework. The article focuses on financial services. The potential of non-discrimination in monetary affairs and macro-economics is discussed elsewhere.[29]

Our approach to this analysis is selective, but we hope illustrative. Instead of discussing the impact of non-discrimination in a general and abstract manner, we consider three concrete areas in which we identify a need for reform. All three areas concern the relationship between the trading and the finance systems. The proposals aim at enabling and stabilizing sound financial regulation while avoiding overt discrimination and protectionism.

A. From Basel to Geneva: Enabling the Adoption of Binding Prudential Standards in the WTO Framework

The GATS framework for financial services has largely 'outsourced' the question of financial services regulation. Paragraph 2 of the Annex on Financial Services exempts prudential standards from the GATS disciplines. This includes measures relating to the protection of investors, depositors, policy holders, to fiduciary obligations, and to the stability of the financial system in general. The so-called prudential carve-out leaves it up to the Members of the WTO to establish regulatory standards (or abandon them).[30] This is important for our argument: WTO Members may adopt prudential measures without interference from WTO law, but they may also refrain from adopting any such measures without violating WTO requirements. This preserves national regulatory autonomy and enables each country to adopt those rules which that country deems appropriate. It 'individualizes' the adoption of regulatory standards, or the obligation to mutually recognize such standards.

The financial crisis demonstrated the importance of appropriate prudential standards. Countries failing to impose adequate minimal capital requirements and related safeguards were much more exposed to it than those operating strong regulation, such as Canada or Australia. The GATS leaves the level of prudential standards and policies entirely to Members. GATS seeks to liberalize markets, but does not seek to harmonize domestic regulation. It safeguards against excessive

---

[28] Anne van Aaken and Jürgen Kurtz, 'Prudence or Discrimination? Emergency Measures, the Global Financial Crisis and International Economic Law', 12 *Journal of International Economic Law* 859 (2009), at 871–73; De Meester, above n 23, at 37–40.

[29] See Chapter 20 by Ernst Baltensperger and Thomas Cottier in this volume.

[30] See Cottier, above n 17, at 7. See also Michael J. Hahn, 'WTO Rules on Trade in Financial Services: A Victory of Greed over Reason?', in Rainer Grote and Thilo Marauhn (eds), *The Regulation of International Financial Markets—Perspectives for Reform* (Cambridge: Cambridge University Press, 2006) 176–205 at 199.

domestic regulation, but does not impose minimal standards.[31] Moreover, countries may operate different standards for foreign and domestic operators. Unlike for MFN, there is no horizontal obligation to operate a level playing field in terms of prudential standards. Nothing prevents a Member from operating stricter standards for foreign operators.

In light of the financial crisis, the question arises whether the GATS should be revisited and foundations should be laid for global minimal prudential standards within the multilateral trading system, in terms of binding obligations on Members, which would need to be applied in a non-discriminatory manner to large multinational banks beyond certain thresholds. The problem of a 'lack of prudential regulation' in the GATS has recently even been recognized by a leading proponent of the multilateral trading system.[32]

The GATS follows the traditional model of trade liberalization and regulation. Liberalization is achieved through international commitments and binding rules, while regulation, left to the domestic level, is subject to certain principles under international law, in particular, necessity. From this perspective, it is argued that carve-out provisions of paragraph 2 of the Annex on Financial Services should continue to be left to individual Members and must not be harmonized. It is argued that the GATS does not amount to an instrument of harmonization and the WTO does not offer a suitable framework to this effect.[33] Prudential standards therefore should be left individualized. Countries are able to adopt regulations suitable to their own economic needs and levels of development in the financial sector.[34] This view assumes that financial stability is a national or regional public good, and overall interests of the global system are better secured by regulatory competition. From another angle, it can be argued that transnational liberalization requires regulatory embedding.[35] This is equally true for financial services. The GATS does not pursue a strict hands-off approach in terms of harmonization, but provides for the possibility of sectoral harmonization under GATS Article VI:4.[36] While this option has so far not been used, except for accounting standards, other WTO agreements have developed more extensive experience and linkages with existing international standards. The Agreement on Technical Barriers to Trade (TBT Agreement) and the Agreement on the Application of Sanitary and Phytosanitary Measures (SPS Agreement) refer to international standards and encourage and

---

[31] Panagiotis Delimatsis, *International Trade in Services and Domestic Regulations—Necessity, Transparency, and Regulatory Diversity* (Oxford: Oxford University Press, 2007), at 84 ff.

[32] Former US Trade Representative Charlene Barshefsky as quoted in 'To Promote Economic Stability, Nations Must Free Themselves from WTO Financial Deregulation Dictates', *Public Citizen*, October 2009, 4.

[33] See e.g. Chapter 11 by Steve Charnovitz in this volume.

[34] Diemo Dietrich, Jasper Finke and Christian Tietje, 'Liberalization and Rules on Regulation in the Field of Financial Services in Bilateral Trade and Regional Integration Agreements', 97 *Beiträge zum Transnationalen Wirtschaftsrecht Halle* (Saale 2010), at 19–25.

[35] See generally Karl Polanyi, *The Great Transformation: The Political and Economic Origins of Our Time*, 9th ed. (Boston: Beacon Press, 2008).

[36] Markus Krajewski, 'Article VI GATS Domestic Regulation', in Rüdiger Wolfrum, Peter-Tobias Stoll and Anja Seibert-Fohr (eds), *WTO—Trade in Services: Max Planck Commentaries on World Trade Law* (Leiden/Boston: Martinus Nijhoff, 2008) 165–96.

grant recourse to them by Members, while not excluding alternative recourse to stricter domestic standards.[37] The linkage of WTO law and standards adopted in other international fora is not alien to the system. To the extent that financial stability is considered a global public good, ways and means to achieve common rules and harmonization do exist within WTO law. Finally, it should be recalled that regulation often entails a mix of international and domestic standards. While some parts may be harmonized in terms of minimal standards, others may be left to regulatory competition. Within the WTO, the Agreement on Trade-Related Aspects of Intellectual Property Rights (TRIPS Agreement) is an example in point.

Keeping these options in mind, this leads us from Geneva to Basel and the standards on financial supervision developed by the Basel committees.[38] At present, there is no legal linkage between the two. Moreover, Basel standards are non-binding. They focus on countries with a highly developed financial sector and do not address the problems of capacity building and institutional constraints in developing countries. As the carve-out is complete ('notwithstanding any other provisions of the Agreement'), there is no requirement to apply prudential standards on an MFN basis, nor to observe national treatment obligations.

Such de-linking raises two problems. First, there is no global system in place which secures level playing fields among all the financial centres, present and emerging. Members may discriminate in recognizing foreign prudential standards, and they can operate different standards for domestic and foreign-controlled operators. Secondly, there are no incentives in WTO law for Members to aim at sound regulatory and supervisory standards in the trading system, and there are no rewards for countries which have adopted such standards. Applying sound prudential standards and thus contributing to the stability of the global financial system is not recognized as a commitment in return for which Members may obtain reciprocal benefits in terms of market access in goods and services of particular interest to them. Could and should the de-linking of Geneva and Basel be overcome? How could this be done?

A number of questions need to be discussed and further researched in this context: for example, is it feasible and possible to recognize the adoption of prudential international standards as a legal commitment or 'concession' in trade negotiations which could in turn be honoured by market access in areas of prime interest to the Member concerned? It is a matter of creating incentives to encourage

---

[37] Rüdiger Wolfrum, Peter-Tobias Stoll and Anja Seibert-Fohr, *WTO—Technical Barriers and SPS Measures: Max Planck Commentaries on World Trade Law* (Leiden/Boston: Martinus Nijhoff, 2007); Stefan Zleptnig, *Non-Economic Objectives in WTO Law: Justification Provisions of GATT, GATS, SPS and TBT agreements* (Leiden: Martinus Nijhoff, 2010).

[38] Basel Committee on Banking Supervision, 'Basel III: A global regulatory framework for more resilient banks and Banking systems', June 2011, at <http://www.bis.org/publ/bcbs189.pdf> (visited on 22 February 2012). See also Robert Howse, Importing Regulatory Standards and Principles into WTO Jurisprudence: the Challenges of Interpreting the GATS Arrangements on Financial Services and Telecommunications, Paper Presented in Vienna, 2009' with See also Robert Howse, '"Importing" Regulatory Standards and Principles into WTO Jurisprudence: the Challenges of Interpreting the GATS Arrangements on Financial Services and Telecommunications' (Presentation given at Services Liberalisation in the EU and the WTO, Vienna, 5–6 March 2009, on file with the authors).

Members to subscribe to common rules defining the level playing field, such as minimal capital requirements of banks. One problem of this approach is, however, that it is built on the other Members' goodwill and that there is no guarantee that market access will be offered in return. The experience with GATS Article IV shows that an approach which builds on voluntarily negotiated concessions is not very effective.[39] One way to avoid this ambiguity would be a plurilateral approach following the model of the Understanding on Commitments in Financial Services, but incorporating regulatory standards. However, it might generally be questioned whether bolstering regulatory reforms should be linked to further market access if—as the 'Stiglitz Commission' and others have suggested[40]—market access is more likely to be part of the problem than part of a solution.

In this context, it might therefore be helpful to consider the basic idea of the Reference Paper on Telecommunications (Reference Paper).[41] This is incorporated in the GATS commitments of the Members as additional commitments and is based on the assumption that a regulatory framework is needed to prevent abuses of dominant market players. In more abstract terms, the Reference Paper embodies a nucleus of transnational regulatory embedding of liberalized markets. It sets a legal standard with which all Members are required to comply in order to prevent and combat the impact of *de facto* monopolies. This approach has also been explored in the field for grid industries and energy-related services.[42] The idea of adopting a legal standard addressing the obligations of Members in regulating specific industries should be further explored for financial services. It is conceivable to create global level playing fields by addressing minimal capital or other requirements within WTO law with which national financial regulations would be obliged to comply.

Alternatively, it may be possible to follow the models of the SPS Agreement and its reference to the Codex Alimentarius standards or the TRIPS Agreement model of incorporating standards from international agreements relating to intellectual property rights. This would contribute to a movement from soft law to more stringently binding rules.[43] While avoiding the problem of voluntary concessions, such an approach would require a change in the treaties themselves, which does not seem likely.

---

[39] WTO Panel Report, *Mexico—Measures Affecting Telecommunications Services (Mexico—Telecoms)*, WT/DS204/R, adopted 1 June 2004, para 7.214.

[40] See UN Commission of Experts, above n 3, para 208; Kevin P. Gallagher, 'Space to Prevent and Mitigate Financial Crises in Trade and Investment Agreements', G24 Discussion Paper No 58, April 2010 at 6.

[41] WTO, Negotiating Group on Basic Telecommunications, 'Telecommunications Services: Reference Paper', 24 April 1996, <http://www.wto.org/english/tratop_e/serv_e/telecom_e/tel23_e.htm> (visited on 14 July 2010).

[42] See Olga Nartova, 'Energy Services and Competition Policies under WTO Law' (Doctoral thesis on file at World Trade Institute, Bern); Olga Nartova, 'Assessment of the GATS' Impact on Climate Change Mitigation', in Thomas Cottier, Olga Nartova and Sadeq Z. Bigdeli (eds), *International Trade Regulation and the Mitigation of Climate Change: World Trade Forum* (Cambridge: Cambridge University Press, 2009) 259–73.

[43] But see Brummer's point that soft law can also trigger compliance: Brummer, above n 18.

The framework of the GATS would allow monitoring and enforcing such standards as they would be subject to dispute settlement under the Dispute Settlement Understanding of the WTO, whether a proper legal standard is adopted or whether it is referred to.

How would these proposals be affected by, or affect, the principle of non-discrimination? Framing a commitment to regulatory standards in the context of negotiations on market access would be compatible with non-discrimination, because any commitments would be applicable on an MFN basis. This might not be the case with every plurilateral approach. While models such as the Understanding on Commitments in Financial Services or the Reference Paper are incorporated into the schedules and therefore also apply on an MFN basis, plurilateral agreements by definition only apply to their Member parties. However, if all Members have an equal possibility to join such an agreement, the underlying function of non-discrimination might be preserved.

The application of legal standards, either pronounced in the agreement or referred to, could be made subject to national treatment. Foreign-owned providers of financial services would thus be essentially subject to the same standards as the domestic financial industry. National treatment does not rule out adopting different standards for different categories of providers, depending upon size and market shares. It would, however, require that all providers within the same group are treated alike.

Incorporating international standards into the WTO framework raises the problem of political economy and the representativeness of the particular standard-setting organization. The approach of WTO law so far is built on the paradigm that only standards of organizations which are open to all WTO Members can be incorporated into the WTO framework.[44] It is questionable whether the Basel Committee on Banking Supervision fulfils this requirement: while in theory the committee is open to all states (there are no formal membership rules), it is *de facto* a club of a few countries, and not open to the rest of the world. Linking Basel to Geneva inevitably implies a review of the legitimacy of the informal processes and exclusiveness in similar ways to when these issues were raised upon the introduction of binding references to international food standards of the Codex Alimentarius Commission.[45] A binding linkage to the WTO implies a review of the Basel process and placing efforts on a broader and essentially global footing. It may be argued that extension of membership is not in the interest of the central banks and financial regulators of industrialized countries. On the other hand, it is evident that future standards need to reach out globally. The financial crisis demonstrated the close interconnections of all countries alike. Future standards need to be able to create level playing fields around the world, including, in particular, emerging economies. We return to the problem of developing countries below.

---

[44] See GATS Article VI:5.
[45] See Joanne Scott, *The WTO Agreement on Sanitary and Phytosanitary Measures: A Commentary* (Oxford: Oxford University Press, 2007); Marsha A. Echols, *Food Safety and the WTO: The Interplay of Culture, Science and Technology* (London: Kluwer Law International, 2001).

B. Mutual recognition, preferential trade agreements, or requiring establishment: How to ensure effective financial market supervision?

In the absence of an incorporation of, or reference to, multilateral regulatory legal standards for financial services in the WTO systems, Members might take recourse to other measures. One way seems to be a trend towards requiring establishment for service suppliers who want to supply their services either through commercial presence or the presence of natural persons (GATS Modes 3 and 4).[46] This submits foreign service suppliers to the regulatory standards of the host Member and excludes the operation of subsidiaries which would remain under the supervision of the home Member. Such requirements are restrictions on market access (GATS Article XVI:2(e)) and may also be violations of the national treatment principle. They will hence only be compatible with the GATS if there are no conflicting commitments. In general, however, such restrictions run against the commitment of market access and non-discrimination. They defy the very idea of cross-border services. Much as in the internal market law of the European Union, ways of combining cross-border trade and oversight need to be developed.[47]

How could countries move forward and combine strict regulatory supervision with giving full market access? One way would be the conclusion of preferential agreements which combine high regulatory standards with preferential market access rights.[48] In such a case, countries could accept financial services suppliers who remain subject to their home regulation because the parties to the agreement are satisfied that they all employ similar regulatory standards. This can be achieved through regional integration agreements as the example of the European Union has shown. However, it is not possible to conclude preferential agreements which cover financial services only for these purposes, because GATS Article V requires that economic integration agreements have substantial sectoral coverage. This excludes preferential agreements which are limited to the financial sector, e.g. by covering only insurance and banking.

As an alternative, Members could enter into mutual recognition agreements on the basis of GATS Article VII:2 and, specifically, paragraph 3 of the Annex on Financial Services. However, it is questionable whether WTO Members can combine this with conditional market access commitments limited to the Members of such an agreement. In the absence of any GATS Article II exemptions, a conditional commitment could violate the MFN principle. Furthermore, Article VII:3 specifically requires that mutual recognition not be a means of discrimination between Members. Some Members have made commitments based on the condition of concluding a mutual recognition agreement. Yet, even if such a limitation would be considered to be compatible with the GATS MFN principle, it could be a violation of the market access principle. According to Articles XVI:2 and XX:1, a Member may only list those measures as exemptions which are specifically

---

[46] GATS Article I:2(c) and (d).
[47] ECJ, Case C-205/84, *European Commission v Federal Republic of Germany* (1986).
[48] See Dietrich et al, above n 34.

mentioned in either of these provisions.[49] It therefore seems that this option might run against GATS principles.

This shows that the application of the non-discrimination principles may hamper efforts of Members to combine tight regulatory standards and supervision with market access commitments which allow for home-country Member control. As a consequence, the abovementioned attempts to incorporate regulatory standards into the schedules may be more compatible with the trading system.

C. Graduation in financial regulation

Progressive liberalization of services through the GATS offers ample flexibility and policy space to Members. It is interesting to observe that the criticism faced by, for example, the TRIPS Agreement with its minimal standards, has not been voiced in the context of services, and the need for special and differential treatment (S&D) does not exist in the same way as it exists in other agreements of the multilateral trading system. Apart from general rules and principles, commitments are tailor-made and, up to now, have essentially reflected the regulatory landscape of domestic law. Current negotiations seek to push these limits, but progress has been slow and difficult. Fifteen years after the entry into force of the GATS, it is evident that the process of liberalization will be slow, comparable to the 50 years it took to lower tariffs from an average of 40 per cent to 4 per cent on industrial goods at the end of the Uruguay Round. The development from addressing border measures, such as tariffs and quotas, to non-tariff barriers increasingly led to the adoption of common rules and minimal standards. This in return triggered the need for S&D in many areas. To the extent that common standards, as suggested above, are developed on financial regulation within the GATS, the same process is likely to emerge in the field of services, and financial services regulation in particular. There will be a need to differentiate according to the differing levels of social and economic development. In shaping international financial regulations, it will be important to consider not only diverging sizes of banking institutions, but also diverging levels of social and economic development.

These concerns can be taken into account in two different ways. Firstly, specific prudential standards may be limited per se to international banking and not extended to domestic operators beyond a certain size. It may be tailored in terms of size and turnovers. This will allow the exclusion of smaller operators and limit harmonized regulations to large and global competitors. Appropriate thresholds need to be developed and applied by appropriate bodies, in particular the Financial Stability Board and those within Basel III, and incorporated or linked to WTO law. Non-discrimination, both in terms of MFN and national treatment, will guarantee fair conditions of competition and level playing fields. All state Members of the WTO will be bound by the standards and will need to apply them to financial operators beyond the thresholds defined. For least developed member countries

---

[49] Panel Report, *Mexico—Telecoms*, above n 39, para 7.353 ff.

and many developed members, this will be relevant only to the extent that operators meet these thresholds. To the extent necessary, appropriate technical co-operation should be provided for in order to implement effective supervision over large financial operators, enabling and empowering the Members' authorities to do so. The threshold of general prudential standards automatically brings about graduation in its own ways, as it only applies to Members with large banks.

Secondly, we suggest further developing the concept of progressive regulation or graduation for harmonized rules on financial services beyond common prudential standards applicable to large multinational corporations wherever they operate. The basic idea is to develop a single regime, but to make the application of specific rules, including the obligation to grant national treatment, dependent upon economic thresholds defining the competitiveness of specific sectors in Member States.[50] Once these levels are reached, the operation of rules would be triggered, while prior to that they would not commit a Member internationally. The model also allows for defining different sets of rules applicable to different levels of competitiveness, all within a single undertaking. We submit that this model could also apply to financial regulation within GATS and outside it. Thus, a revised Understanding on Financial Services, containing such thresholds, could be multilateralized and be applied to all WTO Members reaching the defined thresholds. This approach allows flexibility and predictability in the application of common standards to be combined. Common rules for financial services could be shaped accordingly and rendered applicable to Members whose sectors have reached the critical level of competitiveness. Economic research is required to develop appropriate criteria to this effect. In conclusion, it is possible to limit global rules on prudential standards to global players, thus protecting global public goods while leaving regulation of other operators to the regional or national levels. Within a single undertaking, it is also possible to exclude non-competitive developing country members from being subject to extensive and demanding international regulation.

V. Conclusion

The GATS was negotiated with a view to liberalizing trade in services and to enhancing market access abroad in certain sectors, many of which were subject to traditional restrictions and privileges granted to domestic providers. Domestic regulation of services was made subject to legal disciplines which essentially reflect the principle of proportionality.[51] Regulations should not exceed levels necessary to attain a particular goal. These principles are enshrined in GATS Articles IV, XVI, and XVII. More specifically, the GATS Understanding on Commitments in

---

[50] See Thomas Cottier, 'From Progressive Liberalization to Progressive Regulation', 9 *Journal of International Economic Law* 779 (2006).

[51] Panagiotis Delimatsis, 'Toward a Horizontal Necessity Test for Services: Completing the GATS Article VI:4 Mandate', in Marion Panizzon, Nicole Pohl and Pierre Sauvé (eds), *GATS and the Regulation of International Trade in Services: World Trade Forum* (Cambridge: Cambridge University Press, 2008) 370–96.

Financial Services, in Article 10, encourages Members to remove or limit any significant adverse effects of non-discriminatory measures on financial services. All this reflects the philosophy of deregulation prevailing at the time, and further encouraged governments to limit and dismantle regulations, in particular in the field of financial services. The question arises whether more stringent regulation of the financial sector following the crisis is pre-empted by the GATS' legal framework and its philosophy. We do not think so. The GATS overall is an instrument of sufficient flexibility. It allows Members to tailor appropriate solutions commensurate with regulatory needs. It allows for gradual introduction of national treatment. It equally allows Members to prescribe appropriate prudential standards under the Annex. The GATS inherently allows for the adoption of a post-crisis philosophy which stresses trade regulation as much as liberalization. Much of the balance can be achieved within the present framework. There may not be a need for fundamental reform, if the GATS is read and further developed with a new philosophy in mind. Future amendments should create a framework allowing for the negotiation needed for adopting, incorporating, or referring to appropriate prudential standards and other common regulations for the financial industry within the GATS. Incentives should be created to develop and implement such standards as a matter of binding and enforceable obligations. MFN and the principle of national treatment will play important roles in providing level playing fields. To the extent that common standards are developed, national treatment obligations should be reinforced and made mandatory, rather than in addressing progressive liberalization and market access. At the same time, it will be necessary to develop a framework which is able to take into account different sizes of economic operators and different levels of competitiveness of financial sectors in different Members, and to shape the operation of international standards accordingly. Overall, it is a matter of carefully linking and combining different regulatory regimes and bringing about greater coherence among them. The WTO, specifically the GATS, with its binding and enforceable rules is bound to play a critical role in the process of moving from soft law to hard law and in providing binding international standards for the financial sector. Different avenues and models are available in WTO law to this effect, and additional ones may be developed for positively addressing prudential standards in international law.

16

Financial Services Trade After the Crisis: Policy and Legal Conjectures

*Panagiotis Delimatsis and Pierre Sauvé**

I. Introduction

In September 2009, in the midst of financial turmoil of a severity the world had not witnessed since the 1930s, the G20 leaders reaffirmed their commitment to 'refrain from raising barriers or imposing new barriers to investment or to trade in goods and services'.[1] They further pledged to minimize any negative impact of domestic policies, including fiscal policy and financial sector support schemes, on trade and investment.[2] Still, several measures enacted in the wake of the financial crisis, including subsidies and 'buy, hire and/or lend local' requirements adopted in support schemes in the financial sector and stimulus packages, could be open to legal challenge under World Trade Organization (WTO) rules and investment treaty obligations relating to non-discrimination and transparency.[3]

This chapter explores the various ways in which the financial crisis of 2008–09 and its aftershocks may impact on the future conduct of financial services liberalization and rule-making in a *trade policy setting*. The last three words are italicized for a purpose: in searching for the origins of the extreme turbulence experienced in financial markets of late, one would be hard pressed to find a trace of trade policy. The economic and financial reverberations of the crisis continue to be felt and its regulatory fallout remains uncertain. However, it cannot be likened to the process of progressive dismantling of impediments affecting access to, and operation in, financial markets that was launched in 1999 through the entry into force of the rules regulating financial services enshrined in the General Agreement on Trade in

* The authors are grateful to Juan Marchetti, Costas Stephanou and the participants of the JIEL Conference on 'The Quest for International Law in Financial Regulation' in London on 21 May 2010 for valuable insights and discussions. Any errors are of the authors' alone.
    [1] G-20, 'Leaders' Statement: The Pittsburgh Summit', 24–25 September 2009, para 48, <http://www.pittsburghsummit.gov/mediacenter/129639.htm> (visited 21 October 2010).
    [2] Ibid.
    [3] Organisation for Economic Co-operation and Development, WTO, United Nations Conference on Trade and Development, 'Report on G20 Trade and Investment Measures (September 2009–February 2010)', 8 March 2010.

Services (GATS) and the adoption of the Fifth Protocol[4] To The General Agreement On Trade In Services, S/L/45, 3 December 1997 (and through the numerous preferential trade agreements that have done likewise since then).

This chapter, co-authored by an economist and a lawyer, imparts a deliberately dual narrative to the analysis on offer. It does so with a view to advancing insights— in diagnosis and prescription—that are informed by both big picture policy considerations and the nitty-gritty legal (i.e. rule-making) challenges deriving primarily from the ambiguous and incomplete nature of the GATS and of similar rules governing financial services trade and investment in preferential settings. We consider each of these in turn in the analysis that follows.

II. Policy Conjectures

A. Tracing the origins of the financial crisis

The financial upheaval the world has confronted over the past two years must be seen not so much as a crisis of liberalization—and almost certainly not of trade and investment liberalization—but rather of perverse regulation, lax supervisory practices, and derelict corporate governance.[5] While the origins of the financial crisis cannot be reduced to any single cause nor traced to any single country or class of financial intermediary, the crisis is widely regarded as having taken root in an environment of regulatory incentives encouraging excessive risk-taking, and characterized by undue proximity between market operators and between regulators and regulatees. No attempt at understanding the financial crisis of 2008–09 can be made without also considering the intellectual canvas against which it proceeded, one that long championed the innate virtues of market efficiency, financial innovation and financial market opening, literally as ends in themselves.[6]

Trade historians might take solace from the fact that a financial crisis can be good news for financial market opening. Indeed, looking back only a decade, the Asian financial crisis of 1997–98 and its subsequent spread to other emerging country markets prompted a clear, pro-liberalizing, trade policy response. At the time, several emerging country governments sought to exploit the signalling properties of trade agreements, and notably that of the incipient GATS, by ratcheting up their

---

[4] Fifth Protocol to the General Agreement on Trade in Services, S/L/45, 3 December 1997.

[5] Opinions naturally differ on this point. For instance, a United Nations expert group headed by Nobel laureate Joseph Stiglitz recently concluded that the financial services provisions of the GATS and similar rules found in preferential trade agreements could be seen to 'restrict the ability of governments to change the regulatory structure in ways which support financial stability, economic growth, and the welfare of vulnerable consumers and investors'. See United Nations, 'Report of the Commission of Experts of the President of the United Nations General Assembly on Reforms of the International Monetary and Financial System', September 2009, ch 3, para 208.

[6] Cf. Nouriel Roubini and Stephen Mihim, *Crisis Economics* (London: Penguin, 2010); UK Financial Services Authority, 'The Turner Review—A Regulatory Response to the Global Banking Crisis', March 2009; Viral V. Acharya and Matthew Richardson (eds), *Restoring Financial Stability— How to Repair a Failed System* (New Jersey: Wiley, 2009).

commitment to more open and non-discriminatory financial regimes through legally binding undertakings anchored in schedules of commitments.[7]

There are, alas, reasons to doubt that the latest episode of financial turmoil might generate similar effects. One is that the crisis has only marginally affected some of the world's leading emerging markets. These markets have spent the better part of the last decade strengthening their macro-prudential regimes and cleaning up the balance sheets of leading domestic financial institutions. This time around, the crisis has befallen the countries and institutions arguably least in need of policy signalling. Indeed, the financial crisis took root in countries ranked among the most open to trade and investment in financial services, and whose bound commitments under the GATS and preferential trade agreements (PTAs) typically lock-in the actual level of (largely) non-discriminatory access afforded by domestic regulatory regimes.

An important distinguishing feature of the financial crisis of 2008–09 was its anchoring in a number of advanced industrialized nations. Such countries were long believed to have the most robust macro-prudential regimes and the most sophisticated supervisors enforcing the strictest regulatory regimes. They were also blessed with financial institutions widely seen as operating cutting-edge risk-management systems developed by the best financial engineers money could buy.

B. Direct and indirect contextual considerations

Even though the financial crisis had little to do with trade policy as a central contributing factor, this chapter posits both policy and legal ramifications flowing from its resolution. On the policy side, a number of effects are likely to shape the climate within which trade and investment liberalization in financial services will proceed in future.

For starters, the financial crisis has arguably dented the legitimacy of the traditional *demandeurs* in financial services negotiations. Recent years have seen the marked ascent of a number of emerging country players in the financial field. Such a trend is certain to fuel increasingly offensive market-access interests likely to find expression in trade and investment policy in the coming years, whether in the WTO or under PTAs and bilateral investment agreements (BITs). The fact remains, however, that developed countries, by a large margin, are the main exporters of financial services today and hence they are the predominant *demandeurs* in financial services negotiations. The Organisation for Economic Co-operation and Development (OECD)-centric nature of the financial crisis is likely to complicate the advocacy of further trade-induced financial market opening by its chief protagonists. This problem is likely to be felt more acutely at the WTO level than under PTAs to the extent that individual OECD countries with significant export interests in financial services—e.g. the USA, Japan, Canada, Switzerland and

---

[7] Wendy Dobson, 'Further Financial Services Liberalization in the Doha Round?', No PB02-8 International Economics Policy Brief, 2002, at 6; Sydney J. Key, *The Doha Round and Financial Services Negotiations* (Jackson, TN: AEI Press, 2003).

leading EU Member States—enjoy significantly greater negotiating leverage within bilateral confines than in Geneva discussions.

Secondly, the financial crisis must be situated against the backdrop of a changed, liberalization-adverse ideological environment. Its regulatory fall out coincides with the ongoing prosecution of the Washington Consensus and its advocacy of financial and capital account liberalization. This trial has been proceeding since the conclusion of the Uruguay Round and thus largely predated the onset of the financial crisis. Still, just as the financial crisis has shaken the economics profession and notably the manner in which open economy macro-economics is taught, it is also likely to have marked an important inflection point following a 30-year period of almost theological belief, both in business and policy circles, in the inherent efficiency of markets, the innate virtues of financial innovation and a clear bias towards light(er) regulatory approaches, especially in standard-setting financial centres such as New York or London.

From a trade policy perspective, such a changed ideological climate could affect both the pace and nature of *negotiated* market opening in financial services. This is so even though one may remain relatively sanguine over prospects for continued *unilateral* market opening on the part of the world's key emerging markets, i.e. those countries on the receiving end of most requests for further financial liberalization in a trade policy setting.[8] Indeed, the future relevance of trade and investment rules may well lie as much in preventing governments of OECD countries from succumbing to the (diminished giant) temptation to backslide and undo the edifice of trade and capital mobility painstakingly erected over the past six decades, as in driving the process of financial opening in emerging markets.[9]

C. The trade policy fallout from the financial crisis: possible transmission channels

From the above considerations, five channels linking the financial crisis to the conduct of financial services negotiations can be identified. Each one of these channels calls into question beliefs and policy assumptions that have long formed the basis upon which financial services negotiations have proceeded.

The first channel relates more centrally to investment policy and concerns the optimal degree of foreign presence in domestic financial markets. To the extent that some (typically large) foreign financial operators may be seen as vectors of financial contagion in crisis situations, host-countries may express legitimate concerns that a significant foreign financial presence in domestic markets might heighten macro-

---

[8] The reason for this lies in the growing recognition—measured in continued autonomous policy reforms on the part of many developing country governments—of the central role that a properly regulated, pro-competitive, financial system can play in overall allocative efficiency and medium-term growth prospects.

[9] Cf. Daniel Price, 'The New Face of Anti-Globalization: Economic Recovery and Reform Efforts', in Alexei Monsarrat and Kiron Skinner (eds), *Renewing Globalization and Economic Growth in a Post-Crisis World—The Future of the G-20 Agenda* (Pittsburgh: Carnegie-Mellon University and the Atlantic Council, 2009) 73–6.

prudential risks. In turn, this could legitimize, on prudential grounds, calls for the maintenance or introduction of tighter restrictions on the entry of foreign operators (Mode 3 in GATS parlance), stricter quantitative caps on foreign equity holdings or broader limitations on the permissible scope of post-entry operations by foreign service providers.

The second, closely related, channel concerns the desirability, once more on macro-prudential grounds, of continuing to allow entry of foreign financial institutions through direct branching as opposed to via subsidiaries. The (largely successful) battle to secure access through direct branching has been one of the fiercest fought by OECD governments (and the financial industry) in their quest for financial market opening since the inception of the GATS. Such market opening has also ranked high on PTA radar screens.[10] Yet here again, legitimate concerns of a prudential nature might be expressed regarding the contagion risks that highly leveraged, foreign-established, financial institutions represent for host-countries, all the more so given the limited jurisdictional reach of domestic regulators over foreign branches. Concerns of this nature were heightened by home-country calls for foreign branches to rein in activities abroad and concentrate on lending at home as a counterpart to domestic bailout schemes. Rolling back regulations allowing for entry via direct branching would in many countries require a modification or withdrawal of existing commitments scheduled under the GATS and under PTAs. Trade law would thus appear, in this instance, as a potential rampart against de-liberalization. It may also, *a contrario sensu*, be seen as a potential hurdle to prudential policy design and implementation.

The third channel through which the financial crisis of 2008–09 might be felt in trade policy circles concerns the preference that host-country regulators may henceforth have for commercial presence as a means of ensuring more effective prudential oversight of foreign established financial operators. While such 'forced establishment' requirements might be deemed tantamount to service sector performance requirements—an area where the GATS, unlike the General Agreement on Tariffs and Trade (GATT), imposes no multilateral disciplines,[11] the prudential concerns fuelling such requirements surfaced visibly in proposals regarding the Alternative Investment Fund Managers Directive and the regulation of credit-rating agencies. Any determined move in this direction would affect the modal distribution of services trade commitments, contributing to a further weakening of cross-border trade in financial services (so-called Mode 1). The latter is already the form of trade (alongside the movement of service suppliers) towards which host-country regulators have typically exhibited the greatest precaution in market-opening terms.

The fourth channel through which the financial crisis might affect the future conduct of financial market opening in a trade setting concerns the desirability of

---

[10] Cf. Mona Haddad and Constantinos Stephanou (eds), *Financial Services and Preferential Trade Agreements—Lessons from Latin America* (Washington, DC: World Bank, 2010).

[11] Performance requirements affecting the goods trade are disciplined by the Agreement on Trade-Related Investment Measures (TRIMs Agreement) under the GATT.

using trade agreements, and notably their financial services chapters, to secure the concomitant liberalization of capital account transactions and related limitations on short-term capital movement. While the liberalization of trade in financial services and associated cross-border payments and transfers requires, by definition, that certain restrictions on capital transactions be lifted, a number of countries, most notably the USA, have in recent years shown a marked proclivity to require more sweeping capital account liberalization from their trading partners in the context of financial services negotiations. This trend has been most noticeable in the context of North–South PTAs. The degree to which such pressures might be maintained in the future remains an open question. This is because of the changed US adminis-tration, whose views on financial liberalization may well be more tempered than that of its predecessor, and because countries which maintained greater restrictions on capital transactions (and which took a stricter stance on financial leverage) appear to have weathered the financial storm with greater ease than those which adopted a more liberal policy stance.

The fifth and final channel through which the financial crisis might affect the conduct of trade negotiations in financial services concerns host-country attitudes towards financial innovation and the calls, embedded in the GATS Understanding on Commitments in Financial Services and in numerous PTAs, to treat 'new' financial services favourably in regulatory approval terms (i.e. host-countries should allow trade in financial services that have secured home-country regulatory approval). As noted above, the financial crisis has shaken the long-held belief in the innate virtues of (all forms of) financial engineering, with leading financial market authorities openly questioning the societal value added of much financial innovation.[12]

D. Needed for trade-facilitating and dispute prevention purposes: an internationally coordinated regulatory response

An important challenge confronting the trade and finance communities is whether the—to date primarily national—response to the financial crisis might increase the likelihood of a trade or investment challenge to regulatory measures taken on prudential grounds. Simply stated, are we about to determine the true remit of the GATS prudential carve-out through binding trade and investment arbitration? We believe that the financial crisis may have increased the likelihood that the answer to this question will be in the affirmative. This is so even though judicial activism is not the natural reflex of central bankers and financial supervisors, whose preference lies more with club-like discussion and mediation in Basel at the Bank for International Settlements (BIS) than with adversarial and legally enforceable litigation in Geneva (at the WTO) or under the arbitral proceedings of various tribunals concerned with investment disputes. And this is so even though the scope

---

[12] Prominent examples of such commentaries came from individuals such as Paul Volcker, former Governor of the US Federal Reserve; Mervyn King, the current Governor of the Bank of England; and Lord Turner, head of the United Kingdom's Financial Services Authority.

for successfully prosecuting a financial services complaint under trade law continues to be constrained (as the following section will show) by the incomplete and ambiguous nature of the rules governing trade in financial services.

To date, countries have largely acted according to national impulses, with differing market structures and political climates generating diverse policy proposals. The more such trends predominate, the greater the risk that some jurisdictions may impose regulatory requirements which, while infused with prudential objectives, might still be excessive, unduly burdensome or serve as a cover for industrial policy activism in the financial sector.[13] Trade and investment litigation targeting prudential measures is likely to be significantly less if G20 governments succeed in adopting common reform proposals that move the world in the direction of internationally agreed regulatory reforms in finance.

E. Addressing competitive distortions

A further means to gauge the likely fallout of the financial crisis on trade and investment diplomacy in finance is through the answers to a number of important questions on pro-competitive conduct arising from the unprecedented financial bailouts the world has witnessed. Although a number of policy measures were temporary and subject to early reversal, such as when bailed-out institutions paid back capital infusions to their home-country governments, the scale of recent governmental intervention in financial markets is unlikely to have been competition-neutral in all instances. Such a reality raises complex policy challenges at the interface of trade, investment and competition policy. It also confronts the competing, and at times contradictory, logics of trade and financial policy, with the former anchored in respect for the principle of non-discrimination and the latter principally concerned with principles of soundness and security and the avoidance of systemic market failures in financial markets. Such a clash of regulatory cultures, in turn, raises a number of fundamental questions, some of which might ultimately have to be mediated in a trade policy arena. Such questions include the following:

(1) Should respect for non-discrimination (national treatment and most-favoured nation treatment) always and everywhere trump macro-prudential and financial stability concerns and the measures required to restore or maintain such stability? Simply stated, can financial bailouts ever be fully nationality-blind?

---

[13] As with any major crisis, the policy response to the financial crisis runs the very real risk of regulatory overshooting, with the immediacy of emotion and political expediency succeeding over measured responses. There is already some evidence of this in both the EU and the USA, although in both instances it is important to disentangle legitimate public policy concerns over the compliance costs, fairness and ultimate effectiveness of proposed regulatory fixes from more narrowly commercial lobbying efforts on the part of the financial industry aimed at watering down any significant departures from the pre-crisis regulatory *status quo*. See Chris Giles, 'IMF Fears Rules will Kill Off Securitization', *Financial Times*, 8 October 2009, 3. See also Nikki Tait, 'EU tries to break logjam on hedge funds', *Financial Times*, 14 April 2010, 3 and T. Braithwaite and S. O'Connor, 'US Financial Rules System Faces Overhaul', *Financial Times*, 4 June 2009, 4.

(2) How discriminatory have financial bailouts been in reality? Such an empir-
    ical question clearly points to the central importance of transparency and of
    multilateral monitoring and surveillance, which the WTO has usefully taken
    up more resolutely in the trade and investment fields in the wake of the
    financial crisis in partnership with the OECD and the United Nations
    Conference on Trade and Development (UNCTAD). Yet more credible
    monitoring in the financial field is likely to require closer co-operation and
    coordination among the trade, finance and competition policy communities
    than we have witnessed to date. The fact that the worlds of trade and finance
    already operate through multilateral agencies, whereas the competition
    world does not, could be problematic in this regard.

(3) Does the interconnectedness of financial markets and of financial market
    operators, particularly those involved in wholesale markets, imply that what
    have largely been *de jure* national bailouts have *de facto* most-favoured-
    nation (MFN) effects that may lessen their distortive impact? Once again
    this is largely an empirical challenge that would require the expert opinion of
    financial market specialists from the BIS, the Financial Stability Board (FSB)
    or the International Monetary Fund (IMF) working in concert with their
    trade and competition counterparts.

(4) Potentially anti-competitive effects of financial bailouts are not sufficiently
    documented. In the EU, at the end of December 2009, Directorate General
    for Competition (DG Competition) had to issue 81 advisory notes on the
    competition impact of financial bailouts, 75 of which were deemed unprob-
    lematic from the perspective of the EU's state aid policy. In six cases,
    however, the impact on competition—through excessive market concen-
    tration leading to concerns over possible abuse of dominance—was deemed
    sufficient to prompt demands for remedies, typically in the form of forced
    divestitures.[14] In such instances, might one not assume that cross-border
    trade and investment opportunities could also be compromised and existing
    GATS or PTA commitments potentially nullified or impaired? Thus, the
    risk of bailout-induced problems of market contestability, while generally
    limited, cannot be discounted. Nor can trade and investment litigation be
    discounted, for this very reason. Similarly, the rising level of judicial activism
    witnessed under BITs and PTAs featuring comprehensive investment
    disciplines suggests that scope exists for investor–state lawsuits targeting
    prudential measures in finance as forms of indirect expropriation. The
    likelihood of such litigation is all the greater as few investment chapters
    in PTAs (and even fewer in BITs) feature a prudential carve-out analogous
    to that found in GATS or in the financial services chapters of or annexes
    to PTAs.

---

[14] See Thorsten Beck, Diane Coyle, Mathias Dewatripont, Xavier Freixas, and Paul Seabright,
*Bailing Out the Banks: Reconciling Stabililty with Competition—An Analysis of State-Supported Schemes
for Financial Institutions* (London: Center for Economic Policy Research, 2010).

F. The financial crisis and the unfinished agenda in services rule-making

The regulatory response, both national and international, flowing from the financial crisis and its resolution, is also likely to have repercussions for the unfinished rule-making agenda in services trade. This is particularly so with regard to the need for a fully fledged subsidy regime for trade in services, as well as for embedding a necessity test able to deal with unduly burdensome, disproportionate, inadvertent or disguised domestic regulatory restrictions on trade and investment in services (including financial services).

In the following sections, we explore more fully the legal ramifications of the financial crisis by taking up the issue of how it might revive and inform the quest for more effective multilateral disciplines in these unfinished areas of GATS rule-making. As it happens, these are areas with readymade institutional anchors and negotiating mandates. Coming to our punch line early, we ask: why waste a crisis when useful advances can come from it in good-governance, pro-competitive, rule-making terms?

III. Legal Conjectures

A. Assessing the relevance and effectiveness of existing trade disciplines

Flexibility and softness stand out as two central traits of the supra-national legal framework governing the various measures adopted to remedy the consequences of the financial crisis. The principles and rules adopted under the aegis of the FSB,[15] the BIS and the Basel Committee on Banking Supervision (BCBS) are all neither binding nor enforceable.[16] Meanwhile, the GATS still lacks a comprehensive framework to tackle non- discriminatory, but nonetheless unduly burdensome, regulatory measures; the potentially distortive effects of subsidization in services trade;[17] or the prosecution of anti-competitive practices, among others. Such substantive shortcomings would appear, *prima facie*, to weaken the chances of a successful legal challenge before the WTO adjudicating bodies under current rules. In the meantime, and absent any effective disciplines, it is worth examining under which conditions a non-violation compliant under GATS Article XXIII:3 could be invoked. Other than the extremely onerous features of this provision, which are

---

[15] Cf. FSB, 'Overview of Progress in the Implementation of the G20 Recommendations for Strengthening Financial Stability', 18 June 2010.

[16] See also Mamiko Yokoi-Arai, 'GATS' Prudential Carve Out in Financial Services and its Relation with Prudential Regulation' 57 *International and Comparative Law Quarterly* 613 (2008), at 636. Of course, the softness of a rule does not necessarily imply that it is not respected. This is because of reputation costs and the interest in being a reliable 'member of the club'. See Chris Brummer's contribution in this volume. Also Daniel W. Drezner, *All Politics is Global: Explaining International Regulatory Regimes* (Princeton, NJ: Princeton University Press, 2007).

[17] See Pietro Poretti, *The Regulation of Subsidies within the General Agreement on Trade in Services of the WTO: Problems and Prospects* (Alphen aan den Rijn: Kluwer Law International, 2009).

analogous to GATT Article XXIII:1(b),[18] the existence of specific commitments in the relevant sector is warranted. In the case of financial services, this condition would be easily fulfilled in a complaint raised against a developed country, as most developed countries undertook far-reaching commitments in financial services based on the Understanding on Commitments in Financial Services.

The state of affairs described above need not be unduly worrisome if the measures adopted to promote financial recovery are temporary, as the G20 leaders pledged in Pittsburgh in November 2009. However, it could become a cause for greater concern if the above measures durably distort competitive conditions in the marketplace, affording undue advantages to certain institutions over others or rescuing otherwise unviable institutions from the exigencies of market exit.[19] Equally worrisome are the potentially trade-distorting effects of enticing bailed-out institutions to curtail or with- draw from activities abroad with a view to buttressing domestic lending activities.

The GATS, like all WTO agreements, is an incomplete contract.[20] As befits any agreement in an area that was previously uncharted, the wording of several GATS obligations, for instance, that define services that are excluded from the Agreement's remit or the prudential carve-out applicable to trade in financial services, is drafted in an (often deliberately) ambiguous manner. Meanwhile, several key substantive obligations, notably those on subsidies (Article XV), emergency safeguards (Article X), government procurement (XIII)[21] or domestic regulation (Article VI), which constitute the so-called 'unfinished rule-making agenda of GATS', remain a work in progress 23 years after the launch of the Uruguay Round, in some cases with decidedly slim chances of successful closure.[22]

The financial crisis of 2008–09 underscores the importance of developing effective legal disciplines able to help governments counteract the potentially trade-restrictive effects of financial rescue measures—including those taken on prudential grounds—and to remove the temptation for governments to resort to overtly protectionist financial measures. The question arises of how far the GATS provides them with such means and, if it does not, what can or should be done in future to equip the GATS (and PTAs featuring disciplines on services trade) with the ammunition needed to ensure the continued relevance of trade law in

---

[18] Cf. Panel Reports, *Korea—Measures Affecting Government Procurement (Korea—Procurement)*, WT/DS163/R, adopted 19 June 2000; and *Japan—Measures Affecting Consumer Photographic Film and Paper (Japan—Film)*, WT/DS44/R, adopted 22 April 1998.

[19] See European Commission, 'Temporary Community framework for State aid measures to support access to finance in the current financial and economic crisis', OJ C 83/1 of 7 April 2009.

[20] On the incompleteness of the WTO agreements, see Henrik Horn, Giovanni Maggi and Robert W. Staiger, 'Trade Agreements as Endogenously Incomplete Contracts', National Bureau of Economic Research Working Paper No 12745, December 2006.

[21] As to government procurement, the Understanding on Commitments in Financial Services entails an exception to the overall absence of disciplines on government procurement by requiring that public entities respect MFN and non-discrimination when they purchase financial services.

[22] Cf. Pierre Sauvé, 'Completing the GATS Framework: Addressing Uruguay Round Leftovers', 57(3) *Aussenwirtschaft* 310 (2002).

addressing the regulatory fallout from financial crises whose periodic occurrence is a constant in market economies.

B. The need for clarity on the scope of agreed disciplines

The need for financial authorities to enact prudential regulation in response to the various types of market failures buffeting financial markets is unanimously agreed. Indeed, and paradoxical as it may seem in the wake of the most recent episode of acute financial turmoil, the financial sector ranks in virtually all countries among those subject to the greatest regulatory scrutiny. True to form, the GATS, like trade agreements in general, has little to say on the substantive content of prudential rules or the policy rationales behind their enactment. The remit of trade policy generally lies elsewhere, in determining whether the regulatory objectives that nations set for themselves, and the means to achieve them, are broadly proportionate and necessary according to objective, verifiable criteria and that they do not serve as disguised restrictions to trade or investment. As discussed below, to date the GATS (and PTAs covering services trade) falls short of the above objective by virtue of the inability of WTO Members to reach agreement on the substantive elements of a necessity test for services trade.

As regards the scope of trade disciplines in the services' realm, Article I:3(b) of the GATS (and equivalent provisions found in all PTAs covering trade in services) largely exempts from the Agreement's remit any service provided in the exercise of governmental authority, i.e. public services that are provided on a non-commercial (i.e. not for profit) and non-competitive basis (i.e. not in competition with any other service or service supplier).[23]

The GATS clarifies the sector-specific meaning of Article I:3 in a series of sectoral annexes. In the area of financial services, the Financial Services Annex specifically excludes from the scope of the GATS: (i) activities of central banks and monetary authorities relating to monetary or exchange rate policies; (ii) activities forming part of a statutory system of social security or public retirement plans; and (iii) activities conducted by public entities either for the account or with the guarantee of using governmental financial resources. The Financial Services Annex, however, clarifies that the above activities (with the exception of monetary and exchange rate activities which are clearly monopolistic state prerogatives) would not escape the purview of the GATS if these services are supplied in competition with private financial service suppliers.

The above provisions of the Financial Services Annex clearly raise numerous interpretive questions, not least of which is whether the types of emergency interventions that financial authorities enacted during the financial crisis fall within or outside the scope of monetary and exchange rate policies and whether some of the beneficiaries of financial bailouts—e.g. entities such as Freddie Mac or Fannie

---

[23] GATS Article I:3(b) and (c). Also Eric Leroux, 'What is a "Service Supplied in the Exercise of Governmental Authority" Under Article I:3(b) and (c) of the General Agreement on Trade in Services?', 40(3) *Journal of World Trade* 348 (2006).

Mae—fit the definition of the public services benefitting from the carve-out and the prosecutorial immunity it affords, in principle, to carved-out entities.[24]

C. Determining the scope and limits of the prudential carve-out in GATS

The Financial Services Annex to the GATS complements and, in some in- stances, modifies the scope of various GATS provisions in the area of financial services. As Uruguay Round negotiations pursued the development of a horizontal framework and vertical sectoral provisions in a concurrent manner, negotiators realized, alongside GATS Article XIV on General Exceptions which the framework agree- ment incorporated in a generic, all-inclusive manner, that there was a need for a provision that would exempt from the scope of the GATS those regulatory interventions in the financial sector which responded to prudential concerns. As a result, drafters of the GATS reached agreement on a so-called 'prudential carve-out' in Paragraph 2 of the Financial Services Annex. They did so, however, without defining what this category of measures actually entailed.[25] The legal discipline, entitled 'Domestic Regulation', reads:

(a) *Notwithstanding any other provisions of the Agreement*, a Member shall not be prevented from taking measures for prudential reasons, including for the protection of investors, depositors, policy holders or persons to whom a fiduciary duty is owed by a financial service supplier, or to ensure the integrity and stability of the financial system. Where such measures do not conform with the provisions of the Agreement, they shall not be used as a means of avoiding the Member's commitments or obligations under the Agreement. (emphasis added)

The negotiating history of the GATS reveals that, while WTO Members agreed on the need to insert such an exception into the Financial Services Annex, discussions about the actual scope of the provision under the auspices of the Committee on Financial Services have been few.[26] There are two likely reasons for such relative silence. First, negotiations in financial services concentrated largely on the market opening dimension, such that discussions among Members focused on the actual scope of Articles XVI and XVII of the GATS (market access and national treatment, respectively), rather than on non-discriminatory regulatory measures (Article VI). Second, it appears that several Members took the view that discussing further and perhaps defining the precise remit of the prudential carve-out could

[24] Paragraph 1(b)(iii) of the GATS encompasses a catch-all category of activities performed by a supplier. The most interesting aspects relate to the definition of public entity and the bench-mark that would make a certain activity 'governmental' rather than private. See Armin von Bogdandy and Joseph Windsor, 'Annex on Financial Services', in Rüdiger Wolfrum, Peter-Tobias Stoll and Clemens Feinä ugle (eds), *WTO—Trade in Services: Max-Planck Commentaries on World Trade Law* (Leiden NL: Martinus Nijhoff Publishers, 2008) 618, at 633.
[25] Australia's proposal to define such measures did not have any substantial support from WTO Members. See the Committee on Trade in Financial Services meetings held on 13 April 2000, 25 May 2000, 13 July 2000 and 9 October 2000, S/FIN/M/25–28.
[26] See Juan Marchetti, 'The GATS Prudential Carve-out', in Panagiotis Delimatsis and Nils Herger (eds), *Financial Regulation at the Crossroads—Implications for Supervision, Institutional Design and Trade* (Alphen aan den Rijn: Kluwer Law International, 2011).

actually reduce their regulatory flexibility when enacting such types of measures.[27] Several early assertions that prudential measures should enjoy full prosecutorial immunity under the GATS were rooted in such a perception, which financial supervisors and central banks felt strongly about, but which made trade officials uneasy over the prospect of demands for similar carve-outs in other service sectors. The ultimate compromise reached would submit prudential measures to the WTO dispute settlement provisions, but ensure that any WTO dispute in financial services would involve panellists with the requisite expertise in the financial service issue under dispute.

While there is no WTO jurisprudential guidance regarding the interpretation of the prudential carve-out, its wording clearly suggests that the prudential carve-out is an exception provision with a function similar to that found in GATT Article XX or GATS Article XIV. This means that derogations from any obligation enshrined in the GATS can be justified if the conditions laid down in Paragraph 2 are met. The carve-out covers a potentially broad range of measures so long as it can be shown that they are adopted for prudential purposes. The initial burden of proof lies with the complaining party, who will need to adduce evidence showing the violation of a substantive GATS obligation. Once established, the burden of proof to establish the affirmative defence shifts to the respondent. As with other general exception clauses, Paragraph 2 involves a two-tier test: first, the WTO judiciary will need to examine whether the measure is taken for prudential reasons. A rational relationship between the measure and the objective pursued should be regarded as the minimum required by this provision. This view is corroborated by the last sentence of Paragraph 2(a).[28]

If the above criterion is met, the complaining party will have to prove that such measures still violate relevant GATS provisions. If this is successfully established, it will then be for the respondent to prove that the measures are not used as a means of avoiding its obligations or scheduled commitments. This second tier of the test differs from the second tier of the GATT Article XX test. In the case of the last sentence of Paragraph 2(a), it appears that no demonstration of 'discrimination in application' is required. We submit, however, that a broader discrimination test seems to be implied here and that a delicate balancing exercise between the objective pursued and the alleged discriminatory treatment is warranted. For such a determination, the panellists would probably envisage recourse to other sources, such as the work done within the IMF or the BCBS, to determine the adequacy and necessity of the prudential intervention at stake.

D. Towards a necessity test for services? Addressing the trade-inhibiting effects of non-discriminatory domestic regulatory conduct

It is generally accepted that the bulk of measures taken to strengthen the resilience of domestic financial systems in the aftermath of the crisis were non-discriminatory

---

[27] See Key, above n 7, at 39.
[28] It was argued that the latter sentence also encompasses an intent test. See Bogdandy and Windsor, above n 24, at 635.

in nature.[29] In assessing the possibly adverse impacts that such measures may still have on trade, Article VI of the GATS as well as the prudential carve-out of the Financial Services Annex take centre stage.

In GATS-speak, domestic regulation, as defined in Article VI:4, relates to national measures aimed at ensuring the quality of the service supplied and which do not discriminate (and thus do not fall under the national treatment obligation of GATS Article XVII) nor do they constitute quantitative limitations (and thus do not come under the market access obligation of GATS Article XVI). Due to the intangible nature of services and the lesser relevance (than in goods trade) of the border as a locus of trade regulation in services markets, domestic measures can become the greatest barriers to services trade even in the absence of overt discrimination.[30] In the financial sector, non-discriminatory measures with the potential to significantly restrict trade are not uncommon. Onerous reserve requirements, the impact of which may be felt more acutely by new entrants or less well-established foreign service providers, are one example. The potential trade-restrictive impact of domestic regulations stands in sharp contrast to the weak legal disciplines meant to curtail such practices under Article VI:4 of the GATS. Such a situation inevitably entails greater reliance on the WTO's adjudicating bodies. However, challenging domestic regulatory conduct in services trade, and particularly non-discriminatory conduct, is fraught with controversy, as the *US—Gambling*[31] case demonstrated.

It would appear that the additional disciplines on domestic regulation emerging from the most recent discussions within the GATS Working Party on Domestic Regulation (WPDR) are unlikely to address the above tension satisfactorily. This is because Article VI:4 has a limited scope *ratione materiae*, covering only measures relating to qualification requirements and procedures, licensing requirements and procedures and technical standards. This means that the bulk of the financial recovery measures adopted during and after the financial crisis would be likely to escape the purview of any newly agreed disciplines. This said, such disciplines will assume greater relevance once national laws describing the new regulatory conditions under which financial activities can be pursued (and thus, for instance, under which a licence to provide financial services can be obtained) are adopted.[32]

Absent greater progress under the Article VI:4 work programme, and notably the continuing impasse over the desirability of embedding a necessity test for services trade, the obligations enshrined in Article VI:1, which re- quires that measures of general application affecting trade in services be administered in an objective,

---

[29] See Beck et al., above n 14. See also WTO Secretariat, 'Financial Services', Background Note, S/C/W/312, 3 February 2010.

[30] See Panagiotis Delimatsis, *International Trade in Services and Domestic Regulations—Necessity, Transparency, and Regulatory Diversity* (Oxford: Oxford University Press, 2007).

[31] Panel Report, *United States—Measures Affecting the Cross-Border Supply of Gambling and Betting Services* (*US—Gambling*), WT/DS285/R, adopted 20 April 2005, as modified by Appellate Body Report, WT/DS285/AB/R.

[32] For a discussion of the sometimes far-reaching scope of these disciplines, see Panagiotis Delimatsis, 'Concluding the WTO Services Negotiations on Domestic Regulation—Hopes and Fears', 9(4) *World Trade Review* 643 (2010).

reasonable and impartial manner,[33] could prove beneficial.[34] Whereas this obligation is conditional on the presence of specific commitments, the fact that the
commitments undertaken in the financial sector (notably by developed countries)
tend to be comprehensive suggests that such an obligation may have significant
ramifications for domestic regulatory conduct. Accordingly, any further
strengthening of this discipline involving the codification of criteria with which
to determine the objectivity, impartiality and reasonableness of domestic regulatory
measures (as opposed to their administration) would be welcome. For the time
being, however, the lack of effective disciplines on the potentially trade-restrictive
effects of origin-neutral regulatory measures clearly diminishes the 'bite' of the
GATS and lessens its relevance as an instrument with which to better manage the
latest and future episodes of financial turmoil.

The paradox of the 'necessity' stalemate in the GATS discussions originates in
the reluctance of regulators—above all (but not only) those of the USA—to see
sovereign regulatory decisions subject to the potential scrutiny of unelected, non-
specialist, trade judges.[35] Such a stalemate offers the rare example of a political
economy configuration in which trade rules (or, more precisely, the lack thereof)
are shaped more by the desire of regulators than those of industry. This is all the
more paradoxical in the case of the USA, the world's leading exporter of services
(including financial services) and whose internationally active firms are arguably
most likely to be victims of unduly burdensome regulatory conduct or disguised
restrictions on trade and investment in foreign markets.

The financial crisis offers a readymade opportunity to link the processes of
services trade liberalization with those of regulatory reform and institutional
strengthening, not only domestically, but also across borders.[36] Several ideas were
advanced on how the GATS and prudential standards might, in the future, be
linked.[37] Equally pressing is the need to create stronger co-operation networks
between regulators, which would allow more regular exchanges of information on
domestic and regional reform initiatives and help identify best practices as well as
better manage crises.[38] Such networks should be encouraged within the new, more

[33] Panagiotis Delimatsis, 'Due Process and "Good" Regulation Embedded in the GATS –Disciplining Regulatory Behaviour in Services Through Article VI of the GATS', 10 *Journal of International
Economic Law* 13 (2007); Markus Krajewski, 'Article VI GATS (Domestic Regulation)', in Wolfrum
et al, above n 24, at 165.

[34] Cf. Bart De Meester, 'The Global Financial Crisis and Government Support for Banks: What
Role for the GATS?', 13 *Journal of International Economic Law* 27 (2010), at 52.

[35] This concern may be somewhat less in the area of financial services to the extent that the
Financial Services Annex explicitly provides that any WTO dispute in the sector shall feature panel
expertise drawn from national rosters of financial services specialists.

[36] Currently, we see a fairly nationalistic (or regional, in the case of the EU) approach towards
institutional strengthening. See, for instance, European Commission, 'Regulating Financial Services
for Sustainable Growth', COM(2010) 301 Final, 2 June 2010, at 3. For a tentative criticism, see Iain
Begg, 'Regulation and Supervision of Financial Intermediaries in the EU: The Aftermath of the
Financial Crisis', 47(5) *Journal of Common Market Studies* 1107 (2009).

[37] See the contribution by Thomas Cottier and Markus Krajewski in Chapter 15 of this volume.

[38] Cf. FSB, 'Promoting Global Adherence to International Cooperation and Information Exchange
Standards', 10 March 2010. See also G30, 'Financial Reform—A Framework for Financial Stability',
2009.

inclusive, governance mechanisms of international financial regulation that are emerging in the aftermath of the crisis. At a time when the virtues of multilateral co-operation are assuming renewed prominence, agreements relating to the mutual recognition of prudential measures in accordance with Paragraph 3 of the Financial Services Annex may also become much more appealing as a way of facilitating trade in financial services, promoting regulatory convergence and reducing the scope for trade tensions. In drawing up such agreements, the parties should be encouraged to use international standards (notably those created in Basel) to the greatest extent possible.

E. Disciplining the distortive effects of subsidies in services trade

A cursory review of the rescue measures enacted in the aftermath of the financial crisis suffices to show that many such measures constituted, in one way or another, a form of subsidy that would be routinely open to legal challenge under the GATT.[39] Subsidies carry the potential for severely affecting the nature and extent of competition in finance both within a domestic market and across borders.[40] It is precisely this type of concern that makes the case for promoting greater coordination of regulatory responses to the crisis beyond the nation-state level a compelling one.

Together with tourism and transport services, finance is one of the service sectors where subsidies are most prevalent.[41] The financial crisis has clearly done little to stop this trend. Faced with significant financial turmoil and the prospect of systemic failure among financial institutions deemed too big to fail[42] as well as the concomitant fear of contagion, governments intervened during the crisis by providing financial institutions with staggering (in some cases unlimited) levels of direct support through capital injections and liquidity-guarantee schemes. Such substantial subsidization can distort competition in financial markets and put national beneficiaries in an advantageous position in a post-crisis environment.

In addition, as national banks and governmental institutions have become major shareholders in distressed financial institutions, such institutions could well exert a significant influence on the level of financial globalization and interconnectedness in the post-crisis era. For instance, once national share- holders become sellers after a few years, domestic banks may become less internationalized, or even exclusively domestically owned, if shares end up primarily in the hands of domestic investors, thereby potentially reducing the higher levels of financial market internationalization

---

[39] Around 80 per cent (i.e. over US$9.5 trillion) of the federal relief in the USA alone was provided to services. See Gary N. Horlick and Peggy A. Clarke, 'WTO Subsidy Disciplines During and After the Crisis', in Chapter 17 of this volume.

[40] See WTO Secretariat, above n 29.

[41] See WTO, Working Party on GATS Rules, 'Subsidies for Services Sectors—Information Contained in WTO Trade Policy Reviews', S/WPGR/W/25/Add.5, 27 March 2007.

[42] For those elements that make a bank systematically important, see IMF, BIS, FSB, 'Guidance to Assess the Systemic Importance of Financial Institutions, Markets and Instruments: Initial Consider-ations—Background Paper', October 2009.

prevailing in the years preceding the financial crisis. Important distortionary effects on the allocation of capital within and across borders could thus be seen.[43]

Unfair competitive practices may arise when governmental support for financial institutions is attached to the granting of loans by these institutions to revitalize the national economy. Whereas such support schemes are adopted as emergency measures and are typically temporary[44] (and admittedly several measures of this type have since been withdrawn or banks have foregone the use of guarantees),[45] their continuous application is tempting. In times of prolonged macro-economic instability, pressure exerted by special interest groups for continued state support may mount and indeed be difficult to reverse, particularly in jurisdictions where the financial sector is weakly constrained by competition law.[46] Depending on how a domestic support scheme is structured, severe distortions to the competitive rela-tion- ships of service suppliers in the marketplace can be generated.

While state aid schemes displaying characteristics similar to those described above can be challenged under the WTO Agreement on Subsidies and Counter-vailing Measures in the case of trade in goods, competitive distortions in services markets will remain largely unchallenged owing to the absence of a dedicated set of subsidy disciplines under the GATS. Absent such a regime, on which scant negotiating progress has been achieved since the early days of the Uruguay Round, potentially trade and investment-distorting subsidies of the type applied during the financial crisis can proceed with almost full impunity. This should not be taken to mean that the GATS does not apply to subsidies, which unquestionably constitute measures affecting trade in services under GATS Articles I:1 and XXVIII(a). Thus, in order to escape the scope of Article II, subsidies would have to be included in the list of MFN exemptions of a given Member. By the same token, they cannot be discriminatory unless they are scheduled,[47] limiting eligibil-ity to nationals either sectorally or via so-called horizontal limitations.[48] Otherwise, intervening Members are not allowed to discriminate against foreign, albeit like, financial service suppliers present in their territory.[49]

---

[43] FSB, 'Exit from Extraordinary Financial Sector Support Measures', Note for the G20 meeting of Ministers and Governors on 6–7 November 2009, November 2009.

[44] See also WTO, Trade Policy Review Body, 'Report to the TPRB from the Director-General on Trade-related Developments', WT/TPR/OV/W/3, 14 June 2010.

[45] See European Commission, 'The application of State aid rules to government guarantee schemes covering bank debt to be issued after 30 June 2010', DG Competition Staff Working Document, 30 April 2010, at 3. See also IMF, 'A Fair and Substantial Contribution by the Financial Sector', Final Report for the G-20, June 2010.

[46] In theory at least, the resumption of normal lending activities to the benefit of the economy at large is regarded as a *conditio sine qua non* for the acceptance of otherwise actionable subsidization practices. See European Commission Communication, 'Temporary Community framework for State aid measures to support access to finance in the current financial and economic crisis', OJ C 83/1 of 7 April 2009.

[47] See WTO, 'Guidelines for the Scheduling of Specific Commitments Under the General Agreement on Trade in Services (GATS)', S/L/92, 28 March 2001, para 16.

[48] Cf. WTO, Working Party on GATS Rules, 'Limitiations in Members' Schedules Relating to Subsidies', S/WPGR/W/13/Add.2, 30 August 2004.

[49] Cf. Poretti, above n 17.

As noted above, negotiations on subsidies within the Working Party on GATS Rules have not made any substantial progress to date.[50] This would appear to reflect a clearly revealed policy preference for regulatory inaction on the part of those WTO Members with the deepest pockets. Here again, the financial crisis offers a basis for reconsidering the scope and likely substantive elements for a subsidy regime in services trade whose remit might be either horizontal (i.e. applicable to all sectors) or limited to a specific sector, such as financial services. There are strong reasons to believe that the traffic-light approach espoused in the area of trade in goods could be replicated in the services' realm.

The special and ubiquitous nature of finance, and the possible need for prudential considerations to be allowed to override non-discrimination principles in times of acute financial turmoil, suggest that any subsidy regime for financial services would need to feature a number of defining elements; these include the need for temporary measures; the certainty of policy reversal once crisis conditions abate; the need for governments to apply market interest rates to credit or loan guarantee schemes; the need for adequate multi-lateral surveillance of bailout conditions by multilateral agencies such as the IMF and the FSB working in tandem with the WTO; as well as the need for ensuring that any short-term disbursement of state aid is subject to proper competition-policy scrutiny in the relevant markets likely to be affected by governmental support measures.

IV. Conclusion

While the GATS and trade-induced financial services liberalization are not to blame for the latest financial crisis, such a statement leaves unanswered the question of whether the GATS (and trade law more broadly) can or should play a more critical role in shaping the post-crisis financial architecture. The crisis and the regulatory reforms likely to be enacted in its wake offer a propitious opportunity for revisiting the substance of services trade regulation. This should be done with a view to a substantive strengthening of services trade law that could better manage the downside risks of financial protectionism and offer a more credible platform for confronting the trade and investment disputes whose numbers this chapter considers likely to rise in the coming years. This chapter identified a number of contextual considerations and policy channels, some direct, others less so, likely to shape the climate within which trade and investment liberalization in financial services will proceed in the future. The main policy conclusion drawn is that the crisis is likely to complicate the quest for *negotiated* market opening in financial services, and more so at the WTO than the PTA level.

Each of the policy channels identified questions, beliefs and policy assumptions that have long formed the basis upon which financial services negotiations have proceeded. The first channel relates to investment policy and concerns the optimal

---

[50] See also Rudolf Adlung, 'Negotiations on Safeguards and Subsidies in Services: A Never-Ending Story?', 10 *Journal of International Economic Law* 235 (2007).

extent of foreign presence in domestic financial markets. The second, closely related, channel concerns the desirability of encouraging entry of foreign financial institutions via direct branching as opposed to subsidiaries. The third channel concerns the preference that host-country regulators may henceforth have for commercial presence as a means of ensuring more effective prudential oversight of foreign established financial operators. Such 'forced establishment' requirements would be likely to affect the modal distribution of services trade commitments, contributing to a further weakening of cross-border trade in financial services. The fourth channel concerns the desirability of using trade agreements and their financial services chapters to secure the concomitant liberalization of capital account transactions and related limitations on short-term capital movement. The fifth, and final, channel concerns host-country attitudes towards financial innovation and the calls to treat 'new' financial services favourably in terms of regulatory approval.

The chapter contends that the likelihood of friction at the trade–finance interface has increased as a result of extensive governmental intervention in financial markets, such that judicial activism, including in the investment field, may be expected to increase in the future, resulting in legal challenges of measures enacted on prudential grounds. The resolution of such disputes will require delicate balancing acts and highlights the potentially competing and, at times, contradictory, logics of trade and financial law and policy. They also recall the crucial importance of buttressing currently weak multilateral disciplines on non-discriminatory regulatory conduct, not least because the crisis, and the changed ideological climate it appears to have ushered in, might well fuel regulatory overshooting. They also recall the useful role that competition disciplines operating at the interface of trade and investment law, could play in mitigating the potentially distortive effects of state intervention in financial markets. The chapter draws attention to the inadequacies and shortcomings of existing trade law in services if the GATS and PTAs featuring services disciplines are to play a useful role in addressing the potentially trade and investment-restrictive and competition-impairing effects of the extensive financial rescue measures taken in the wake of the crisis of 2008–09. As currently drafted, existing service sector disciplines are either too vague or insufficiently developed to assume such a role.

The post-crisis period affords a unique opportunity to clarify the scope of GATS law in financial services; to establish with greater precision the remit of the prudential carve-out; and to complete long-stalled rule-making journeys on the key outstanding GATS disciplines of necessity and subsidies without which the law of services trade runs the very genuine risk of remaining a construct more theoretical than real.

17

WTO Subsidies Discipline During and After the Crisis

Gary N. Horlick and Peggy A. Clarke

I. Introduction

The strengths and weaknesses of the World Trade Organization (WTO) Agreement on Subsidies and Countervailing Measures (SCM Agreement)[1] were identifiable before the global financial crisis which erupted in 2007. The crisis highlighted both the strengths and the weaknesses of the SCM Agreement and WTO law, and perhaps paradoxically, will make it more difficult to fix its weaknesses. It also raised issues of whether it was in the interest of the global economy to restrict all manner of goods subsidies or whether, at certain times, certain types of subsidies may be trade-enhancing rather than trade-distorting.

The massive subsidies to the financial services industry raise a fundamental question about the notion of subsidies and subsidy discipline. One of the great triumphs of the SCM Agreement was the single definition of 'subsidy' hitherto lacking from the 1979 General Agreement on Tariffs and Trade (GATT) Subsidies Code. But politicians, left to their own devices, will tend to over-subsidize and to grant too much protection to domestic producers, through protective measures such as countervailing duties (CVDs). The SCM Agreement sets up rules which are not strict enough to eliminate the use of CVDs as protectionism, and disciplines on subsidies that are too loose to prevent politicians from over-subsidizing. The dynamics for subsidies to services may differ, but negotiators need to examine whether the same tension is likely to emerge.

The SCM Agreement covers trade in goods, and not services.[2] The General Agreement on Trade in Services (GATS), in Article XV, mandates the negotiation of disciplines on subsidies. Much work has been done on a draft agreement on

---

[1] GATT Secretariat, *The Results of the Uruguay Round of Multilateral Trade Negotiations, the Legal Texts* (Geneva, 1994) 231.

[2] As the WTO *EC—Bananas* case demonstrates, the same enterprise producing a single good can be providing both a good and a service. See WTO Appellate Body Report, *European Communities— Regime for Importation, Sale and Distribution of Bananas (EC—Bananas)*, WT/DS27/AB/R), adopted 25 September 1997.

services subsidies,[3] but the Members failed to complete it.[4] The significance of this omission is apparent from the calculation that at least $9.782 *trillion* of the $11.97 trillion in federal crisis relief in the USA alone was provided to services (as much as $7.537 trillion to financial services and $2.25 trillion to home building)[5]—not counting the very low interest rates that the USA considers countervailable subsides when allegedly maintained by China.

   This raises the interesting question of whether the lack of WTO discipline on subsidies for services during the crisis was a problem or not. And that in turn raises the question of why one wants discipline on subsidies in the WTO.[6] The driving force seems to be a desire to let market forces reward the most efficient producer (of goods and services) without state intervention, although, as we shall see, there are other motives at work as well. We will return soon enough to issues of discipline on subsidies for services. But we will first review the SCM Agreement disciplines on subsidies for goods, the relevance of those disciplines during the crisis and the outlook. We do not discuss here whether the SCM Agreement rules in general are a reasonable approach to subsidies discipline. Sykes has written cogently on the subject.[7]

II. Existing SCM Agreement

A. Export subsidies

The most successful WTO subsidy discipline has been the ban (for developed and most developing Members) on export subsidies (except for agriculture). This type of subsidy is considered to be so pernicious that it is prohibited without a

---

   [3] See e.g. Report by the Chairperson of the Working Party on GATS Rules, S/WPGR/10, 30 June 2003 (providing a brief summary of the work done).

   [4] The main areas of non-agreement were subsidy definition, modal applications and countervailing mechanisms—but far greater gaps were bridged in negotiating the SCM Agreement, so a more probable explanation is that either there was lack of political will to complete the deal and/or the lack of a 'round' to provide enough tradeoffs and momentum. See Pietro Poretti, *The Regulation of Subsidies within the General Agreement on Trade in Services of the WTO: Problems and Prospects* (Alphen aan den Rijn, Netherlands: Kluwer Law International, 2009). See also Chapter by Steve Charnovitz and Chapter 16 by Panagiotis Delimatsis and Pierre Sauvé, in volume.

   [5] Gary Hufbauer, Luca Rubini and Yee Wong, 'Swamped by Subsidies: Averting a US-EU Trade War after the Great Crisis', Policy Note, 24 July 2009. It should be noted that these numbers are disputed. Others have argued that much of the money included in the calculation by Hufbauer et al would not be considered subsidies by the WTO. 'Do Bailouts For Banks And Detroit Mean Boeing vs. Airbus Should Be Suspended?', Inside U.S. Trade, 5 August 2009.

   [6] The work on services subsidies is not modeled on the subsidies discipline for goods found in the SCM Agreement. Numerous Members have suggested that the definition of a subsidy and the scope of any disciplines provided must be different than that contained in the SCM Agreement with respect to subsidies for goods. They argue for an approach that expands the definition of a subsidy to include certain other forms of government intervention besides a financial contribution. See e.g. Communication from Chile: The Subsidies Issue, S/WPGR/W/10, 2 April 1996.

   [7] Alan O. Sykes, 'The Questionable Case for Subsidies Regulation: A Comparative Perspective', Stanford University School of Law, Law & Economics Research Paper Series, Paper No 380, <http://papers.ssrn.com/sol3/papers.cfm?abstract_id=1444605> (visited 29 June 2010).

complaining Member needing to show any adverse effects. While export subsidies may well be trade-distortive, the impetus for the successful prohibition may owe as much to the widespread use of export subsidies in the past, and to the consequent attraction of a 'seller's cartel' (since the benefit of the subsidy went mainly to foreign purchasers, an agreement by all Members to eliminate them made sense for each country). This discipline seems to have held up fairly well in the crisis. None of the reported 'crisis measures'[8] seems to be an explicit export subsidy within the meaning of Article 3.1 of the SCM Agreement, although Organisation for Economic Co-operation and Development (OECD) countries as a whole reportedly increased export financing (which would be WTO-consistent) to try to keep trade flowing. Even before the crisis, the prohibition seemed to be working well, with very few completely new export subsidies, and numerous successful WTO challenges to ones pre-existing the WTO.[9]

The two most obvious exceptions to the discipline had proven to be problems *before* the crisis:

(1) The WTO dispute resolution system has been erratic in detecting *de facto* prohibited export subsidies. In *Australia—Leather*, a loan not explicitly provided as a stimulus to exports was found to be a prohibited export subsidy by a panel because the sales needed to meet the terms of the subsidy eligibility would necessarily include exports,[10] while in *Canada—Aircraft* a government program was found *not* to be a prohibited export subsidy because it was not explicitly tied to exports even though the government knew or should have known that 99 per cent of the final subsidized products would be exported.[11] Footnote 4 SCM to the Agreement notes that the mere fact of exportation does not mean that it was required. That footnote was included to take account of the lack of domestic markets for small countries such that any subsidies would go to production which was predominantly for export. But Canada is neither a small country nor an undiversified economy, so the Appellate Body ruling in *Canada—Aircraft* permits numerous *de facto* export subsidies to escape undisciplined. While such *de facto* considerations may be a feature in some of the crisis measures,

---

[8] For analysis and listings of the crisis measures, see Global Trade Alert, <http://www.globaltradealert.org> (visited 27 August 2010).

[9] See WTO Panel Report, *Australia—Subsidies Provided to Producers and Exporters of Automotive Leather (Australia—Leather)*, WT/DS126/R, adopted 16 June 1999; WTO Appellate Body Report, *Brazil—Export Financing Programme for Aircraft (Brazil—Aircraft)*, WT/DS46/AB/R, adopted 20 August 1999; WTO Appellate Body Report, *Canada—Measures Affecting the Export of Civilian Aircraft (Canada—Aircraft)*, WT/DS70/AB/R, adopted 20 August 1999; WTO Appellate Body Report, *USA—Tax Treatment for 'Foreign Sales Corporation' (US—FSC)*, WT/DS108/AB/R, adopted 20 March 2000; and WTO Appellate Body Report, *Canada—Certain Measures Affecting the Automotive Industry (Canada—Autos)*, WT/DS139, 142/AB/R, adopted 19 June 2000.

[10] *Australia—Leather*, above n 9, paras 9.63–9.69. It should be noted that neither party appealed this panel decision for whatever reason.

[11] WTO Appellate Body Report, *Canada—Aircraft—Recourse by Brazil to Article 21.5 of the DSU*, WT/DS70/AB/RW, adopted 4 August 2000, para 49.

they are not readily apparent in any of them, and, in any event, no Member has complained (although that is not the legal standard).[12]

(2) Item (k) of Annex I[13] of the SCM Agreement permits subsidized export credits if they are within the OECD arrangements on export Credit financing.[14] The OECD arrangments are a clear example of sellers' cartels agreeing how much can be given away to their customers. The *Brazil—Aircraft* and *Canada—Aircraft* cases (in each of which retaliation has been authorized but not used), at least implicitly, extend item (k)'s Paragraph 2 grandfathering permission to subsidize to non-OECD WTO Members. While this has not been a feature of crisis measures so far, it may become more of a focus if export credit financing is used as a stimulus measure. For example, the USA recently proposed to increase the Export–Import Bank's credit available for small- and medium-sized businesses from the current $4 billion to $6 billion in the next year and to redirect $30 billion in Troubled Asset Relief Program (TARP) loans to small businesses as part of the Administration's export initiative.[15] More troubling is that, as interpreted, item (k) imposes disciplines on any Member that seeks to use export credits, on the basis of terms negotiated by only some of the WTO Members, and that those terms reflect a changing standard.[16] Proposals have been made in the Doha talks to eliminate or modify item (k), although the push behind those proposals (e.g. by Brazil and India) could wane if those countries are permitted to use the item (k) rules and economic circumstances make the same financing terms available to them.

A group of relatively poor developing Members is permitted to use explicit export subsidies in certain circumstances in accordance with Article 27.3 of the SCM Agreement; an exemption which has been extended several times.[17] This has the perverse effect of allowing developing countries to bid against each other in offering subsidies to investors and consumers in developed countries. These poor developing Members, however, are not large traders; therefore, the permission does not have a significant distorting effect on most trade.

---

[12] The conventional practice in Geneva that 'it must be alright if no one has complained' can be found nowhere in the WTO Agreement.

[13] There may be other flaws lurking in Annex I, which was incorporated from Annex A of the 1979 GATT Subsidy Codes without sufficient changes to prevent conflicts with the 1994 SCM Agreement.

[14] See 'The OECD Arrangement on Guidelines for Officially Supported Export Credits', <http://www.oecd.org/officialdocuments/displaydocumentpdf/> (visited 29 June 2010).

[15] See Darrell A. Hughes, 'Obama Urges Export-Import Bank to Up Small-Firm Loans', *Wall Street Journal*, 4 February 2010.

[16] *Brazil—Aircraft*, above n 9, paras 7.24–7.33 (found that all countries must meet the OECD standard but that the standard at issue was whatever the OECD had decided at the time the credit was granted, not at the time the WTO was negotiated).

[17] In 2007, because of the continual extensions, the General Council adopted procedures for extensions subject to annual review. See Article 27.4 of the Agreement on Subsidies and Countervailing Measures Decision of 27 July 2007, WT/L/691, 31 July 2007. An annex to this decision lists the countries and specific programs covered by this decision.

B. Import-substitution subsidies

Import-substitution subsidies under Article 3.1(b) of the SCM Agreement had not been the subject of much discussion prior to the crisis.[18] The crisis measures taken in the automotive sector, however, have shone a spotlight on this problem. One leading subsidy practitioner, in an unpublished memorandum written on behalf of a client, claimed that a Member could give subsidies to a manufacturer contingent on producing automobiles within the Member's territory, without thereby running afoul of Article 3.1(b), because the grant would not be contingent on use of domestic inputs.

In *Canada—Autos* the Appellate Body read into Article 3.1(b) of the SCM Agreement a condemnation of *de facto* (as well as explicit, *de jure*) import-substitution subsidies, even though the text contains no such language.[19] (According to one of the drafters, the initial omission of *de facto* was indeed a mistake, but the decision not to correct it prior to signing was deliberate.)[20] The Appellate Body found that a program could violate the Article 3.1(b) prohibition if the value-added content was such that a company *would* need to use at least some domestic goods to meet the content requirement.[21] Some years later, in *US— Foreign Sales Corporation Tax*, Article 21.5 proceedings, the Appellate Body concluded that a government program which conditioned receipt of the benefits on use of domestic value added, even if the value added included services as well as goods, was prohibited under GATT 1994, Article III:4, as long as it created an incentive to use domestic over imported goods.[22]

The spotlight on import-substitution was intensified in 2009 when President Sarkozy of France appeared to condition receipt of French government funds by French auto companies on their keeping auto plants in France open while closing

---

[18] The *Indonesia—Auto* case arguably dealt with import-substitution subsidies, but the facts of the case were so unusual that the decision has not had much impact. (Indonesia conceded that the local content requirement for eligibility for the subsidy at issue would fall under Article 3.1(b) but argued successfully that Indonesia's status as a developing country meant that the program was not prohibited at that time.) See WTO Panel Report, *Indonesia—Certain Measures Affecting the Automobile Industry (Indonesia—Auto)*, WT/DS54, 55, 59, 64/R, adopted 23 July 1998. In addition, the *Canada—Autos* case also addressed import- substitution subsidies; however, the facts did not permit a full analysis of the issue (because the Appellate Body reversed a finding of the Panel that the law at issue did not involve an import-substitution subsidy and, in so doing, found that the Panel had not provided enough factual analysis to enable the Appellate Body to decide the issue). See *Canada—Autos*, above n 9. In the *US—Upland Cotton* case, the Appellate Body agreed with the Panel that because Step 2 payments were made only to consumers of domestic cotton, they constituted import- substitution subsidies prohibited under SCM Agreement, Article 3.1(b) and that the prohibition extended to products falling under the Agreement on Agriculture. See: WTO Appellate Body Report, *USA—Subsidies on Upland Cotton (US—Upland Cotton)*, WT/DS267/AB/R, adopted 21 March 2005.

[19] *Canada—Autos*, above n 9, para 143.

[20] Interview by Gary Horlick with one of the people most involved with the drafting.

[21] Ibid.

[22] WTO Appellate Body Report, *USA—Tax Treatment for 'Foreign Sales Corporations'—Recourse to Article 21.5 of the DSU by the European Communities' (US—FSC Art. 21.5)*, WT/DS108/AB/RW, adopted 29 January 2002, paras 220–22.

them elsewhere.[23] The appearance of this conditional receipt, however, led to an outcry in the EU and potential scrutiny from the European Commission for consistency with state aid measures.[24] Similarly, in the negotiations leading up to both the US and Japanese cash-for-clunkers programs, efforts were made to limit the beneficiaries to domestically-produced cars, although both such efforts were generally defeated in the final programs.[25] In this context, it is worth noting that Article III:8 of GATT 1994 excludes national treatment and permits the payment of direct subsidies to domestic producers only. Such actions are not prohibited unless they require something (such as local content rules) which may violate the prohibition of import-substitution subsidies or rules on investment.[26] Thus, conditioning payments on a commitment to maintain local employment would not appear to be prohibited. A requirement to keep domestic production facilities open is more troubling; the larger the Member, the more likely that local physical inputs will be used, arguably triggering the prohibition of Article 3.1(b) of the SCM Agreement.

The use of overt import-substitution subsidies has been relatively limited in the economic crisis, with most taking the form of 'buy national' provisions in more general subsidies, which may or may not violate the import-substitution subsidy prohibitions.[27] Such provisions may be disciplined in other contexts.[28] Members that have joined the Government Procurement Agreement are constrained in the 'buy national' provisions they can enact. For example, the regulations implementing the American Recovery and Reinvestment Act specifically exempt from the 'Buy America' provisions the goods and services of countries with which the USA has relevant treaty obligations (such as members of the Government Procurement Agreement).[29] Nonetheless, even if not prohibited, such buy-national provisions could give rise to actionable subsidies. China, in its recent final CVD decision on *Grain-Oriented Electrical Steel from the USA* found that the 'Buy America' provision in various US laws requiring the use of US-produced iron and steel provided a

---

[23] See e.g. 'Volvo Group Balks at Conditions Tied to French Aid to Renault Trucking Subsidiary', BNA Daily Report for Executives, 12 February 2009; 'Renault Agrees to Maintain Partial Production of Clio in France', 17 January 2010, <http://www.France24.com> (visited 23 April 2010).

[24] On EU disciplines see Chapter 18 by Marsden and Kokkoris in this volume.

[25] See e.g. 'Japan Changes Its Cash-For-Clunkers Program To Allow In U.S. Autos', Inside U.S. Trade, 19 January 2010; Press Release, 'Ambassador Bruton Urges Congress to Refrain from Discrimination in Car Scrappage Legislation', 22 April 2009, <http://www.insidetrade.com> (visited 23 April 2010).

[26] See SCM Agreement, Article 3.1(b) and Agreement on Trade-Related Investment Measures Annex, para 1(a).

[27] See e.g. Global Trade Alert at <http://www.globaltradealert.org> (visited 27 August 2010).

[28] Even if measures do not violate SCM Agreement, Article 3.1(b), they may violate the national treatment requirements of GATT 1994, Article III:4 if they create a preference for the use of domestic goods over imported goods. See ibid, at paras 220–22.

[29] *Requirements for Implementing Sections 1512, 1605, and 1606 of the American Recovery and Reinvestment Act of 2009 for Financial Assistance Awards—Interim Final Guidance*, 2 C.F.R. Part 176, 74 US Federal Register 18449 ff, 23 April 2009.

countervailable subsidy because it enabled the US producers to charge the government above-market prices for the steel.[30]

C. Domestic subsidies

Most subsidies are domestic subsidies, i.e. measures that are neither contingent on exportation nor on the use of domestic over imported goods. The purpose of such domestic subsidies is to support production within a country either by supporting the production of the goods or by increasing the demand for such goods. Despite the thousands of pages listing subsidies reported by the Members collectively pursuant to Article 25.4 of the SCM Agreement, there have been very few cases addressing such subsidies, notably *US—Upland Cotton* (which implicates the Agreement on Agriculture). The most recent cases involving such domestic/ production subsidies are the *US—Large Civil Aircraft* and *EC—Large Civil Aircraft* cases,[31] the ramifications of these two cases will fill in a lot of the blanks on domestic production subsidies. Where domestic subsidies have been addressed in the context of disputes involving CVD proceedings, they have focused on the definitional aspects of subsidies such as the nature of financial contribution, entrustment and direction, the recipient of the benefit and the measure of benefits.[32]

Unlike export and import-substitution subsidies, harmful trade effects are not presumed by domestic subsidies and must be demonstrated by anyone challenging the existence of such actionable subsidies. Perhaps, this is because subsidies are widely recognized as a useful and popular tool of governments for distribution of money. Thus, there is little or no impetus to ban such subsidies or even to curtail their use.[33] Nevertheless, long-term use of such subsidies is likely to distort trade by preventing the closure of inefficient production facilities and leading to overcapacity. The SCM Agreement provides discipline by enabling action if trade harm can be demonstrated. That action may be multilateral in the context of a WTO challenge on the grounds that the subsidies are causing serious prejudice to another Member's interests or it may be unilateral through the imposition of CVDs (CVDs may also be imposed to address harm caused by export and import-substitution

---

[30] Notice dated 12 April 2010, in Chinese at <http://gpj.mofcom.gov.cn/aarticle/c/201004/20100406864469.html> (visited 27 August 2010). The USA may challenge this in the WTO.

[31] WTO Appellate Body Report, *United States—Measures Affecting Trade in Large Civil Aircraft—Second Complaint*, WT/353/AB/R, circulated 12 March 2012; WTO Appellate Body Report, *European Communities—Measures Affecting Trade in Large Civil Aircraft*, WT/316/AB/R, adopted 1 June 2011.

[32] For example, WTO Panel Report, *Mexico—Definitive Countervailing Measures on Olive Oil from the European Communities*, WT/DS341/R, adopted 21 October 2008; WTO Appellate Body Report, *Japan—Countervailing Duties on Dynamic Random Access Memories from Korea*, WT/DS336/AB/R, adopted 17 December 2007; WTO Appellate Body Report, *USA—Final Countervailing Duty Determination With Respect To Certain Softwood Lumber From Canada*, WT/DS257/AB/R, adopted 17 February 2004; WTO Appellate Body Report, *USA—Countervailing Measures Concerning Certain Products from the European Communities*, WT/DS212/AB/R, adopted 8 January 2003.

[33] The EU has a highly developed internal discipline on subsidies, through Directorate General for Competition. The USA and most other nations have little or no discipline.

subsidies—but again, a showing of injury is required). Action has mostly been unilateral through the imposition of CVDs, with little evidence that these duties led to a withdrawal of domestic subsidies (logically, that would only occur if the exporter sold 100 per cent of the subsidized production in the country imposing the CVD).

When the SCM Agreement first entered into force, it contained provisions reflecting Members' desires to provide different disciplines for different types of subsidies. Hence, Article 6.1 SCM of the Agreement defined certain types of subsidies for which serious prejudice was presumed, but unlike the prohibition on export and import-substitution subsidies, that presumption was rebuttable. They were:

- where the total *ad valorem* subsidization[34] exceeded 5 per cent of the company's income;
- subsidies to cover operating losses sustained by an industry;
- subsidies to cover operating losses sustained by an enterprise, other than one-time, non-recurrent measures designed to provide time to develop long-term solutions and to avoid acute social problems; and
- direct forgiveness of debt.

The SCM Agreement also provided that three types of subsidies were not actionable, i.e. there was a non-rebuttable presumption that the subsidies led to no trade harm (or at least that the benefits of these actions outweighed any trade harm caused). Thus, as long as the subsidy met the criteria in Article 8, subsidies for research and development, regional development and to comply with environmental laws were not actionable. However, these provisions (both the rebuttable presumption of serious prejudice and the irrebuttable presumption of no harm) were controversial and were implemented on a trial basis for five years. Although no disputes arose under either provision, in the aftermath of the Seattle Ministerial, the provisions were allowed to lapse (if they had not lapsed, the Article 6.1 presumption might have had a great impact on agricultural trade—and Doha negotiations—with the lapse of the 'peace clause' in the Agreement on Agriculture).[35]

III. What is to be Done?

We do not propose to fight the last war by suggesting disciplines on subsidies based on specific stimulus or bail-out packages. The next crisis will not mirror the past. Therefore, this section discusses possible subsidy disciplines for the general

---

[34] These subsidies were also to be measured using a different standard than that applied in other contexts. Annex IV provides that the total ad valorem subsidization was to be measured as a cost to the government, rather than the benefit to the recipient standard used in other contexts under the SCM Agreement.

[35] The non-decision to allow Articles 6.1 and 8 to lapse through inertia was not well thought out. This outcome could have been avoided by making the lapse depend on 'reverse consensus' or something less than lapse based on one Member's objection.

categories—subsidies on goods including export subsidies, import-substitution subsidies and domestic subsidies and subsidies on services—which we hope will advance subsidy discipline, whatever the future holds.

A. Export subsidies

As discussed above, export subsidies seem to be well disciplined. While there may be some discussion about when a *de facto* export subsidy occurs, in general, export subsidies are not widely used. The discipline appears to have held up so far during the crises and countries have rarely resorted to such subsidies. Therefore, perhaps no immediate changes to the export regime are required. Nevertheless, it would behoove Members to resolve the issues of item (k)—by extending its protections to all Members and ensuring that all Members have a say in the terms (or, perhaps, by deleting it).

B. Import subsidies

As discussed above, while the crisis has certainly led to national preferences to keep subsidies within their borders, there has been little use of explicit import-substitution subsidies. Years from now, it may prove that there was considerable use of *de facto* import-substitution, but so far peer pressure has prevented the most visible abuses. Because the extent of any such use is not now known, it is difficult to determine whether current levels of discipline are sufficient. Thus, more information is needed before deciding whether new or alternative disciplines should be adopted. One minor change would be to explicitly add *de facto* import-substitution to the SCM Agreement, Article 3 prohibition. Members may also wish to consider further disciplining the payment of subsidies to domestic producers to eliminate requirements that productive facilities be retained in one country at the expense of productive facilities in another.

C. Domestic subsidies

Perhaps not surprisingly, the most common type of measure taken to address the economic crisis was a domestic subsidy—although in many different forms, such as tax breaks, direct investment in failing companies, low-interest or no-interest loans, provisions of funds and incentives to purchasers to buy these items (e.g. cash-for-clunkers programs). Nevertheless, the use of such stimulus money was lopsided. Only the wealthier economies could afford to provide significant subsidies to their manufacturing sector (or to their services sector for that matter), thus the use of large domestic subsidies in this crisis was largely limited to the developed countries and a few of the emerging economies.

The domestic subsidy area, therefore, should be the focus of any reforms. Within the area of domestic subsidies, as discussed above, the Members in the SCM Agreement tried the experience of creating deep-amber (Article 6.1) and green-lighted (Article 8) subsidies. A return to this approach might work well, although the criteria and specific subsidies should be revised to reflect additional experiences.

As part of the ongoing Doha negotiations, the USA presented a proposal for new prohibited subsidies,[36] and then approximately one year later presented a revised proposal—which contained many changes largely reversing the initial proposal.[37] The US proposal's obvious attempt to avoid condemning those subsidies if they do not 'increase capacity' was no doubt spurred by the desire of the USA to insulate its 'emergency' loans to steel companies in the USA, which total several hundred million dollars.[38] We are aware of no other examples in the USA at the time of the proposal where there was a subsidy of the type that the USA proposed to prohibit, although there may be a few. In short, the USA proposed to maintain the ability of industrialized countries to subsidize 'sunset' industries, even if those companies are uncreditworthy, unequityworthy or running losses. Typically, the big subsidies in the USA are for companies building new plants, mostly provided at the state level, such as the competition that went on between Louisiana and Alabama to subsidize a new $3 billion steel mill. Because these are start-ups, none of them would have losses or appear uncreditworthy (with the obvious exceptions of the recent investments in General Motors and Chrysler, US governments do not make equity investments in manufacturing companies). Finally, the failure of the USA to propose a prohibition on subsidies greater than 5 per cent (as exists in Article 6.1, SCM Agreement) may reflect the USA understanding that such a prohibition would hit the USA agricultural programs if the USA does not succeed in obtaining a 'peace clause' or other carve-out options for agriculture.

Subsidies, however, can be an effective tool of economic and fiscal policy in times of extreme economic stress. Economists also recognize that subsidies can be used to encourage behavior when the external costs of a desired behavior are so great as to

[36] Paper from the USA, 'Expanding the Prohibited "Red Light" Subsidy Category', TN/RL/GEN, 16 January 2006. The USA proposed to prohibit the Article 6.1 'dark-amber' subsidies and urged Members to expand the prohibitions still further to include other items, such as government equity investments in companies with poor financial prospects unable to attract commercial financing ('unequityworthy' in US countervailing duty parlance). The EU responded by indicating reluctance to address new issues through prohibition and that any new disciplines should focus on the actual trade effects of the measure, rather than presumed trade effects. Submission of the European Communities, 'Subsidies', TN/RL/GEN/135, 24 April 2006.

[37] Proposal from the USA, 'Expanding the Prohibited "Red Light" Subsidy Category Draft Text', TN/RL/GEN/146, 5 June 2007. This paper eliminated the prohibition on subsidies exceeding 5 per cent *ad valorem* and when subsidies were made for 'prudential reasons pursuant to laws and regulations of general application, including the protection of investors, depositors, policy holders or persons to whom a fiduciary duty is owed by a financial service supplier, or to ensure the integrity and stability of the financial system.' This latter change appears remarkably prescient in light of the steps the USA took in late 2008 and throughout 2009.

[38] This concept that the effect on capacity is relevant contradicts the position long-taken by the US Department of Commerce in countervailing duty cases, wherein the Department countervails subsidies provided to close facilities and reduce capacity. See e.g. *Carbon Steel Products from the United Kingdom*, 47 U.S. Federal Register 39384, 39392 (Department Commerce, 7 September 1982) (finding funds used for plant closures and redundancies still benefited company as a whole; impact on capacity was not relevant to subsidy analysis).

discourage this behavior in the absence of such incentives. Therefore, any reform should also include a new group of green-lighted subsidies. We suggest that the following may make sense given the world's experience in recent years.

- R&D: Research and development is an area where some incentives could be useful because R&D can be so expensive that a company cannot expect to recover the costs. Therefore, companies invest less in R&D than is desirable. Thus, some form of carve-out for a limited level of R&D subsidy may be useful, but any such provision should be better drafted than the default language of Article 8 of the SCM Agreement, to try to avoid subsidizing research that would occur anyhow.

- Regional development: Many poorer developing countries experience extreme disparities in the costs of investment in different regions of the country and extreme variations in income and employment opportunities in those same areas. Therefore, some form of carve-out for regional development subsidies, perhaps limited to the developing country Members defined in Annex VII, would be likely to benefit trade flows.

- Natural disaster recovery: In recent years the world has experienced numerous natural disasters of such magnitude that recovery from them requires extraordinary investment.[39] In crafting such a provision, the Members would need to find a method of determining which disasters are so large as to require such special treatment and when the recovery period had ended. Any such carve-out should be narrowly crafted (if possible) to permit subsidies to restore what was destroyed, rather than to expand capacity or modernize functioning but obsolete production facilities. Such recovery subsidies should also only be permitted for a limited period after a disaster (subsidies are notoriously difficult to end once provided, even if the original reason for the subsidy has ceased to apply).

- Environmental: The Article 8 provision on environmental subsidies was broad based and provided little discipline, covering as it did up to 20 per cent of the cost of adapting to new environmental regulations.[40] However, as with R&D, environmental measures can have large externalities such that subsidies could be effective in encouraging environmental investment without distorting trade. The provision should not be the existing Article 8 provision. Any provision should not undermine the 'polluter pays' concept. If exceptions to polluter pays are to be permitted, the exceptions should be narrowly defined. Another possible area for agreement on environmental subsidies is where those subsidies arise from explicit action agreed upon by virtually all WTO Members—defined

---

[39] For example, the 2004 tsunami, Hurricane Katrina, and the recent earthquakes in Haiti and Chile.

[40] This provision was the result of a last-minute proposal by Mexico (drawn from a 1989 EC proposal). See Gary N. Horlick and Peggy A. Clarke, 'The 1994 WTO Subsidies Agreement', 17(4) *World Competition* 41 (1994), at 47 and n 34.

as representing more than 95 per cent (or more, but less than 100%) of the world's trade[41]—such as a global climate change agreement.

- Small: In practical terms, small subsidies will not have much effect, so subsidies below a certain *de minimis* level (1, 2 or 3 per cent?) could be ignored as not having much effect, or as being 'washed out' by other factors, such as currency fluctuations, while subsidies above that level should be disciplined much more than they are now. The vestiges of this idea are reflected in the now-defunct provisions of SCM Agreement, Article 6.1(a), providing for a 'presumption of serious prejudice' for subsidies in excess of 5 per cent of value.[42]

We do not propose a green-light category for subsidies in times of extreme financial crisis because we consider it unlikely that one could be sufficiently narrowly crafted (through temporal restrictions and/or a definition of what would be considered an adequate economic downturn) to avoid creating such a large loophole as to eliminate any effective discipline on domestic subsidies. Perhaps the solution for 'crisis subsidies' is a procedural one, using the SCM Agreement Committee or Permanent Group of Experts to approve time-limited, specific subsidy proposals on an emergency basis (i.e. quickly) during a crisis such as occurred in late 2008 and early 2009, with an EU-style prohibition on any subsidies not notified.

D. Subsidies to services

In an economic crisis created by a failure of liquidity in the financial sector, most major economies intervened with substantial money infusions into their banking and financial services sectors. Many economists considered that such intervention prevented the crisis from deepening still further into a widespread, long-term depression.[43] Thus, there may be a benefit to permitting intervention in financial

---

[41] We suggest an extreme definition of 'virtually all' because the actions should be universally agreed. However, we suggest that it requires less than 100 per cent of trade because one extremely small country should not be able to control global environmental policy through the exercise of a veto.

[42] This should not be confused with the negligibility concept already found in SCM Agreement, Articles 11.9 and 27(b). A good argument can be made that imports below a certain level should not be the subject of CVD cases (0.5 per cent of market share?), especially for developing countries. Some very low level of market share is so unlikely to cause injury—especially if split among many companies—that those companies should not have to pay the cost of defense of a case, nor be subject to duties. Therefore, a properly drafted 'negligibility' exception should be included. This is particularly the case for developing country exporters. Such a provision was included in the 'Dunkel' draft of the Agreement on the Implementation of Art. VI GATT (Anti-Dumping Agreement), but negotiators, pushed by the USA, Australia and the EU, rather strangely agreed on the bizarre provision found in Article 5.8 of the current Anti-Dumping Agreement that an exporter with less than 3 per cent of *import share* is excluded *ex ante*— unless other countries with less than 3 per cent of import share collectively have 7 per cent of import share. This creates a very strong incentive to add as many small countries as possible to the case, thus forcing more and more small exporters to defend themselves. It also means that product markets with low import penetration, and thus arguably needing less protection, are more easily made a site for CVD cases, because 3 per cent of the total imports will be low, while for markets with high import penetration, 3 per cent of total imports will be quite high, and, thus, imports below the 3 per cent will also be quite high.

[43] See e.g. IMF, World Economic Outlook, October 2009, at 1; 'Chapter 3: Market Interventions During the Financial Crisis: How Effective and How to Disengage?', in IMF, Global Financial Stability Report, October 2009.

services, at a minimum. However, such permission would have to be narrowly constrained or there would continue to be no discipline on subsidies to services. While the Members have been unable to agree to subsidy disciplines for services, some form of discipline should be concluded. Services continue to account for a growing portion of world trade, and subsidies can be as disruptive and distortive in the services sectors as they are in trade in goods. Any subsidy discipline, however, would have to be coordinated with the regulatory rules and have 'prudential' carve-outs.[44] Subsidies also need to be taken into account in constructing new international financial regulations, e.g. derogations from regulations could well have the same effect as a subsidy.

As with subsidies on goods, it may be worth examining different types of subsidies to different services industries and determining if some are obviously harmful to trade and should be prohibited or if there is a class where harm can be presumed subject to rebuttal. It may also be possible to enable the use of certain types of subsidies in extreme economic situations, subject to time constraints and a need for prior notice so that other countries have the opportunity to argue either that the economic situation does not give rise to the exception on normal disciplines or that the type of subsidy proposed is unnecessarily trade restrictive.

Several Members have provided proposals that examine the nature of services and define subsidies differently from the way it is done with respect to goods, given the different nature of services and service commitments (and given experience with the definitions of the SCM Agreement). The proposals define government actions that may not involve a 'financial contribution' in the SCM Agreement sense as a subsidy.[45] They also suggest carve-outs for subsidies provided for certain policy goals as opposed to ones that afford an artificial competitive advantage.

We suggest that one area of focus for such carve-outs be services aimed at advancing the economic development of the least developed countries. For example, it may be that certain service sectors are critical to the development of an economic infrastructure such that their advancement would expand, rather than distort trade. Service sectors that come to mind include: logistics services, capital markets, and communication services. Nonetheless, any such carve-out must be carefully crafted to avoid discriminating against potential investors or otherwise creating distortions.

---

[44] This would be an example of the difficulty of untangling the 'real' amount of the 'net' subsidy from the 'gross' subsidy (although the US Department of Commerce tried to do so in CVD cases until it became politically unpopular in 1983). Bank 'bail-outs' are part of a package, which can include costly capital and other regulatory controls—and also rock-bottom interest rates, which can transfer money from savers to banks. See Sykes, above n 7, at 24.

[45] See e.g. Communication from Chile: 'The Subsidies Issue', S/WPGR/W/10, 2 April 1996; Report by the Chairperson on the Working Party on GATS Rules, 'Negotiations on Subsidies', S/WPGR/10, 30 June 2003.

IV. Conclusion

While recent reactions to the global financial crisis raised some issues, in the main subsidy discipline held, although the long-term effects of the stimulus packages are still to be determined. Nevertheless, there are weaknesses to subsidy discipline, some highlighted by the crisis, others widely acknowledged prior to the crisis, which should be reduced or eliminated.

Most obviously, an effort should be made to repair the flaws, which have become apparent in the SCM Agreement disciplines on export subsidies (to make sure the discipline is not evaded by larger Members giving 'non-export subsidies' for production, 99 per cent of which is known to be exported), import- substitution subsidies (such as subsidies to keep open those factories that will be likely to use local parts) and 'domestic subsidies' (where better calibration is needed of what disciplines should be applied). Beyond the text, a deeper reconsideration of the economics of subsidies disciplines (such as the questions raised by Sykes) and the political economic issues raised by the tension between the need for some-but different-disciplines on both subsidies and CVDs is called for.

18

The Role of Competition and State Aid Policy in Financial and Monetary Law

Philip Marsden and Ioannis Kokkoris

I. Introduction

During the economic crisis, most governments intervened in markets to support their banking industry on the basis that most of the players were 'too big to fail' or at least the sector as a whole was too important to be weakened. Few governments allowed their intervention to be disciplined in any way by competition policy considerations.[1] The urgency and potential for disaster were too great, and the need to act to save a sector on which other industries rely meant that competition policy was relegated to being a distant bystander in the proceedings. This is true even for the European Union (EU), which is unique in actually having the power to direct such interventions by controlling aid from states to private companies. The EU largely rubber-stamped almost all of the interventions made by Member States to support their domestic banking industries.[2]

The special rules for the financial services sector are quite permissive as it is. During this crisis, the European Commission signalled its intention to be pragmatic in the assessment of state aid while the crisis persisted.[3] The Commission has

---

[1] Member States primarily injected capital in banks and raised deposit guarantees to assure the public and to prevent runs on banks. For example, UK, *Rescue aid to Bradford & Bingley*, NN 41/2008; Ireland, *Guarantee scheme for banks in Ireland*, NN 48/2008; Denmark, *Liquidity support scheme for banks in Denmark*, NN 51/2008; Spain, *Prolongation for the Fund for the Acquisition of Financial Assets in Spain*, N 337/2009.

[2] By 16 December 2009, of the 81 decisions adopted by the European Commission only 6 were conditional decisions after a formal investigation procedure. Between 2002 and 2007, the amount of state aid to industry and services decreased annually by 2 per cent on average (€65 billion). The financial crisis led to an explosion of state aid. Total state aid (excluding railways) granted by the Member States amounted to €279.6 billion in 2008. The level of state aid almost quintupled in 2008 compared to 2007 almost exclusively as a result of crisis aid to the financial sector. The Commission approved, between October 2008 and October 2009, measures amounting to around €3632 billion. See further Ioannis Kokkoris and Rodrigo Olivares-Caminal, *Antitrust Policy Amidst Financial Crises* (Cambridge: Cambridge University Press, 2010).

[3] The European Commission issued a number of communications related to the assessment of state aid during the crisis. Communication from the Commission, The application of state aid rules to measures taken in relation to financial institutions in the context of the current global financial crisis, OJ 2008 C 270/8 (First Banking Communication); Communication from the Commission, The

been willing to apply more lenient rules in view of the gravity of the situation such that banks that receive public funds for restructuring may not be required to undertake divestments to the same extent as other undertakings that received aid for the same purpose in the past.[4]

The statistics reveal that Member States' notifications of state aid have largely been approved unconditionally.[5] As the new rules[6] are very lenient, the few cases where the Commission has raised concerns relate to measures that were so complex that the devised solutions could not fit well into any set of EU rules and thus the Commission had to initiate the relevant investigations.

The degree to which the EU 'bent with the wind' may make it seem highly unlikely that the EU would be a potential model for designers of an international legal order to control state aid. This would be unfortunate, however, since the very fact that the EU had state aid controls, and could conduct reviews of each national aid programme. Even if the EU's own disciplinary influence was minor, it still contributed to the ordered release of aid in a transparent manner and with the least anti-competitive outcomes—both important constraints absent in other jurisdictions. As such, this chapter considers how competition policy, in particular the 'failing firm' defence in merger control and its state aid policy, is applied to this financial crisis. It begins by describing the most elaborate use of the failing firm arguments during the crisis—that of the UK in the Lloyds/HBOS transaction[7]— and goes on to examine the use of European state aid provisions to the financial sector.

II. Failing Firm Defence Amid Crises

In periods of crisis, the question arises as to the potential sensitivity and flexibility of the competition authorities when assessing mergers. Should the conditions for the application of the failing firm defence, or more generally the competition policy rules themselves, be relaxed during difficult economic times?

A. EU

The failing firm defence refers to the effect on competition of concentrations where one (or both) of the merging parties (the acquirer and/or the target) are failing or

---

recapitalisation of financial institutions in the current financial crisis: limitation of aid to the minimum necessary and safeguards against undue distortions of competition, OJ 2009 C 10/2 (Recapitalisation Communication); Communication from the Commission, The treatment of impaired assets in the Community banking sector, OJ 2009 C 72/1 (Impaired Asset Communication); Communication from the Commission—The return to viability and the assessment of restructuring measures in the financial sector in the current crisis under the State aid rules, OJ 2009 C 195/9 (Restructuring Communication).

[4] See further Kokkoris and Olivares-Caminal, above n 2, at Ch 7 (on state aid).
[5] <http://cc.europa.eu/competition/state_aid/studies_reports/studies_reports.html>.
[6] The 'new rules' comprise several communications from the European Commission, see above n 3.
[7] The Merger of Lloyds TSB Group plc and HBOC plc.

will fail, due to poor financial performance.[8] In the EU, the failing firm defence is addressed in the merger guidelines.[9] The case-law has provided further impetus, albeit weak, to the development of the defence in both jurisdictions.

The previous European Community Merger Regulation (ECMR)[10] did not include any reference to the failing firm defence. However, the defence had been invoked[11] and dealt with[12] in a number of decisions and judgments. In vigorously competitive markets, mergers involving failing firms may often enhance general welfare either through increasing the efficiency of existing capacity, redeploying that capacity to socially more valued uses, or preserving jobs and having other socially beneficial advantages.[13] If one of the companies in the merger is a 'failing firm' and would leave the market anyway, then the merger may be deemed not to significantly impede effective competition. The basic requirement is that the deterioration of the competitive structure that follows the merger cannot be said to be caused by the merger.[14]

The Commission considers the following three criteria[15] as relevant for the application of a failing firm defence. First, if not taken over by another undertaking, the allegedly failing firm would in the near future be forced out of the market because of financial difficulties. Second, there is no less anti-competitive alternative purchase than the notified merger. Third, in the absence of a merger, the assets of the failing firm would inevitably exit the market. Once the conditions for the application of the failing firm defence are fulfilled, the merger would not be considered to cause a significant impediment to effective competition in the common market. The three criteria outlined in the EU Guidelines appear to be the cumulative requirements for proving lack of causality between the merger and the worsening of the competitive structure that it would otherwise create.[16]

---

[8] Vincenzo Baccaro, 'Failing Firm Defence and Lack of Causality: Doctrine and Practice in Europe of Two Closely Related Concepts', 25 *European Competition Law Review* 1 (2004), at 11.

[9] Guidelines on the assessment of non-horizontal mergers under the Council Regulation on the control of concentrations between undertakings, OJ 2008 C65 (Guidelines).

[10] Council Regulation (EEC) No. 4064/89, OJ L 395.

[11] Cases include: European Commission, Case IV/M.053 *Aerospatiale- Alenia/de Havilland* (1991) OJ L 334/42; European Commission, Case IV/M.774, *Saint-Gobain/Wacker-Chemie/NOM* (1997) OJ L 247/1; European Commission, Case IV/M.890—*Blokker/Toys 'R' Us* (1998) OJ L 316/1; European Commission, Case IV/M.993—*Bertelsmann/Kirch/Premiere* (1999) OJ L 053/1; European Commission, Case IV M.1221 *Rewe/Meinl* (1999) OJ L 274/1; European Commission, Case COMP/M.2810 *Deloitte & Touche/Andersen UK*; European Commission, Case COMP/M.2824 *Ernst & Young/Andersen Germany* (2002); European Commission, Case COMP/M.2816 *Ernst & Young/Andersen France* (2002).

[12] Cases include: European Commission, Case IV/M308 *Kali und Salz/MdK/Treuhand* (1994) OJ L 186/30; on appeal ECJ, Cases C-68/94 and C-30/95 *France v Commission, Societe Commerciale es Potasses et de l'Azore (SCPA) v Commission* (1998) ECR I-1375.

[13] Gary Hewitt, 'The Failing Firm Defence', 1 OECD *Journal of Competition Law and Policy* 2 (1999), at 115.

[14] Guidelines, above n 9, para 89.

[15] Ibid, para 90.

[16] See Baccaro, above n 8.

Thus, if one of the parties is financially failing, the EU Guidelines would permit an otherwise anti-competitive merger.[17] The rationale is that the competitive structure would deteriorate equally absent the merger. The future market structure would be equally detrimental to competition irrespective of whether the deal is cleared or blocked. Thus, there is no link of causality between the merger and the negative effects on competition and therefore no legal ground for prohibiting the merger. The Commission made it clear in the *Kali und Salz*[18] decision that the acceptance of the failing firm defence is an exceptional situation. Normally, there would be a presumption that a concentration which results in a significant impediment to effective competition is the cause of this deterioration in the competitive structure. The burden of proof that the requirements of the failing firm defence are fulfilled and that there is no causal link between the merger and the deterioration of the competitive structure is upon the parties.

Baccaro suggests an additional criterion to the criteria for failing firm defence: the lack of causality as regards the deterioration of the competitive structure of the market should be satisfied if a failing division defence is invoked.[19] The importance of proving lack of causality is even greater in the case of a claimed 'failing division'.[20] Otherwise, every merger involving an allegedly unprofitable division could be justified under merger control law by the declaration that, without the merger, the division would cease to operate.

B. UK

When one of the parties involved in a merger is failing, certain pre-merger conditions of competition may not prevail. In this regard, the parties, for example, argued that particular care should be taken regarding HBOS, which if it failed would have had disastrous consequences for financial stability. The Office of Fair Trading (OFT) decided that it was not appropriate in this case to apply the failing firm defence, since it was unrealistic that HBOS would have been allowed to fail or its assets to exit the market.

The UK HBOS/Lloyds merger[21] is a clear example of the intervention of the UK government in a competition authority's assessment of mergers in exceptional circumstances. In this case, the government intervened to allow the merger despite the potential for competition concerns. The government took into account the bad financial situation of HBOS, along with the disadvantages that a failure of a bank

---

[17] Firms on the verge of liquidation may not meet the criterion of anticipated exit from the market. Firms already in liquidation are more likely to satisfy the criterion. It should be noted that decisions by a profitable parent company to shut down its loss-making subsidiaries are not likely to be accepted as a credible failing firm defence.

[18] See European Commission, Case IV/M308 above n 12.

[19] Failing division defence refers to cases where a division rather than the whole firm is in severe financial status. See Baccaro, above n 8, at 16.

[20] Case COMP/M.2876—*Newscorp/Telepiu`*, OJ 2004 L 110/73, at 212.

[21] For more information on the HBOS/Lloyds merger, search the website of the OFT, <http://www.oft.gov.uk> (visited 26 June 2010).

entails in terms of loss of consumer confidence and financial instability, and cleared the merger.[22]

In order to intervene and to allow the merger, the UK government developed an additional provision requiring maintenance of the stability of the UK financial system to be introduced as a policy exception—along with the existing national security exception—which circumvented the requirement to refer relevant merger situations to the Competition Commission (CC) under Section 58 of the Enterprise Act 2002.[23] Lord Mandelson thus cleared the merger on public interest grounds,[24] rather than referring the merger to the CC, ranking competition concerns behind financial stability.[25]

The treatment of the Lloyds/HBOS merger has been deemed a 'rather pragmatic approach adopted by some Member States, most notably the United Kingdom'.[26] A change in the approach towards mergers, during a crisis, is clearly illustrated by comparing Lloyds/HBOS to an earlier UK banking case. In 2001, the Secretary of State for Business adopted a diametrically opposite view in the planned acquisition of Abbey National by Lloyds. As an OECD Report highlights the dramatic shift observed in the case of Lloyds/HBOS reflects the extraordinary difficulty of the situation and the consequent subordination of competition concerns to stability concerns, at least in the short run.[27]

C. USA

In the USA, pursuant to the relevant legislation regarding failing firm defence, a merger is not likely to create or enhance market power or facilitate its exercise if the following circumstances apply:[28]

---

[22] It should be stressed that, in this particular case, the failing firm defence was not applicable and therefore was not the basis for the clearance of the merger.

[23] The UK government could usually only intervene in merger control decisions only with respect to national security and media-related mergers. 'Summary Record of the discussion on Competition and Financial Markets', DAF/COMP/M(2009)1/ANN2, 10 April 2009, 'Introduction and Round-table 1 on Principles: Financial Sector Conditions and Competition Policy', at 179, <http://www.oecd.org> (visited 26 June 2010).

[24] Under the Enterprise Act 2002, the Secretary of State can intervene on public interest grounds and decide on public interest grounds to either (i) clear a merger despite a substantial lessening of competition, or (ii) prohibit a merger, or subject it to conditions. Such an intervention and subsequent decision need not be even where such intervention is justified by competition concerns alone. Department of Business, Enterprise and Regulatory Reform, 'Decision by Lord Mandelson, the Secretary of State for Business, not to refer to the Competition Commission the merger between Lloyds TSB Group plc and HBOS plc under Section 45 of the Enterprise Act 2002', 31 October 2008, <http://www.berr.gov.uk/files/file48745.pdf> (visited 26 June 2010).

[25] Department of Business, Enterprise and Regulatory Reform, 'Peter Mandelson Gives Regulatory Clearance to Lloyds TSB Merger with HBOS', Press release 2008/253, 31 October 2008.

[26] Damien Gerard, 'Managing the Financial Crisis in Europe: Why Competition Law is Part of the Solution, Not of the Problem', Global Competition Review, December 2008, <http://papers.ssrn.com/sol3/papers.cfm?abstract_id=1330326> (visited 5 August 2010).

[27] OECD Report, Competition and Financial Markets: Key Findings, 2009, at 32, <http://www.oecd.org/dataoecd/9/22/43067294.pdf> (visited 26 September 2010).

[28] US Department of Justice and the Federal Trade Commission, Horizontal Merger Guidelines, revised 8 April 1997, Section 5.1.

(i) the allegedly failing firm would be unable to meet its financial obligations in the near future;

(ii) it would not be able to reorganize successfully under Chapter 11 of Title 11 of the US Code (known as the 'Bankruptcy Code');

(iii) it has made unsuccessful good-faith efforts to elicit reasonable alternative offers of acquisition of the assets of the failing firm that would both keep its tangible and intangible assets in the relevant market and pose a less severe danger to competition than does the proposed merger; and

(iv) absent the acquisition, the assets of the failing firm would exit the relevant market.

These criteria are less stringent than the equivalent criteria under the European counterpart (ECMR), since they do not require that the target company's market share must be obtained by the acquirer if the failing firm exits the market.[29]

D. Discussion

The assessment of a merger involving a failing firm is therefore not the same as that of a normal transaction involving healthy firms. First, where a merging firm is failing, pre-merger competitive conditions should not be used as a benchmark since the *status quo* pre-merger is clearly not relevant. If anything, the *status quo* is exit of the failing firm and a reduction in competition. Such exit could be more harmful than the merger itself.[30] Relatedly, if the merger or acquisition of a failing firm is not allowed and the failing firm exits the market, any technical or productive achievements of the failing firm will be lost. Secondly, when a failing firm is involved in a merger, competition authorities may grant particularly generous treatment to claimed efficiencies. Thus, the failing firm defence carries most weight when it can be shown that the merger enables productive assets to continue in productive use.

To explain further, if one of the parties to a merger is failing, pre-merger conditions of competition might not prevail even if the merger were prohibited. In such a case, the counterfactual might need to be adjusted to reflect the likely failure of one of the parties and the resulting loss of rivalry. For example, once a bank or a financial institution of the size of HBOS or Lehman Brothers is involved, there are very few banks big and strong enough to act as an acquirer and hence the

---

[29] US Cases where the failing firm defence was invoked include: *International Shoe Co. v Federal Trade Commission*, 280 US 291 (1930); *United States v General Dynamics Corp.* 415 US 486 (1974); *Citizen Publishing Co. v United States*, 394 US 131 (1969); *Federal Trade Commission v Arch Coal, Inc.*, 329 F. Supp. 2d 109, (DDC 2004); *United States v Lever Brothers Co. and Monsanto Chemical Company*, 216 F.Supp. 887 DCNY 196 (1963); *United States v Blue Bell Inc. and Genesco Inc.* 395 F.Supp. 538, (DC Tenn. 1975); *Erie Sand and Gravel Company v Federal Trade Commission* 291 F.2d 279 (CA 3 1961); *American Press Association v United States*, 245 Fed 91 (CA 7) (1917); *Brown Shoe v United States*, 370 US 294 (1962).

[30] OFT, 'Mergers, Substantive Assessment Guidance', at 34, <http://www.oft.gov.uk/shared_oft/mergers/642749/OFT1254.pdf> (visited 26 June 2010).

choice open to the authorities is extremely limited. When one presents itself, the choice seems to be between allowing the target to fail, with an elimination or dispersion of its assets across the market, or seeing them go to the acquirer and being put to more productive use, albeit with some concern for competition.

Considering the likely anti-competitive outcome of allowing a merger involving a failing firm and the counterfactual of blocking the merger and the firm exiting the market, a more lenient policy towards the failing firm defence also allows severely distressed as well as imminently failing firms to survive and may yield social benefits and promote more effective competition in the long run.

In certain cases, however, competition authorities should exercise great caution in accepting failing firm defence arguments. If under-performing, inefficient and poorly managed firms are bailed out simply because of the crisis and the fact that they are large employers, then the message to industry will be simply to ensure that they become too big to fail and that they need not be concerned about being efficient. Central banks had long struggled to avoid allowing the too-big-to-fail thesis to become a moral hazard and had attempted to avoid any definition of whether an institution fell into that category. As Sir Callum McCarthy, former Chair of the UK's Financial Services Authority, argued 'the general view is that there is a real problem with the "too-big-to-fail" concept and that it would be perfectly rational for depositors and counterparties to trade preferentially with larger firms, thus squeezing out the smaller ones. Preventing that would be a real issue in terms of competition policy'.[31]

The financial services market has certain unique characteristics that make *ex ante* regulation prudent. It is indeed one of the most regulated sectors because banks are crucial to a well-functioning economy. Problems in the financial sector inevitably affect the performance of other markets for goods and services and the economy as a whole.[32] That said, banks have unique characteristics which make them more vulnerable to instability than firms in other sectors.[33] Instability can arise for a variety of reasons. For example, banks are vulnerable to runs or panics. Banks are also susceptible to instability because they are subject to inter-bank contagion. Instability can also arise from excessive risk taking, especially where, in this sector, the risk of failure of financed investment is mostly carried by depositors, while profits which arise from successful investments accrue to banks.[34]

In certain circumstances, the social cost of rescuing the relevant institutions will be less than the ruinous cascade effects that may surge through the financial sector.

---

[31] Speech of Sir Callum McCarthy 'Summary Record of the discussion on Competition and Financial Markets', *Roundtable 4 on Going Forward: Adaptation of Competition Rules, Processes and Institutions to Current Financial Sector Issues*, DAF/COMP/M(2009)1/ANN5, 10 April 2009, <http://www.oecd.org> (visited 26 June 2010).

[32] There is a high social cost associated with their failure. Presentation of Xavier Vives, 'Competition and Stability in Banking: A New World for Competition Policy?', IESE Business School, Amsterdam, 5 March 2009.

[33] See also Elena Carletti and Xavier Vives, 'Regulation and Competition Policy in the Banking Sector' in Xavier Vives (ed), *Competition Policy in the EU: Fifty Years on from the Treaty of Rome* (Oxford: Oxford University Press, 2009).

[34] See Kokkoris and Olivares-Caminal, above n 2, at Ch 7.

This is the state of being too big to fail, which both the Federal Trade Commission (FTC) and Department of Justice have identified as an outcome that antitrust law could and should prevent.[35]

If some banks are not to be allowed to fail, this naturally suggests that those banks can consider themselves less at risk than others.[36] This clearly distorts the market because such banks will have an *ex ante* competitive advantage over smaller less connected banks; indeed, they can take greater risks which themselves can cause crises. The too-big-to-fail doctrine or its recent expanded version should thus be used only in exceptional circumstances because the cure is worse than the disease. The knowledge that the authorities will allow a bank, even a big bank, to fail is an important mechanism of market discipline.[37]

Discretion by the central bank authorities thus creates a necessary uncertainty. Therefore, the 'great task' of central banks has to be performed before the crises. To achieve this, strict supervision is required, as well as an improvement in the accounting standards, to reflect the 'real' situation of the banks. Financial disclosure is increasingly favoured by the banks, their supervisors, and international organizations as an instrument promoting transparency without adding undue regulatory burdens or creating competitive distortions for banks *vis-à-vis* other financial institutions.[38]

In a speech concerning the financial crisis, Neelie Kroes, then European Commissioner for Competition Policy, argued: 'The Commission is committed to continue applying the existing rules, taking full account of economic environment... That means the Commission can and will take into account the evolving market conditions and, where applicable, the failing firm defence.'[39]

In times of crisis, the emergency created by the financial distress requires fast and effective measures. Authorities must be able to act effectively and in the shortest time possible. Therefore, competition rules must be flexible and an indulgent application must be acceptable when the considerations at hand are more important than the blind application of the texts. In other words, the violation of the regulations, or at least their application with more flexibility than usual, constitutes less damage than would be caused by their strict application.

We should also note that 'in declining industry situations it is more likely that firms flailing today will be failing tomorrow'.[40] *Flexibility* implies that a competi-

---

[35] 'Interview with Thomas Rosch, Commissioner, Federal Trade Commission', 23 Antitrust 32 (2009), at 41.

[36] See Philip Molyneux, 'Banking Crises and the Macro-economic Context', in Rosa M. Lastra and Henry N. Schiffman (eds), *Bank Failures and Bank Insolvency Law in Economies in Transition* (London: Kluwer Law International, 1999), at 4.

[37] Rosa M. Lastra, *Central Banking and Banking Regulation* (London: Financial Markets Group, London School of Economics, 1996) 123.

[38] Ibid, at 112.

[39] Speech of Neelie Kroes (European Commissioner for European Policy), 'Dealing with the Current Financial Crisis', Brussels, 6 October 2008, <http://europa.eu/rapid/pressReleasesAction.do?reference=SPEECH/08/498> (visited 26 June 2010).

[40] Oxera, 'Failing, or Just Flailing? The Failing-Firm Defence in Mergers', *Oxera Agenda: Advancing Economics in Business*, March 2009, <http://www.oxera.com/cmsDocuments/Agenda_Mar%2009/Failing%20firm%20defence.pdf> (visited 26 June 2010).

tion authority accepts the defence despite the fact that the alleged failing firm is not likely to exit the market in the near future but is in a degree of financial distress that makes it difficult for it to engage in real and effective competition.

During a financial crisis affecting a whole economy, the various markets, consumers, employees, and competitors are all affected. If the credit market has ceased to function effectively, then firms struggle to obtain financing. Normally, banks or other providers of finance would play a crucial role in sorting the efficient from the inefficient players. Hence, competition and any supporting competition rules fail to achieve their original goal in the presence of a stronger and much more urgent priority. Consequently, for a short time only or until the problem is resolved, it is completely understandable to substitute competition rules, with 'exceptional' rules decided by the supervising governments on a case-by-case basis, in order to provide a solution that benefits the economy in general including consumers, shareholders (of the failing firms), and employees. For all of these reasons, the exceptional 'public interest' notion should include 'financial stability'.

In general, the financial crisis does not mean that there should be a change in the fundamentals of competition law since drastic and excessive changes would be dangerous to the structure of the economy. Instead, where there are adjustments to the scope of competition review in a crisis, these should be communicated clearly and particularly to trading partners. The OECD Report states that international cooperation in setting and enforcing competition policy, especially in relation to failing firm defences, is essential for ensuring consistency in troubled times, speeding up the enforcement process, and giving clarity to enforcement activities.[41]

III. EU State Aid Enforcement Amid Crises

During the recent financial crisis, the European Commission initially implemented its usual state aid provision to allow national aid measures in favour of banks on the basis of it being 'aid to remedy a serious disturbance in the economy of a Member State'.[42] The EU legal framework on state aid applied was relevant to the action taken following the financial crisis.

A. The Legal Framework

There are two steps in the process of enforcing EU state aid control. Initially, a decision should be made as to whether the measure is state aid within the meaning defined in Article 107(1) of the Treaty on the Functioning of the European Union (TFEU). In the second step, once the measure is classified as 'state aid', a decision should be made on whether this state aid is 'compatible with the EU market',

---

[41] OECD, 'Summary Record of the Discussion on Competition and Financial Markets', *Introduction and Roundtable 1 on Principles: Financial Sector Conditions and Competition Policy*, DAF/COMP/M(2009)1/ANN2, 10 April 2009, <http://www.oecd.org> (visited 26 June 2010).
[42] TFEU Article 107(3)(b).

hence, if it can be exempted from the ban under the provisions of TFEU Article 107(3). Only if the state aid is not compatible with the European market, will the Commission ban it.

Neither the TFEU nor any secondary legislation defines state aid. Therefore, what measures constitute state aid under the TFEU is not always clear. State aid measures can sometimes be effective tools for achieving objectives of common interest (including services of general economic interest, social and regional cohesion, employment, research and development, sustainable development, and promotion of cultural diversity) and for correcting 'market failures'. State aid may therefore be compatible with the TFEU, provided that it fulfils clearly defined objectives of common interest and does not distort competition to an extent contrary to the common interest.[43]

A measure will be regarded as state aid if it gives the firm an economic or financial advantage it would not otherwise have enjoyed,[44] i.e. under 'normal market conditions'.[45] The Commission adopted and has renewed its Community Guidelines on state aid.[46] As early as 1961, the European Court of Justice (ECJ) stated that 'the concept of aid is . . . wider than that of a subsidy because it embraces not only positive benefits, such as subsidies themselves, but also interventions which are normally included in the budget of an undertaking and which, without therefore being subsidies in the strict meaning of the word, are similar in character and have the same effect'.[47]

The 'market economy investor principle' (MEIP) is used for determining if state aid is present.[48] This principle means that the measure is not state aid if a government behaves as a private investor, and the measure constitutes state aid if a private investor would not undertake it.[49] In the most recent crisis, due to the breakdown of financial markets, obtaining the necessary capital injections or guarantees from private market players was unlikely. Since private markets did not function properly, state interventions under these conditions were contrary to the behaviour of private market participants. Thus, the MEIP may not hold in such circumstances.

---

[43] See ECJ, Case C-142/87 *Belgium v Commission* (1990) ECR I-959, para 56; ECJ, Case C-39/94 *Syndicat Français de l'Express International v Commission* (1996) ECR I-3547, para 36.

[44] See ECJ, Case 61/79 *Amministrazione delle Finanze v Denkavit Italiana* (1980) ECR 1205.

[45] ECJ, Case C-39/94 *SFEI v La Poste* (1996) ECR I-3547, para 60.

[46] See for example, Commission Guidelines on State Aids for Research and Development, EE C 45, 17 February 1996, at 5, and EE C 111, 8 May 2002, at 3; Commission Guidelines on State Guarantees, EE C 71, 11 March 2000, at 14; Commission Guidelines on State Aids for Environmental Protection, EE C 37, 3 February 2001, at 3; Commission Guidelines on Regional State Aids, EE C 74, 10 March 1998, at 9, as amended, EE C 258, 9 September 2000, at 5; Commission Guidelines on State Aids in the Agricultural Sector, EE C 28, 1 February 2000, at 2, etc. Revised Guidelines came into effect in 2004, see (EE C 244, 1.10.2004, at 2).

[47] See ECJ, Case 30/59 *Steenkolenmijnen v High Authority* (1961) ECR 3, at 19.

[48] Commission (EC), 'Communication on Government Capital Injections', (Bulletin) EC 9-1984.

[49] See ECJ, Case C-305/89 *Italy v Commission* (*Alfa Romeo*) (1991) ECR I-1603, para 19 ff; ECJ, Case C-482/99 *France v Commission* (*Stardust Marine*) (2002) ECR I-4397, para 69 ff; specifically for state guarantees, see also the European Commission, Notice on the Application of Articles 87 and 88 of the EC Treaty to State Aid in the Form of Guarantees, OJ 2008 C 155/10. See ECJ, Case 234/84 *Belgium v Commission* (1986) ECR 2263, para 14.

State aid is generally prohibited and only admissible in exceptional circumstances under the conditions set out in TFEU Article 107(2) and (3). Pursuant to TFEU Article 108(3) all new aid measures must be notified and approved by the Commission prior to their implementation. The burden of proof lies therefore with the Member States to show that the proposed aid meets the conditions for its approval.[50] According to Article 107(2), aid satisfying the conditions is automatically compatible with the common market, not bestowing any discretion to the Commission. The automatic exemption from the general ban on state aid does not, nevertheless, exonerate the Member States from their duty to notify the Commission.[51] Article 107(2)(a) exempts 'aid having a social character, granted to individual consumers, provided that such aid is granted without discrimination related to the origin of the products concerned'.[52] Article 107(2)(b) renders compatible with the common market aid to make good the damage caused by natural disasters or exceptional circumstances. The aid is meant to counterbalance the harm, i.e. to neutralize the damage and the loss of profit suffered and not to overcompensate the recipients.[53]

The Commission has established a balancing test pursuant to which it asks:

Is the aid measure aimed at a well-defined objective of common interest? The aid must be an appropriate means to attain an objective mentioned in Article 107 (3) TFEU (growth, employment, regional cohesion, environment, energy security).

Is the aid well designed to deliver the objective of common interest, that is to say, does the proposed aid address the market failure or other objective? The aid must be proportionate in order to limit distortions of competition and must be the 'least distortive' form of aid.

According to the current Community legislative regime, rescue and restructuring state aid given to companies in difficulty, for example, companies that face bankruptcy or need to restructure, is compatible with EC law only under strict conditions. If the firm receiving state aid operates internationally, the distortion spreads to other countries.

B. Weathering the storm

It soon became obvious that, in times of crisis, more is needed than simply applying the basic rules. The Commission adopted four Banking Communications concerning state aid measures for banks in times of crisis.[54] The first three Communi-

---

[50] See ECJ, Case C-364/90 *Italy v Commission* (1993) ECR I-2097.

[51] See Pietro Crocioni, 'Can State Aid Policy Become More Economic Friendly?' 29 *World Competition* 89 (2006), <http://www.accessmylibrary.com/coms2/summary_0286-14439637_ITM> (visited 26 June 2010).

[52] See for example European Commission, 'Commission approves changes to social aid for air travel between mainland Portugal and the Autonomous Region of Madeira', Press Release IP/07/1900, 11 December 2007.

[53] See ECJ, Case C-73/03 *Spain v Commission*, (2004) Judgment of 11 November 2004.

[54] See First Banking Communication, above n 3; Recapitalisation Communication, above n 3; Impaired Asset Communication, above n 3; Restructuring Communication, above n 3. For further analysis of these, see further: Ulrich Soltész and Christian von Köckritz, 'From State Aid Control to the

cations set out the requirements for certain aid measures and determined the necessity and the extent of the restructuring required for certain banks. A final Restructuring Communication then set out the details of the necessary follow-up measures for banks that had recourse to state aid to overcome the crisis.

On 13 October 2008, the Commission published a communication on the application of state aid rules to measures taken in relation to financial institutions.[55] According to the communication, support schemes introduced by the Member States, such as guarantees to cover their liabilities or recapitalization schemes, would be approved by the Commission following an accelerated procedure if they fulfilled conditions which guarantee that they are well-targeted and proportionate to the objective of stabilizing financial markets and contain certain safeguards against unnecessary negative effects on competition.

The Commission emphasized the exceptional character of this exemption and that it cannot be used in other sectors in the absence of a risk that would have an immediate impact on the economy of the Member State as a whole and that the measures be applied only as long as the crisis situation persists. Therefore, reviews should be carried out at least every six months whereby Member States are required to report to the Commission assessing the continued justification and any potential need for adjustment. In addition, aid must be limited to the strict minimum, and a significant contribution from the beneficiaries and/or the sector should be ensured. In order to avoid an undue distortion of competition, Member States must include a combination of behavioural constraints, or appropriate provisions enforcing behavioural constraints, in order to ensure that the beneficiary does not engage in aggressive expansion. Another instrument for avoiding distortions of competition is adjustment measures for the sector as a whole and/or the restructuring or liquidation of individual beneficiaries.

The Commission expects Member States to inform it of their intentions and to notify their measures as early as possible—and in any event before the implementation of the measures in question. Extraordinarily, the Commission provided that such notifications could be dealt with, if necessary, very promptly (even within 24 hours).

In December 2008, the Commission adopted the communication on the recapitalisation of financial institutions in the current crisis.[56] The common objectives of this communication are the restoration of the financial stability of the banks, ensuring the lending to the real economy, and avoiding the systemic risk of possible insolvencies.

State measures must therefore be proportional and temporary and they have to distinguish between fundamentally sound and less well-performing banks. The Commission pointed out that it will pay particular attention to the risk profile of the beneficiaries and that it will need a basis for a differentiation of remuneration

---

Regulation of the European Banking System—DG COMP and the Restructuring of Banks', 6 *European Competition Journal* 285 (2010).

[55] First Banking Communication, above n 3.
[56] Recapitilisation Communication, above n 3.

rates for different banks, such as a requirement for compliance with regulatory solvency requirements and prospective capital adequacy, pre-crisis spreads and ratings.[57]

The Recapitalisation Communication refers to the safeguards against possible abuses and distortions of competition. High remuneration requires fewer safeguards; however, these may be necessary to prevent aggressive commercial expansion financed by state aid, and mergers and acquisitions should be organized on the basis of a competitive tendering process.

State aid proved to be an important tool in coping with the crisis, but it was not sufficient to prevent structural reform of some banks. In addition to restructuring measures, on 25 February 2009, the Commission deemed it expressly necessary to provide guidance so that some banks could 'cleanse' their balance sheets of impaired or 'toxic' assets.[58]

The Commission offered specific guidance on the application of state aid rules to asset relief. Asset relief can be a measure to safeguard financial stability and underpin the supply of credit to the real economy, as it would directly address the uncertainty regarding the quality of banks' balance sheets and revive confidence in the sector. Not only immediate objectives of safeguarding financial stability should be pursued, but long-term considerations, such as behavioural safeguards and restructuring, should be also included in a government intervention. In order to give incentives for banks to participate in asset relief with public policy objectives, an enrolment window limited to six months from the launch of the scheme by the government should be introduced. Participation in the scheme may be mandatory or voluntary. In the latter situation, additional incentives may be provided to the banks to encourage take-up. However, the principles of transparency and disclosure, fair valuation, and burden sharing must be respected. Behavioural constraints should always condition the access to asset relief.[59]

The Restructuring Communication[60] complements the previous guidance on the assessment of state aid for banks concerning guarantees, recapitalization, and the treatment of impaired assets. This communication, adopted on 14 August 2009, outlines how the competition rules will be applied to support financial stability, as the return of banks to long-term viability is the best guarantee for stability and for their sustained ability to lend to the economy. The restructuring plans submitted by Member States should be comprehensive, detailed, based on coherent concepts, and must include a comparison with alternative options. When a bank cannot be restored to viability, the restructuring plan will indicate how to wind it up in an orderly fashion.

In December 2008, the Commission adopted a communication setting up an EU Framework for state aid measures to support access to finance in the current

---

[57] See further Kokkoris and Olivares-Caminal, above n 2.

[58] Impaired Asset Communication, above n 3. Communication on the Treatment of Impaired Assets in the EU Banking Sector OJ C 72, 26 March 2009, at 1–22.

[59] See Kokkoris and Olivares-Caminal, above n 2, at Ch 6.

[60] Restructuring Communication, above n 3, at Ch 6.

financial and economic crisis[61] which allowed Member States to grant aid under existing instruments for all sectors of the economy through higher limits on grants, credit guarantees, risk capital, and loans.

One of the most important state aid cases is that of the Lloyds Banking Group (LBG). The Commission approved a package of financial support measures to the banking industry in the UK.[62] The UK notified a restructuring plan for LBG on 16 July 2009, in respect of the recapitalization measures that the bank had received six months earlier. LBG's need for state aid was largely due to the acquisition of HBOS (discussed above) and the latter's subsequent financial difficulties. Prior to its takeover, HBOS was on the brink of collapse because of its high-risk lending practices and excessive use of leverage. The takeover offer was conditional upon the receipt of the large amount of government aid necessary to rescue HBOS. In January 2009, LBG received a state recapitalization of £17 billion which resulted in the UK government having an equity ownership of LBG of 43.5 per cent. The aid allowed Lloyds TSB to acquire HBOS and significantly increase its market shares. In addition, the acquisition eliminated a challenger in markets which were already concentrated.

In order to ensure that LBG re-emerges as a stable, profitable bank, measures have concentrated on reducing the balance sheet of LBG, its risk profile and its funding gap. In addition, these measures will result in the disposal or running down of non-core businesses and activities in the corporate, whole- sale, personal, and small business segments.

The Commission imposed detailed requirements on the group. LBG is required to conduct a tendering procedure for the sale of the Divestment Business, which must be adequately publicized. It will also undertake an asset reduction programme to achieve a £181 billion reduction in a specified pool of assets by 31 December 2014. The Commission also provided a detailed account of the features that the prospective buyer should have.

The Commission set out in detail the precise divestment package and what was required of the buyer, in order to ensure that the divested entity will provide an appropriate means of increasing competition in the concentrated UK retail banking market. With the TSB brand, the Lloyds TSB Scotland branches, the C&G branches, and supplementary branches assuring proportional geographical coverage, the carved-out entity will constitute a sufficiently attractive target for some competitors wishing to enter the UK market.

IV. Concluding Remarks

This chapter has introduced the small but important policy area of competition policy to the mix of subjects addressed in this issue, not because it is a solution to

---

[61] Communication from the Commission, Temporary Framework for State Aid Measures to Support Access to Finance in the Current Financial and Economic Crisis, OJ 2009 C 16/01.
[62] *Financial Support Measures to the Banking Industry in the UK*, N 507/2008, 13 October 2008.

the problem, but because it seems to help a bit. No one would suggest that the world's trading partners adopt European state aid control or try to agree a common approach to the merger of failing firms. Neither would be possible, particularly in more *laissez faire* economies, nor is such really necessary. Indeed, as pointed out at the start of this chapter, for example, state aid control did not really 'control' all that much—essentially the authorities approved what was necessary—though it contributed to an ordered release of aid with, what is to be hoped, were minimal competitive distortions.

Also noteworthy is that while state aid is one aspect of competition policy, this does not mean that such an instrument is incapable of being transformed in some way to the international stage. It is true that, in the WTO context, members were not able to agree on entering into negotiations of possible international competition rules. That alone does not rule out the possibility of an international regulatory review of the state-aid component of competition policy. State aid, after all, is not about business practices; it is, by definition, aid by a government and functions as a 'measure' that can and should be reviewable through WTO consultation or dispute settlement proceedings.

This may not necessarily lead to any form of international notification mechanism, as arguably, such a mechanism would not be particularly effective when states have to act quickly. Indeed, international notification through government channels may act a lot more slowly in these circumstances than officials tracking daily developments in the financial press. In any event, it is unlikely that there would be anything that an international body could do—during the time that such aid is being considered—to discipline its release. This flash of *realpolitik* may not sit well in a journal searching for international law in financial regulation, but it is a fact of life nonetheless.

Nor is it necessarily crucial that some international mechanism be created to prohibit such aid, *ex ante* or even *ex post*. After all, if a state deems aid to be needed in extreme circumstances, then it will grant it and worry about the ramifications, in terms of treaty obligations, later. Some form of international review *ex post* is conceivable however. The very existence of a possible review may exert some form of discipline on the more egregiously discriminatory forms of aid that might arise.

Of course, difficult questions remain: What would prevent the provision of state aid which distorts competition? A requirement for repayment? That can hardly be a discipline, since it is required anyway. Fines against the state? That does not seem appropriate when most international rules require only compensatory mechanisms which 'right the wrong' or restore the balance of international commitments, rather than something more punitive. The reality is that aid will be discriminatory and harmful to non-recipients and trading partners. What then might be done?

Just as the important international law principle of non-discrimination should certainly be something which disciplines the release of aid, or reviews its propriety *ex post*, so too can international regulators learn from the state aid model itself.

For example, there are clear disciplines within the review of state aid to ensure that such funds are not used by the recipient to aggressively expand its offering, or to engage in predatory pricing, or otherwise act anti-competitively. Those are fundamental principles of fairness, one could argue, which both underpin competition on the merits and the legitimate use of public funds.

State aid, by definition, is distortive and is only necessary when companies are crying out for a remedy that the market cannot provide. Distortion then needs to be as small as possible; the aid should be proportionate to the problem, and there should be some form of disciplines on its use to ensure that 'unfair competition' does not result.[63]

An international discussion of possible mechanisms should include the sorts of principles that come from the European state aid model, rather than trying to incorporate the model itself.

In general, the financial crisis has not brought about a change in the fundamentals of competition law as they apply to the failing firm defence. The Commission can use its margin of discretion flexibly in its assessment of the defence, hereby taking account of crisis market conditions. In exercising this discretion in crisis situations, competition authorities and courts in the EU must be pragmatic and consider the grounds on which the failing firm defence was introduced into the merger regulations and always apply it in order to achieve those same original goals.

When considering a merger involving a firm that is failing during—and perhaps due to—a crisis, the effects on jobs and consumers should also be borne in mind. Such social costs must be taken into account by governments *ex ante* when adopting the general formulation of the failing company defence, rather than taking social costs into account on an individual basis.[64]

In a volume such as this, with so many contributions from financial, trade and regulatory experts, it is quite clear that—as in the real world—competition policy issues play only a very small part in the face of larger or more systemic and structural failure. Competition policy is about preventing market failure, of course, but it can only go so far, and that the crisis we faced was too big for one narrow policy tool to handle it alone. To that end, perhaps policies that address the impact of competition, concentration and stability in the financial services sector could consider the effect that such policies could have on the broader economy, not only in the home jurisdiction where regulation is imposed, but in other countries around the world. Governments could take into account the viability of firms and sectors as a whole. A rigorous competitive effects analysis of failing firm mergers and state aid measures is helpful to ensure that valid claims of difficult market conditions are carefully considered and evaluated.[65]

---

[63] See Rolf Weber, 'State Interventions and Competition Distortion in Financial Markets', 6 *Schweizerische Zeitschrift für Wirtschaftsrecht* 428 (2009).

[64] Edward Correia, 'The Failing Company Defence', <http://www.ftc.gov/opp/global/final.htm> (visited 15 March 2009).

[65] Lizabeth Leeds, 'The Failing Firm Defence', *Federal Trade Commission Hearings on Changing Nature of Competition in a Global and Innovation-Drive Age*, 14 November 1995, <http://www.ftc.gov/opp/global/GC111495.htm> (visited 26 June 2010).

19

International Regulatory Reform and Financial Taxes

Kern Alexander

I. Introduction

The costs of the financial crisis of 2007–09 are rising exponentially and will impose huge economic and social costs on both developed and developing countries for generations to come. The crisis has also made it extremely difficult for developed countries to honour their pledges made at the Gleneagles G7 Summit in 2005 to increase their financial support for global public goods such as the United Nations (UN) Millennium Development Goals (MDGs). Governments will thus be obliged to generate additional revenue, and to shape taxation accordingly. This chapter examines the effectiveness and feasibility of several financial taxes, including a bank balance sheet tax, a currency transaction tax (CTT) and a broader financial transaction tax (FTT).[1] The chapter argues that financial taxes are becoming part of the international regulatory landscape and will eventually become an integral component of prudential regulatory regimes. The chapter also suggests that financial taxes can serve as innovative sources of finance to pay for the social costs of financial crises while also providing for global public goods.[2]

Financial policymakers are debating whether and how to use financial taxes to enhance the regulation of financial markets.[3] Financial taxes can have three main objectives: (i) to limit excessive risk-taking; (ii) to provide an insurance or resolution fund for systemically important institutions; and (iii) to help pay for global public goods. It should be emphasized that these three objectives are separable,

---

[1] A financial transaction tax is a generic term covering a number of possible taxes that could apply to certain securities investments, derivative contracts or other financial products including commodities.

[2] Global public goods can be defined as goods or services that are not provided by the market because of market failure and which governments can therefore justify providing on efficiency grounds in order to enhance economic and social outcomes. See generally Anthony B. Atkinson, 'Innovative Sources to Meet a Global Challenge', in A.B. Atkinson (ed), *New Sources of Development Finance* (Oxford: Oxford University Press, 2005) 1–3.

[3] See International Monetary Fund, 'A Fair and Substantial Contribution by the Financial Sector', Final Report for the G-20, IMF Final Report, <http://www.imf.org/external/np/g20/pdf/062710b.pdf> (visited 25 July 2010).

both in their economic rationale and in practice. The first objective, limiting excessive risk-taking, is derived from the desire to price risk efficiently. In this case, how the funds are used subsequently is not of primary concern. Second, the proposition that such funds might be used to build an insurance fund is an entirely separate argument related not to mitigating the riskiness of financial transactions but to pricing accurately the implicit insurance provided to institutions deemed too big or too inter-connected to fail. The provision of assistance to those most affected by ill-chosen risk-taking is a third component of an efficient pricing strategy. Hence the objective of efficient pricing may be pursued by adopting all three goals at once, or by pursuing them separately.

II. Bank Balance Sheet Taxes

A. Domestic efforts

Sweden adopted a so-called 'stability fee' in 2009 that was a direct levy on Swedish banks and credit institutions to provide a fund to pay for the resolution of failed Swedish banks.[4] Banks were required to pay the levy on an annual basis at an initial rate of 0.018 per cent of each institution's liabilities, excluding equity capital and certain subordinated debt, based on audited balance sheets.[5] The government injected an initial 15 billion kronor into the fund with banks making their first payments into the fund following government auditing of their balance sheets in 2010. In 2011, the bank levy increased to 0.036 per cent of liabilities and the government has expressed interest in introducing a risk weighted charge in the future. Banks with riskier assets would pay a higher percentage. Such a tax on bank liabilities may result, however, in banks being double-charged on their liabilities if they have retail or wholesale deposits which often require reserve requirements at the central bank. The Swedish levies are allocated to a stability fund managed by the Swedish National Debt Office. The government plans to continue levying the fee over a period of 15 years until the revenue generated reaches 2.5 per cent of Swedish gross domestic product (GDP).[6]

The Swedish stability fee serves as a model for other countries. The Obama administration proposed a similar fee in March 2010 that it called a 'financial crisis responsibility fee', to be imposed at a rate of 0.15 per cent on the largest US banks in order to repay US taxpayers for the costs of the US bank bailout programme. Congress rejected the Obama bank tax in the Dodd–Frank Act by requiring regulators to impose several different assessments on the largest US banks and non-bank financial institutions to cover the costs of the government's expanded

---

[4] See Anders Borg, 'Letter to G20 Finance Ministers' (Ministry of Finance, Sweden, 2010, on file with the author).

[5] Ibid.

[6] The Swedish government estimates 2.5 per cent of GDP to be the cost to the Swedish economy of a full-scale banking crisis. Ibid.

supervisory and resolution responsibilities.[7] Unlike other countries, which are adopting bank taxes designed to curb future risk-taking, the US assessments are retrospective in effect because they are designed mainly to reimburse taxpayers for the direct costs of the government's bank bailouts and to establish a fund to support the future resolution of financial institutions.

Germany, France and the UK announced that they too would adopt a levy or stability tax on bank balance sheets.[8] The UK government proposed in its 2010 budget a graduated tax on bank liabilities and equity where the banking group's aggregated liabilities exceed £20 billion. The tax came into force from the 1 January 2011 and is based on all liabilities and equity excluding tier-1 capital, insured retail deposits, repurchase agreements on sovereign debt and retail insurance reserves.[9] Due to the uncertain market conditions an initial rate of 0.05 per cent was imposed in 2011 increasing to 0.075 per cent in 2012 with a reduced rate for longer maturity funding (i.e. greater than 1 year) at 0.025 per cent in 2011 rising to 0.0375 per cent in 2012.[10] An improvement in the resilience of the Banking Sector led this initial rate to be scraped and the higher rate being applied for 2011.[11] A shortfall in projected revenue caused the rate to be revised up to 0.088 per cent with a reduced rate of 0.044 per cent as of 1 January 2012.[12] Significantly, unlike the Swedish and US bank taxes, the German, French and UK taxes are not considered to be insurance against bank failure and liability to pay the tax does not indicate that the bank is too big to fail. The revenues generated from the levy are not intended to pay for future bank bailouts or indirect interventions. Instead, they are meant to be charges on the broader economic and systemic risks posed by the banking sector. The different design and objectives of these national bank taxes may affect bank risk-taking differently across jurisdictions, which suggests that more cross-border coordination is needed among national authorities to ensure that these taxes achieve their objectives and are not circumvented through arbitrage.

B. International initiatives

The Group of 20 (G20) Heads of State requested the International Monetary Fund (IMF) to examine the desirability and feasibility of various types of financial taxes

[7] The Wall Street Reform and Consumer Protection Act of 2010 (Dodd–Frank Act), Pub. L.111–203 (21 July 2010).

[8] HM Treasury, 'Bank Levy', Press Release and Joint Statement of the UK, French and German Governments, 4 June 2010 (announcing that the UK government would impose a bank levy from 1 January 2011 and that the UK, French and German governments would impose similar bank balance sheet levies). The UK levy would be based on the 'consolidated balance sheet' of banking groups and the 'aggregated subsidiary and branch balance sheets of foreign banks and banking groups operating' in the UK where these institutions have 'relevant aggregated liabilities' of £20 billion or more. See HM Treasury, *Financial Times*, 8 June 2010, 12.

[9] Ibid.

[10] HM Treasury, 'Government introduces bank levy', <http://www.hm-treasury.gov.uk/press_01_11.htm> (visited on 5 March 2012).

[11] HM Treasury, 'Bank levy rates to be increased raising £800m more in 2011', <http://www.hm-treasury.gov.uk/press_14_11.htm> (visited on 5 March 2012).

[12] HM Treasury, 'Bank Levy: Rate Change', <http://www.hmrc.gov.uk/tiin/tiin637.pdf> (visited on 5 March 2012).

and to report its conclusions to the G20.[13] The IMF issued its report in June 2010 recommending that countries consider adopting two taxes: a 'Financial Stability Contribution' (FSC) and a 'Financial Activities Tax' (FAT).[14] The FSC is a balance sheet tax that would be based on the bank's total liabilities minus equity, insured deposits and insurance policyholder reserves, with most of the proceeds going to a bank resolution fund. In contrast, the FAT would be levied on the profits and remuneration of financial institutions and the proceeds would go to the general revenue fund.[15] The FSC is primarily designed as an insurance fund to pay retrospectively for the resolution or bailout of a large systemically important or too-interconnected-to-fail bank or financial institution. In contrast, the FAT would primarily be applied prospectively to deter excessive risk-taking.

The IMF's recommended financial stability contribution is similar to the financial stability tax discussed above that Sweden adopted in 2009 and which was based on bank liabilities and equity. The G20 and the Financial Stability Board are considering proposals that would recommend that countries adopt a balance sheet tax and levy similar to the IMF's proposals. These taxes, however, have met with resistance from some developed countries and many developing countries because they might impose disproportionate costs on countries whose economies rely more on bank finance.[16] Moreover, some G20 countries which had regulated their banks more strictly before the crisis and hence did not provide direct bailouts to their banks (i.e. Canada, China, India and Japan) have opposed a balance sheet tax and have led opposition to the adoption of such a tax on an international basis. Indeed, these countries influenced the text of the G20 Toronto Summit Communiqué to state that each country would be free to adopt whatever tax measures it deemed appropriate for the needs of its economy and financial system. Another criticism of the bank balance sheet tax is that it will fail to deter banks from engaging in excessive risk-taking and will not generate adequate revenue to pay for a resolution fund because most banks will avoid the tax by shifting risky assets and liabilities off balance sheet to affiliates and related entities located outside the taxing jurisdiction. These weaknesses of the proposed bank balance sheet tax suggest that policy-makers should consider the merits of an FTT that would be applied by national governments and collected by banks and dealers with the support of transnational clearing and settlement houses.

---

[13] The G20 Pittsburgh Communiqué stated that the IMF should 'prepare a report for our next meeting [June 2010] with regard to the range of options countries have adopted or are considering as to how the financial sector could make a fair and substantial contribution toward paying for any burden associated with government interventions to repair the banking system.' See G20, 'Leaders' Statement: The Pittsburgh Summit', 24–25 September 2009, para 16. See also IMF Final Report, above n 3, at 1.

[14] See IMF Final Report, above n 3.

[15] Ibid, at 2–3.

[16] Developing countries usually have under-developed capital markets and rely mainly on a bank-led finance system. See Gerald M. Meier and James E. Rauch, *Leading Issues in Economic Development*, 7th ed. (New York: Oxford University Press, 2000) 138–46.

III. FTTs

The recent crisis has raised questions about the possibility of a Tobin or transactions tax to restrain the explosive growth of financial transactions in recent years. In considering such a tax, it should be borne in mind that most countries do not impose a sale or value-added tax on financial services transactions.[17] The idea behind an FTT has been attributed to Nobel Laureate James Tobin who proposed a CTT in the 1970s primarily to limit the destabilizing influence of the growing volume of very short-term foreign exchange transactions and to enhance control over the financial aspects of macro-economic policy.[18] Since Tobin's original proposal, the idea of an FTT has been developed by economists and civil society groups as a possible source of revenue to finance global development objectives.[19] Recently, the global financial crisis has brought the issue back on the agenda with the G20's efforts to rebuild the financial architecture. Unlike the pre-crisis literature, proposals for an FTT have gained considerable traction, both as a financial stability instrument and as a way to pay for global public goods, such as the UN MDGs and climate-change policies.

This section suggests that the effectiveness and feasibility of an FTT will depend on how well it satisfies the following criteria: (i) achieves a balance of economic benefits in terms of risk mitigation that does not significantly distort the market nor undermine liquidity; (ii) generates adequate revenue to pay for public goods; (iii) is collected and monitored through clearing and settlement infrastructure subject to central bank oversight; and (iv) complies with applicable international law.

A. The economic rationale

In considering the merits of an FTT, one should bear in mind that the object of economic activity is to produce goods and services. Financial transactions are the means by which the production of goods and services is funded. In the 1960s, international trade grew by 8.2 per cent a year, which, together with long-term investment flows, was financed by foreign exchange transactions that were roughly

---

[17] The European Commission is examining an EU financial transaction tax, while the European Parliament has generally endorsed the broad outlines of a tax and the need for EU institutions to develop a unified position on the issue. Commission of the European Communities, 'Innovative Financing at a Global Level', Commission Staff Working Document, SEC (2010) 409, 1 April 2010 and European Parliament, 'Motion for a Resolution to Wind-Up the Debate by the Commission Pursuant to Rule 110 (2) of the Rules of Procedure on Financial Transaction Taxes—Making Them Work', B7 0000/2009, 8 January 2010.

[18] See James Tobin, 'A Proposal for International Monetary Reform', 4 Eastern Economic Journal 153 (1978), at 154. See also James Tobin, *The New Economics One Decade Older, The Eliot Janeway Lectures on Historical Economics in Honour of Joseph Schumpeter* (Princeton: Princeton University Press, 1974).

[19] Mahbubul Haq, Inge Kaul, Isabelle Grunberg (eds), *The Tobin Tax: Coping with Financial Volatility* (New York: Oxford University Press, 1996).

double the value of the trade deals themselves.[20] In recent years, however, the volume and value of transactions have grown much more rapidly than the underlying production and trade. Between 2000 and 2007, while growth in international trade slowed to just 5.8 per cent per year, the value of foreign exchange transactions rose to more than 80 times the value of the underlying trade and long-term investment.[21]

Similarly, the growth of derivatives markets and in particular of credit default swaps (CDSs) has grown dramatically with the total notional value of such contracts rising from just over $1 trillion in 1986 to around $516 trillion in 2007.[22] The CDS market was at the centre of the financial distress in September 2008 when Lehman Brothers collapsed. The collapse of Lehman Brothers and its aftermath demonstrates that the risk to the economy as a whole was not just a function of complexity and the interconnectedness of transactions, but also of the sheer size of the transactions themselves, relative to the underlying trade or loans on which they were written. For example, Lehman's over-the-counter (OTC) CDS book had a notional value of $72 billion, yet Lehman's net exposure to OTC credit default contracts is estimated to have been only about $5.2 billion.[23]

The ever-growing amount of financial transactions that are based upon a relatively small amount of underlying assets has led some to suggest that policymakers should give serious consideration to an FTT.[24] The focus on transaction taxes reflects that the proliferation of financial transactions themselves has become a concern of regulators and that a significant portion of transactions has been characterized as 'socially useless'.[25] The excessive growth of financial transactions imposes a risk on society as a whole. Those who impose that risk should pay for it. If they do not, then risk is mispriced. This raises an important question: if financial transactions have grown too large and pose serious risks to financial stability, can an FTT reduce the value and volume of transactions to a more efficient level without undermining liquidity and financial development?

Academic opinion is strongly divided over what utility FTTs have in curbing excessive risk-taking and generating sustainable sources of revenue. Proponents of FTTs view financial markets as characterized by excessive trading activity and

---

[20] See Kern Alexander, John Eatwell, Avinash Persaud and Robert Reoch, 'Crisis Management, Burden Sharing, and Solidarity Mechanisms in the EU' IP/A/ECON/FWC/2010, Report to the European Parliament, 2010, at 31–3.

[21] Ibid.

[22] Bank for International Settlements, 'Semiannual OTC Derivatives Statistics at end-June 2008', <http://www.bis.org/statistics/derstats.htm> (visited 25 July 2010).

[23] The Bank for International Settlements Estimated in June 2008 that the value of CDSs outstanding in major financial markets was $57.3 trillion. Ibid. In late 2008, the US Depository Trust and Clearing Corporation revealed that the value of CDS transactions was ten times greater than the value of the underlying risk being insured. See Depository Trust and Clearing Corporation, 'Trade Information Warehouse Data', <http://dtcc.com/products/derivserv/data_table_i.php> (visited 25 July 2010).

[24] Adair Turner, 'What Do Banks Do, What Should They Do and What Public Policies are Needed to Ensure Best Results', March 2010, <http://www.fsa.gov.uk/pubs/speeches/at_17mar10.pdf> (visited 25 July 2010).

[25] Ibid, at 1.

short-term speculation, and consider that such speculation generates volatility not only in short-term asset prices, but also in long-term asset prices marked by persistent and dramatic departures from equilibrium.[26] Keynes observed that this could lead to the 'predominance of speculation over enterprise' with the result that 'enterprise becomes the bubble on a whirlpool of speculation'.[27] Accordingly, a tax on transactions in securities and other financial instruments would increase the cost of speculative trading, especially for trades with shorter durations, and this would have a stabilizing effect on asset prices. Moreover, the tax would generate revenue needed to assist governments with fiscal consolidation, especially during times of crisis.

Opponents of transaction taxes generally believe that a high number of transactions—both short- and long-term—are necessary for the price discovery process to work and for the efficient distribution of risk. More transactions lead to a smoothing in asset-price movements towards equilibrium,[28] and short-term trading is necessary to allow effective hedging and should not, therefore, be limited. Any increase in transaction costs (i.e. a tax) would limit parties' ability to hedge risk, thus reducing liquidity and increasing short-term volatility of asset prices. An alternative, and fundamentally contradictory point, is that globalized and liberalized financial markets make it very difficult to implement a FTT and will result in evasion and circumvention of the FTT, thereby substantially reducing its effectiveness and its revenue-raising capacity.

B. Global public goods

The crisis has also made it extremely difficult for developed countries to honour their pledges taken at the Gleneagles G7 Summit in 2005 to increase their financial support for global public goods and in particular to achieve the UN MDGs.[29] At

---

[26] Lawrence H. Summers and Victoria P. Summers, 'When Financial Markets Work Too Well: A Cautious Case for a Securities Transaction Tax', 3 *Journal of Financial Services Research* 261 (1989); Joseph E. Stiglitz, 'Using Tax Policy to Curb Short-Term Trading', 3 *Journal of Financial Services Research* 101 (1989); J. Bradford de Long, Andrei Sheleifer, Lawrence H. Summers, and Robert J. Waldmann, 'Positive Feedback Investment Strategies and Destabilizing Rational Speculation', 45(2) *The Journal of Finance* 379 (1990); and Stephan Schulmeister, 'A General Financial Transaction Tax: A Short Cut of the Pros, Cons and a Proposal', <http://www.makefinancework.org/IMG/pdf/schulmeister_eng.pdf> (visited 25 July 2010).

[27] J.M. Keynes, *The General Theory of Employment, Interest and Money* (London: Macmillan, 1936) 158–9. Keynes also observed that to limit excessive speculation on the stock exchange 'a substantial Government transfer tax on all transactions might prove the most serviceable reform available'. Ibid, at 160.

[28] Karl F. Habermeier, Andrei A. Kirilenko, 'Securities Transaction Taxes and Financial Markets', 50 IMF Staff Papers 165 (special issue), 2003. See also John Grahl and Photis Lysandrou, 'Sand in the Wheels or Spanner in the Works? The Tobin Tax and Global Finance', 27(4) *Cambridge Journal of Economics* 597 (2003).

[29] UN General Assembly Resolution, 'United Nations Millennium Declaration', A/Res/55/2, 18 September 2000. The MDGs consist of eight specific goals: (i) eradicating extreme poverty; (ii) achieving universal primary education; (iii) promoting gender equality and empowering women; (iv) reducing child mortality; (v) improving maternal health; (vi) combating HIV/AIDS, malaria and other diseases; (vii) ensuring environmental sustainability; and (viii) developing a global partnership for development.

the Gleneagles Summit, the G7 Heads of State promised increased financial support for poverty reduction in the world's poorest countries and to raise Official Development Assistance to 0.7 per cent of gross national product. These financial commitments, however, have not been met. The World Bank has estimated that since 2005 the resource gap between the financial commitments made by developed countries and their actual expenditures and support levels for global public goods grew substantially and would reach an estimated range of between US$324 and 336 billion per year sometime between 2012 and 2017.[30] Even if the global economy improves, the resource gap for developed countries will remain substantial, thus making it difficult for developed countries to fulfil their financial commitments to achieve the MDGs. Consequently, developed countries are considering alternative and innovative sources of finance to pay for their MDG commitments and other global public goods.

IV. CTT

The foreign exchange market (FX market) is crucial for the functioning of the global financial system because it is the largest and most liquid of the asset class markets. In the post-crisis environment, it has taken on an even greater significance because of the recognized importance of liquidity to the successful operation of the global financial system. Despite the recent economic downturn and associated financial distress in most countries, the average daily turnover in the global foreign exchange market has increased dramatically from just over US$3 trillion a day in 2007 to US$4 trillion a day in 2010 (Fig. 19.1).[31] The vast majority of the market (about 90 per cent) consists of spot transactions, outright forwards and forex swaps, while non-traditional foreign exchange derivatives and other products (i.e. currency swaps and options) comprise about 10 per cent of the market (Fig. 19.1). Most of these trades can be settled within seven days, which suggests that they are predominantly speculative and have little connection to underlying trade. Although foreign exchange markets generally operated efficiently in the recent crisis, there were considerable disruptions to the foreign exchange swap market before and after the Lehman Brothers' collapse.[32] Traditionally, most of these transactions were carried out by interbank dealers—the largest investment banks and their dealers— but in 2010 the proportion of transactions carried out by interbank dealers dropped to 39 per cent while the proportion of transactions carried out by 'other financial

---

[30] Organisation for Economic Co-operation and Development, 'Economic Outlook No 86', <http://www.oecd.org/document/18/0,3343,en_2649_34109_20347538_1_1_1_37443,00.html> (visited 25 July 2010).

[31] Bank for International Settlements, 'Triennial Central Bank Survey for Foreign Exchange and Derivatives Market Activity in April 2010—Preliminary Global Results, September 2010, at 3. Although trading volumes dropped in 2008–09 in the aftermath of the Lehman Brothers' collapse, daily volumes are now expected to grow further because of increased investment in emerging economies and commodity-producing countries and advances in computer trading systems.

[32] See N. Baba and F. Packer, 'From Turmoil to Crisis: Dislocations in the FX Swap Market Before and After the Failure of Lehman Brothers', BIS Working Papers No 285, July 2009.

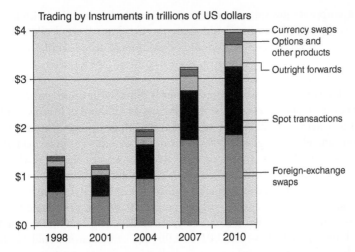

Fig. 19.1. Global foreign exchange market

Source: BIS

institutions', such as mutual funds, insurance companies, pension funds, hedge funds and central banks, rose significantly to 42 per cent. A much smaller proportion of trades (13 per cent) were carried out by nonfinancial businesses, such as manufacturing and airline companies.[33]

A CTT could work as follows: it would be assessed on individual foreign exchange transactions by interbank dealers and other financial intermediaries in the foreign exchange market and monitored and possibly collected by the main international foreign exchange settlement house, the Continuous Link Settlement Bank (CLS Bank),[34] with support from central banks through their real-time gross-settlement systems. National authorities could then collect the tax from the CLS Bank in cooperation with central banks and with access to information provided by data cooperatives such as the Society for Worldwide Interbank Financial Telecommunications (SWIFT).[35] The financial intermediaries and dealers would pay the tax and if there were no intermediary in the process (e.g. intra-group payments

---

[33] See Triennial Central Bank Survey, above n 31, at 3.

[34] The Continuous Link Settlement System (CLS) and the Continuous Link Settlement Bank International (CLS Bank) were established in 2002 by the 17 leading central banks, which issue the world's reserve currencies and a group of leading banks and financial institutions. The CLS Bank holds the deposits of its member banks denominated in the currencies of its participating central banks in the CLS system so that if one member bank cannot fulfil its counterparty obligation to another CLS member, then the CLS Bank can draw on the defaulting member's relevant currency deposit to cover the obligation owed to the non-defaulting CLS member. In 2009, the CLS Bank settled approximately 55 per cent of the value of foreign exchange transactions. The other main settlement method is traditional correspondent banking which settles about 32 per cent of the value of forex transactions.

[35] SWIFT operates a worldwide voluntary financial messaging network which exchanges information between banks and other financial institutions in order to facilitate interbank payments, but it does not clear and settle payments and therefore could not collect or deduct tax on transactions. See <http://www.swift.com> (visited 25 July 2010).

within a corporate group) then the taxpayer would become liable itself (i.e. the holding company). A country could apply the CTT on all wholesale transactions conducted by intermediaries (banks and other brokers) based within that country, independently of where the transactions are negotiated, the location of transferor or transferee or the place of settlement.

The CTT is similar to the Tobin tax, but is different in important respects: the Tobin tax was intended to slow the flow of cross-border capital ('throw sand in the wheels') to enhance the ability of national authorities to conduct monetary policy and to prevent an exchange-rate crisis. This meant that the Tobin tax had to be at a high enough rate (0.50 or 1.0 per cent) to change investor behaviour, which led to the criticism that under certain circumstances it would significantly limit liquidity in the market, which could exacerbate a crisis.[36] Instead, a CTT could be assessed at a low enough rate (0.01 per cent –1 basis point or 0.005 per cent – one-half a basis point) so as not to limit liquidity unduly, while deterring only those transactions with such low spreads (less than 0.01 or 0.005 per cent) that it would not have an appreciable effect on liquidity nor on underlying economic activity.

A. How high should the CTT rate be?

In considering the rate at which the tax should be levied, it will be necessary to consider two factors: (i) how much the market will decline given the tax rate charged, and (ii) the market's capacity to pay the tax without unduly limiting liquidity. Schmidt estimates a fall in volume of transactions of 14 per cent if the rate of one-half of a basis point (0.005 per cent) is levied.[37] The market's capacity to pay the tax will depend in part on the depth of liquidity in the market and ability of dealers and clients to circumvent and avoid the tax. Some studies suggest significant 'market dampening' and 'leakage' would lead to a market reduction of 25 per cent.[38]

Proponents of the CTT estimate that a low tax rate can generate substantial revenue even if only applied to a few reserve currencies (sterling and euro).[39] The most comprehensive and realistic estimates of how much money a CTT can raise across the major currencies are from Schmidt and Baker.[40] Based on 2007 data, Schmidt estimates that a coordinated CTT levied at 0.005 per cent (one-half a basis point) applied to the leading reserve currencies would yield US$33.41 billion a year.[41] In contrast, a coordinated CTT at the same rate on all the major currencies except the dollar would yield US$21.24 billion a year, and a coordinated tax on

---

[36] Grahl and Lysandrou, above n 28, at 598–600.

[37] Rodney Schmidt, *The Currency Transaction Tax: Rate and Revenue Estimates* (Toronto: United Nations/North-South Institute, 2008) 14.

[38] Dean Baker, 'The Benefits of a Financial Transaction Tax', <http://www.cepr.net/documents/publications/financial-transactions-tax-2008–12.pdf> (visited 25 July 2010).

[39] See Machiko Nissanke, 'The Tobin Tax for Development Finance' in Atkinson (ed), above n 2, at 72; see also Heikki Patomaki and Katarina Sehm-Patomaki, *The Tobin Tax: How to Make it Real* (Helsinki: The Network Institute for Global Democratisation, 1999).

[40] See Schmidt, above n 37, at 14–17, and Baker, above n 38.

[41] Schmidt's estimates for a CTT on the US dollar as one leg against all other currencies amounted to: US$28.8 billion, while a CTT on the euro alone as one leg against all other currencies would yield

only the euro and sterling would yield US$16.52 billion a year. His estimates are more realistic and much lower than what other CTT proponents had estimated because he gives more weight to market dampening as a result of the tax.[42] Most of the volume reductions that result from the tax derive from the loss of short-term trading, such as algorithmic trading, that responds to very small spreads of less than one basis point which would be smaller than the estimated tax. On the other hand, his revenue estimates can be considered more optimistic because he minimizes the risk of avoidance and circumvention because of the expected effect of centralized settlement in the CLS Bank system which would make it very difficult to avoid paying the tax.[43]

Schmidt's higher estimates should be contrasted with those of other CTT and FTT advocates who adopt similar methodologies but give more weight to avoidance and circumvention. For instance, Baker estimated a CTT yield of only US $7.8 billion that took into account a higher level of market reduction of 25 per cent based on a tax rate of 0.01 per cent (one basis point).[44] Nissanke uses BIS data from 2001 to estimate that a global CTT at a rate of 0.02 per cent applied to wholesale transactions would yield between US$30 and US$35 billion while at a rate of 0.01 per cent, it would yield between US$17 and US$31 billion a year.[45] Schmidt's estimate of $33.41 billion a year appears to be a realistic assessment of the capacity of the CTT to raise revenue based on the depth and liquidity of the foreign exchange markets and the institutional consolidation that is occurring in centralized settlement of foreign exchange transactions.[46]

In addition, the adoption of a CTT, and its rate, would have important implications for certain international financial centres, such as the UK's City of London which serves as the world's leading foreign exchange trading centre, with nearly 36.7 per cent of the value of foreign exchange transactions taking place each day.[47] UK policy-makers would understandably be concerned that such a tax might cause the migration of much of this business to other jurisdictions. At a 0.005 per cent rate, however, it is difficult to show that a UK CTT of 0.005 per cent— equivalent to a £500 charge for a £10 million transaction—would undermine London's status as the *world's* leading centre for foreign exchange trading.

US$12.29 billion, and similarly on the yen alone against all other currencies would yield US$5.59 billion, and sterling alone against all other currencies would yield US$4.98 billion. Ibid.

[42] For example, this should be compared with the much higher estimate of US$176 billion a year. J. Frankel 'How Well Do Markets Work: Might a Tobin Tax Help?' in Haq et al, above n 19, at 41–82.

[43] In light of the BIS Triennial Central Bank Survey 2010 survey, these estimates are rather cautious because they are based on average daily foreign exchange turnover of US$3 trillion a day, and not on the 2010 survey's much higher turnover of US$4 trillion a day.

[44] See Baker, above n 38.

[45] See Nissanke above n 39.

[46] See Schmidt, above n 37.

[47] London is followed by the USA (18 per cent), Japan (6.2 per cent), Singapore (5.3 per cent), Switzerland (5.2 per cent), Hong Kong (4.7 per cent), Australia (3.8 per cent), France (3.0 per cent), Denmark (2.4 per cent), Germany (2.1 per cent). Triennial Central Bank Survey, above n 31, at 2.

B. Technical feasibility and incidence

In considering the implementation and incidence of CTT, previous studies support the viability of administering such a tax in modern foreign exchange settlement systems.[48] The CLS Bank, along with the CLS infrastructure, could permit CTTs to be imposed at a relatively low level, which has little effect on the relative costs of the transaction. For the CLS Bank to collect the tax, it would need the support of participating central banks, which issue the leading reserve currencies, to monitor wholesale gross-currency transactions through their real-time gross-settlement (RTGS) payment systems. Some central bankers, however, might emphasize that there is nothing in their mandate that would authorize them to support the CLS Bank in collecting a CTT. Understandably, central bankers charged with financial stability are very concerned about undermining market stability, and would there-fore be concerned about any process that drove participants away from well-established and well-run existing markets, which might hinder liquidity and significantly raise transaction costs. This point is reinforced by the belief that the CLS Bank had performed well during the crisis and especially during the week in September 2008 when Lehman Brothers collapsed when it settled effectively $26.3 trillion in foreign exchange payments despite disruptions in the foreign exchange swap market. Although central banks would probably like to see more use of the CLS Bank in settling forex transactions, because of the high transparency of the transactions and reduced settlement risk, they might have concerns with it collect-ing a CTT because this might drive transactions away from the CLS System, thereby increasing settlement risk.

Nevertheless, in an age when authorities have effectively nationalized the bulk of banking systems and where governments and central banks have purchased sub-stantial quantities of hard to value private instruments, if regulators believe using a central settlement system promotes financial stability, then using such a system can be made mandatory for instruments to be legally valid or there could be higher capital-adequacy requirements for those not settling their trades in the central settlement system because, by settling outside the system, they are taking greater risks and possibly increasing systemic risk.

On the other hand, the incidence of the tax may create private costs that offset the social benefits from requiring the trade to be settled in a particular system. Foreign exchange trade encompasses a huge amount of different commercial activities with differing motivations. While foreign exchange speculation is one type of commercial activity taking place on the market, a large number of trade, investment, savings and pensions activities—conducted by individuals and business entities at the retail and wholesale levels—involve the foreign exchange markets. As such, a large proportion of 'activity' on the foreign exchange market is already taxed in numerous ways. Also, foreign exchange trading supports international trade in goods and services and a tax on currency transactions might hinder international

---

[48] See Schmidt, above n 37, at 4.

trade itself by increasing the cost of trade finance, especially for developing countries. It is uncertain whether it is desirable to try and exclude from the CTT those transactions that primarily support international trade because it might be difficult to differentiate between foreign exchange speculation and hedging transactions and currency transactions that are incidental to international trade. On the other hand, the size of the levy being proposed is unlikely to make any material difference to a corporate or real goods trade transaction. It may be useful to note that legal and banking fees on many of these transactions often amount to well in excess of 1.0 per cent or 100 basis points. In large, cross-border corporate finance transactions, banks charge advisory fees, arrangement fees and commitment fees, and each of these is a large multiple of a basis point. In trade finance transactions, banking fees are similar, amounting to many multiples of a basis point.

Some critics, however, are sceptical that the tax would have a 'negligible effect'. While the proposed size of the levy (0.005 per cent or 0.5 basis points) appears very low, it is not low relative to the spreads for the most liquid exchange rates in the foreign exchange market such as euro/$, £/$, Sfr/$and $/¥. In times of low volatility, spreads for these currencies were reported to stand at around one basis point, in which case a 0.5 basis point levy would be very significant. Nevertheless, it should be noted that the spread is not a reflection of trading profitability, but reflects the price of liquidity. Banks make profit from trading foreign exchange partly by charging for this liquidity, but primarily by following trends in the market place and in their customers' business.

Regarding the burden of the tax, it should be observed that in terms of information the foreign exchange market is primarily a wholesale market. Retail transactions are a very small proportion of total transactions. The burden of the tax will fall on those carrying out thousands of transactions over short periods of time—this is decidedly not retail, it is wholesale and is primarily algorithmic trading. For instance, a pension fund investor will execute transactions in a long-term fund a few times a year, while a hedge fund would do so hundreds of times.

V. FTT

A transaction tax could be applied to a broader range of financial assets—equities, bonds, swaps, options and an array of derivative instruments. Many developed and developing countries, such as Brazil and Japan, already impose broad-based taxes on futures and derivatives transactions and stocks and bonds, and some countries such as the UK have narrower taxes on equity shares traded on an exchange.[49] A broader FTT could potentially raise substantial sums to defray the costs of financial crises and reduce the growing public resource gaps identified by international organizations. A broader FTT could be based on most instruments in OTC markets, such

---

[49] See IMF Final Report, above n 12, Appendix 5.

as interest rate swaps and currency swaps and options, and certain exchange-traded derivatives and futures.[50]

Although the tax could be levied at a rate similar to the CTT, it could be applied at different rates to reflect different risks posed by the instruments and different liquidity requirements in the markets in which the instruments trade. Dealing and trading in instruments outside the forex markets often involves a broader range of players located in multiple jurisdictions who use different clearing and settlement institutions and are exposed to different counterparty and market risks. To this end, Spahn has proposed that different tax rates apply to different counterparties (regulated banks, other financial institutions and private capital and non-financial corporations and public institutions) depending on their size and the systemic risk that they pose.[51] This proposal assumes that some categories of counterparty (e.g. hedge funds) or transactions (e.g. certain derivative products) are more prone to speculative trading than others. Such a multi-tiered tax regime should aim to identify the desirable level of reduction in trading activities, which should be large enough to eliminate short-term speculative trading, but not so large as to limit unduly or hamper the normal functioning of markets.

Econometric analysis has estimated how much a broad FTT can raise across a wide number of financial instruments (including bonds, exchangetraded, centrally cleared and OTC derivatives).[52] For instance, Schulmeister incorporates conservative parameters for market dampening, avoidance and circumvention. Although his estimates are rather cautious, they provide probably the most accurate estimate to date of the market impact of a FTT at tax rates of 0.5, 0.1 or 0.01 per cent. Based on his methodology, if the lowest tax rate of 0.01 per cent is applied to all exchange-traded and OTC derivatives, the estimated revenue would be between $100 and $120 billion a year.[53] The broader FTT, unlike the CTT, would generate substantially higher revenue and would achieve regulatory objectives because it would be focused mainly on instruments with shorter term positions that consist of higher levels of leverage which pose greater systemic risk.

Recent regulatory initiatives in Europe and the USA will require most OTC derivatives and futures contracts to be traded and cleared on an organized exchange and/or clearing house. It would be advantageous to implement a FTT through centralized clearing and settlement structures. The trend towards centralized clearing and settlement of derivatives and foreign exchange transactions has made it much more feasible to implement a FTT on a global basis. Clearing houses already have sophisticated reporting processes for withholding tariffs and other

---

[50] The average daily value of the global OTC derivatives market is approximately US$24 trillion per year (including credit default swaps, commodity contracts, equity derivatives, interest rate contracts, and FX contracts). Alexander et al, above n 20, at 52.

[51] Paul B. Spahn, 'On the Feasibility of a Tax on Foreign Exchange Transactions', <http://www.wiwi.uni-frankfurt.de/profs/spahn/tobintax/Tobintax.pdf> (visited 25 July 2010).

[52] Stephan Schulmeister, 'A General Financial Transaction Tax: A Short Cut of the Pros, Cons and a Proposal', WIFO Working Papers No 344, 2009.

[53] Schulmeister's parameters show that the lower tax rate of 0.01 per cent would generate more revenue in absolute terms than the higher tax rates of 0.10 and 0.50 per cent largely because of market dampening at the higher rates.

charges and costs for dealers and other users and maintain up-to-date data on all cleared transactions.[54] This type of centralized clearing and settlement network can provide vital information for use in assessing and reporting the applicable amount of tax owed for an FTT. Moreover, future regulatory reforms will provide incentives such as lower capital charges for intermediaries to clear their derivatives trades through clearing houses and therefore a small transaction tax of 0.01 per cent (one basis point) or 0.005 per cent (one-half of one basis point) would be a small price to pay for the cost savings and reduced risk of clearing trades through clearing houses.

For both the FTT and CTT, an international mechanism for distribution of the proceeds will have to be agreed by the participating states. Once collected, the revenue could be distributed first to the national authorities of the jurisdiction where the market participants paid the tax. These governments might then have an obligation to use a pre-agreed portion of the revenue for domestic regulatory programmes, or to reimburse the government for direct assistance to the financial sector. They would then distribute a pre-agreed portion of the revenue to international aid organizations to be used to promote the UN MDGs and reduce existing official sector resource gaps in support of overseas development programmes. In addition, some of the revenue could be designated for a global solidarity fund to pay for climate change initiatives and provide other global public goods. In this way, financial tax revenue could be used both to achieve regulatory objectives and provide global public goods.

VI. The FTT/CTT and WTO Obligations

Foreign exchange and OTC market activity has become much more global with the proportion of cross-border transactions increasing to 65 per cent in 2010 from 62 per cent in 2007.[55] The significant increase in cross-border trading activity in the financial markets raises some important issues regarding how a CTT or a FTT may impinge on World Trade Organization (WTO) commitments. The WTO General Agreement on Trade in Services (GATS) and its Annex on Financial Services provide the international legal framework for the regulation of cross-border trade in financial services. Although the jurisdictional scope of the GATS does not cover the liberalization of cross-border capital flows, it does cover cross-border money transfers or payments that are necessary for Members to fulfil their specific commitments on market access and national treatment.

Under Article XI(1) of the GATS, a Member may not restrict 'international transfers and payments for current transactions relating to its specific commitments.' In other words, restrictions on capital flows or payments that are necessary to make a payment for cross-border trade in a services sector or subsector that is

[54] Robert Barnes, 'Counterparty Clearing House User Choice: An Evolving European Landscape', <http://www.oxera.com/cmsDocuments/Agenda_March%2010/Counterparty%20clearing%20 house%20user%20choice.pdf> (visited 25 July 2010).
[55] BIS Triennial 2010 Survey, above n 31, at 4.

subject to a GATS market access or national treatment commitment is not permitted under the GATS. Article XI provides:

Article XI: Payments and Transfers

1. Except under the circumstances envisaged in Article XII, a Member shall not apply restrictions on international transfers and payments for current transactions relating to its specific commitments.

Significantly, this prohibition on restrictions on international transfers and payments relates *only* to specific commitments made by WTO Members to liberalize their services sectors. For instance, where a Member has not made a liberalization commitment for a particular services sector, the Article XI prohibition would not apply. States have discretion through the WTO negotiation process to liberalize their services sectors on a sector-by-sector basis. Regarding financial services, most developed countries adopted in 1997 the Understanding on Commitments in Financial Services that sets out a blue- print for making liberalization commitments in financial services. The Understanding allows its 31 signatory members (counting the EU as one) to opt for a higher and more robust set of market-access and national treatment commitments.

The relevance of Article XI for the analysis of the CTT and FTT is that most developed countries and some developing countries that are WTO Members (i.e. the USA, the EU, Japan and some sub-Saharan African countries) have made substantial market-access commitments in many of their services sectors, thereby incurring an obligation under Article XI(1) not to impose *any restrictions* (including taxes or charges) on 'international transfers and payments' that relate to the provision of these cross-border services (including financial services). Although it is not clear whether the CTT and FTT are discriminatory measures under WTO jurisprudence, they could be interpreted as restrictions on cross-border transfers and payments related to specific commitments in violation of a Member's market access commitments under Article XVI GATS. The Annex on Financial Services, however, permits Members to depart from their GATS liberalization commitments (including the Article XI obligation not to impose restrictions on international transfers and payments) by adopting measures for a prudential reason that protect investors, depositors, policyholders or to maintain the stability and integrity of the financial system.[56] This is known as the 'prudential carve-out' and it is intended to provide member governments discretion to adopt measures for a prudential reason that may have the effect of departing from their liberalization commitments in services sectors.

The FTT and CTT would arguably qualify for the 'prudential carve-out' because they can potentially be designed to achieve prudential regulatory objectives in the

---

[56] Annex on Financial Services, Article 2(a). It states in relevant part: 'Notwithstanding any other provisions of the Agreement, a Member shall not be prevented from taking measures for prudential reasons, including for the protection of investors, depositors, policy holders, or persons to whom a fiduciary duty is owed by a financial service supplier, or to ensure the integrity and stability of the financial system.'

form of curbing excessive risk-taking, providing funds for bank resolution pro-grammes and paying for the social costs of financial crises. However, if the FTTs or CTTs are designed largely to raise revenue to pay for global public goods, such as the UN MDGs and climate-change measures, unrelated to regulatory objectives, they will have difficulty withstanding a legal challenge by a WTO Member under Article XI of the GATS.[57]

VII. Conclusion

The chapter examines the advantages and disadvantages of several types of financial taxes, including a bank balance sheet tax, a CTT and a broader FTT. The chapter suggests that FTTs, especially those applied to currency transactions and exchange-traded and OTC derivatives, could serve regulatory objectives while raising sus-tainable revenue to assist governments in paying for the social costs of financial crises and providing global public goods. Nevertheless, financial policy-makers should consider what type of financial tax is most appropriate for their jurisdictions and then adopt international principles with other national authorities to govern their implementation in order to minimize arbitrage and circumvention.

---

[57] Cf. also on prudential carve out in GATS Chapter 15 by Cottier and Krajewski, in this volume.

PART V

MONETARY REGULATION

20

The Role of International Law in Monetary Affairs

*Ernst Baltensperger and Thomas Cottier**

I. Introduction

A stable currency and well-functioning, efficient financial markets are cornerstones of economic and social systems. In particular, a stable currency is one of our most valuable public goods, comparable to well-functioning systems of law, public order or public finance and taxation. Malfunctioning, disordered currencies hamper economic performance and growth and can lead to extremes of economic and political decay.

A crucial question concerns the regulatory and institutional framework best suited to provide a sound monetary and financial environment. How should money be regulated, both at the national and at the international level? What are the proper institutional arrangements, in particular the roles of law and of informal networks of coordination? The recent financial and sovereign debt crisis brought to the forefront the complexity of this question. The interaction of domestic and international fora, of monetary policies and regulation of the financial sector and services, the impact of international trade, of fiscal policies and public debt leave us with a tangle of issues which are difficult to grasp, and extremely difficult to address in a coherent manner on the national, regional and international levels.

Monetary affairs, next to taxation, amount to one of the last and most solid bastions of national sovereignty.[1] Outside Europe, currencies have remained major attributes and symbols of statehood and national or regional identity.[2] While other policy areas have moved into modes of cooperation and even integration, monetary

* The authors are most grateful to Tetyana Payosova, MLaw, Research Fellow, Department of Economic Law, World Trade Institute for her assistance in preparing the paper, and to Rosa M. Lastra, co-editor, for her review and valuable comments.

[1] Rosa M. Lastra, *Legal Foundations of International Monetary Stability* (Oxford: Oxford University Press 2006) 4–5; Tullio Treves, 'Monetary Sovereignty Today', in Mario Giovanoli (ed), *International Monetary Fund: Issues for the New Millennium* (Oxford: Oxford University Press, 2000) 111–18, at 111.

[2] See for the role of the euro in the formation of European identity: Thomas Cottier and Nathaniel Greene, 'The Symbolic and Political Significance of the Euro', in *L'intégration Européenne: Historique et Perspectives* (European Integration: History and Perspectives) (Zürich: Schulthess, 2002) 163–77.

policies and the management of currencies have remained one of the strongholds of formally independent decision-making by national central bankers. The Eurozone of 16 Member States of the European Union is currently the only case in which sovereignty has been formally transferred in recent years to the regional level and it has a common and shared system of central banks with the European Central Bank at its heart. Almost all the other countries of the world operate under national sovereignty and informal modes of multilayered governance with allocations of powers and functions much less clearly defined and framed and largely left to the political process.

Following the financial crisis of 2007–09 and the impending challenges of massive public debt, traditional perceptions of sovereignty in monetary affairs need to be revisited. The crucial question is to what extent effective and preventive monetary policies call for enhanced international cooperation beyond current levels. How can the law contribute to achieving stability and prosperity in the field? We address the competitive relationship of different currencies and explore, on that basis, the potential of non- discrimination and of enhanced procedural obligations in the coordination of currencies. In doing so, we hope to encourage further research.

II. Economic Foundations: the Provision of Money and Monetary Services

A. The central bank monopoly

Given the importance of money in defining and expressing national sovereignty, issues of monopoly and competition in the provision of currencies and monetary services play a major role in the discussion of monetary affairs and their regulation. There is a presumption in favor of competition and free trade among many economists. At the same time, certain elements of monopoly in money and finance have a long-standing and strong tradition. Even as unambiguous a liberal and pro-market economist as Milton Friedman accepted the monopoly of government in currency issue and monetary policy.[3] 'There is probably no other area of economic activity with respect to which government intervention has been so uniformly accepted', he stated in his seminal contribution 'A Program for Monetary Stability'. He asked whether money and credit can be left to the free market, and answered the question explicitly in the negative:

These, then, are the features of money that justify government intervention: the resource cost of a pure commodity currency and hence its tendency to become partly fiduciary; the peculiar difficulty of enforcing contracts involving promises to pay that serve as a medium of exchange and of preventing fraud in respect to them; the technical monopoly character of a purely fiduciary currency which makes essential the setting of some external limit on its

---

[3] Milton Friedman, *Essays in Positive Economics* (Chicago: University of Chicago Press, 1953) 8, 217.

amount; and, finally, the pervasive character of money which means that the issuance of money has important effects on parties other than those directly involved and gives special importance to the preceding features.[4]

Historically, the emergence of local monopolies for particular currencies can be explained by the seignorage revenue that accrues from the creation of money. Since the beginning of coinage, it was known that the right to create money was linked to corresponding revenues. When metallic coins were used, this revenue accrued either from fees the coin minter could levy or from the difference between the value of the metal and its purchasing power. In medieval times, only certain feudal lords or 'seigneurs' were entitled to the right of coinage, which was usually granted by the emperor or the king (hence the term 'seignorage').[5]

The use of currencies led to competition between different currencies and coins, in particular if political domains of power and governance were strongly fractioned. This raised the question of the advantages and disadvantages of such diversity of currency and types of money, and of the competition associated with it. Uncounted examples of such competition are known from monetary history, interpreted as evidence for its feasibility in some cases and as proof of its inefficiency in others. With the advent of the nation state in Europe, however, central governments were conferred the exclusive right of coinage almost everywhere. In many places, this put an end to the coexistence of different currencies in circulation and allowed the central government to claim the entire profit from creating money for itself.

The introduction of paper money in the form of bank notes offered the additional opportunity to only partially cover the note issue with metal (usually gold or silver), so that the issuing bank could invest the uncovered part of its outstanding notes in interest-bearing assets. Hence, it allowed the bank to make a profit in excess of the income from seignorage due to coinage. The possibility of making profits by issuing notes was one reason why the right to issue was conferred to central governments over time. Today, this right is vested in the central bank in most countries. The abolition of mandatory metal coverage for central bank money issue, which is characteristic of practically all monetary systems today, allows central banks, in principle, to issue this money through buying interest-bearing assets and to vary their nominal quantity in a discretionary way. In such a system of paper money, the value of money depends crucially on the credibility of the central bank and on its commitment to keep the quantity of money stable, relative to the level of economic activity.

Over time, despite the central bank monopoly, the private financial sector has created better and better substitutes for central bank money in the form of demand

[4] Milton Friedman, *A Program for Monetary Stability*, The Millar Lectures Number Three (New York City: Fordham University Press, 1960) 8. See also an earlier work of one of the authors, Ernst Baltensperger, 'Monopoly and Competition in Money and Credit', in Ulrich Bindseil, Justus Haucap and Christian Wey, *Institutions in Perspective: Festschrift in Honour of Rudolf Richter on the Occasion of his 80th Birthday* (Tübingen: Mohr Siebeck, 2006) 205–18, at 206.
[5] See Ernst Baltensperger and Thomas J. Jordan, 'Seignorage und Notenbankgewinn', 4 *Quartalsheft der Schweizerischen Nationalbank* 43 (1998).

deposits and other highly liquid liabilities. There is usually more or less pronounced competition between the issuers of such private money. However, it is a key property of these private forms of money that they are always convertible into government money at a fixed price (convertibility, duty of redemption). In this sense, these types of obligation represent money 'derived' from government money. For this reason, competition between issuers of bank money is of a different kind to competition between issuers of 'original' money.

B. Monopoly abuse and the argument for currency competition

In 1976, Hayek, based upon previous work, sparked a controversy about the advantages and disadvantages of currency competition, i.e. competition between alternative 'original' monies.[6] Hayek's argument has its roots in the obvious risk that monopoly, even a currency monopoly, can lead to inefficiency and the temptation of abuse and has often done so, particularly in the context of the pure paper money systems which came to prevail during the twentieth century. This is reflected in numerous instances of inflation that characterize this era.[7] Hayek argued that abolishing the currency monopoly of government and allowing for private, competing currencies offers the best chance to end these abuses. He was thinking of autonomous ('original') currencies of the paper money type. He thought that 'convertibility' was necessary for a monopolist, but not for competing suppliers who can only stay in business if they supply a money at least as attractive as that of their competitors. In his view, every supplier would determine the quality of its product indirectly by regulating the quantity of its money supply, and competition would take over the role of the convertibility requirement.[8]

1. Pros and cons of competition and monopoly

Hayek's contribution on currency competition resulted in a relatively broad academic debate on the subject during the 1970s and 1980s.[9] This discussion has since calmed down. It has remained without any practical influence. However, it has an important bearing on international regulation of money. The academic debate focused on a variety of problems of the currency competition proposal,

---

[6] Friedrich August von Hayek, *Denationalisation of Money—The Argument Refined*, 2nd ed. (London: The Institute of Economic Affairs, 1978). The concern goes back to his work *Monetary Nationalism and International Stability* (London: Longmans, 1937) or even before, as one of his students at the London School of Economics, Vera [Lutz] Smith (who married Friedrich Lutz), published her thesis Vera C. Smith, The Rationale of Central Banking (London: PS King, 1936), in 1936, paying special attention to the role of note issue. See generally, Rosa M. Lastra, *Central Banking and Banking Regulation* (London: LSE, Financial Markets Group, 1996) 252–7. But see also Benjamin Klein, 'The Competitive Supply of Money', 6 *Journal of Money, Credit and Banking* 421 (1974).

[7] See e.g. Peter Bernholz, *Regimes and Inflation. History, Economic and Political Relationships* (Cheltenham: Edward Elgar, 2003).

[8] See Hayek, above n 6, at 192.

[9] Some significant works of the *laissez faire* proponents in this area include: Klein, above n 6; Lawrence H. White, *Free Banking in Britain: Theory, Experience and Debate, 1800–1845* (Cambridge: Cambridge University Press, 1984).

which made it look very questionable as a feasible, practical arrangement. Major difficulties of the proposal relate to:

(1) the cost of information, transaction, accounting and storage of multiple currency systems and the cost advantages of a single currency;

(2) the network and scale effects of money: a currency is more valuable to its potential users the greater the number of users and the probability that potential partners in trade will accept it without question (money as a 'public good');

(3) the 'time inconsistency problem' tempting the money supplier to deviate from his previously announced promises, undermining his credibility and the trust in his product;

(4) the notion that private money must almost necessarily be accompanied by a promise of convertibility (into gold, a bundle of goods or another 'dominant' money) in order to be acceptable, and that government is the only agent which can create the credibility required for a paper money without convertibility (a 'fiat money system'), due to its monopoly to tax;

(5) the view that given the above-mentioned network and scale effects on currency competition, even if it works as it should according to Hayek, it would ultimately lead to a single currency (or a very limited number of currencies), so that a monopoly situation would arise anew (money as a 'natural monopoly').

In its overall conclusion, this debate resulted in a defence by a majority of views of the government monopoly in the provision of money.[10] The idea of money as a national symbol (an expression of national sovereignty) further tended to strengthen this view. However, it should be noted that this does not answer the fundamental concern which led Hayek to advance his proposal in the first place: the problem of potential abuse of monopoly, the time inconsistency problem and the temptation to deviate from announced promises, apply to the currency monopoly of the government as much (if not more) than to competitive suppliers. So, if competition does not solve this problem, protection against the (undoubtedly existing) perils of a currency monopoly must be sought along other lines. This is why Friedman in his proposal in 1960 emphasized that the government monopoly must be a *regulated monopoly*, and made a concrete proposal for the realization of such a regulation in the form of a constitutional rule—his famous money growth rule.[11] Over the past decade, the idea that the mandates of central banks must be anchored in law, ideally at the constitutional level, has gained widespread support for reasons along these lines.

---

[10] See for instance Charles Goodhart, *The Evolution of Central Banks* (Cambridge, MA: MIT Press, 1988).

[11] See Friedman, above n 4.

2. The coexistence of currency regimes

Despite its advantages, there are *limits to the argument in favour of a currency monopoly*. If there were none, why stop short of a universal, world monopoly for money issuance? The arguments that favour a currency monopoly are not applicable only to competition between various small, local currencies (as in medieval times) or different private units of money within a country. In principle, they can also be used as a justification of a *union of different national currencies* (and they were used accordingly at the foundation of the European Monetary Union). Ultimately, this would lead us to a *single world currency*—an idea that was discussed at the inception of the International Monetary Fund (IMF, or Fund) (Keynes' 'bancor'),[12] but which, for good reasons, has received virtually no support since then. The following limitations, in particular, come to mind:

(1) There may be limits to the network and scale effects mentioned above in support of monopoly. A currency area may require a certain size, but it may not need to encompass the whole world or entire continents. Possibly, a global economy with a limited number of national (or, as in the case of the euro, regional) currencies competing with each other may represent an ideal mix balancing the advantages and disadvantages of both monopoly and competition.

(2) As long as the world is politically organized along the lines of sovereign nation states with social, economic and fiscal autonomy, there are good reasons to define monetary autonomy along the same lines. Monetary unions short of common economic and fiscal policies lack sustainability and stability. They either fail or move towards transfers of fiscal and regulatory powers to the union. The European Monetary Union is the prime example of this process.[13]

(3) In his seminal contribution on optimal currency areas, Mundell has drawn attention to the fact that next to its benefits, a single currency may also have significant costs in a world characterized by heterogeneous, region-specific rigidities and frictions (such as lack of factor mobility, limited wage and price flexibility). The entire world can hardly be an 'optimal currency area' in the sense of Mundell.[14]

---

[12] Keynes considered the creation of a new international currency, which he named 'bancor', that would support other international policies regarding trade, investment and development. See Keith Horsefield (ed), *The International Monetary Fund 1945–1965, Volume III: Documents* (Washington, DC: International Monetary Fund, 1969) 3–18 and 19–36. See generally Lastra, above n 1, at 345–379 with further references.

[13] See on regional monetary unions: International Law Association, Committee on International Monetary Law, *Report of the Seventy-Third Conference*, Rio de Janeiro, 2008, at 407–412, <http://www.ila-hq.org/en/news/index.cfm/nid/C687CFE8-BE13-463C-83636151B231A1C7>. Further discussion on monetary unions: Francesco Paolo Mongelli, 'On the Benefits and Costs of a Monetary Union', Center for Economic Policy Research, Policy Insight No 46, March 2010.

[14] Robert Mundell, 'A Theory of Optimal Currency Areas', 51 *American Economic Review* 657 (1961), at 658–9.

In conclusion, there are strong arguments for the coexistence of a number, albeit limited, of independent national and/or regional currencies. Such coexistence will also very likely characterize the future. Currencies have grown historically and are difficult to attack and replace by competing currencies, provided they satisfy certain minimal quality requirements. The fact that different currencies are, directly and indirectly, competing in some way through international financial markets and the international effects of national economic policies helps to limit the range of national monopolies, at least to some extent.

Even so, the problem of the optimal control and regulation of central bank monopolies, as addressed by Friedman, remains. It is not settled by the facts of international currency competition. The problem first appears at the *national level*. Currency monopolies have the potential to abuse, even if they are in the hands of government. This is particularly true for government monopolies in a paper money standard, which technically cannot become insolvent because they can issue any amount of money they wish. This is why they require public regulation. From today's perspective, this is best done *via constitutional and legal norms and requirements which oblige the central bank to comply with a precise mandate*. Over the past two decades, significant progress in applying and implementing this idea has been made, both in theory and in practice.

III. From National to International Regulation of Money: The Need for Coordination

The problem discussed above also appears at the international level: there is an obvious need for international coordination of some kind in today's globalized economy. But this is not specific to our age. International coordination of monetary systems and policies has a long history, ranging from loose forms of informal cooperation to fixed exchange rate arrangements and even attempts at full monetary union between independent, sovereign states.

A. Alternative structures of international coordination

1. Competition between independent central banks: the flexible exchange rate system

One of the prototypes among different systems of international money is a flexible exchange rate arrangement with fully autonomous national (or regional) central banks, each issuing its specific ('original') money and determining the relative value of this money via its policy of issue (i.e. the resulting relative scarcity of its product and the rate of inflation implied by it). In the 1950s and 1960s, in view of the increasing difficulties of the fixed exchange rate system of Bretton Woods in force at that time, a broad array of academic economists made the case for such a system, arguing that it would lead to smooth and automatic adjustment of international financial imbalances and thus represents an ideal instrument for international coordination (e.g. Friedman,[15] Sohmen[16] and Lutz[17] to name but a few). The system of flexible exchange rates adopted after the breakdown of the old arrangement in 1973 has prevailed ever since. It has, however, never worked as smoothly and elegantly as promised by academic blueprints. Almost from the beginning, it was characterized by numerous episodes of excessive exchange rate fluctuation and foreign exchange market turbulence. Nevertheless, the system has great advantages. The major advantages are that (i) it leaves monetary policy as an independent tool of macroeconomic policy and adjustment to the national (or regional) central banks and their governments, and (ii) it preserves an element of competition (and thus checks to potential abuse) in the world money system. Still, annoyance with exchange rate disturbances and the degree of exchange rate uncertainty associated with it has led to a search for additional instruments of coordination, in particular, currency boards, aimed at dampening exchange rate volatility and the planning uncertainty resulting from it.[18] Obviously, what is required is a more or less explicit harmonization and coordination of the goals and procedures of the various central banks involved.

2. Harmonization of goals and procedures through loose international arrangements

International cooperation can assume many different forms. Loose, ad hoc forms of coordination among the concerned governments in periods of stress have been the usual approach in the past few decades. Formalized, 'systematic' coordination has been restricted to not very effective monitoring through international organizations, especially in the form of IMF 'exchange rate surveillance'.[19]

In the past two decades, such an informal approach has been helped greatly by a developing consensus on the appropriate goals of monetary policy. Price stability received increasingly widespread support as the primary, long-term goal of monetary policy, with policies aiming at ('low' rates of) inflation becoming the dominant strategy among central banks. Short-run cyclical stabilization of the real economy was regularly added as a second central objective. Some controversy has remained about the relative weight and position of these two objectives ('hierarchical' central bank mandates of the European Central Bank (ECB), the Bank of England, or the Swiss National Bank (SNB), versus the US Federal Reserve's dual or multiple mandate including growth, employment and the stability of the financial system). But this did not prevent a major worldwide shift from the inflation-prone monetary environment of the preceding decades to a culture of (much more) monetary stability. Central bank independence, along with the principles of transparency

---

[15] Milton Friedman, 'The Case for Flexible Exchange Rates' in Friedman, above n 3, at 157–203.
[16] Egon Sohmen, *Flexible Exchange Rates* (Chicago: University of Chicago Press, 1961).
[17] Friedrich A. Lutz, 'The Case for Flexible Exchange Rates', VII *Banca Nazionale del Lavoro Quarterly Review* 175 (1954).
[18] See Lastra, above n 1, at 73–9.
[19] See, on IMF exchange rate surveillance, Lastra, above n 1, at 399–404.

and accountability, were at the same time widely established as fundamental elements of a successful framework for the conduct of monetary policy. This convergence in monetary policies was essential for the dramatic decline of financial and real volatilities observed over the 1990s and 2000s until the outbreak of the recent financial crisis, referred to by many as the 'great moderation' (and mistakenly viewed as the coming of a 'new economic age'). However, note that this consensus is fragile. It has been severely strained by the financial crisis of the past three—years and its fallout, and it is likely to be even more tested in the future. As already mentioned, the hierarchy of price stability and cyclical stabilization as prime goals of monetary policy, despite legal codification in particular in the German Bundes-bank Act, Swiss law and the Maastricht Treaty, has never been unambiguously recognized. The very definition of inflation and of which numerical inflation target is appropriate (and consistent with price stability) is unsettled.[20] Considerations of financial sector stability are suggested as additional goals of monetary policy. The immense levels of public indebtedness and the dismal fiscal situation of many governments are likely to put pressure on monetary policy in many countries. The concept of central bank independence is itself increasingly being questioned. Consequently, international divergence in monetary policy could well become more frequent again. The need for international coordination might appear in a different light under these changed conditions, and a more formalized approach to the quest for this coordination might seem desirable. But the same developments will make this quest even more demanding than before.

3. Harmonization through international agreements

Coordination could be achieved through a *formal international agreement on the goals and procedures of monetary policy* among participants of equal standing. It will usually take place under the auspices of an existing international organization, such as the IMF or the Bank for International Settlements (BIS) or a newly created one. This institution could serve as a mere platform for discussion and exchange (like the BIS in the Basel process on international banking regulation), or could itself be given an active and material role (like the IMF in the plans of those who see it as the future issuer of a new global currency). We may distinguish between symmetric and asymmetric models.

(a) *Symmetric models.* Models of coordination can be symmetric, with equal decision rights for all participants. An ideal case of a symmetric solution would be a formal international agreement on the goals and procedures of monetary policy among all major countries and with equal standing for all (an 'international monetary charter'). One possibility would be to install an institution such as the *IMF as coordinator and supervisor with a formal mandate* (reaching beyond its current exchange rate surveillance). The IMF would draw up a charter of rules (goals and procedures) for sound monetary policy. All members would commit to

---

[20] See Rosa M. Lastra and Geoffrey Wood, 'The Crisis of 2007–2009: Nature, Causes and Reactions', Chapter 1 of this volume.

observe these rules, and they would agree on a set of decision mechanisms, supervisory procedures and sanctions for cases of violation. In lieu of the IMF, the BIS or possibly a new and separate institution along the lines of the World Trade Organization (WTO) in international trade regulation, could be given this role. However, the IMF would be likely to prevail as a candidate, given that it already exists, has a very broad membership, formal legitimacy, and operates in precisely this area.

Symmetry would also exist in the case of a common adoption of a particular monetary regime, e.g. the gold standard, or in the extreme situation of a single 'world money' issued by a world central bank governed equally by all. The international gold standard was an example of coordination through law. In principle, it was a regulation at the level of national law: adoption of common national standards regulating the respective national currencies, with an implicit understanding of this common structure by all participants. Only in the case of a monetary union, such as the Latin Currency Union, was explicit international coordination at the legal level involved.[21] In order to work, such an arrangement must be based on a common set of principles governing monetary and general economic policies (monetary stability, fiscal stability, free trade and mobility). The break-up of the gold standard historically reflects the end of international consensus on these principles.

Symmetric coordination could, finally, be achieved through the *adoption of a single currency on a worldwide scale* (a '*world monetary union*', '*world money*'). This is a utopian idea with no serious chance of realization in the short term. Its disadvantages would probably be excessive.[22] Its long-run stability would be highly doubtful, too. But it is occasionally suggested, usually with the IMF as the money issuer and manager, as a possible approach.

(b) *Asymmetric models.* Alternatively, coordination within an international agreement could work through *adoption of a 'lead country', or a small number of lead countries, and subordination of the remaining partners* to the monetary policy decisions of the leader(s). Given existing inequalities in size and power in the global economy, asymmetric models have a greater likelihood of realization than symmetric ones. Historical examples are thus easier to find. A prime example was the arrangement of Bretton Woods, the system of fixed (but—under certain conditions— adjustable) exchange rates in force in the first few decades after World War II, with the US dollar as lead currency under the gold standard.[23] But such a system is feasible and sustainable only with sufficient trust in the lead country and its currency. Bretton

---

[21] See e.g. Barry Eichengreen and Marc Flandreau (eds), *The Gold Standard in Theory and History*, 2nd ed. (London: Routledge, 1997).

[22] See at page 4 above.

[23] The par value regime, often referred to as the Bretton Woods regime, was a two-tier system of convertibility, also known as the gold-dollar standard. According to this par value regime, the value of currency of each participating member was defined in terms of gold or alternatively in terms of the US dollar of 1 July 1944, which had a fixed gold value (one ounce of gold was equal to $35). For a history of the regime see, *inter alia*, Lastra, above n 1, at 356–64; and Andreas F. Lowenfeld, 'The International Monetary System: A Look Back Over Seven Decades', Chapter 3 of this volume.

Woods worked fairly well, as long as the US maintained a responsible monetary policy course consistent with expectations of long-term price stability, and hence with stable exchange rate patterns (apart from structural changes in the real world economy requiring real exchange rate adjustments, which presents no problem). But it became unstable as soon as the USA shifted (for various reasons) to an inflationary policy course in the 1960s and 1970s. Under these conditions, the dollar could no longer provide a sufficiently firm anchor to the world monetary system. Speculation and monetary disturbance arose as a consequence of this shift, and the system did not survive this unstable environment for long. Earlier attempts at fixed exchange rates and monetary union (such as the Latin Currency Union under French leadership in the decades before World War I) eventually declined for similar reasons. Calls for a 'New Bretton Woods' have been heard again and again since the original version broke down in 1973. But it is very difficult to see which single currency on its own would be sufficiently credible today to give us much hope for a revival of such an approach.

Asymmetric approaches with an oligopoly of a small number of core participants and passive behaviour of all the remaining partners have not infrequently been advanced in the international discussion. In the 1980s, for example, proposals by McKinnon[24] and by Williamson[25] received much attention. McKinnon's plan at the time envisaged a coordinated management of the 'world money supply' by US, German and Japanese monetary authorities, with the aim of maintaining price level stability and keeping exchange rates between the US dollar, the Deutsch Mark and the yen within narrow bands through appropriate exchange market interventions. Today, McKinnon would probably select the US dollar, the euro and the Chinese renminbi. Williamson's idea involved steering worldwide nominal demand through the appropriate coordination of national monetary and fiscal policies while establishing narrow target zones for exchange rates. A practical, but only partially effective and short-lived example fitting this mould was the Plaza Accord of 1985.[26]

A world central bank dominated by one country, or a small group of countries, would be equally asymmetric. On a world scale, proposals of this type have no history of implementation. Agreements on monetary policy goals, among the diversity of partners found are extremely difficult to achieve. Corresponding 'cartel agreements' risk either being too loose and vague to create sufficient constraint and trust, or else being unstable, as individual participants have incentives to deviate from the agreement, as long as the others play according to the rules. In a regional

---

[24] Ronald McKinnon, 'Monetary and Exchange Rate Policies for International Financial Stability: A Proposal', 2 *Journal of Economic Perspectives* 83 (1988); Ronald McKinnon, *An International Standard for Monetary Stabilization* (Washington, DC: Institute for International Economics, 1984).

[25] John Williamson, 'Comment on McKinnon's Monetary Rule', 2 *Journal of Economic Perspectives* 113 (1988); see also Hali J. Edison, Marcus H. Miller, and John Williamson, 'On Evaluating and Extending the Target Zone Proposal', 9(1) *Journal of Policy Modeling* 199 (1987).

[26] G8, 'Announcement of the Ministers of Finance and Central Bank Governors of France, Germany, Japan, the United Kingdom, and the USA' (Plaza Accord), 22 September 1985, <http://www.g8.utoronto.ca/finance/fm850922.htm> (visited 10 July 2010).

context, attempts of this kind have more chance of success. For instance, the European Monetary Union can be interpreted in this way. Of course, as the current problems of the euro show, long-term stability and success are difficult to maintain even at the level of a regional agreement.

B. On the difficulty of reaching and maintaining international agreements on monetary policy goals and procedures

A central condition for a credible, sustainable solution, regardless of the particular symmetric or asymmetric informal or formal mode of coordination, is the basic consensus on the possibilities, goals and procedures of monetary policy. Without such common foundations, any system will sooner or later break up. An asymmetric regime, such as the system of Bretton Woods, requires that the 'passive' partners respect the major policy decisions of the lead partner; otherwise, they will not be content with their passive role for long. Bretton Woods did indeed break down when this condition ceased to be met in the course of the 1960s and 1970s. A symmetric system even more obviously requires mutually consistent views on fundamental principles of monetary policy.

Broad international agreement on goals and procedures of monetary policy is extremely difficult to achieve and maintain, if something more than general statements without much content is sought. Agreements on principles and goals in vague and loose terms are easier to reach. But they are not very helpful in generating trust and confidence (they may even have the opposite effect, if they are too obviously vague), and thus are not sufficient to provide the required anchor for the stability and expectation of long-run survival of a monetary arrangement. Major obstacles are the following:

(1) The *fragility of the consensus on goals and procedures* already described above. In fact, diversity of views on monetary policy goals and procedures has a long history, and the convergence of the last two decades may represent the exception, rather than the rule. So, more disagreement may reappear.

(2) Despite the recent consensus, as already mentioned, there is disagreement about the relative roles and weights of price level stability and cyclical stabilization and about the appropriate *numerical targets* (appropriate inflation target; inflation target consistent with 'price stability').

(3) Even if an agreement with a well-formulated, strict and credible mandate or charter could be reached, *time inconsistency considerations* create serious enforcement problems. Participants have (potentially strong) *incentives to deviate* from agreed upon behavior, as long as other participants stick to the rules, be it for reasons of cyclical stimulation or as a means of real debt relief. This undermines the credibility and stability of the system and reduces the likelihood of an acceptable agreement to begin with.

Regulation through international law is difficult enough in the area of trade. There is more agreement among relevant participants (academics and practitioners) on the principle advantages of free trade ('gains from trade') than there is on 'stable money', low inflation, and the advantages of monetary stability. Direct linkages to fiscal policy (monetary stability is undermined by lack of fiscal discipline in the long run), where divergence is even greater, increase the heterogeneity of views further. It is true that Bretton Woods in 1944 was less controversial than the comparable initiative in international trade, the International Trade Organization (Havana Charter), which failed [success in the trade area came later in a more modest form with the General Agreement on Tariffs and Trade (GATT)]. However, it must be seen that Bretton Woods still reflected the spirit of the international gold standard with its implicit consensus on central economic policy principles. This consensus has gone and is difficult to resurrect.

C. Disciplining national monopolies through international currency competition

An international, worldwide monopoly in money with no fear of competition from any other source would probably be the worst kind of monopoly we can imagine. There is little reason to believe that it would be able and willing to create a stable and trustworthy currency and maintain it over an extended period. Incentives to deviate from an initial 'stability promise' would be strong and credibility difficult to establish. Elements of competition and contestability would be sorely missed. An agreement in the form of an 'international cartel' dominated by a few big players (mainly the USA, China, the EU and Japan) would have quite similar effects. It would be extremely difficult to establish a trustworthy, stable currency under such a system, and politically the system would almost certainly prove unstable. Maintenance of a sufficient number of independent national or regional currencies therefore is crucial as a means of control and discipline of monopoly abuse in the field of money. However, the quest for international monetary stability makes it highly desirable to have them all subject to a strong commitment to common basic policy objectives.

An international agreement on common monetary policy objectives (and stable exchange rates), to be successful and permanent, requires as a precondition a mutual understanding on certain parameters of economic policy in other areas, in particular, factor and product market flexibility (price flexibility, unhindered mobility) and fiscal responsibility. An eroding willingness to respect these conditions typically induces attempts to stabilize the system through administrative controls in other fields, especially restrictions on trade and international movement of capital and labor. In the Bretton Woods era (and partly before then), this was increasingly a problem. Thus the system of Bretton Woods was never a particularly successful example of international monetary coordination. The present build-up of great international imbalances reflects the fact that there is insufficient flexibility in the world economic system. It is possible to react by allowing for more flexibility in exchange rates (i.e. in the area of money), or by restricting trade and factor mobility. In terms of economic costs, the second option is probably much worse. It would be desirable to reestablish international consensus on all these objectives. If this is not feasible, it may be best to allow for some range of exchange rate adjustment (i.e. for more modest goals in international monetary coordination).

IV. Framing Currency Competition in International Law

Past experience and the prospects of addressing monetary affairs in terms of international law and international agreements set out above help to identify the proper potential role of international law in the field. Given the constraints imposed by the existence of different currencies and legacies of national sovereignty, we submit that the emphasis of international monetary law should be on framing fair competition and interaction of different currencies. The law may contribute to this both in terms of substance and procedure in achieving agreed objectives required to bring about currency competition. We recall the relevance of international trade regulation and investment protection as a prerequisite for effective currency competition in international relations.

A. The contribution of international trade regulation and investment protection

International law is not devoid of substance relevant to monetary affairs. Short of common economic policies and given the difficulties of addressing monetary policies in international law, it is evident that the principles and rules regulating and stabilizing trade and the open market are of paramount importance to the monetary system. Competition between currencies depends upon an open and stable trading system. On substance, and apart from creating an appropriate organizational framework for monetary policy, the multilateral trading system and a wide network of preferential trade agreements perhaps amount to the most important contribution of contemporary substantive international law to monetary affairs.

Recourse to tariffs and quantitative restrictions was the primary reaction to the Great Depression, leading to a decline in international trade and a worldwide recession. This experience, and lessons drawn from it, provided the basis for stabilizing trade policies by international agreements. The 1934 Reciprocal Trade Act of the USA formed the basis of subsequent bilateral agreements, the concept of which was essentially multilateralized by the GATT. Building upon GATT, principles and trade rules have been developed over the past 60 years. The contrast to monetary affairs could not be stronger: while trade rules focus on substantive principles and issues, leaving procedures in today's WTO and within bilateral and regional agreements (except for the EU) at low organizational levels, monetary affairs focus on decision-making and allocation of powers with very little law in substance. And yet, the two regimes need to be mutually supportive. International trade requires a stable monetary regime, and the monetary regime requires, for reasons discussed above, a stable and predictable trading order. Securing a relatively open and stable trading system has been a major contribution of international law and policy over the 15 years since the WTO was founded. Empirical research shows that rent-seeking protectionism and recourse to trade remedies in relation to growing trade has gradually decreased.[27] The financial crisis of 2007–09 has not triggered extensive recourse to protectionist measures.[28] This is in strong contrast to the Great Depression, and it is fair to say that the WTO system has weathered the storm reasonably well. The stability of the trading system contributed to limiting the damage done by the financial crisis, and provided its main basis in international law for a recovery of the world economy in 2010. Without it, the financial crisis might have included an outright breakdown of the international monetary system. The same is true for international investment law. Its principles and rules prevent governments from taking outright protectionist measures, unduly impeding the mobility of capital. Albeit less detailed than trade rules, investment protection assumes an important role in stabilizing relations and bringing about greater predictability. Other areas of international law stabilizing the relations of nations may assist in this role, knitting the fabric within which monetary policies operate.

B. What role for law in international monetary affairs?

Framing competition among competing currencies is a primary task, in accordance with the findings discussed above. The role of law in achieving these goals mainly consists in establishing and maintaining a structural and procedural architecture with the independence of monetary authorities from direct political control at its heart. Yet, there is very little that it contributes directly in terms of substantive law.[29] In recent times, monetary policies have been economic policies and were firmly dominated by economic methodology. Indeed, upon leaving the gold standard and the fixed exchange rates, there was very little left for a regulatory and legal approach to monetary affairs. The law plays a larger role in flanking policies: trade regulation (goods and services), investment, fiscal (taxation), lending and spending (subsidies and public procurement) and financial markets, but is not so involved in the core areas of monetary affairs: interest rates and supply of money, monetary intervention and exchange rate policies. And what is true for domestic law is even more so for international law. Given the difficulties described in finding an international consensus, it comes as no surprise that there are hardly any substantive rules on the subject. However, even the procedural and structural rules are weak. The law does not play a role in achieving overarching goals of

---

[27] National Board of Trade, 'Open Trade or Protectionism?', Stockholm 2009, <http://www.kommers.se/upload/Analysarkiv/Publikationer/open%20trade%20or%20protectionism.pdf> (visited 17 June 2010).
[28] WTO, Trade Policy Review Board (TPRB), 'Report to the TPRB from the Director-General on Trade-Related Developments', WT/TRP/OV/W/3, 14 June 2010, para 13.
[29] See Lastra, above n 1; Andreas F. Lowenfeld, *International Economic Law*, 2nd ed. (Oxford: Oxford University Press, 2008) 598–803.

monetary policy and in bringing about and stabilizing the competitive relationship among different currencies.

The question arises of the extent to which these monetary operations can and should be framed in legal terms beyond the general framework of international law (trade and investment) and domestic law (property, contracts, torts). Regulation of monetary affairs does not seem to be unique. It is about meaningfully regulating a monopoly and as to how different monopolies should interact and compete at the international level.

First, it is essentially a matter of defining a proper mix of law and economic policies within a defined framework. Little is known, it seems, about whether and how complex issues could and should be addressed in law. The relationship between law and economics requires further research and exploration. New modes and instruments may be designed to respond to the challenges more appropriately. The problem lies less in matters of principle than in matters of degree. The law should define the framework and scope of conduct within which market-based allocations of resources operate. With a view to enhancing transparency and predictability—the essence of legal security—one could examine how a future global system could and should employ legally defined thresholds of interventions and boundaries. Such a system would thus define—as in previous snake models—margins of appreciation within which economic policies are based on market forces and economics, while international law would define the thresholds to which central banks would be accountable. Operations would thus be framed in terms of international law. Non-compliance would trigger responsibilities and actions by appropriate international bodies, ranging from naming and shaming to full-fledged monetary sanctions.

Secondly, the relationship of substantive rules and procedural rights and obligations needs to be explored. How far can procedure substitute for substance and to what extent does it depend upon substantive rules? To what extent might procedures secure competition among different currencies?

These considerations result in the following basic questions:

(1) How can monetary policy in terms of substance, and beyond institutional design and allocation of decision-making powers, be addressed in legal terms?

(2) How can monetary policy in terms of substance, and beyond institutional design and allocation of powers, be addressed by international law?

(3) What is and should be the role of procedural rules and of dispute settlement in international monetary law? How do they relate to substantive law?

(4) How should powers be allocated among international institutions in the field? This is the question of horizontal allocation of powers and architecture at the level of international law.

(5) How should the relationship between the international and the national levels be defined?

This question relates to vertical allocation of powers within the overall architecture of the system.

Obviously, the answers to these questions depend upon perceptions of national sovereignty and political will to engage in international cooperation and even integration. In addressing them conceptually and in research, it may be useful to take the following into account.

1. Recourse to the doctrine of multilayered governance

In addressing these questions, recourse could be made to models developed on multilayered governance, largely induced by problems encountered in the regula-tion of international trade and in the field of human rights protection. According to these models of consitutionalization, it is essentially a matter of appropriate and functional allocation of powers, both horizontally and vertically.[30] These alloca-tions need to match criteria of legitimacy and modes of decision-making on different layers. While all layers are informed by the same legal principles and foundations—as they are essentially human operations at all levels and institutions—different factors of legitimacy, in particular democracy, justice, equality, non-discrimination, human rights, legal security, stability and peaceful relations, are not evenly allocated to all layers alike. Thus, the factors legitimizing the monetary system will remain stability and peaceful relations in a competitive relationship, while democracy or human rights cannot play a significant role in this field. These issues need to be addressed in manifold facets, including a review of the goals of monetary policy, and it is impossible to provide general answers at the outset of the quest for international law.

2. What can we learn from competition law?

The coexistence of different national monopolies recalls legal disciplines established for dealing with monopolies in competition policy: the obligation to operate them in a non-discriminatory and transparent manner, to limit rights to the extent necessary to achieve the policy goals of the instrument and the importance of protecting others from abuse of dominant positions and the abuse of rights.[31] How could such principles play a role in bringing about accountability and legitimacy of monetary policies? To what extent is the principle of denying the abuse of rights, based upon the principle of good faith, relevant in the field? What could be the potential of transferring these principles to monetary law? Could this provide a basis

---

[30] See further, on the issue of multilayered governance, Thomas Cottier 'Multilayered Governance, Pluralism and Moral Conflict', 16(2) *Indiana Journal of Global Legal Studies* 647 (2009); Thomas Cottier and Maya Hertig, 'The Prospects of 21st Century Constitutionalism', 7 *Max Planck Yearbook of United Nations Law* 261 (2003); Thomas Cottier, 'Challenges Ahead in International Economic Law', 12 *Journal of International Economic Law* 3 (1999).

[31] See Christopher Bellamy and Graham D. Child, *Common Market Law of Competition*, 4th edition (London: Sweet & Maxwell, 1993); Ivo van Bael and Jean-Francois Bellis, *Competition Law of the European Community*, 5th ed. (Alphen: Kluwer Law International, 2010).

for addressing fundamental imbalances which are induced by recourse to monopoly powers in setting exchange rates, pegging them to another currency beyond certain bounds? How could they be rendered more specific and operational? Recourse to principles of competition policy and the law of monopolies and subsidization exercised in public interests (*service public*) does not seem to offer a sufficient answer to the challenges of financial regulation.[32] Yet, the underlying idea of monopoly powers exercised by nation states through their central banks could be further explored. It necessarily entails the need to address these disciplines on the level of international law. It also leads to the broader question of how disciplines developed in international trade regulation could be put to work in framing currency competition.

In this context, it would also be appropriate to examine the extent to which principles of graduation should be used to reflect particular needs and the constellations of developing countries and emerging economies.[33] The essence of graduation consists in linking rights and obligations to the levels of competitiveness achieved. It is conceivable that a number of rights and obligations and disciplines would only take effect upon the achievement of certain levels of competitiveness. Economic indicators to assess and define thresholds could be commonly developed and used in the field of trade and financial regulation as well as monetary affairs. Graduation would allow the focus to be put on major currencies in regulation without unduly harming others. It may help to bring about a consensus among industrialized, emerging, and developing countries.

3. What can we learn from trade regulation?

Given the close relationship between trade and the monetary system, one would expect the two regulatory fields to adhere to coherent and compatible principles. The very purpose of the international monetary system of the IMF and the BIS consists in supporting an open international trading system and securing financial stability among the different currencies of the world with which payments for international transactions in goods and services are made. Both share the common goal of creating conditions of equal opportunity in the world market. They are complementary and mutually dependent. They are the two sides of the same coin. What can finance learn from trade regulation? There are many aspects worth considering, ranging from principles and rules to procedures and dispute settlement.[34]

---

[32] See Philip Marsden and Ioannis Kokkoris, 'The Role of Competition and State Aid Policy', Chapter 18 of this volume.

[33] See Thomas Cottier, 'From Progressive Liberalization to Progressive Regulation', 9 *Journal of International Economic Law* 779 (2006), at 794 ff.

[34] See Gary Hufbauer and Erika Wada, 'Can Financiers Learn from Traders?', 2 *Journal of International Economic Law* 567 (1999).

V. The Role of Non-Discrimination in Monetary Affairs

A. Unconditional non-discrimination

In the quest for international monetary law, the principle of non-discrimination immediately springs to mind. In trade, it is of the utmost importance in bringing about fair conditions of competition. Does this apply equally to competition between currencies?

Legally, unconditional non-discrimination amounts to a prohibition on adopting differential treatment on the basis of specific factors, such as nationality or origin of like or competing products or persons. Like human rights, such as non-discrimination on the basis of sex or age, it is defined more narrowly than the principle of equality of law which does not limit recourse to any reasonable distinction among different factual constellations. Beyond equality, the principle of non-discrimination is a cornerstone of the multilateral trading system. It increasingly shapes—by means of the WTO agreement on trade in services—international financial regulations. It entails both unconditional most-favored nation (MFN) treatment and progressive allocation of national treatment, i.e. the principle of granting treatment no less favourable to foreign services.[35] It is one of the main elements in creating a level playing field.

To what extent could the rules of non-discrimination contribute to greater coherence instead of fragmentation? To what extent can it inform fair competition and level playing fields among currencies? The topic is of particular interest in the context of decisions made by central banks and international monetary organizations. It is interesting to recall at this point that an illustrious group of economists, including Paul Samuelson and Milton Friedman, called for *objective and non-discriminatory rules* in addressing the impact of restrictive monetary policies.[36] The importance of securing fair and equal treatment for all affected by the policies adopted remains important today, even though overall conditions have altered. It would seem that financial regulation and monetary affairs are closely related, and one cannot be fundamentally different from the other.

Nevertheless, despite a close and vulnerable relationship of trade and monetary affairs in international law and policy, underlying principles of operation differ considerably. Trade regulation has traditionally focused on liberalization while monetary law is about stabilization.[37] A different function may explain why non-discrimination is not a well-established topic in monetary affairs. The literature does not reveal a close and operative relationship between the two.[38] It is hardly mentioned, and it is not a topic upon which debate evolves. Discussions relate to

---

[35] See Thomas Cottier and Markus Krajewski, Chapter 15 of this volume .
[36] Paul A. Samuelson et al, 'Monetary Policy to Combat Inflation', 42 *American Economic Review* 384 (1952), at 387 (recommendation III).
[37] See Hufbauer and Wada, above n 34, at 569 ff.
[38] See Lastra, above n 1.

currency manipulation and export subsidy disciplines,[39] or to the impact of imposing non-discriminatory trade and investment policies and conditionalities in lending agreements. It would seem that monetary policy follows distinct mechanisms, and that principles of non-discrimination are not suitable for the subject in a comparable manner to that in which they dominate trade policy and regulation. The rules pertaining to the IMF do not refer at all to MFN or national treatment. The same holds true for the BIS. The provisions on the European Monetary Union are not framed in terms of non-discrimination, although, arguably, they are subject to the fundamental principles of non-discrimination on the basis of nationality. Indeed, it would seem that the classical functions of central banks do not lend themselves to the operation of classical non-discrimination.

Firstly, monetary policies in an international context are highly contextual; they respond to particular constellations, the origin of which may be in a particular currency and thus call for appropriate action with respect to a particular exchange rate constellation or inflation experience. Imbalances may exist with respect to one, but not in relation to other countries and currencies. Setting interest rates, defining the cost of money and supply of money, are responses to the particular needs of a particular economy. Selective and thus discriminatory action seems to be inherent to the operation of central banks. Likewise, policies and measures adopted by international institutions, in particular the IMF, are highly situational. Measures and conditions adopted in support of individual Member States in distress respond to the particular circumstances. They cannot prejudge action with regard to others where the same conditions do not prevail and different types of measures may be required. No case is like the other. Unlike in international trade regulation, it is not a matter of granting equal conditions of competition for foreign products (goods and services) or persons, but of stabilizing the monetary system of a particular country and of the international system as a whole. The macroeconomic perspective is different from that of international trade governance. The legal culture varies. Both the roles of government and of international institutions are different. In trade, governments are obliged to secure non-discriminatory market access and policies within the framework of the WTO and other international trade agreements. In monetary affairs, they are not currently subject to hard and fast rules unless they accept support under bilateral or multilateral lending arrangements. In recent decades, this has resulted in a dual system, obliging developing and emerging countries dependent upon Fund assistance, and leaving industrialized countries outside effective international disciplines. The Basel Accords amount to no less than soft law, albeit central banks share a strong interest in voluntary compliance, not always shared by the community of commercial banks.[40]

---

[39] See the discussion on China's exchange rate policy in: Simon J. Evenett (ed), 'The US-Sino Currency Dispute: New Insights from Economics, Politics and Law', Centre for Economic Policy Research, April 2010, at 109 ff, <http://www.voxeu.org/reports/currency_dispute.pdf> (visited 11 July 2010).

[40] Klaus Peter Follak, 'International Harmonization of Regulatory and Supervisory Frameworks', in Mario Giovanoli (ed), *International Monetary Fund: Issues for the New Millennium* (Oxford: Oxford University Press, 2000) 291–322, at 306.

Secondly, marked differences also exist with respect to the function of international institutions. The WTO is a framework of hard and fast rules, subject to dispute settlement, and agreed rights and obligations can be enforced by means of withdrawing trade concessions. Rules apply to Members in their mutual relations, and not between the WTO as an organization and the Members. The WTO has no functions in running trade policy or intervening in support of countries in distress. The IMF, on the other hand, defines the relationship between the Fund and its Members. Rights and obligations mainly relate to that relationship. In doing so it provides a rather loose legal framework offering ample policy space and is equipped as an agent of governments to intervene and support countries in distress. Shared functions of the two institutions are limited to debate and monitoring domestic policies.

Principles of non-discrimination in monetary law may therefore be explored and applied to the extent that relations among states are concerned. Sovereign states enact laws that prejudice foreign nationals, implicitly or explicitly. Orders freezing assets—imposed unilaterally—are an example of the coercive power of the state within its own territory, when certain security or political considerations prevail. Other examples of unilateral decisions taken by sovereign states include the confiscation of monetary assets (expropriation without compensation) and the repudiation of external debt obligations. Mann argued that monetary sovereignty needs to be exercised by the state in accordance with the principles of customary international law.[41] At present, neither national treatment nor a set of disciplined exceptions framing recourse to discriminatory measures is in place in financial and monetary affairs as a matter of treaty law. National treatment can play an enhanced role. In some areas, exceptions may even be excluded. For example, central banks must be allowed to operate differential interest rates for domestic and foreign banks. Support measures should not depend upon the nationality of the institution, but rather upon its relevance to the economy. Again, it is a matter of developing a doctrine and methodology of national treatment, of defining principles and exceptions comparable to those that have evolved within the law of GATT and the WTO.

To the extent that the principles should address the role and conduct of international organizations *vis-à-vis* states, they are not suitable per se. National treatment does not apply to international organizations, and equal treatment of states largely depends upon whether they meet certain conditions and commonalities. It is inherently limited to conditional MFN.

B. The principle of equality and conditional MFN

While non-discrimination in monetary law, unlike in trade and investment law, does not seem suitable as a general legal concept, the question arises as to whether

---

[41] Frederick A. Mann, *The Legal Aspects of Money*, 5th ed. (Oxford: Clarendon Press, 1992). See also Lastra, above n 1, at 14 ff.

the broader principle of sovereign equality of states, equality as a general principle of law, might not play a more prominent role in rendering the monetary system more stable, predictable and coherent. Clearly, members of the IMF or the European Monetary Union are entitled in principle to the same treatment. Comparable situations should be dealt with in comparable manners; different situations need to be dealt with differently, in accordance with the fundamental principles of equality before the law of Aristotelian origin. Beyond that stage, it cannot possibly be left to the governing bodies to decide arbitrarily whether to grant support in one, but not in another case, e.g. for political reasons or because domestic policies do not respond to the ideals of the Washington Consensus or any other set of informally adopted policy preferences. Overall, policies need to be coherent and predictable and be applied coherently to all Members where comparable conditions prevail. There is ample room to differentiate on the basis of factual differences, case-by-case, taking into account appropriate economic factors and indicators.

In terms of non-discrimination, this could translate into the application of conditional MFN. States are entitled to equal treatment to the extent that they meet the same conditions as others. The IMF thus would be obliged to treat members alike to the extent that they meet the applicable conditions. Beyond the general principle of sovereign equality of states and of equal treatment, the potential of conditional MFN could and should be explored in the international law of monetary affairs. The extent to which both international organizations and states should be subject to this principle in order to achieve greater coherence and consistency in framing competition between different currencies should be examined.

VI. Procedural Rights and Obligations

Article IV of the IMF Articles of Agreement (IMF Agreement) oblige Members to cooperate with the Fund and with other Members with a view to achieving the essential goals of the system:

Recognizing that the essential purpose of the international monetary system is to provide a framework that facilitates the exchange of goods, services, and capital among countries, and that sustains sound economic growth, and that a principal objective is the continuing development of the orderly underlying conditions that are necessary for financial and economic stability, each member undertakes to collaborate with the Fund and other members to assure orderly exchange arrangements and to promote a stable system of exchange rates.

The Agreement entails a number of obligations. In relation to currency competition, Article IV(iii) is of particular importance:

In particular, each member shall:
    (iii) avoid manipulating exchange rates or the international monetary system in order to prevent effective balance of payments adjustment or to gain an unfair competitive advantage over other members; . . .

Neither the IMF Agreement nor its instruments give procedures for how these obligations can and should be implemented beyond consultations of Members and the Fund.[42] At this stage, there is no obligation to engage in consultations, negotiations and dispute settlement. The lack of procedural avenues for implementing these provisions is of particular relevance in addressing imbalances and the problem of under- or over-valued currencies. There are no procedures available to mandatorily address and solve such problems within the IMF. Members can simply refuse to discuss the matter before the appropriate bodies of the Fund. According to IMF Article XXVI(2), if a Member fails to fulfil any of its obligations under the IMF Agreement (including an obligation of bilateral surveillance and an obligation to avoid currency manipulations) the Fund may declare the member ineligible to use the general resources, then suspend voting rights and finally suspend membership. However, are these sanctions an efficient tool? Most probably it is not easy to prove the violation of an obligation (also because of the vague language of the IMF Agreement) and there are no clear, transparent and binding procedures for investigations.

They can oppose and block fact-finding and research in the field by the staff, and thus prevent a debate of the matter within the IMF. Such traditional emphasis on national sovereignty leads affected Members to contemplate seeking redress in the multilateral trading system of the WTO. It is argued that undervaluation of national currencies of exporting countries in relation to the currency of importing countries amounts to an export subsidy which is subject to the imposition of import duties to set off such effects.[43] Whether or not such currency policies can be covered by the Agreement on Subsidies and Countervailing Measures is still an open question. Nor is it clear to what extent this matter can and should be taken within Article XV of the General Agreement on Trade in Services. Linkages of monetary policy and law to trade policy and law, in particular the WTO, are complex and need to be further explored.[44] Yet, the possibility of having unilateral recourse to countervailing duties under the Agreement on Subsidies and Countervailing Measures, Track II,[45] forces exporters to challenge these measures in WTO dispute settlement. Since the examination and the review by a panel and, upon

---

[42] See IMF, 'Article IV of the Fund's Articles of Agreement: An Overview of the Legal Framework', Legal Department, 28 June 2006, <http://www.imf.org/external/np/pp/eng/2006/062806.pdf> (visited 10 July 2010) and the decisions of the IMF Executive Board on surveillance: 'On Surveillance over Exchange Rate Policies', Decision No 5392-(77/63), 29 April 1977, and 'Bilateral Surveillance over Members' Policies', 15 June 2007, <http://www.imf. org/external/np/sec/pn/2007/pn0769.htm#decision> (visited 21 October 2010). For an example concerning China, see Robert W. Staiger, Alan O. Sykes, 'Currency Manipulation and World Trade', National Bureau of Economic Research Working Paper 14600, 2008, at 25, <http://www.nber.org/papers/w14600> (visited 10 July 2010).

[43] This has been the case with the perceived undervaluation of the Chinese Renminbi Yuan in the US which led in October 2011 to the US Senate passing a bill that would see imports from countries that the US believed had artificially suppressed currencies being subject to additional countervailing duties tariffs. See, 'US currency bill passes Senate vote', <http://www.ft.com/intl/cms/s/0/5a6bd3ca-f3fc-11e0-b221-00144feab49a.html#axzz1oFPYwdMC> (visited on 6 March 2012).

[44] See e.g. Deborah E. Siegel, 'Legal Aspects of the IMF/WTO Relationship: The Fund's Articles of Agreement and the WTO Agreements', 96 *American Journal of International Law* 561 (2002).

[45] Articles 10–23 of the Agreement on Subsidies and Countervailing Measures.

appeal, by the Appellate Body takes, in practice, some three years, and compliance does not entail retroactive measures such as compensation, the avenue may be used, or the threat of using it may be made, in order to bring about adjustment in currency competition.

It is evident that adjusting currencies is not a task which should primarily be assigned to, and pursued by means of trade regulation. This should be at the heart of the law of currency competition and Article IV(iii) of the IMF. Appropriate procedures need to be developed within the IMF to provide obligations to engage in consultations, negotiations and possibly dispute resolution. The extent to which matters relating to currency valuations are justiciable and suitable for legal dispute settlement is an open question. Yet the experience of dispute resolution under WTO law should encourage the development of appropriate mechanisms within the IMF, obliging members to work towards a solution based upon mandatory fact-finding by the Fund. As in trade, recourse to national sovereignty and unilateral policies no longer offers appropriate answers and creates undue burdens upon the trading system and dispute settlement in the WTO.

VII. Summary and Conclusions

This chapter has sought to explore the potential and future role of international law in monetary affairs beyond setting and defining the constitutional framework for decision-making and allocation of powers in monetary institutions. It tentatively puts forward a number of questions for debate. It is based on the finding that the global monetary system is founded upon globally competing monetary monopolies and sovereign rights. While such an arrangement poses difficult challenges and is volatile, it is preferable to centralization, and attempts to build a global currency for the age of globalization are discouraged. The world is better off with a number of currencies which reflect differences in the cultures, and economic and social policies of different countries and continents. Competition amounts to a major check on the operation of these monopolies. International law should contribute towards framing conditions of competition, and defining objectives, standards and procedures to prevent and remedy the abuse of monopolies and of rights.

A number of reflections are offered on how to enhance the role of law beyond the current state of affairs and move towards the rule of law. Monetary policy should be based upon agreed objectives and principles and implemented in accordance with agreed rules. This does not exclude appropriate margins of discretion and adjustment to particular circumstances. The rules of the Fund and other monetary institutions need to reflect an appropriate balance of substantive and procedural rights and obligations of all Members alike. The financial crisis of 2007–09 shows that efforts to bring about and monitor appropriate disciplines for industrialized countries are of prime importance in the effort to fill current lacunae in international monetary law.

In doing so, recourse should be made to the doctrine of multilayered governance, and powers and rules should be properly allocated vertically and horizontally with a view to bringing about a framework of competition between different national currencies and thus between national monopolies. First, disciplines of competition policy could perhaps inspire this effort. The doctrine of abuse of dominant positions and of abuse of rights may serve as a starting point from which to refine the legal framework within which international organizations and central banks could operate. Principles of non-discrimination, inspired by other parts of international economic law, in particular trade and investment regulation, may have the potential to bring about objective and more predictable terms of reference for monetary policy. The principles of non-discrimination and of equality before the law offer important foundations. Disciplines on non-discrimination and conditional MFN could find a place not only in policy-making, but also in the future architecture of the international monetary system. Appropriate guarantees should be introduced in international law and be monitored by international organizations, subject to reporting, monitoring and possibly dispute settlement. Developing procedural avenues appears to be most promising. They should be examined in shaping future rules of engagement for international institutions, in particular the Fund and the BIS, in terms of monitoring, transparency, naming and shaming, structural adjustment programs and lending. This is a promising field which lawyers, economists and scholars in international relations should jointly enter.

21

Financial Stability and Monetary Policy: Need for International Surveillance

*Gary Hufbauer and Daniel Danxia Xie**

I. Introduction

In the wake of the Great Crisis of 2008, regulatory proposals have emphasized the micro-prudential space: greater bank liquidity and more bank capital, strict supervision of too-big-to-fail financial firms, 'living wills', new resolution mechanisms, compensation that tracks risk. Proposed reforms also address troublesome problems created by cross-border financial institutions and international financial networks. An important ingredient is missing from this menu. Micro-prudential reforms that focus on financial firms are essential, but it is equally important to reform the macro-economic behavior of central banks. New evidence shows a strong link between loose monetary policy and greater risk-taking by banks and other financial institutions. Regulatory failures in the USA and Europe may have been the proximate cause of the crisis, but massive monetary policy errors set the stage.

In this chapter, we suggest that the monetary policy framework should be expanded to take explicit account of financial stability as a policy objective for central banks—a policy objective in addition to inflation and output. To fulfill this objective, we commend a new measure of monetary aggregates, De Facto Money (DFM). DFM attempts to measure the quantity of a broad set of liquid assets, as a useful indicator of systematic financial risk in the economy. Empirical evidence for the USA indicates that DFM can be useful for identifying asset booms and moderating asset busts.

We also present cross-country evidence for the 2000s that shows the connection between DFM and the international background of the Great Crisis. For that exercise, a panel data set of 18 countries explores correlations between the DFM dimension of monetary policy and current account balances. The panel regressions indicate that loose monetary policies—defined in terms of their wealth effects—are robustly related to current account deficits. In their summit meetings, G20

* The views expressed are the opinions of the authors, not necessarily the views of the Institute.

countries have stressed that global imbalances should be curtailed to ward off the next crisis. It follows that greater emphasis on financial stability, especially in the boom phase of the economic cycle, should be explored as an instrument for achieving this policy objective.

Monetary policy has historically belonged squarely in the realm of national sovereignty, and has not been a subject of international surveillance. As US Treasury Secretary John Connally famously said, when the Bretton Woods system of fixed exchange rates was collapsing: 'The dollar is our money and your problem'.[1] As a consequence of the Great Crisis, however, the downside risks of financial globalization now challenge the conventional assignment of monetary policy strictly to national authorities. Cross-country spillover effects call for surveillance of national monetary policies, especially for 'systemically important countries'.

II. Booming Wealth and Private Risk-Taking

We are certainly not the first to critique the role of loose monetary policy, during the period 2002–05, for setting the stage of the Great Crisis. John B. Taylor was an early and prominent critic of the Federal Reserve. Taylor used a simulation exercise to indicate that tighter monetary policy could have slowed the huge housing boom in the USA.[2]

In fact, well before the bubble, Bernanke and Gertler,[3] and then Bernanke, Gertler, and Gilchrist proposed a 'financial accelerator' model in which monetary policy pumps up the financial sector.[4] These research papers illustrate how frictions within the credit markets can amplify shocks to the macroeconomy. In good times, private actors underestimate risk, load up on assets, and enlarge their debt burdens. In bad times, risk premiums soar, and deteriorating credit market conditions worsen the economic downturn. Borio and Zhu emphasized the explicit 'risk-taking channel' of monetary policy—easier money by the central banks, higher risk by private lenders.[5]

In a similar spirit, Rajan argued that loose monetary policy can induce asset managers to 'search for yield', bending constraints such as contract structures and

---

[1] John Connally made this comment to European finance ministers in 1971.

[2] John B. Taylor, 'Housing and Monetary Policy', <http://www.stanford.edu/'"'johntayl/Housing%20and%20Monetary%20Policy–Taylor–Jackson%20Hole%202007.pdf> (visited 5 August 2010).

[3] Ben Bernanke and Mark Gertler, 'Agency Costs, Net Worth, and Business Fluctuations', 79 *American Economic Review* 14 (1989).

[4] Ben Bernanke, Mark Gertler and Simon Gilchrist, 'The Financial Accelerator in a Quantitative Business Cycle Framework', in John B. Taylor and Michael Woodford (eds), *Handbook of Macroeconomics* (Amsterdam: Elsevier, 1999) 1341–93.

[5] Claudio Borio and Haibin Zhu, 'Capital Regulation, Risk-Taking and Monetary Policy: A Missing Link in the Transmission Mechanism?', Bank for International Settlements Working Papers No 268, December 2008, <http://www.bis.org/publ/work268.htm> (visited 5 August 2010).

other institutional features.[6] Cukierman even mentioned Madoff as an example of outright fraud facilitated by easy access to credit.[7]

Seminal research by Jiménez et al showed the impact of low interest rates on the appetite of Spanish banks for credit risk. Under expansive monetary policy, Spanish banks relaxed their lending standards and extended loans to borrowers with weak credit histories.[8]

The Bank for International Settlements (BIS) further confirmed the risk-taking channel of monetary policy, using a large new cross-country data set.[9] Drawing on this data set, Gambacorta found robust evidence that the default probability for banks increased in countries where interest rates remained low for a lengthy period prior to the crisis.[10] In their latest research, Altunbas, Gambacorta, and Marques-Ibanez explored a detailed database of European and American banks, and confirmed that enduring low interest rates contributed to higher risk-taking behavior.[11] To round out the story, Schularick and Taylor provide long-run historical evidence of the linkage between fast credit growth and financial crises.[12]

To summarize, an academic consensus is forming around the idea that prolonged easy money can set the stage for financial crisis. Of course, central bankers are quick to proclaim 'not on my watch'. Bernanke is a prominent example.[13] But these self-serving declamations are not turning the tide of academic analysis.

[6] Raghuram Rajan, 'Has Financial Development Made the World Riskier?', <http://www.imf.org/external/np/speeches/2005/082705.htm> (visited 5 August 2010). Adrian and Shin carry the analysis further and explore connections between monetary policy and the cyclical behavior of the balance sheets of financial institutions. Tobias Adrian and Hyun Song Shin, 'Money, Liquidity, and Monetary Policy', 99 *American Economic Review* 600 (2009). Tobias Adrian and Hyun Song Shin, 'Financial Intermediaries and Monetary Economics', in Benjamin Friedman and Michael Woodford (eds), *Handbook of Monetary Economics* (Amsterdam: North Holland, 2010).

[7] Alex Cukierman, 'Reflections on the Crisis and on its Lessons for Regulatory Reform and for Central Bank Policies', *Journal of Financial Stability* (2010), <http://www.tau.ac.il/''alexcuk/pdf/Bocconi-Revised%20&%20Expanded-12-09.pdf> (visited 4 November 2010).

[8] Gabriel Jiménez et al., 'Hazardous Times for Monetary Policy: What do Twenty-Three Million Bank Loans Say About the Effects of Monetary Policy on Credit Risk-Taking?', Bank of Spain (Banco de España) Working Papers No 0833, <http://www.bde.es/webde/SES/Secciones/Publicaciones/PublicacionesSeriadas/DocumentosTrabajo/08/Fic/dt0833e.pdf> (visited 5 August 2010). Smaller Spanish banks were found to be more affected by loose monetary policy than larger ones, at 8, DocumentosTrabajo/08/Fic/dt0833e.pdf

[9] 'International Banking and Financial Market Developments', BIS Quarterly Review, December 2009, <http://www. bis.org/publ/qtrpdf/r_qt0912.htm> (visited 5 August 2010).

[10] Leonardo Gambacorta, 'Monetary Policy and the Risk-taking Channel', BIS Quarterly Review, Special Features, December 2009, at 43, <http://www.bis.org/publ/qtrpdf/r_qt0912.htm> (visited 5 August 2010).

[11] Yener Altunbas, Leonardo Gambacorta and David Marques-Ibanez, 'Does Monetary Policy Affect Bank Risk-taking?', BIS Working Papers No 298, March 2010, <http://www.bis.org/publ/work298.htm> (visited 5 August 2010).

[12] Moritz Schularick and Alan M. Taylor, 'Credit Booms Gone Bust: Monetary Policy, Leverage Cycles and Financial Crises, 1870–2008', National Bureau of Economic Research Working Paper No 15512, November 2009, <http://www.jfki.fu-berlin.de/faculty/economics/team/persons/schularick/Schularick_Taylor_Credit_Booms_Gone_Bust.pdf> (visited 5 August 2010).

[13] Speech of Ben Bernanke, 'Monetary Policy and the Housing Bubble', Annual Meeting of the American Economic Association, Atlanta, Georgia, 3 January 2010, <http://www.federalreserve.gov/newsevents/speech/bernanke20100103a.htm> (visited 5 August 2010).

III. The Mainstream Monetary Regime

The great inflation of the 1970s and early 1980s turned mainstream economists and central bankers alike into inflation hawks. New Zealand pioneered the adoption of inflation targeting (IT) as its monetary policy framework in 1989. Since then, IT has been popularly adopted in both developed and developing countries. In fact, IT has become the dominant monetary regime, with various degrees of formality. Developed countries with explicit targets often identify 2–3 per cent as the desirable range of inflation: the UK uses 2.5 per cent , Korea uses 2.5–3.5 per cent, Sweden uses 2 per cent (±1 per cent) and Spain uses 2 per cent . With or without explicit targets, central bankers settled on the view that, when inflation was acceptably low, all was well in the economic kingdom. As Blanchard, Giovanni dell'Ariccia, and Paolo Mauro put the consensus:

we thought of monetary policy as having one target, inflation, and one instrument, the policy rate. So long as inflation was stable, the output gap was likely to be small and stable and monetary policy did its job . . . There was an increasing consensus that inflation should not only be stable, but very low. . . .[14]

Bernanke et al published the first systematic study of IT and found that IT countries typically enjoyed lower inflation, lower inflation expectations, and lower nominal interest rates.[15] Moreover, temporary shocks to the price level had a smaller 'pass-through' effect on inflation. Based on their findings, Bernanke et al list the following principles for an IT framework:

- Explicit central bank commitment to low and stable inflation as the overriding objective
- Public disclosure of the official inflation target over a defined time horizon
- Mechanisms that compel the central bank to comply with its commitment.

A later study by Truman likewise reported that, after adopting this 'benevolent' monetary regime, IT countries generally achieved lower inflation levels and higher gross domestic product (GDP) growth rates.[16] Before the Great Crisis, nearly all empirical studies confirmed the fine performance of IT.

This happy consensus was shattered by the events of 2008 and 2009. Buiter for one argues that the narrow focus of monetary policy on IT distracted the authorities from the equally important goal of financial stability.[17] The former Chief

---

[14] Olivier Blanchard, Giovanni dell'Ariccia and Paolo Mauro, 'Rethinking Macroeconomic Policy', IMF Staff Position Note, SPN/10/03, 12 February 2010, at 3–4, <http://www.imf.org/external/pubs/ft/spn/2010/spn1003.pdf> (visited 5 August 2010).

[15] Ben Bernanke et al., *Inflation Targeting: Lessons from the International Experience* (Princeton, NJ: Princeton University Press, 1999).

[16] Section 3 of Edwin Truman, *Inflation Targeting in the World Economy?* (Washington, DC: Peterson Institute for International Economics, 2003).

[17] Willem Buiter, 'The Unfortunate Uselessness of Most "State of the Art" Academic Monetary Economics', 6 March 2009, <http://www.voxeu.org/index.php?q=node/3210> (visited 5 August 2010).

Economist of the Central Bank of Iceland, Gudmundsson confessed: 'I was a great fan of IT. However, experience has brought with it a better appreciation of the challenges that come with it. Iceland was the first country that I am aware of to suspend IT because of a financial crisis'.[18]

IV. The Political Economy of Financial Crisis

Conservative economists sometimes argue that financial crises are an efficient way of wiping out weak companies, leading to a post-crisis boost in productivity. This view does not sit well with a public that must bear the cost of high unemployment and lost retirement wealth. In democracies, and even in some autocracies, political pressures to arrest financial distress are considerable. Central banks will, over time, reflect public preferences. In the early 1980s, inflation was the major concern, and IT eventually became the dominant monetary policy. In the early 2010s, financial stability looks like a bigger concern and this may set the stage for a new approach to monetary policy. As Feldstein points out:

> The Fed has been subject to substantial, and I believe justified, criticism for its failure to prevent the behavior in those institutions that contributed directly to the recent financial crisis . . . . . . In the years before the meltdown that began in 2006 and 2007, Fed officials frequently indicated that bank capital was quite adequate and not a cause for concern.[19]

While central bank independence has come to be regarded as the Holy Grail of monetary policy, the taxpaying public, unemployed workers, and impoverished retirees will all be heard when central bank errors contribute to financial crises.[20] This suggests that Financial Stability—capital F, capital S—will be added to IT as an explicit policy objective.

V. Rethinking the Monetary Policy Framework

In an unpublished paper, Xie proposed that the new monetary policy framework should reflect a broad definition of aggregate assets to track DFM.[21] DFM measures the quantity of all liquid assets in the economy, expressed in the national currency unit, such as dollars, euros, yen, or yuan. The goal of Financial Stability

---

[18] Már Gudmundsson, 'Challenges to Inflation Targeting: Raising Some Issues', BIS Papers No 51, <http://www.bis.org/publ/bppdf/bispap51b.pdf> (visited 5 August 2010).

[19] Martin Feldstein, 'What Powers for the Federal Reserve?', 48(1) *Journal of Economic Literature* 134 (2010). Feldstein goes on to recite a familiar list of remedies for Wall Street excess (tighter supervision of the large bank holding companies, etc.).

[20] Alberto Alesina and Andrea Stella, 'The Politics of Monetary Policy', National Bureau of Economic Research Working Paper No 15856, April 2010, <http://www.nber.org/papers/w15856. pdf?new_window=1> (visited 5 August 2010).

[21] Daniel Danxia Xie, 'Beyond Inflation Targeting in the Post Crisis World: Towards a New Monetary Regime' (Unpublished mimeo, Peterson Institute for International Economics, Washington, DC, 2009, on file with the authors).

can then be defined in terms of moderating fluctuations in DFM. In comparison with two or three decades ago, most assets are more tradable and more liquid than they were owing to the creation of new financial products, advances in information technology, much lower transaction costs, and a high degree of global financial integration.

Thanks to these innovations, a growing proportion of assets have come to share the attributes of traditional money (M1, M2, and M3).[22] Moreover, the shadow banking system has grown so large that it rivals the traditional banking system which is safeguarded by deposit insurance in many countries. In a financial crisis, the absence of deposit insurance for a shadow bank (think Northern Rock, Bear Stearns, and AIG) hardly means that the institution can be allowed to fail, wiping out creditors as well as shareholders.

Our proposal emphasizes Xie's augmented measure, DFM, in order to take account of the liquidity characteristics of a broad spectrum of assets, including traditional bank assets, bonds and shares, real estate, and new financial instruments (like mortgage-backed securities). Since different categories of assets have different degrees of liquidity, ideally we would like to sum up the total of liquidity-weighted assets in the economy. Equation (1) provides a simple definition of DFM:

$$DFM = \sum_{i=1}^{n} Liquidity_i \cdot V_i$$

In equation (1), V_i denotes the total value of asset category i, and $Liquidity_i$ measures the degree of liquidity of this type of asset, on a scale from zero to one. For example, bank deposits, certificates of deposit and money market funds might have a liquidity index of 1.0, bonds might have 0.9, stocks 0.7, and residential real estate 0.5.

To illustrate the calculation of DFM in the USA, we make the strong assumption that all assets have the same degree of liquidity. This assumption gives too much weight to real estate relative to stocks and bonds (even though real estate is much more liquid now than it was two decades ago). With this assumption we can borrow the wealth account data constructed by Jorgenson, and Landefeld and Jorgenson.[23] The wealth account is the sum of the reproducible and tangible assets held by households and non-profit organizations (NPOs), and the government. It includes an adjustment for the net international investment position of the

---

[22] There are small variations in the definition of monetary aggregates for different countries, but the definitions are very similar. For the USA, M1: The total of currency in circulation, checking accounts, and currency held as bank reserves; M2: In addition to M1, bank savings accounts, money market accounts, retail money market mutual funds, and certificates of deposit under $100,000; M3: In addition to M2, all other Certificate of Deposit (CD)s, time deposits over $100,000; institutional money market mutual funds; deposits of Eurodollars, and repurchase agreements (repos).

[23] Dale W. Jorgenson, 'A New Architecture for the US National Accounts', 55(1) *Review of Income and Wealth* 1–42 (2009); Dale W. Jorgenson and J. Steven Landefeld, 'Blueprint for Expanded and Integrated U.S. Accounts: Review, Assessment, and Next Steps', in Dale W. Jorgenson, J. Steven Landefeld, and William D. Nordhaus (eds), *A New Architecture for the U.S. National Accounts* (Chicago: University of Chicago Press, 2006) 13–112.

USA. Averaged over the decade from 1990 to 2000, data shows that 39 per cent of total US wealth was in equity, bonds, and mutual funds, while 22 per cent was in residential housing. Another 20 per cent of US wealth was held by the government. For our purposes, wealth held by the government is excluded.[24]

Figure 21.1 plots the GDP growth rate, the inflation rate (measured by the Consumer Price Index, or CPI), the M2 growth rate, and the growth rate of private US wealth for the USA from 1973 to 2009.[25] We see no large anomalies in the GDP growth rate or inflation rate between 1993 and 2006. However, the growth rates of M2 and wealth accelerated after 1993.[26]

Period averages are summarized in Table 21.1. From Figure 21.1 and Table 21.1, we can see that during the 2003–06 periods, GDP, CPI, M1 and M2 generally grew at slower speeds than during the 1996–99 period, and the speeds were comparable to the 1992–95 averages. Note, however, the unusual feature of the 2003–06 period: wealth growth reached 12.2 per cent annually, much faster than inflation or GDP. Column (6) shows the difference between wealth growth rates and inflation rates; column (7) shows the difference between wealth growth rates and GDP growth rates. The period 2003–06 stands out among the past three decades. The large gap between wealth growth and either inflation or GDP growth indicates conditions leading to a crisis. Meticulous calculations by Taylor likewise imply a deviation from the eponym Taylor Rule[27] from 2003 to 2006.[28] However, excessive monetary ease shows up more clearly in the gap between wealth growth and the sum of inflation and GDP growth rates for this period, as shown in column (8).

VI. Cross-Country Comparisons

Global imbalances are often cited as a factor contributing to the Great Crisis (e.g. Bernanke), Obstfeld and Rogoff, and Bergsten and Subramanian).[29] Obstfeld and

[24] Government wealth, such as military bases, national parks and office buildings is highly illiquid and plays little role in financial volatility.
[25] Wealth figures from 2002 to 2009 are based on our own calculations. The source of the figures for 1973–2001 is the Federal Reserve Board.
[26] The growth of M3 also accelerated after 1993, but the Federal Reserve discontinued this M3 series in 2006.
[27] The Taylor rule stipulates how much the nominal interest rate should be changed in response to weighted divergences between: (i) the actual inflation rate and the target inflation rate; and (ii) the actual level of GDP and the potential level of GDP.
[28] See Taylor, above n 2; John B. Taylor, 'The Financial Crisis and the Policy Responses: an Empirical Analysis of What Went Wrong', National Bureau of Economic Research Working Paper No 14631, January 2009, at 5, <http://www.nber.org/papers/w14631.pdf?new_window=1> (visited 5 August 2010).
[29] Speech of Ben Bernanke, 'Financial Reform to Address Systemic Risk', The Council on Foreign Relations, Washington, DC, 10 March 2009, <http://www.bis.org/review/r090313a.pdf> (visited 18 July 2012); Maurice Obstfeld and Kenneth Rogoff, 'Global Imbalances and the Financial Crisis: Products of Common Causes', <http://elsa.berkeley.edu/""obstfeld/santabarbara.pdf> (visited 5 August 2010); Fred Bergsten and Arvind Subramanian, 'America Cannot Resolve Global Imbalances on Its Own', *Financial Times*, 19 August 2009, <http://www.iie.com/publications/opeds/oped.cfm?

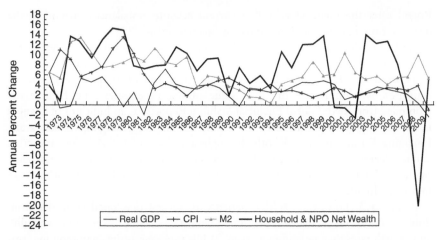

Fig. 21.1. US growth rates of GDP, CPI, M2 and wealth, 1973–2009

Table 21.1. US Growth Rates of GDP, CPI, Ml, M2, and Wealth, 1977–2006

Periods	GDP (1)	CPI (2)	Ml (3)	M2 (4)	Wealth (5)	Wealth—CPI (6)	Wealth—GDP (7)	Wealth—(CPI + GDP) (8)
1977–81	3.1	9.8	7.4	8.8	12.2	2.3	9.1	−0.8
1982–91	3.0	4.1	7.6	6.8	7.5	3.4	4.5	0.4
1992–95	3.2	2.9	6.1	1.9	6.0	3.1	2.7	−0.1
1996–99	4.4	2.3	−0.1	6.2	11.3	9.0	6.9	4.7
2003–06	3.0	2.9	2.9	5.1	12.2	9.3	9.2	6.4

Source: U.S. Bureau of Economic Analysis, The Federal Reserve Board, and Jorgenson and Landefeld (2006, 2009).
Note: For the purpose of this table, wealth is defined as the net worth of households and NPO with an adjustment for the net international investment position.

ResearchID=1283> (visited 5 August 2010). For a deeper debate about global imbalances, contrast the views represented by Obstfeld and Rogoff, and Bergsten, who all think that large current account imbalances are not sustainable in the long run, with the views supported by Dooley, Folkerts-Landau, and Garber and Caballero, Farhi, and Gourinchas, as well as Cooper, who all argue that current account imbalances can be a global equilibrium solution to differing savings and investment preferences in different countries, and can be sustained for long periods. Maurice Obstfeld and Kenneth Rogoff, 'Global Current Account Imbalances and Exchange Rate Adjustments', *Brookings Papers on Economic Activity* 1 (2005) 67–146. Michael Dooley, David Folkerts-Landau, and Peter Garber, *International Financial Stability: Asia, Interest Rates, and the Dollar* (New York: Deutsche Bank Global Research, 2005). Ricardo Caballero, Emmanuel Farhi, and Pierre-Olivier Gourinchas, 'An Equilibrium Model of "Global Imbalances" and Low Interest Rates' 98 *American Economic Review* 1 (2008) 358–93. Richard N. Cooper, 'Living with Global Imbalances', Brookings Papers on Economic Activity 2 (2007) 91–107.

Rogoff offer the nuanced view that current account imbalances 'magnified the ultimate causal factors behind the recent financial crisis'.[30]

With this view in mind, it is worth exploring the relationship between global imbalances and monetary policy. We start with a cross-region comparison for the years before and during the Great Crisis. Due to the lack of comparable data across countries, we simply use the total value of bonds, equities, and bank assets (compiled from IMF Global Financial Stability Reports) as an indicator of changes in DFM. Figure 21.2 illustrates the experience in five emerging market areas. Emerging Europe registered both the highest growth of DFM before the crisis and the deepest recession afterwards.[31] Asset growth in emerging Europe was fueled by the bank lending channel, which empirically shows the highest correlation to an imminent financial crisis.

Figure 21.3 shows the DFM experience of several developed countries from 2002 to 2008. Generally, the developed countries exhibit lower DFM volatility and growth rates than emerging markets. While Greece was the champion in terms

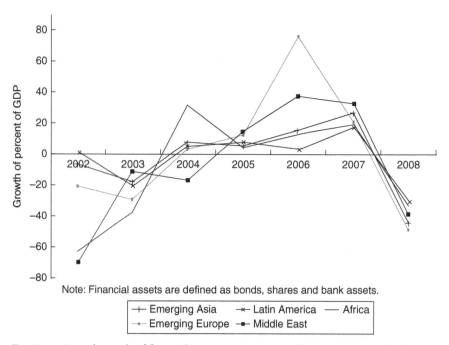

Note: Financial assets are defined as bonds, shares and bank assets.

| —+— Emerging Asia | —×— Latin America | —— Africa |
| —•— Emerging Europe | —■— Middle East | |

Fig. 21.2. Annual growth of financial assets in emerging markets, as percent of GDP

---

[30] See Obstfeld and Rogoff (2005), ibid, at 10.

[31] See Morris Goldstein and Daniel Xie, 'The Impact of the Financial Crisis on Emerging Asia', presented at the conference on Asia and the Global Financial Crisis, Santa Barbara, 18–20 October 2009, <http://www.frbsf.org/economics/conferences/aepc/2009/09_Goldstein.pdf> (visited 5 August 2010).

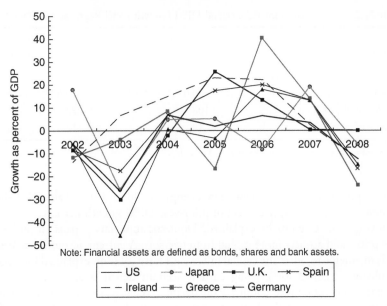

Note: Financial assets are defined as bonds, shares and bank assets.

| ——— US | —○— Japan | —■— U.K. | —×— Spain |
| — — Ireland | —■— Greece | —▲— Germany | |

Fig. 21.3. Annual growth of financial assests in developed countries, as per cent of GDP

of DFM volatility and growth, Ireland, Spain, and the UK all experienced significant DFM growth before the crisis.

Our data set for 18 Organisation for Economic Co-operation and Development (OECD) countries includes as one crucial variable DFM, for which our proxy measure is the total value of bonds, equities, and bank assets (compiled from IMF Global Financial Stability Reports).[32]

We use panel regression with so-called 'fixed effects' to control both omitted variables and country-specific characteristics.[33]

Column (1) of Table 21.2 shows the panel regression results where the current account balance is the dependent variable, and the corresponding DFM growth rate and its lagged value are independent variables. These empirical results reveal a robust negative correlation between past DFM growth and current account positions. Faster DFM growth in the lagged year is strongly correlated with a larger current account deficit (or a smaller current account surplus) in the present year.

Exchange rate movements may explain a good part of changes in current account balances. To control for this effect, we single out the Euro area countries and rerun the regressions. Since the Euro area countries have a single currency, this experi-

---

[32] The database also includes current account data for the corresponding countries (from the IMF WEO database).

[33] For an explanation of the 'fixed effects' regression model, see Jeffrey M. Wooldridge, *Econometric Analysis of Cross Section and Panel Data* (Cambridge, MA: MIT Press, 2001).

Table 21.2. Current Account Balance and DFM Growth Panel Regression 2000–08

Independent variables	(1) 18 OECD countries	(2) 12 Euro countries
Current year DFM growth rate	0.005 (−0.009)	0.008 (−0.012)
Lagged year DFM growth rate	−0.024** (−0.01)	−0.029** (−0.013)
Number of observations	108	72
Number of countries	18	12

Note: Standard errors in parentheses; **P < 0.05; *P*: Probability.

ment implicitly removes exchange rate changes. Column (2) of Table 21.2 shows the new results: the negative effect of prior-year DFM growth persists.

How can these results be explained? Domestic monetary expansion pushes up asset prices and attracts more capital from overseas. A current account deficit then needs to emerge to offset the capital inflow, as Harry Johnson explained long ago.[34] An obvious channel for a rising current account deficit is appreciation of the exchange rate—for those countries on flexible exchange rate regimes. However, even for countries with fixed rate regimes—those in the Euro area, for example— the negative relationship between DFM growth and the current account balance persists. This implies that a second channel is general economic expansion fueled by capital inflows, which in turn enlarges the current account deficit.[35]

An interesting piece of evidence to support the negative relation between the current account position and lagged DFM growth is that China may witness a smaller current account deficit in 2010. One explanation for this surprising phenomenon could be the recent strength of housing prices due to super-loose monetary policy in 2009.

VII. Alternative Monetary Targets

A few scholars and policymakers have begun to reconsider the received tenets of monetary policy, in light of the most serious economic crisis since the Great Depression of the 1930s. Blanchard dell'Ariccia, and Mauro, for example, suggest the possibility of increasing the desired inflation targets, aiming to make more room for monetary easing[36] in containing the next economic crisis.[37]

---

[34] Harry G. Johnson, 'The Monetary Approach to Balance of Payments Theory', 7 *Journal of Financial and Quantitative Analysis* 1555 (1972).

[35] A caveat is that our panel data set only covers developed countries, which means that major developing countries like China, India, and Brazil are not included due to the difficulties of data collection. The experience of these developing countries may differ from the results reported here.

[36] To stimulate economic activity, central bank might reduce interest rates and boost money supply.

[37] See Blanchard, dell'Ariccia, and Mauro, above n 14, at 5.

Other researchers have proposed revisions to the way in which inflation is measured in the present IT framework. For example, they would include selected asset prices in the price index to warn of the next bubble. However, unlike consumption goods, the role of asset expansion cannot be entirely captured by a price index. For example, new financial products may be created that have little influence on the average level of asset prices, but still greatly expand the gross value of tradable and liquid assets. Moreover, financial innovation keeps creating new products that might be overlooked by financial supervisors in the early stages and not integrated into the price index until a crisis finally happens. Collateralized debt obligations (CDOs) would be an example.

To achieve the policy objective of Financial Stability, in addition to IT, additional policy targets and instruments are needed, not just an adjustment of existing targets and instruments. As for targets, we have sketched DFM and the way that the concept is summarized in equation (1) above is certainly measured better than we have done in this chapter.

Turning to instruments, various micro-economic controls are available, in addition to the standard central bank suite of short-term policy interest rates and M1 levels. For example, more stringent liquidity and capital requirements for banks, beyond Basel III, are widely discussed, and these can be varied in response to changes in financial stability conditions. An obvious instrument for the housing sector is the mortgage down-payment requirement. Margin requirements can be adjusted to moderate stock and bond market booms. For derivatives, the authorities can insist on central clearing houses, which in turn can enforce initial margin and variation margin requirements. Another instrument is to regulate the extent of credit card debt by imposing maximum interest rates, which in turn will induce banks to raise their standards for issuing credit cards.[38] All these tools are clearly within the legal powers of central banks and other financial supervisors.

VIII. International Surveillance

If the new monetary policy framework we suggest is so good, and if instruments for DFM targeting are readily available, why don't countries by their own initiative seek to moderate financial fluctuations by better control of national DFM levels? What is the rationale for international surveillance? Our short answer is that the combination of rising asset values and low inflation is a central banker's dream. Under the legendary Alan Greenspan, years of loose monetary policy created a vast real-estate boom that ended in tears. During the good times, Greenspan was

---

[38] Quite often, the credit card default rate is around 10 per cent annually, which implies that credit card interest rates must be at least 15 per cent for the issuing firms to make money on outstanding balances. On 30 April 2010, Senator Sheldon Whitehouse Democrat-Rhode Island (D-RI) offered an amendment to the financial regulatory bill to force national card issuers to comply with anti-usury laws in each state where their customers reside. If enacted, this measure would dramatically curtail the issue of high-risk credit cards. In preference to this approach, we favor granting the Federal Reserve the power to cap credit card interest rates.

crowned 'the greatest central banker in history' by no less a figure than Alan Blinder.[39] The inevitable tears were confined neither to Wall Street nor the boundaries of the US economy. Owing to global financial integration, damage was spread far and wide. In earlier but smaller episodes—the Latin American debt crisis of the 1980s, and the Asian and Russian crises of the 1990s—damage was also global.

National central banks are neither omniscient nor immune to the pleasures of rising asset values. Moreover, national monetary authorities are unlikely to give sufficient weight to the global consequences of 'feel-good' policies at home. Even if central bankers are assigned explicit objectives—a combination of low inflation, full employment, and financial stability—they might put insufficient weight on financial stability. From time to time, central bankers need forceful warnings from their foreign peers.

For purposes of global financial stability, country size matters. A few large countries bear nearly all the responsibility for stabilizing global asset values. Any system of international financial surveillance needs to worry about the USA, the EU, Japan, China, India, Brazil, and a very few others. This group is the core of the G20, the latest global steering group which came together in the midst of the Great Crisis.[40]

The empirical results derived in the last section suggest that international trade and monetary surveillance are complementary actions. Obstfeld and Rogoff, for example, have proposed that current account balances should be a consideration in the formation of monetary policy.[41] According to our empirical analysis, if excess monetary expansion is avoided, by adopting a DFM target reinforced by international monetary surveillance, large and persistent current account deficits could be mitigated.

At the G20 Summit, held in London in April 2009, the Financial Stability Forum of the BIS was enlarged to include all G20 countries, and renamed the Financial Stability Board (FSB), with the implication of stronger powers and broader representation. However, so far the FSB has only played a consultative role, with a focus on micro-prudential issues. Despite its grand name, the FSB is not the right forum for international surveillance of Financial Stability, in the sense that we conceive this objective.

Instead the International Monetary Fund (IMF) is the prime candidate for the task of macro-financial surveillance. The IMF already has extensive experience in designing 'early warning' indicators. So far, however, the IMF has been singularly ineffective in warding off looming financial crises. Rather, the IMF's role has historically been to discipline smaller countries after a crisis erupts. We are suggesting

---

[39] Alan S. Blinder, *The Quiet Revolution: Central Banking Goes Modern* (New Haven, CT: Yale University Press, 2004).

[40] The G20 held its inaugural meeting in Washington in November 2008, with two meetings since then—London in April 2009 and Pittsburgh in September 2009. The G20 has essentially eclipsed the G8 as the steering forum for the world economy. The next meetings are scheduled for Toronto in July 2010 and Seoul in November 2010.

[41] See Obstfeld and Rogoff (2005), above n 29, at 10.

that the IMF should widen its ambitions to play a 'crisis avoidance' role for 'systemically important countries', namely the big G20 nations.

The DFM framework that we have proposed, with suitable refinements, should be used by the IMF to monitor anomalous financial imbalances in important countries and then blow the whistle. As a first step this would require enhancement of the two IMF data reporting systems: the SDDS (Special Data Dissemination Standard) and the GDDS (General Data Dissemination System). Wealth accounts and flow of funds accounts would be needed for the important IMF members. A benchmark threshold can then be set between the DFM growth rate and a combination of GDP and inflation growth rates, drawing on empirical evidence from previous boom and bust episodes. When the DFM growth rate for an important country exceeds the benchmark threshold, the IMF should sound the alarm.

IX. Conclusions

The Great Crisis has motivated both scholars and officials to think about tools for containing the next global financial crisis. Loose monetary policy was among the causes of the Great Crisis. At present, the mainstream monetary policy regime, which focuses on price stability, is not well equipped to detect the beginning of an asset bubble, which in turn sets the stage for a financial crisis. The huge social cost of a financial crisis should, however, compel policymakers to include Financial Stability as a major policy objective. We propose the DFM framework, which quantifies a broad set of liquid assets, as the basis for measuring Financial Stability. Empirical evidence shows that DFM can anticipate conditions that presage a financial crisis. Cross-country comparisons illustrate that future fragility is correlated to contemporary rapid expansion of DFM. Empirical evidence thus lends strong support to including DFM as an additional target for central banks to monitor, and thereby promote financial stability. To implement this new monetary framework, central banks need to invoke more instruments than traditional short-term policy interest rates and M1 controls. The new instruments must include control over bank capital and liquidity requirements, mortgage down payments, and maximum credit card interest rates.

Spillover of financial crisis is an inevitable side effect of globalization. International surveillance is needed because national central banks typically enjoy the upside of an asset cycle, and typically discount the negative spillover effects from a domestic crisis. The IMF is the ideal candidate to carry out the surveillance task.

22

Enhancing the IMF's Regulatory Authority

*Sean Hagan**

I. Introduction

Perhaps not surprisingly, the recent financial crisis has given renewed relevance to the International Monetary Fund (the Fund) as a financial institution. Over the past two years, there has been a large increase in the number of member countries whose adjustment programs have received financial support from the Fund. Moreover, the Fund has revised its instruments so as to increase the flexibility and effectiveness of its financial support.[1] Finally, as the demand for Fund financing has increased, the Fund has taken steps to increase the resources available to it, the most recent one being the agreement to increase the amounts that it can draw upon under the New Arrangements to Borrow from US$60 billion to 550 billion.[2]

Less visible—but no less important—has been the discussion of the steps needed to enhance the Fund's effectiveness as a regulatory institution. From the outset of the global financial crisis in 2008, there has been a recognition that measures are needed both at the national and international levels to strengthen the regulatory and policy framework that underpins the global economic and financial system, with a view to both minimizing the chances of financial crises occurring in the future and mitigating their effect when they do occur.[3] In that context, the reform of the Fund's regulatory authority in a number of different areas is under consideration and this chapter provides an analysis of the key issues that arise in that context.[4] As

---

* The views expressed in this chapter are those of the author and do not necessarily reflect the views of the Fund.
[1] Of particular importance in this area has been the establishment of the Flexible Credit Line; see International Monetary Fund (IMF), 'GRA Lending Toolkit and Conditionality: Reform Proposals', 13 March 2009, <http://www.imf.org/external/pp/longres.aspx?id=4321> (visited 5 August 2010).
[2] While the Executive Board of the Fund has approved this increase, it will not become effective until ratified by the signatories; see IMF, 'Proposed Decision to Modify the New Arrangements to Borrow', 25 March 2010, <http://www.imf.org/external/pp/longres.aspx?id=4455> (visited 5 August 2010); see also IMF Press Release No 10/145, 'IMF Executive Board Approves Major Expansion of Fund's Borrowing Arrangements to Boost Resources for Crisis Resolution', 12 April 2010, <http://www.imf.org/external/np/sec/pr/2010/pr10145.htm> (visited 5 August 2010).
[3] This recognition is reflected, e.g. in the various G20 Communiqués that have been issued since the onset of the crisis, <http://www.g20.org/pub_communiques.aspx> (visited 5 August 2010).
[4] This discussion is based, in part, on two papers prepared by the staff of the Fund in August 2009, regarding the mandate of the Fund, see 'The Fund's Mandate—The Legal Framework' (the Legal

discussed below, while some of the contemplated reforms can be accommodated under the Articles of Agreement, the Fund's charter, others may require an amendment of this international treaty.

II. The Fund's Existing Mandate: An Overview

To place the ongoing discussion of the reform of the Fund's regulatory authority in context, it is helpful to provide an overview of the Fund's existing mandate. The powers conferred upon the Fund under the Articles can be divided into three categories: (i) *regulatory powers*, relating primarily to the Fund's responsibility to monitor and promote the observance of members' obligations under the Articles; (ii) *financial powers*; and (iii) *advisory powers*. The underlying theme that unifies both the scope and content of these powers is the promotion of the stability of the international monetary system; i.e. the arrangements that directly control the balance of payments of member countries. The most important powers in each of these categories are briefly summarized below.

A. Regulatory powers

1. Bilateral surveillance

Although the par value system was abrogated at the time of the Second Amendment of the Fund's Articles,[5] Article IV, Section 1 of the Fund's Articles continues to give primacy to exchange rates and exchange rate policies, the general obligation of members set forth in Article IV being the promotion of a 'stable system of exchange rates'.[6] Although the Articles specifically recognize that domestic policies must also be scrutinized by the Fund, the objective of this scrutiny is to assess the extent to which these domestic policies contribute to—or undermine—the external stability of the member and, thereby, the stability of the overall exchange rate system.[7] Pursuant to Article IV, Section 3(b), the Fund is required to oversee members' compliance with its obligations under the Articles and this oversight responsibility provides the basis for periodic Article IV Consultations with individual members, which normally take place annually.[8]

Framework Paper), <http://www.imf.org/external/np/pp/eng/2010/022210.pdf> (visited 5 August 2010); and 'The Fund's Mandate—An Overview' (the Overview Paper), <http://www.imf.org/external/np/pp/eng/2010/012210a.pdf> (visited 5 August 2010).

[5] The Second Amendment of the Articles of Agreement became effective on 1 April 1978.

[6] Articles of Agreement, Article IV, Section 1.

[7] The scope of members' domestic obligations under Article IV, Section 1 is discussed in greater detail in Section IV of this chapter.

[8] The Executive Board of the Fund has adopted general decisions regarding the periodicity of Article IV Consultations, see Selected Decisions and Selected Documents of the International Monetary Fund, 34 Issue, Washington, DC, 31 December 2009, 64–6 (Selected Decisions).

2. Multilateral surveillance

Separately, Article IV, Section 3(a) of the Fund's Articles also requires the Fund 'to oversee the international monetary system in order to ensure its effective operation'. This oversight responsibility is generally referred to as 'multilateral surveillance' and provides the basis for the Fund's analysis of developments and risks in the international economic and financial system.[9] Importantly, and unlike Article IV, Section 1—which provides the basis for bilateral surveillance—Article IV, Section 3(a) does not establish any substantive obligations regarding the policies of member countries. It does, however, create the procedural obligation of requiring members to consult with the Fund to the extent that the Fund determines that such a consultation is necessary in order for it to discharge its oversight responsibility.

3. Jurisdiction over current international payments and transfers

Under Article VIII, members may not, without the approval of the Fund, impose restrictions on the 'making of payments and transfers for current international transactions'.[10] Importantly, the Fund's responsibility in this area excludes restrictions on capital movements; indeed, the Articles specifically recognize that '[m]embers may exercise such controls as are necessary to regulate international capital movements'.[11] This exclusion reflects the view—prevailing when the Fund was established—that speculative capital movements had contributed to the instability of the pre-war system.

4. Provision of information

Article VIII, Section 5 provides that the Fund may require members to furnish it with such information as it deems necessary for its activities. In particular, while the Articles list the minimum information that must be provided, the Fund is empowered to request additional information, a power that it exercised in 2003 with the adoption of the current framework for information.[12] As will be discussed in this chapter, this obligation is subject to an important exception: 'Members shall be under no obligation to furnish information in such detail that the affairs of individuals or corporations are disclosed.'[13]

---

[9] Among the most important work products in this area are the World Economic Outlook and Global Financial Stability Report, which are issued every six months. The most recent publications of these products are IMF, 'World Economic Outlook: Rebalancing Growth', April 2010, <http://www.imf.org/external/pubs/ft/weo/2010/01/pdf/text.pdf> (visited 5 August 2010) and IMF, 'Global Financial Stability Report: Meeting New Challenges to Stability and Building a Safer System', April 2010, <http://www.imf.org/external/pubs/ft/gfsr/2010/01/pdf/text.pdf> (visited 5 August 2010).

[10] Articles of Agreement, Article VIII, Section 2(a).

[11] Articles of Agreement, Article VI, Section 3.

[12] See 'Strengthening the Effectiveness of Article VIII, Section 5', Selected Decisions, above n 8, 534–42.

[13] Articles of Agreement, Article VIII, Section 5(b).

B. Financial powers

The Fund is empowered to make its general resources available to members in order to assist them in resolving their balance of payments problems. The Articles require that the Fund make these resources available on a conditional basis; i.e. based upon an assessment that the member will use the financing provided by the Fund to resolve—rather than delay the resolution of—the problem and will do so in a manner that ensures adequate safeguards for the Fund.[14] These requirements—which reinforce one other—provide the basis for Fund conditionality, and although the design of the Fund's policies on conditionality have evolved over the years, they have been anchored by the relevant purpose set forth in Article I which provides, in part, that the Fund's general resources should be made available to members so that they can 'correct maladjustments in their balance of payments without resorting to measures destructive of national or international prosperity'.[15]

C. Advisory powers

In addition to the above, the Fund has the authority to perform, upon request, financial and technical services, provided that these services are consistent with the Fund's purposes.[16] In contrast to the Fund's regulatory authority, these powers are voluntary for both the member (they are only provided if requested) and for the Fund (the Fund is under no obligation to honor the request). Over the years, these advisory powers have been used extensively by the Fund to both complement and enhance its regulatory and financial powers. For example, for the past 10 years the Fund has conducted a periodic detailed analysis of individual members' financial

---

[14] The relevant provision is Article V, Section 3(a), which reads:

> The Fund shall adopt policies on the use of its general resources, including policies on stand-by or similar arrangements, and may adopt special policies for special balance of payments problems, that will assist members to solve their balance of payments problems in a manner consistent with the provisions of this Agreement and that will establish adequate safeguards for the temporary use of the general resources of the Fund.

[15] Articles of Agreement, Article I (v). In addition to this authority, it was decided at the time of the Second Amendment that the quota subscriptions that had been paid with gold could be retained by the Fund and used—subject to decisions adopted by an 85 percent majority—for limited purposes. One such purpose was to provide balance of payments financing 'on special terms to developing members', see Articles of Agreement, Article V, Section 12(f)(ii). This power has provided the basis for the Fund's concessional financing assistance, given through, *inter alia*, the Poverty Reduction and Growth Trust, see Selected Decisions, above n 8, 216–31. Separately, the Fund is authorized to allocate Special Drawing Rights (SDRs) to members of the Fund that are also participants of the SDR Department. An allocation may only be made if the Fund has made the determination that there is a long-term global need to supplement reserve assets and, once such a determination is made, the allocation must be made to all participants as a uniform percentage of their quotas. In contrast with the Fund's general resources, and consistent with the reserve quality of SDRs, a member has the right to use them (i.e. through designation) to resolve balance of payments problems on an unconditional basis.

[16] Article V, Section 2(b), which was introduced at the same time as the Second Amendment, reads as follows: If requested, the Fund may decide to perform financial and technical services, including the administration of resources contributed by members, that are consistent with the purposes of the Fund. Operations involved in the performance of such financial services shall not be on the account of the Fund. Services under this subsection shall not impose any obligation on a member without its consent.

systems, referred to as the Financial Sector Assessment Program (FSAP).[17] These assessments are conducted on a voluntary basis and, accordingly, are a technical service provided by the Fund within the meaning of Article V, Section 2(b).

III. Enhancing Financial Sector Surveillance

As noted above, the Fund conducts bilateral surveillance of its member countries through the periodic (normally annual) consultation process. The obligations that are required to be monitored by the Fund during the consultation process are set forth in Article IV, Section 1 of the Articles, which reads as follows:

Recognizing that the essential purpose of the international monetary system is to provide a framework that facilitates the exchange of goods, services, and capital among countries, and that sustains sound economic growth, and that a principal objective is the continuing development of the orderly underlying conditions that are necessary for financial and economic stability, each member undertakes to collaborate with the Fund and other members to assure orderly exchange arrangements and to promote a stable system of exchange rates. In particular, each member shall:

(1) endeavor to direct its economic and financial policies toward the objective of fostering orderly economic growth with reasonable price stability, with due regard to its circumstances;

(2) seek to promote stability by fostering orderly underlying economic and financial conditions and a monetary system that does not tend to produce erratic disruptions;

(3) avoid manipulating exchange rates or the international monetary system in order to prevent effective balance of payments adjustment or to gain an unfair competitive advantage over other members; and

(4) follow exchange policies compatible with the undertakings under this Section.

As is evident from the text, while the general obligation under Article IV relates to the external policies of members (collaboration 'to assure orderly exchange arrangements' and the promotion of a 'stable system of exchange rates'), Article IV envisages that members' performance of this general obligation will be supported by their observance of more specific obligations relating to domestic policies, set forth in Article IV, Section I (i) and (ii). This text reflects an important assumption regarding the relationship between domestic policies and exchange rates; namely, that the overall stability of the exchange rate system is enhanced by the pursuit of appropriate domestic policies.[18] In 2007, the Fund adopted a decision (the 2007 Decision) that is designed to provide further operational guidance regarding the scope of surveillance and, among other things, the range of domestic policies that will be the subject of particular scrutiny during the Article IV process.[19] As noted in the 2007 Decision, the Fund focuses on those policies that have a significant impact

[17] The FSAP is discussed in greater detail in Section IV of this chapter.
[18] For a comprehensive legal analysis of Article IV, see IMF, 'Article IV of the Fund's Articles of Agreement: An Overview of the Legal Framework', <http://www.imf.org/external/np/pp/eng/2006/062806.pdf> (visited 5 August 2010).
[19] See Selected Decisions, above n 8, 37–47.

on a member's own 'external stability', which is defined as a 'balance of payments position that does not, and is not likely to, give rise to disruptive exchange rate movements'. Importantly, the decision provides that, in light of this focus, the policies that will always be a subject of scrutiny during the Article IV process include not only exchange rate policies, but also monetary, fiscal and financial sector policies. The underlying premise is that a member's own external instability can give rise to systemic instability; i.e. instability of the overall system of exchange rates.[20]

Of course, the financial crisis that erupted in 2008 has only reinforced the important relationship between a member's domestic financial policies and the stability of the overall system. It is generally recognized that weaknesses in the financial regulatory frameworks of important financial centers, including the USA and the UK, were a key factor behind the financial instability and macroeconomic dislocation that swept through the global economy. As is evidenced in successive G20 Communiqués, it is because weaknesses in the financial sector played such an important transmission role during the crisis that the international community has placed such emphasis on establishing international best practices in this area.[21]

A. Upgrading the FSAP

Consistent with the above focus, in April 2010 the IMF's Executive board confirmed that it was considering fully integrating the Fund's FSAP into the bilateral surveillance process. In September 2010 an agreement was reached where it became mandatory for systematically important financial sectors in 25 jurisdictions to be assessed, every five years, by the FSAP on their financial stability.[22] As suggested by its name, the FSAP involves in-depth assessments of members' financial sector regulatory frameworks. The program was initiated following the Asian financial crisis in recognition of the important linkages between the financial sector and macroeconomic stability. Among other things, the FSAP analyzes the extent to which a member's financial sector regulatory framework is consistent with international best practice in key areas.[23]

---

[20] The relevant text of the 2007 Decision reads:

> The scope of bilateral surveillance is determined by members' obligations under Article IV, Section 1. Members undertake under Article IV, Section 1 to collaborate with the Fund and other members to assure orderly exchange arrangements and to promote a stable system of exchange rates (hereinafter 'systemic stability'). Systemic stability is most effectively achieved by each member adopting policies that promote its own 'external stability'—that is, policies that are consistent with members' obligations under Article IV, Section 1 and, in particular, the specific obligations set forth in Article IV, Sections 1(i) through (iv). 'External stability' refers to a balance of payments position that does not, and is not likely to, give rise to disruptive exchange rate movements. Except as provided in paragraph 7 below, external stability is assessed at the level of each member.

Ibid, at 39.

[21] For a list of relevant Communiqués, see G20, above n 3.

[22] See, IMF Press Release 'IMF Expanding Surveillance to Require Mandatory Financial Stability Assessments of Countries with Systemically Important Financial Sectors', <http://www.imf.org/external/np/sec/pr/2010/pr10357.htm> (visited 6 March 2012)

[23] The FSAP is reviewed—and adjusted—periodically. The Executive Board paper that provides the basis for the most recent review is: IMF and World Bank, 'The Financial Sector Assessment

Until now, the FSAP had been voluntary for members and, accordingly, had constituted an exercise of the Fund's advisory rather than regulatory powers. Making it part of bilateral surveillance means that the Fund will have the authority to require members to (i) provide the information that the Fund needs to conduct the assessment and (ii) engage in the type of consultation process regarding its findings that is typical of the bilateral surveillance process. As is apparent from the text of Article IV, Section 1, the Articles provide a clear legal basis for this approach; specifically, members are required to 'seek to promote stability by fostering orderly underlying economic and financial conditions and a monetary system that does not tend to produce erratic disruptions'.[24]

The FSAP is a time-consuming and resource-intensive exercise. The question had been posed, therefore, whether it was possible, as a legal matter, to require FSAP assessments only with respect to the Article IV Consultations with those members that have financial sectors of systemic importance. The Fund's Legal Department confirmed that such an approach would be possible since it would not violate the principle of uniformity of treatment.[25] Specifically, it has always been recognized that this principle allows for differentiation among members as long as the differentiation is based on criteria that are relevant to the power being exercised. In this case, given that the overall objective of bilateral surveillance, as reflected in the text of Article IV itself, is to ensure that the stability of the international monetary system is not undermined by domestic or external policies of individual members—it is entirely appropriate for the Fund to give priority to those members whose policies are more likely to have an impact on this system.

B. The provision of information

The Fund has long recognized that the quality of its surveillance is entirely dependent, in turn, on the quality of the information that it receives from its members. Accordingly, as discussions have evolved regarding the need for the Fund to deepen its surveillance of the financial sector, the question has arisen as to whether the Fund has the information it needs to be effective in this area. In particular, the experience of the most recent financial crisis demonstrates the importance of understanding the linkages between—and the changing pattern of exposure among—a number of large complex financial institutions. The difficulty is that the Articles limit the Fund's authority to obtain such information. Specifically, while Article VIII, Section V provides that the Fund 'may require members to furnish it with such information as it deems necessary for its activities', this provision also includes an important exception to the Fund's authority in this area, inasmuch as it provides that '[m]embers shall be under no obligation to furnish information in such detail that the affairs of individuals or corporations

---

Program After Ten Years: Experience and Reforms for the Next Decade', <http://www.imf.org/external/np/pp/eng/2009/082809b.pdf> (visited 5 August 2010).

[24] Articles of Agreement, Article IV, Section 1(ii).
[25] See the Legal Framework Paper, above n 4, at 7.

are disclosed'.[26] Accordingly, short of an amendment of the Articles, the only way the Fund could obtain such information would be on a voluntary basis. For this reason, consideration could be given to the feasibility of the Fund entering into memoranda of understanding with both national and regional authorities.[27]

IV. Multilateral Surveillance

While the conduct of bilateral surveillance with individual members is central to the Fund's regulatory role, the global crisis has demonstrated the need for a multilateral perspective when assessing risk to the overall system.[28] Indeed, given the integration of financial markets, the collective destruction of global wealth can be out of proportion to the failings of one member's financial sector oversight. Accordingly, within the Fund, there has been a desire to enhance the design and implementation of multilateral surveillance, an activity which is based on the Fund's responsibility under the Articles to 'oversee the international monetary system in order to ensure its effective operation'.[29] It should be noted that this provision already provides the basis for certain work products of the Fund that supply analysis and forecasts of economic and financial developments, notably the World Economic Outlook and the Global Financial Stability Report. However, there is recognition that this analysis needs to be supplemented by the Fund entering into a multilateral dialogue with members regarding both the spillover effects of members' policies and the vulnerabilities of the system as a whole.

From a legal perspective, the Fund's reliance on multilateral surveillance enables it to fill a gap that arises from the limited scope of bilateral surveillance. As noted above, a member's obligations under Article IV include those regarding the pursuit of domestic stability, the concern being that domestic instability may give rise to systemic instability. However, there is an emerging recognition that there may be cases where a member's domestic policies, while being completely supportive of domestic stability, may nevertheless give rise to systemic instability.[30] Since such policies are not inconsistent with the member's obligations under Article IV, it would not be appropriate for them to be the primary focus of the Fund's bilateral surveillance with that member.[31] However, given the systemic impact of these policies, it would be possible for the Fund, relying on its authority to oversee the international monetary system, to assess the impact of these policies and discuss

---

[26] Articles of Agreement, Article VIII, Section 5(b).

[27] For further suggestions relating to exchange rate problems, based upon a functional comparison with WTO law on subsidization see the Chapter 20 by Baltensperger and Cottier in this volume.

[28] For a general discussion of the policy considerations underlying the enhancement of multi-lateral surveillance, see the Overview Paper, above n 4.

[29] Articles of Agreement, Article IV, Section 3(a).

[30] For example, while low interest rates in the USA may be entirely appropriate given the underlying economic conditions of that country, such interest rates may adversely affect the economies of other countries.

[31] For a comprehensive discussion of the scope of members' obligations regarding domestic policies, see the Legal Framework Paper, above n 4, at 7–8.

them not only with the member carrying them out but also with the members affected by them.

Importantly, the scope of members' obligations with respect to multilateral surveillance is more limited than with respect to bilateral surveillance. In the case of bilateral surveillance, the Fund is assessing the extent to which the members are adhering to the substantive obligations set forth in Article IV, Section 1; i.e. the obligations regarding the conduct of the specified domestic and external policies. With respect to multilateral surveillance, however, the Articles do not specify any substantive policy obligation that members must adhere to in support of the Fund's efforts to 'oversee the international monetary system'. Rather, members' obligations are procedural in nature: they are required to consult with the Fund when the Fund determines that such consultation is necessary in order for it to discharge its oversight function in this area. Similarly, the member would be required to provide the Fund with such information as the Fund considers necessary in order to conduct effective multilateral surveillance.[32]

V. The Regulation of Capital Movements

A key purpose of the Fund is to support the expansion of international trade[33] and, to that end, the Articles give the Fund a regulatory role with respect to the payments that are associated with the trading system. More specifically, pursuant to Article VIII, Section 2(a), members may not, as a general rule, impose restrictions on the 'making of payments and transfers for current international transactions.' This general rule is subject to important exceptions. First, the Articles include transitional arrangements, which permit a country to maintain and adapt to changing circumstances those restrictions that were in place when it became a member of the Fund until such time as its balance of payments situation enable them to be removed.[34] Secondly, the Articles give the Fund the authority to

---

[32] See the Legal Framework Paper, above n 4, at 9–12.

[33] Indeed, this mandate is expressed in two of the purposes set forth in Article I; namely:

The purposes of the International Monetary Fund are:
(ii) To facilitate the expansion and balanced growth of international trade, and to contribute thereby to the promotion and maintenance of high levels of employment and real income and to the development of the productive resources of all members as primary objectives of economic policy.
. . . .
(iv) To assist in the establishment of a multilateral system of payments in respect of current transactions between members and in the elimination of foreign exchange restrictions which hamper the growth of world trade.

[34] The full text of Article XIV, Section 2 reads:

A member that has notified the Fund that it intends to avail itself of transitional arrangements under this provision may, notwithstanding the provisions of any other articles of the Agreement, maintain and adapt to changing circumstances the restrictions on payments and transfers for current international transactions that were in effect on the date on which it became a member. Members shall, however, have continuous regard in their foreign exchange policies to the purposes of the Fund, and, as soon as conditions permit, they

approve the imposition of new restrictions and, over the years, the Fund has developed approval policies which permit members to impose restrictions for balance of payments reasons on a temporary and nondiscriminatory basis.[35]

Unlike other aspects of the Fund's regulatory authority, the scope of this obligation has not changed since the Fund was established in 1945. It reflects not only the priority that was placed on the promotion of international trade but also certain assumptions regarding the allocation of responsibilities among different international organizations. While other international fora (originally the General Agreement on Tariffs and Trade and subsequently the World Trade Organization) were charged with the liberalization of trade in goods and services, the Fund was required to ensure that members liberalized the payments and transfers associated with such trade.

Importantly, the Fund's responsibility in this area explicitly excludes restrictions on payments transfers relating to capital movements.[36] Specifically, Article VI, Section 3 recognizes that '[m]embers may exercise such controls as are necessary to regulate international capital movements'. This exclusion reflects the view—prevailing when the Fund was established—that speculative capital movements had contributed to the instability of the pre-war system and that extensive capital controls would be in place for the foreseeable future, with the future growth in the global economy being driven by trade flows. Since that time, however, international capital movements have come to play a critical role in the global economy, presenting members with significant benefits—but also significant risks.

With respect to the potential benefits, capital account liberalization can lower the cost of capital for emerging market economies and can facilitate the development of domestic financial markets. To the extent that capital flows take the form of foreign direct investment, such flows can have a particularly positive impact on the host country's economy, by facilitating the transfer of technology and know-how and the expansion of exports. Furthermore, by allowing consumers to borrow when

shall take all possible measures to develop such commercial and financial arrangements with other members as will facilitate international payments and the promotion of a stable system of exchange rates. In particular, members shall withdraw restrictions maintained under this Section as soon as they are satisfied that they will be able, in the absence of such restrictions, to settle their balance of payments in a manner which will not unduly encumber their access to the general resources of the Fund.

[35] See Selected Decisions, above n 8, 517–18. In addition, the Fund has adopted a policy that permits members to impose and maintain exchange restrictions for reasons of national security, see Selected Decisions, above n 8, 512–13.

[36] The way in which a current transaction is defined as being 'international' is derived from the Fund's mandate regarding the balance of payments of its members. Since the transactions that affect a member's balance of payments are normally those entered into between residents and non-residents, it is these transactions that are treated as 'international' for the purposes of this obligation. Since the foreign affiliate of a foreign investor is considered a resident of the host country where it is incorporated, this definition has important implications with respect to the degree of investment protection that the Fund's Articles provide. Specifically, transactions between a foreign affiliate and other companies located in the host country (and any payments arising from these transactions) would constitute transactions between two residents and, therefore, would not be considered 'international' within the meaning of this provision. However, the repatriation of profits by the foreign affiliate to its non-resident parent firms would be 'international' within the meaning of the Fund's Articles.

their income falls and repay when their income rises, capital account liberalization can promote longer term economic stability. Finally, the integration of a country's economy into international financial markets can have an important disciplining effect on economic policy-making.

Notwithstanding these benefits, experience demonstrates that capital account liberalization can create risks to macroeconomic and financial stability. Under certain circumstances, capital inflows may fuel a sharp expansion of credit, resulting in inflationary pressures and an appreciated exchange rate that, in turn, can result in a deteriorating current account balance. Where the financial sector is underdeveloped or where the regulatory and supervisory framework is weak, the liberalization of capital flows—particularly short-term flows—can result in financial instability. Indeed, a key problem with short-term flows is their volatility: given their sensitivity to domestic and foreign interest-rate differentials, changes in exchange rate expectations and overall market sentiment, these flows can reverse suddenly and such 'sudden stops' can lead to a full-scale balance of payments crisis.

In recognition of the major role—for better or for worse—that capital flows can play in the global economy, the Fund considered an amendment of its Articles during the 1990s that would give the Fund jurisdiction over international capital movements.[37] In some respects, the overall approach followed was consistent with that applicable to the current account: members would have a general obligation to liberalize capital movements and this obligation would be qualified by the existence of transitional arrangements and approval policies. However, given the potential risks arising from capital movements, there was recognition that a more elaborate safeguard would be needed, particularly with respect to the design of the Fund's approval policies, where care was taken to ensure that they were adequately flexible and generous to take into consideration the range of circumstances that could arise. In the end, these efforts to amend the Articles were abandoned based on the judgment that there was inadequate support among the membership. While the loss of momentum was due, in part, to the general reluctance of a small number of members to convey additional authority to the Fund, a key factor was the onset of the Asian Crisis. In particular, there was a concern that the crisis was caused, in large part, by excessive short-term borrowing that had been made possible by the premature opening of the capital accounts of the relevant countries. Although, when studied closely, it is clear that the proposed amendment would have included safeguards to address these risks, there was a perception that it would have increased pressure on liberalization, something which, at the time, was very controversial.[38]

[37] In September 1997, the Interim Committee of the Fund set forth a statement inviting the Fund's Executive Board to complete its work on an amendment that would give the Fund jurisdiction over international capital movements; this statement is often referred to as the 'Hong Kong Declaration', see IMF, 'Communiqué of the Interim Committee of the Board of Governors of the International Monetary Fund', Hong Kong, 21 September 1997, <http://www.imf.org/external/np/cm/1997/cm970921.htm> (visited 5 August 2010).
[38] Indeed, the Hong Kong Declaration specifically referred to the need to temper liberalization with safeguards to ensure financial stability:

Perhaps ironically, the financial crisis of 2008–09 has created new momentum for a more proactive role to be played by the Fund in the area of capital movements. As in the case of the Asian crisis, there is a sense that a number of central and eastern European members liberalized their restrictions on capital movements too early, resulting in excessive borrowing and, in turn, macroeconomic instability. This time, however, the focus is decidedly on the regulation rather than the liberalization of capital movements. While the proposal designed in the 1990s was, as indicated above, sensitive to the risks posed by the free movement of capital, it is unlikely that the membership will support any amendment that creates a general obligation to liberalize—no matter how meaningful the qualifications. An alternative approach would be one that addresses capital movements exclusively through the lens of the stability of the international monetary system. Indeed, depending on its design, this approach may not require an amendment of the Fund's Articles. Specifically, it has been recognized that the right of members to regulate capital movements under Article VI is subject to some limitations. In particular, members must exercise their right to regulate capital movements in a manner that is consistent with their obligation to collaborate with the Fund and other members to promote a stable system of exchange rates.[39] Indeed, this was recognized when the first decision on surveillance was adopted at the time of the Second Amendment.[40] For this reason, it would be open for the Fund to establish policies pursuant to Article IV, Section 1 that provide guidance to members as to: (i) what conditions should be in place before a member liberalizes its capital account, and (ii) when the imposition of controls on outflows or inflows may be an appropriate response to balance of payments or macroeconomic pressures. In the conduct of bilateral surveillance, the Fund would assess the extent to which members' actions are consistent with these

> International capital flows are highly sensitive, inter alia, to the stability of the international monetary system, the quality of macroeconomic policies, and the soundness of domestic financial systems. The recent turmoil in financial markets has demonstrated again the importance of underpinning liberalization with a broad range of structural measures, especially in the monetary and financial sector, and within the framework of a solid mix of macroeconomic and exchange rate policies. Particular importance will need to be attached to establishing an environment conducive to the efficient utilization of capital and to building sound financial systems solid enough to cope with fluctuations in capital flows. This phased but comprehensive approach will tailor capital account liberalization to the circumstances of individual countries, thereby maximizing the chances of success, not only for each country but also for the international monetary system.

See 'Statement of the Interim Committee on the Liberalization of Capital Movements Under an Amendment of the Articles', ibid, para 2.

[39] IMF, 'The Fund's Mandate—The Legal Framework', 22 February 2010, para 35, <http://www.imf.org/external/np/pp/eng/2010/022210.pdf> (visited 21 October 2010).

[40] The 1977 Surveillance Decision included, among the indicators that 'might indicate the need for discussion' with a member 'the introduction or substantial modification for balance of payments purposes of restrictions on, or incentives for, the inflow or overflow of capital.' See Executive Board Decision, 'Surveillance over Exchange Rate Policies', Decision No 5392-(77/63), adopted 2 April 1977, para 2 (iii) (b). This provision was also included in the 2007 (Surveillance) Decision, para 15(iii)(b).

recommendations.[41] The Fund could also take up the systemic role of capital movements—and the impact of controls on such movements—in the context of multilateral surveillance.

Whatever approach is followed, there is an emerging concern that there is inadequate attention being paid at the international level to the relationship between capital account liberalization and the stability of the international monetary and financial system. Indeed, capital account liberalization often takes place in the context of bilateral and regional arrangements that give investor protection priority over financial stability. Given that the Fund is charged with providing financing to address crises that may be caused by premature liberalization, it may be particularly appropriate for the Fund to play a central role in determining when liberalization supports—or undermines—the stability of members and the overall system.

---

[41] However, this assessment of consistency would be for the purposes of policy discussions with members. The failure of a member to observe these policies would not, in itself, lead to a finding of breach of obligation.

PART VI
CONCLUSIONS

Conclusions

Thomas Cottier and Rosa M. Lastra

I. Introduction

The global financial crisis and the ensuing great recession have had a severe impact around the world, in particular this time the developed world. Banking and financial crises often mutate into sovereign debt crises, which in turn can trigger further banking crises. Our understanding of financial markets and regulation has been challenged by the events of the last three years. Prior to the crisis, monetary and financial law operated upon two premises: the first being that national law reigns supreme (though in the EU supranational norms underpin the process of regional integration), the second that market discipline or self-regulation was sufficient. The premise that financial markets were best left to their own devices has now been seriously contested. Notwithstanding the prizes awarded to the theory of rational expectations and to the efficient market hypothesis, individuals (and individual institutions) that 'rationally' expect the worst and behave accordingly, lead in their collective behaviour to the 'irrationality' of financial markets. The herd phenomenon, the downward debt spiral, the domino effect are examples of what Galbraith referred to as the 'insanity' of financial markets in times of crisis.[1] The dichotomy between global markets and national law became acute at the peak of the financial crisis: institutions like Lehman Brothers live globally, but die nationally. In response to the crisis there is now a public demand for regulation, and—in a global market—that regulation must be by definition of an international character. In this book we have argued that we must change our approach to monetary law and financial regulation. We need to 'internationalize' the law of money and finance and go much beyond the weak and largely outdated rules of the International Monetary Fund (IMF), the Bank of International Settlement (BIS) and predominantly informal concertations among national authorities.

The absence of effective disciplines on financial and monetary law in international law contrasts with the multilateral trading system which emerged under the General Agreement on Tariffs and Trade (GATT) and has been enshrined since

[1] John Kenneth Galbraith, *A Short History of Financial Euphoria* (New York: Whistle Books in Association with Viking, 1993)

1995 under the umbrella of the World Trade Organization (WTO). Financial and monetary regulation was set out after World War II within a comprehensive international organization of the IMF, but gradually failed, in particular after the 1971 suspension of the gold standards, to effectively address monetary affairs among industrialised nations. The task of the IMF turned towards assistance of developing countries while monetary concertation of industrialised countries moved into informal concertation within a number of variable clubs, such as the G7 or G10. Trade regulation, on the other hand, began—after the rejection of the Havana Charter—without the insignia of an international organization. GATT built trade law over five decades and nine Rounds of multilateral negotiations and an informally adopted panel system for dispute settlement. The advent of the WTO in 1995 and with it a binding dispute settlement system, the rule based or, at least rule-oriented, system reached so far unprecedented levels of agreed limitations to national sovereignty and international regulation. These strikingly contrasting developments, described by Gadbaw[2] and Lowenfeld[3] in this volume, partly rely upon the nature of the subject matter. While trade regulation is largely motivated and informed by needs to secure market access and non-discrimination for goods and services sold abroad, and thus inherently a matter to be addressed in international law, financial and monetary affairs do not comprise reciprocity and immediate interdependence in a comparable manner. Competitive advantages of domestic operators can be achieved by supervision and unilateral measures and policies, both in terms of financial regulation and monetary policies. They have often shown traits of beggar your neighbour, for example in exchange rate policy. Secondly, shared policies of liberalization in trade, finance and monetary affairs required governmental efforts in trade negotiations and international commitments while abstention was sufficient in the other areas. Thirdly, and perhaps most importantly, central banks and lenders of last resort in key jurisdictions, in particular the US and the EU, UK and Switzerland, enjoy full independence from government and the political process with a view to successfully combating inflation and deflations in monetary policy. They operate outside normal channels of governance. They follow their own standards of accountability and often show a lack of transparency in policy formulation and communication. Such independence implies that on transnational cooperation international arrangements do not find their way into properly binding international agreements the conclusion of which is exclusively reserved to government and subject to approval by parliament. The lack of proper treaty making in monetary affairs and the predominance of soft law instruments and network governance among like minded institutions addressed shortly may thus be explained by a combination of these factors. The lack of international regulation of financial markets, on the other hand, may best be explained by unilaterally attainable goals of enhancing competitiveness and the long-standing power of large banks able to strongly influence governments to practice a hands-off approach considerably different from trade policy. Before

---

[2] See R. Michael Gadbaw in this volume at Chapter 2.
[3] See Andreas F. Lowenfeld in this volume at Chapter 3.

this background, soft law in financial monetary affairs is at the heart of the debate and of a number of contributions to this volume.

The purpose of this concluding chapter, building upon the papers first published in the Special Issue of the *Journal of International Economic Law* on the Quest for International Law in Financial Regulation and Monetary Affairs (Issue 13.3) and reprinted in this volume with an updated introduction, is to cast some light on the role that international law should play in the regulation of money and finance. It offers a reflection of the main ideas and lessons that can be extracted from the different contributions to Issue 13.3 and also presents some alternative views.

II. Towards Multilevel Governance

Whether and how financial and monetary affairs should be addressed on the international level calls, in our view, for an analytical and normative framework which allows to answer these questions in a more convincing manner than mere recourse to economic interests of operators. A strong conceptual divide between international and domestic law facilitates an equally strong divide between domestic and international regulation in finance, discussed by Tietje and Lehmann in this volume.[4] It equally allowed stressing sovereignty and national monopolies in monetary affairs as the chapter by Baltensperger and Cottier shows.[5]

We submit that the matter should henceforth taking recourse to the emerging doctrines of multilevel or multilayered governance, expounded in this volume by Rolf H. Weber[6] as well as Christian Tietje and Matthias Lehmann.[7] This doctrine essentially argues that all layers of governance—both domestic and international—are not fundamentally different and share common values and goals of public governance. This is equally and perhaps particularly true in finance and monetary affairs. Weber highlights financial stability, trust and market integrity as public goods shared on all levels of governance.[8] Financial stability emerges, as Trachtman expounds, as a new and hitherto often neglected prime goal and public good.[9] It has to be pursued and achieved on all levels of governance alike. It forms a common foundation for coordinated and concerted efforts on all levels of governance alike.

The financial and debt crisis recalls that financial stability, transparency, trust and market integrity are of key importance. These values underlying the regulatory framework of financial and monetary affairs are goals and principles at the same time. They define what overall should be achieved in combining different layers of governance and they inform, as principles, the details and implementation of regulation on all these layers. They in return depend upon transparency of operations as a mainstay in implementing these principles on all levels of governance

---

[4] See Christian Tietje and Matthias Lehmann in this volume at Chapter 7.
[5] See Ernst Baltensperger and Thomas Cottier in this volume at Chapter 20.
[6] See Rolf H. Weber in this volume at Chapter 8.
[7] See above n 4.
[8] See above n 6.
[9] See Joel P. Trachtman in this volume at Chapter 10.

alike, whether local, domestic, regional or global. There is no fundamental difference and divide between different levels of governance when it comes to underlying
goals and principles. The fact that financial services have been mainly regulated, so
far, in domestic law and was largely ignored beyond soft law in international affairs
stems from a combination of national sovereignty and powerful influences in the
banking sector expounding neo-liberal beliefs, both of which kept the matter from
effective international control and monitoring up to today. The same holds true for
monetary affairs albeit the level of regulation generally is much less prominent and
policies are largely left to economists both in domestic and international fora. The
financial and debt crisis shows that the overall framework largely based upon
competing domestic regulations and largely absent of effective international disciplines is deficient and unable to achieve the overall goals and principles described
above. International or global law is bound to play a stronger role in these fields.
The question is where and how.

   Allocation of regulatory powers to different levels of governance in the pursuit of
shared goals and principles should take place in response to the question of how and
where best public goods and goals can be achieved. While local public goods are
best addressed locally, regional and global goods need regulation on the regional
and global level respectively. The need for international law in finance is advocated
by many of the contributions to this volume. However, this does not simply imply
wholesale international harmonization to the detriment of domestic law. Tietje and
Lehmann argue that a uniform global financial regime increases the risk of global
failures and—based upon Multilevel Governance—suggest that there are times
when competition between legal regimes is desirable:

The relationship between international harmonization and regulatory competition cannot
be an 'either/or' one: it has to be an 'at the same time' one. (...) The question is not
whether we need international cooperation—we certainly do—but what is the optimal
degree.[10]

They then go on to elaborate in which areas harmonization is needed (e.g. with
regard to restructuring rules for banks and bail-out regimes) and in which other
areas different regimes provide a better answer (where they controversially include
capital rules).

   In conclusion, there is no single answer as to how financial stability, transparency, trust and market integration can best be achieved; it much depends on the
regulatory context and the details of the subject matter. It is a matter of assessing
and deciding how and by which instrument this can best be achieved. It calls both
for harmonization and regulatory competition, and a combination thereof. The
question entails both the level of governance and the legal nature of measures which
should be adopted in pursuit of the public good addressed. It also assists in
revisiting the prevailing view that soft law is most suitable in international financial
and monetary affairs.

---

[10] See above n 4.

We first turn to financial stability. We then address proper normative forms of regulation and the phenomenon of soft law widely discussed in this book.

III. Financial Stability and the Rationale of International Financial Regulation

It is clear by now that insufficient attention to financial stability considerations by inflation-centred central bankers and too narrow a focus on micro-prudential supervision by the supervisory authorities, led to inadequate systemic risk control.[11] That systemic risk was either ignored or downplayed is considered to be one of the defining features of the crisis, as pointed out in the chapter by Lastra and Wood. Regulation—Hal S. Scott observes in his chapter—must be above all about systemic risk reduction.

A distinction is made between regulation and supervision,[12] a point that is examined in several chapters, including the ones by Garicano and Lastra[13], Tietje and Lehmann.[14] Regulation refers to the establishment of rules, to the process of rule-making and includes legislative acts and statutory instruments issued by the competent authorities nationally and supra-nationally, international rules (often 'soft law' in the field of banking and finance) and rules issued by self-regulatory organisations and private bodies or 'clubs', such as a cooperative bankers association. Financial regulation draws from national, supranational and international sources. While regulation refers to the establishment of rules, supervision (micro-prudential supervision) refers to the oversight of financial firms' behaviour, in particular risk monitoring and risk control.[15]

In the aftermath of the crisis a consensus has emerged as regards the need to supervise systemic risk via macro-prudential supervision. The latter presents the view of the 'forest' while the micro dimension focuses upon 'individual trees'. This differentiation between micro-prudential supervision (focusing upon individual institutions) and macro-prudential supervision (focusing upon systemic risk and the soundness of the system as a whole) has led to a number of institutional developments on the international level, including the establishment of Councils for Financial Stability, such as the Financial Stability Oversight Council in the USA (created by the Dodd–Frank Act 2010) and the European Systemic Risk Board

---

[11] See Lastra, Inaugural Lecture on the Quest for International Financial Regulation, 23 March 2011, at <http://www.law.qmul.ac.uk/podcast/lastra2011.html> (visited on 15 March 2012).

[12] See Rosa Lastra, *Central Banking and Banking Regulation*, Financial Markets Group, London School of Economics, London, 108–44 (1996).

[13] Luis Garicano and Rosa M. Lastra in this volume at Chapter 4.

[14] See above n 4.

[15] Supervision in a broad sense can be understood as a process with four stages or phases: first, licensing, authorisation or chartering (entry into the business), secondly, supervision *stricto sensu* (they essential component of any supervisory process), thirdly, sanctioning or imposition of penalties in the case of non-compliance with the law, fraud, bad management or other types of wrongdoing, and, finally, crisis management, which comprises lender of last resort, deposit insurance and bank insolvency proceedings.

(which became operational in January 2011). It has also led to a revamping of the supervisory structure in the UK with new legislation that is to transfer many supervisory responsibilities back to the Bank of England, and establish within the Bank, a Financial Policy Committee charged with the pursuit of financial stability. The chapter by Garicano and Lastra presents a template for the design of adequate macro-prudential supervision.[16]

The understanding of financial stability requires an understanding of market failures and, in turn, this requires an adequate inter-disciplinary dialogue between law and economics. This is one of the key themes that permeates through the book.[17] The loss of confidence and trust in functioning financial markets— explored by Lastra and Wood—remains a puzzle for bankers, politicians and regulators today and in every other previous crisis.[18] It is the existence of market failures and deficiencies, notably negative externalities and information asymmetries that provides the rationale of regulation. Externalities or spillovers are the costs to society of banking failures. Indeed, the costs to society of a crisis are very large— as we know from recent experience—and, by far, exceed the private costs to individual financial institutions; that is why a key aim of regulation should be to internalize these externalities. Information asymmetries or deficiencies—a feature of the services industry in general—refers to the fact that the provider of the service knows much more than the consumer of the service. In banking these problems are particularly acute and the phenomenon of bank runs is well known. Furthermore, excessive group think—a point made by Langevoort[19] and Garicano and Lastra[20]—exacerbated the information problem. The aim of banking and financial laws should be to protect individuals (depositors, investors, policy-holders), to ensure the smooth conduct of the business (fair, efficient and transparent markets) and to safeguard the payment system and the stability of the financial system at large, preventing and containing systemic risk and systemic crises.

The quest for international law in money and finance is a logical response to the increasing globalization of financial markets. It is also a response to the need to prevent and contain contagious systemic risk, a risk that does not respect geographic boundaries. The crisis showed that national financial markets cannot be looked at in isolation. A fragmented global regulatory and accounting regime gives rise to regulatory arbitrage ('forum shopping'), loopholes and shadow institutions and markets; it also increases transaction costs and can lead to financial protectionism.

---

[16] See above n 13.

[17] That markets need rules to function well has been argued by Nobel Laureates Ronald Coase and Douglass North. But long before Coase and North, the importance of the law for functioning markets had been recognised. Adam Smith, the founding father of Economics as an autonomous subject, wrote in 1776: 'Commerce (...) can seldom flourish long in any state which does not enjoy a regular administration of justice, in which the people do not feel themselves secure in the possession of their property, in which the faith of contracts is not supported by the law, and in which the authority of the state is not supposed to be regularly employed in enforcing the payment of debts from all those who are able to pay'.

[18] See Rosa M. Lastra and Geoffrey Wood in this volume at Chapter 1.

[19] See Donald C. Langevoort in this volume at Chapter 14.

[20] See above n 13.

Incompatible or conflicting rules from country to country increase the regulatory costs and can create new risks. Regulatory competition can also lead to a race to the bottom.

Though the financial crisis was global, the solutions to the mounting problems were mostly national. Some of these solutions—including unprecedented liquidity assistance and massive government support and intervention—were quite extraordinary and, in the absence of adequate laws, emergency legislation or new rules were expeditiously introduced in several countries. Using an analogy with fire departments, while every effort was made to extinguish the fire during the crisis, in the aftermath of the financial crisis we need to re-examine the fire regulations and to consider how well (or how badly) the institutions did. In many cases we may conclude that the adequate response is not necessarily more regulation, but better supervision and enforcement or greater transparency or better international coordination. As Garicano and Lastra point out, the failure was often in the 'how' to supervise and not in the 'who', since all structures failed to adequately supervise financial institutions.[21] We should also beware of the excesses of regulation and the dangers of over-regulating a given sector or type of institutions, creating incentives for businesses to move outside the regulatory framework. Any regulatory perimeter brings its own shadows and loopholes, a point that Goodhart and Lastra emphasize in their chapter on 'border problems'.[22]

Confidence and trust are preconditions for a market economy to function efficiently (the term credit comes from the Latin *credere*: to trust, to believe), and such trust that underlies all transactions, that is the foundation of enterprise and development, is supported by a legal framework. Christine Kaufman and Rolf Weber view transparency as 'a pre-condition for building confidence since it is the very essence of any expectation'.[23] An alternative view is offered by Garicano and Lastra, who argue that a downside of transparency concerns panics, since the belief in a panic is self-fulfilling.[24] Indeed, there is also a psychological element in the transmission mechanism of any crisis; modern financial innovation and information technology has added to the speed of transmission.

Financial stability is a goal that transcends national boundaries and thus exposes the limitations of the principle of sovereignty. Like a tsunami that does not respect territorial frontiers, episodes of instability travel fast in a world of interconnected markets and financial transactions. As Tietje and Lehmann point out, what is different when it comes to many financial law measures, is their extraterritorial character.[25] Extra-territoriality—a key theme in international law and in insolvency law—is also a key theme to understand the legal foundations of financial stability.

---

[21] Ibid.
[22] See Charles A.E. Goodhart and Rosa M. Lastra in this volume at Chapter 9.
[23] See Christine Kaufmann and Rolf H. Weber in this volume at Chapter 13.
[24] See above n 13.
[25] See above n 4.

IV. Global Finance and National Law

It is the dichotomy between global financial markets and institutions and national law, policies and regulation that more clearly illustrates the need to internationalise the law of money and finance. Indeed, at the national level, financial law is mostly governed by hard law rather than soft law, which suggests that the real challenge in moving forward in the quest for international law in monetary affairs and financial regulation lies precisely in the resolution of this dichotomy.

In the quest for international law in financial regulation we need a combination of general principles (such as non discrimination and transparency)—which represent a mix of ethics and efficiency that withstand the passage of time—with more prescriptive technical rules that can be adjusted to new circumstances with flexibility. In accordance with the principle of subsidiarity and regulatory competition some global standards may be not only impractical but undesirable. The same may be true for avoiding unnecessary risks inherent to uniform regulation. Yet there are a number of concepts—credibility, confidence, fairness—that should permeate through all the different layers of regulation and influence the behaviour of bankers and financiers. Regulation should be designed in good times, when rapid credit expansion and exuberant optimism cloud the sound exercise of judgment in risk management, rather than in bad times, in response to a crisis. The biblical story of Joseph offers instructive lessons in this regard. We must also remember that markets are part of the solution since it is well functioning markets that generate growth.

It is argued that some aspects of the new *lex financiera* and the emerging international architecture should be sanctioned by a Treaty. Nothing less than a Treaty is legally binding from a formal point of view. Perhaps the 'core values' of non-discrimination and transparency as a prerequisite for both good governance and sound financial regulation, as Christine Kaufmann and Rolf H. Weber point out, and fairness could form the basis of formal international law in the field of money and finance.[26]

Drawing on the lessons of history, it was in the context of World War II that countries were ready to make the sacrifices needed in terms of sovereignty by signing a number of international treaties that gave rise to international organizations such as the United Nations, the International Monetary Fund and the World Bank. John Maynard Keynes had wisely stated that in order to win the war we needed to 'win the peace'. It was this understanding that also inspired Henry Morgenthau (then US Treasury Secretary) to proclaim in the opening remarks of the Bretton Woods conference in New Hampshire in July 1944 that 'prosperity like peace is indivisible'.[27] Neither Keynes nor Morgenthau were thinking only in

---

[26] See above n 23.

[27] See 'Address by the Honorable Henry Morgenthau, Jr, at the Inaugural Plenary Session 1 July 1944,' in *United Nations Monetary and Financial Conference, Bretton Woods, New Hampshire, 1–22 July 1944: Final Act and Related Documents* (Washington: US Government Printing Office, 1944).

territorial/national terms: they were thinking in international terms. And we also need now to think in international terms to solve some of the problems of our times. Kaufman and Weber point out that 'sound financial regulation is not an objective in itself but a means to an end'.[28] They recall how Franklin Roosevelt and Winston Churchill agreed in 1941 that stable monetary and financial systems were one of the pillars of the peaceful post-war order.

The dichotomy between global finance and national law is particularly acute in the resolution of cross border banks and systemically important financial institutions (SIFIs). Financial institutions, though global in ambitions and often in international presence, are still subject to the control of national authorities. Banking remains a sensitive sector at the core of a nation's concerns. Regardless of how much a bank expands internationally, it is still recognized as a legal entity under the domestic laws of the place of incorporation. Constitutional and cultural differences, national habits and, at times, national oligopolies often obstruct international coordination, and may hinder other regional efforts, as evidenced by the EU experience.

The dichotomy between national law and international markets and institutions is particularly relevant in the case of resolution and insolvency. Financial institutions may claim to be global when they are alive; they become national when they are dying. The bankruptcy of Lehman Brothers is a clear example of this dichotomy. If at the national level, bank crisis management is complex (with the involvement of several authorities and the interests of many stakeholders), this complexity is far greater in the case of cross border bank crisis management. In any financial crisis, it is necessary to have a clear and predictable legal framework in place to govern how a financial institution would be reorganized or liquidated in an orderly fashion so as not to undermine financial stability. We do not have such a framework yet with regard to cross-border banks (nor for any cross-border financial institution), neither at the European level nor at the international level, though the recent release by the Financial Stability Board of international standards on effective resolution regimes is a step in the right direction.[29] The capital standards, in particular Basel I, contributed to the international soft law agreement that was then widely implemented in many jurisdictions around the globe. The challenge is now to implement the FSB resolution standards—endorsed by the G20 Heads of State at its summit in Cannes on 4 November 2011—to achieve regulatory and legislative convergence in this key area.[30]

The fear of failure needs to always be present in banking and finance, as Lastra and Wood emphasize.[31] Risk is at the essence of finance and, by definition, risk

---

[28] See above n 23.
[29] See 'Key Attributes of Effective Resolution Regimes for Financial Institutions', Financial Stability Board October 2011, <http://www.financialstabilityboard.org/publications/r_111104cc.pdf> (visitied on 15 March 2012).
[30] Hal S. Scott elaborates upon capital regulation. With regard to cross border resolution of banks and other financial institutions, see generally Rosa M. Lastra, *Cross Border Bank Insolvency* (Oxford: Oxford University Press, 2011).
[31] See above n 18.

brings return but risk also entails failure. We need market discipline in regulation, but we also need market discipline in protection. As Lee Buchheit put it in his testimony to the House of Lords in 2009:

The fundamental principle of the capitalist system is that within the constraints of the law, and regulation if it is a regulated entity, every enterprise is free to pursue its affairs as it sees fit. No one guarantees that you will not fail, but by the same token, no one places any artificial constraint on your ability to succeed. The sanction that capitalism imposes on imprudence, incompetence, some times bad luck, is failure. It is the brooding presence of that sanction that keeps managers on their toes, that keeps them acting in a prudent way.[32]

Financial regulation needs to be redesigned to respond to the needs of international financial markets. Global problems—and the crisis was indeed a global problem— require global solutions. The limitations of sovereignty as an organising territorial principle that forms the anchor of the nation state are all too clear when it comes to global finance. And the system of incentives that govern financial institutions must also be redrawn. Capitalism relies on the lure of wealth (privatisation of gains) and the discipline imposed by the fear of bankruptcy (privatisation of losses).

The financial crisis has triggered a revolution in regulatory thinking. For markets to prosper, markets need rules and international financial markets need international rules. We need an effective system for the cross border resolution of banks and other financial institutions, and in order to achieve it, we need international law. The question of who will enforce it remains a daunting challenge, though the IMF is well placed to adopt a role as a 'global sheriff' with regard to international financial stability. Sean Hagan reflects in his contribution about the changing and expanding mandate of the Fund as an international financial institution.[33]

The quest for international law in financial regulation does present complex and difficult challenges. But since the world's economic and financial problems will not solve themselves, we should echo Einstein's words: 'We can't solve problems by using the same kind of thinking we used when we created them'.

V. Soft Law Versus Hard Law

The reliance on soft law and soft institutions to govern international money and finance is in stark contrast to the law and institutional framework that govern international trade. As explained in the Introduction, when it comes to monetary and financial issues, we have a black hole in terms of 'hard' international law. We do have a large number of international soft law rules, but little hard law. The corpus of international monetary and financial law has been heavily reliant upon soft law, with the one relevant exception of the law of the IMF, in particular the

---

[32] See Lee Buchheit, 'The Future of EU Financial Regulation and Supervision' Report of the House of Lords' European Union Committee, June 2009, Vol. II, Evidence, H.R. Paper 106-II, p. 5.

[33] See Sean Hagan in this volume at Chapter 22.

Articles of Agreement of the International Monetary Fund. The regulatory function at the international level is shared by a variety of actors, including informal groupings of an international character such as the Financial Stability Board, the Basel Committee on Banking Supervision, the International Organization of Securities Commissions (IOSCO) and the International Association of Insurance Supervisors (IAIS), professional associations—such as the International Swaps and Derivatives Association (ISDA)—and other entities. International financial soft law is often a 'top-down' phenomenon with a two-layer implementation scheme. The rules are agreed by international financial standard setters and national authorities must implement them in their regulation of the financial industry. The financial intermediaries are the 'final' addresses of those rules. Standards and uniform rules, however, can also be designed by the financial industry itself. Self-regulation, by definition, has a 'bottom-up' character, comprising rules of practice, standards, master agreements, usages as well as rules and principles agreed or proposed by scholars and experts.

The lack of formal commitments and formal rules works well in good times, but not in a crisis. In the words of Chris Brummer, 'the predominance of international soft law in finance does not, however, imply its perfection'.[34] What is needed in a crisis is certainty, clarity, predictability and *ex ante* knowledge as to the *loci* of power and the rules and processes that must be followed. This typically requires hard law, not soft law, as well as an adequate institutional framework.

Chris Brummer and Joseph Norton elaborate upon the issues of legitimacy and representation in the international financial law making process. While soft law is harder in practice and more influential than generally assumed, Brummer calls for more robust monitoring of regulatory rules oversight.[35] The increasingly important role of the G20 and the mandate of the Financial Stability Board ought to be examined under the prism of greater legitimacy and fairer representation, including emerging economies and developing countries in such process. Norton's paper extrapolates lessons from the regulation of sovereign wealth funds and suggests the need for new procedures and processes in international financial regulation.[36]

Whether we need a new institutional structure or a revamping of the current structure with a new mandate focused on financial stability issues remains an issue of intense debate. Indeed while some think the IMF should assume a leading role in the international financial architecture, i.e. reform of the current system, as advocated by the IMF General Counsel,[37] others would prefer a new structure, gravitating around the FSB and the G20. What ever the solution, the current soft law approach is no longer suitable to produce the public goods of financial stability, trust and market integration. A bolder approach is called for.

The move towards formalization of law (from informal to formal law) is a perennial trait in the history of law. The evolution of international law and of

[34] See Chris Brummer in this volume at Chapter 5.
[35] Ibid.
[36] See Joseph J. Norton in this volume at Chapter 6.
[37] See above n 33.

commercial law, to cite two relevant examples, provides clear evidence in this regard. The primary sources of international law are conventional law (treaty law), customary law and the general principles of law, as recognised by Article 38 of the Statute of the International Court of Justice. Customary international law results when states follow certain practices generally and consistently. Customary law, however, can evolve into conventional law. Indeed, important principles of customary international law have become codified in the Vienna Convention of the Law of the Treaties, thus acquiring the characteristic of 'conventional law'. The birth and development of formal commercial law was influenced by the medieval *lex mercatoria*, that is by the mercantile codes and customs which reflected the usages of trade, the international maritime and commercial practice at the time. Many of the uncodified usages of trade that constituted the *lex mercatoria* eventually became formal law.[38]

Financial and monetary law being a relatively novel subject compared with other more established areas of law is navigating towards greater formalisation. The crisis has accelerated that trend and the emerging *lex financiera* is international in character.

John Maynard Keynes in the debate that led to the establishment of the International Monetary Fund famously stated: 'Perhaps the most difficult question is how much to decide by rule and how much by discretion'.[39] That challenge remains in the current process of internationalization of the law of money and finance. The rules versus discretion debate that has dominated monetary policy and administrative law for so many decades finds a new dimension when it comes to the understanding of this emerging *lex financiera*.

To begin, it is important to realise that rules and discretion are not mutually exclusive, since rules may grant discretion (for example a rule on monetary or supervisory independence grants a degree of discretion to the central bank in the pursuit of its tasks). Also, it is not a matter of fundamental difference between hard and soft law. While soft law rules tend to allow for a greater margin for discretion and offer a higher degree of flexibility and pragmatism than hard law rules, they may also entail rigid standards (such as Basel III), as formal, hard law may grant extensive discretion in operation and implementation. It is rather a divide between a rule-based or rule-oriented approach and a policy-based approach. The discretionary, policy-based powers granted to central banks have been a defining feature of the financial crisis. It is the prompt and immediate nature of the assistance provided by central banks that makes them uniquely capable of managing a crisis. However, that very discretion granted to central bankers in the exercise of their lender of last resort role is now being increasingly curtailed after the crisis. For example, the

---

[38] Sir Roy Goode recalls in his writings that the *lex mercatoria* or law merchant (which was international rather than English and which was administered by its own mercantile courts) was given full recognition by the common law courts (absorbed in the common law itself). The fertility of the business mind and the fact that a practice which begins life by having no legal force acquires over time the sanctity of law are key factors to which the commercial and financial lawyer must continually be responsive.

[39] John Maynard Keynes, 'Proposals for an International Currency (Clearing) Union', 1942.

Dodd–Frank Act 2010 restricts the room for manoeuvre of the Federal Reserve System in the interpretation of Section 13.3 of the Federal Reserve Act, the arcane legal provision that provided the legal basis for the emergency liquidity assistance and rescue packages that the Fed helped put together.

Yet, there is no fundamental divide between a rule-based or a rule-oriented approach and discretion. The latter often is part of the law, and depends upon regulatory density chosen. The law readily modulated rules and discretion as appropriate to take into account the relevant circumstances which often cannot be foreseen and remain unpredictable. A fundamental divide rather exists between a rule-based approach and those voices arguing the matter should be left to markets and government intervention be limited to discretionary policies. We submit that a rule-based approach establishes a proper framework within which discretion may be exercised to a certain extent. The law shapes the scope of policy space available. This is true both for financial and for monetary affairs. Both can and need to be addressed in international law. Both may be inspired by the idea of providing an appropriate regulatory framework for competition. Again, it is not a matter of wholesale harmonization, but of asking which elements inherently need common denominators in order to provide a proper framework for competition.

As to financial regulation, it is not a matter of proposing single and uniform harmonised rules across the board. It is rather a matter of defining those elements which are necessary to bring about and allow proper regulatory competition between different systems, as Tietje and Lehman argue.[40]

Decentralization should take place to the utmost extent possible in order to avoid undue risks of policy failures. At the same time, it is a matter of identifying inherently common rules which in a global system should be shared. Minimal capital requirements for large operators, for example, are indispensable parameters for competition. Other inherently shared elements entail common prudential standards currently entailed in Basel II and III and additional disciplines on disclosure and transparency as Scott argues.[41] It calls for future principles of taxation of capital flows in international law, such as a Tobin tax discussed by Kern Alexander.[42] Common rules relating to the problem of moral hazard and the Too Big To Fail problem and its variants (too interconnected to fail, too complex to fail, etc.) equally need to be addressed on a global level. While competition law and policy, as it currently stands, was of little importance in addressing the financial crisis according to Philip Marsden and Ioannis Kokkoris,[43] the underlying ideas could well be put to work to develop specific rules on merger controls for international banking and financial corporations. Finally, and not particularly addressed in this volume is the need to develop shared rules and principles on international bankruptcy relating to financial institutions, as mentioned above when referring to the FSB Key Attributes of Effective Resolution Regimes.

---

[40] See above n 4.
[41] See Hal S. Scott in this volume at Chapter 12.
[42] See Kern Alexander in this volume at Chapter 19.
[43] See Philip Marsden and Ioannis Kokkoris in this volume at Chapter 18.

Competition law and policy could also inspire future rules addressing the relationship of different currency regimes. We submit with Baltensperger and Cottier that international monetary law should be inspired by disciplines of competition law as national currencies find themselves in a competitive relationship. Moreover, they amount to monopolies which may be abused and therefore call for an appropriate regulatory framework. It is doubtful that this can be achieved on the basis of soft law. Both competition law and international trade regulation rely upon hard law in addressing monopolies both in domestic and international law.

The shift towards a greater role for hard law will not remain without an impact on treaty-making powers. The chapter by Baltensperger and Cottier further argues that the lack of independent treaty making powers by central banks is one of the main reasons for recourse to soft law.[44] The enhanced role of central banks in the current debt crisis beyond traditional tasks, including oversight over financial sector in a number of countries such as UK, calls for enlarged accountability which may need translation into more formal international commitments. To the extent that independence of central banks and lenders of last resort should be combined with hard law, we need to review current treaty making powers. New avenues need to be sought for central banks which combine independence and new formal treaty making powers. National statutes establishing independence reserve institutions should explicitly define and limit the scope of powers and tasks that the institution is entitled to engage in international treaties. It should be commensurable to domestic regulatory powers assigned. Such parallelism will allow centrals bank to engage in international agreements which form part of international law and could be made subject to international adjudication and enforcement. Moreover, transparency requirements in terms of formal and informal consultations made prior to setting policies and engaging in international commitments should be established. International Agreements transgressing these goals should remain with the Government and democratic processes of accountability. The allocation of powers in financial and monetary affairs between government, parliament and central banks will amount to one of the most important challenges in coming years. Lessons may be learned from other areas of international law and relations, in particular trade regulation.

VI. Linking Trade, Financial and Monetary Affairs

Trade, monetary affairs and financial regulation have so far evolved along completely separate tracks. Both the chapters by Michael Gadbaw[45] and Andreas Lowenfeld[46] offer an extensive account of a fragmented world. At the same time, it is evident that the there is a close triangle between these different areas of international law, including investment protection. Baltensperger and Cottier

---

[44] See above n 5.   [45] See above.   [46] See above.

expound that an open and rule-based multilateral trading system amounts to the most important contribution to an open exchange rate regimes and competition among different currencies.[47] Stable exchange rates, in turn, are a prerequisite to an open trading system. Distorted rates give rise to protectionist measures in trade and investment. Growths and trade flows determine, in the long run, the amount and costs of money and credit. Prior to the financial crisis, a long period of growth short of inflation due to inexpensive exports by China allowed central banks to embark in expansive monetary policies resulting in inexpensive money which triggered highly speculative transactions. Trade and monetary affairs are the two sides of the same coin.

The same holds true for financial regulation. Inadequate prudential regulation and excessive scope for speculation threaten the supply of liquidity which is essential in the operation of international trade. The slump of international trade by 10 per cent induced by the financial crisis was mainly due to lack of liquidity at the time. Likewise, the lack of appropriate prudential regulation—for example the risk weightings assigned to different asset categories in the capital rules agreed in the Basel I accord—distorts competition and may lead to protectionism. It can also induce spill-over effects into other economies as it threatens the long-term process of liberalization and the provision of market access for foreign operators which, by allowing for competition, generally deploys beneficial welfare effects. The General Agreement on Trade in Services (GATS) was built upon the premises of progressive trade liberalization. It entails, in Article VI, standards of necessity and proportionality addressing excessive regulation. These disciplines remain of importance, as Panagiotis Delimatsis and Pierre Sauvé expound.[48] However, it is equally relevant with Cottier and Krajewski to revisit the Agreement's carve-out for prudential standards and to seek making appropriate and positive prudential standards a prerequisite for liberalization.[49] Committing to appropriate prudential standards is a contribution to the public good of financial stability which should, in return, be honoured by enhanced market access for banks operating under such agreed standards. Linkages also need to be further developed in the field of subsidies. The various stimuli programmes on both sides of the Atlantic were in violation of the WTO Agreement on Subsidies and Countervailing Duties as illustrated by Gary N. Horlick and Peggy A. Clarke.[50] No action was taken in the light of the pending crisis, and provisions violating investment rules of the Trade Related Investment Measures (TRIMs) Agreement (buy national) were impaired. The Agreement does not provide for sufficient policy space for a Keynesian response to crisis; it does not entail exceptions, while allowing circumvention of disciplines with loop holes which should be closed. The agreement does not entail appropriate disciplines and criteria which could and should guide governments in designing subsidy programmes upon economic crisis.

---

[47] See above n 5.
[48] See Panagiotis Delimatsis and Pierre Sauvé in this volume at Chapter 16.
[49] See Thomas Cottier and Markus Krajewski in this volume at Chapter 15.
[50] See Gary N. Horlick and Peggy A. Clarke in this volume at Chapter 17.

Future trade negotiations therefore need to take into account the goals and principles of financial stability and market integrity, as well as transparency. Disciplines need to be developed which both anticipate and prevent the building up of a crisis, and which are able to address them in law.

VII. Institutional Linkages

Future regulations both in monetary and financial affairs inevitably will establish linkages with the trading system, and trade measures taken for reasons of financial or monetary policy may therefore be subject to WTO dispute settlement. It will be necessary to develop appropriate procedures interfacing different institutions. Thus, WTO dispute settlement should be in a position to refer issues of financial and monetary affairs to the appropriate bodies. Under the Dispute Settlement Understanding, Panel and the Appellate Body are in a position to seek expert advice in the process of fact finding. They can turn to other international organizations for advice and guidance. What however, is called for is the possibility to refer certain questions to appropriate institutions for legal determination which in return would provide an appropriate basis for assessing the trade measure taken by panels and the Appellate Body. These procedures are currently missing and need to be developed.[51] The IMF, for example, is not in a position to make authoritative findings in matters relating to exchange rate policies within Article IV of the Fund which may form the basis for trade restrictive measures challenged before the WTO. Appropriate mechanism should be developed enabling the IMF to properly deal with the problem from the point of view of monetary law. Improved legal linkages are important to overcome the present fragmentation and to avoid over-stretching the WTO dispute settlement in matters linked to financial regulation and monetary affairs.

The challenges of interfacing different but closely interconnected policy areas in dispute settlement show the need for work not only in terms of substantive rules beyond soft law, but also, and perhaps foremost, for the development of appropriate procedural channels which allow addressing the interface of trade, finance and monetary affairs in a future architecture of international economic law.

---

[51] Cf. Thomas Cottier and Tetyana Payosova, Challenges in International Monetary Law, in Inge Govare, Reinhard Quick, Marco Bronkers (eds), *Trade and Competition in the EU and Beyond*, (Cheltenham: Edward Elgar, 2011) at 35.

Bibliography

Abbott, K.W. and Snidal, D. 'Hard and Soft Law in International Governance' 54 *International Organization* 421 (2000)

Acharya, V.V. and Richardson, M. *Restoring Financial Stability: How to Repair a Failed System* (New Jersey: John Wiley & Sons, 2009)

Adrian, T. and Shin, H.S. 'Financial Intermediaries and Monetary Economics', in B. Friedman and M. Woodford (eds), *Handbook of Monetary Economics* (Amsterdam: North Holland, 2010)

Adrian, T. and Shin, H.S. 'Money, Liquidity, and Monetary Policy' 99 *American Economic Review* 600 (2009)

Akerlof, G.A. and Kranton, R.E. 'Identity and the Economics of Organizations' 19 *Journal of Economic Perspectives* 9 (2005)

Akerlof, G.A. and Kranton, R.E. 'It is Time to Treat Wall Street Like Main Street', *Financial Times* (24 February 2010)

Akerlof, G.A. and Shiller, R. *Animal Spirits; How Human Psychology Drives the Economy and Why it Matters for Global Capitalism* (Princeton and Oxford: Princeton University Press, 2009)

Alesina, A. and Stella, A. 'The Politics of Monetary Policy', National Bureau of Economic Research Working Paper No 15856, April 2010, <http://www.nber.org/papers/w15856.pdf?new_window=1> (visited 5 August 2010)

Alexander, K. *Economic Sanctions: Law and Public Policy* (London: Macmillan/Palgrave, 2009)

Alexander, K. 'The Need for Efficient International Financial Regulation and the Role of a Global Supervisor', in E. Ferran, and C.A.E. Goodhart (eds), *Regulating Financial Services and Markets in the 21st Century* (Oxford: Hart Publishing, 2001)

Alexander, K., Dhumale, R. and Eatwell, J. *Global Governance of Financial Systems: The International Regulation of Systemic Risk* (Oxford: Oxford University Press, 2006)

Alexander, K., John Eatwell, Avinash Persaud and Robert Reoch, 'Crisis Management, Burden Sharing, and Solidarity Mechanisms in the EU', IP/A/ECON/FWC/2010, Report to the European Parliament (2010)

Allen, W.A. and Wood, G. 'Defining and achieving financial stability' 2 (2) *Journal of Financial Stability* 152–72 (2006)

Altunbas, Y., Gambacorta L. and Marques-Ibanez, D. 'Does Monetary Policy Affect Bank Risk-taking?', BIS Working Papers No 298, March 2010, <http://www.bis.org/publ/work298.htm> (visited 5 August 2010)

Anand, A. and Green, A.J. 'Why is This Taking So Long? The Move Toward a National Securities Regulator' 60(2) *University of Toronto Law Journal* 663 (2010)

Anderson, T. and Sousa, R. (eds), *Reacting to the Spending Spree: Policy Changes We Can Afford* (Stanford: Hoover Institution Press, 2009)

Andrews, E.L. 'Greenspan concedes errors on regulation', *New York Times*, 23 October 2008, <http://www.nytimes.com/2008/10/24/business/economy/24panel.html> (visited 30 September 2010)

Arner, D.W. *Financial Stability, Economic Growth, and the Role of Law* (Cambridge: Cambridge University Press, 2007)

Arner, D.W. and Taylor, M.W. 'The Global Financial Crisis and the Financial Stability Board: Hardening the Soft Law of International Financial Regulation?', Asian Institute of International Financial Law, Working Paper No 6, 2009, <http://papers.ssrn.com/sol3/papers.cfm?abstract_id=1427084> (visited 20–21 July 2010)

Avgouleas, E. 'The Global Financial Crisis, Behavioural Finance and Financial Regulation: In Search of a New Orthodoxy' 9 *Journal of Corporate Legal Studies* 23 (2009)

Baba, N. and Packer, F. 'From Turmoil to Crisis: Dislocations in the FX Swap Market Before and After the Failure of Lehman Brothers', BIS Working Papers No 285, July 2009

Baccaro, V. 'Failing Firm Defence and Lack of Causality: Doctrine and Practice in Europe of Two Closely Related Concepts' 25 *European Competition Law Review* 1 (2004)

Baltensperger, E. and Jordan, T.J. 'Seignorage und Notenbankgewinn' 4 *Quartalsheft der Schweizerischen Nationalbank* 43 (1998)

Bart De Meester, 'The Global Financial Crisis and Government Support for Banks: What Role for GATS?' 13 *JIEL* 27 (2010)

Barth, J.R., Caprio, G. and Levine, R. 'Bank Regulation and Supervision: What Works Best?' 13 *Journal of Financial Intermediation* 205 (2004)

Barth, J.R., Caprio, G. and Levine, R. *Rethinking Bank Regulation; Till Angels Govern* (New York: Cambridge University Press, 2006)

Barth, J.R. et al, 'An International Comparison and Assessment of the Structure of Bank Supervision', Working Paper, February 2002, <http://ssrn.com/abstract=306764> (visited 10 May 2010)

Basel Committee on Banking Supervision, 'International Convergence of Capital Measurement and Capital Standards: A Revised Framework', June 2004 (Basel II)

Basel Committee on Banking Supervision, 'International Framework for Liquidity Risk Measurement, Standards, and Monitoring', Consultative Document, December 2009

Beck, T., Coyle, D., Dewatripont, M., Freixas, X. and Seabright, P. *Bailing Out the Banks: Reconciling Stabililty with Competition—An Analysis of State-Supported Schemes for Financial Institutions* (London: Center for Economic Policy Research, 2010)

Bengt Holmstrom and Paul Milgrom, 'The Firm as an Incentive System' 84(4) *American Economic Review* 972 (1994)

Benston, G.J. *The Separation of Commercial and Investment Banking: the Glass-Steagall Act Revisited and Reconsidered* (New York: Oxford University Press, 1990)

Bergsten, F. and Subramanian, A. 'America Cannot Resolve Global Imbalances on Its Own', *Financial Times*, 19 August 2009, <http://www.iie.com/publications/opeds/oped.cfm?ResearchID=1283> (visited 5 August 2010)

Bernanke, B., Gertler, M. and Gilchrist, S. 'The Financial Accelerator in a Quantitative Business Cycle Framework', in John B. Taylor and Michael Woodford (eds), *Handbook of Macroeconomics* (Amsterdam: Elsevier, 1999) 1341–93

Billio, M., Getmansky, M., Lo, A. and Pelizzon, L. 'Measuring Systemic Risk in the Finance and Insurance Sectors' (MIT Sloan School, Working Paper 4774-10, 17 March 2010)

Bismuth, R. 'Financial Sector Regulation and Financial Services Liberalization at the Crossroads: The Relevance of International Financial Standards in WTO Law', 44 *Journal of World Trade* 489 (2010)

Black, J. 'The Death of Credit, Trust—and Principles Based Regulation?', *Risk and Regulation*, Financial Crisis Special, Centre for Analysis of Risk and Regulation (CARR), December 2008, 8

Black, J. 'Managing the Financial Crisis—The Constitutional Dimension', LSE Law, Society and Economy Working Papers 12/2010, at 38, <http://ssrn.com/abstract=1619784> (visited 20 July 2010)

Blanchard, O., dell'Ariccia, G. and Mauro, P. 'Rethinking Macroeconomic Policy', IMF Staff Position Note, SPN/10/03, 12 February 2010, at 3–4, <http://www.imf.org/external/pubs/ft/spn/2010/spn1003.pdf> (visited 5 August 2010)

Blinder, A. and Wyplosz, C. 'Central Bank Talk: Committee Structure and Communication Policy', Mimeo, Prepared for the session 'Central Bank Communication' at the ASSA Meeting in Philadelphia, 9 January 2005, <http://www.aeaweb.org/annual_mtg_%20papers/2005/0109_1015_0702.pdf>

Blinder, A.S. *The Quiet Revolution: Central Banking Goes Modern* (New Haven: Yale University Press, 2004)

Borio, C. and Zhu, H. 'Capital Regulation, Risk-Taking and Monetary Policy: A Missing Link in the Transmission Mechanism?', Bank for International Settlements Working Papers No 268, December 2008, <http://www.bis.org/publ/work268.htm> (visited 5 August 2010)

Brandeis, L.D. 'What Publicity Can Do', in Other People's Money: And How the Bankers Use It (Mansfield Centre: Martino Publishing, 2009, first published 1914 by McClure Publications) 92–108

Brummer, C. 'How International Financial Law Works (and How it Doesn't)', 99 *Georgetown Law Journal* 257 (2011), <http://papers.ssrn.com/sol3/papers.cfm?abstract_id=1542829> (visited 11 October 2010)

Brummer, C. 'Territoriality as a Regulatory Technique: Notes from the Financial Crisis', 79 *University of Cincinnati Law Review* 257 (2010)

Buchheit, L. 'Did we Make Things too Complicated', 27 *International Financial Law Review* 24 (2008), at 24–6, <http://www.iflr.com> (visited 9 August 2010)

Buiter, W. 'The Unfortunate Uselessness of Most "State of the Art" Academic Monetary Economics', 6 March 2009, <http://www.voxeu.org/index.php?q=node/3210> (visited 5 August 2010)

Calomiris, C.W. 'The Subprime Turmoil: What's Old, What's New and What's Next' 15 *Journal of Structured Finance* 6–52 (2009)

Carletti, E. and Vives, X. 'Regulation and Competition Policy in the Banking Sector' in X. Vives (ed), *Competition Policy in the EU: Fifty Years on from the Treaty of Rome* (Oxford: Oxford University Press, 2009)

Carrasco, E. 'Global Financial and Economic Crisis Symposium: The Global Financial Crisis and the Financial Stability Forum: The Awakening and Transformation of an International Body' 19, *Transnational Law & Contemporary Problems* 19 (2010)

Chander, A. and Costa, R. 'Clearing Credit Default Swaps: A Case Study in Global Legal Convergence' 10 *Chicago Journal of International Law* 639 (2010)

Chan-Lau, J.A., Mathieson, D.J. and Yao, J.Y. 'Extreme Contagion in Equity Markets', IMF Staff Papers, Volume 51(2), 2004

Claessens, S., Dell'Ariccia, G., Igan, D. and Laeven, L. 'Lessons and Policy Implications from the Global Financial Crisis', IMF Working Paper, WP/10/44, 2010

Cottier, T. 'Challenges ahead in International Economic Law' 12 *Journal of International Economic Law* 3 (2009)

Cottier, T. 'From Progressive Liberalization to Progressive Regulation' 9 *Journal of International Economic Law* 779 (2006)

Cottier, T. 'Multilayered Governance, Pluralism and Moral Conflict' 16 *Indiana Journal of Global Legal Studies* 647 (2009)

Cottier, T. and Mavroidis, P. 'Regulatory Barriers and the Principle of Non-Discrimination in WTO Law: An Overview', in T. Cottier and P. Mavroidis (eds), *Regulatory Barriers and the Principle of Non-Discrimination in World Trade Law* (Ann Arbor: The University of Michigan Press, 2000)

Cottier, T. and Oesch, M. *International Trade Regulation: Law and Policy in the WTO, the European Union and Switzerland* (Berne/London: Stämpfli Publishers/Cameron May, 2005)

Cremer, J., Garicano, L. and Prat, A. 'Language and the Theory of the Firm' 122 *Quarterly Journal of Economics* 373 (2007)

Crocket, A. 'Rebuilding the Financial Architecture' 46(3) *Finance & Development* 18–19 (2009)

Cukierman, A. *Central Bank Strategy, Credibility and Independence: Theory and Evidence* (Cambridge, MA: Massachusetts Institute of Technology Press, 1992)

Cukierman, A. 'Reflections on the Crisis and on its Lessons for Regulatory Reform and for Central Bank Policies', *Journal of Financial Stability* (2010), <http://www.tau.ac.il/""alexcuk/pdf/Bocconi-Revised%20&%20Expanded-12-09.pdf> (visited 4 November 2010)

Cukierman, A., Web, S.B., and Neyapti, B. 'Measuring the Independence of Central Banks and Its Effect on Policy Outcomes' 6 *World Bank Economic Review* 353 (1992)

Cunningham, L. 'A Prescription to Retire the Rhetoric of "Principles-based Systems" Corporate Law, Securities Regulation and Accounting', 66 *Vanderbilt Law Review* 1411 (2007)

Dam, K. 'The Subprime Crisis and Financial Regulation: International and Comparative Perspectives' 10 *Chicago Journal of International Law* 581 (2010)

Davidoff, S.M. and Zaring, D. 'Regulation by Deal: The Government's Response to the Financial Crisis' 61 *Administrative Law Review* 463 (2009)

Davies, H. and Green, D. *Global Financial Regulation: The Essential Guide* (Cambridge: Polity Press, 2008)

Delimatsis, P. *International Trade in Services and Domestic Regulations—Necessity, Transparency, and Regulatory Diversity* (Oxford: Oxford University Press, 2007)

Delimatsis, P. 'Toward a Horizontal Necessity Test for Services: Completing the GATS Article VI:4 Mandate', in M. Panizzon, N. Pohl and P. Sauvé (eds), *GATS and the Regulation of International Trade in Services: World Trade Forum* (Cambridge: Cambridge University Press, 2008)

Demirgüc-Kunt, A. and Kane, E.J. 'Deposit Insurance Around The Globe—Where Does It Work?', World Bank Policy Research Working Paper No 2679, 2001

Dieter, H. 'The Stability of International Financial Markets: A Global Public Good?', in S.A. Schirm (ed), *New Rules for Global Markets—Public and Private Governance in the World Economy* (Basingstoke/Hampshire: Palgrave MacMillan, 2004)

Dietrich, D., Finke, J. and Tietje, C. 'Liberalization and Rules on Regulation in the Field of Financial Services in Bilateral Trade and Regional Integration Agreements', 97 *Beiträge zum Transnationalen Wirtschaftsrecht Halle* (Saale 2010)

Dodd–Frank Wall Street Reform and Consumer Protection Act, Pub. L. 111–203 (2010) (the Dodd–Frank Act)

Drezner, D.W. *All Politics is Global: Explaining International Regulatory Regimes* (Princeton: Princeton University Press, 2007)

Eichengreen, B. and Kenen, P.B. 'Managing the World Economy under the Bretton Woods System: An Overview' in Peter B Kenen (ed), *Managing the World Economy: Fifty Years After Bretton Woods* (Washington, DC: Institute for International Economics, 1994)

Ernst-Ulrich Petersmann, *Constitutional Functions and Constitutional Problems of International Economic Law* (Fribourg: University Press, 1991)

Ferguson, R. 'Alternative Approaches to Financial Supervision and Regulation' 16(2) *Journal of Financial Services Research* 297 (1999)

Ferran, E. 'Principles-based, Risk-based Regulation and Effective Enforcement', in M. Tison (ed) *Perspectives in Company Law and Financial Regulation* (Cambridge: Cambridge University Press, 2009)

Financial Services Authority, 'The Turner Review: A Regulatory Response to the Global Banking Crisis', March 2009 <http://www.fsa.gov.uk/pages/Library/Corporate/turner/index.shtml>

Financial Stability Board, 'Financial Stability Board Principles for Sound Compensation Practices', 2 April 2009, <http://www.financialstabilityboard.org/publications/r_0904b.pdf> (visited 16 July 2010)

Financial Stability Forum, 'Principles for Cross-border Cooperation on Crisis Management', 2 April 2009, <http:www.financialstabilityboard.org/publications/r_0904c.pdf>

Flannery, M. 'No Pain, No Gain? Effecting Market Discipline via Reverse Convertible Debentures', in H.S. Scott (ed), *Capital Adequacy Beyond Basel: Banking Securities and Insurance* (Oxford: Oxford University Press, 2005)

Follak, K.P. 'International Harmonization of Regulatory and Supervisory Frameworks', in M. Giovanoli (ed), *International Monetary Fund: Issues for the New Millennium* (Oxford: Oxford University Press, 2000)

Ford, C. 'New Governance, Compliance and Principles-based Regulation' 45 *American Business Law Review* 1 (2008)

Friedman, M. *Essays in Positive Economics* (Chicago: University of Chicago Press, 1953)

Friedman, M. *A Program for Monetary Stability, The Millar Lectures Number Three* (New York City: Fordham University Press, 1960)

Gadbaw, R.M. 'The WTO as a Systemic Regulator', *The Globalist*, 16 February 2010, <http://www.theglobalist.com/storyid.aspx?StoryId=8214> (visited 3 August 2010)

Gambacorta, L. 'Monetary Policy and the Risk-taking Channel', *BIS Quarterly Review, Special Features*, December 2009, <http://www.bis.org/publ/qtrpdf/r_qt0912.htm> (visited 5 August 2010)

Garicano, L. 'Hierarchies and the Organization of Knowledge in Production' 108(5) *Journal of Political Economy* 874 (2000)

Gerding, E. 'Code, Crash and Open Source: The Outsourcing of Financial Regulation to Risk Models and the Global Financial Crisis', 84 *Washington Law Review* 127 (2009)

Gilpin, R. *Global Political Economy: Understanding the International Economic Order* (Princeton: Princeton University Press, 2001)

Giovanoli, M. 'The Reform of the International Financial Architecture After the Global Crisis', 42 *New York University Journal of International Law & Politics* 81 (2010)

Giovanoli, M. and Devos, D. (eds), *International Monetary and Financial Law: The Global Crisis* (Oxford: Oxford University Press, 2010)

Goldstein, M. and Xie, D. 'The Impact of the Financial Crisis on Emerging Asia', presented at the conference on Asia and the Global Financial Crisis, Santa Barbara, 18–20 October 2009, <http://www.frbsf.org/economics/conferences/aepc/2009/09_Goldstein.pdf> (visited 5 August 2010)

Goodhart, C. 'The Background to the 2007 Financial Crisis', 4 *Journal of International Economics and Economic Policy* 331 (2008)

Goodhart, C. 'The Boundary Problem in Financial Regulation', Appendix A, in M. Brunnermeier, A. Crockett, C. Goodhart, A.D. Persaud and H.S. Shin (eds), *The Fundamental Principles of Financial Regulation* (11th Geneva Report on the World

Economy) (Geneva: International Center for Monetary and Banking Studies and Centre for Economic Policy Research, 2009) Appendix A

Goodhart, C. *The Evolution of Central Banks* (Cambridge, MA: MIT Press, 1988)

Goodhart, C. 'How Should We Regulate the Financial Sector?', in R. Layard and P. Boone (eds), *The Future of Finance: The LSE Report* (London: The London School of Economics and Political Science, 2010) 153–76

Goodhart, C. *Monetary Theory and Practice: The UK Experience* (London: MacMillan, 1984)

Goodhart, C. 'The Organizational Structure of Banking Supervision', LSE Financial Markets Group Special Paper 127, 2000, at 30–1

Goodhart, C. 'What Weight Should be Given to Asset Prices in the Measurement of Inflation?', 111 (472) *The Economic Journal* (2001), F335–56, available at <http://www.jstor.org/stable/2667880> (visited 9 August 2010)

Goodhart C. and Schoenmaker, D. 'Institutional Separation between Supervisory and Monetary Agencies' in C. Goodhart (ed), *The Central Bank and the Financial System* (Cambridge, MA: MIT Press, 1995) 333–414

Grabosky, P.N. 'Using Non-Governmental Resources to Foster Regulatory Compliance', 8(4) Governance 527 (1995)

Grahl, J. and Lysandrou, P. 'Sand in the Wheels or Spanner in the Works? The Tobin Tax and Global Finance', 27(4) *Cambridge Journal of Economics* 597 (2003)

Green, J. 'Inside Man', Atlantic Monthly, April 2010 <http://www.theatlantic.com/magazine/archive/2010/04/inside-man/7992/>

Grote, R. and Marauhn, T. (eds), *The Regulation of International Financial Markets— Perspectives for Reform* (Cambridge: Cambridge University Press, 2006)

Habermeier, K.F. and Kirilenko, A.A. 'Securities Transaction Taxes and Financial Markets', 50 IMF Staff Papers 165 (Special Issue), 2003

Haddad, M. and Stephanou, C. (eds), *Financial Services and Preferential Trade Agreements— Lessons from Latin America* (Washington, DC: World Bank, 2010)

Hagan, S. 'Restructuring Corporate Debt in the Context of Systemic Crisis', 73 *Law and Contemporary Problems* 4 (2010)

Hammer, C., Kunzel, P. and Petrova, I. 'Sovereign Wealth Funds: Current Institutional and Operational Practices', IWG Working Paper No 08/254, 2008, <http://www.iwg-swf.org/pubs/eng/swfsurvey.pdf> (visited 20–21 July 2010)

Haq, M., Kaul, I. and Grunberg, I. (eds), *The Tobin Tax: Coping with Financial Volatility* (New York: Oxford University Press, 1996)

Hart, O. and Zingales, L. 'A New Capital Regulation for Large Financial Institutions' (Center for Economic Policy Research, Discussion Paper No. DP7298, September 2009), <http://faculty.chicagobooth.edu/luigi.zingales/research/papers/a_new_capital_regulation.pdf> (visited 5 March 2010)

Hayek, F.A. *Denationalisation of Money—The Argument Refined*, 2nd ed. (London: The Institute of Economic Affairs, 1978)

Horlick, G.N. and Clarke, P.A. 'The 1994 WTO Subsidies Agreement', 17(4) *World Competition* 41 (1994)

Huertas, T. *Crisis: Cause, Containment and Cure* (Basingstoke: Palgrave Macmillan, 2010)

Hufbauer, G. and Wada, E. 'Can Financiers Learn From Traders?', 2 *Journal of International Economic Law* 567 (1999)

IMF, 'The Fund's Mandate—The Legal Framework', 22 February 2010, <http://www.imf.org/external/np/pp/eng/2010/022210.pdf> (visited 21 October 2010)

IMF, 'IMF Expanding Surveillance to Require Mandatory Financial Stability Assessments of Countries with Systemically Important Financial Sectors', Press Release No 10/357, 27 September 2010, <http://www.imf.org/external/np/sec/pr/2010/pr10357.htm> (visited 18 October 2010)

International Monetary Fund, 'A Fair and Substantial Contribution by the Financial Sector', Final Report for the G-20 (Washington DC, IMF, 27 June 2010)

IWG, 'International Working Group of Sovereign Wealth Funds Reaches a Preliminary Agreement on Draft Set Generally Accepted Principles and Practices—"Santiago Principles"', 2 September 2008, <http://www.iwg-swf.org/pr/swfpr0804.htm> (visited 20–21 July 2010)

Jackson, H.E. 'Centralization, Competition, and Privatization in Financial Regulation', 2(2) *Theoretical Inquiries in Law (Online Edition)* Article 4 (2001), <http://www.bepress.com/til/default/vol2/iss2/art4> (visited 3 July 2010)

Jackson, H.E. 'Variation in the Intensity of Financial Regulation: Preliminary Evidence and Potential Implications', 24 *Yale Journal on Regulation* 253 (2007)

Jackson, J.H. 'Global Economics and International Economic Law', 1 *Journal of International Economic Law* 1 (1998)

Jackson, J.H. 'International Economic Law: Complexity and Puzzles', 10 *Journal of International Economic Law* 3 (2007)

Jackson, J.H. 'Sovereignty-Modern: A New Approach to an Outdated Concept', 97 *American Journal of International Law* 782 (2003)

Jackson, J.H. *Sovereignty, the WTO, and Changing Fundamentals of International Law* (Cambridge: Cambridge University Press, 2006)

Jackson, J.H. *The World Trade Organization—Constitution and Jurisprudence* (London: Routledge, 1998)

Jackson, P. et al, 'Capital Requirements and Bank Behavior: The Impact of the Basel Accord', Basel Committee on Banking Supervision Working Paper No 1, April 1999

Jiménez, G. et al, 'Hazardous Times for Monetary Policy: What do Twenty-Three Million Bank Loans Say About the Effects of Monetary Policy on Credit Risk-Taking?', Bank of Spain (Banco de España) Working Papers No 0833, <http://www.bde.es/webbde/Secciones/Publicaciones/PublicacionesSeriadas/DocumentosTrabajo/08/Fic/dt0833e.pdf> (visited 5 August 2010)

Johnson, S. *13 Bankers: The Wall Street Takeover and the Next Financial Meltdown* (New York: Pantheon Books, 2010)

Jorgenson, D.W. 'A New Architecture for the US National Accounts', 55 (1) *Review of Income and Wealth* 1–42 (2009)

Kaletsky, A. 'The Benefits of the Bust', *Wall Street Journal*, 19–20 June 2010

Karmel, R.S. and Kelly, C. 'The Hardening of Soft Law in Securities Regulation', 34 *Brooklyn Journal of International Law* 883 (2009)

Kaufmann, C. 'Clearing House Interbank System' in C. Tietje and A. Brouder (eds), *Handbook of Transnational Economic Governance Regimes*, (Leiden: Martinus Nijhoff, 2009)

Kaufmann, C. 'International Law in Recession? The Role of International Law when Crisis Hits: Food, Finance and Climate Change' in U. Fastenrath et al (eds.), *From Bilateralism to Community Interest, Essays in Honour of Bruno Simma* (Oxford: Oxford University Press, 2011)

Kaufmann, C. and Ciesolka, M. 'Wann baute Noah die Arche—Vermögensverwaltung als Akteurin einer nachhaltigen Marktentwicklung' in P.R. Isler and R. Cerutti (eds),

Vermögensverwaltung III, (Zürich: Schriftenreihe Nr. 105 des Europainstitutes an der Universität Zürich, 2010)

Kay, J. 'Narrow Banking. The Reform of Banking Regulation', available at <http://www. johnkay.com/wp-content/uploads/2009/12/JK-Narrow-Banking.pdf> (visited 9 August 2010)

Keynes, J.M. *The General Theory of Employment, Interest and Money* (London: Macmillan, 1936)

Kindleberger, C.P. *Manias, Panics and Crashes: A History of Financial Crises* (London: Macmillan, 1978)

Kokkoris, I. *The Treatment of Non-Collusive Oligopoly Under the ECMR and National Merger Control* (Oxford: Routledge, 2011)

Kokkoris, I. and Olivares-Caminal, R. *Antitrust Policy in the Wake of Financial Crises* (Cambridge: Cambridge University Press, 2010)

Kotlikoff, L.J. *Jimmy Stewart is Dead: Ending the World's Ongoing Financial Plague with Limited Purpose Banking* (Chichester: John Wiley & Sons, 2010)

Krajewski, M. 'Article VI GATS Domestic Regulation', in R. Wolfrum, P.T. Stoll and A. Seibert-Fohr (eds), *WTO—Trade in Services: Max Planck Commentaries on World Trade Law* (Leiden/Boston: Martinus Nijhoff, 2008)

Krajewski, M. 'Democratic Legitimacy and Constitutional Perspectives of WTO Law', 35 *Journal of World Trade* 167 (2001)

Kroes, N. (European Commissioner for European Policy), 'Dealing with the Current Financial Crisis', Brussels, 6 October 2008, <http://europa.eu/rapid/pressReleasesAction.do? reference=SPEECH/08/498> (visited 26 June 2010)

Kuritzkes, A. and Scott, H. 'Markets are the Best Judge of Bank Capital', FT.COM, 23 September 2009, <http://www.ft.com/cms/2ca160b0-a870-11de-9242-00144feabdc0. html> (visited 5 March 2010)

Langevoort, D.C. 'The SEC, Retail Investors and the Institutionalization of the Securities Markets', 95 *Virginia Law Review* 1025 (2009)

Langevoort, D.C. 'Steps Toward the Europeanization of US Securities Regulation, with Thoughts on the Evolution and Design of a Multinational Securities Regulator', in M. Tison et al (eds), *Perspectives in Company Law and Financial Regulation* (Cambridge: Cambridge University Press, 2009)

Langevoort, D.C. 'Structuring Securities Regulation in the European Union: Lessons from the US Experience', in G. Ferrarini and E. Wymeersch (eds), *Investor Protection in Europe: Corporate Law Making, the MiFID and Beyond* (Oxford: Oxford University Press, 2006)

Lannoo, K. 'Challenges to the Structure of Financial Supervision in the EU', in G.G. Kaufmann (ed), *Bank Fragility and Regulation: Evidence from Different Countries* (New York: Elsevier, 2000)

Lannoo, K. 'Supervising the European Financial System', Centre for European Policy Studies Policy Brief No 21, May 2002

Lastra, R.M. *Central Banking and Banking Regulation* (London: Financial Markets Group, London School of Economics and Political Science, 1996)

Lastra, R.M. *Legal Foundations of International Monetary Stability* (Oxford: Oxford University Press 2006)

Lastra, R.M. 'Lender of Last Resort, An International Perspective', 48 *International and Comparative Law Quarterly* 340 (1999)

Lastra, R.M. 'The Role of the IMF as a Global Financial Authority' in *European Yearbook of International Economic Law*, Vol. 2 (2011) 121–36

Lastra, R.M. and Shams, H. 'Public Accountability in the Financial Sector', in E. Ferran and C.A.E. Goodhart (eds), *Regulating Financial Services and Markets in the 21st Century* (Oxford: Hart Publishing, 2001) 165–88

Leroux, E. 'Trade in Financial Services under the World Trade Organization', 36 *Journal of World Trade* at 413 (2002)

Lichtenstein, C.C. 'Lessons for the 21st Century Central Bankers: Differences between Investment and Depositary Banking', in M. Giovanoli and D. Devos (eds), *International Monetary and Financial Law: The Global Crisis* (Oxford: Oxford University Press, 2010)

Litan, R.E. 'Economics: Global Finance', in P.J. Simmons and Chantal de Jonge Oudraat (eds), *Managing Global Issues: Lessons Learned* (Washington: Carnegie Endowment, 2001)

Litan, R.E. 'Taking the Dangers Out of Bank Deregulation', 4(4) *The Brookings Review* 3 (1986)

Llewellyn, D. 'The Economic Rationale for Financial Regulation', UK FSA Occasional Paper 1, 1999

Lowenfeld, A.F. *International Economic Law*, 2nd ed. (Oxford: Oxford University Press, 2008) 598–803

Ludlow, P. *The Making of the European Monetary System: A Case Study of the Politics of the European Community* (London: Butterworths, 1982)

McKinnon, R. *An International Standard for Monetary Stabilization* (Washington, DC: Institute for International Economics, 1984)

McKinnon, R. 'Monetary and Exchange Rate Policies for International Financial Stability: A Proposal', 2 *Journal of Economic Perspectives* 83 (1988)

Miron, J.A. 'Financial Panics, the Seasonality of the Nominal Interest Rate, and the Founding of the Fed', 76 (1) *The American Economic Review* (1986), 125–40

Molyneux, P. 'Banking Crises and the Macro-economic Context', in R.M. Lastra and H. N. Schiffman (eds), *Bank Failures and Bank Insolvency Law in Economies in Transition* (London: Kluwer Law International, 1999)

Mundell, R. 'A Theory of Optimal Currency Areas', 51 *American Economic Review* 657 (1961), at 658–9

Nicolaïdis, K. and Trachtman, J.P. 'From Policed Regulation to Managed Recognition: Mapping the Boundary in GATS', in P. Sauvé and R. Stern (eds), *GATS 2000: New Directions in Services and Trade Liberalization* (Washington, DC: The Brookings Institution, 2000)

Norton, J.J. *Devising International Bank Supervisory Standards* (Dordrecht: Martinus Nijhoff, 1995)

Norton, J.J. '"NIFA-II" or "Bretton Woods- II"?: The G-20 (Leaders) Summit Process on Managing Global Financial Markets and The World Economy—Quo Vadis?', 11 *Journal of Banking Regulation* 261 (2010)

Norton, J.J. 'A suggested First Step for Moving Toward a "Next Generation" of Viable and Effective Long-term Financial Sector Legal Reform: Taking Stock of the "First Generation" of Reform,' Monograph in World Bank (LVP) Series on Legal and Judicial Reform, Law & Development Working Paper Series, No 4 (Washington, DC: World Bank, 2007), <http://siteresources.worldbank.org/INTLAWJUSTICE/Resources/LDWP4_FinSecLegRef.pdf> (visited 18 July 2012)

O'Driscoll Jr., J.P. 'The Gulf Spill, the Financial Crisis and Government Failure', *Wall Street Journal*, 14 June 2010

Obstfeld, M. and Rogoff, K. 'Global Imbalances and the Financial Crisis: Products of Common Causes', <http://elsa.berkeley.edu/""obstfeld/santabarbara.pdf> (visited 5 August 2010)

Patomaki, H. and Sehm-Patomaki, K. *The Tobin Tax: How to Make it Real* (Helsinki: The Network Institute for Global Democratisation, 1999)

Paulson, H.M. *On the Brink: Inside the Race to Stop the Collapse of the Global Financial System* (New York: Business Plus, 2010)

Plender, J. 'Just Targeting Symptoms of the Crisis is too Neat', *Financial Times*, 25 February 2010

Poretti, P. *The Regulation of Subsidies within the General Agreement on Trade in Services of the WTO: Problems and Prospects* (Alphen aan den Rijn, Netherlands: Kluwer Law International, 2009)

Posner, R.A. *The Crisis of Capitalist Democracy* (Cambridge, MA: Harvard University Press, 2010)

Posner, R.A. *A Failure of Capitalism: The Crisis of '08 and the Descent into Depression* (Cambridge, MA: Harvard University Press, 2009)

Quintyn, M. and Taylor, M.W. 'Regulatory and Supervisory Independence and Financial Stability', IMF Working Paper, WP/02/46, 2002

Rajan, R. 'Has Financial Development Made the World Riskier?', <http://www.imf.org/external/np/speeches/2005/082705.htm> (visited 5 August 2010)

Raustiala, K.R. 'The Architecture of International Cooperation: Transgovernmental Networks and the Future of International Law', 43(1) *Virginia Journal of International Law* 1 (2002)

Reinhart, C.M. and Rogoff, K.S. *This Time is Different: Eight Centuries of Financial Folly* (Princeton and Oxford: Princeton University Press, 2009)

Report of the High Level Group on Financial Supervision in the EU, Brussels, 25 February 2009, (de Larosière Report), <http://ec.europa.eu/internal_market/finances/docs/de_larosiere_report_en.pdf> (visited 3 August 2010)

Romano, R. 'The Political Dynamics of Derivative Securities Regulation', 14 *Yale Journal on Regulation* 279 (1997)

Roubini, N. and Mihim, S. *Crisis Economics* (London: Penguin, 2010)

Ruddy, B. 'The Critical Success of the WTO; Trade Policies of the Current Economic Crisis', *Journal of International Economic Law* 2010; 13: 475–95

Sah, R.K. and Stiglitz, J.E. 'The Architecture of Economic Systems: Hierarchies and Polyarchies', 76(4) *American Economic Review* 716 (1986)

Sauvé, P. 'Completing the GATS Framework: Addressing Uruguay Round Leftovers', 57(3) *Aussenwirtschaft* 310 (2002)

Schaeck, K. and Čihák, M. 'Banking Competition and Capital Ratios', IMF, Working Paper No. WP/07/216, 28 March 2010), <http://ssrn.com/abstract=1579625> (visited 5 March 2010)

Schinasi, G. *Safeguarding Financial Stability: Theory and Practice* (Washington, DC: International Monetary Fund, 2006)

Schinasi, G.J. 'Defining Financial Stability', IMF Working Paper, WP/04/187, 2004

Schmidt, R. *The Currency Transaction Tax: Rate and Revenue Estimates* (Toronto: United Nations/North-South Institute, 2008)

Schularick, M. and Taylor, A.M. 'Credit Booms Gone Bust: Monetary Policy, Leverage Cycles and Financial Crises', 1870–2008, National Bureau of Economic Research Working Paper No 15512, November 2009, <http://www.jfki.fu-berlin.de/faculty/economics/team/persons/schularick/SchularickTaylor_Credit_Booms_Gone_Bust.pdf> (visited 5 August 2010)

Schulmeister, S. 'A General Financial Transaction Tax: A Short Cut of the Pros, Cons and a Proposal', WIFO Working Papers No 344, 2009

Schwartz, A.J. 'Real and Pseudo-Financial Crises', in F. Capie and G. Wood (eds), *Financial Crises and World Banking Policy* (New York: St. Martin's Press, 1986)

Scott, H.S. *The Global Financial Crisis* (New York: Foundation Press, 2009)

Scott, H.S. 'The Reduction of Systemic Risk in the United States Financial System', 33 *Harvard Journal of Law and Public Policy* 671 (2010)

Scott, H.S. and Shinsaku Iwahara, 'In Search of a Level Playing Field: The Implementation of the Basel Accord in Japan and the United States', Group of Thirty Occasional Paper No 46, 1994

Scott, K. 'Criteria for Evaluating Failure Resolution Plans' mimeo presented at 'Ending Government Bailouts as We Know Them' Policy Workshop, Stanford University, 10 December 2009

Siegel, D.E. 'Legal Aspects of the IMF/WTO Relationship: The Fund's Articles of Agreement and the WTO Agreements', 96 *American Journal of International Law* 561 (2002)

Smith, R.C. and Walter, I. *Global Banking* (New York: Oxford University Press, 2003)

Sorkin, A.R. *Too Big to Fail* (New York: Viking, 2009)

Spahn, P.B. 'On the Feasibility of a Tax on Foreign Exchange Transactions', <http://www.wiwi.uni-frankfurt.de/profs/spahn/tobintax/Tobintax.pdf> (visited 25 July 2010)

Steil, B. and Hinds, M. *Money, Markets and Sovereignty* (New Haven: Yale University Press, 2009)

Stiglitz, J.E. 'Using Tax Policy to Curb Short-Term Trading', 3 *Journal of Financial Services Research* 101 (1989)

Summers, L.H. and Summers, V.P. 'When Financial Markets Work Too Well: A Cautious Case for a Securities Transaction Tax', 3 *Journal of Financial Services Research* 261 (1989)

Tarullo, D.K. *Banking on Basel: The Future of International Financial Regulation* (New York: Peterson Institute for International Economics, 2008)

Taylor, J.B. 'The Dodd-Frank Financial Fiasco', *Wall Street Journal* (1 July 2010)

Taylor, J.B. 'Housing and Monetary Policy', <http://www.stanford.edu/""johntayl/Housing%20and%20Monetary%20Policy–Taylor–Jackson%20Hole%202007.pdf> (visited 5 August 2010)

Taylor, M.W. 'Assessing the Case for Unified Sector Supervision', London School of Economics Financial Markets Group Special Papers 134, 2001

Thomas, R.S. and Cotter, J.F. 'Measuring Securities Market Efficiency in the Regulatory Setting', 63 *SUM Law & Contemporary Problems* 105 (2005)

Thornton, H. *An Enquiry into the Nature and Effects of the Paper Credit in Great Britain* [1802] (London: George Allen & Unwin, 1939)

Tietje, C. 'The Duty to Cooperate in International Economic Law and Related Areas', in J. Delbrück (ed), *International Law of Cooperation and State Sovereignty* (Berlin: Veröffentlichungen des Walther-Schücking-Instituts für Internationales Recht an der Universität Kiel Nr. 139, 2002) 45–65

Tietje, C., Nowrot, K. and Wackernagel, C. 'Once and Forever? The Legal Effects of a Denunciation of ICSID', *Band 74 von Beiträge zum transnationalen Wirtschaftsrecht*, (Halle-Witterberg: Institute of Economic Law, 2008)

Tobin, J. 'Financial intermediation and deregulation in perspective', 3(2): 19–29 *Bank of Japan Monetary and Economic Studies* (1985)

Tobin, J. 'A Proposal for International Monetary Reform', 4 *Eastern Economic Journal* 153 (1978)

Trachtman, J.P. *The Economic Structure of International Law* (Cambridge, MA: Harvard University Press, 2008)

Trachtman, J.P. 'International Regulatory Competition, Externalization and Jurisdiction', 34 *Harvard International Law Journal* 47 (1993)

Treves, T. 'Monetary Sovereignty Today', in M. Giovanoli (ed), *International Monetary Fund: Issues for the New Millennium* (Oxford: Oxford University Press, 2000) 111–18

Turner, A. 'What Do Banks Do, What Should They Do and What Public Policies are Needed to Ensure Best Results', March 2010, <http://www.fsa.gov.uk/pubs/speeches/at_17mar10.pdf> (visited 25 July 2010)

Van Aaken, A. and Kurtz, J. 'Prudence or Discrimination? Emergency Measures, the Global Financial Crisis and International Economic Law', 12 *Journal of International Economic Law* 859 (2009)

Walker, M. and Fidler, S. 'IMF Chief Urges Coordinated Finance Rules', *Wall Street Journal* (30–31 January 2010)

Weber, R.H. 'Financial Stability—Structural Framework and Development Issues', 6(4) *International and Comparative Corporate Law Journal* 1 (2008)

Weber, R.H. 'Mapping and Structuring International Financial Regulation—A Theoretical Approach', 20(5) *European Banking Law Review* 651 (2009)

Weber, R.H. *Shaping Internet Governance: Regulatory Challenges* (Zürich: Schulthess and Springer, 2009)

Weber, R.H. 'State Interventions and Competition Distortion in Financial Markets', 6 *Schweizerische Zeitschrift für Wirtschaftsrecht* 428 (2009)

Weber, R.H. and Arner, D. 'Toward a New Design for International Financial Regulation', 29(2) *University of Pennsylvania Journal of International Law* 391 (2007)

Westbrook, D.A. *Out of Crisis: Rethinking our Financial Markets* (Boulder: Paradigm Publishers, 2009)

Whitehead, C.K. 'Reframing Financial Regulation', 90 *Boston University Law Review* 1 (2010)

Wood, G. and Kabiri, A. 'Firm Stability or System Stability: the Regulatory Delusion' in J.R. Labrosse, R. Olivares-Caminal and D. Singh (eds.), *Managing Risk in the Financial System* (Cheltenham: Edward Elgar, 2011)

Index